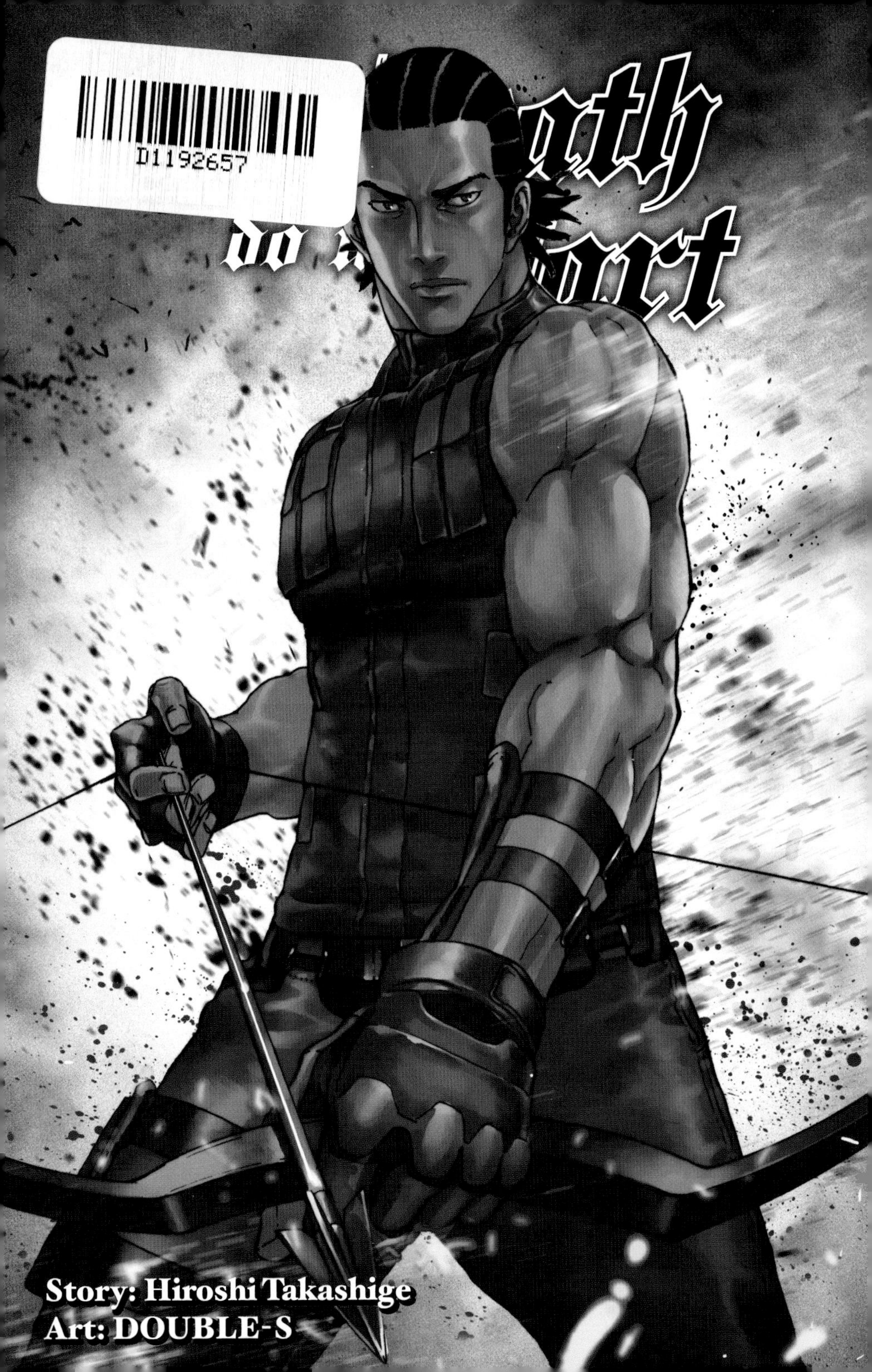
ath
do
art
Story: Hiroshi Takashige
Art: DOUBLE-S

Until Death do us Part

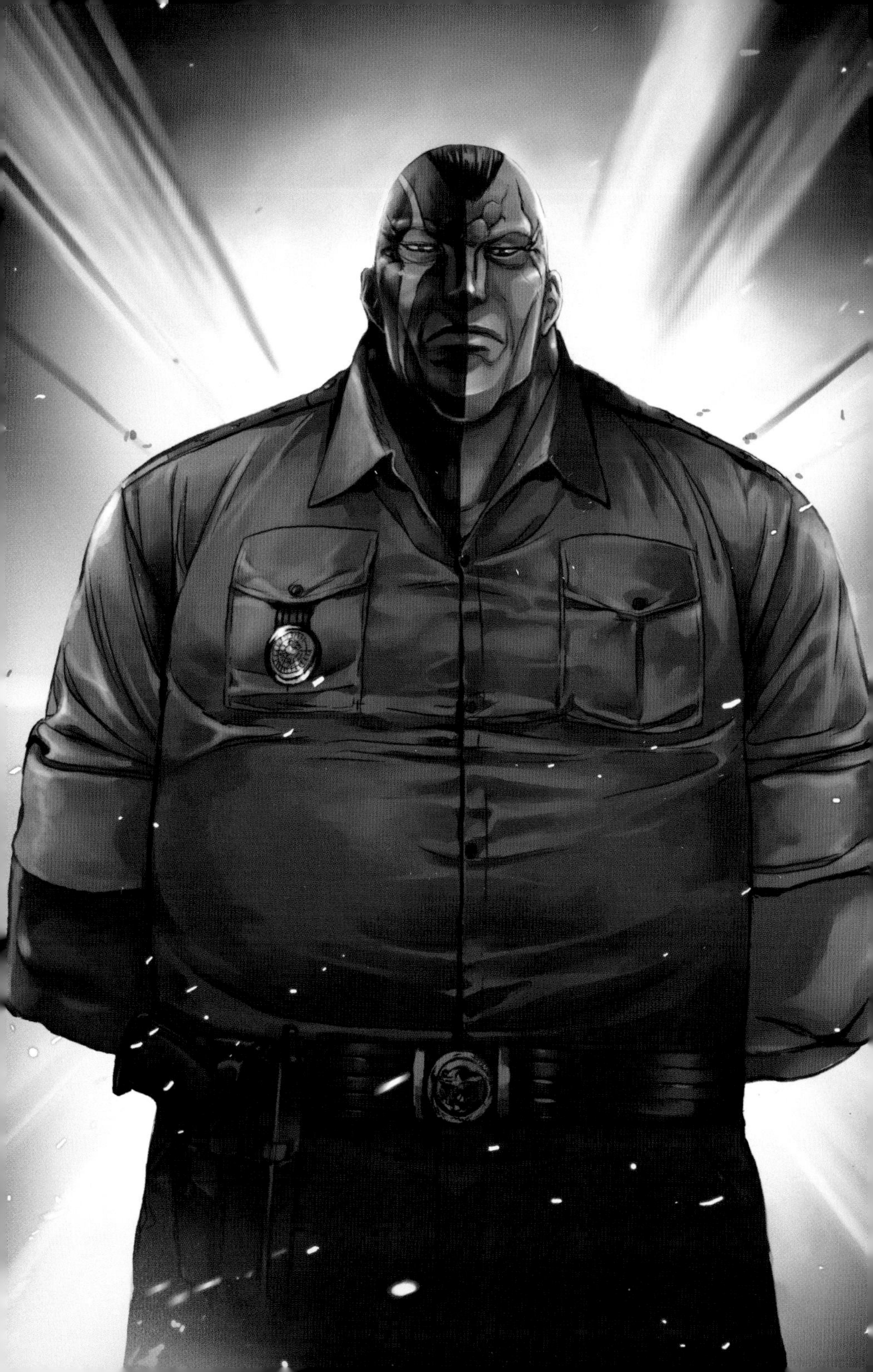

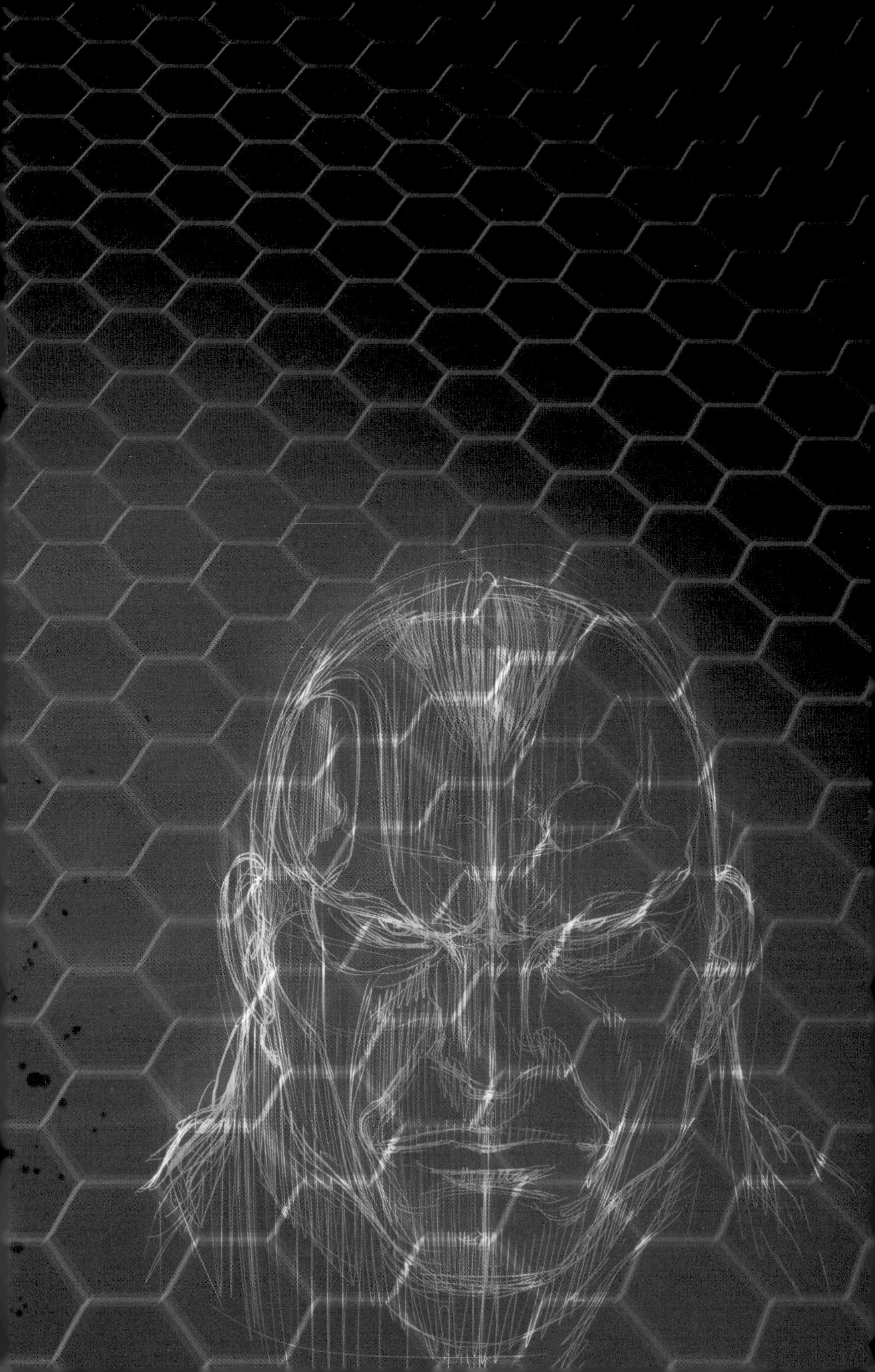

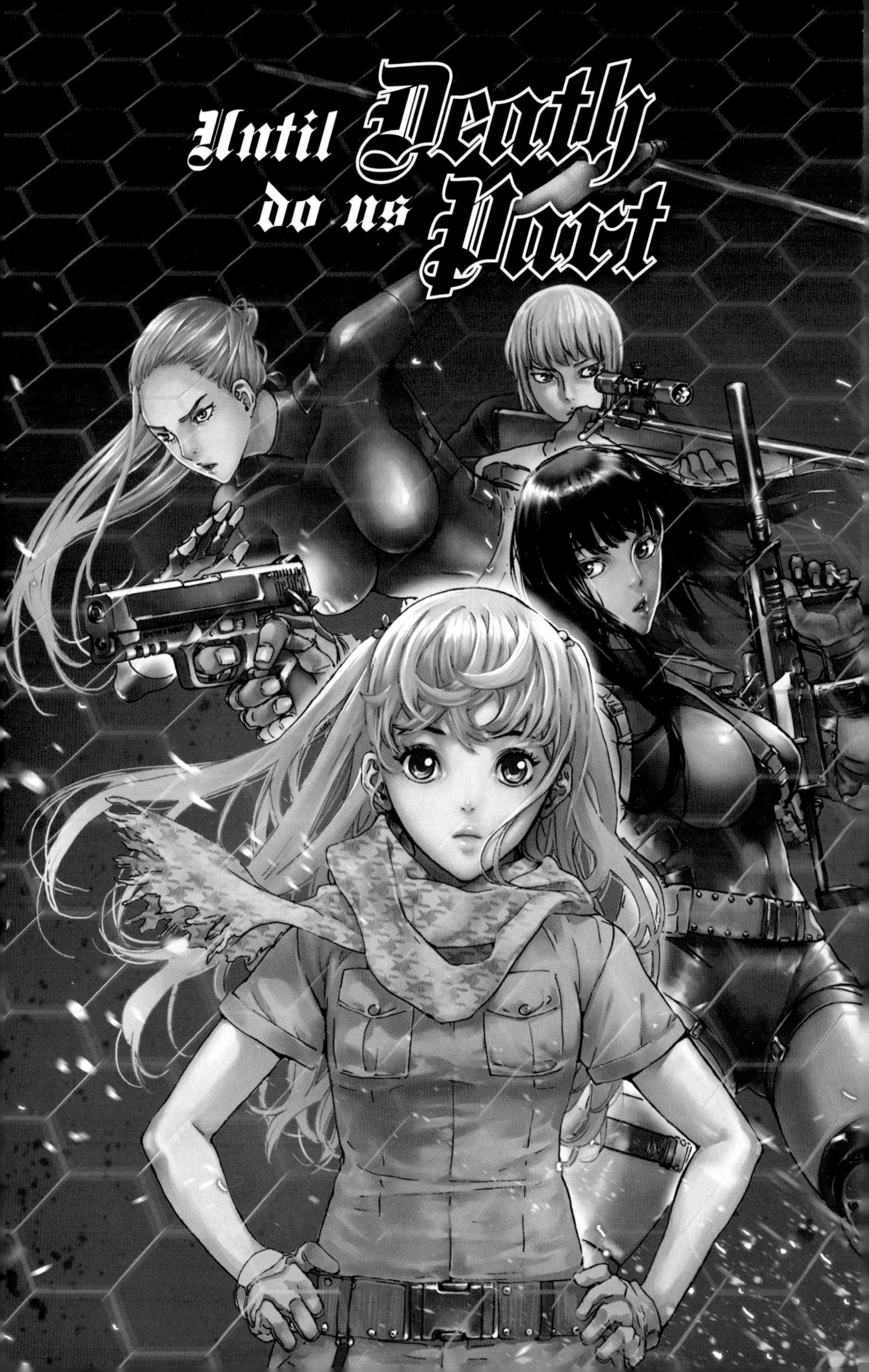
Until Death do us Part

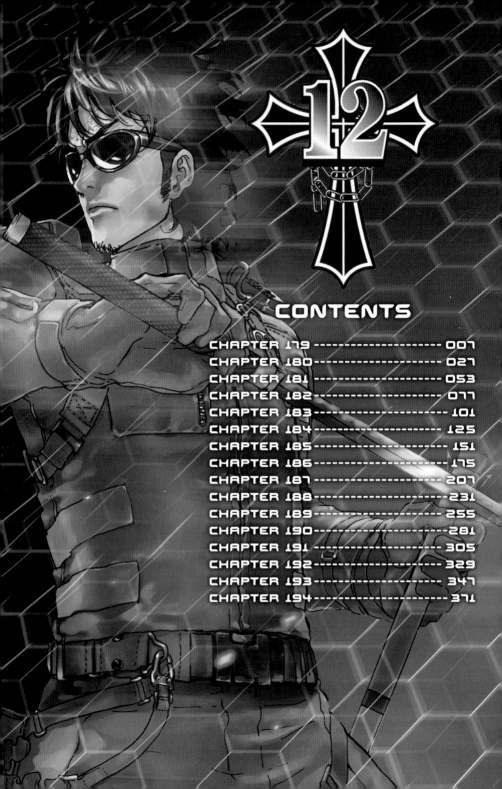

12

CONTENTS

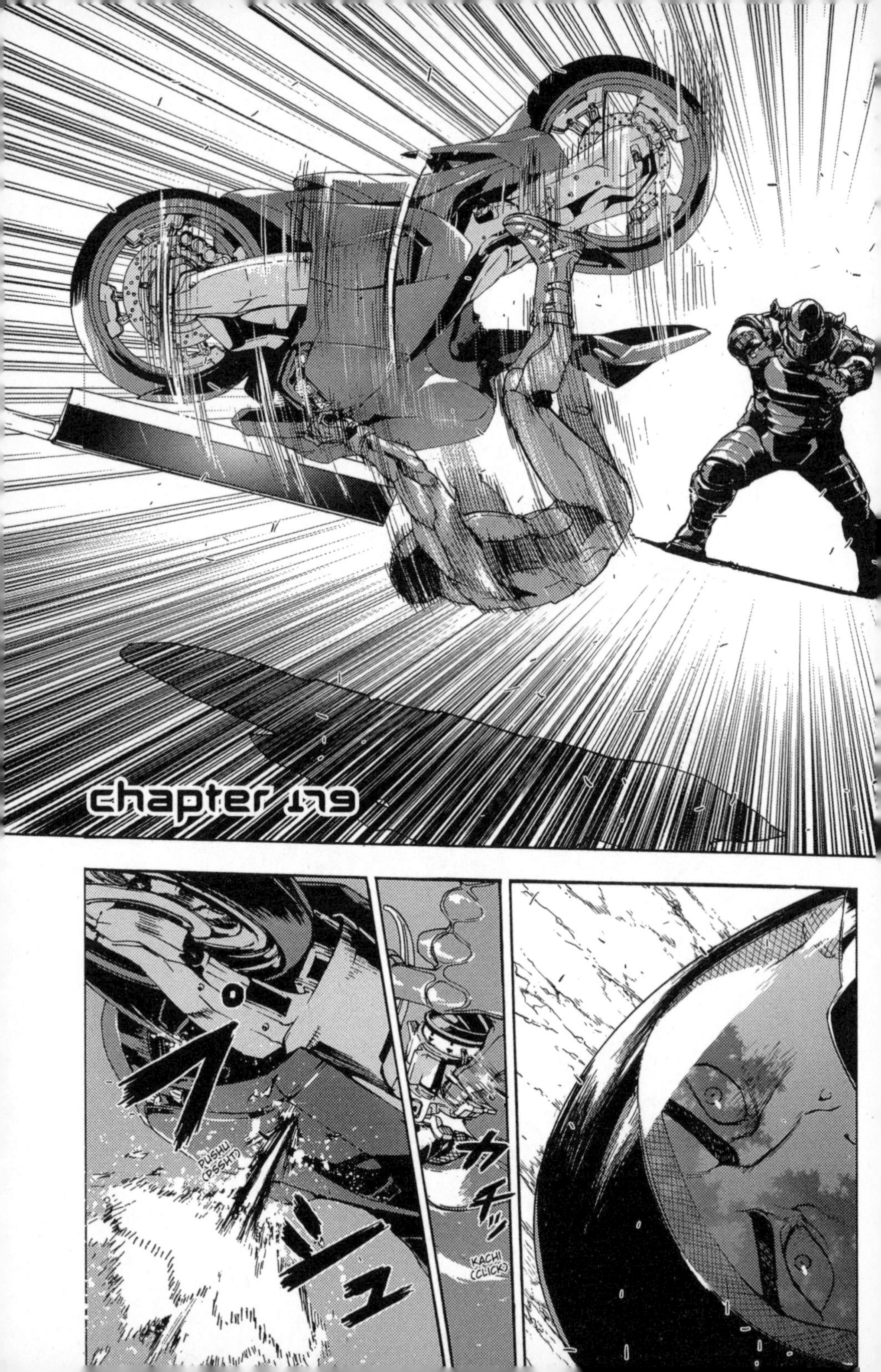
chapter 179
KACHI (CLICK)
PUSHU (PSSHT)

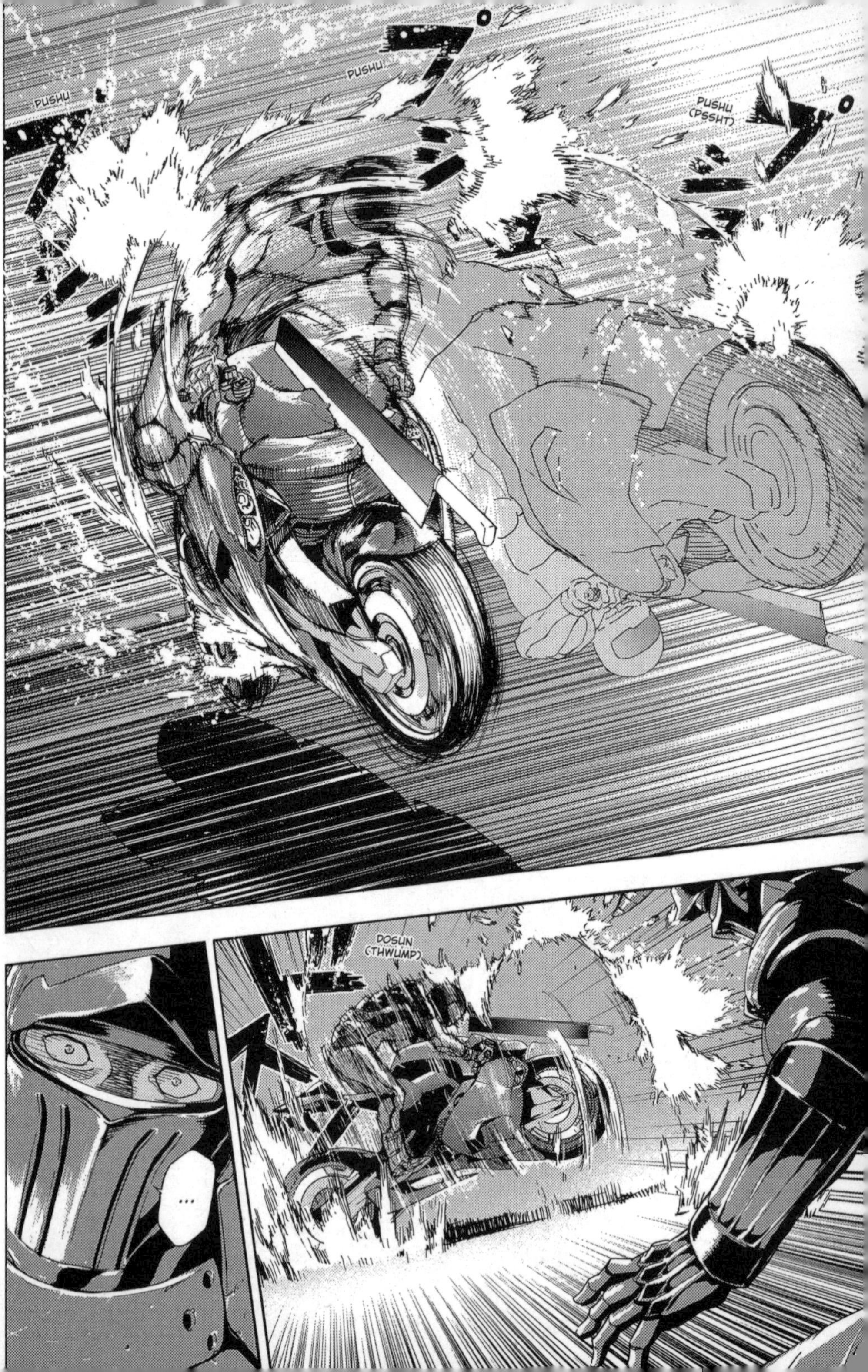
PUSHU (PSSHT)
PUSHU
PUSHU
DOSUN (THWUMP)
...

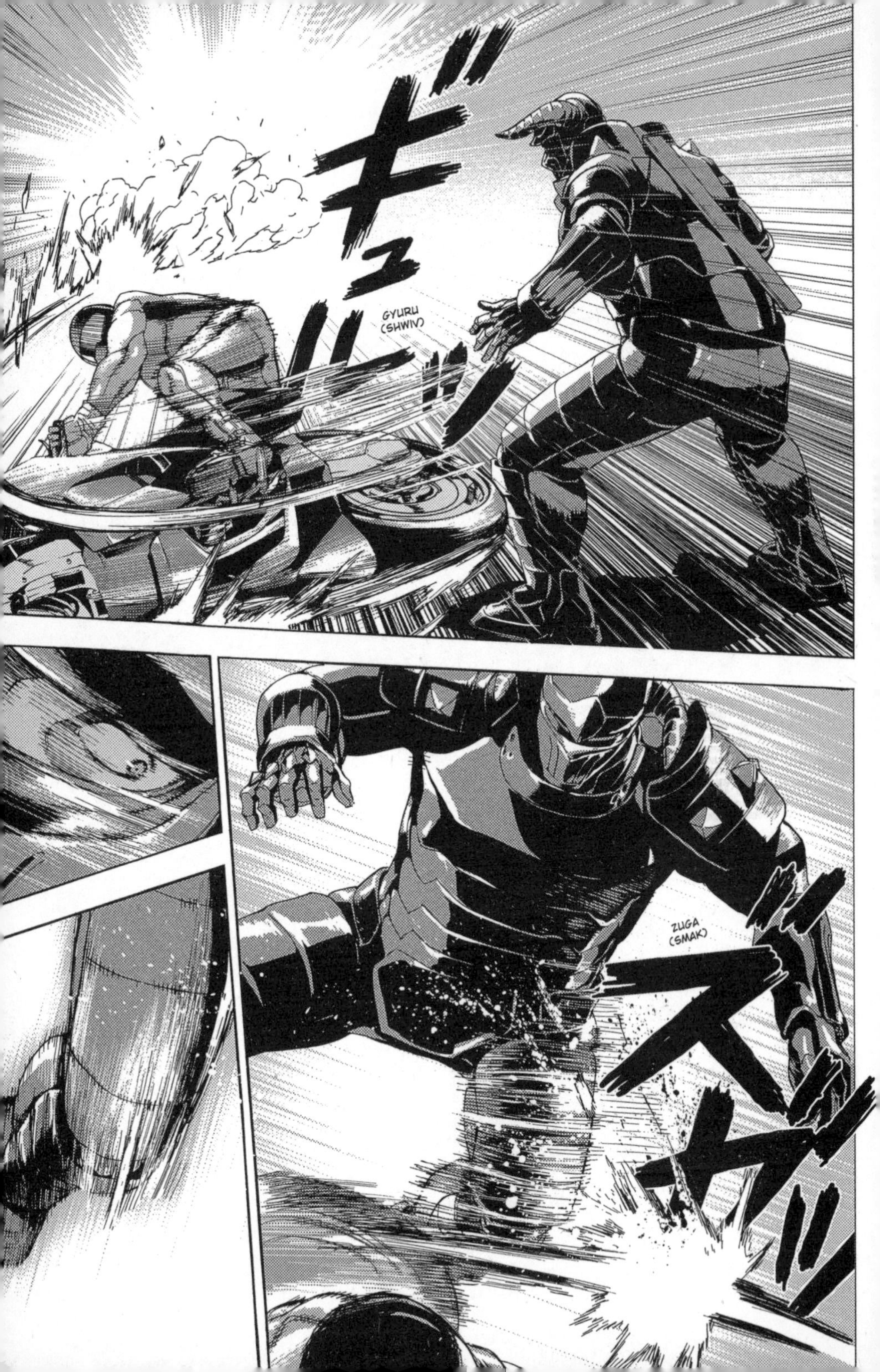
GYURU
(SHWIV)
ZUGA
(SMAK)

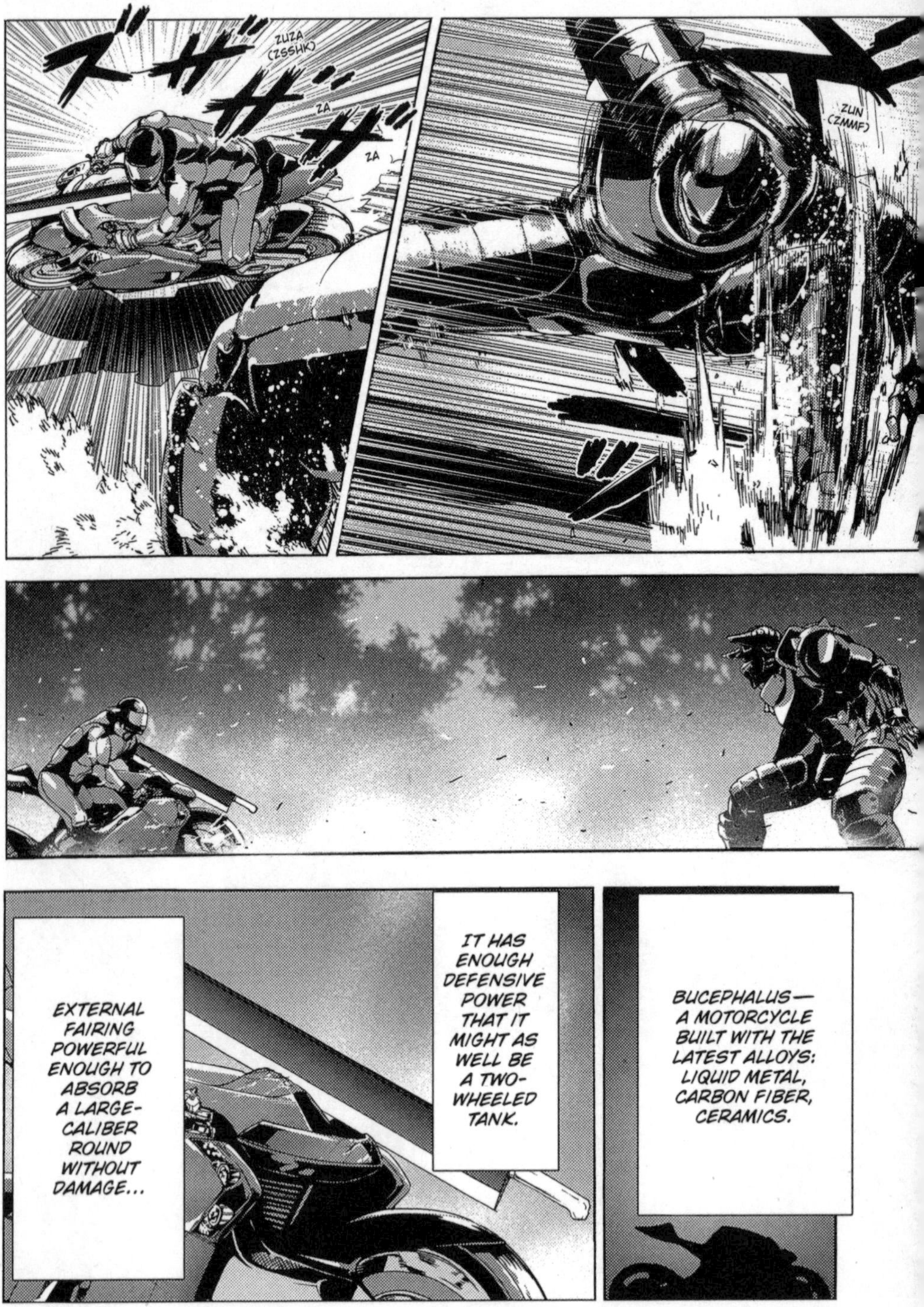
ZUN (ZMMF)
ZUZA (ZSSHK)
ZA
ZA
BUCEPHALUS—A MOTORCYCLE BUILT WITH THE LATEST ALLOYS: LIQUID METAL, CARBON FIBER, CERAMICS.
IT HAS ENOUGH DEFENSIVE POWER THAT IT MIGHT AS WELL BE A TWO-WHEELED TANK.
EXTERNAL FAIRING POWERFUL ENOUGH TO ABSORB A LARGE-CALIBER ROUND WITHOUT DAMAGE...

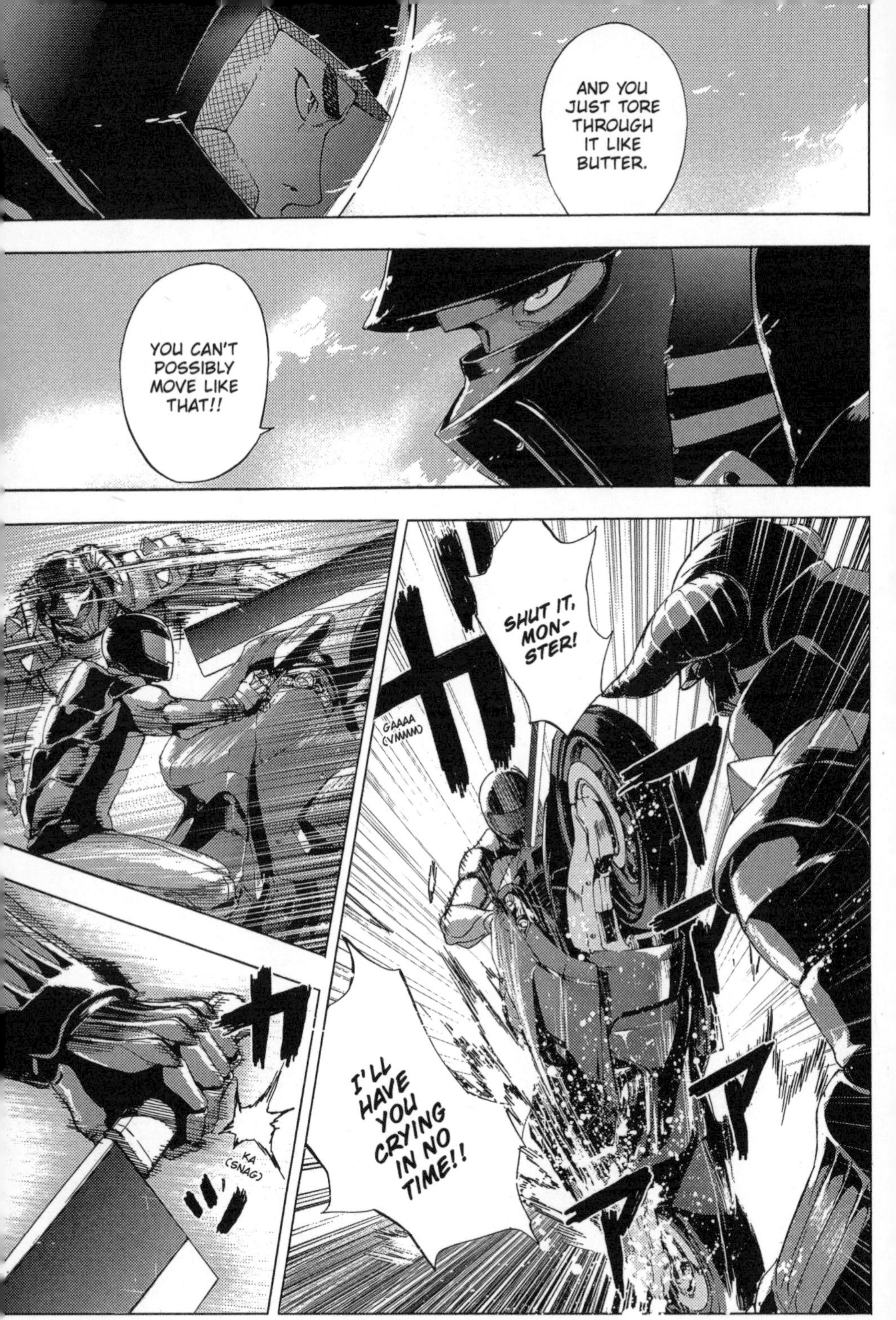
AND YOU JUST TORE THROUGH IT LIKE BUTTER.
YOU CAN'T POSSIBLY MOVE LIKE THAT!!
SHUT IT, MON-STER!
GAAAA (VMMMM)
I'LL HAVE YOU CRYING IN NO TIME!!
KA (SNAG)

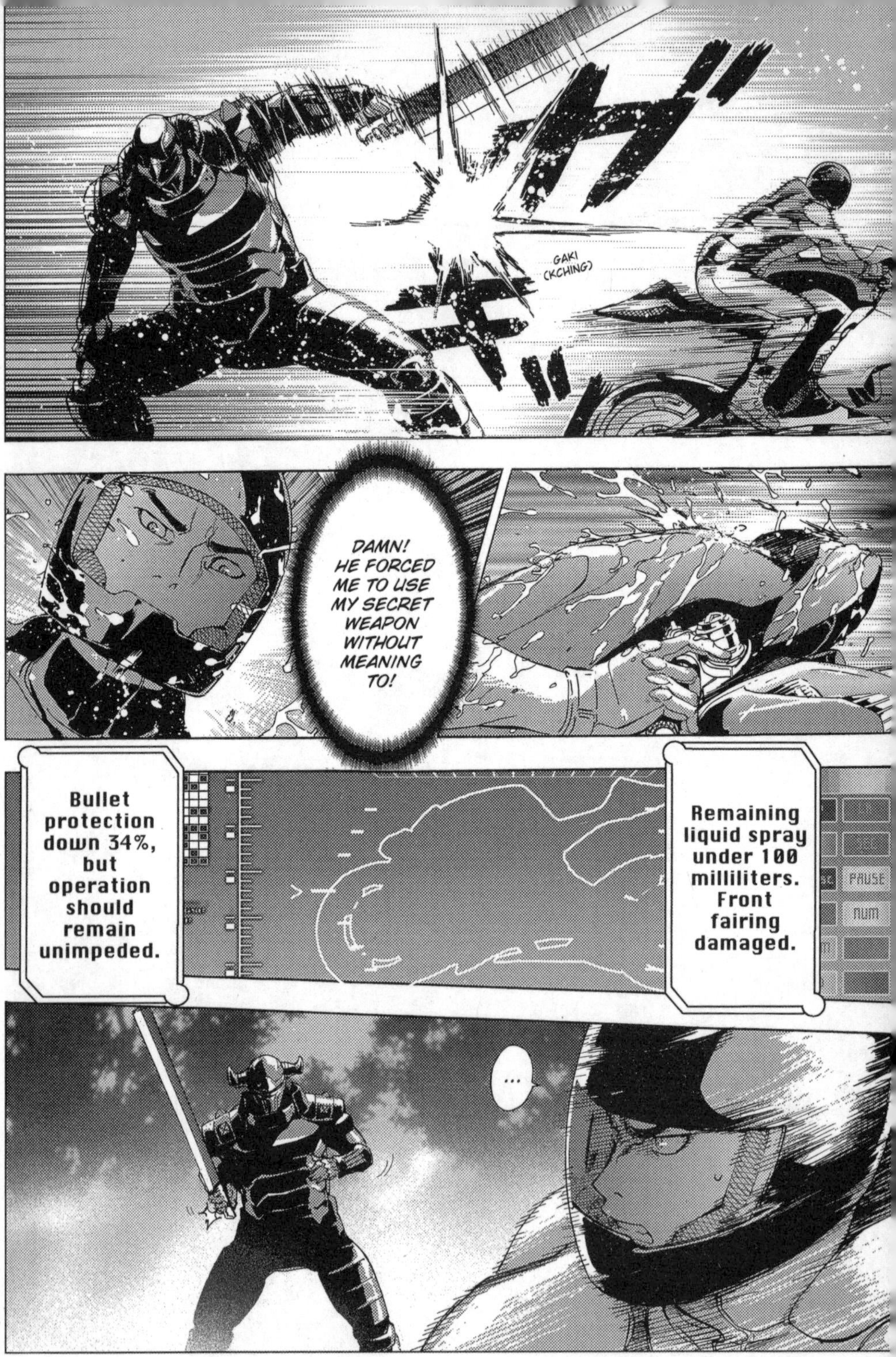
GAKI (KCHING)
DAMN! HE FORCED ME TO USE MY SECRET WEAPON WITHOUT MEANING TO!
Remaining liquid spray under 100 milliliters. Front fairing damaged.
Bullet protection down 34%, but operation should remain unimpeded.
PAUSE
NUM
...

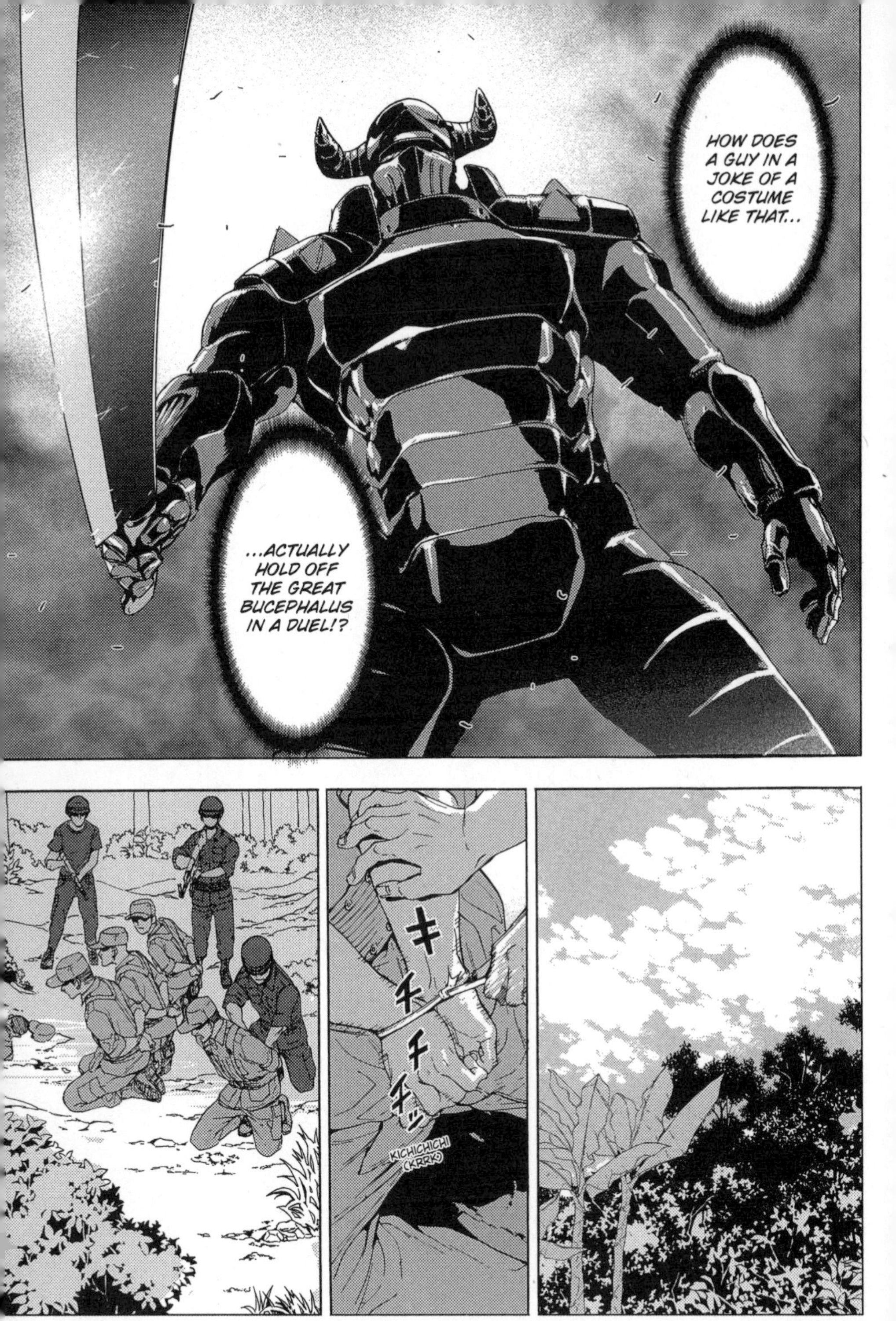
HOW DOES A GUY IN A JOKE OF A COSTUME LIKE THAT...
...ACTUALLY HOLD OFF THE GREAT BUCEPHALUS IN A DUEL!?
キチチチッ
KICHICHICHI (KRRK)

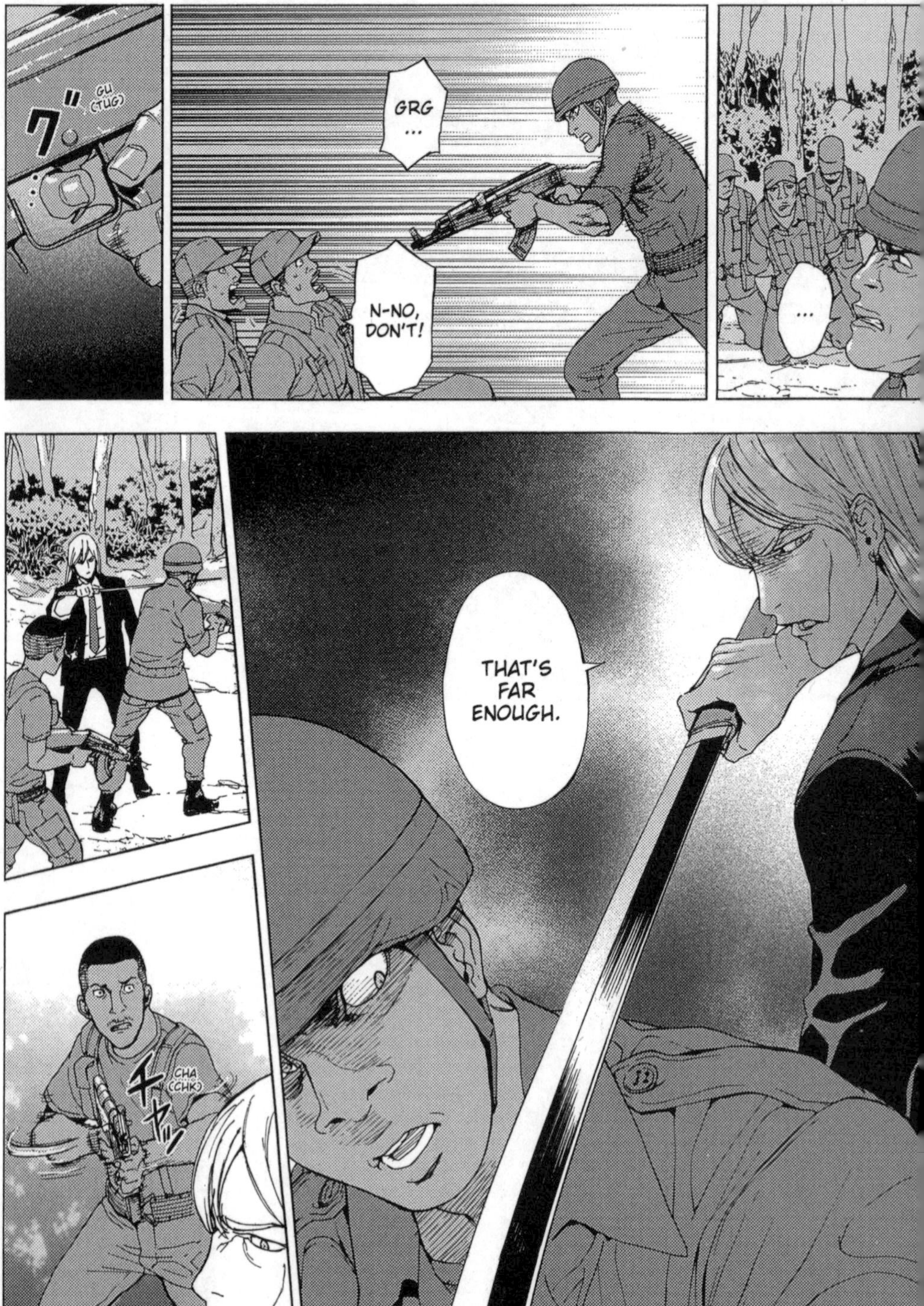
...
GRG ...
N-NO, DON'T!
GU (TUG)
THAT'S FAR ENOUGH.
CHA (CHK)

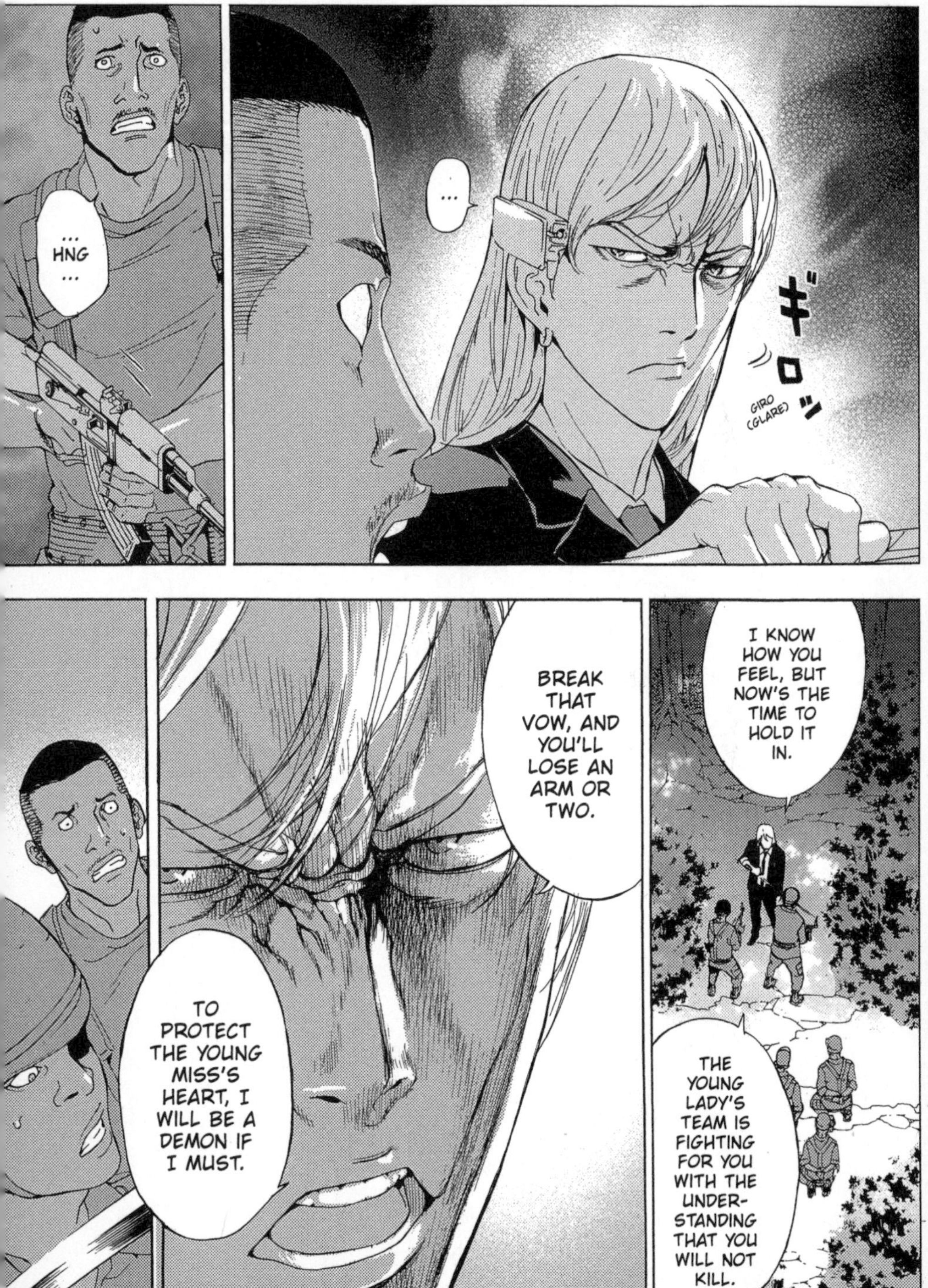
...
ギロッ
GIRO (GLARE)
... HNG ...
I KNOW HOW YOU FEEL, BUT NOW'S THE TIME TO HOLD IT IN.
THE YOUNG LADY'S TEAM IS FIGHTING FOR YOU WITH THE UNDER-STANDING THAT YOU WILL NOT KILL.
BREAK THAT VOW, AND YOU'LL LOSE AN ARM OR TWO.
TO PROTECT THE YOUNG MISS'S HEART, I WILL BE A DEMON IF I MUST.

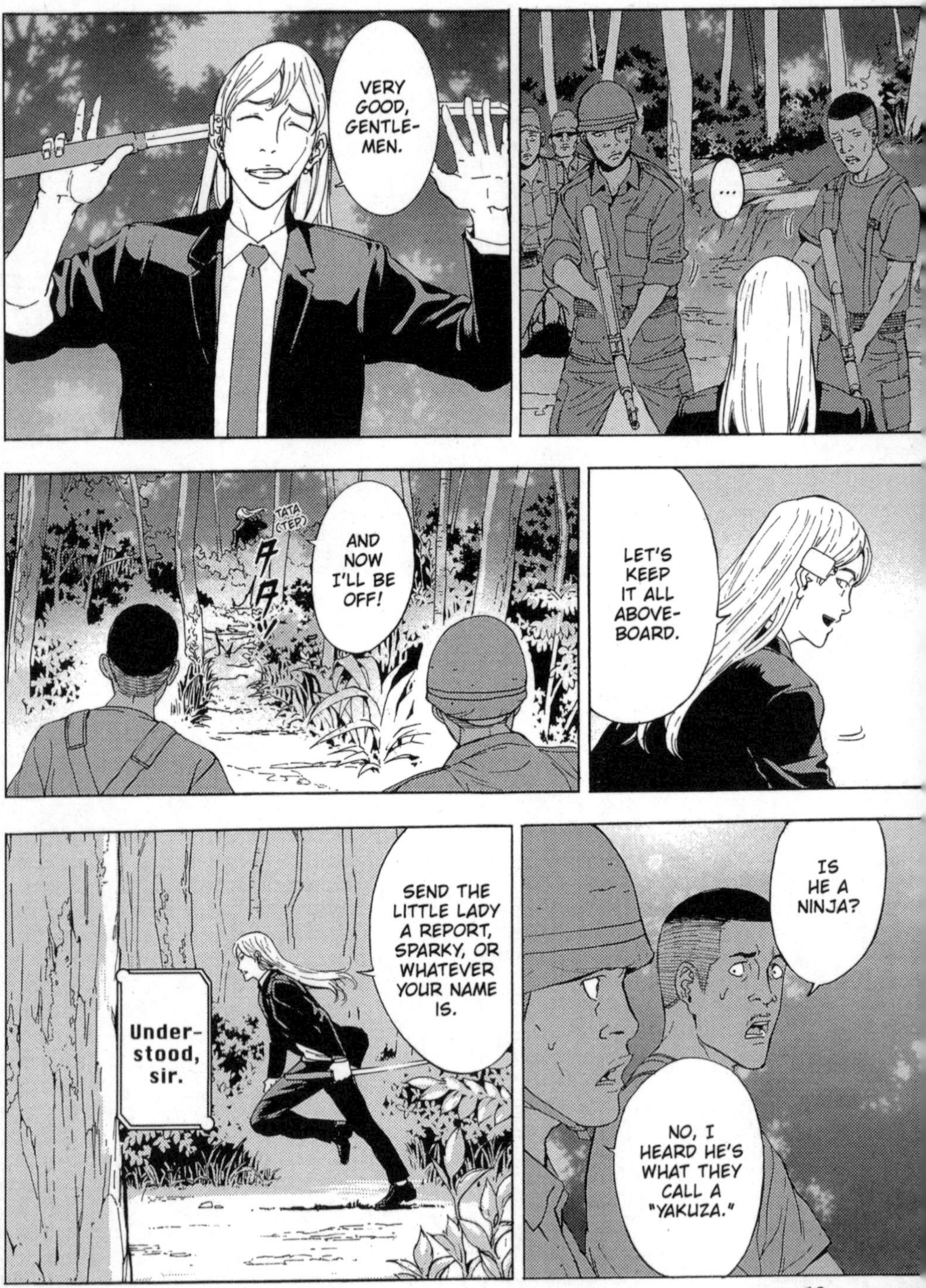
...
VERY GOOD, GENTLE-MEN.
LET'S KEEP IT ALL ABOVE-BOARD.
TATA (TEP)
AND NOW I'LL BE OFF!
IS HE A NINJA?
NO, I HEARD HE'S WHAT THEY CALL A "YAKUZA."
SEND THE LITTLE LADY A REPORT, SPARKY, OR WHATEVER YOUR NAME IS.
Under-stood, sir.

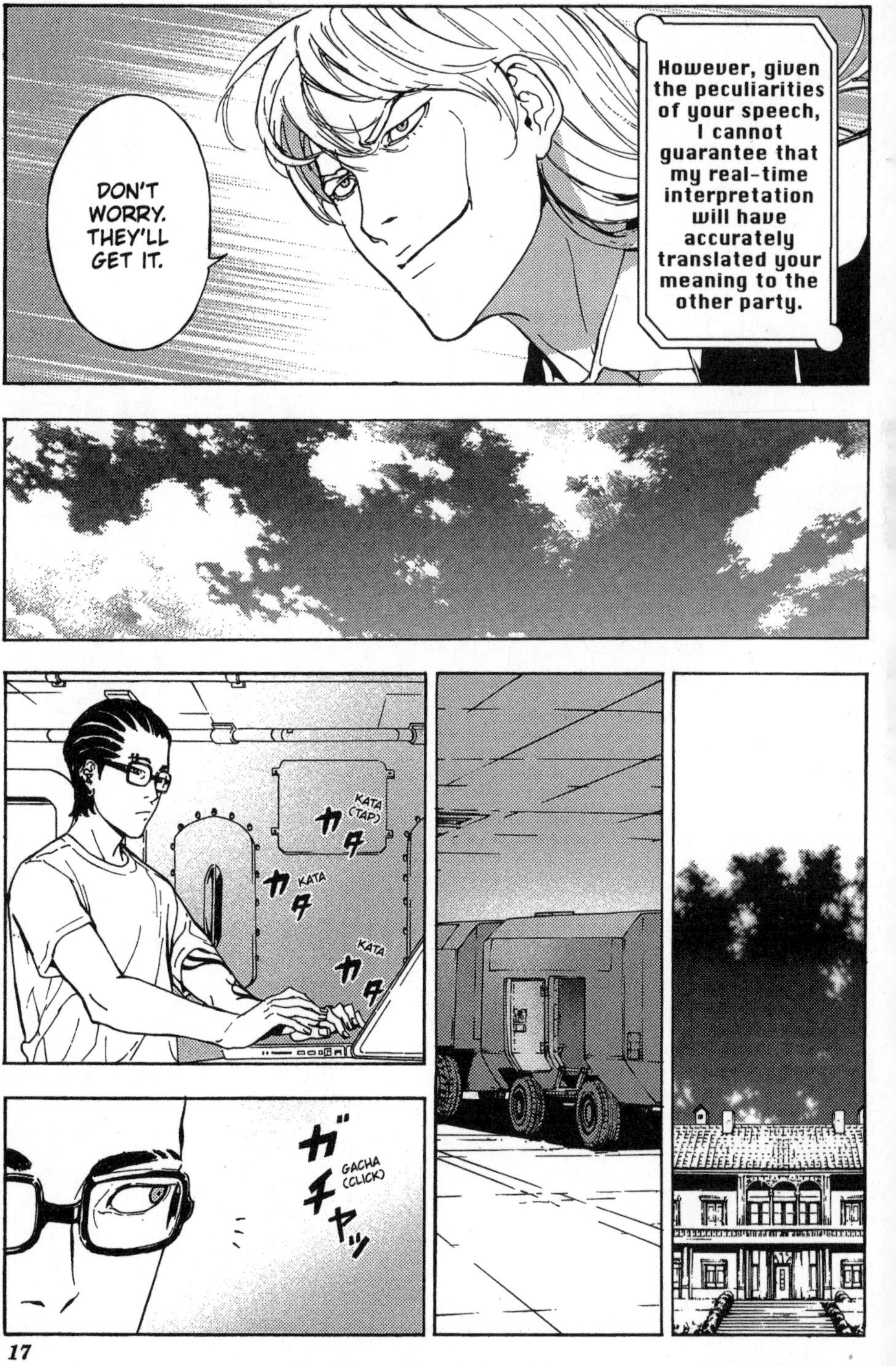
However, given the peculiarities of your speech, I cannot guarantee that my real-time interpretation will have accurately translated your meaning to the other party.
DON'T WORRY. THEY'LL GET IT.
カタ
KATA (TAP)
カタ
KATA
カタ
KATA
ガチャッ
GACHA (CLICK)

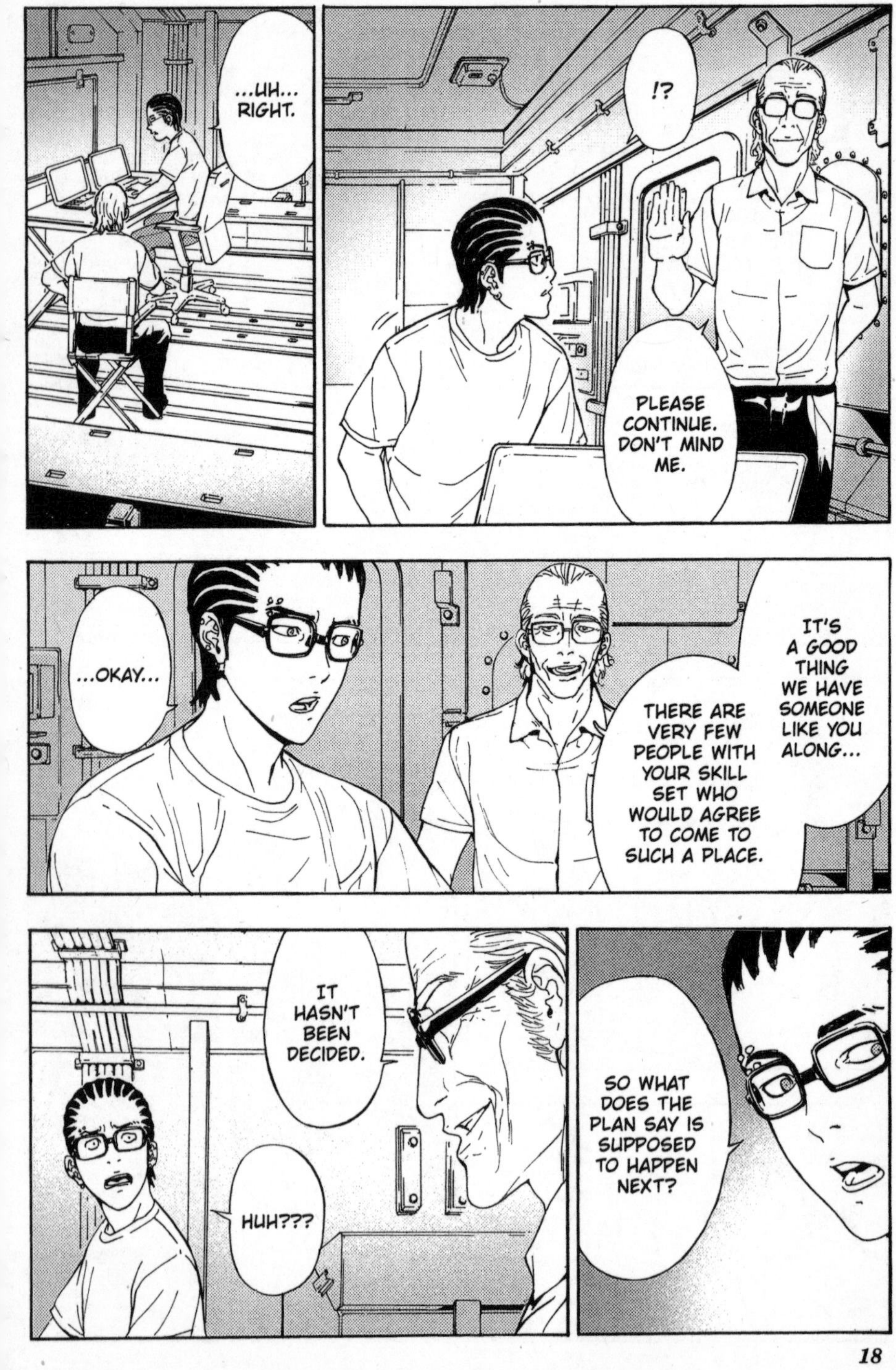
!?
PLEASE CONTINUE. DON'T MIND ME.
...UH... RIGHT.
IT'S A GOOD THING WE HAVE SOMEONE LIKE YOU ALONG...
THERE ARE VERY FEW PEOPLE WITH YOUR SKILL SET WHO WOULD AGREE TO COME TO SUCH A PLACE.
...OKAY...
SO WHAT DOES THE PLAN SAY IS SUPPOSED TO HAPPEN NEXT?
IT HASN'T BEEN DECIDED.
HUH???

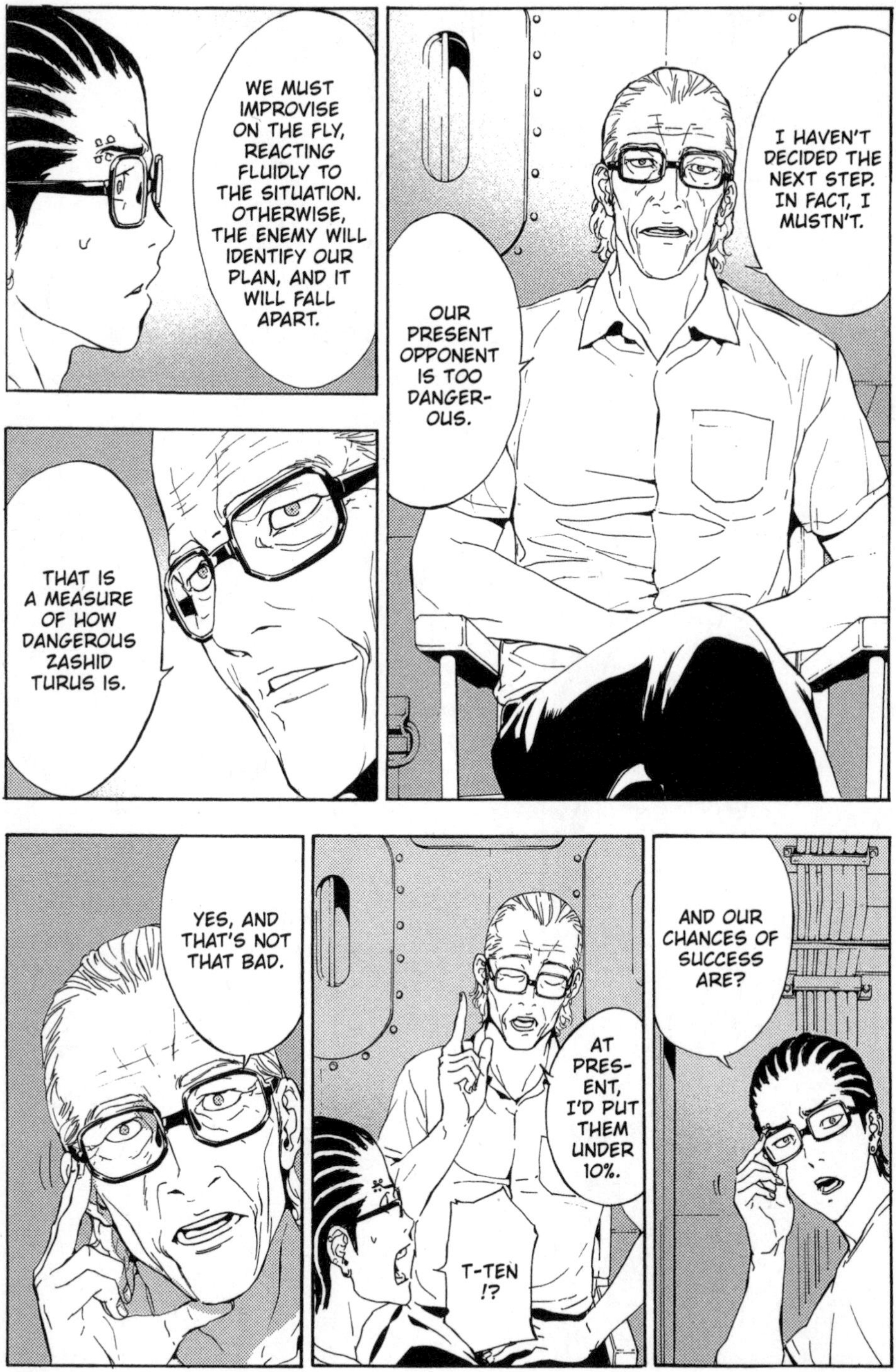
I HAVEN'T DECIDED THE NEXT STEP. IN FACT, I MUSTN'T.
OUR PRESENT OPPONENT IS TOO DANGER-OUS.
WE MUST IMPROVISE ON THE FLY, REACTING FLUIDLY TO THE SITUATION. OTHERWISE, THE ENEMY WILL IDENTIFY OUR PLAN, AND IT WILL FALL APART.
THAT IS A MEASURE OF HOW DANGEROUS ZASHID TURUS IS.
AND OUR CHANCES OF SUCCESS ARE?
AT PRES-ENT, I'D PUT THEM UNDER 10%.
T-TEN !?
YES, AND THAT'S NOT THAT BAD.

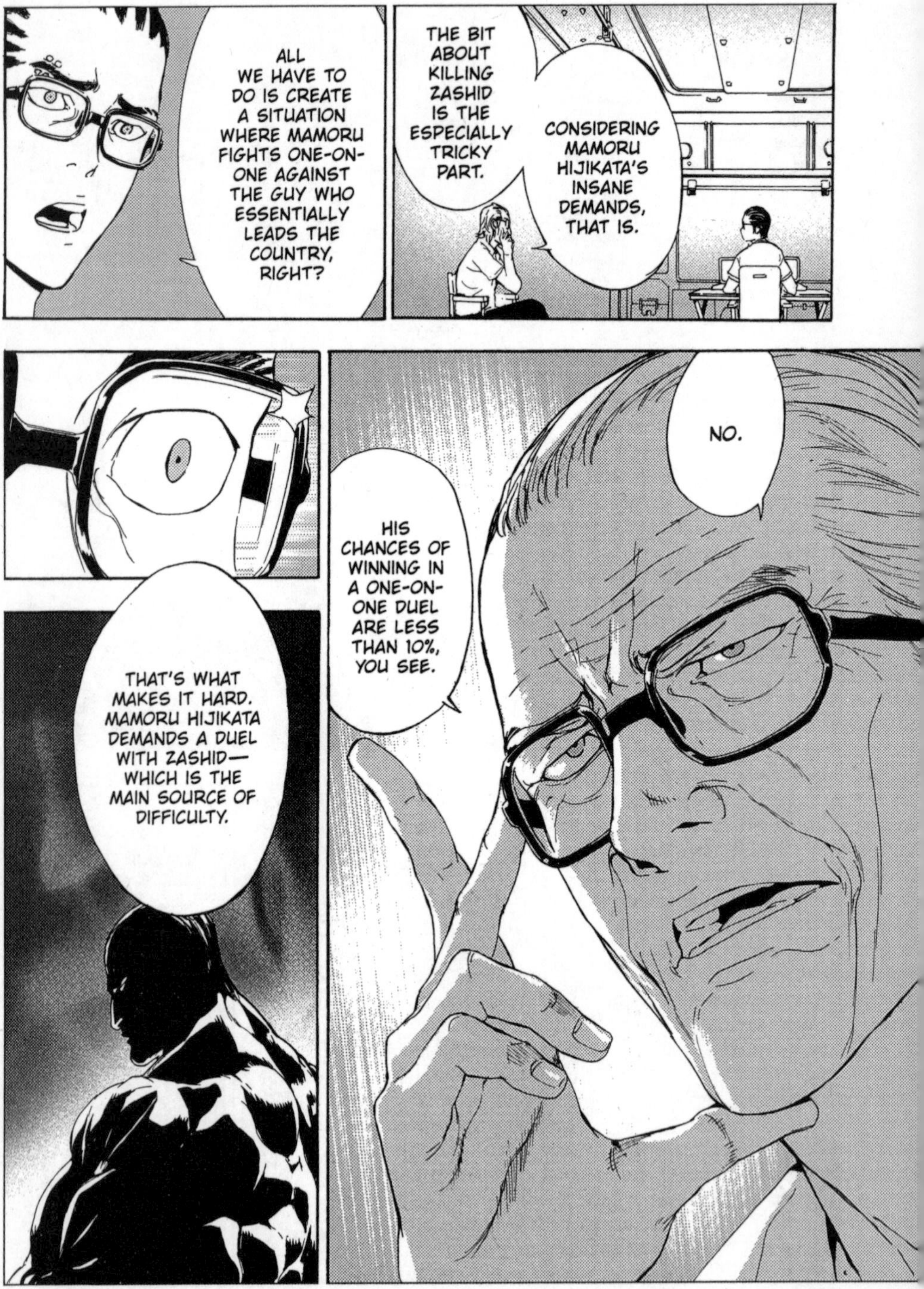
THE BIT ABOUT KILLING ZASHID IS THE ESPECIALLY TRICKY PART.
CONSIDERING MAMORU HIJIKATA'S INSANE DEMANDS, THAT IS.
ALL WE HAVE TO DO IS CREATE A SITUATION WHERE MAMORU FIGHTS ONE-ON-ONE AGAINST THE GUY WHO ESSENTIALLY LEADS THE COUNTRY, RIGHT?
NO.
HIS CHANCES OF WINNING IN A ONE-ON-ONE DUEL ARE LESS THAN 10%, YOU SEE.
THAT'S WHAT MAKES IT HARD. MAMORU HIJIKATA DEMANDS A DUEL WITH ZASHID—WHICH IS THE MAIN SOURCE OF DIFFICULTY.

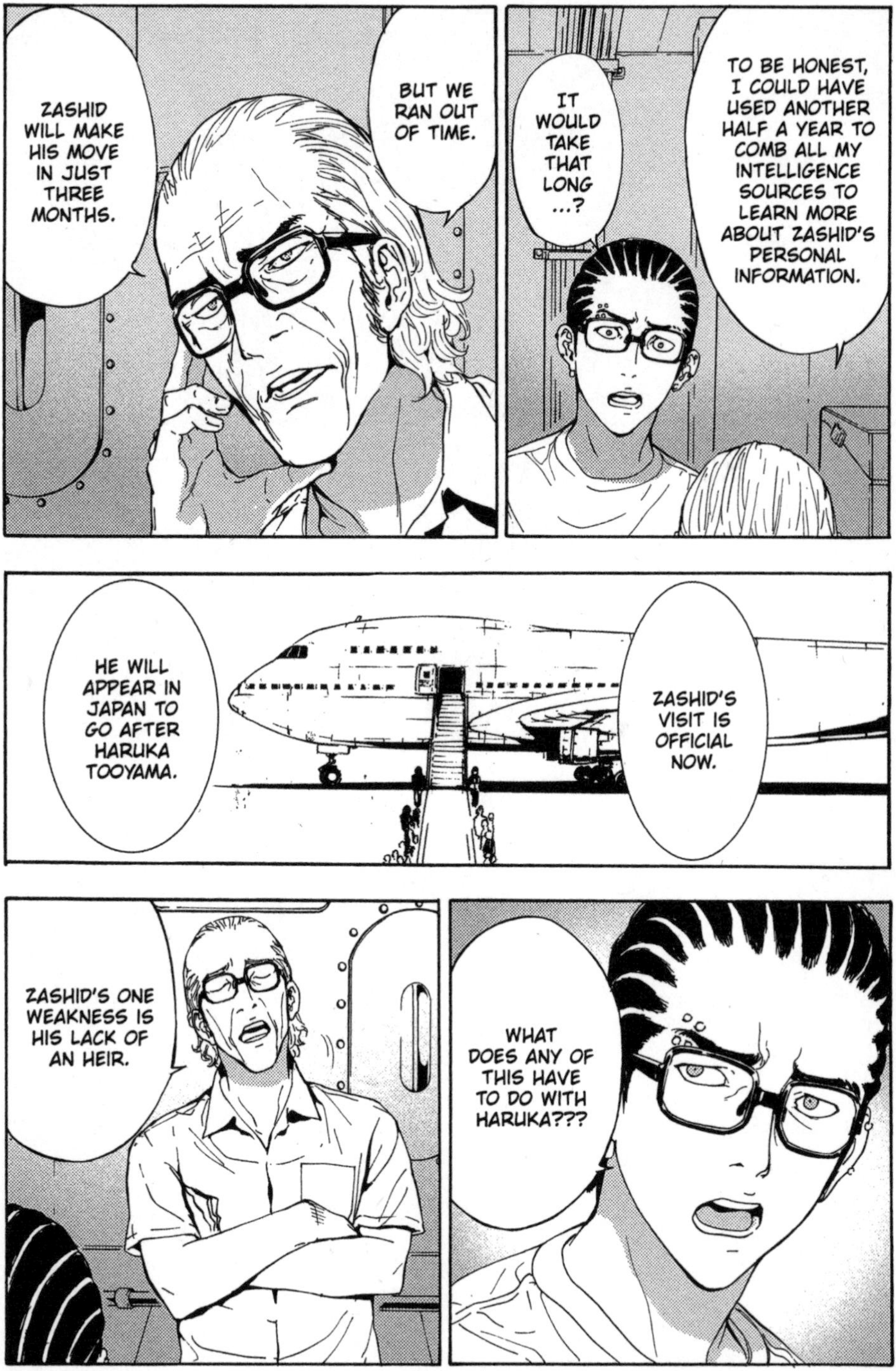
TO BE HONEST, I COULD HAVE USED ANOTHER HALF A YEAR TO COMB ALL MY INTELLIGENCE SOURCES TO LEARN MORE ABOUT ZASHID'S PERSONAL INFORMATION.
IT WOULD TAKE THAT LONG ...?
BUT WE RAN OUT OF TIME.
ZASHID WILL MAKE HIS MOVE IN JUST THREE MONTHS.
ZASHID'S VISIT IS OFFICIAL NOW.
HE WILL APPEAR IN JAPAN TO GO AFTER HARUKA TOOYAMA.
WHAT DOES ANY OF THIS HAVE TO DO WITH HARUKA???
ZASHID'S ONE WEAKNESS IS HIS LACK OF AN HEIR.

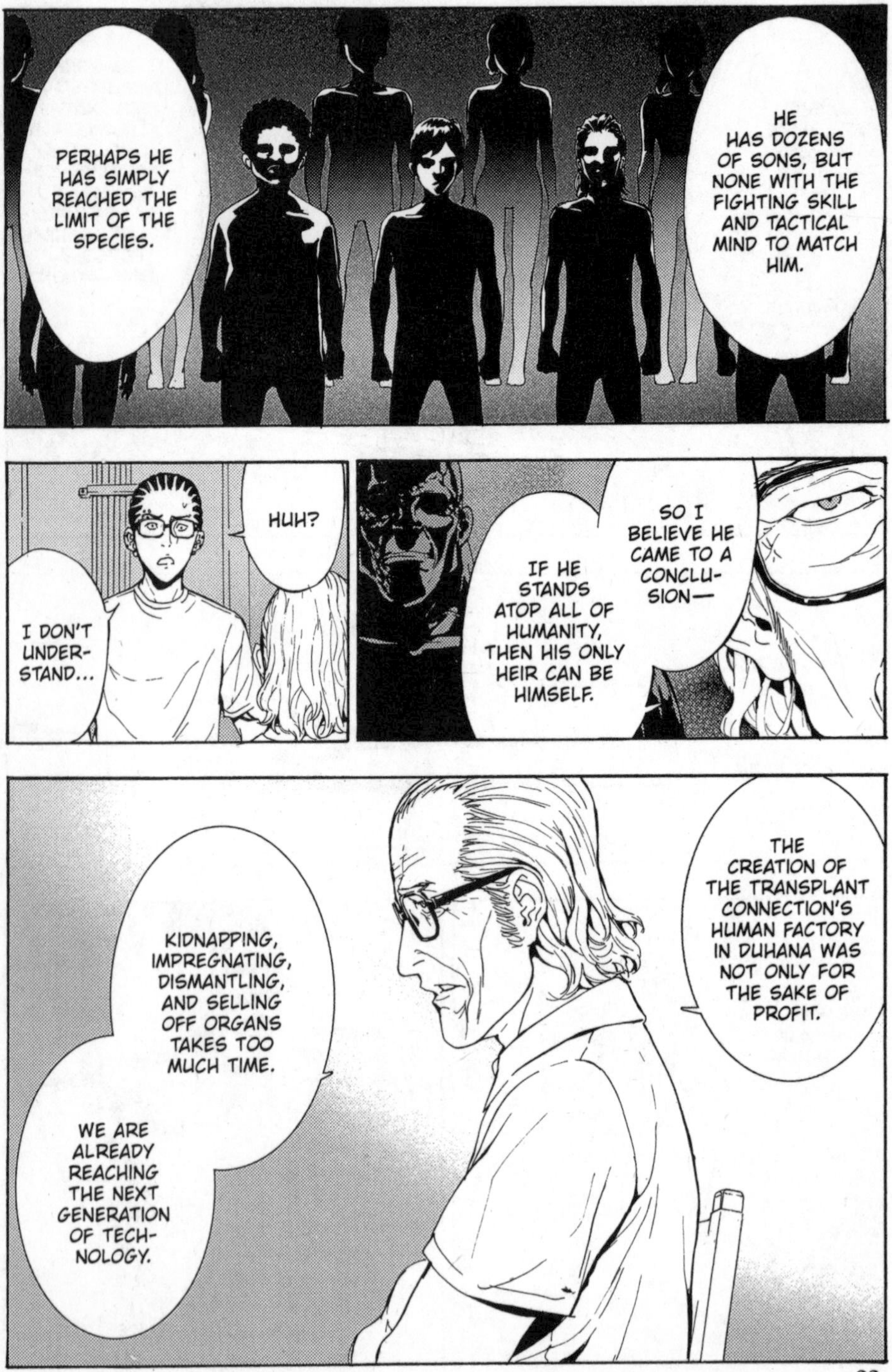
HE HAS DOZENS OF SONS, BUT NONE WITH THE FIGHTING SKILL AND TACTICAL MIND TO MATCH HIM.
PERHAPS HE HAS SIMPLY REACHED THE LIMIT OF THE SPECIES.
SO I BELIEVE HE CAME TO A CONCLU-SION—
IF HE STANDS ATOP ALL OF HUMANITY, THEN HIS ONLY HEIR CAN BE HIMSELF.
HUH?
I DON'T UNDER-STAND...
THE CREATION OF THE TRANSPLANT CONNECTION'S HUMAN FACTORY IN DUHANA WAS NOT ONLY FOR THE SAKE OF PROFIT.
KIDNAPPING, IMPREGNATING, DISMANTLING, AND SELLING OFF ORGANS TAKES TOO MUCH TIME.
WE ARE ALREADY REACHING THE NEXT GENERATION OF TECH-NOLOGY.

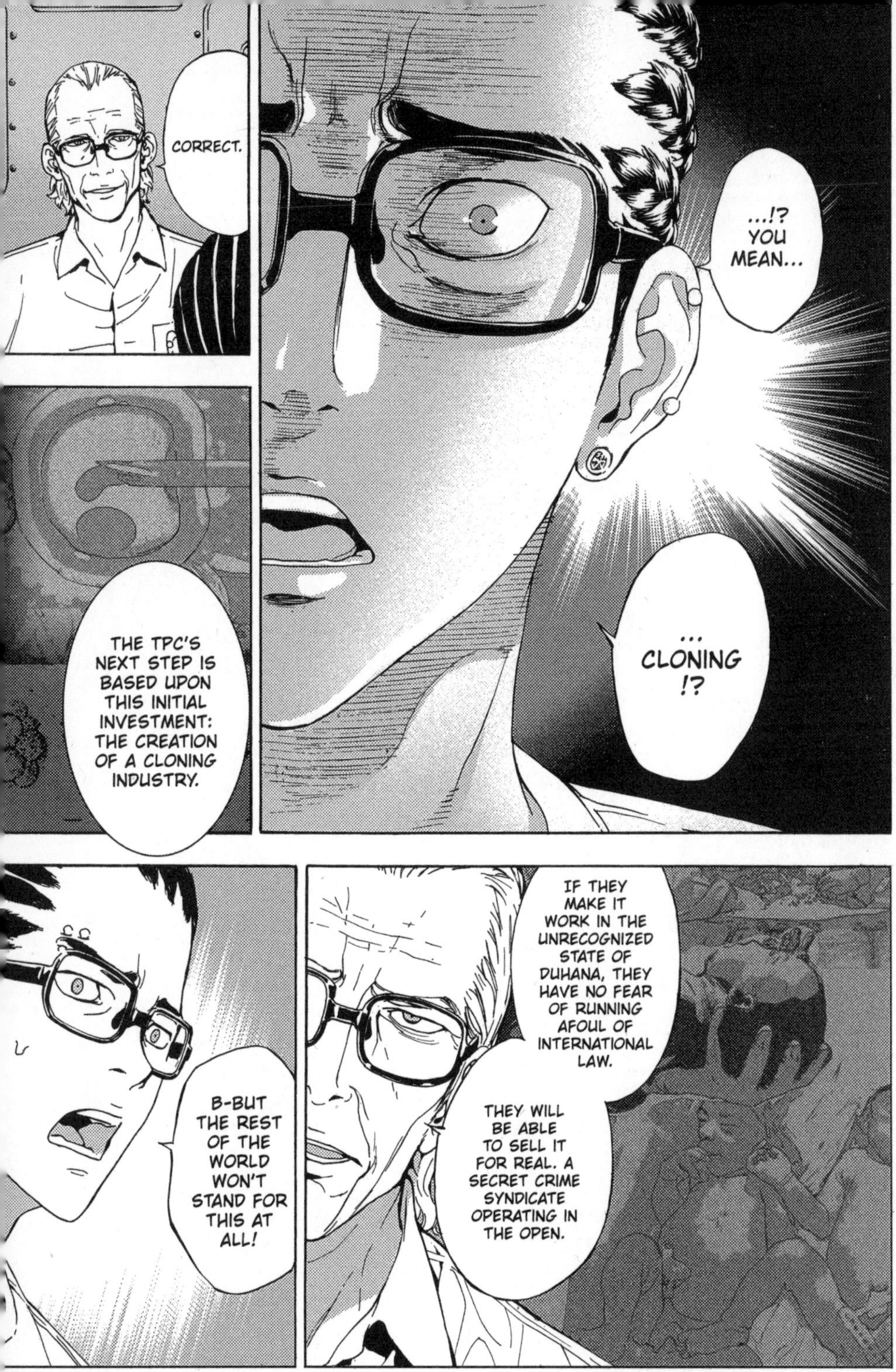
...!? YOU MEAN...
...CLONING!?
CORRECT.
THE TPC'S NEXT STEP IS BASED UPON THIS INITIAL INVESTMENT: THE CREATION OF A CLONING INDUSTRY.
IF THEY MAKE IT WORK IN THE UNRECOGNIZED STATE OF DUHANA, THEY HAVE NO FEAR OF RUNNING AFOUL OF INTERNATIONAL LAW.
THEY WILL BE ABLE TO SELL IT FOR REAL. A SECRET CRIME SYNDICATE OPERATING IN THE OPEN.
B-BUT THE REST OF THE WORLD WON'T STAND FOR THIS AT ALL!

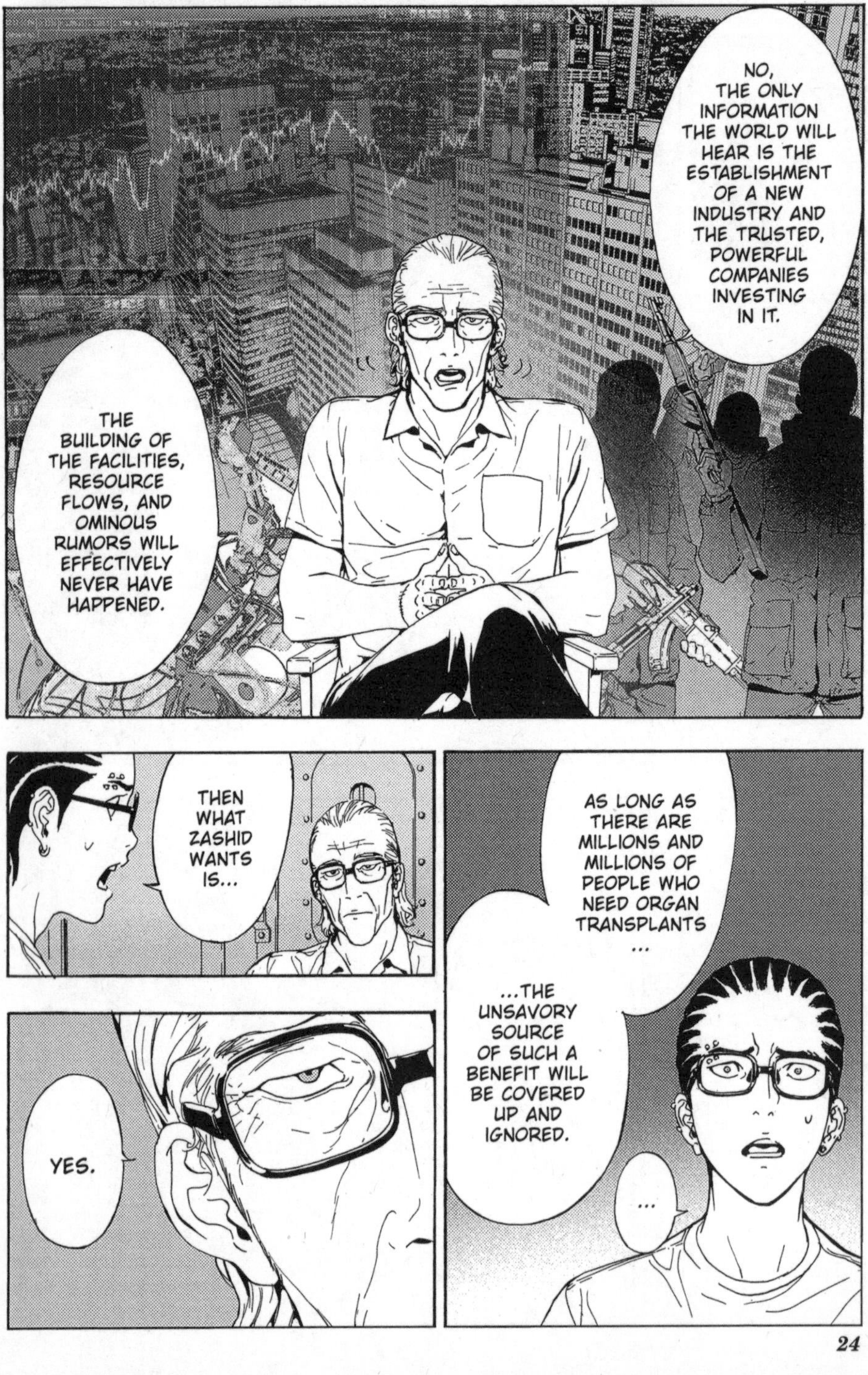
NO, THE ONLY INFORMATION THE WORLD WILL HEAR IS THE ESTABLISHMENT OF A NEW INDUSTRY AND THE TRUSTED, POWERFUL COMPANIES INVESTING IN IT.
THE BUILDING OF THE FACILITIES, RESOURCE FLOWS, AND OMINOUS RUMORS WILL EFFECTIVELY NEVER HAVE HAPPENED.
AS LONG AS THERE ARE MILLIONS AND MILLIONS OF PEOPLE WHO NEED ORGAN TRANSPLANTS ...
...THE UNSAVORY SOURCE OF SUCH A BENEFIT WILL BE COVERED UP AND IGNORED.
...
THEN WHAT ZASHID WANTS IS...
YES.

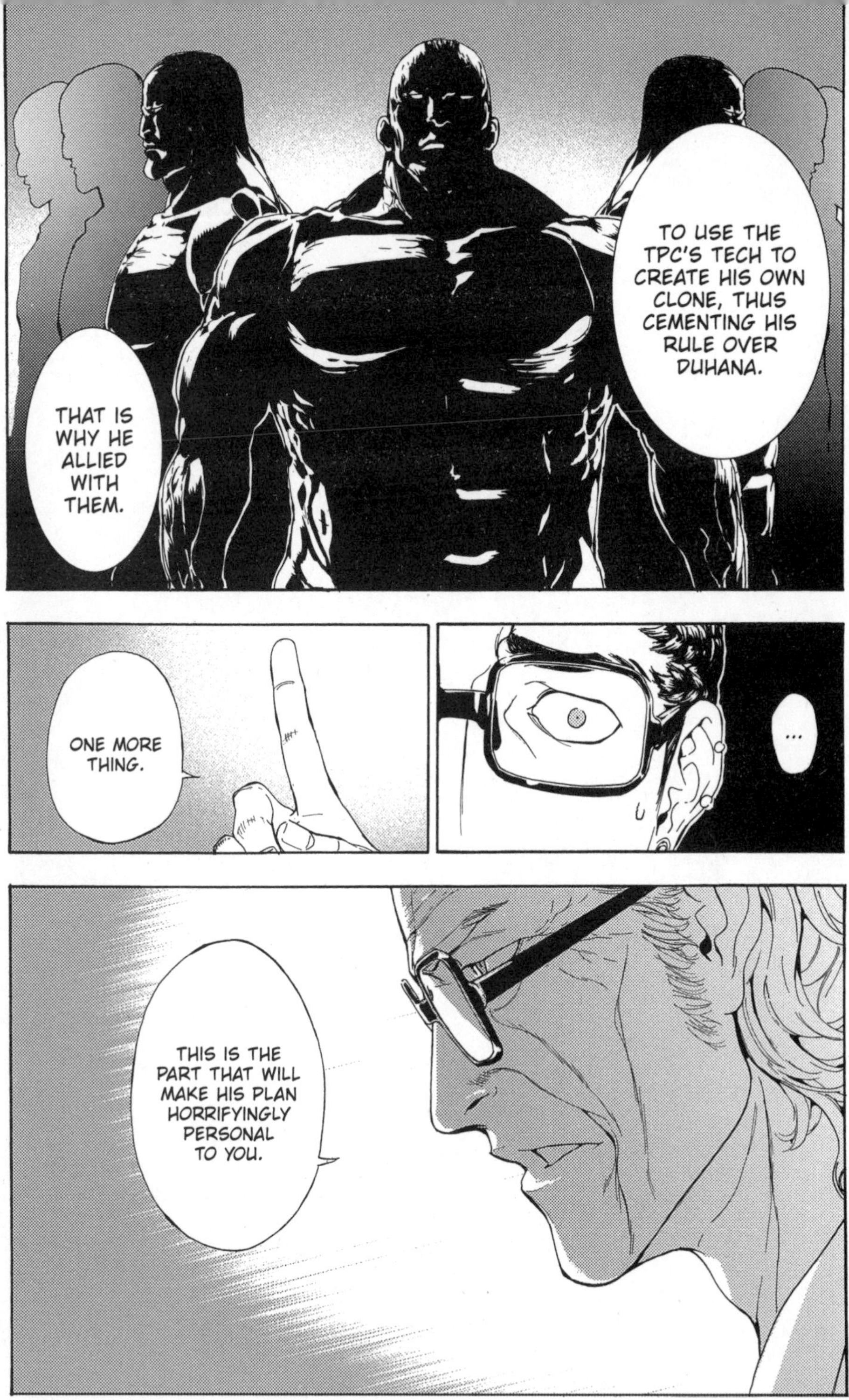
TO USE THE TPC'S TECH TO CREATE HIS OWN CLONE, THUS CEMENTING HIS RULE OVER DUHANA.
THAT IS WHY HE ALLIED WITH THEM.
...
ONE MORE THING.
THIS IS THE PART THAT WILL MAKE HIS PLAN HORRIFYINGLY PERSONAL TO YOU.

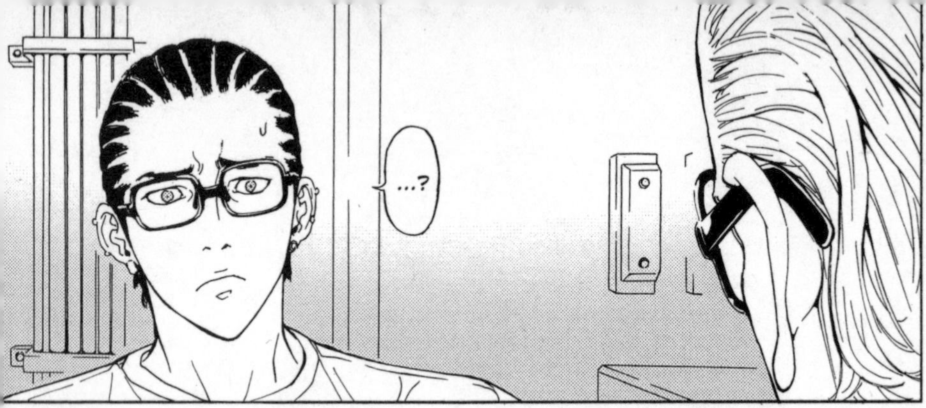
...?
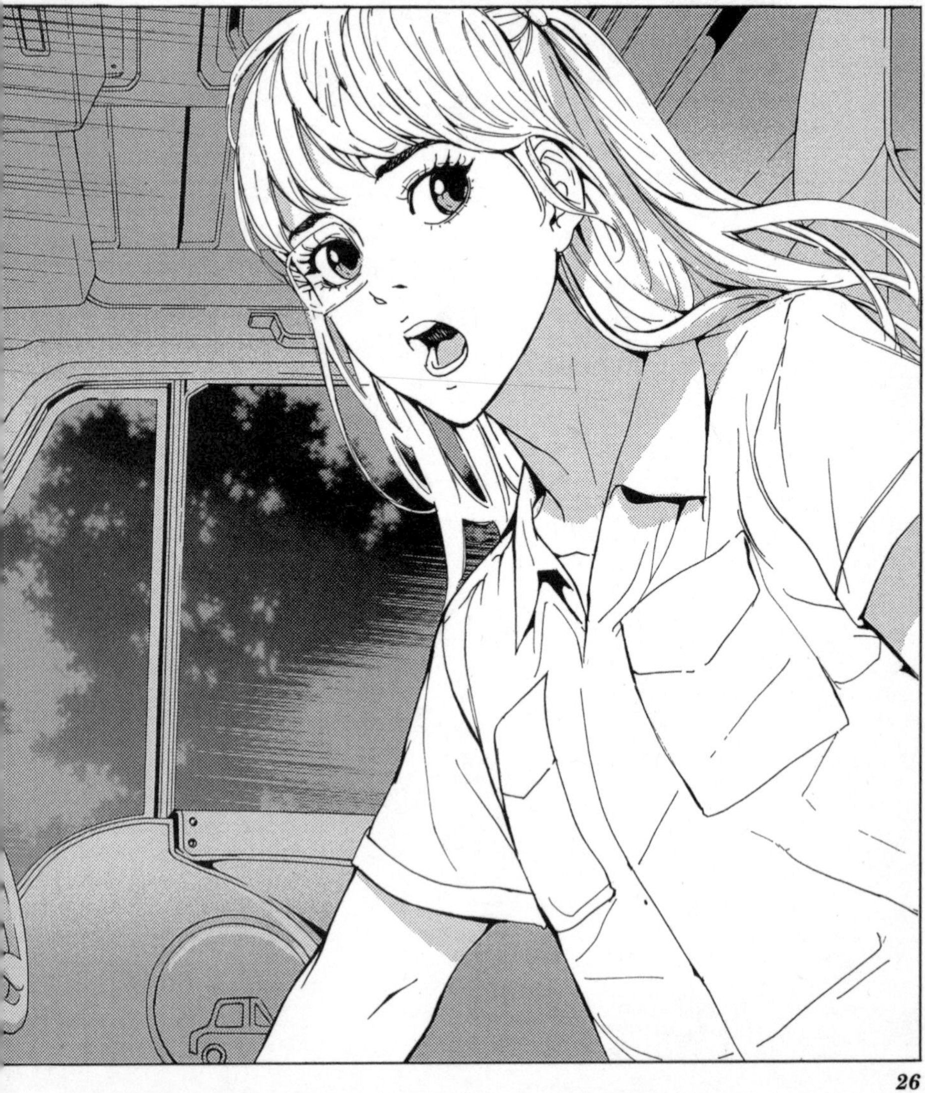

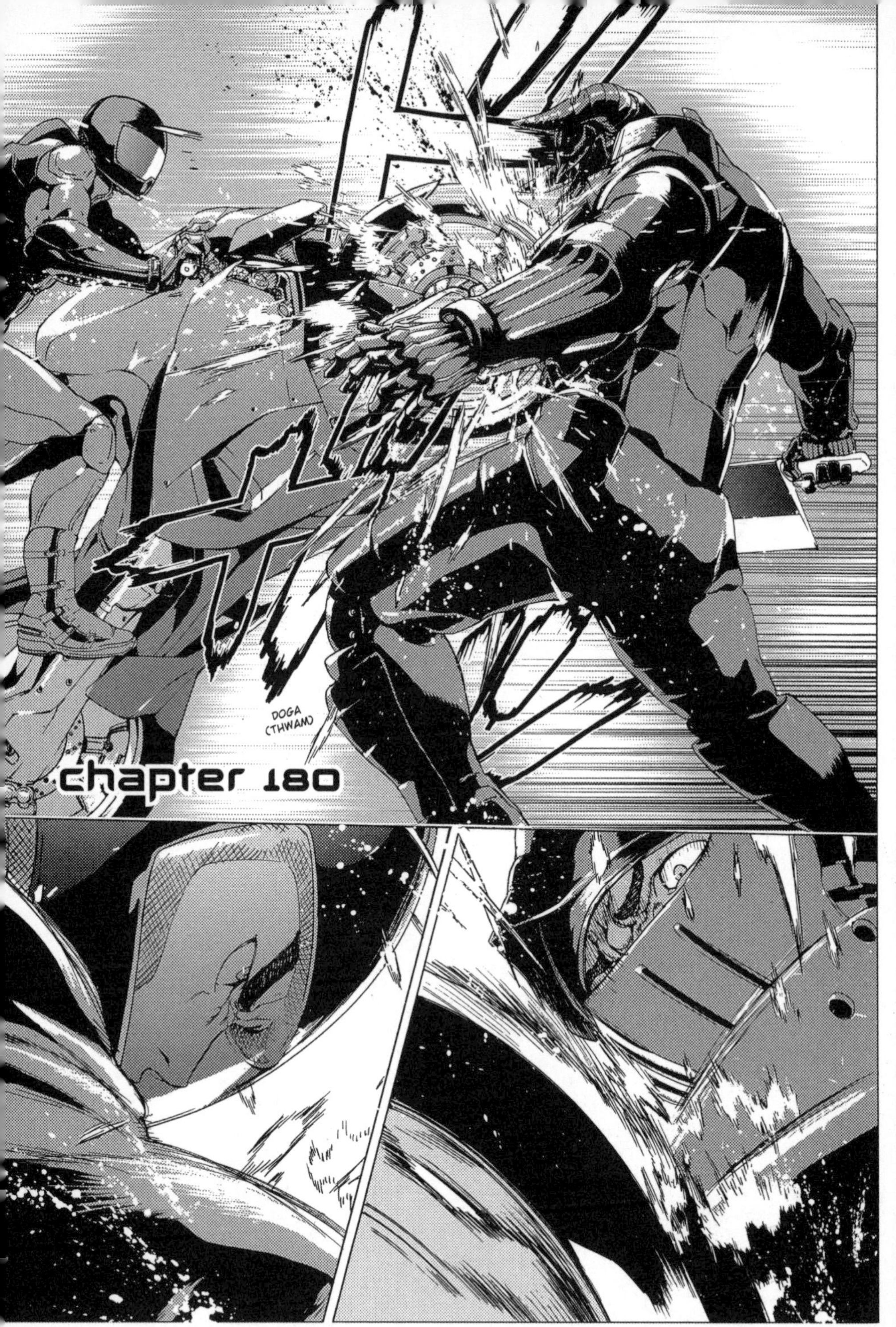
chapter 180
DOGA
(THWAM)

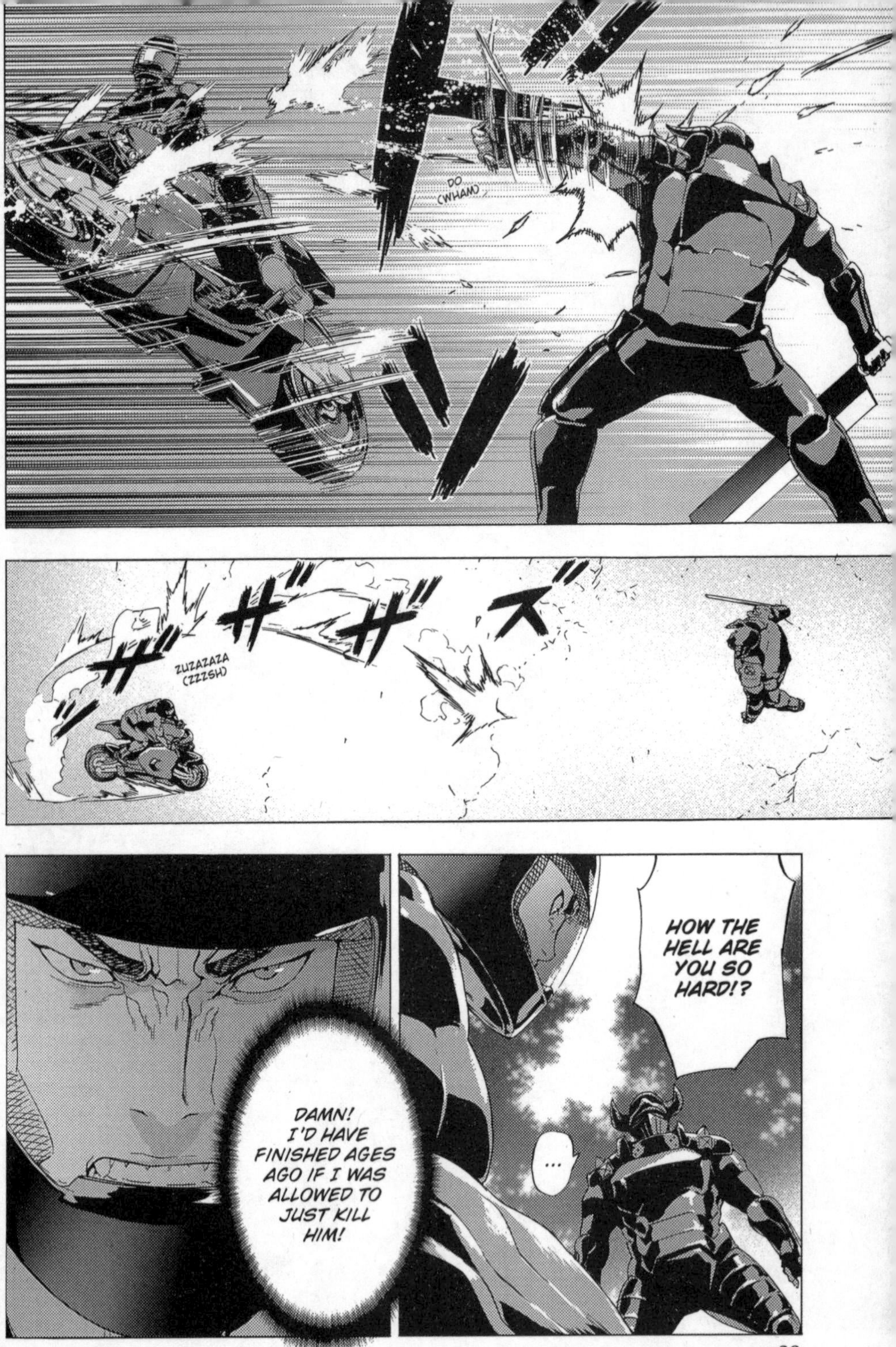
DO (WHAM)
ZUZAZAZA (ZZZSH)
HOW THE HELL ARE YOU SO HARD!?
...
DAMN! I'D HAVE FINISHED AGES AGO IF I WAS ALLOWED TO JUST KILL HIM!

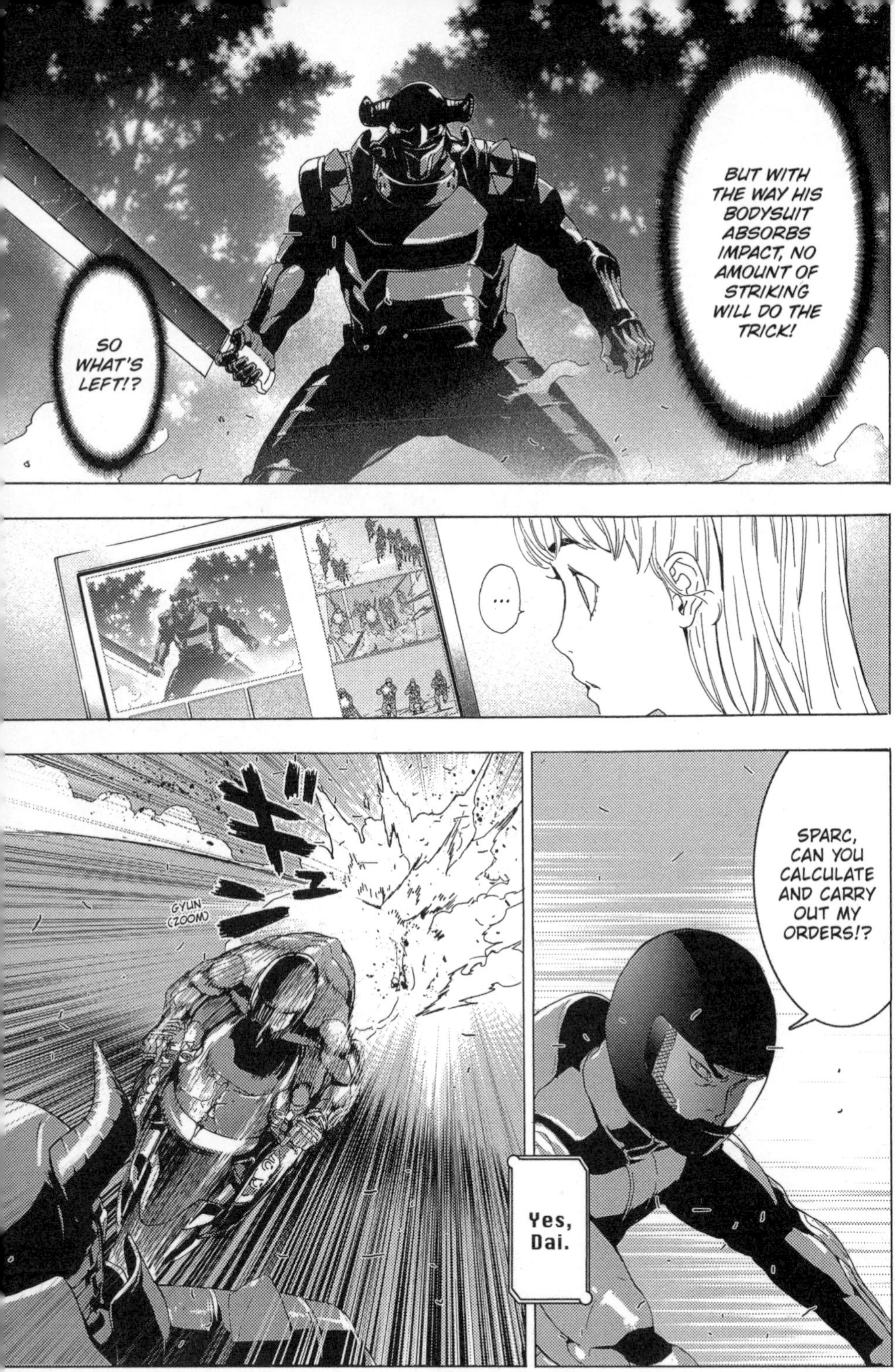
BUT WITH THE WAY HIS BODYSUIT ABSORBS IMPACT, NO AMOUNT OF STRIKING WILL DO THE TRICK!
SO WHAT'S LEFT!?
...
SPARC, CAN YOU CALCULATE AND CARRY OUT MY ORDERS!?
Yes, Dai.
GYUN (ZOOM)

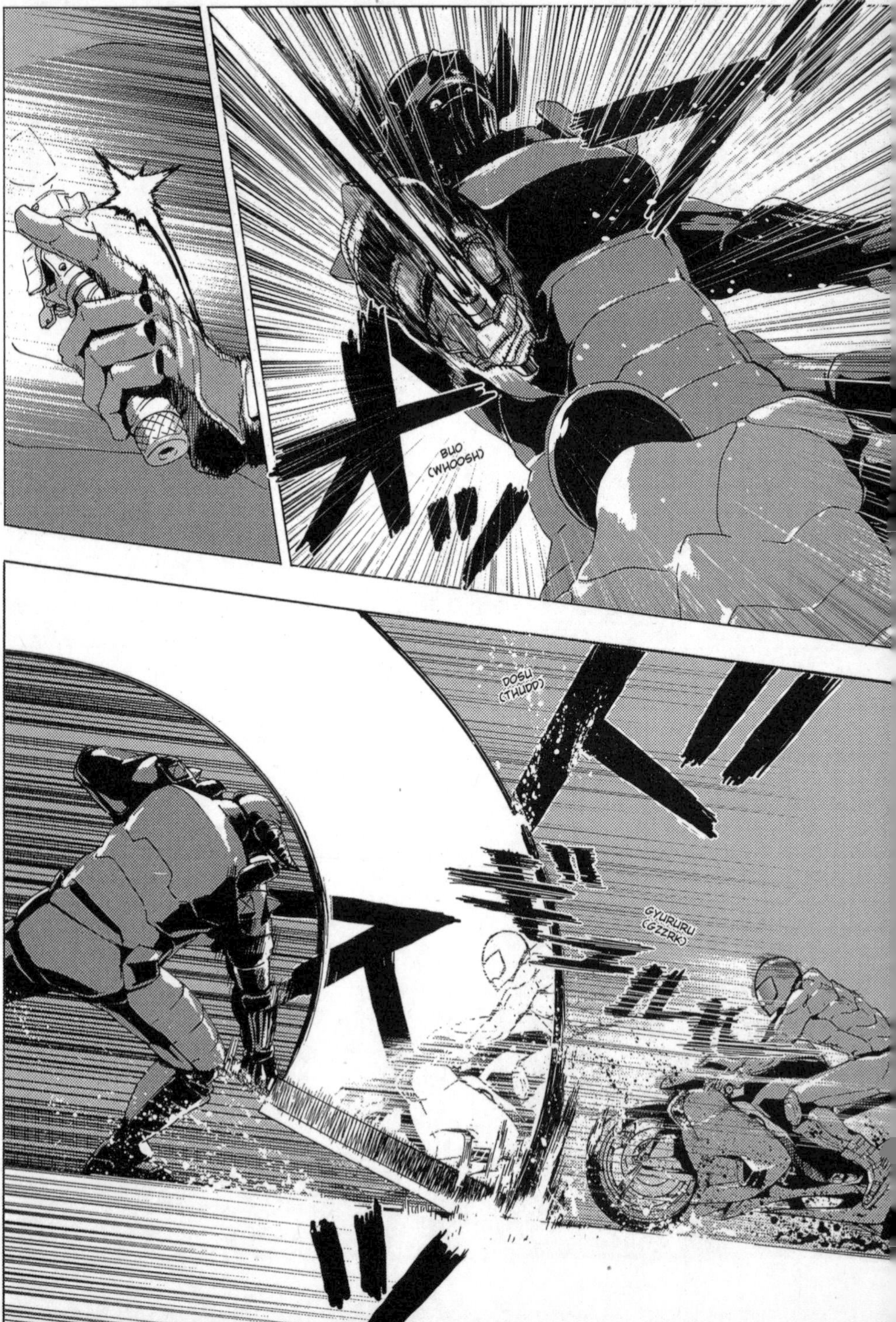
BUO
(WHOOSH)
DOSU
(THUDD)
GYURURU
(GZZRK)

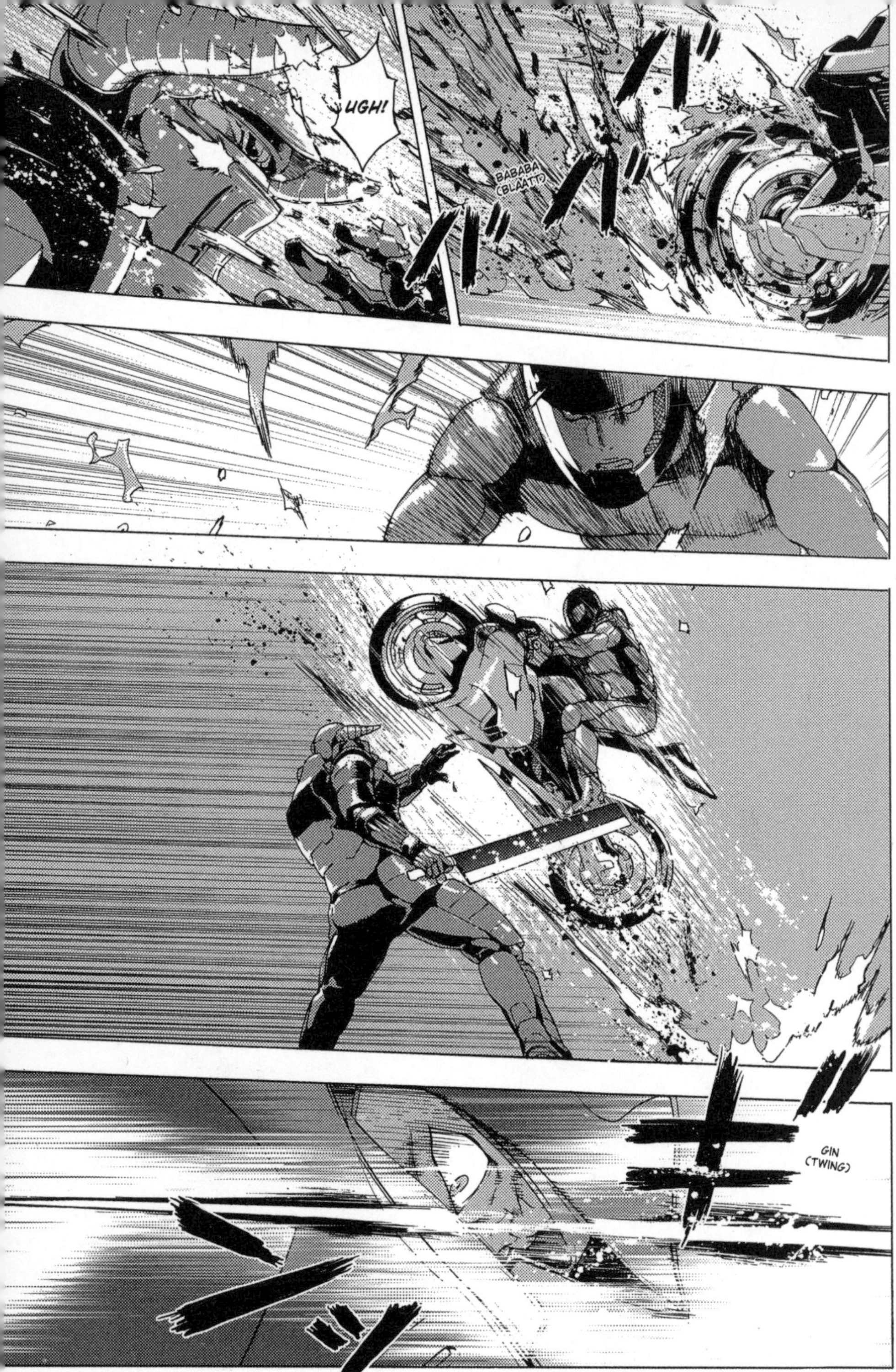
BABABA
(BLAATT)
UGH!
GIN
(TWING)

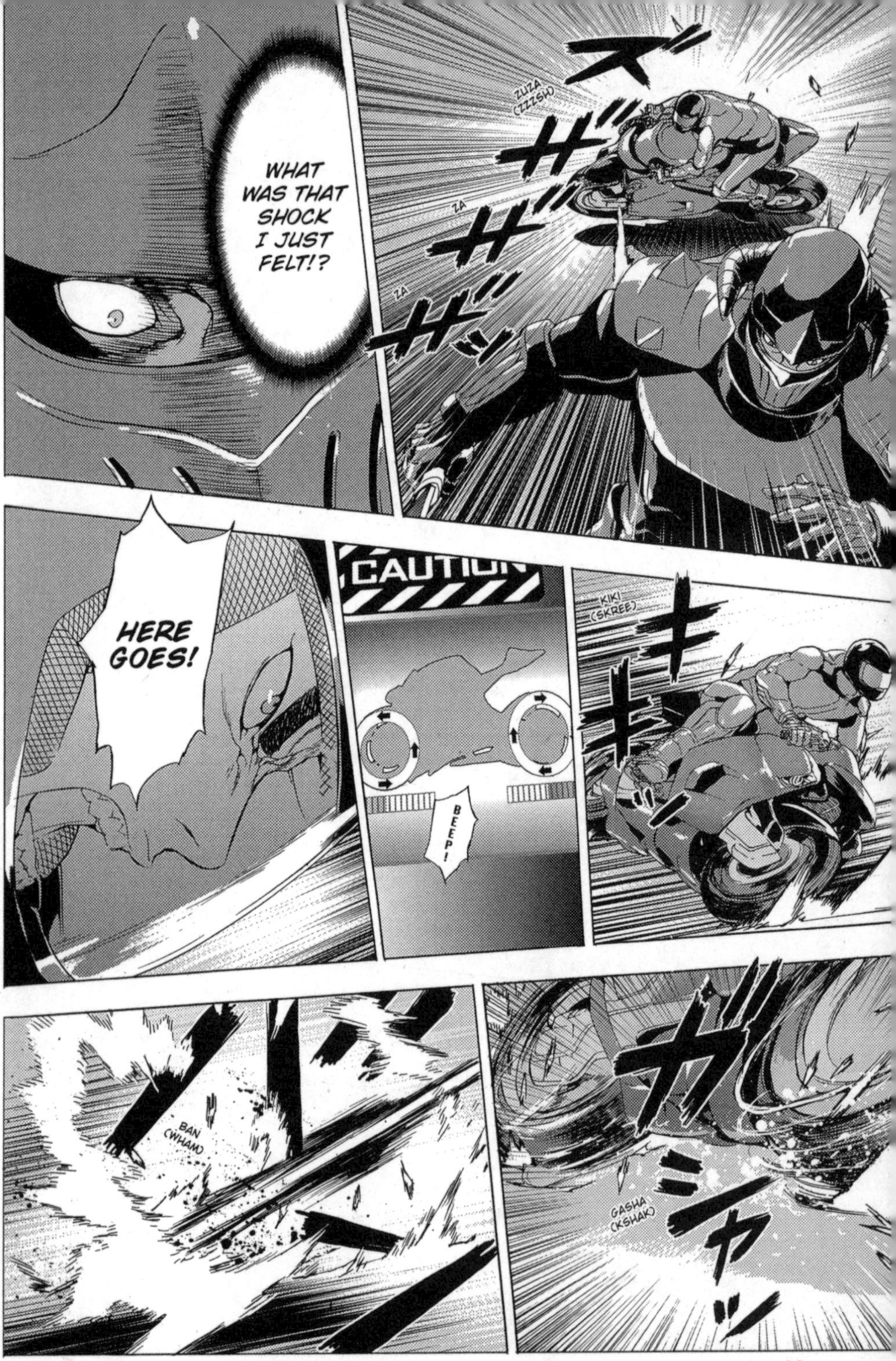
ZUZA (ZZZSH)
ZA
ZA
WHAT WAS THAT SHOCK I JUST FELT!?
KIKI (SKREE)
BEEP!
CAUTION
HERE GOES!
GASHA (KSHAK)
BAN (WHAM)

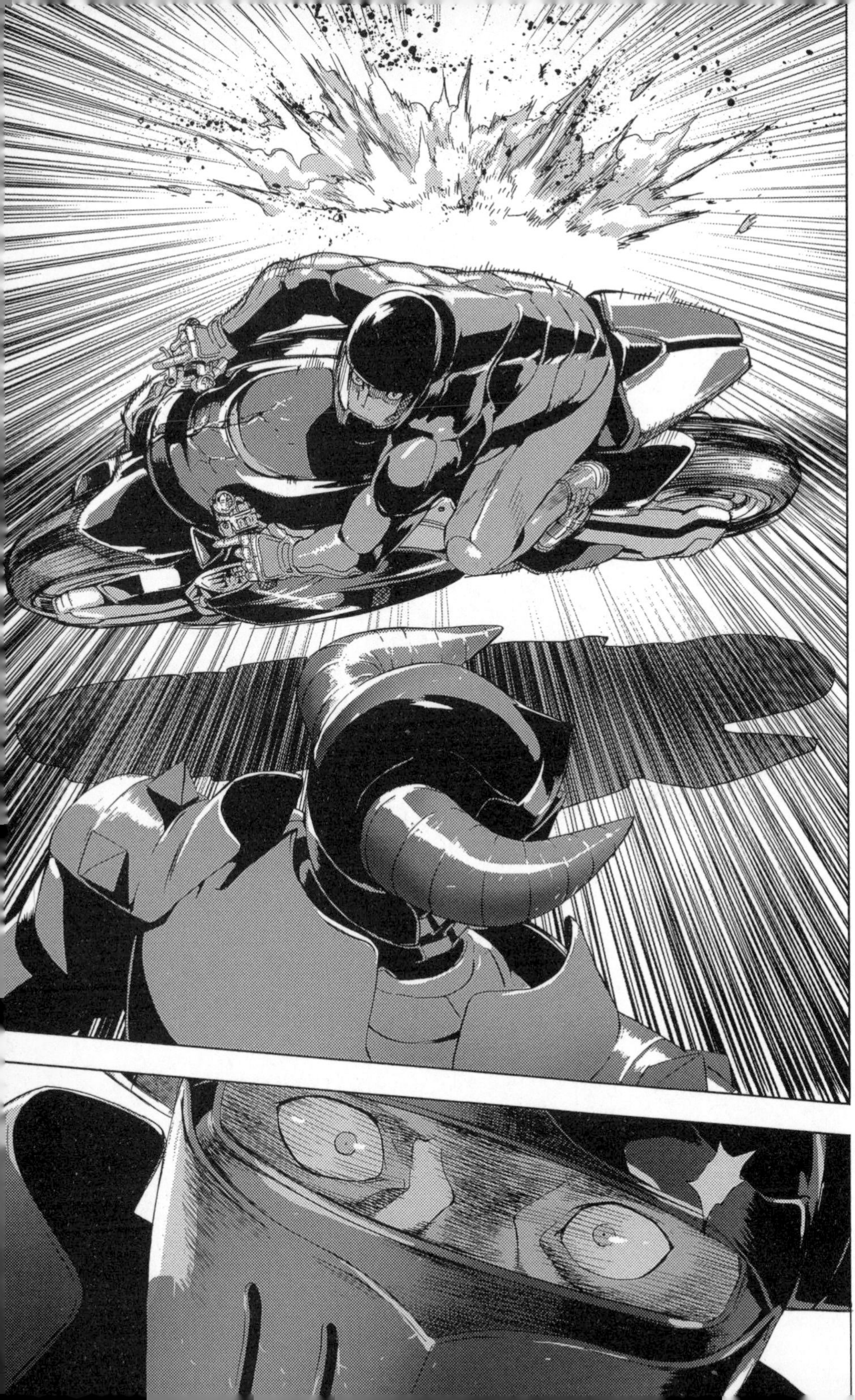

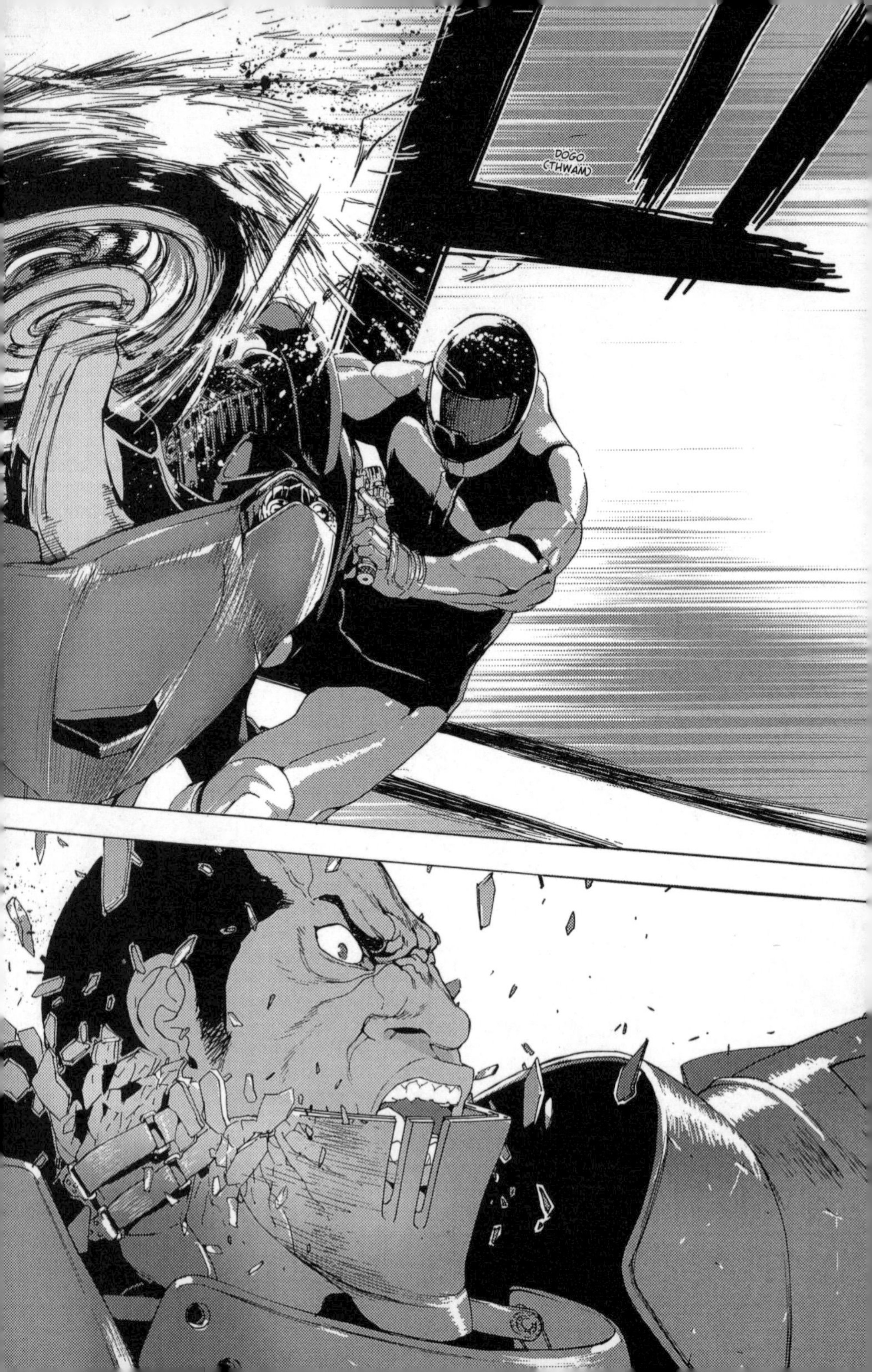
DOGO
(THWAM)

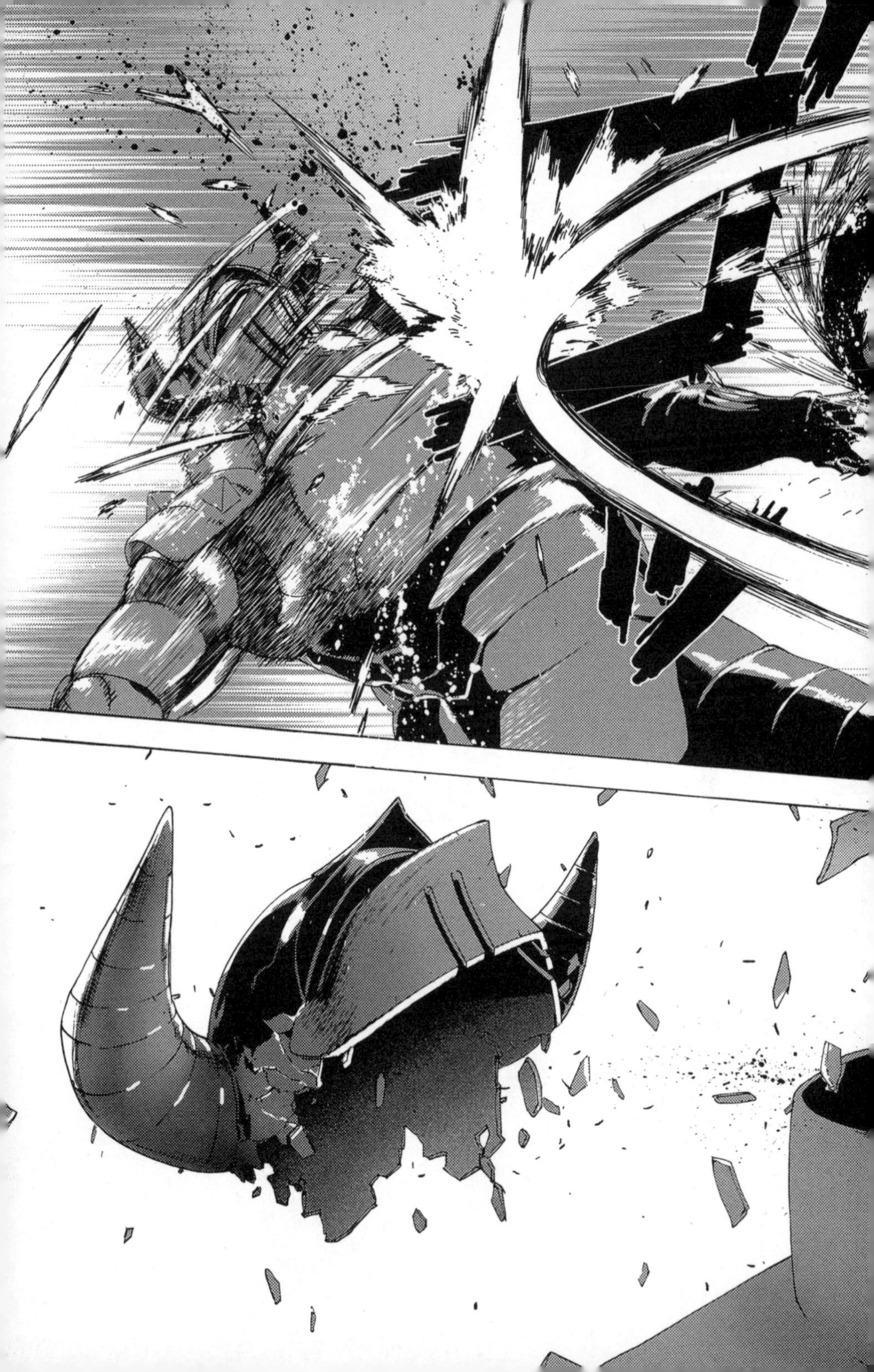

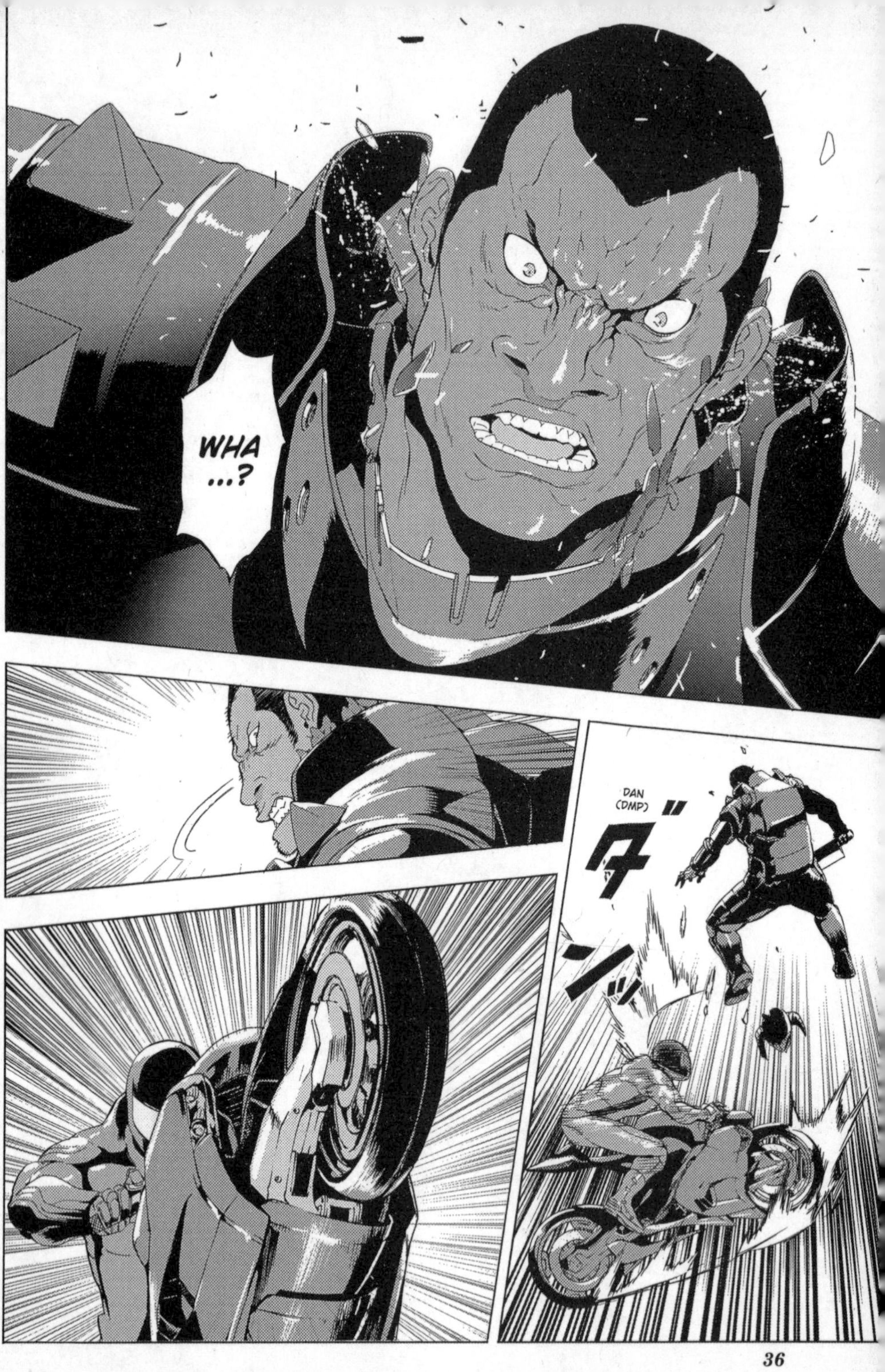
WHA ...?
ダン
DAN (DMP)

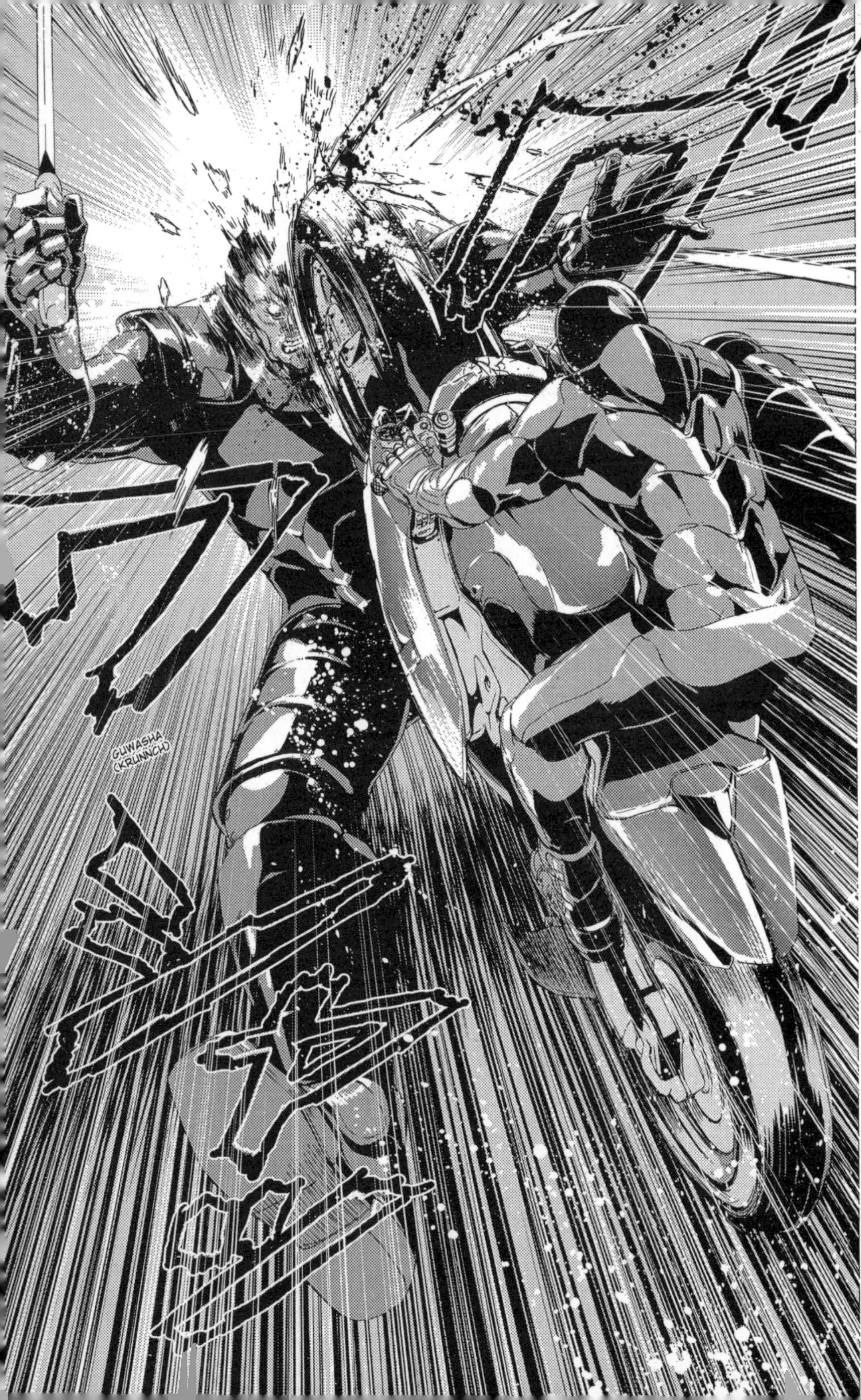
GUWASHA (KRUNNCH)

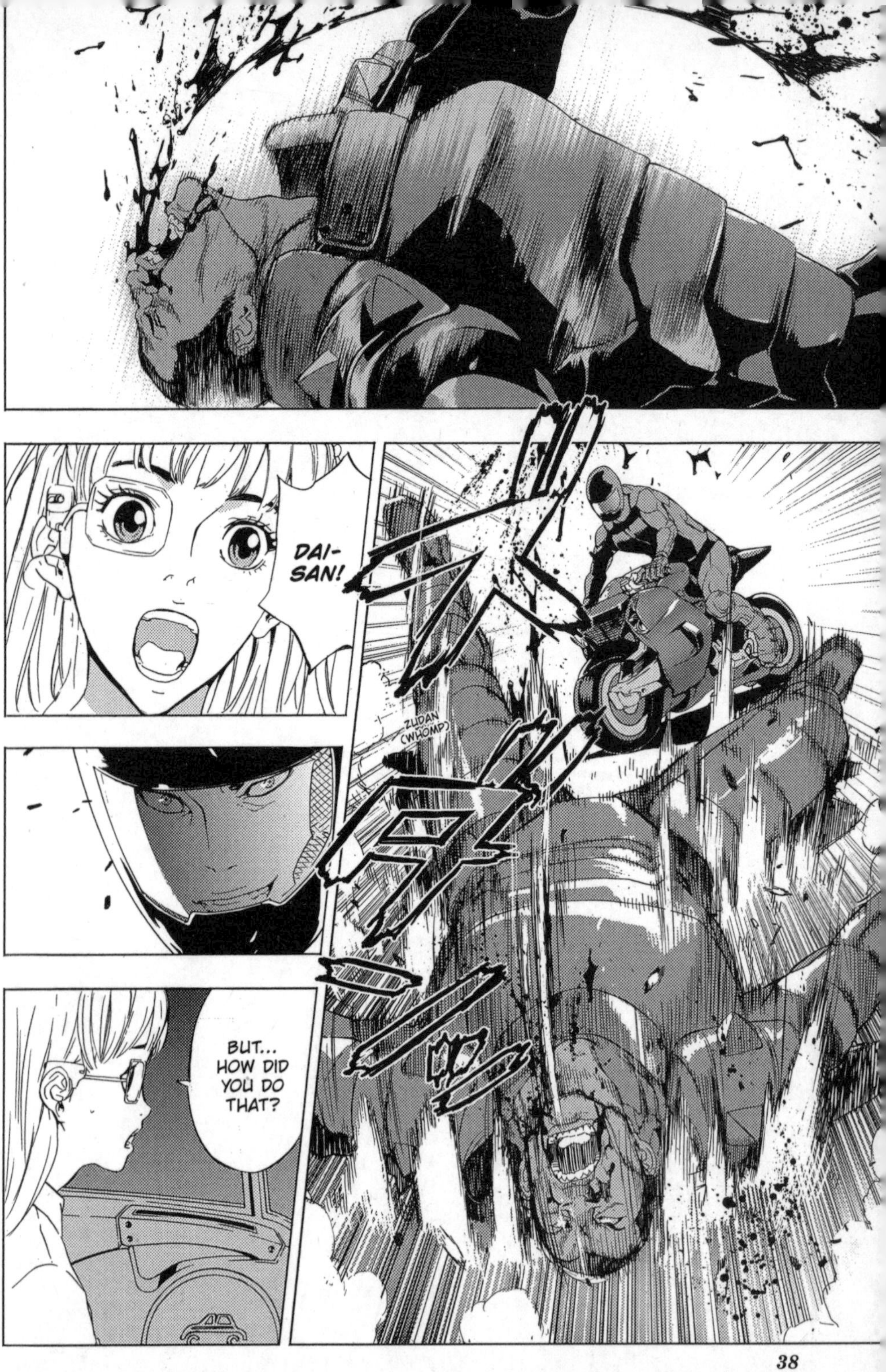
ZUDAN (WHOMP)
DAI-SAN!
BUT... HOW DID YOU DO THAT?

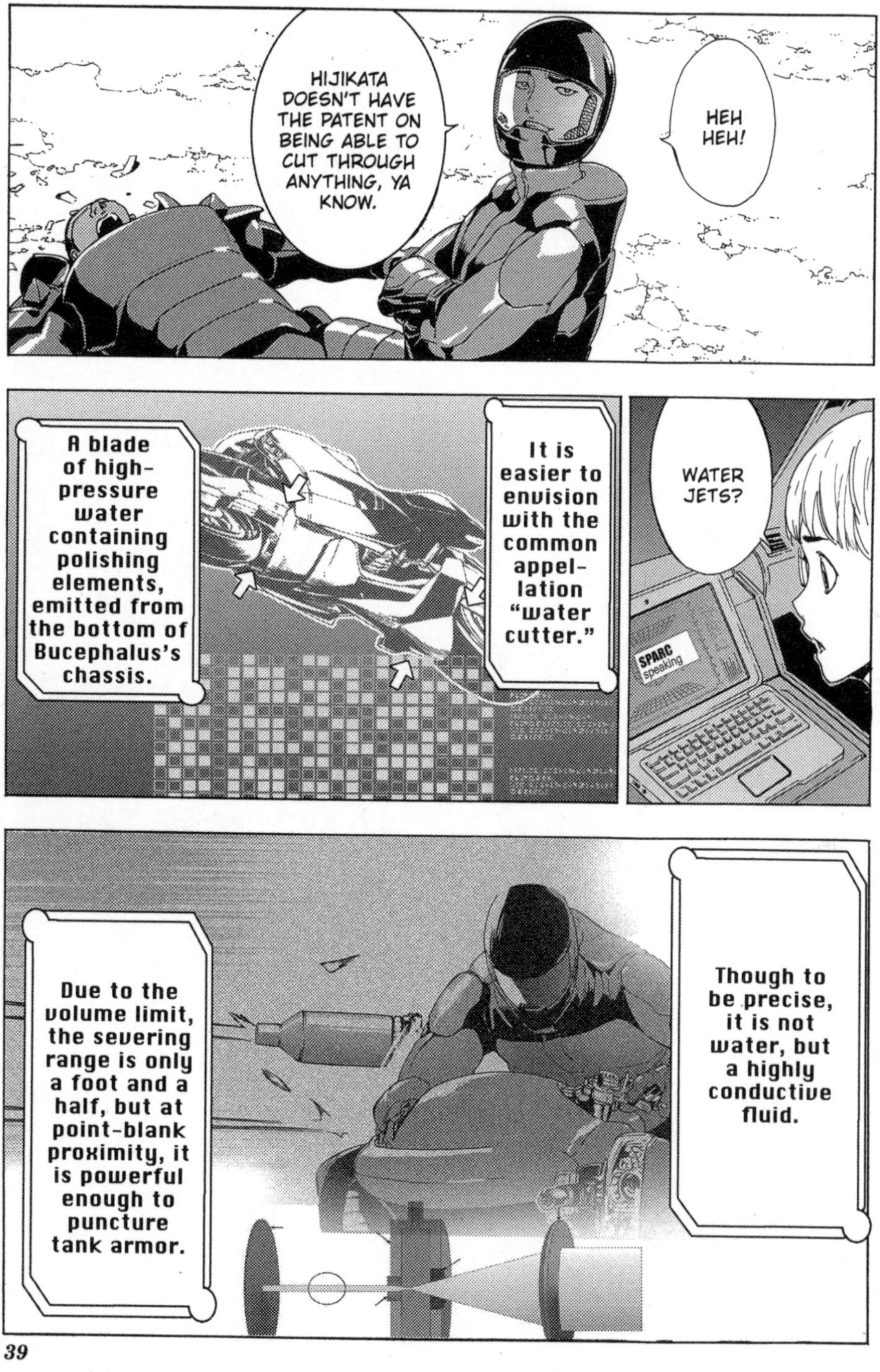
HEH HEH!
HIJIKATA DOESN'T HAVE THE PATENT ON BEING ABLE TO CUT THROUGH ANYTHING, YA KNOW.
WATER JETS?
SPARC speaking
It is easier to envision with the common appellation "water cutter."
A blade of high-pressure water containing polishing elements, emitted from the bottom of Bucephalus's chassis.
Though to be precise, it is not water, but a highly conductive fluid.
Due to the volume limit, the severing range is only a foot and a half, but at point-blank proximity, it is powerful enough to puncture tank armor.

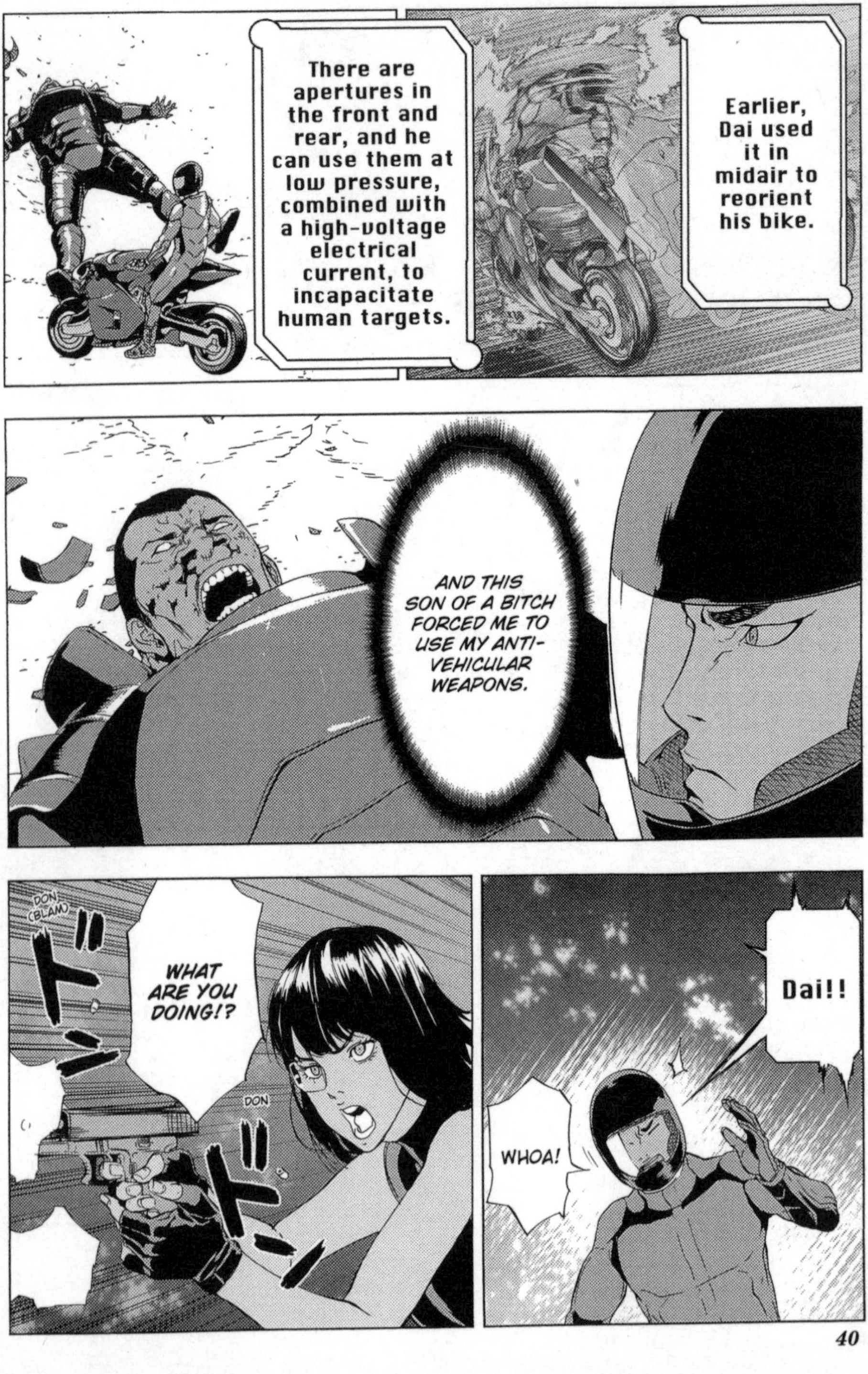
Earlier, Dai used it in midair to reorient his bike.
There are apertures in the front and rear, and he can use them at low pressure, combined with a high-voltage electrical current, to incapacitate human targets.
AND THIS SON OF A BITCH FORCED ME TO USE MY ANTI-VEHICULAR WEAPONS.
Dai!!
WHOA!
DON (BLAM)
WHAT ARE YOU DOING!?
DON

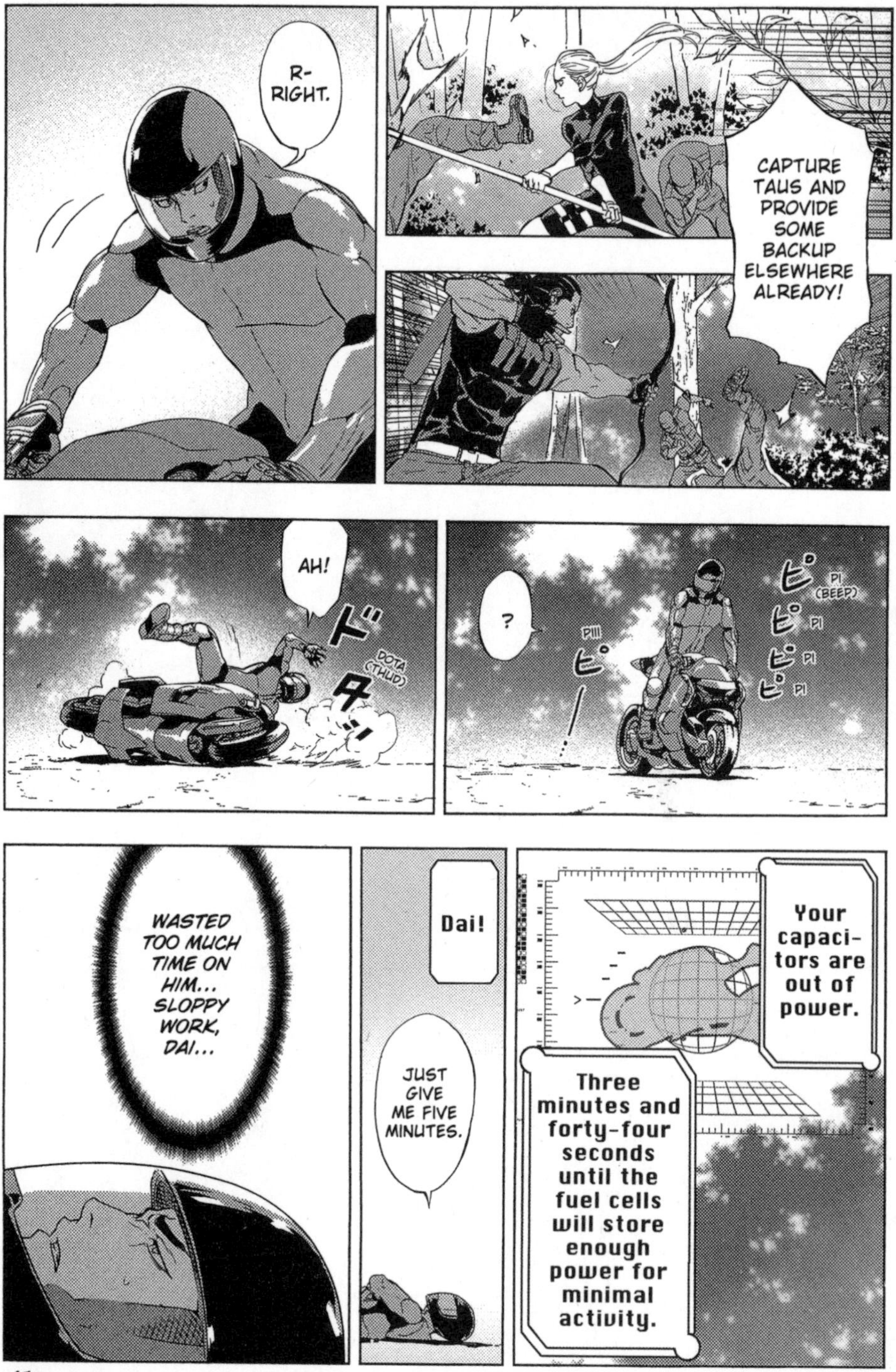
CAPTURE TAUS AND PROVIDE SOME BACKUP ELSEWHERE ALREADY!
R-RIGHT.
ピ PI (BEEP)
ピ PI
ピ PI
ピ PI
ピ PIII
?
AH!
ドタッ DOTA (THUD)
Your capaci-tors are out of power.
Three minutes and forty-four seconds until the fuel cells will store enough power for minimal activity.
Dai!
JUST GIVE ME FIVE MINUTES.
WASTED TOO MUCH TIME ON HIM... SLOPPY WORK, DAI...

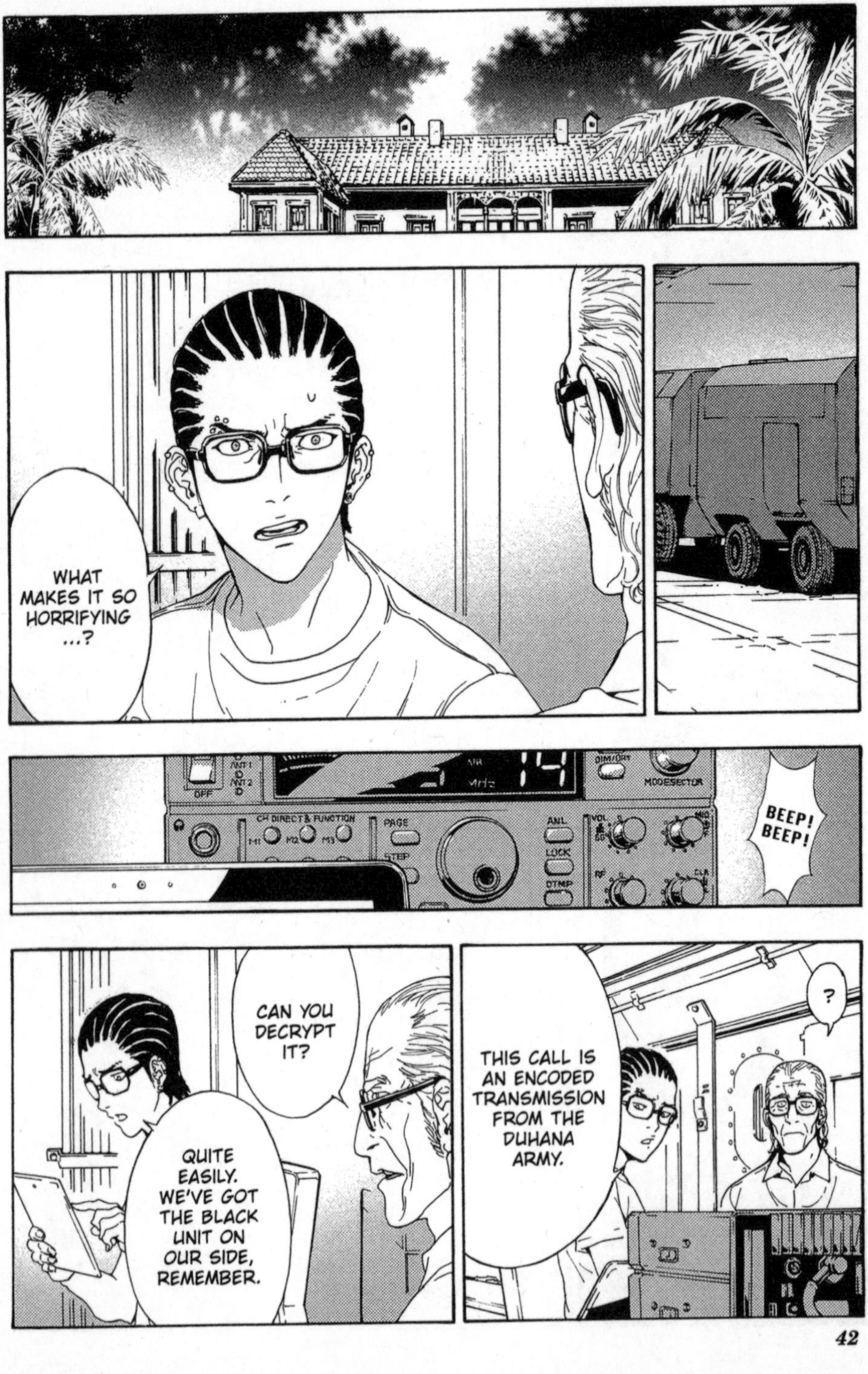
WHAT MAKES IT SO HORRIFYING ...?
BEEP! BEEP!
?
THIS CALL IS AN ENCODED TRANSMISSION FROM THE DUHANA ARMY.
CAN YOU DECRYPT IT?
QUITE EASILY. WE'VE GOT THE BLACK UNIT ON OUR SIDE, REMEMBER.

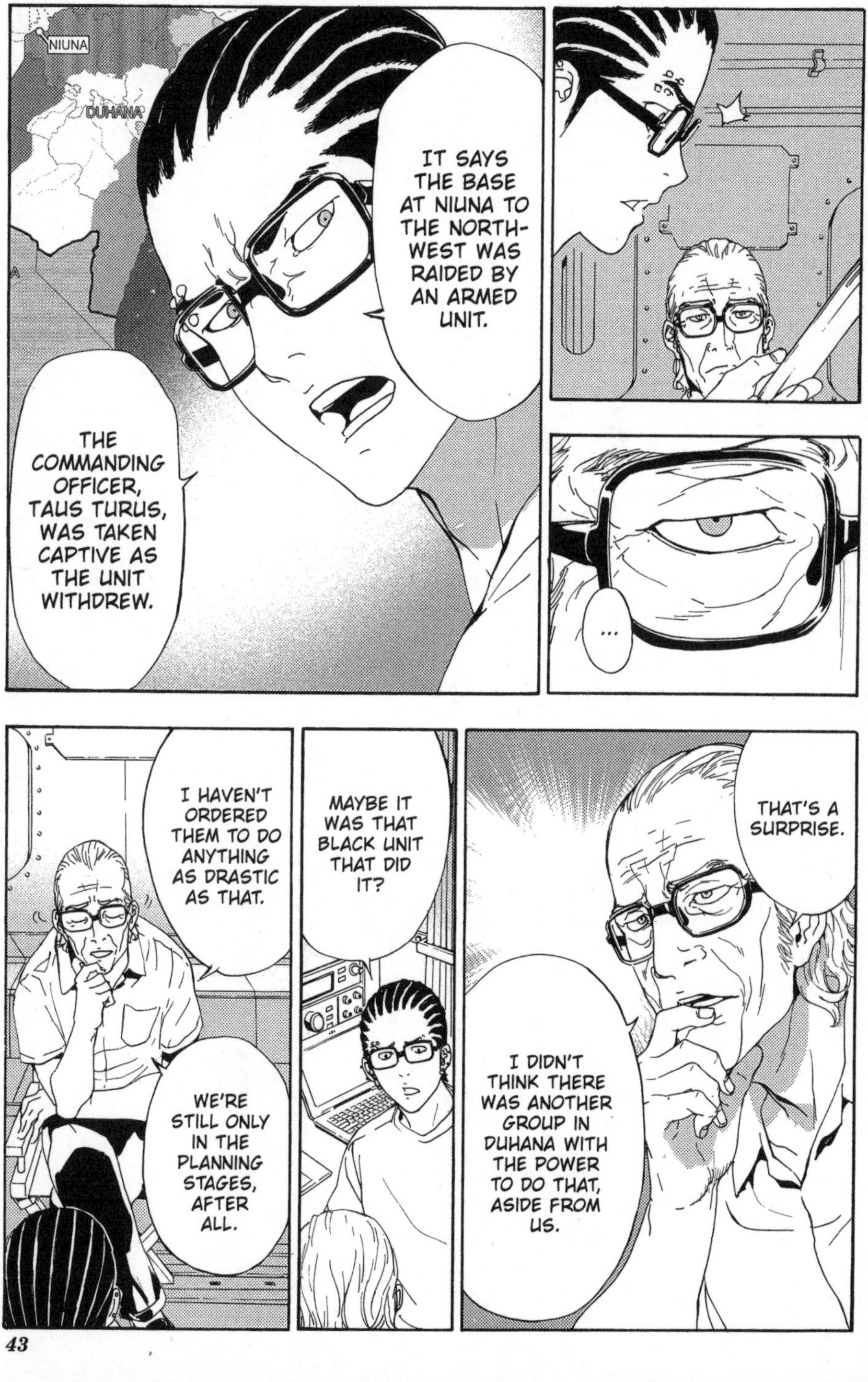
...
NIUNA
DUHANA
IT SAYS THE BASE AT NIUNA TO THE NORTH-WEST WAS RAIDED BY AN ARMED UNIT.
THE COMMANDING OFFICER, TAUS TURUS, WAS TAKEN CAPTIVE AS THE UNIT WITHDREW.
THAT'S A SURPRISE.
I DIDN'T THINK THERE WAS ANOTHER GROUP IN DUHANA WITH THE POWER TO DO THAT, ASIDE FROM US.
MAYBE IT WAS THAT BLACK UNIT THAT DID IT?
I HAVEN'T ORDERED THEM TO DO ANYTHING AS DRASTIC AS THAT.
WE'RE STILL ONLY IN THE PLANNING STAGES, AFTER ALL.

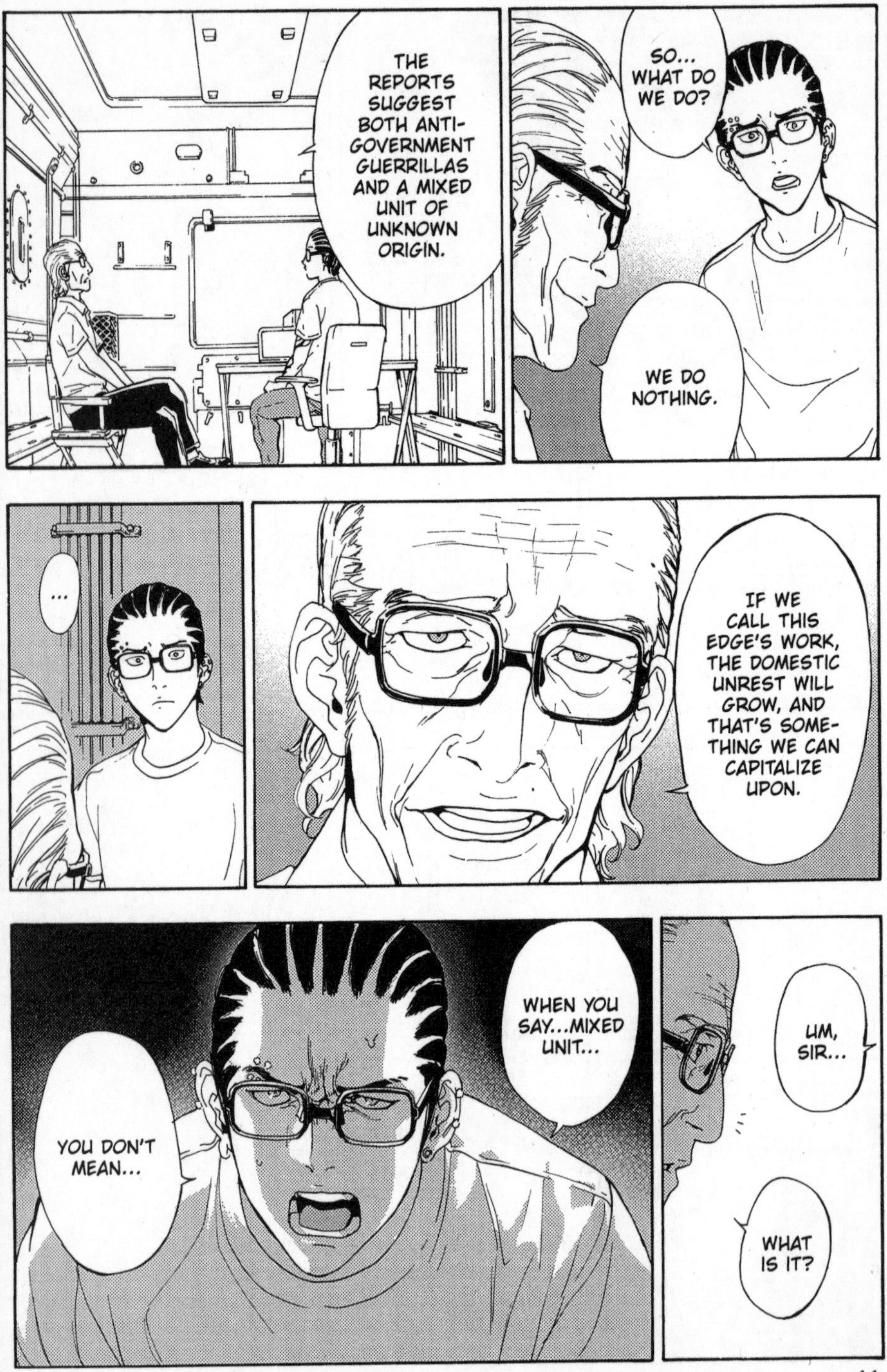
SO... WHAT DO WE DO?
WE DO NOTHING.
THE REPORTS SUGGEST BOTH ANTI-GOVERNMENT GUERRILLAS AND A MIXED UNIT OF UNKNOWN ORIGIN.
IF WE CALL THIS EDGE'S WORK, THE DOMESTIC UNREST WILL GROW, AND THAT'S SOME-THING WE CAN CAPITALIZE UPON.
...
UM, SIR...
WHAT IS IT?
WHEN YOU SAY...MIXED UNIT...
YOU DON'T MEAN...

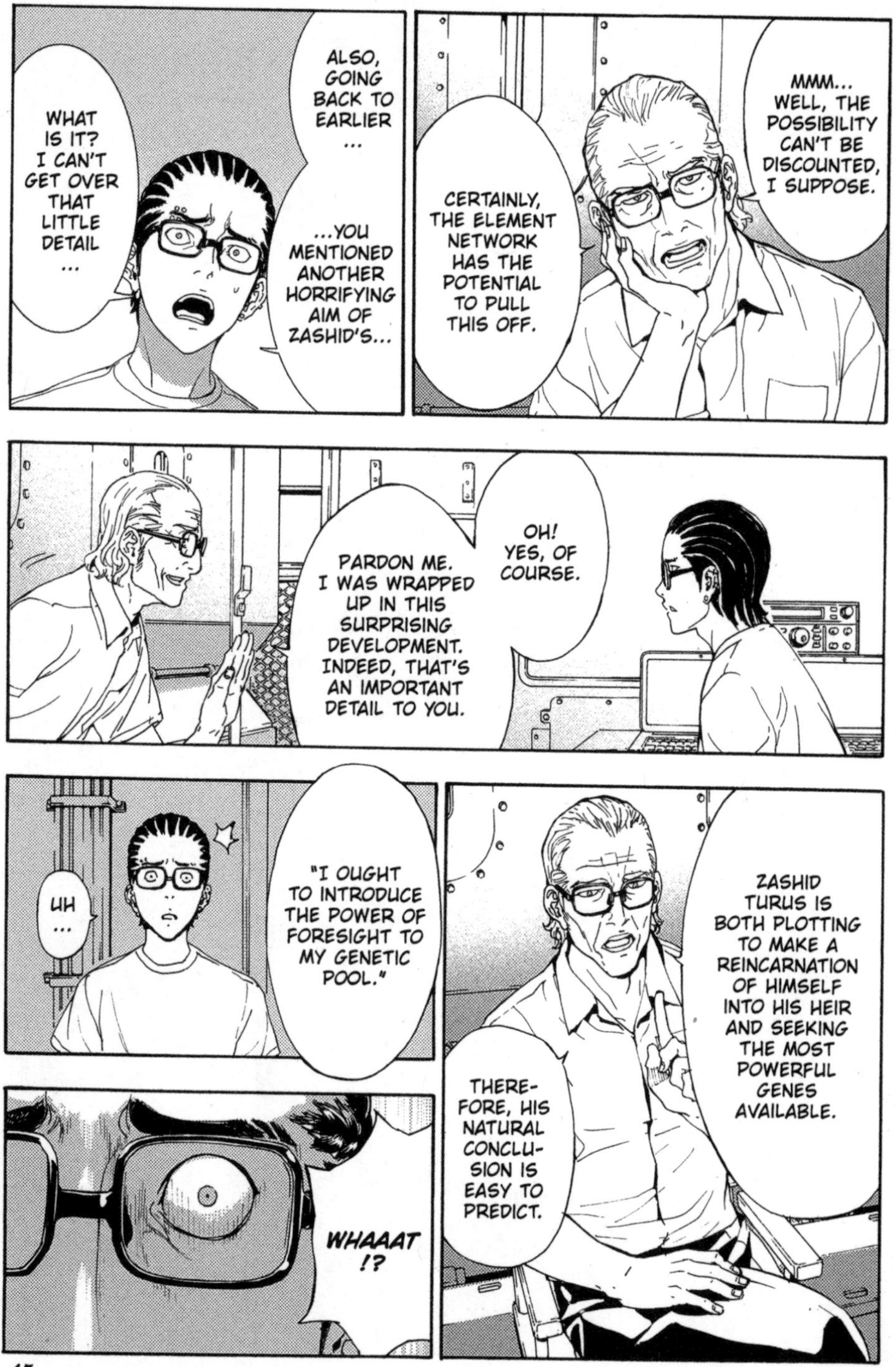
MMM... WELL, THE POSSIBILITY CAN'T BE DISCOUNTED, I SUPPOSE.
CERTAINLY, THE ELEMENT NETWORK HAS THE POTENTIAL TO PULL THIS OFF.
ALSO, GOING BACK TO EARLIER ...
...YOU MENTIONED ANOTHER HORRIFYING AIM OF ZASHID'S...
WHAT IS IT? I CAN'T GET OVER THAT LITTLE DETAIL ...
OH! YES, OF COURSE.
PARDON ME. I WAS WRAPPED UP IN THIS SURPRISING DEVELOPMENT. INDEED, THAT'S AN IMPORTANT DETAIL TO YOU.
ZASHID TURUS IS BOTH PLOTTING TO MAKE A REINCARNATION OF HIMSELF INTO HIS HEIR AND SEEKING THE MOST POWERFUL GENES AVAILABLE.
THERE-FORE, HIS NATURAL CONCLU-SION IS EASY TO PREDICT.
"I OUGHT TO INTRODUCE THE POWER OF FORESIGHT TO MY GENETIC POOL."
UH ...
WHAAAT !?

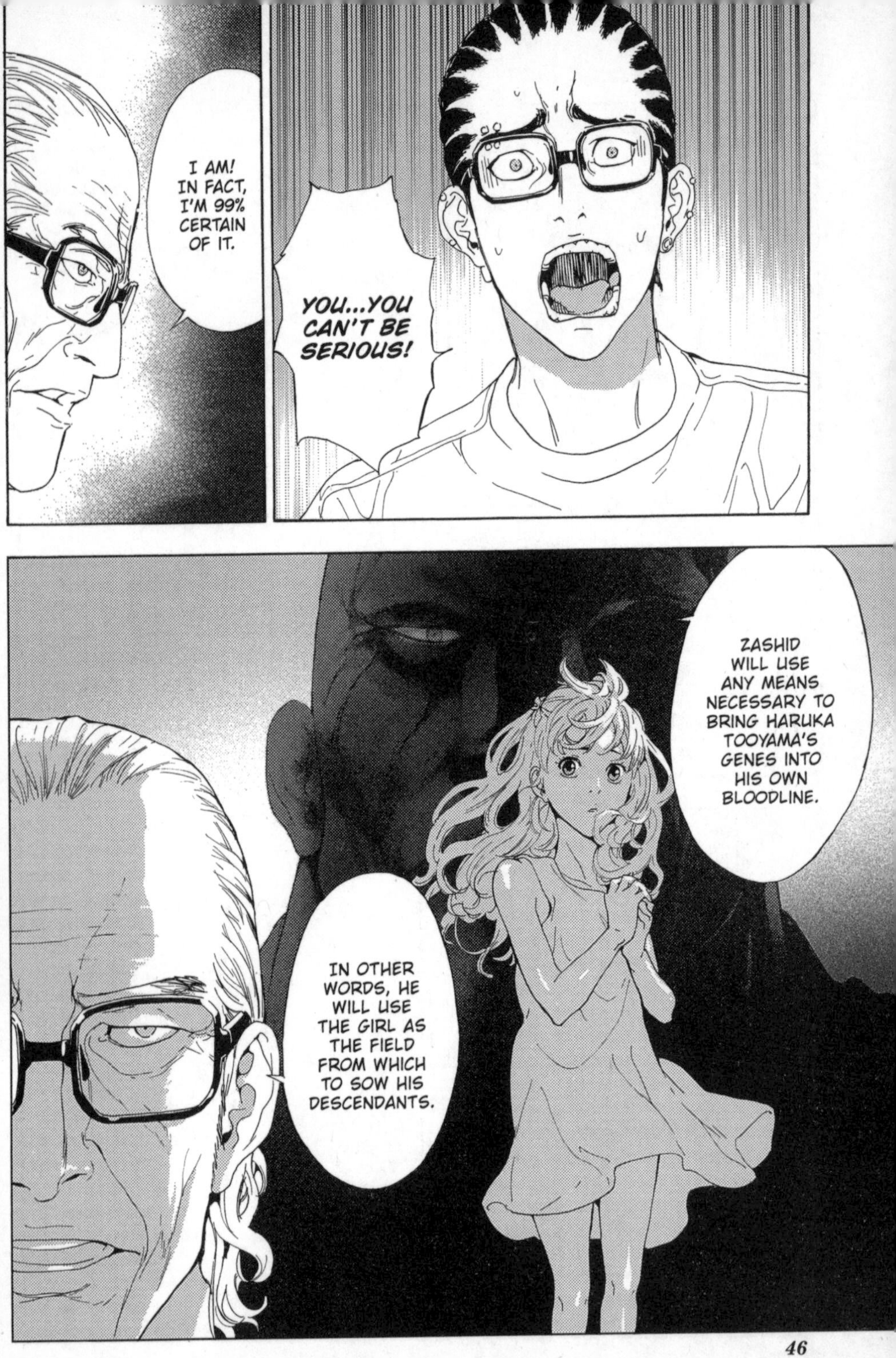
YOU...YOU CAN'T BE SERIOUS!
I AM! IN FACT, I'M 99% CERTAIN OF IT.
ZASHID WILL USE ANY MEANS NECESSARY TO BRING HARUKA TOOYAMA'S GENES INTO HIS OWN BLOODLINE.
IN OTHER WORDS, HE WILL USE THE GIRL AS THE FIELD FROM WHICH TO SOW HIS DESCENDANTS.

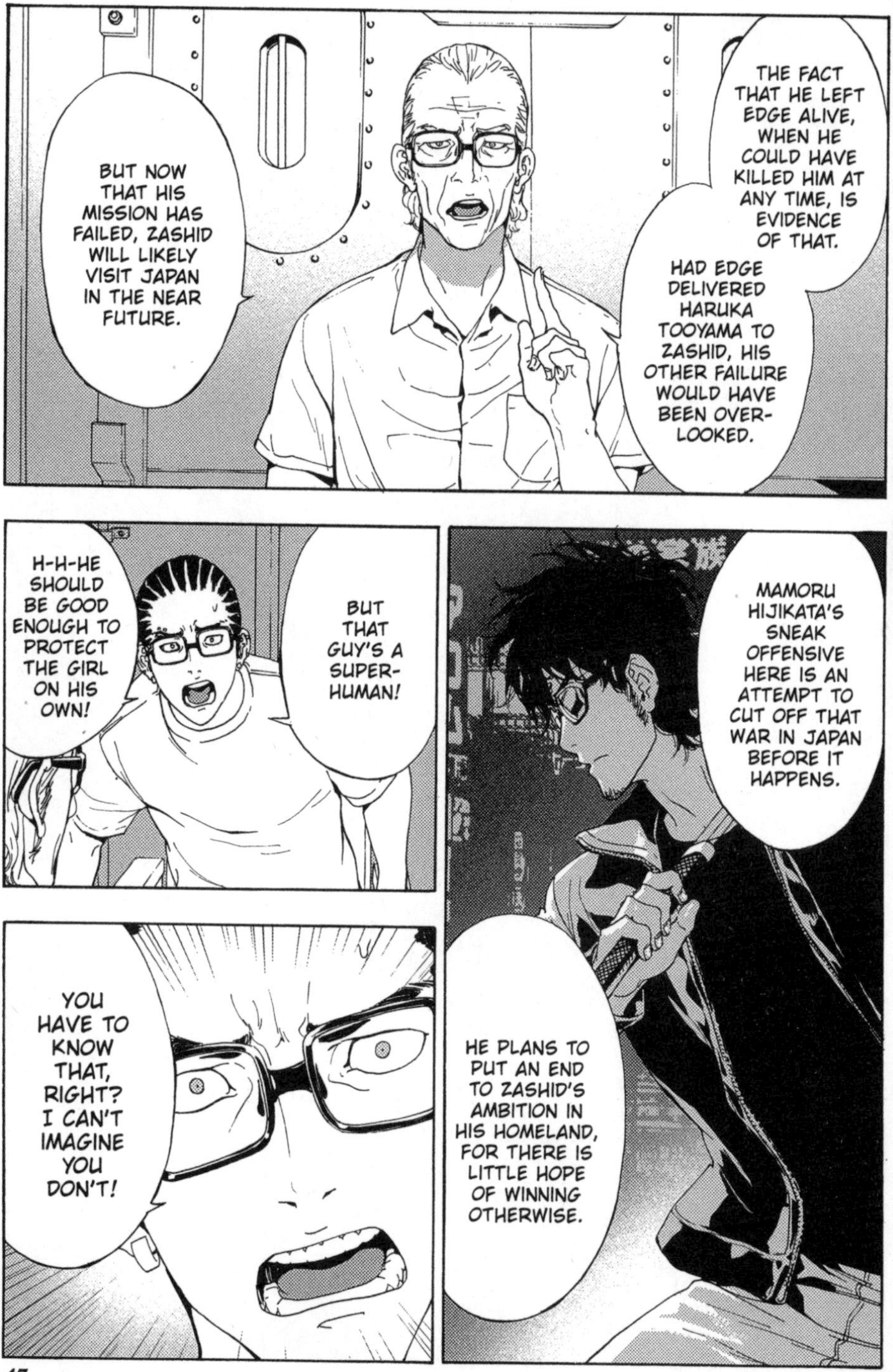
THE FACT THAT HE LEFT EDGE ALIVE, WHEN HE COULD HAVE KILLED HIM AT ANY TIME, IS EVIDENCE OF THAT.
HAD EDGE DELIVERED HARUKA TOOYAMA TO ZASHID, HIS OTHER FAILURE WOULD HAVE BEEN OVER-LOOKED.
BUT NOW THAT HIS MISSION HAS FAILED, ZASHID WILL LIKELY VISIT JAPAN IN THE NEAR FUTURE.
MAMORU HIJIKATA'S SNEAK OFFENSIVE HERE IS AN ATTEMPT TO CUT OFF THAT WAR IN JAPAN BEFORE IT HAPPENS.
HE PLANS TO PUT AN END TO ZASHID'S AMBITION IN HIS HOMELAND, FOR THERE IS LITTLE HOPE OF WINNING OTHERWISE.
BUT THAT GUY'S A SUPER-HUMAN!
H-H-HE SHOULD BE GOOD ENOUGH TO PROTECT THE GIRL ON HIS OWN!
YOU HAVE TO KNOW THAT, RIGHT? I CAN'T IMAGINE YOU DON'T!

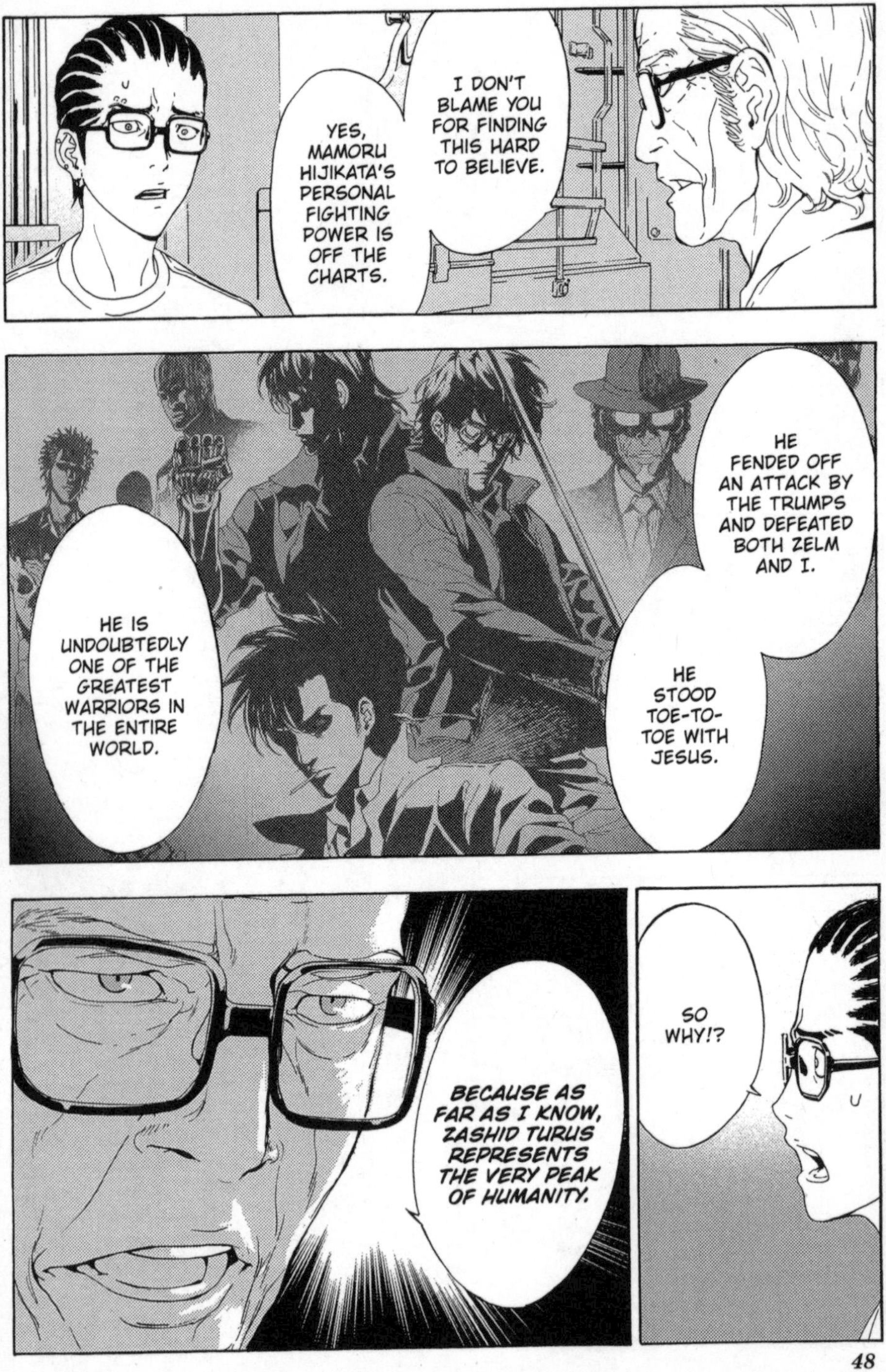
I DON'T BLAME YOU FOR FINDING THIS HARD TO BELIEVE.
YES, MAMORU HIJIKATA'S PERSONAL FIGHTING POWER IS OFF THE CHARTS.
HE FENDED OFF AN ATTACK BY THE TRUMPS AND DEFEATED BOTH ZELM AND I.
HE STOOD TOE-TO-TOE WITH JESUS.
HE IS UNDOUBTEDLY ONE OF THE GREATEST WARRIORS IN THE ENTIRE WORLD.
SO WHY!?
BECAUSE AS FAR AS I KNOW, ZASHID TURUS REPRESENTS THE VERY PEAK OF HUMANITY.

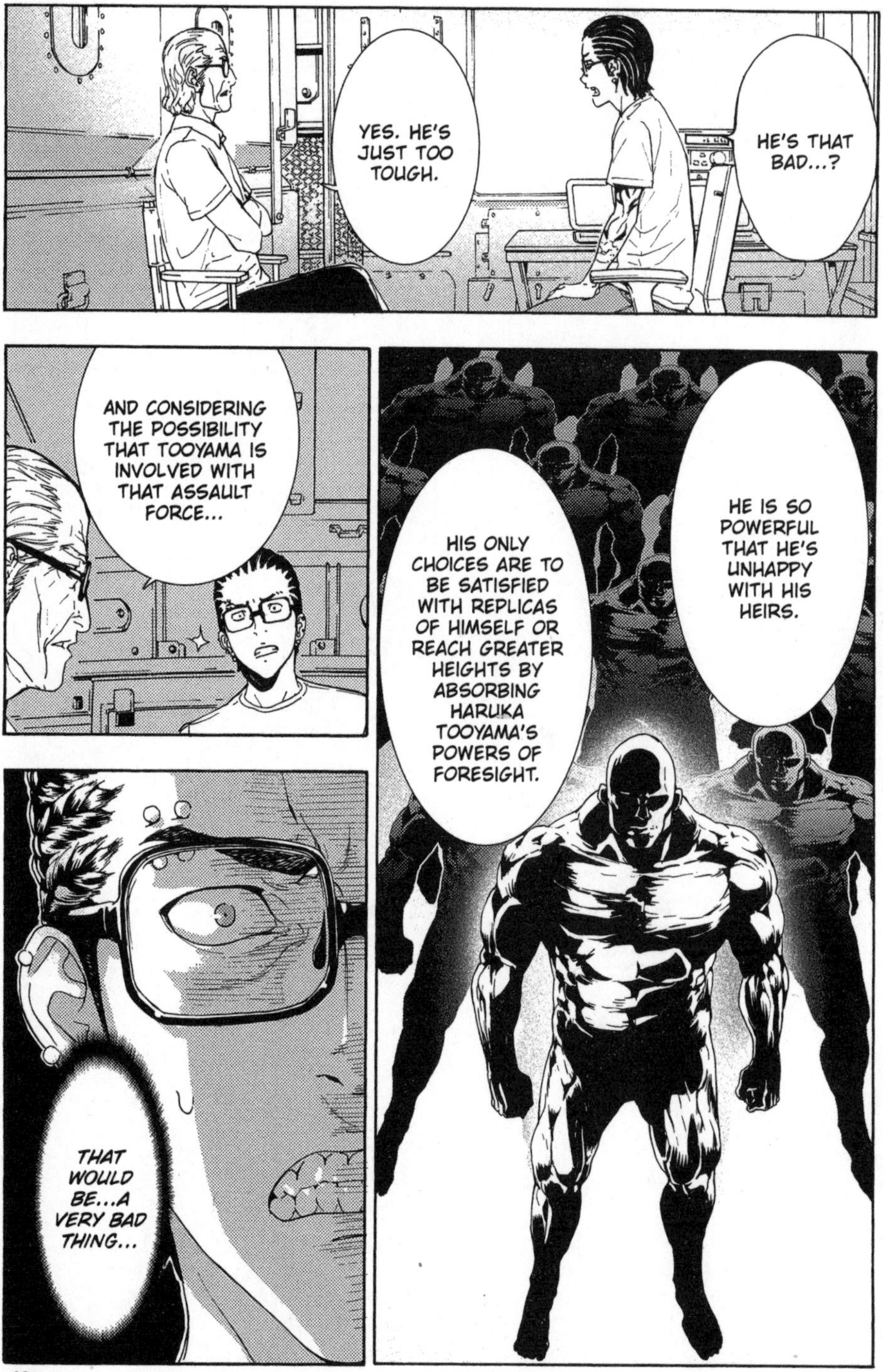
HE'S THAT BAD...?
YES. HE'S JUST TOO TOUGH.
HE IS SO POWERFUL THAT HE'S UNHAPPY WITH HIS HEIRS.
HIS ONLY CHOICES ARE TO BE SATISFIED WITH REPLICAS OF HIMSELF OR REACH GREATER HEIGHTS BY ABSORBING HARUKA TOOYAMA'S POWERS OF FORESIGHT.
AND CONSIDERING THE POSSIBILITY THAT TOOYAMA IS INVOLVED WITH THAT ASSAULT FORCE...
THAT WOULD BE...A VERY BAD THING...

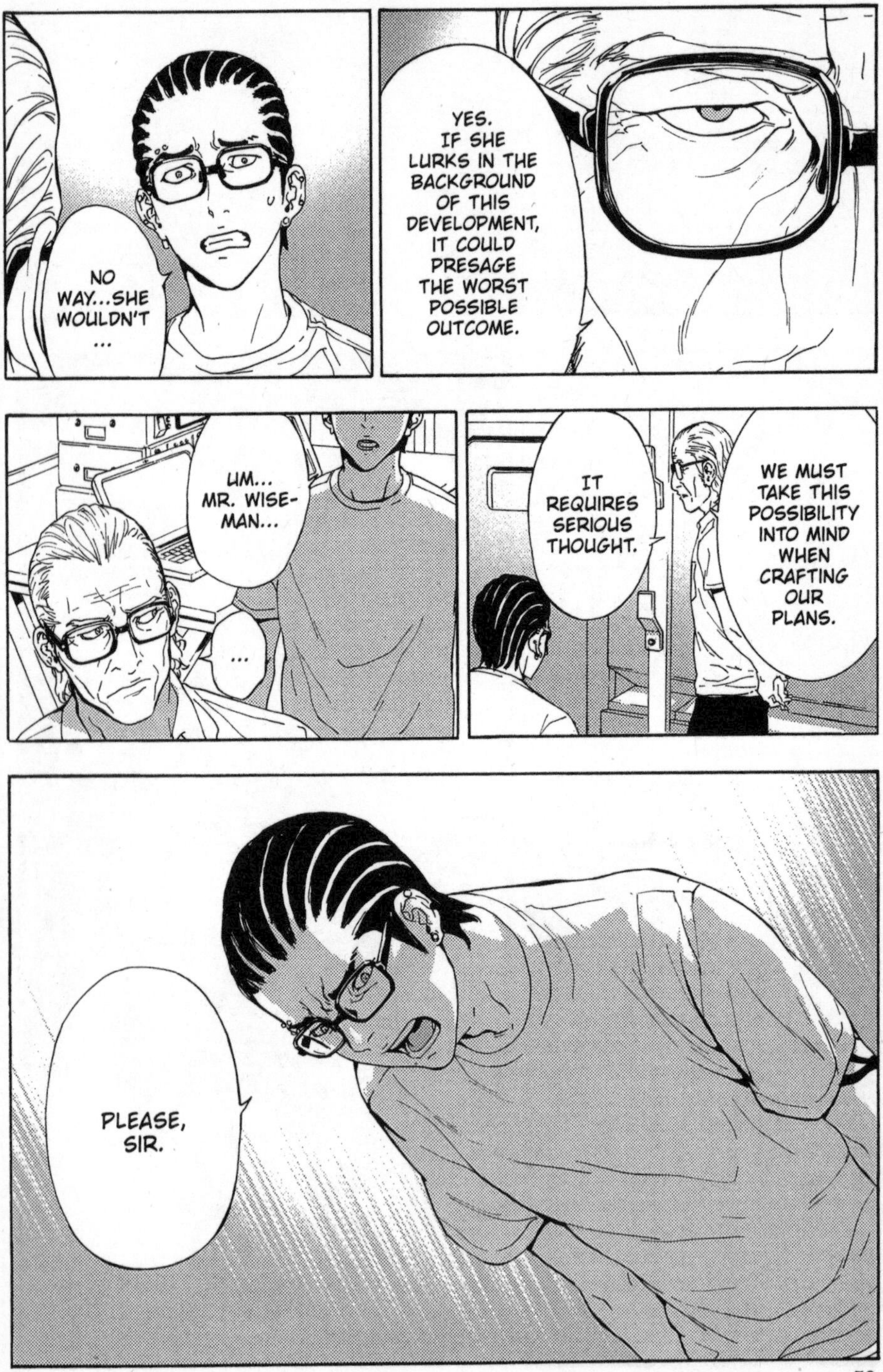
YES. IF SHE LURKS IN THE BACKGROUND OF THIS DEVELOPMENT, IT COULD PRESAGE THE WORST POSSIBLE OUTCOME.
NO WAY...SHE WOULDN'T ...
WE MUST TAKE THIS POSSIBILITY INTO MIND WHEN CRAFTING OUR PLANS.
IT REQUIRES SERIOUS THOUGHT.
UM... MR. WISE-MAN...
...
PLEASE, SIR.

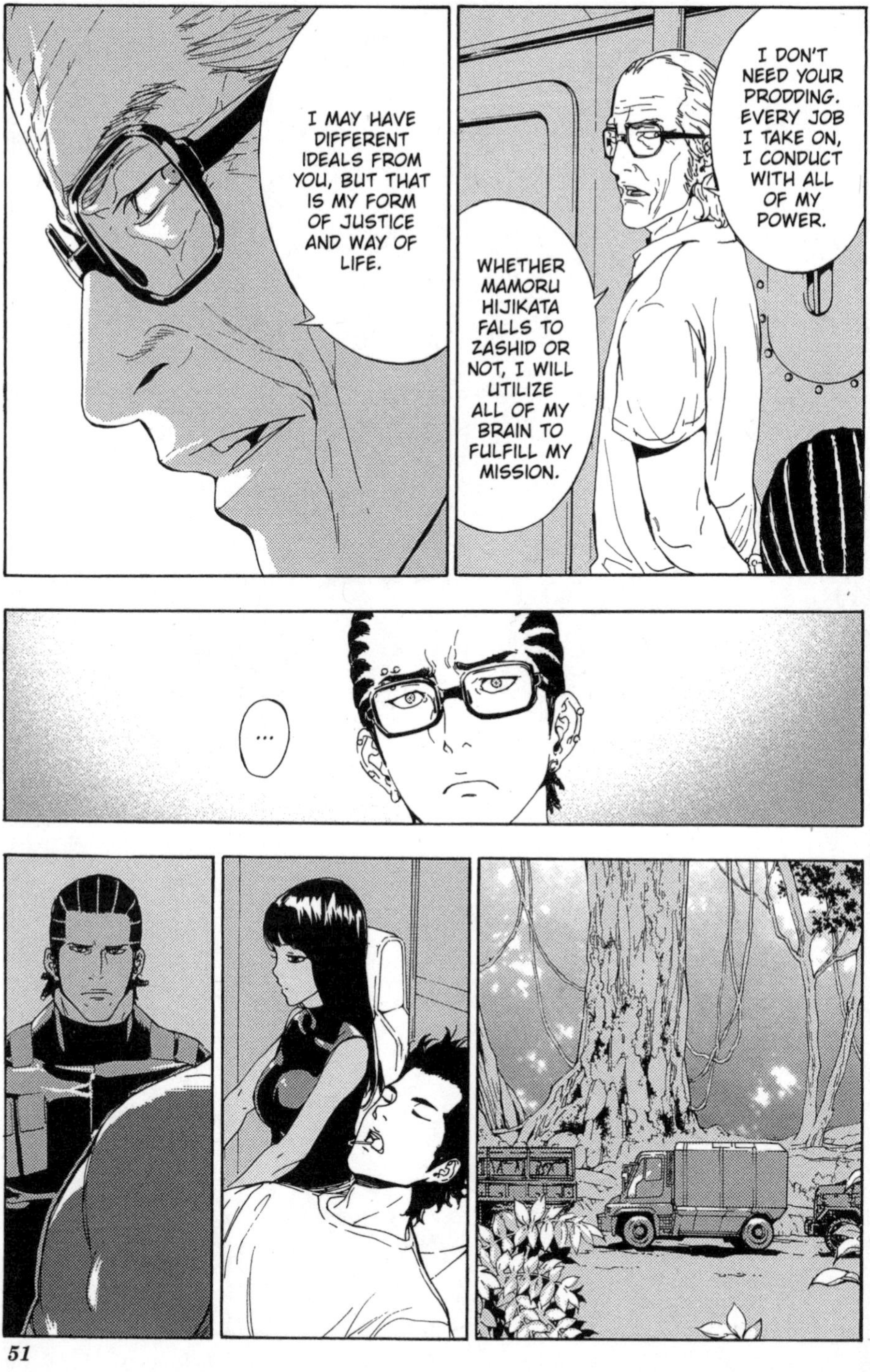
I DON'T NEED YOUR PRODDING. EVERY JOB I TAKE ON, I CONDUCT WITH ALL OF MY POWER.
WHETHER MAMORU HIJIKATA FALLS TO ZASHID OR NOT, I WILL UTILIZE ALL OF MY BRAIN TO FULFILL MY MISSION.
I MAY HAVE DIFFERENT IDEALS FROM YOU, BUT THAT IS MY FORM OF JUSTICE AND WAY OF LIFE.
...

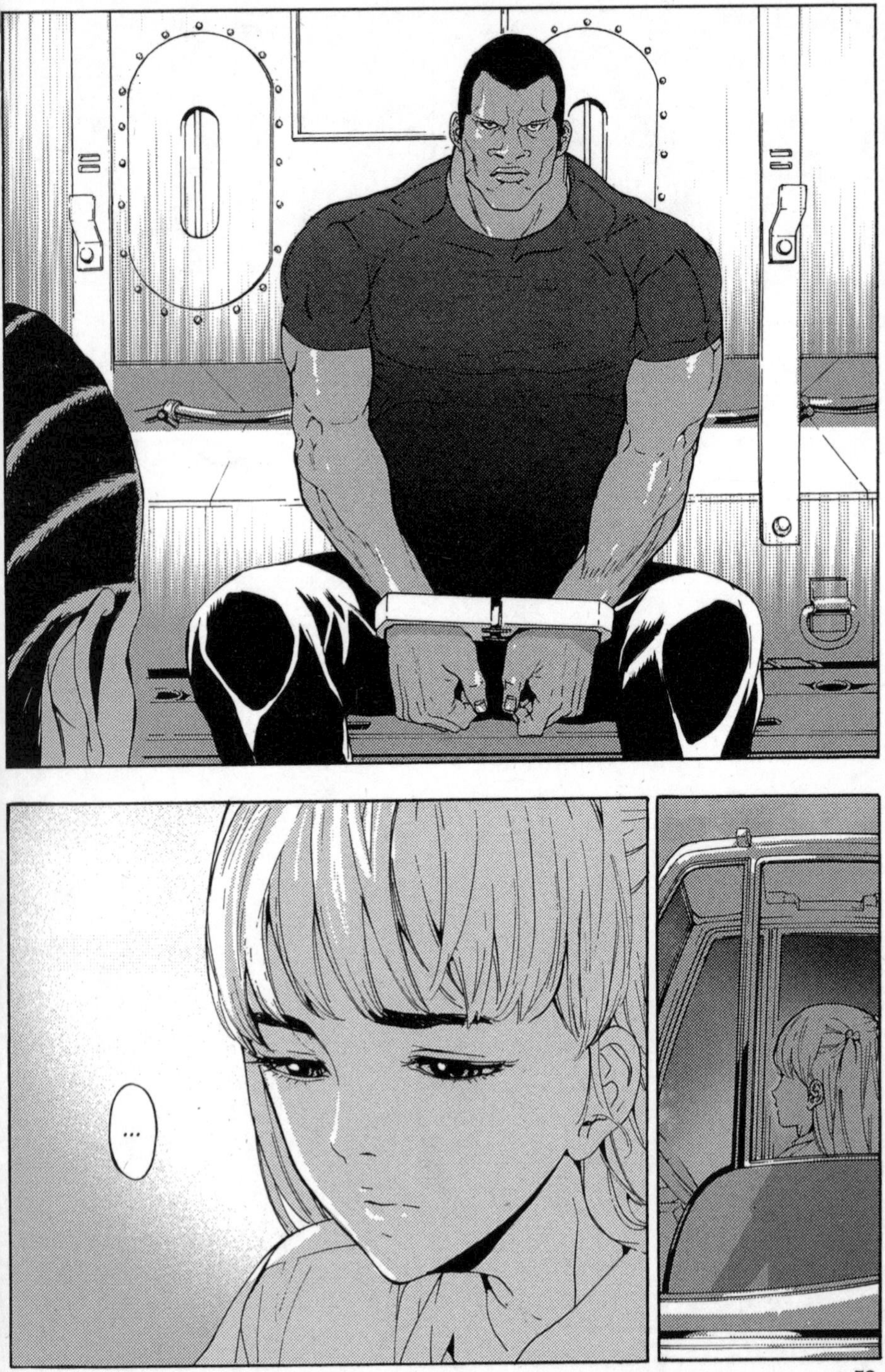
...

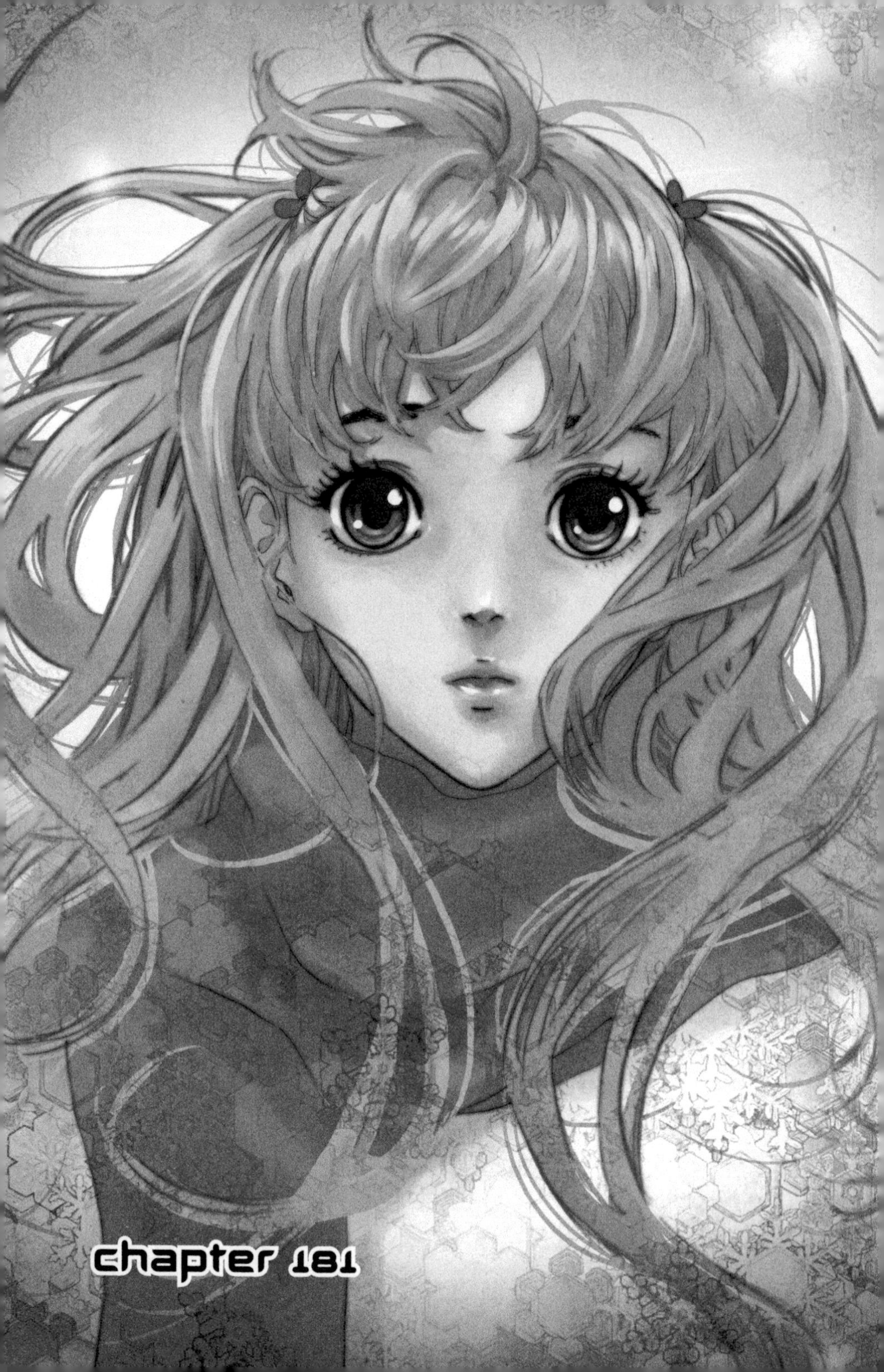
chapter 181

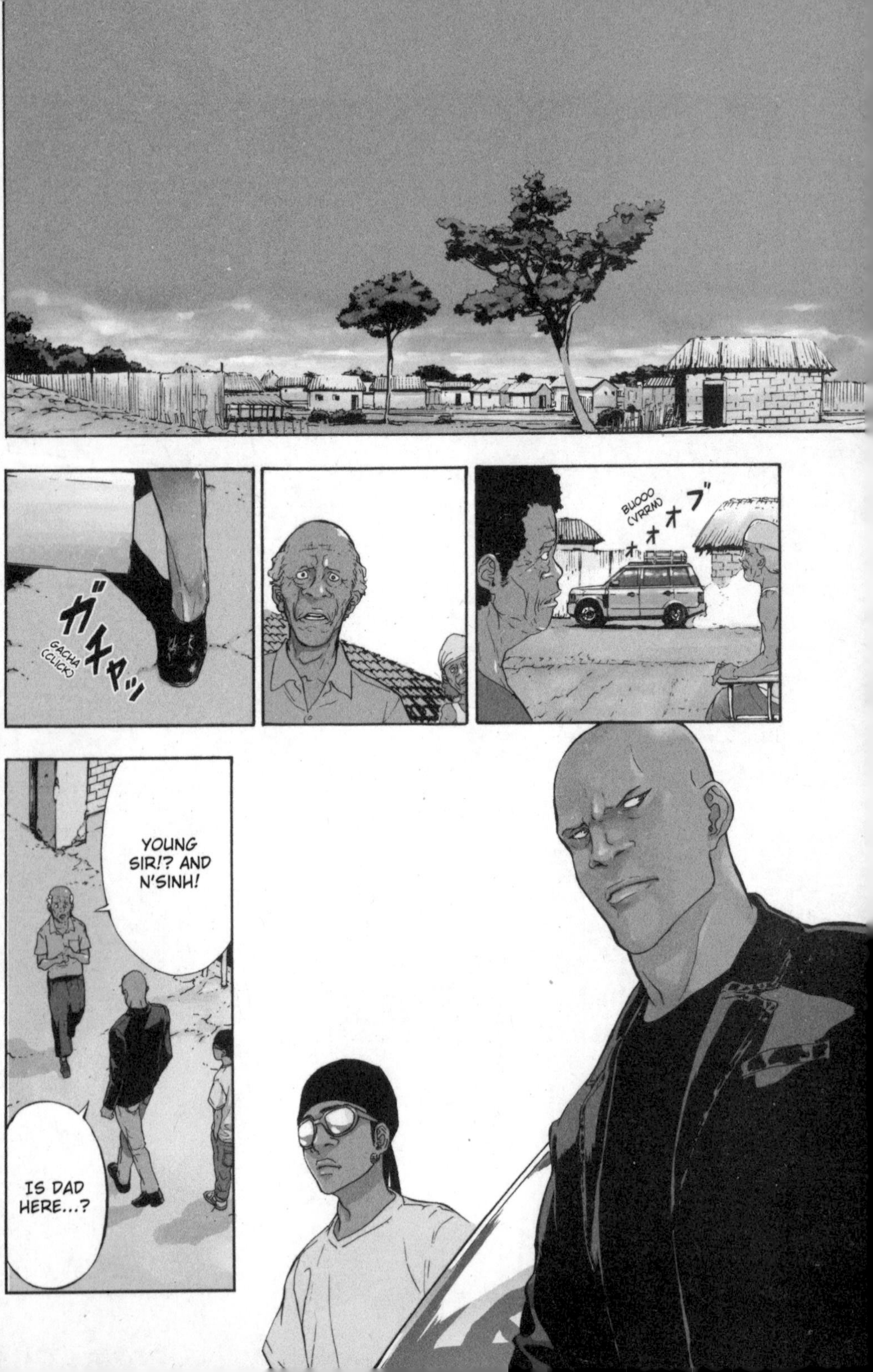
BUOOO (VRRM)
ブオオオ
ガチャッ
GACHA (CLICK)
YOUNG SIR!? AND N'SINH!
IS DAD HERE...?

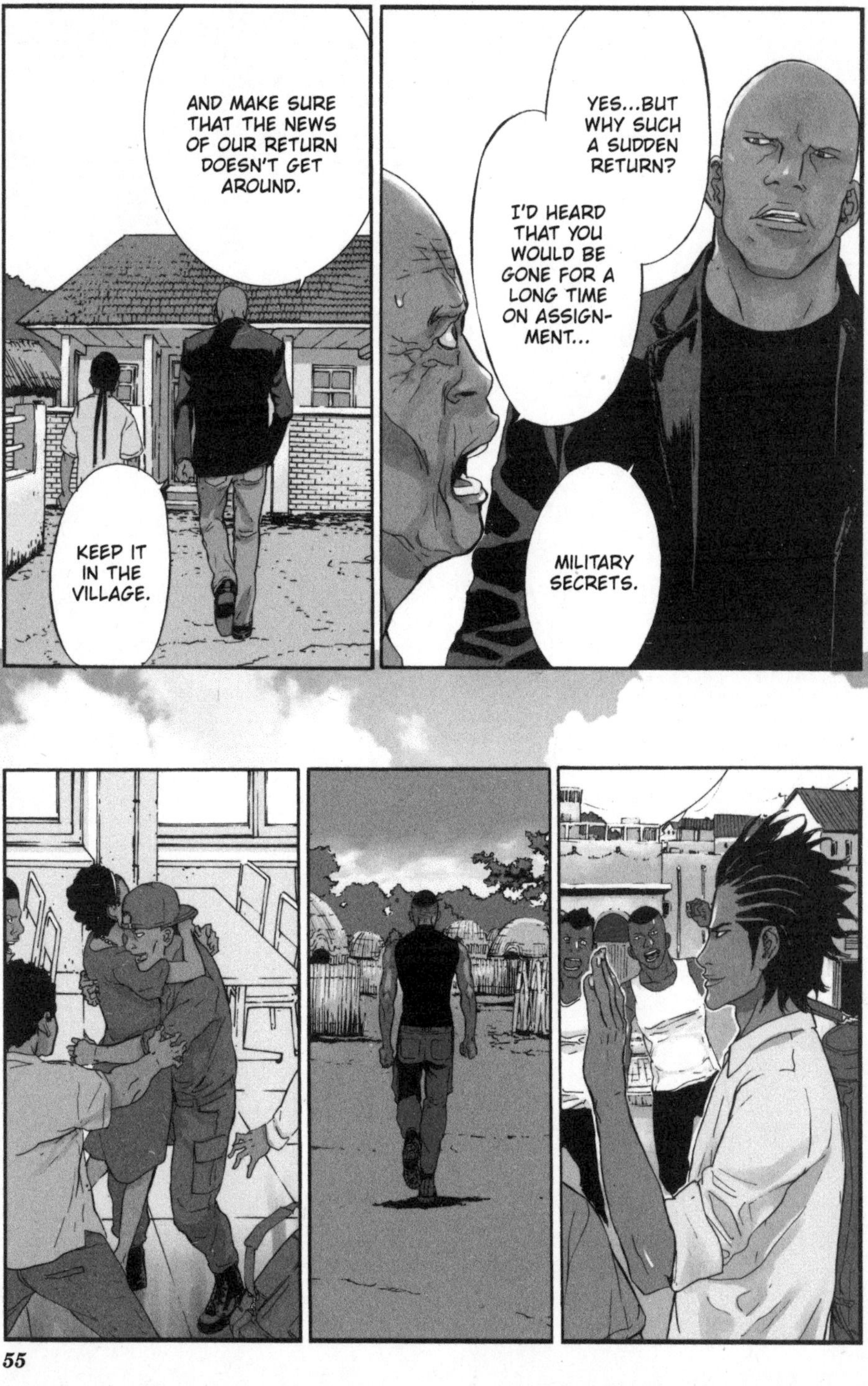
YES...BUT WHY SUCH A SUDDEN RETURN?
I'D HEARD THAT YOU WOULD BE GONE FOR A LONG TIME ON ASSIGN-MENT...
MILITARY SECRETS.
AND MAKE SURE THAT THE NEWS OF OUR RETURN DOESN'T GET AROUND.
KEEP IT IN THE VILLAGE.

Until Death do us Part

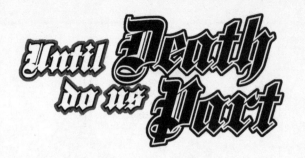

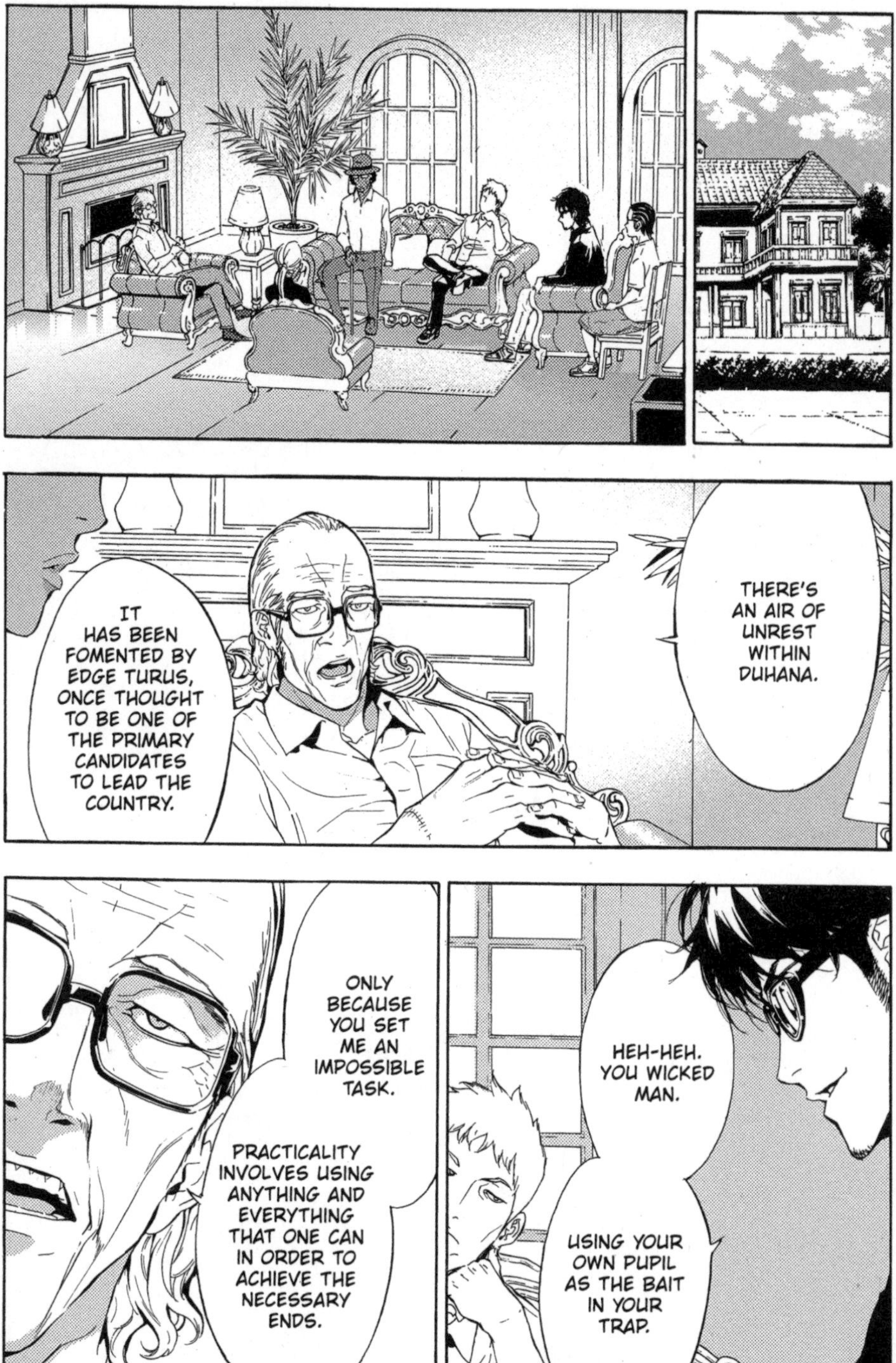
THERE'S AN AIR OF UNREST WITHIN DUHANA.
IT HAS BEEN FOMENTED BY EDGE TURUS, ONCE THOUGHT TO BE ONE OF THE PRIMARY CANDIDATES TO LEAD THE COUNTRY.
HEH-HEH. YOU WICKED MAN.
USING YOUR OWN PUPIL AS THE BAIT IN YOUR TRAP.
ONLY BECAUSE YOU SET ME AN IMPOSSIBLE TASK.
PRACTICALITY INVOLVES USING ANYTHING AND EVERYTHING THAT ONE CAN IN ORDER TO ACHIEVE THE NECESSARY ENDS.

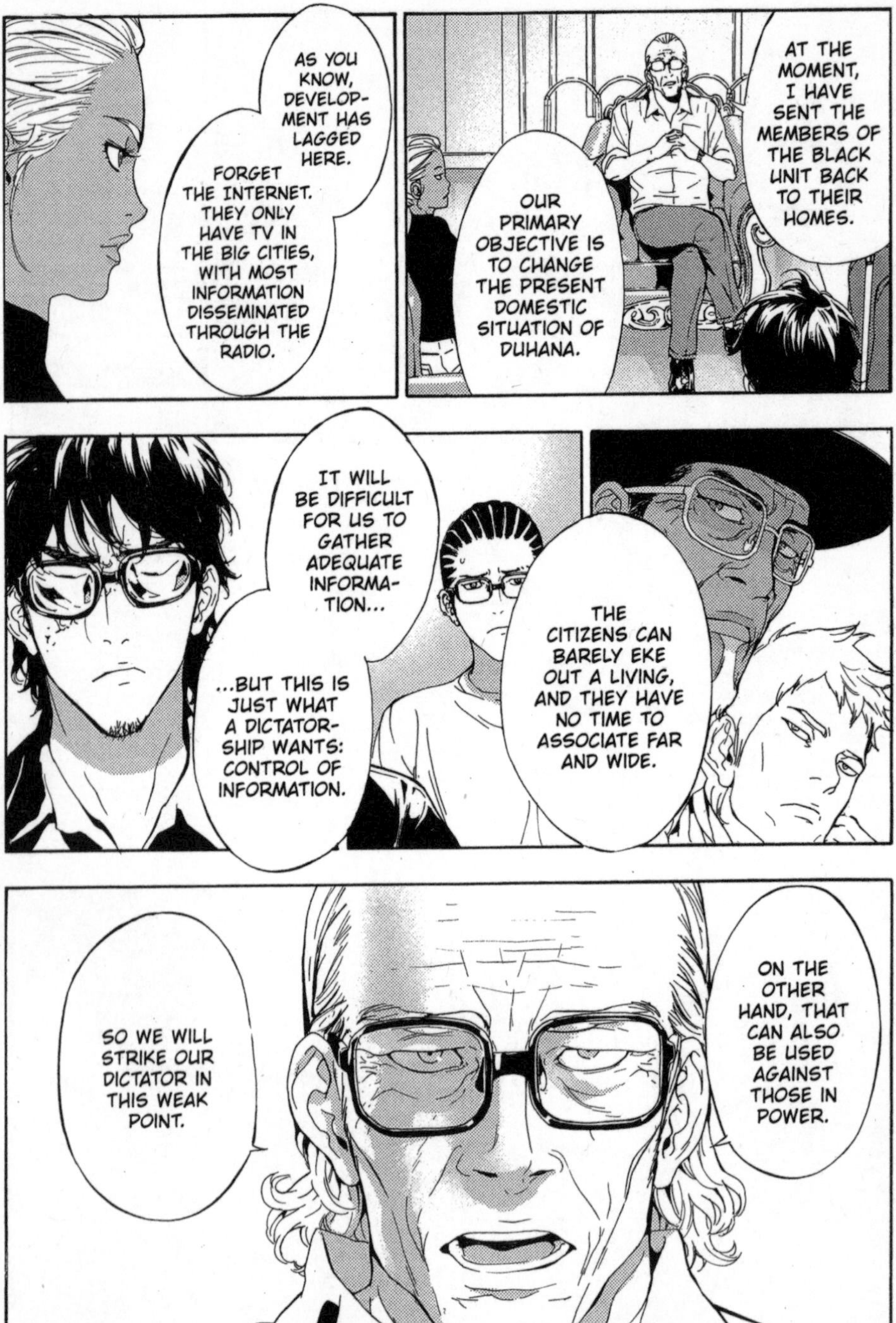
AT THE MOMENT, I HAVE SENT THE MEMBERS OF THE BLACK UNIT BACK TO THEIR HOMES.
OUR PRIMARY OBJECTIVE IS TO CHANGE THE PRESENT DOMESTIC SITUATION OF DUHANA.
AS YOU KNOW, DEVELOPMENT HAS LAGGED HERE.
FORGET THE INTERNET. THEY ONLY HAVE TV IN THE BIG CITIES, WITH MOST INFORMATION DISSEMINATED THROUGH THE RADIO.
THE CITIZENS CAN BARELY EKE OUT A LIVING, AND THEY HAVE NO TIME TO ASSOCIATE FAR AND WIDE.
IT WILL BE DIFFICULT FOR US TO GATHER ADEQUATE INFORMATION...
...BUT THIS IS JUST WHAT A DICTATORSHIP WANTS: CONTROL OF INFORMATION.
ON THE OTHER HAND, THAT CAN ALSO BE USED AGAINST THOSE IN POWER.
SO WE WILL STRIKE OUR DICTATOR IN THIS WEAK POINT.

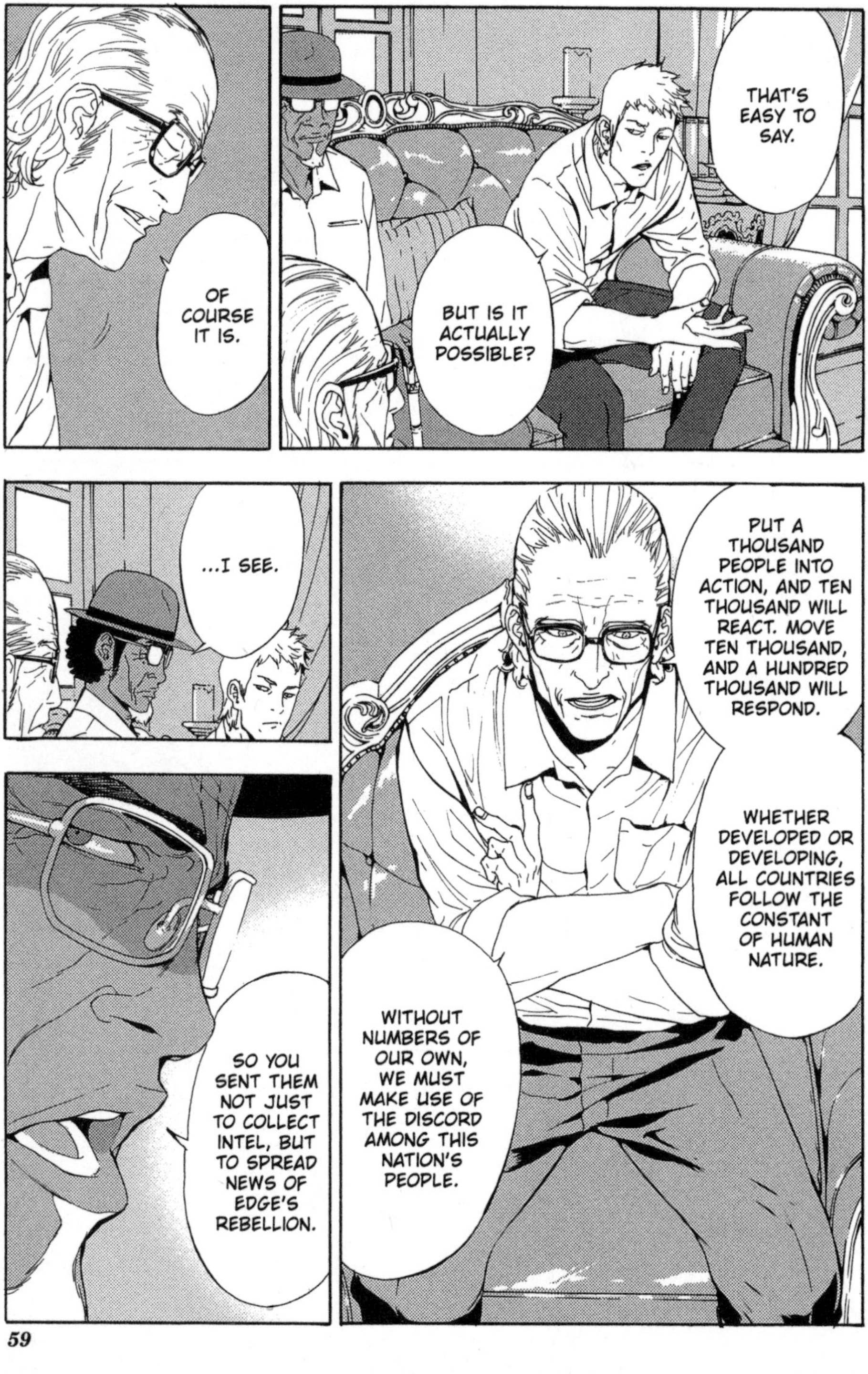
THAT'S EASY TO SAY.
BUT IS IT ACTUALLY POSSIBLE?
OF COURSE IT IS.
PUT A THOUSAND PEOPLE INTO ACTION, AND TEN THOUSAND WILL REACT. MOVE TEN THOUSAND, AND A HUNDRED THOUSAND WILL RESPOND.
WHETHER DEVELOPED OR DEVELOPING, ALL COUNTRIES FOLLOW THE CONSTANT OF HUMAN NATURE.
WITHOUT NUMBERS OF OUR OWN, WE MUST MAKE USE OF THE DISCORD AMONG THIS NATION'S PEOPLE.
...I SEE.
SO YOU SENT THEM NOT JUST TO COLLECT INTEL, BUT TO SPREAD NEWS OF EDGE'S REBELLION.

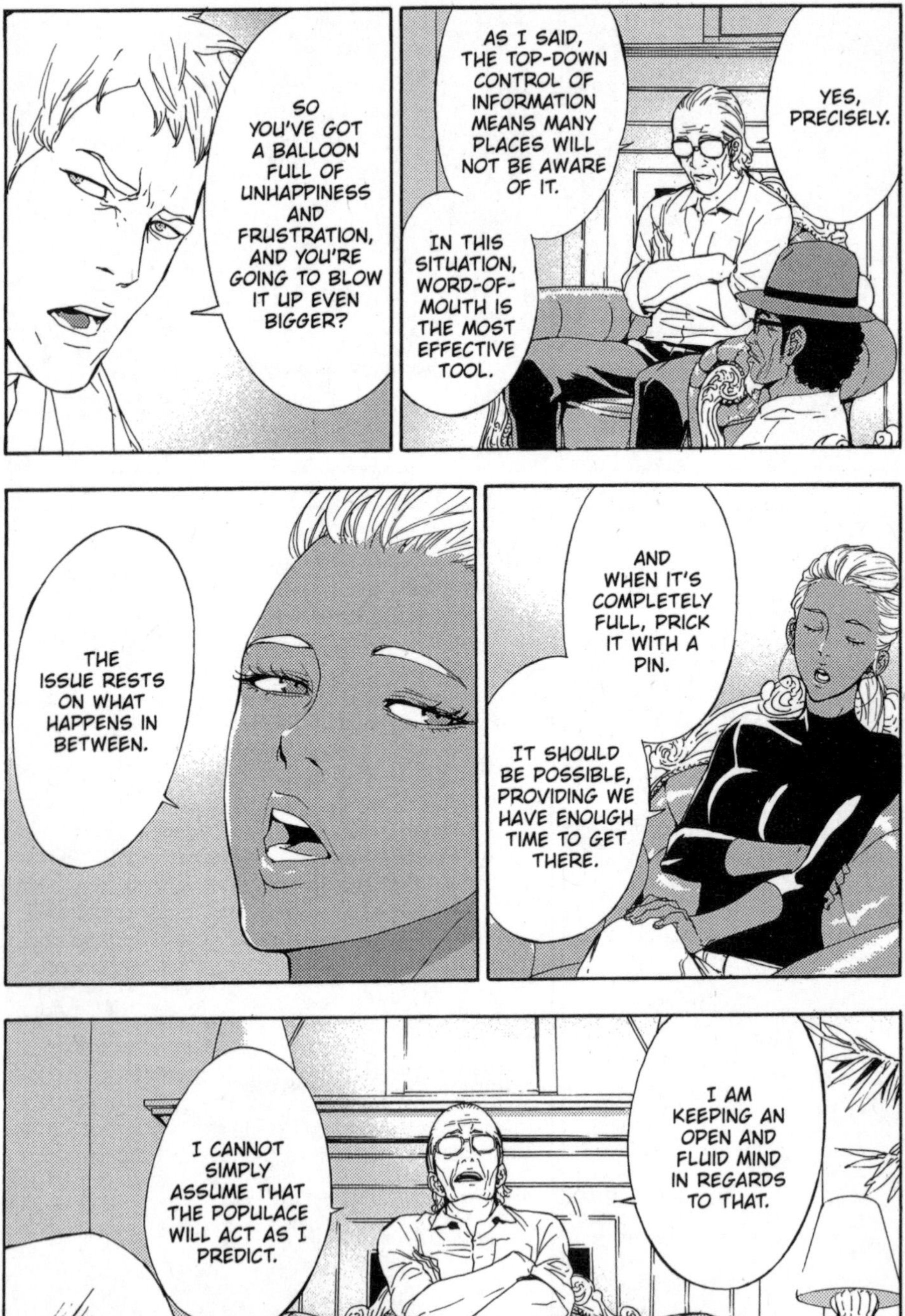
YES, PRECISELY.
AS I SAID, THE TOP-DOWN CONTROL OF INFORMATION MEANS MANY PLACES WILL NOT BE AWARE OF IT.
IN THIS SITUATION, WORD-OF-MOUTH IS THE MOST EFFECTIVE TOOL.
SO YOU'VE GOT A BALLOON FULL OF UNHAPPINESS AND FRUSTRATION, AND YOU'RE GOING TO BLOW IT UP EVEN BIGGER?
AND WHEN IT'S COMPLETELY FULL, PRICK IT WITH A PIN.
IT SHOULD BE POSSIBLE, PROVIDING WE HAVE ENOUGH TIME TO GET THERE.
THE ISSUE RESTS ON WHAT HAPPENS IN BETWEEN.
I AM KEEPING AN OPEN AND FLUID MIND IN REGARDS TO THAT.
I CANNOT SIMPLY ASSUME THAT THE POPULACE WILL ACT AS I PREDICT.

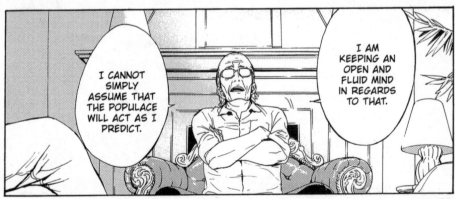

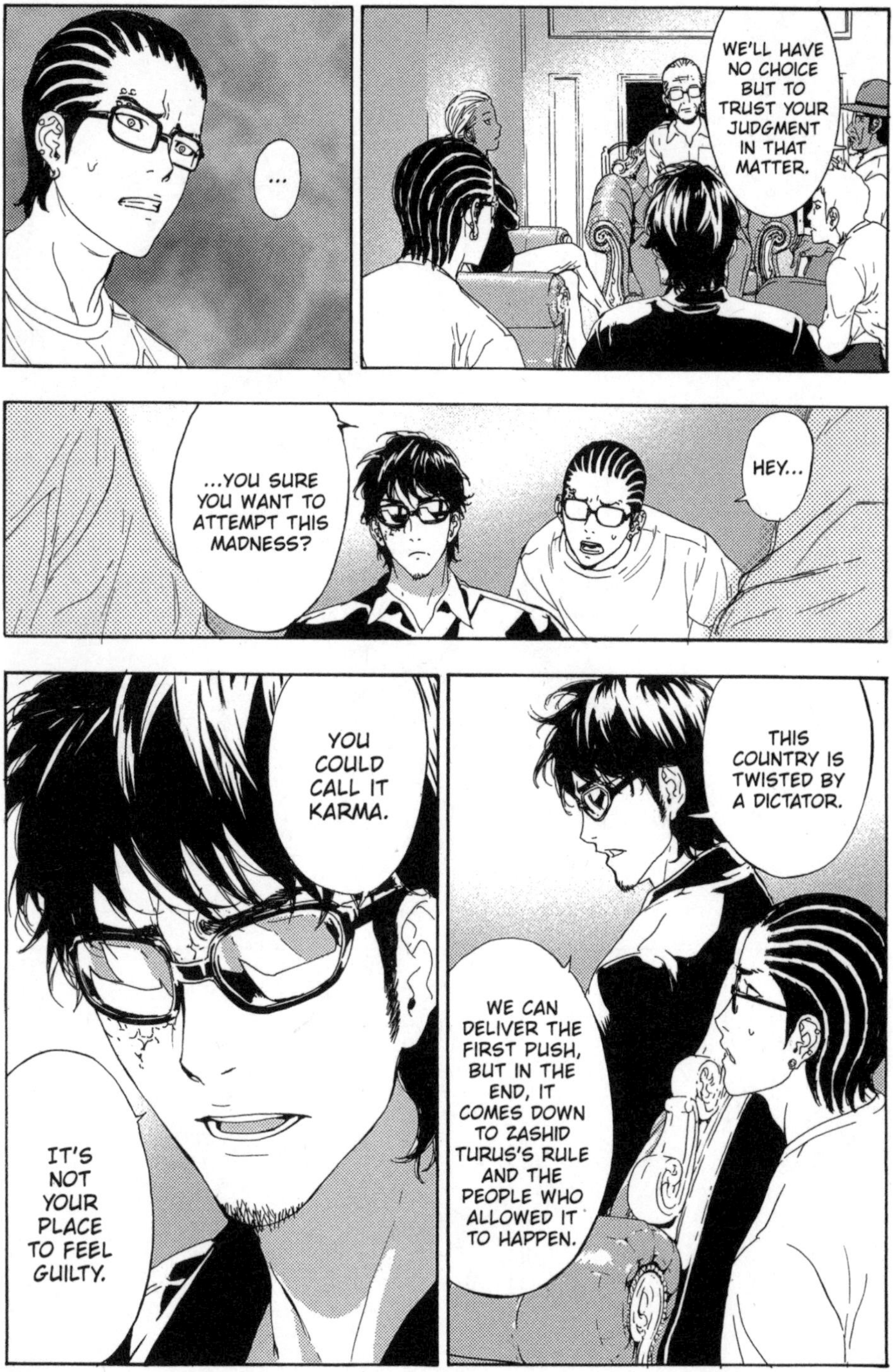
WE'LL HAVE NO CHOICE BUT TO TRUST YOUR JUDGMENT IN THAT MATTER.
...
HEY...
...YOU SURE YOU WANT TO ATTEMPT THIS MADNESS?
THIS COUNTRY IS TWISTED BY A DICTATOR.
WE CAN DELIVER THE FIRST PUSH, BUT IN THE END, IT COMES DOWN TO ZASHID TURUS'S RULE AND THE PEOPLE WHO ALLOWED IT TO HAPPEN.
YOU COULD CALL IT KARMA.
IT'S NOT YOUR PLACE TO FEEL GUILTY.

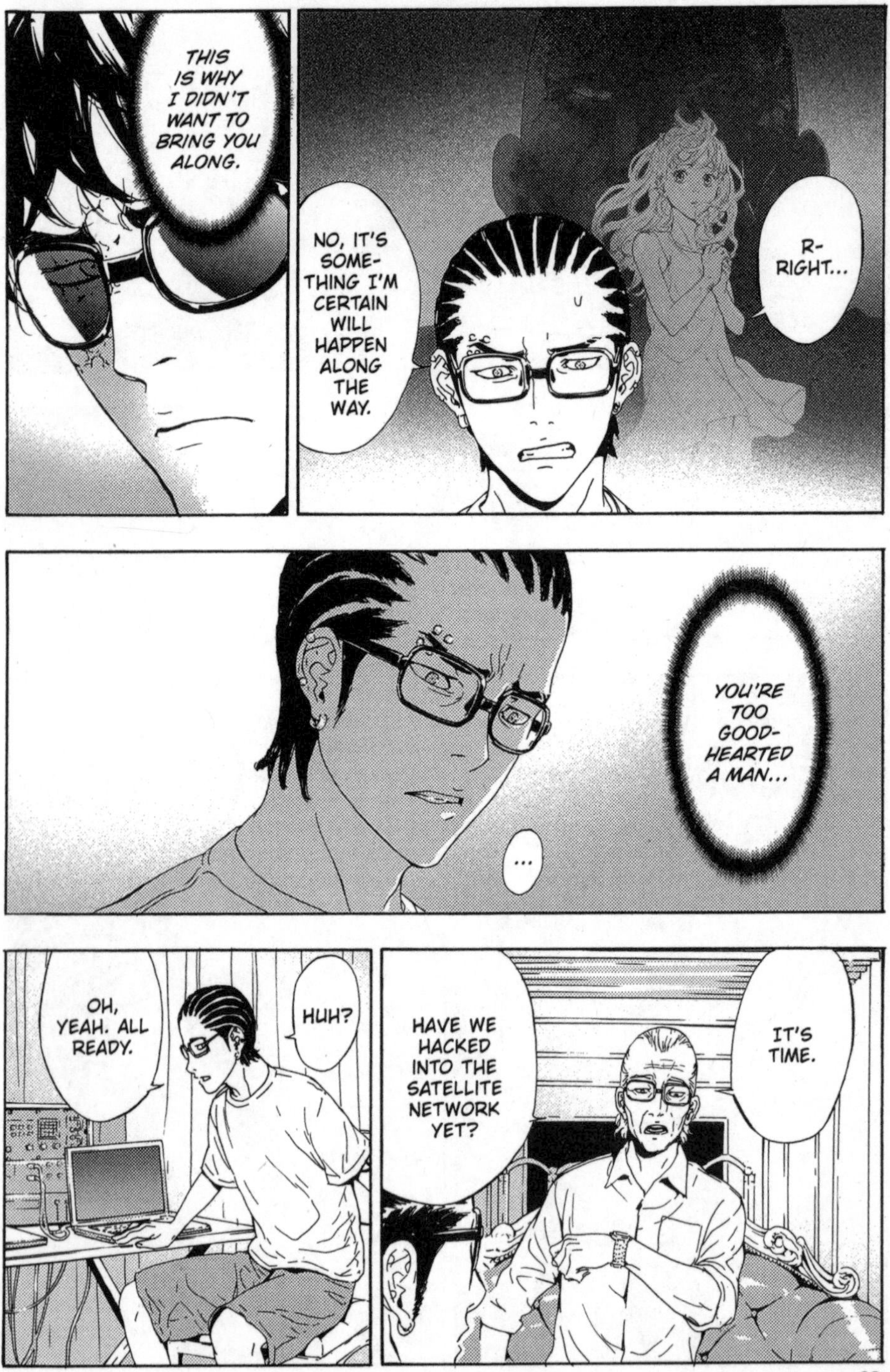
R- RIGHT...
NO, IT'S SOME-THING I'M CERTAIN WILL HAPPEN ALONG THE WAY.
THIS IS WHY I DIDN'T WANT TO BRING YOU ALONG.
YOU'RE TOO GOOD-HEARTED A MAN...
...
IT'S TIME.
HAVE WE HACKED INTO THE SATELLITE NETWORK YET?
HUH?
OH, YEAH. ALL READY.

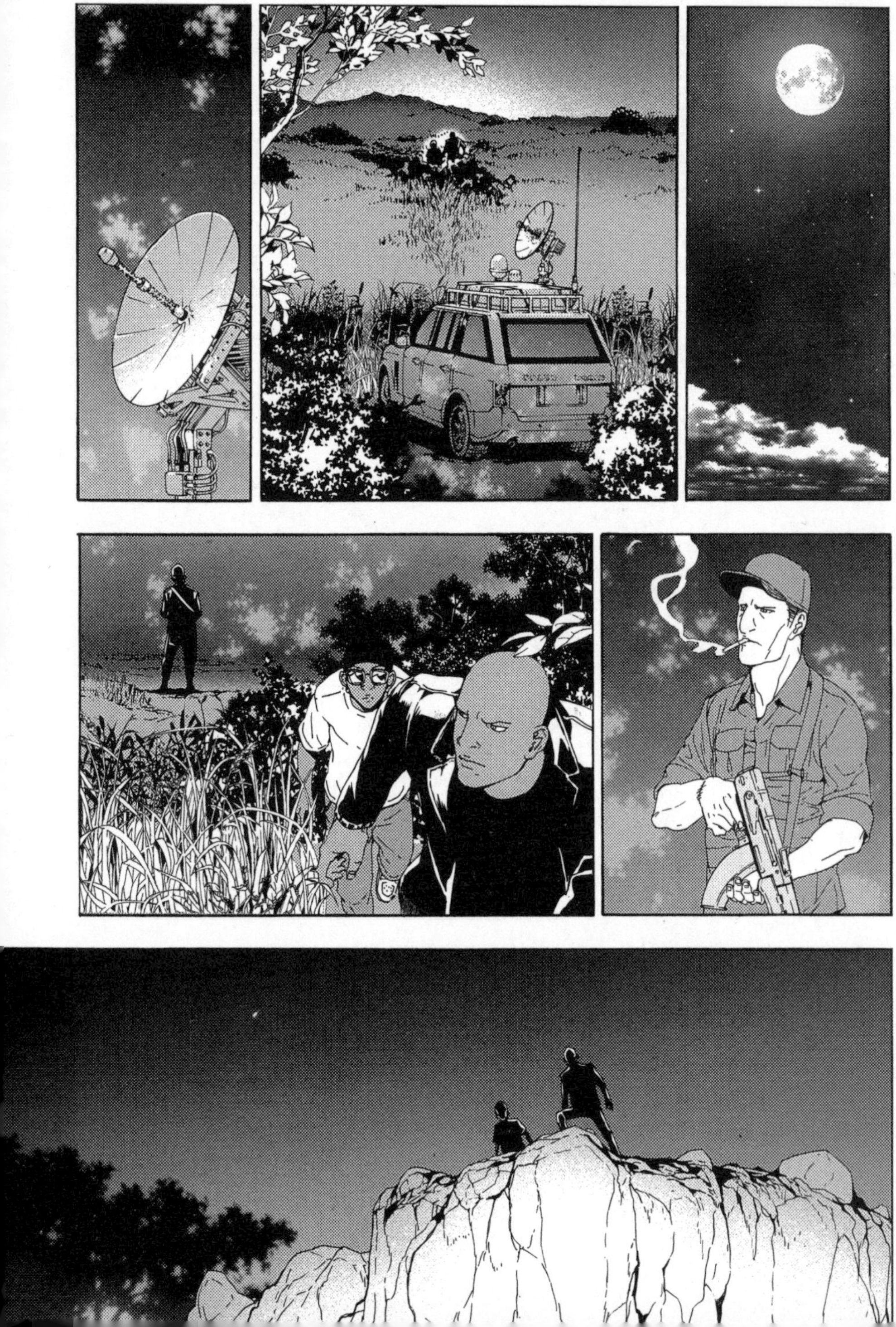

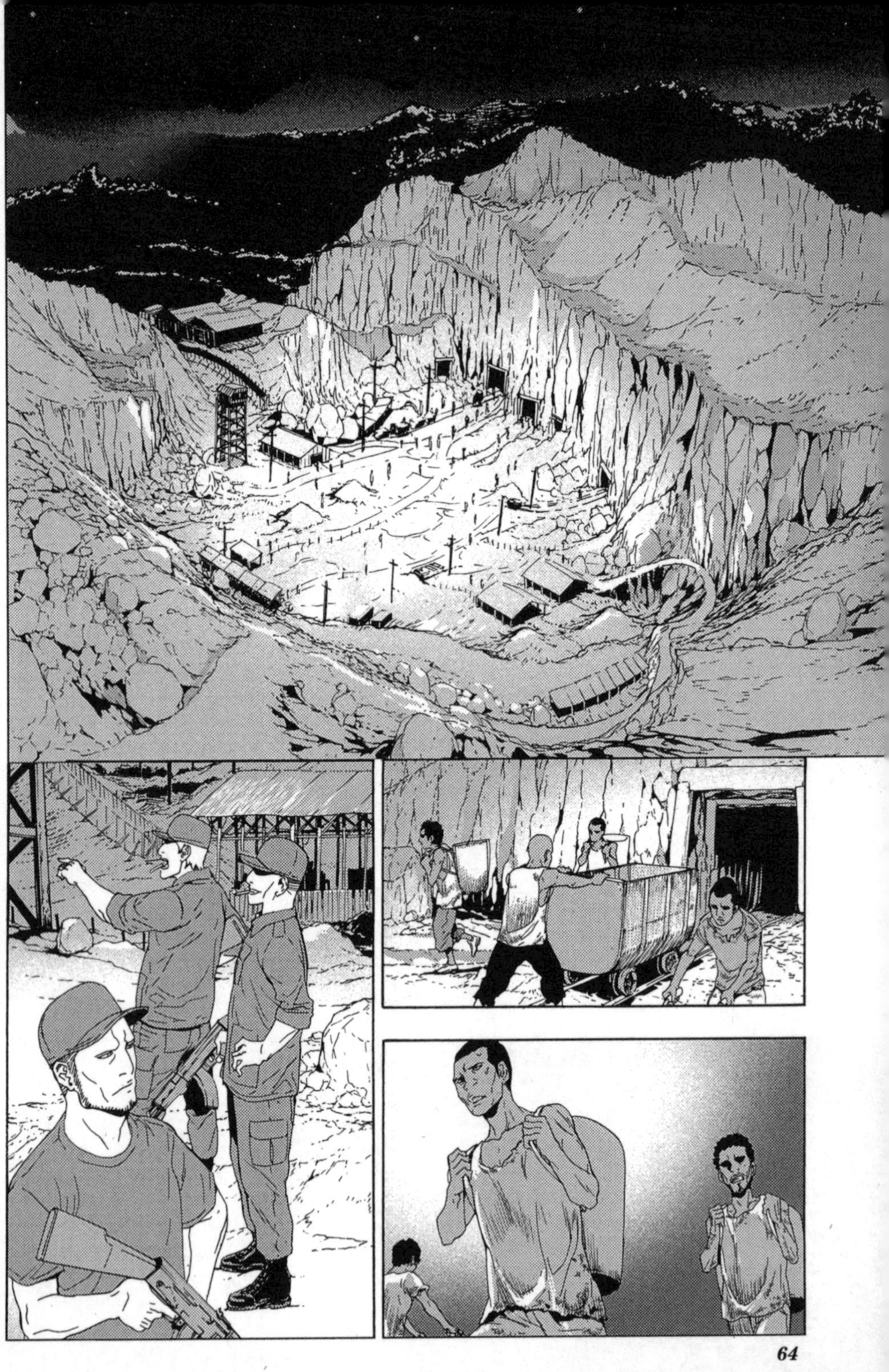

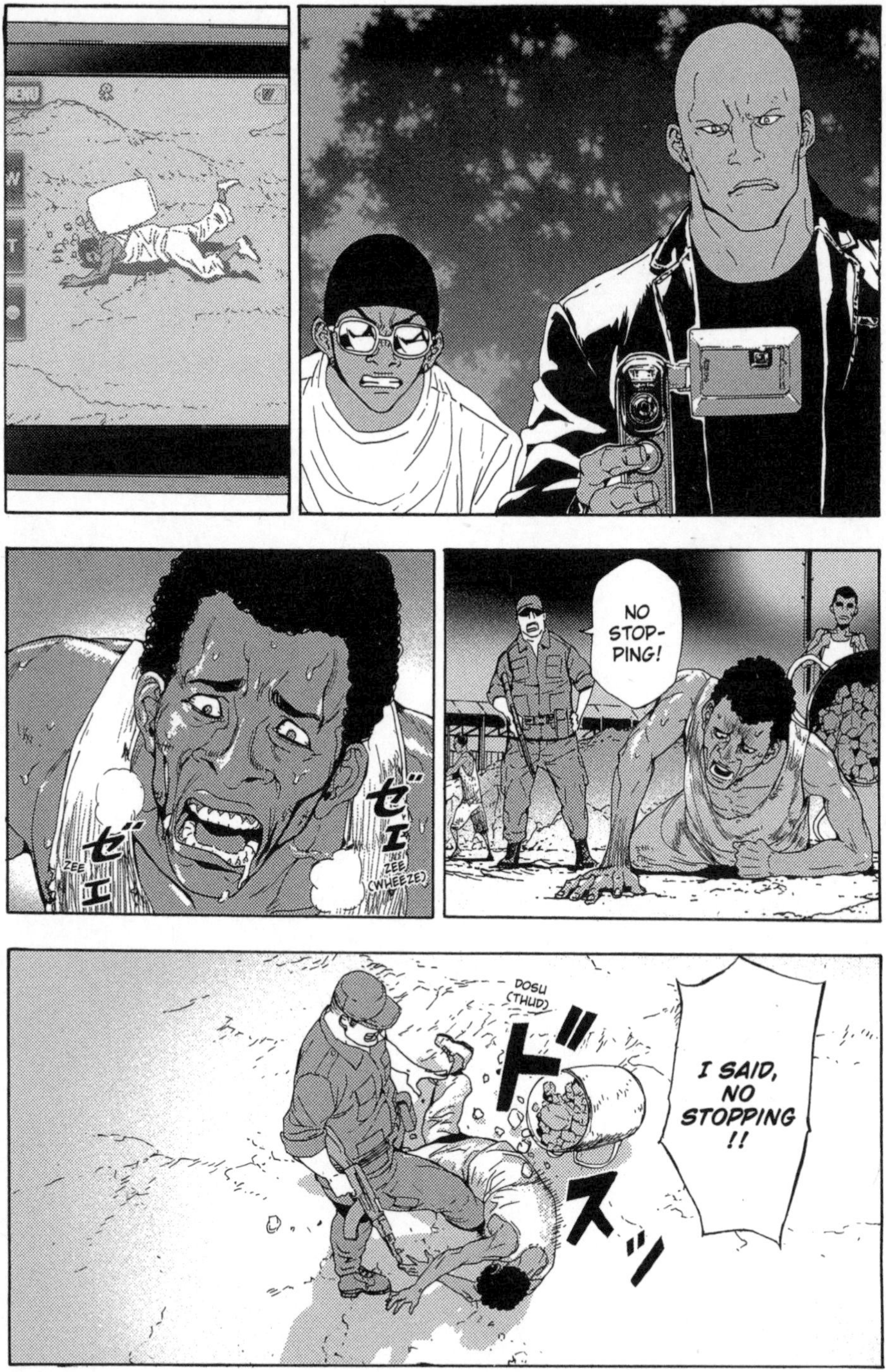

NO STOP-PING!
ゼェ
ZEE (WHEEZE)
ゼェ
ZEE
I SAID, NO STOPPING !!
DOSU (THUD)
ドズッ

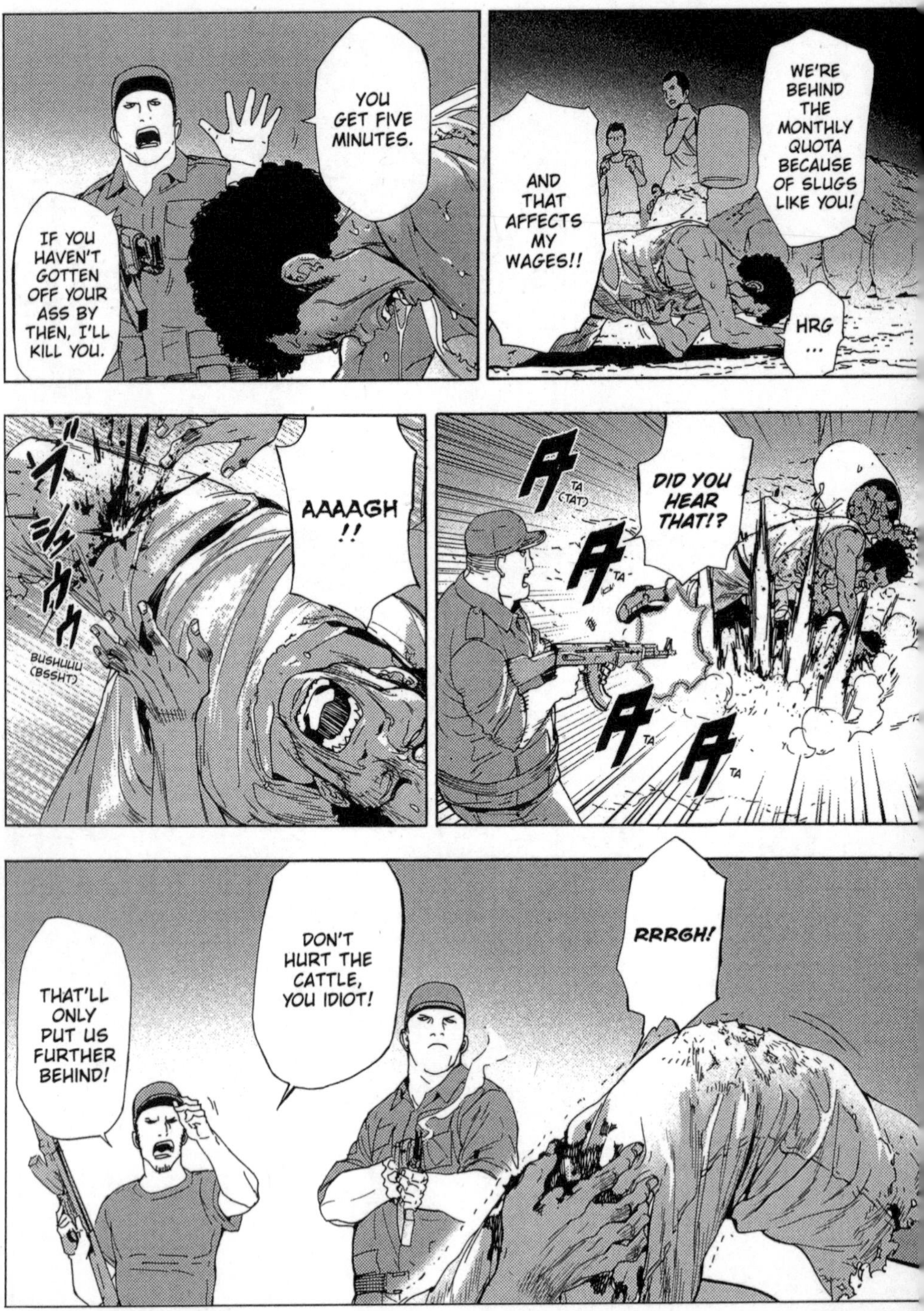
WE'RE BEHIND THE MONTHLY QUOTA BECAUSE OF SLUGS LIKE YOU!
AND THAT AFFECTS MY WAGES!!
HRG ...
YOU GET FIVE MINUTES.
IF YOU HAVEN'T GOTTEN OFF YOUR ASS BY THEN, I'LL KILL YOU.
TA (TAT)
DID YOU HEAR THAT!?
TA
TA
TA
AAAAGH !!
BUSHUUU (BSSHT)
RRRGH!
DON'T HURT THE CATTLE, YOU IDIOT!
THAT'LL ONLY PUT US FURTHER BEHIND!

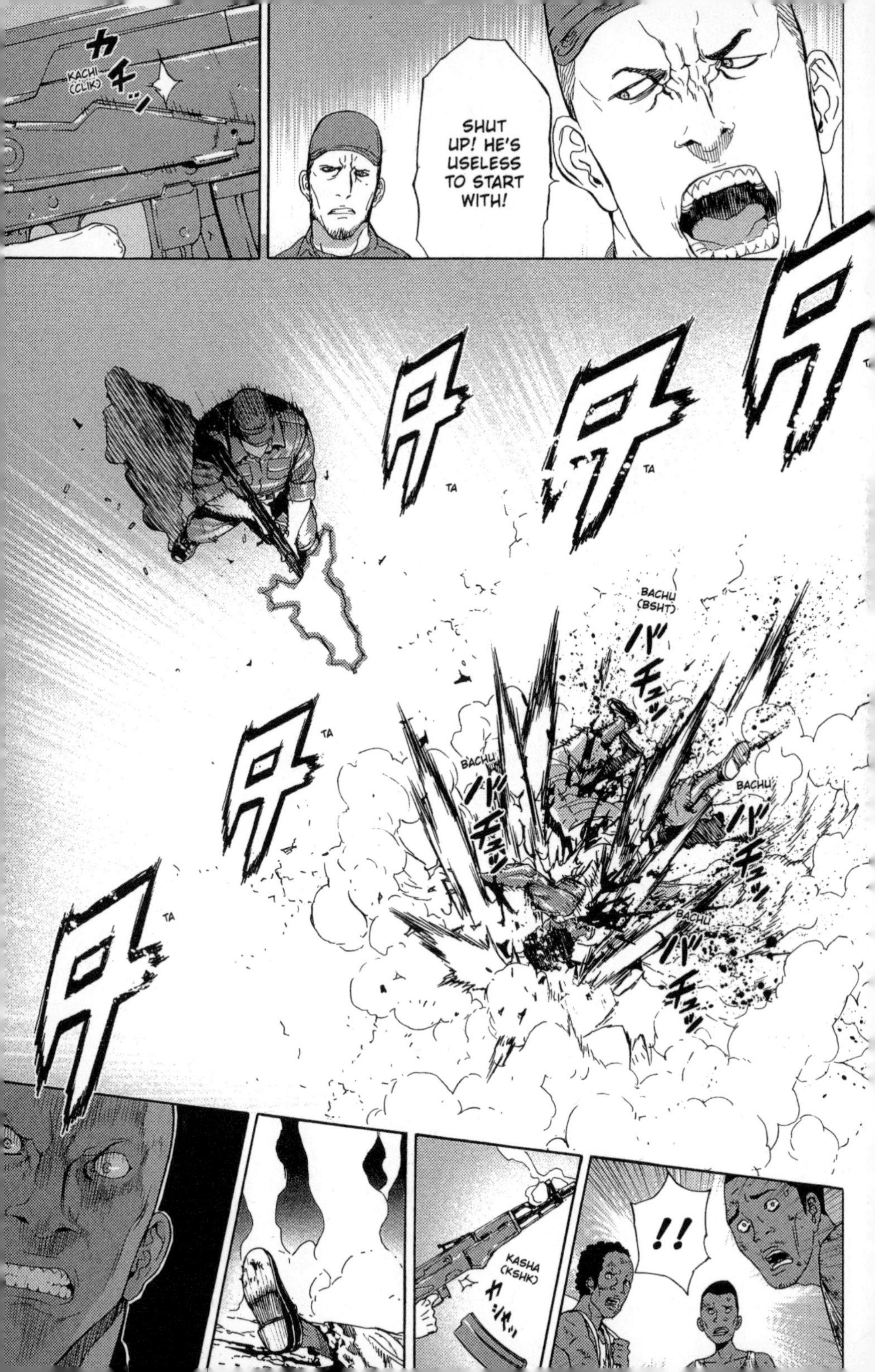
SHUT UP! HE'S USELESS TO START WITH!
カチッ
KACHI (CLIK)
TA
TA
TA
BACHU (BSHT)
バチュッ
BACHU
バチュッ
BACHU
バチュッ
BACHU
バチュッ
TA
TA
!!
KASHA (KSHK)
ガシャッ

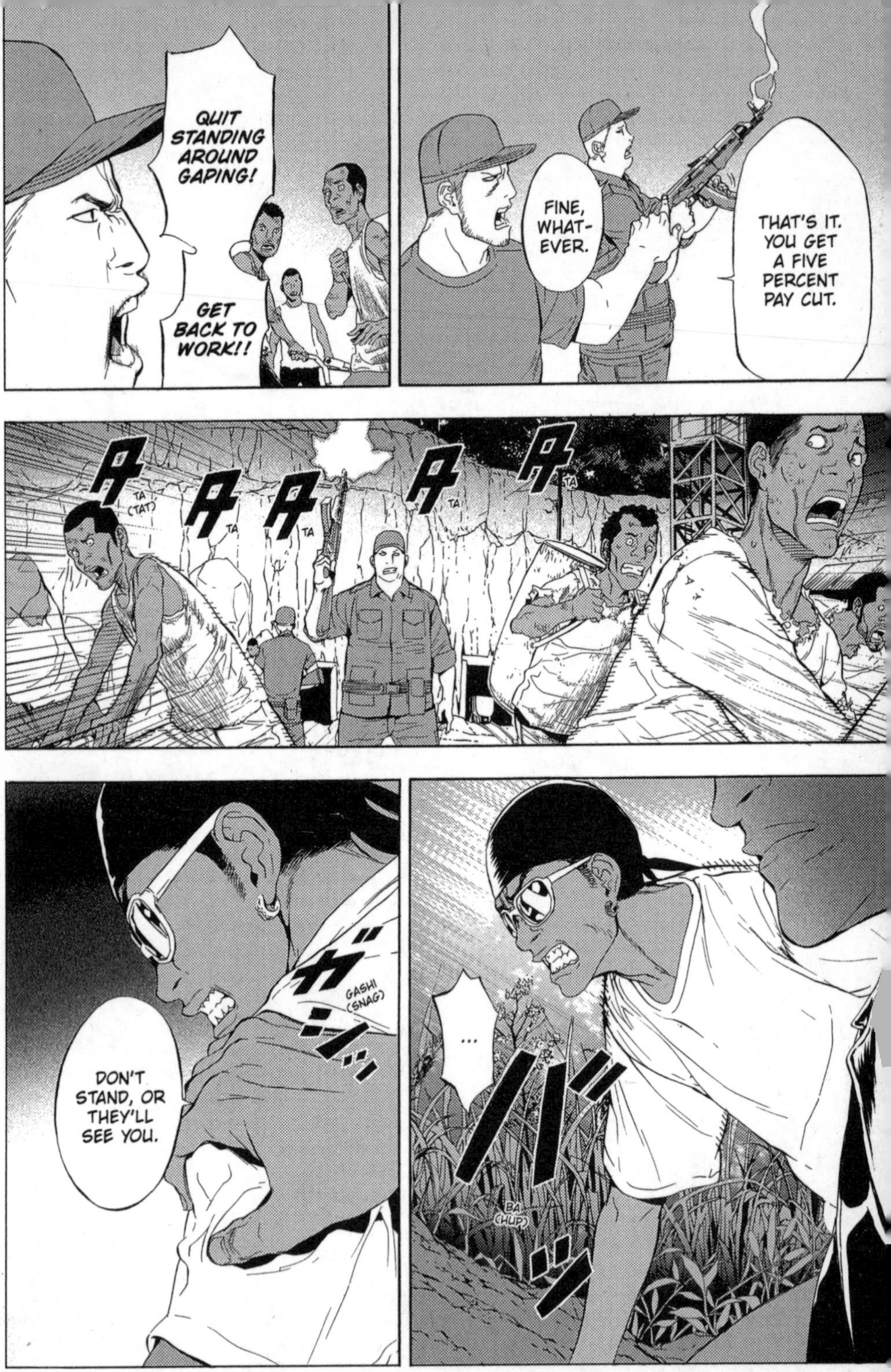
THAT'S IT. YOU GET A FIVE PERCENT PAY CUT.
FINE, WHATEVER.
QUIT STANDING AROUND GAPING!
GET BACK TO WORK!!
TA
TA
TA
TA
TA (TAT)
...
BA (HUP)
GASHI (SNAG)
DON'T STAND, OR THEY'LL SEE YOU.

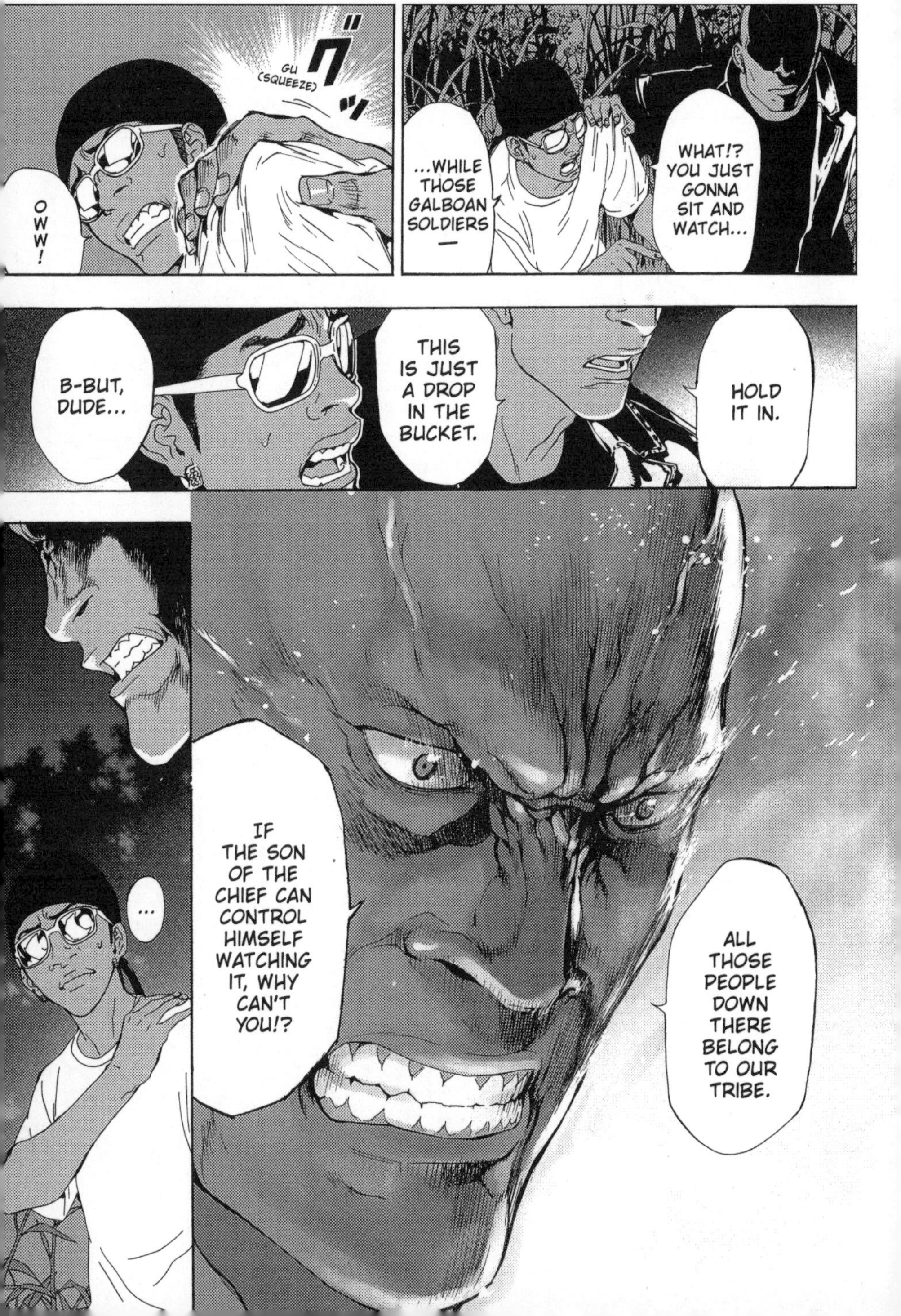
WHAT!? YOU JUST GONNA SIT AND WATCH...
...WHILE THOSE GALBOAN SOLDIERS —
GU (SQUEEZE)
OWW!
HOLD IT IN.
THIS IS JUST A DROP IN THE BUCKET.
B-BUT, DUDE...
ALL THOSE PEOPLE DOWN THERE BELONG TO OUR TRIBE.
IF THE SON OF THE CHIEF CAN CONTROL HIMSELF WATCHING IT, WHY CAN'T YOU!?
...

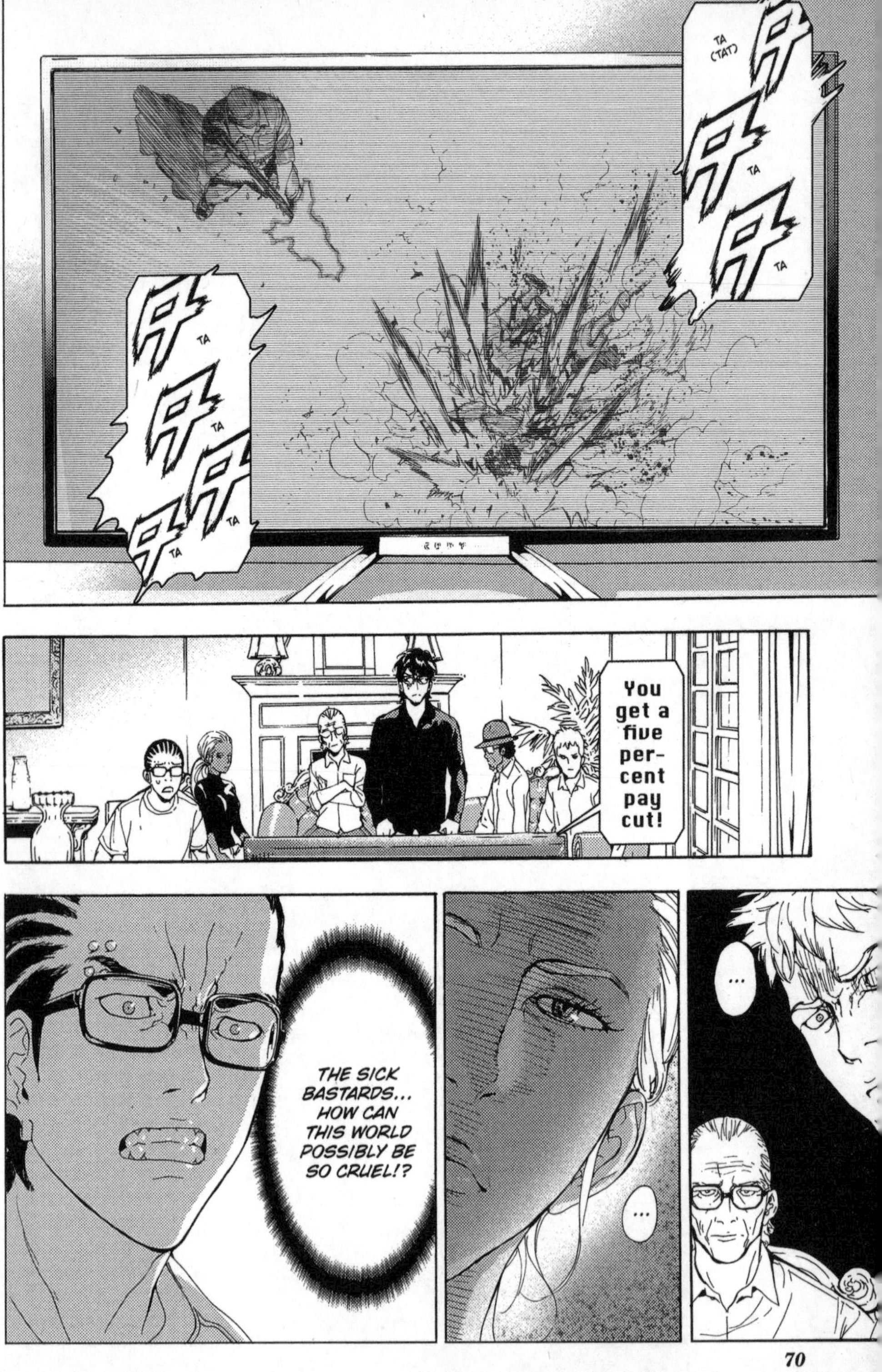
TA (TAT)
TA
TA
TA
TA
TA
TA
You get a five per-cent pay cut!
...
...
THE SICK BASTARDS... HOW CAN THIS WORLD POSSIBLY BE SO CRUEL!?

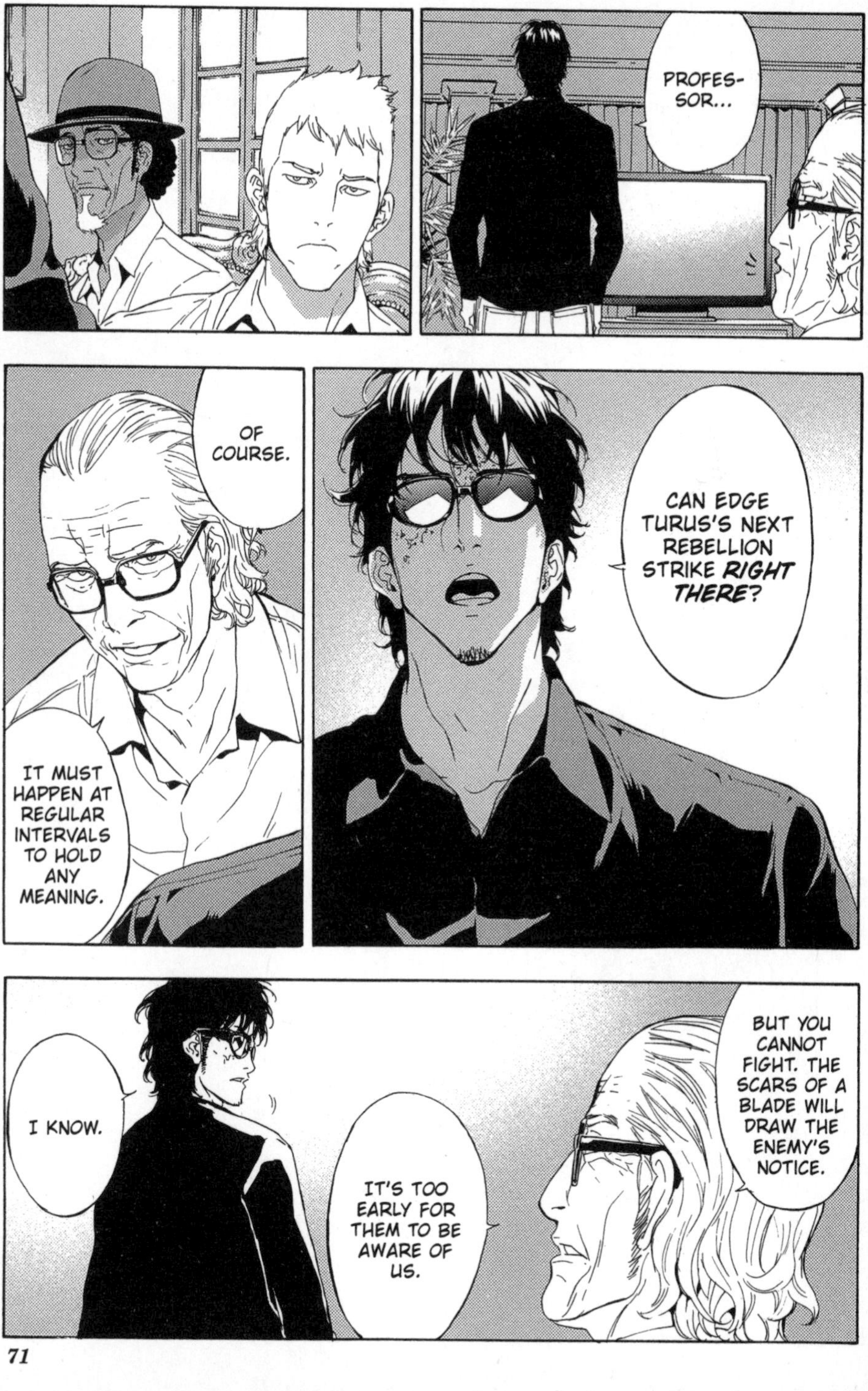
PROFES-SOR...
CAN EDGE TURUS'S NEXT REBELLION STRIKE *RIGHT THERE*?
OF COURSE.
IT MUST HAPPEN AT REGULAR INTERVALS TO HOLD ANY MEANING.
BUT YOU CANNOT FIGHT. THE SCARS OF A BLADE WILL DRAW THE ENEMY'S NOTICE.
IT'S TOO EARLY FOR THEM TO BE AWARE OF US.
I KNOW.

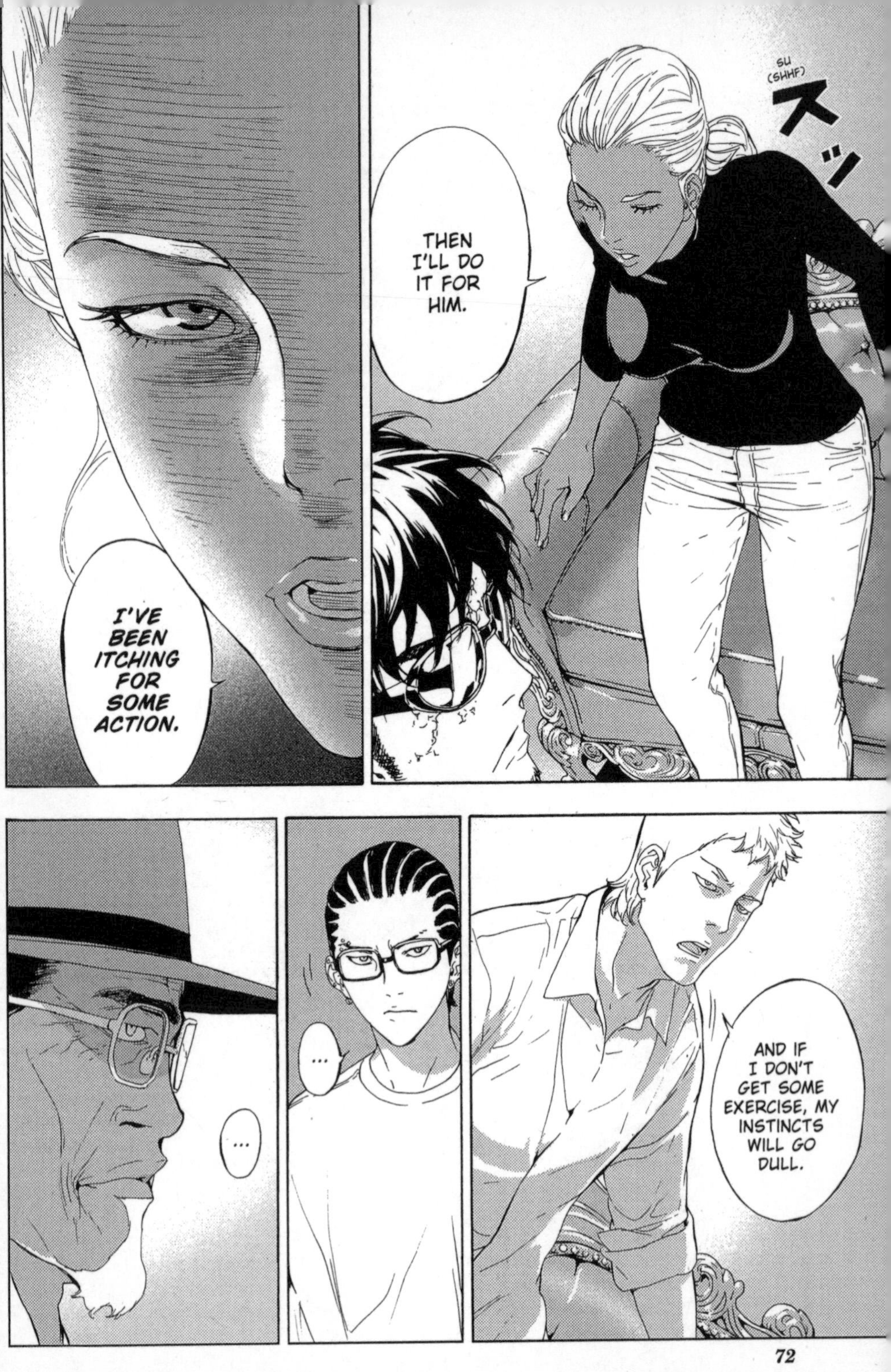
SU (SHHF)
スッ
THEN I'LL DO IT FOR HIM.
I'VE BEEN ITCHING FOR SOME ACTION.
AND IF I DON'T GET SOME EXERCISE, MY INSTINCTS WILL GO DULL.
...
...

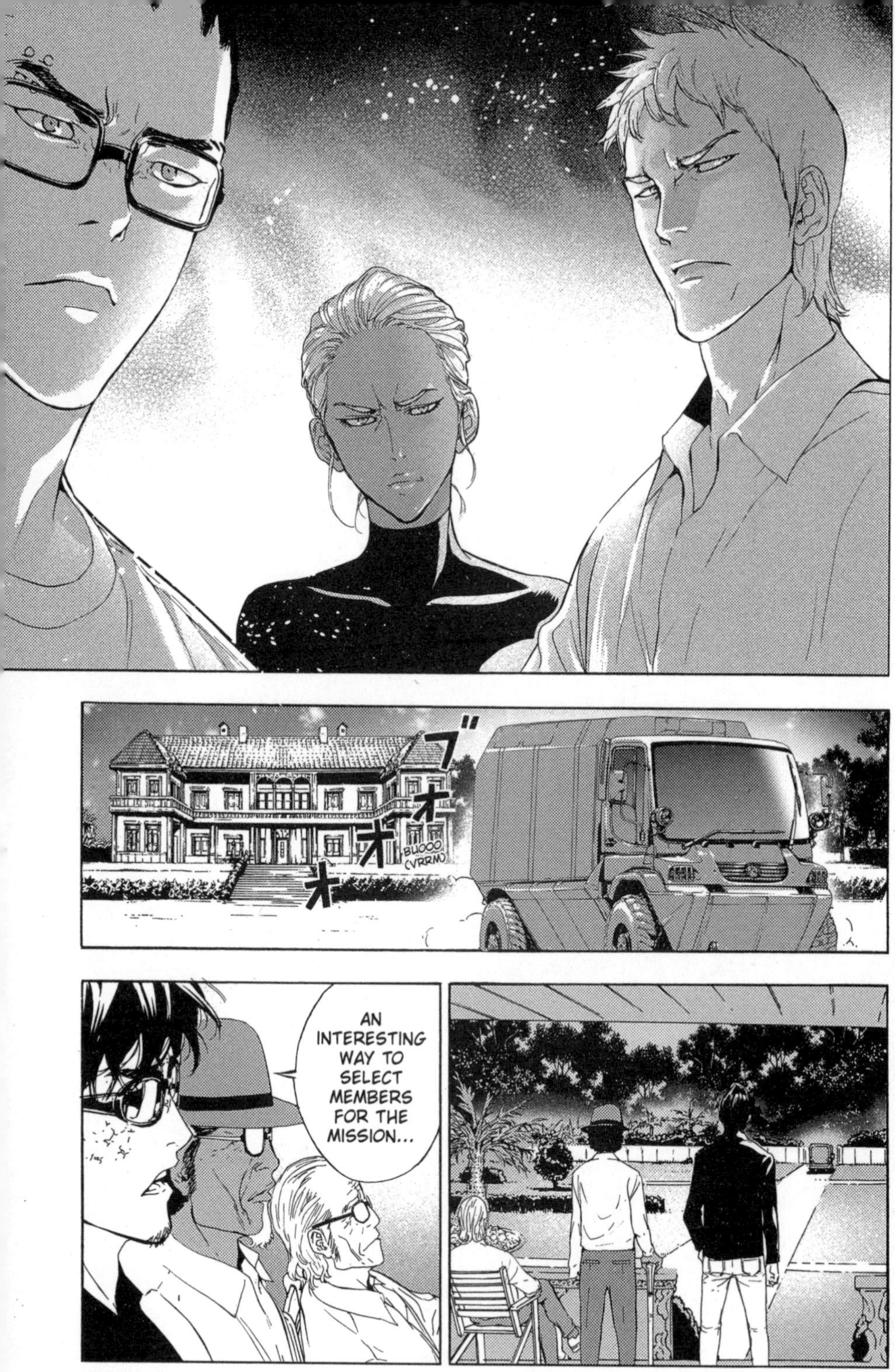
BUOOO (VRRM)
AN INTERESTING WAY TO SELECT MEMBERS FOR THE MISSION...

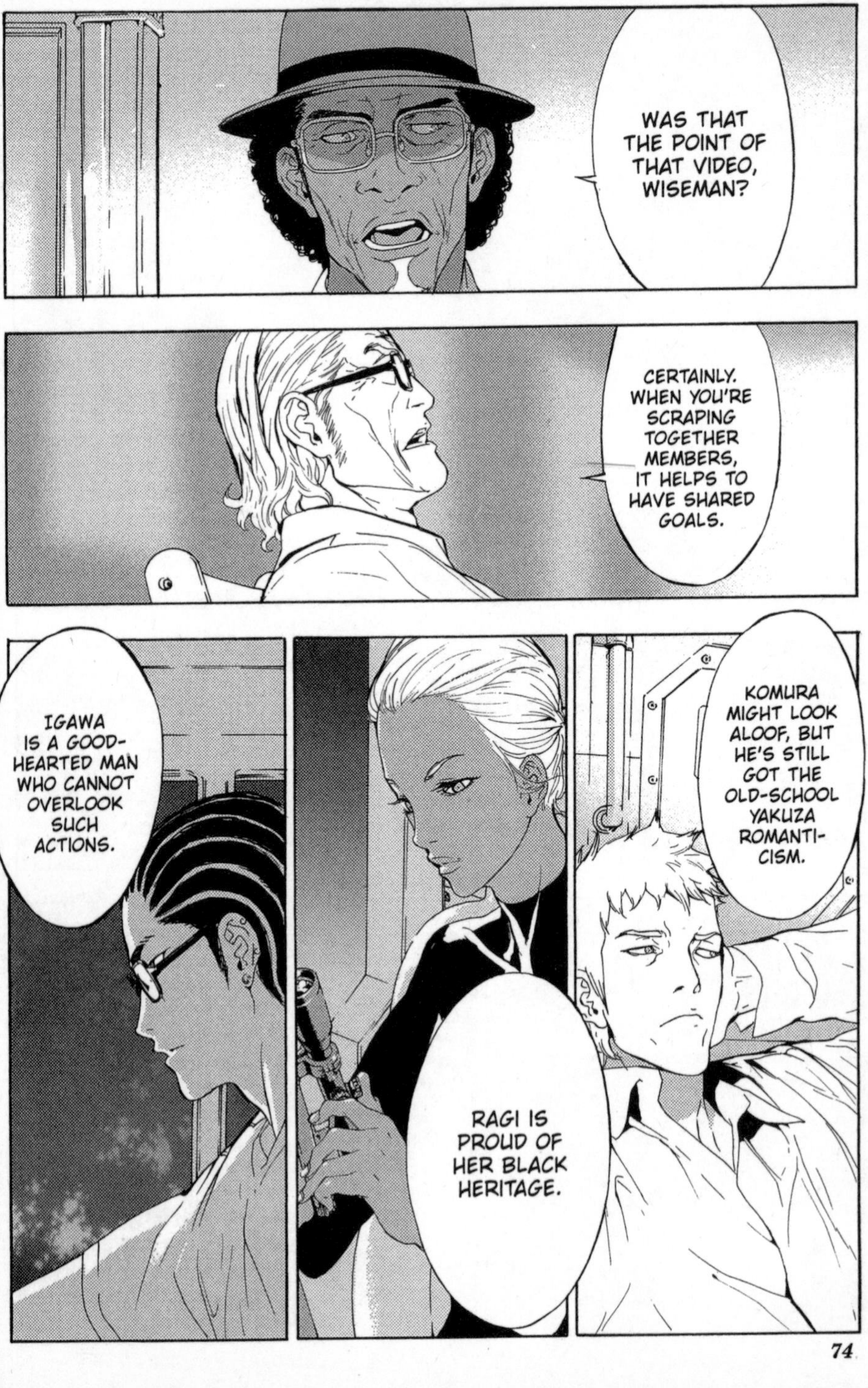
WAS THAT THE POINT OF THAT VIDEO, WISEMAN?
CERTAINLY. WHEN YOU'RE SCRAPING TOGETHER MEMBERS, IT HELPS TO HAVE SHARED GOALS.
KOMURA MIGHT LOOK ALOOF, BUT HE'S STILL GOT THE OLD-SCHOOL YAKUZA ROMANTI-CISM.
RAGI IS PROUD OF HER BLACK HERITAGE.
IGAWA IS A GOOD-HEARTED MAN WHO CANNOT OVERLOOK SUCH ACTIONS.

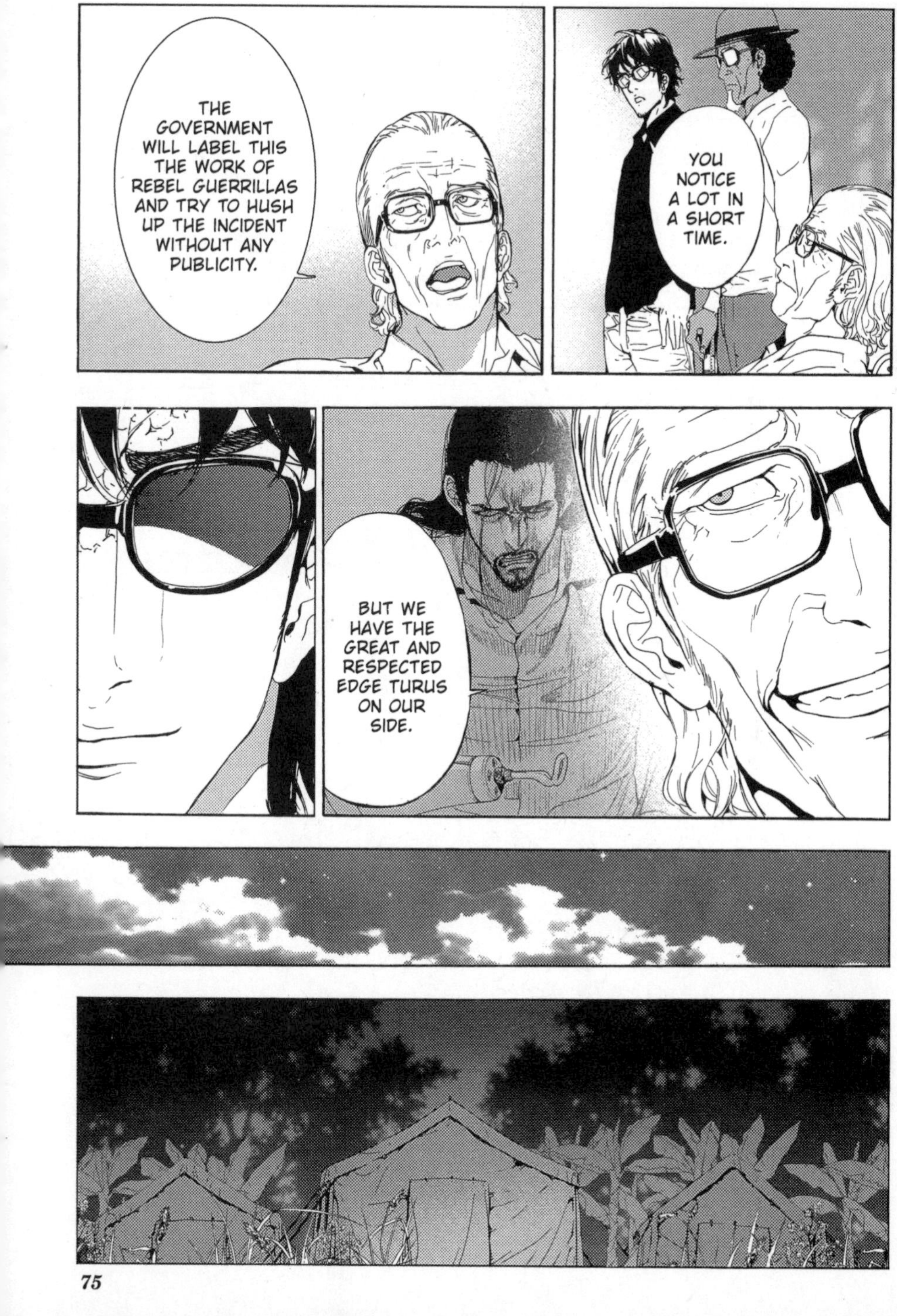

YOU NOTICE A LOT IN A SHORT TIME.
THE GOVERNMENT WILL LABEL THIS THE WORK OF REBEL GUERRILLAS AND TRY TO HUSH UP THE INCIDENT WITHOUT ANY PUBLICITY.
BUT WE HAVE THE GREAT AND RESPECTED EDGE TURUS ON OUR SIDE.

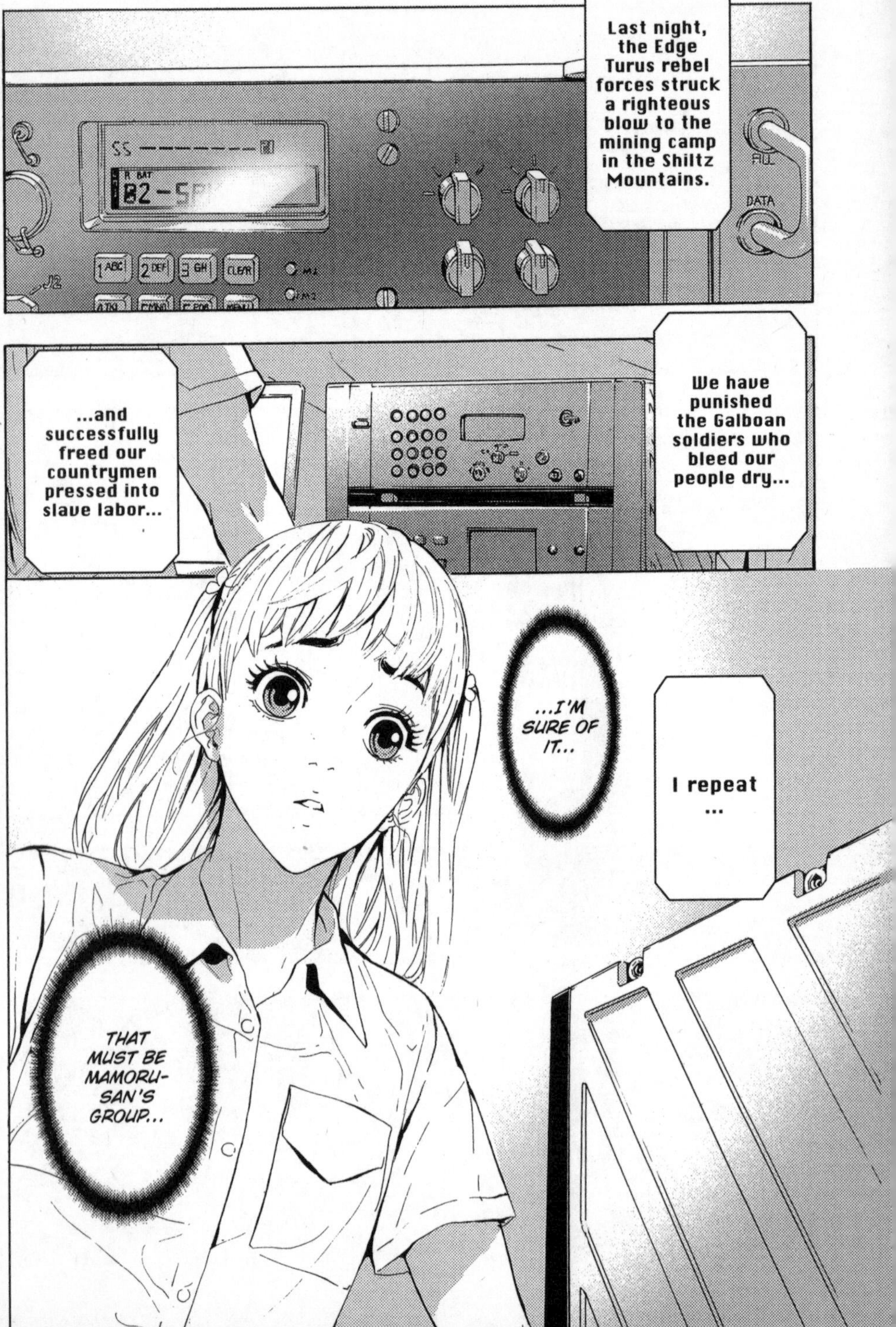
Last night, the Edge Turus rebel forces struck a righteous blow to the mining camp in the Shiltz Mountains.
We have punished the Galboan soldiers who bleed our people dry...
...and successfully freed our countrymen pressed into slave labor...
I repeat ...
...I'M SURE OF IT...
THAT MUST BE MAMORU-SAN'S GROUP...

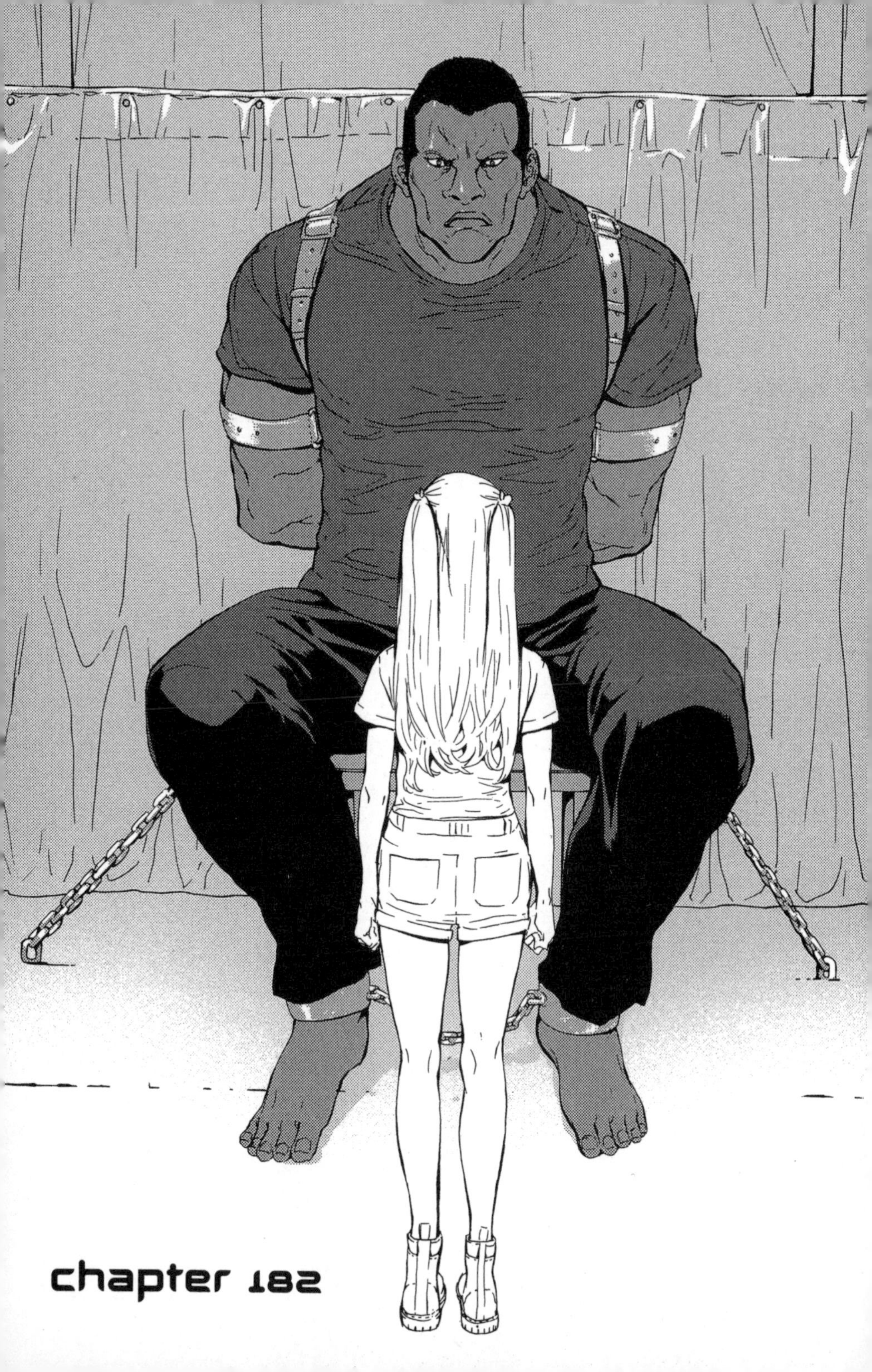
chapter 182

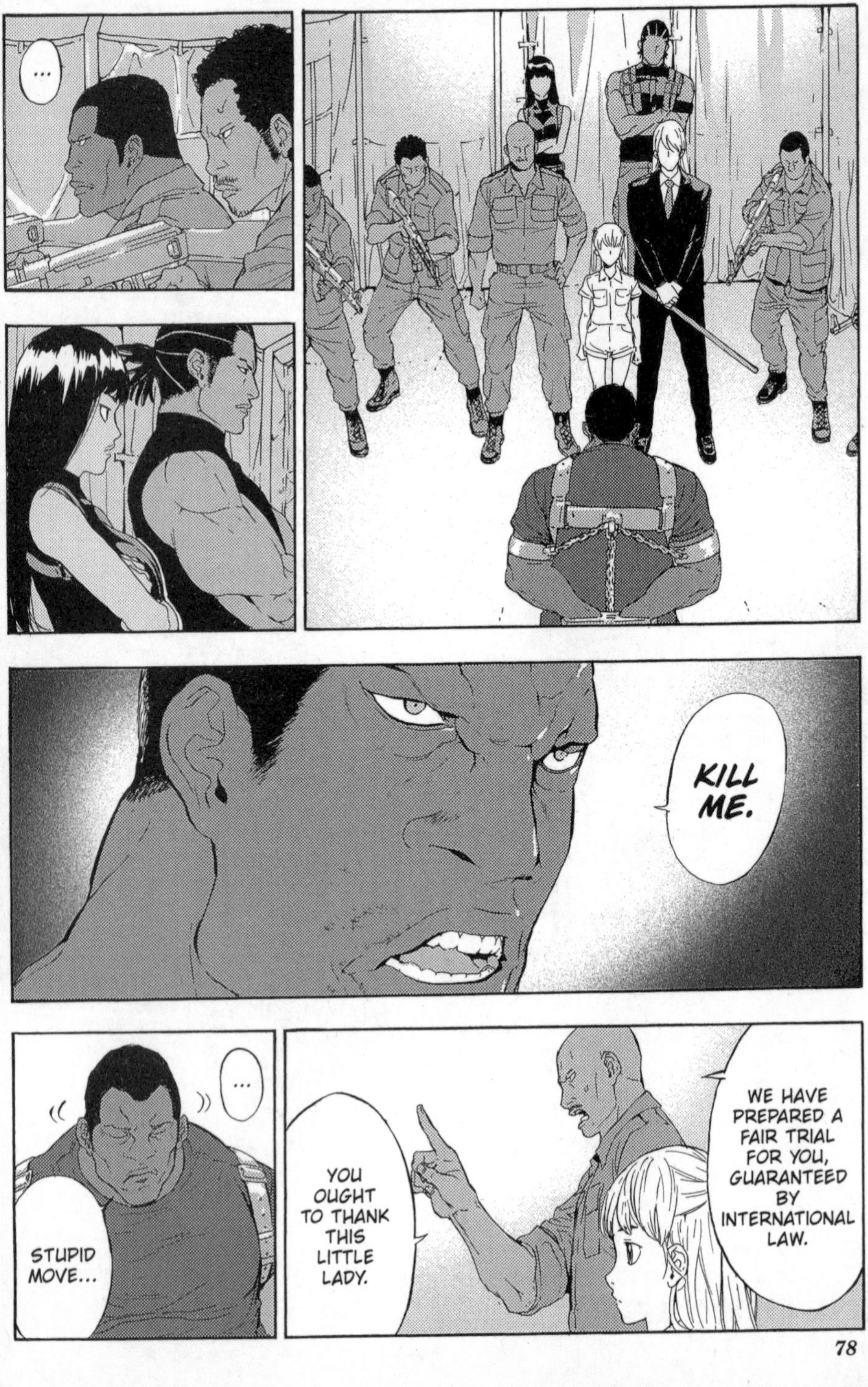
...
KILL ME.
WE HAVE PREPARED A FAIR TRIAL FOR YOU, GUARANTEED BY INTERNATIONAL LAW.
YOU OUGHT TO THANK THIS LITTLE LADY.
...
STUPID MOVE...

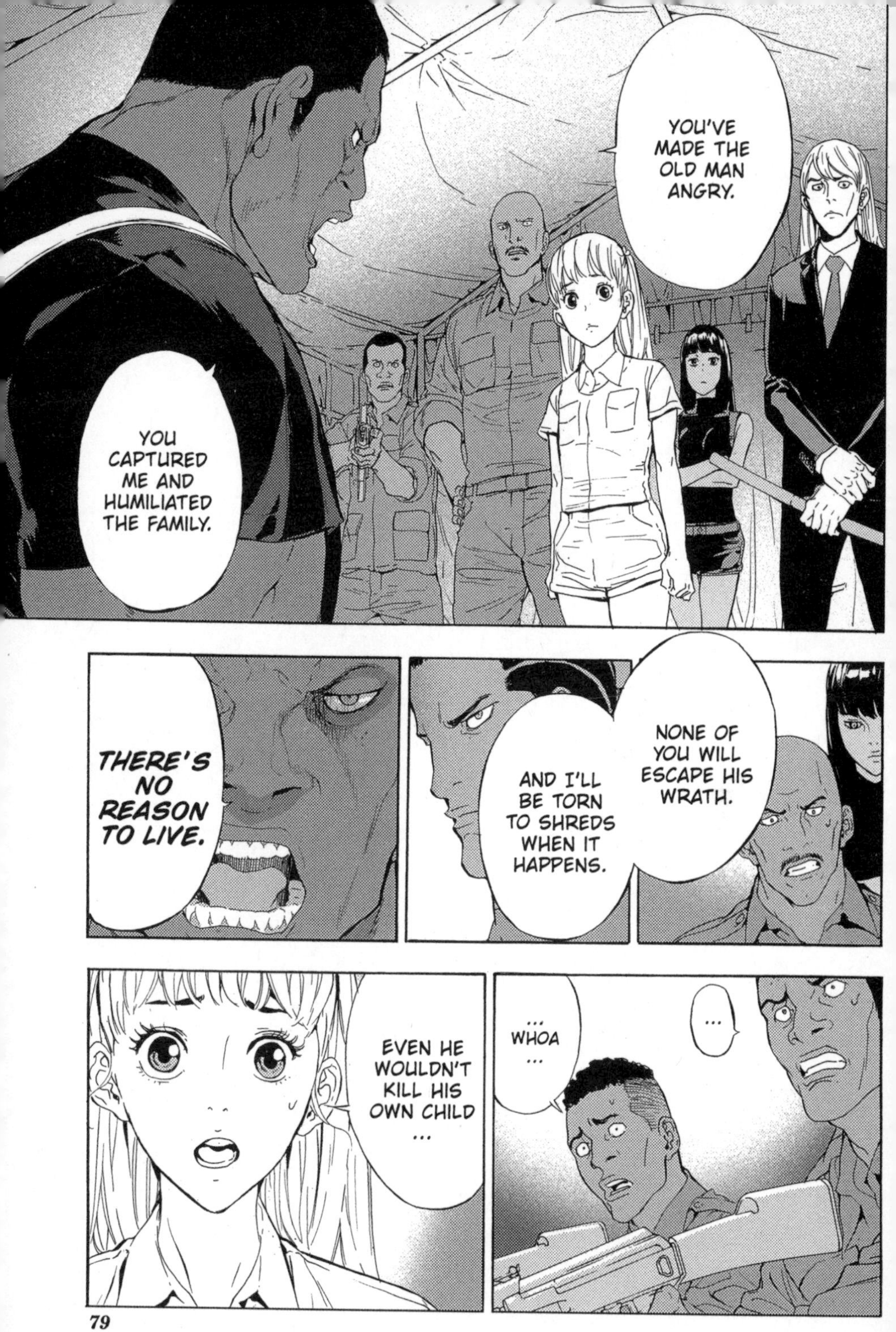
YOU'VE MADE THE OLD MAN ANGRY.
YOU CAPTURED ME AND HUMILIATED THE FAMILY.
NONE OF YOU WILL ESCAPE HIS WRATH.
AND I'LL BE TORN TO SHREDS WHEN IT HAPPENS.
THERE'S NO REASON TO LIVE.
...
... WHOA ...
EVEN HE WOULDN'T KILL HIS OWN CHILD ...

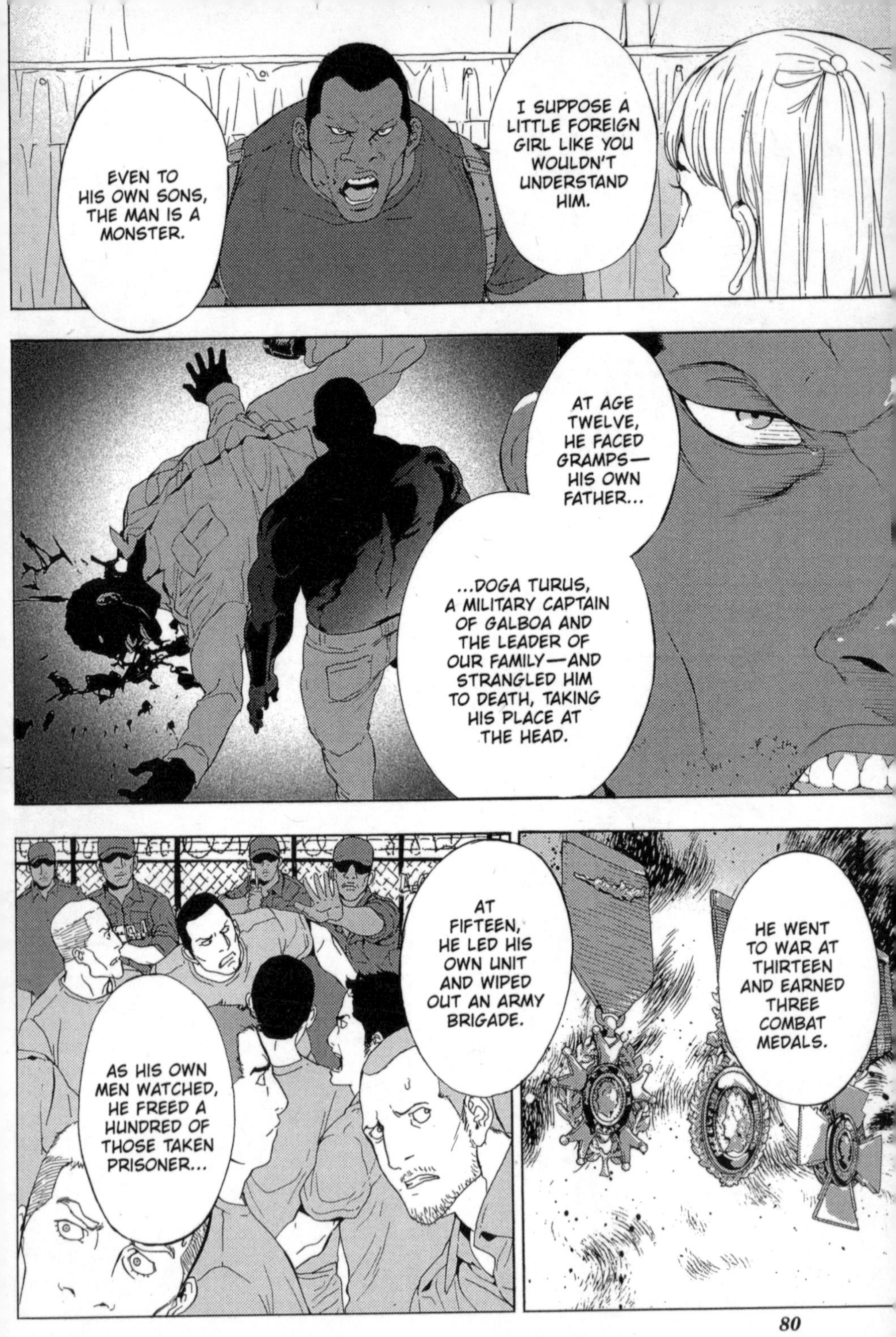
I SUPPOSE A LITTLE FOREIGN GIRL LIKE YOU WOULDN'T UNDERSTAND HIM.
EVEN TO HIS OWN SONS, THE MAN IS A MONSTER.
AT AGE TWELVE, HE FACED GRAMPS— HIS OWN FATHER...
...DOGA TURUS, A MILITARY CAPTAIN OF GALBOA AND THE LEADER OF OUR FAMILY—AND STRANGLED HIM TO DEATH, TAKING HIS PLACE AT THE HEAD.
HE WENT TO WAR AT THIRTEEN AND EARNED THREE COMBAT MEDALS.
AT FIFTEEN, HE LED HIS OWN UNIT AND WIPED OUT AN ARMY BRIGADE.
AS HIS OWN MEN WATCHED, HE FREED A HUNDRED OF THOSE TAKEN PRISONER...

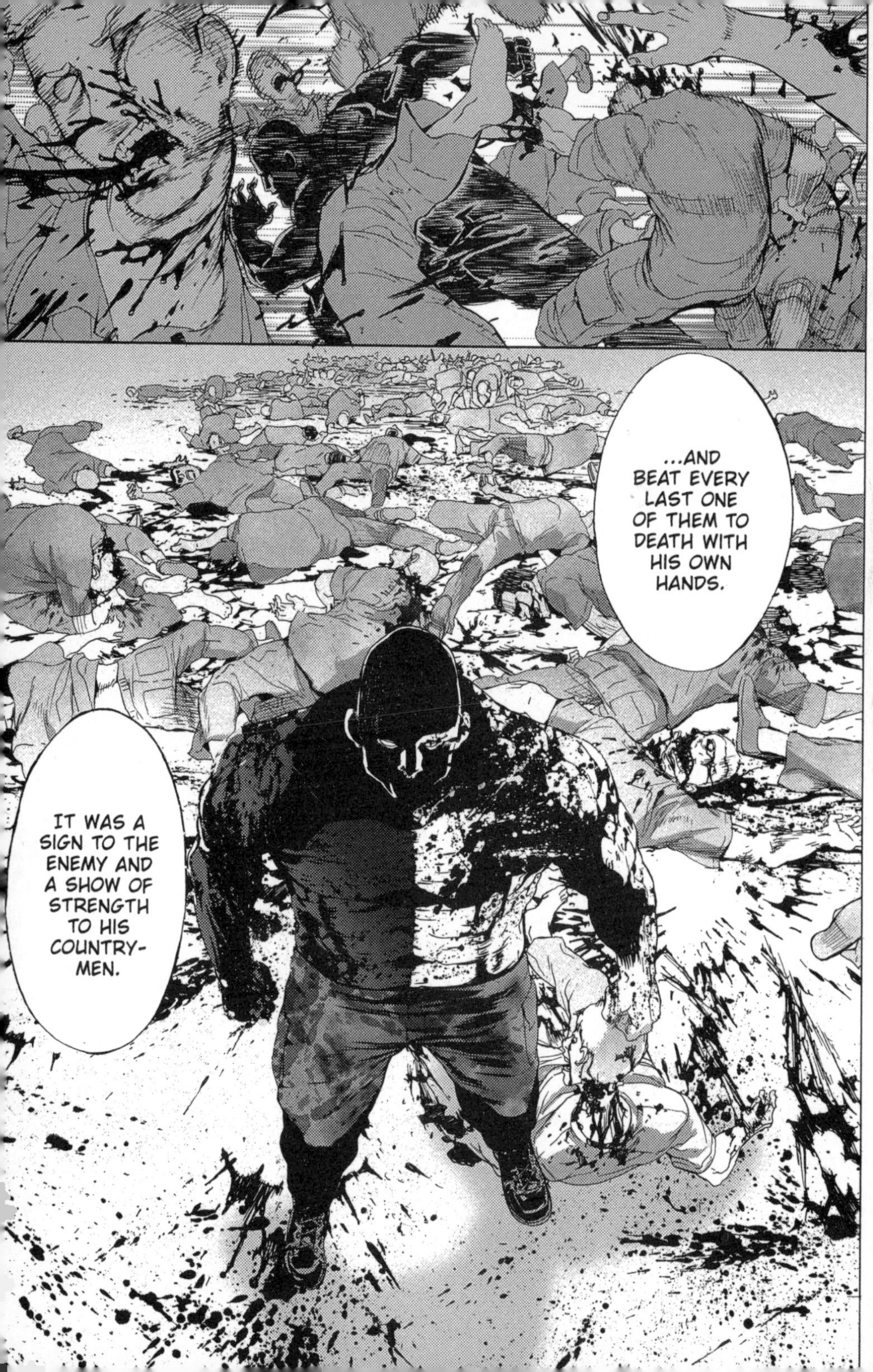
...AND BEAT EVERY LAST ONE OF THEM TO DEATH WITH HIS OWN HANDS.
IT WAS A SIGN TO THE ENEMY AND A SHOW OF STRENGTH TO HIS COUNTRY-MEN.

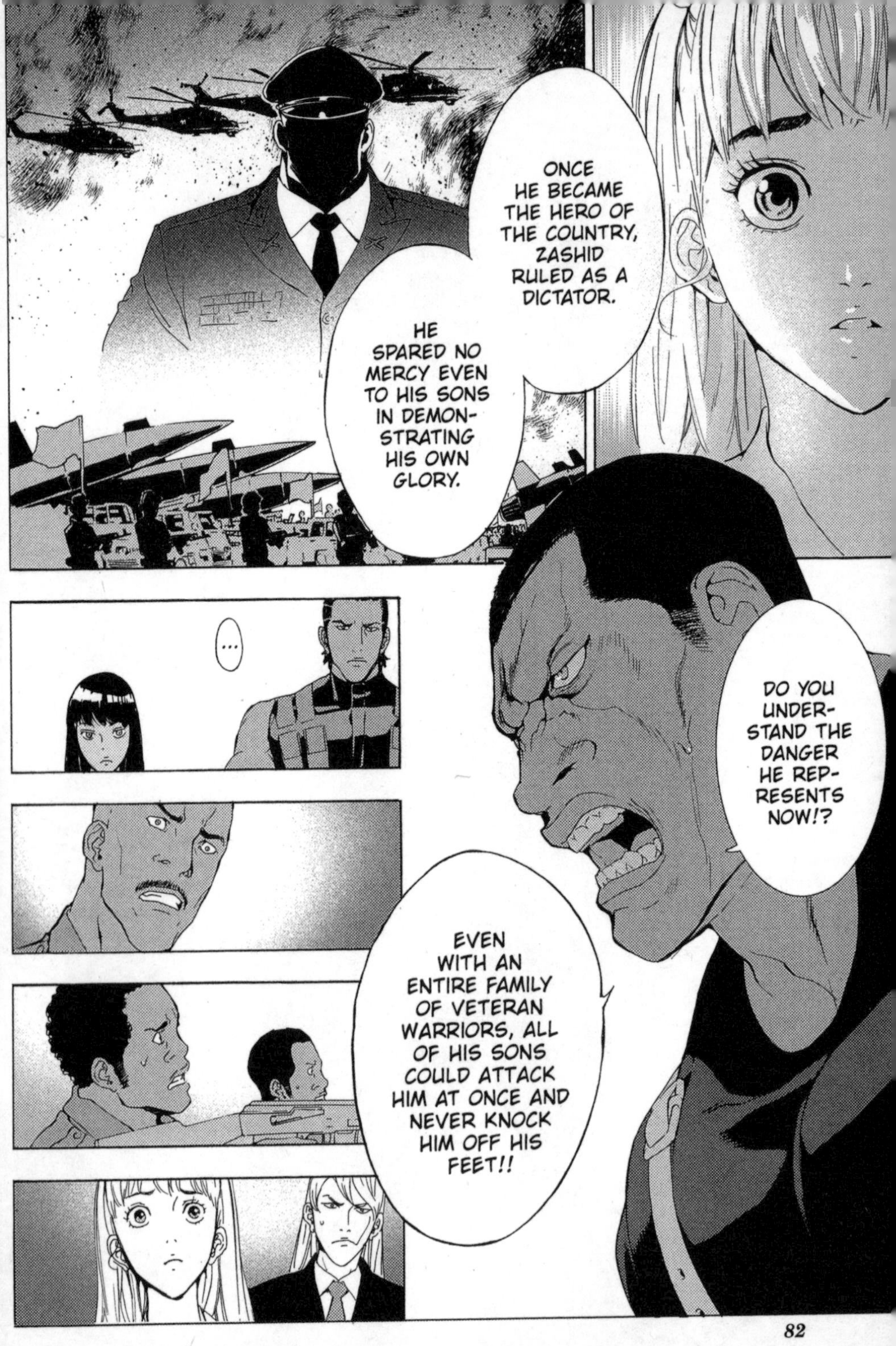
ONCE HE BECAME THE HERO OF THE COUNTRY, ZASHID RULED AS A DICTATOR.
HE SPARED NO MERCY EVEN TO HIS SONS IN DEMON-STRATING HIS OWN GLORY.
DO YOU UNDER-STAND THE DANGER HE REP-RESENTS NOW!?
EVEN WITH AN ENTIRE FAMILY OF VETERAN WARRIORS, ALL OF HIS SONS COULD ATTACK HIM AT ONCE AND NEVER KNOCK HIM OFF HIS FEET!!
...

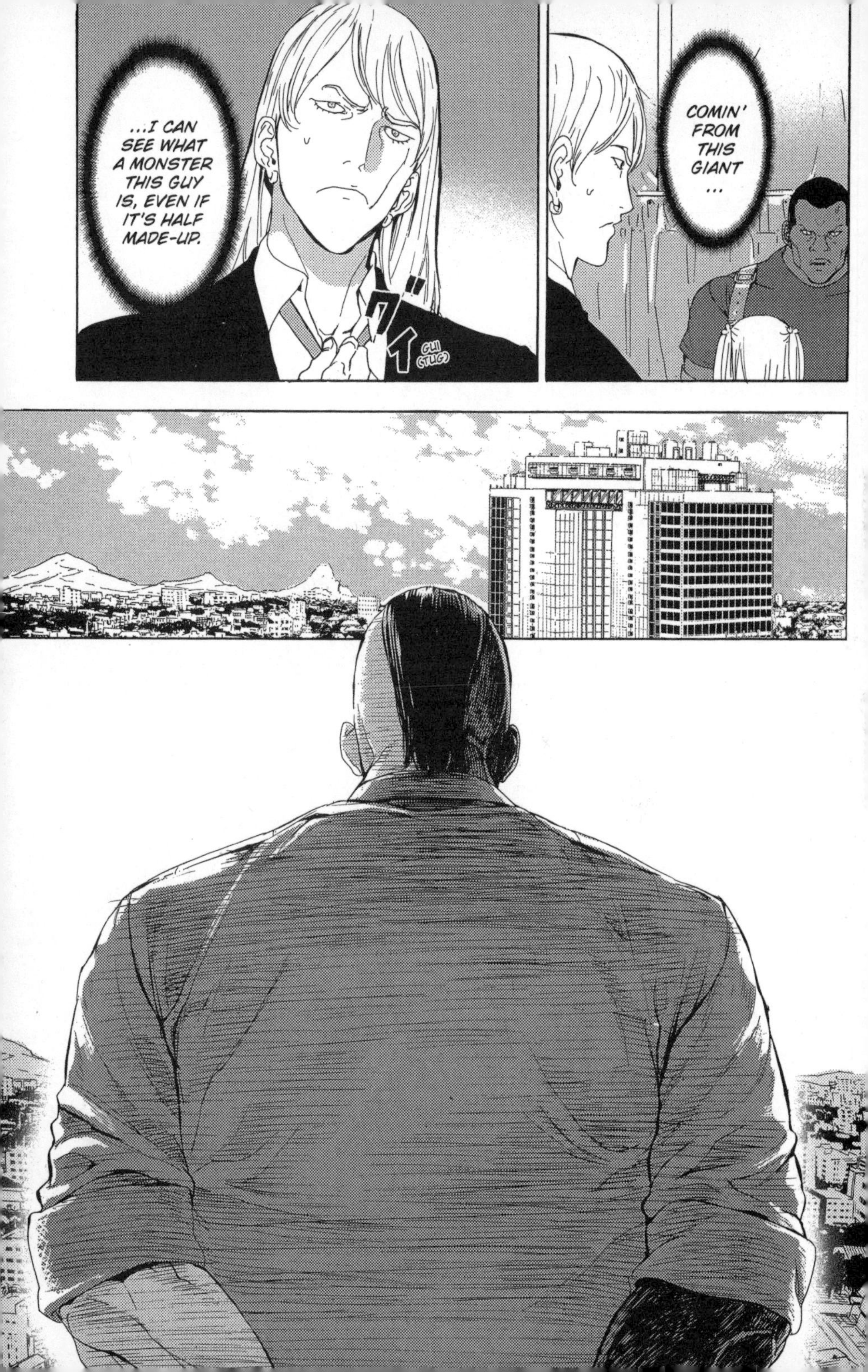
COMIN' FROM THIS GIANT ...
...I CAN SEE WHAT A MONSTER THIS GUY IS, EVEN IF IT'S HALF MADE-UP.
グイ
GUI (TUG)

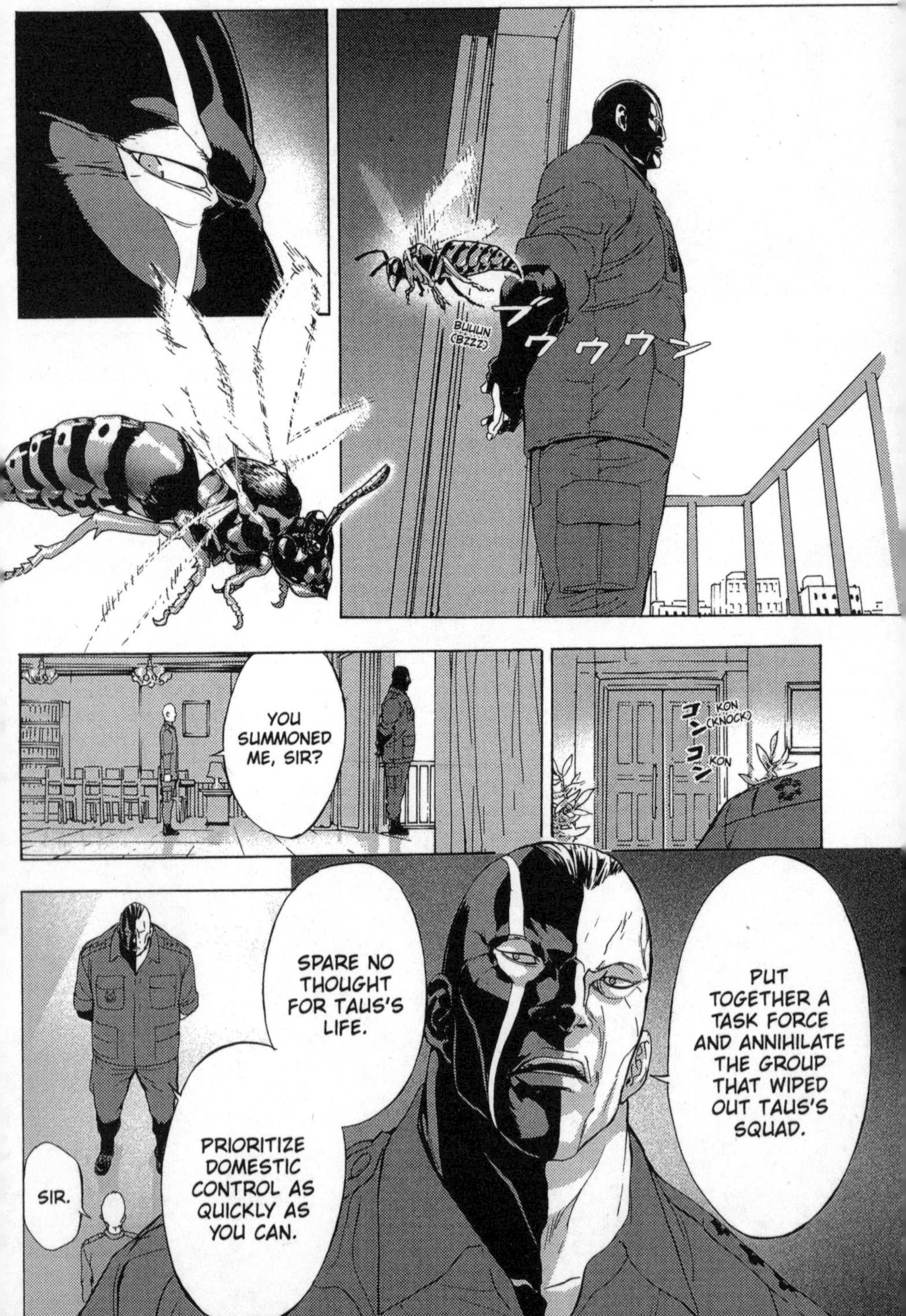

BUUUN (BZZZ)
ブウウウン
KON (KNOCK)
コンコン
KON
YOU SUMMONED ME, SIR?
PUT TOGETHER A TASK FORCE AND ANNIHILATE THE GROUP THAT WIPED OUT TAUS'S SQUAD.
SPARE NO THOUGHT FOR TAUS'S LIFE.
PRIORITIZE DOMESTIC CONTROL AS QUICKLY AS YOU CAN.
SIR.

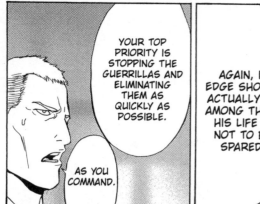

AND ORDER THAT THIS MYSTERIOUS GROUP CLAIMING TO BE EDGE'S MEETS THE SAME FATE.
AGAIN, IF EDGE SHOULD ACTUALLY BE AMONG THEM, HIS LIFE IS NOT TO BE SPARED.
YOUR TOP PRIORITY IS STOPPING THE GUERRILLAS AND ELIMINATING THEM AS QUICKLY AS POSSIBLE.
AS YOU COMMAND.
EXCEL-LENCY!
THERE'S A WASP!
A SIMPLE WANDERING INSECT FROM THE MEDITER-RANEAN, NO MORE.
BUT THEIR STINGS HAVE RE-SULTED IN FATALITIES!
LET US BE CAUTIOUS AND RETIRE ...
...TO ANOTHER ROOM!
ANY HEAD OF STATE WHO FLEES A LITTLE BEE IS A LAUGHING-STOCK.
B-BUT...
WHOA!

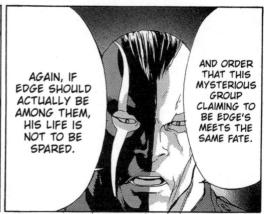

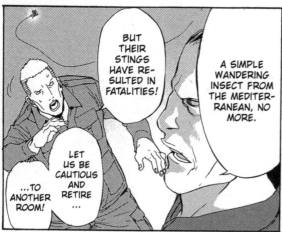

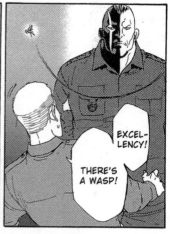

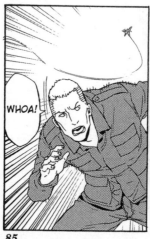

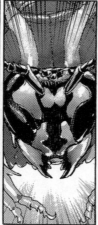

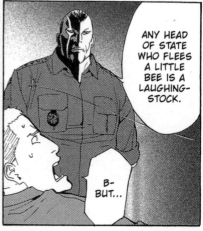

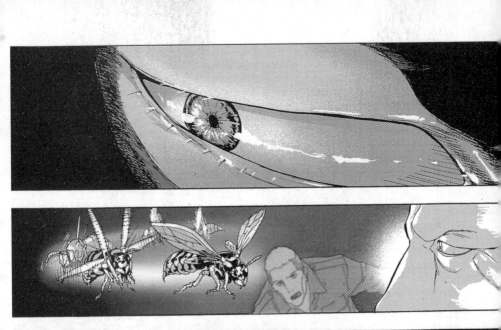

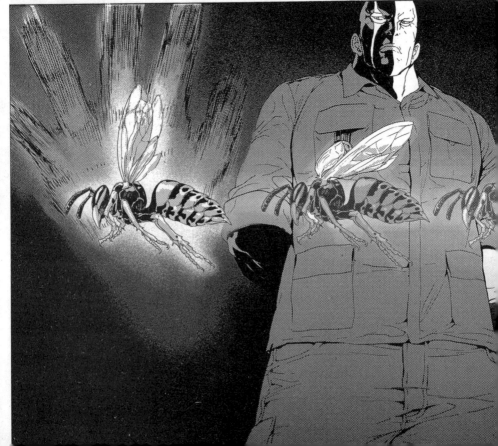

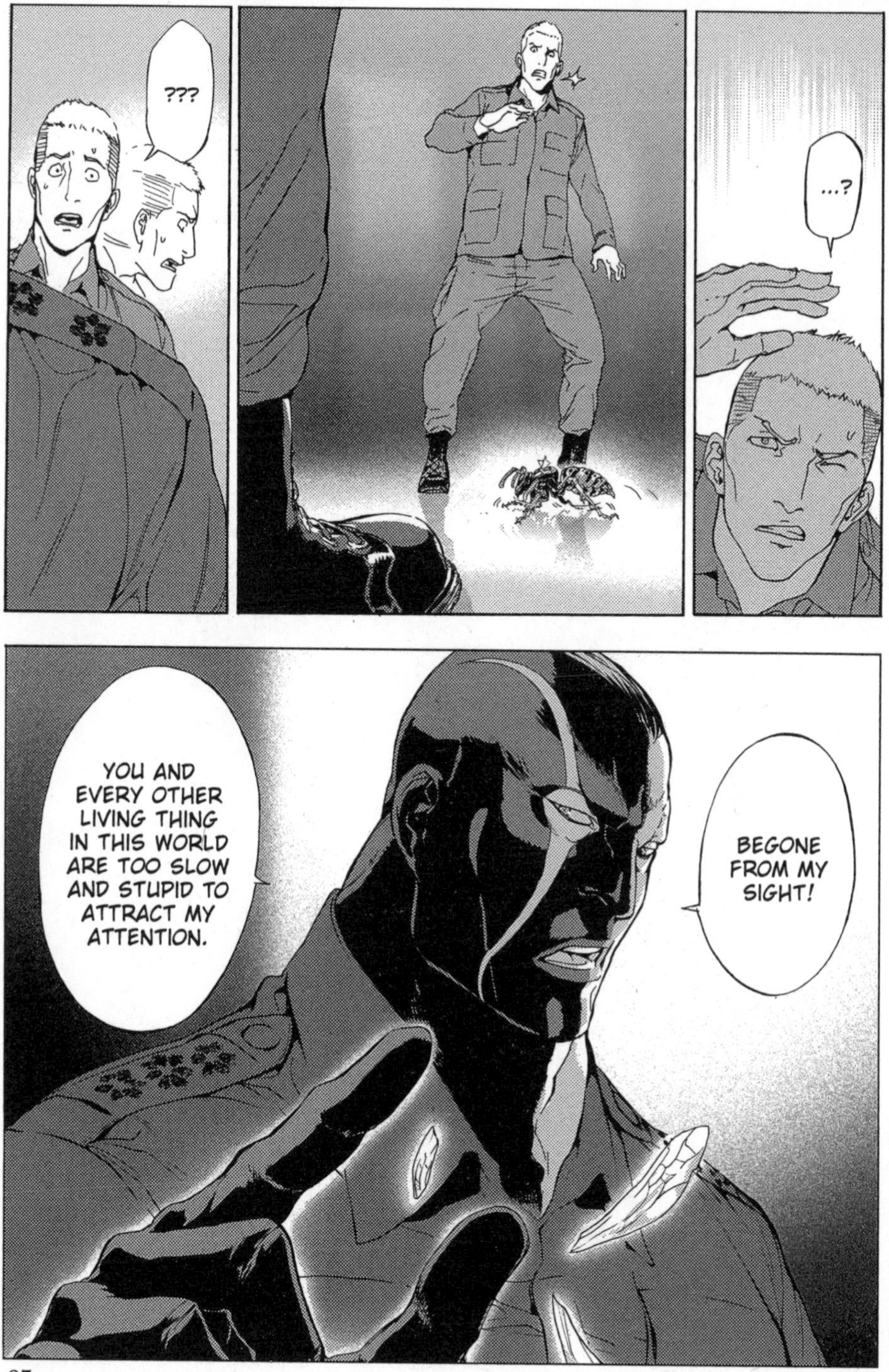
...?
???
BEGONE FROM MY SIGHT!
YOU AND EVERY OTHER LIVING THING IN THIS WORLD ARE TOO SLOW AND STUPID TO ATTRACT MY ATTENTION.

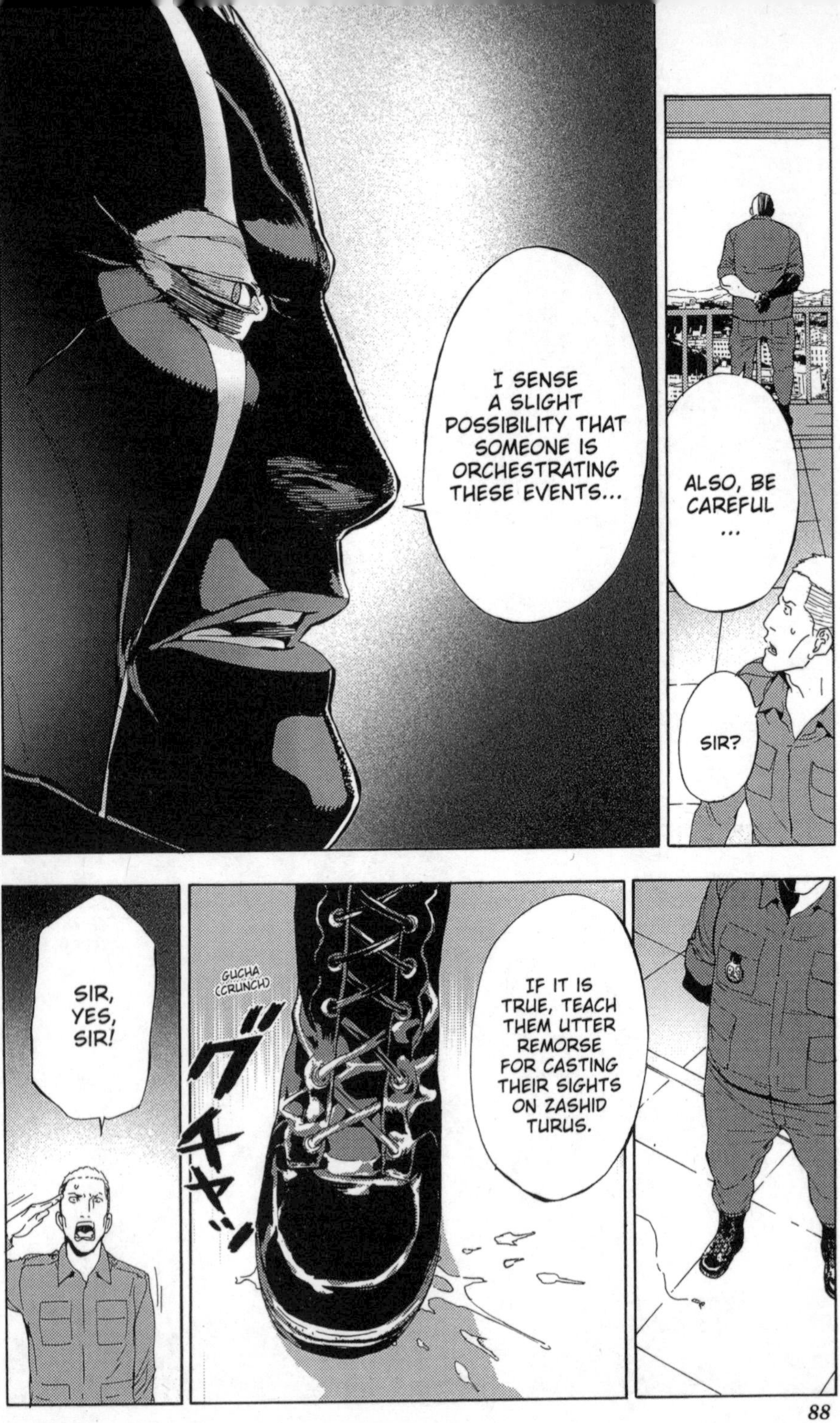
ALSO, BE CAREFUL ...
SIR?
I SENSE A SLIGHT POSSIBILITY THAT SOMEONE IS ORCHESTRATING THESE EVENTS...
IF IT IS TRUE, TEACH THEM UTTER REMORSE FOR CASTING THEIR SIGHTS ON ZASHID TURUS.
GUCHA (CRUNCH)
グチャッ
SIR, YES, SIR!

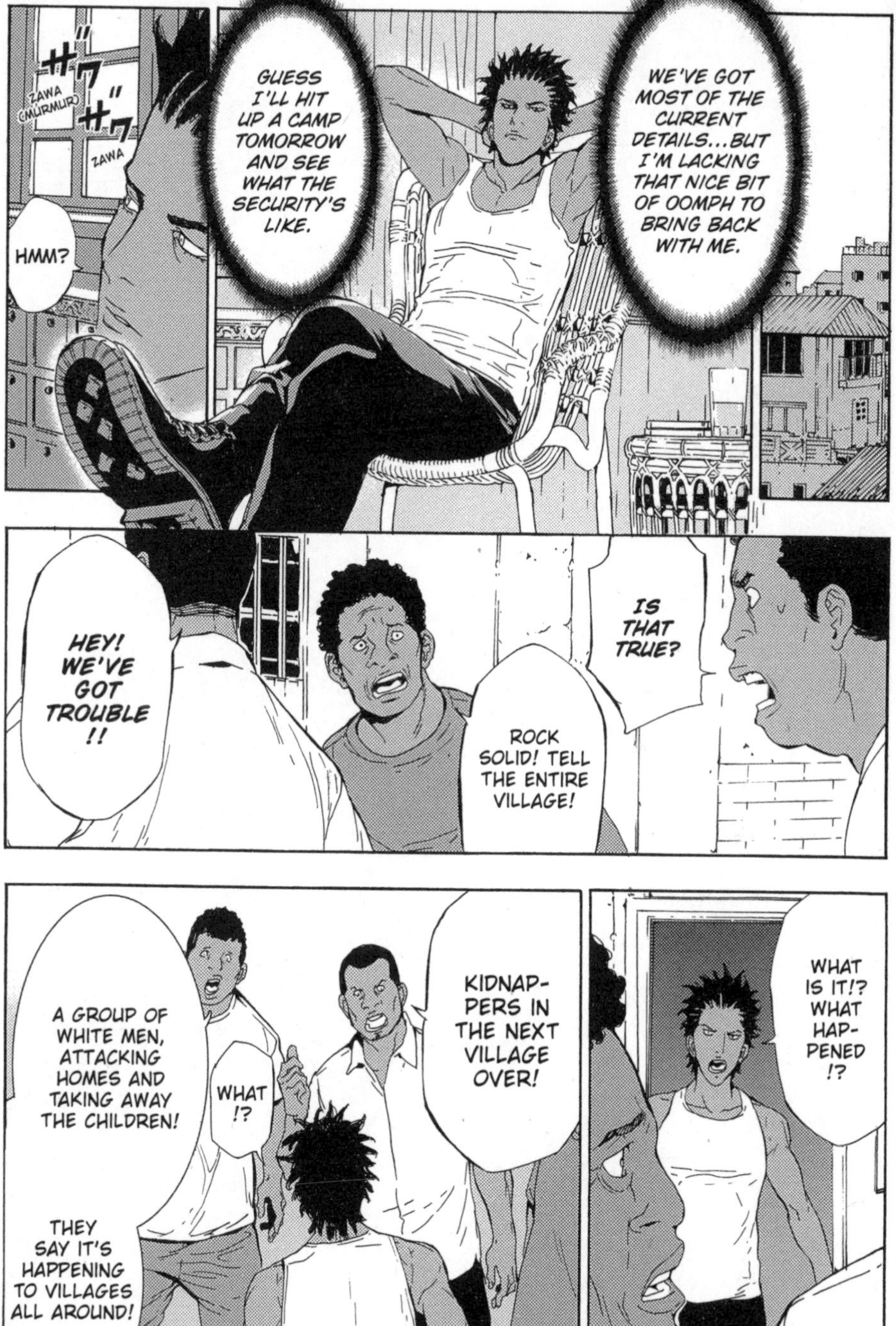
WE'VE GOT MOST OF THE CURRENT DETAILS...BUT I'M LACKING THAT NICE BIT OF OOMPH TO BRING BACK WITH ME.
GUESS I'LL HIT UP A CAMP TOMORROW AND SEE WHAT THE SECURITY'S LIKE.
ザワ ZAWA (MURMUR)
ザワ ZAWA
HMM?
HEY! WE'VE GOT TROUBLE!!
IS THAT TRUE?
ROCK SOLID! TELL THE ENTIRE VILLAGE!
WHAT IS IT!? WHAT HAPPENED!?
KIDNAPPERS IN THE NEXT VILLAGE OVER!
A GROUP OF WHITE MEN, ATTACKING HOMES AND TAKING AWAY THE CHILDREN!
WHAT!?
THEY SAY IT'S HAPPENING TO VILLAGES ALL AROUND!

GASHA
(KSHAK)

BATAN
(SLAM)

バ
タ
ン

TSK! LEAVE THIS JOB TO THE SOLDIER!

TAKE YOUR FAMILIES INTO THE JUNGLE FOR A FEW DAYS.

MAKE SURE EVERYONE KNOWS ABOUT THIS.

THIS'LL BE A WORTHY TALE TO TELL.

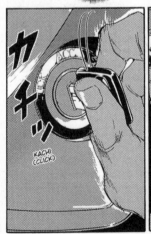
カ
チ
ッ

KACHI
(CLICK)

DO
(BOOM)

BUOOO
(VRRM)

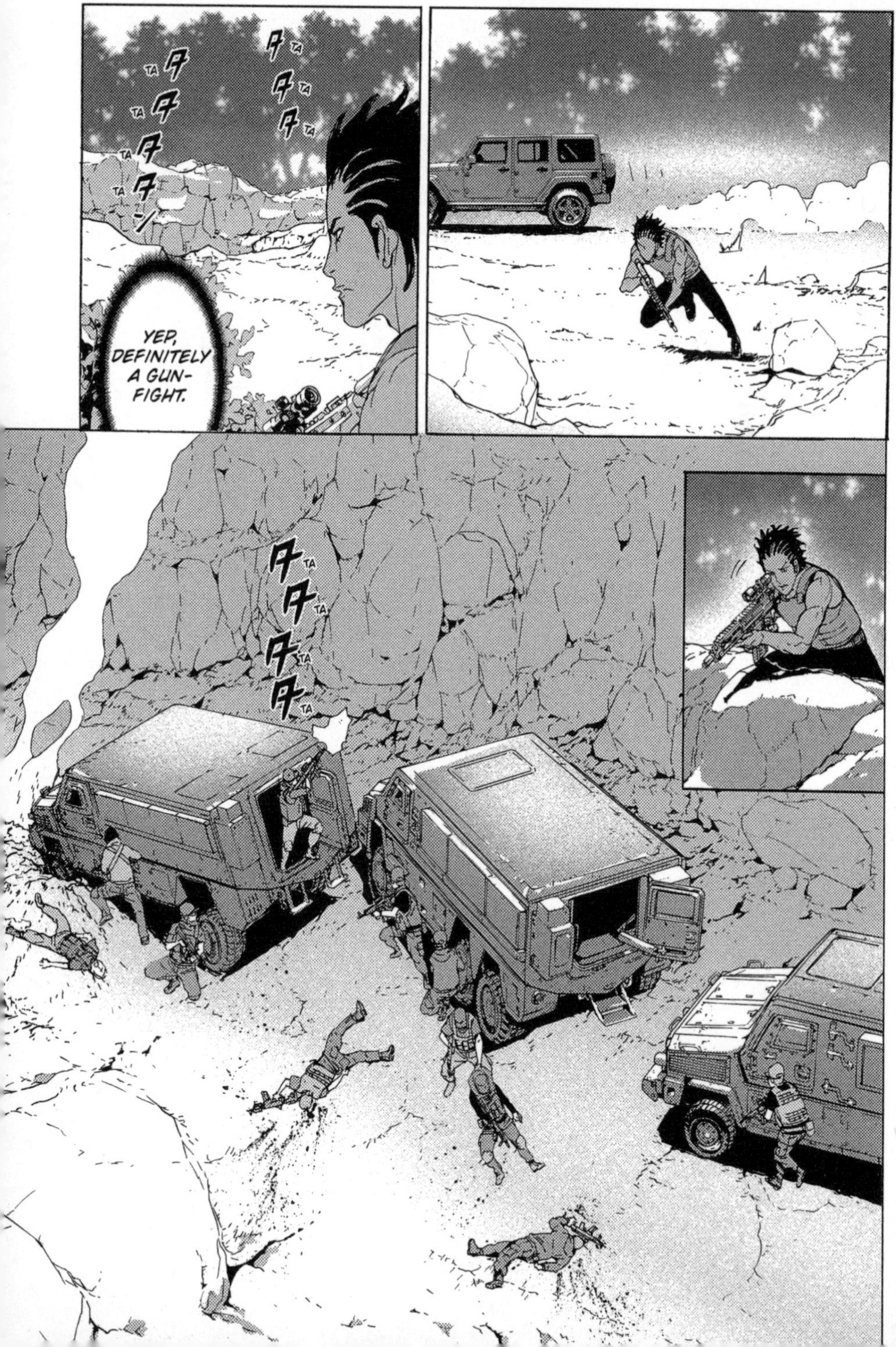
TA TA TA TA
TA TA TA
YEP, DEFINITELY A GUN-FIGHT.
TA TA TA TA

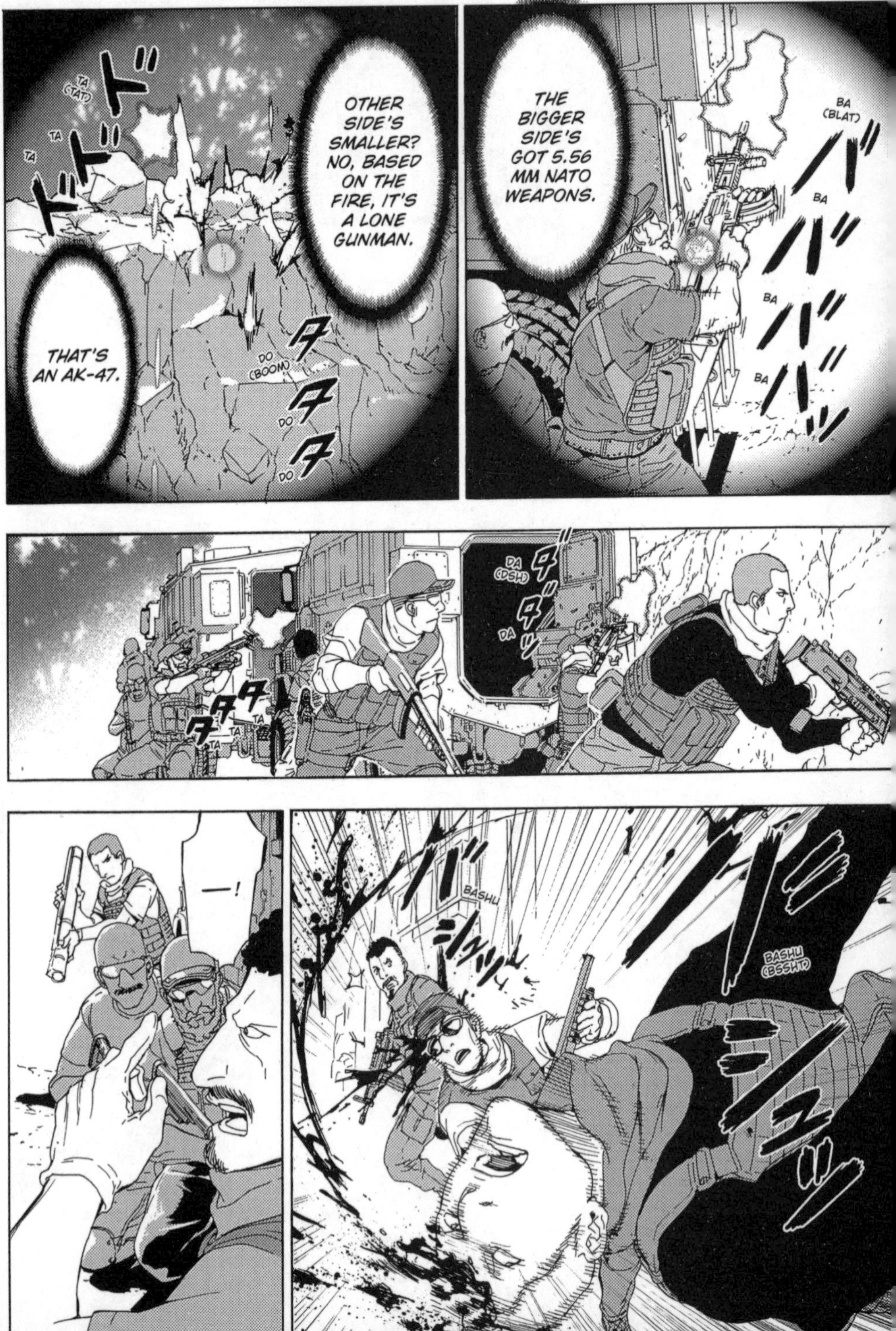
BA (BLAT)
BA
BA
BA
THE BIGGER SIDE'S GOT 5.56 MM NATO WEAPONS.
OTHER SIDE'S SMALLER? NO, BASED ON THE FIRE, IT'S A LONE GUNMAN.
TA (TAT)
TA
TA
DO (BOOM)
DO
DO
THAT'S AN AK-47.
DA (DSH)
DA
TA
TA
TA
BASHU (BSSHT)
BASHU
—!

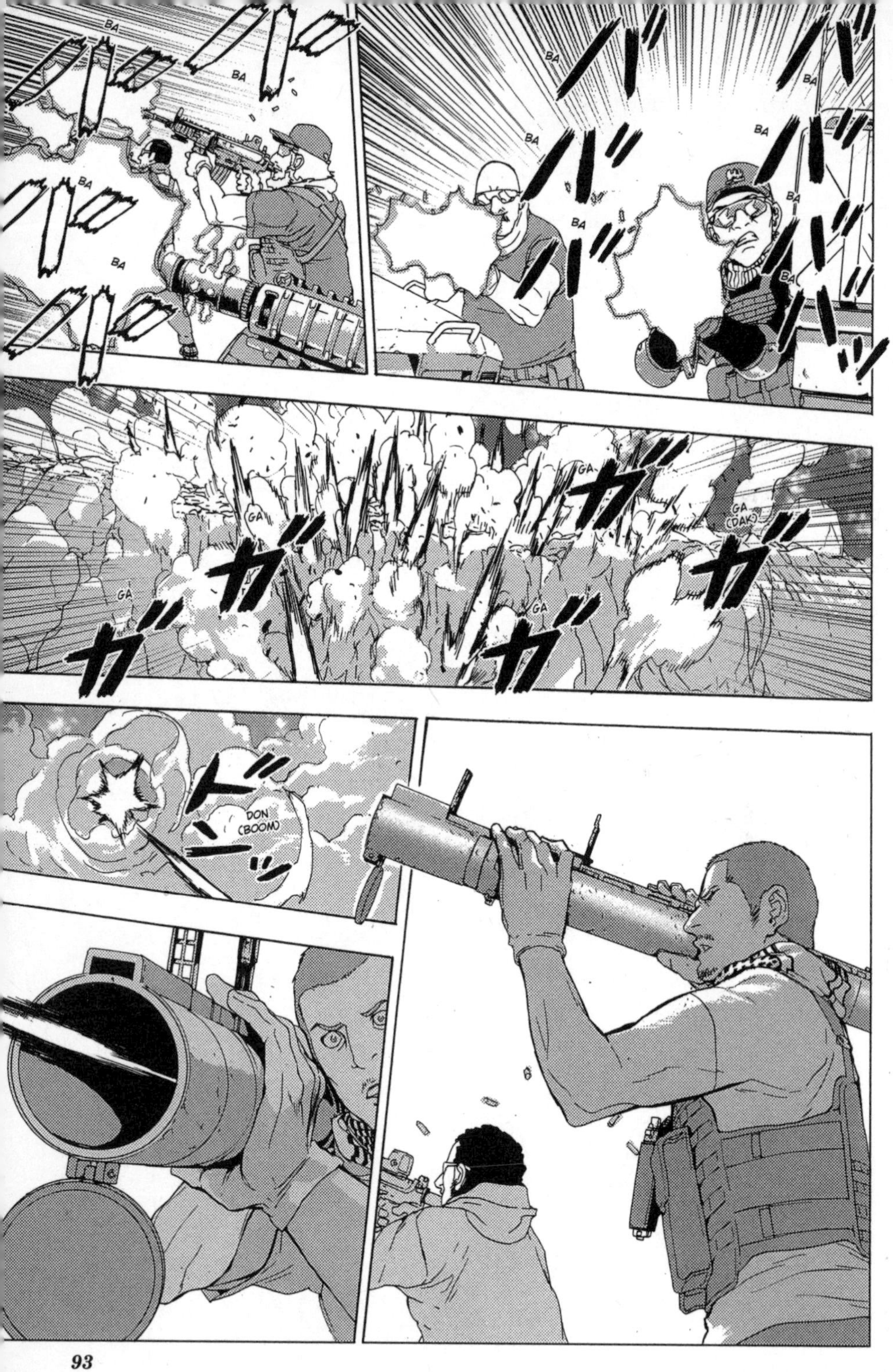
BA
BA
BA
BA
BA
BA
BA
BA
BA
BA
BA
GA (DAK)
GA
GA
GA
GA
DON (BOOM)

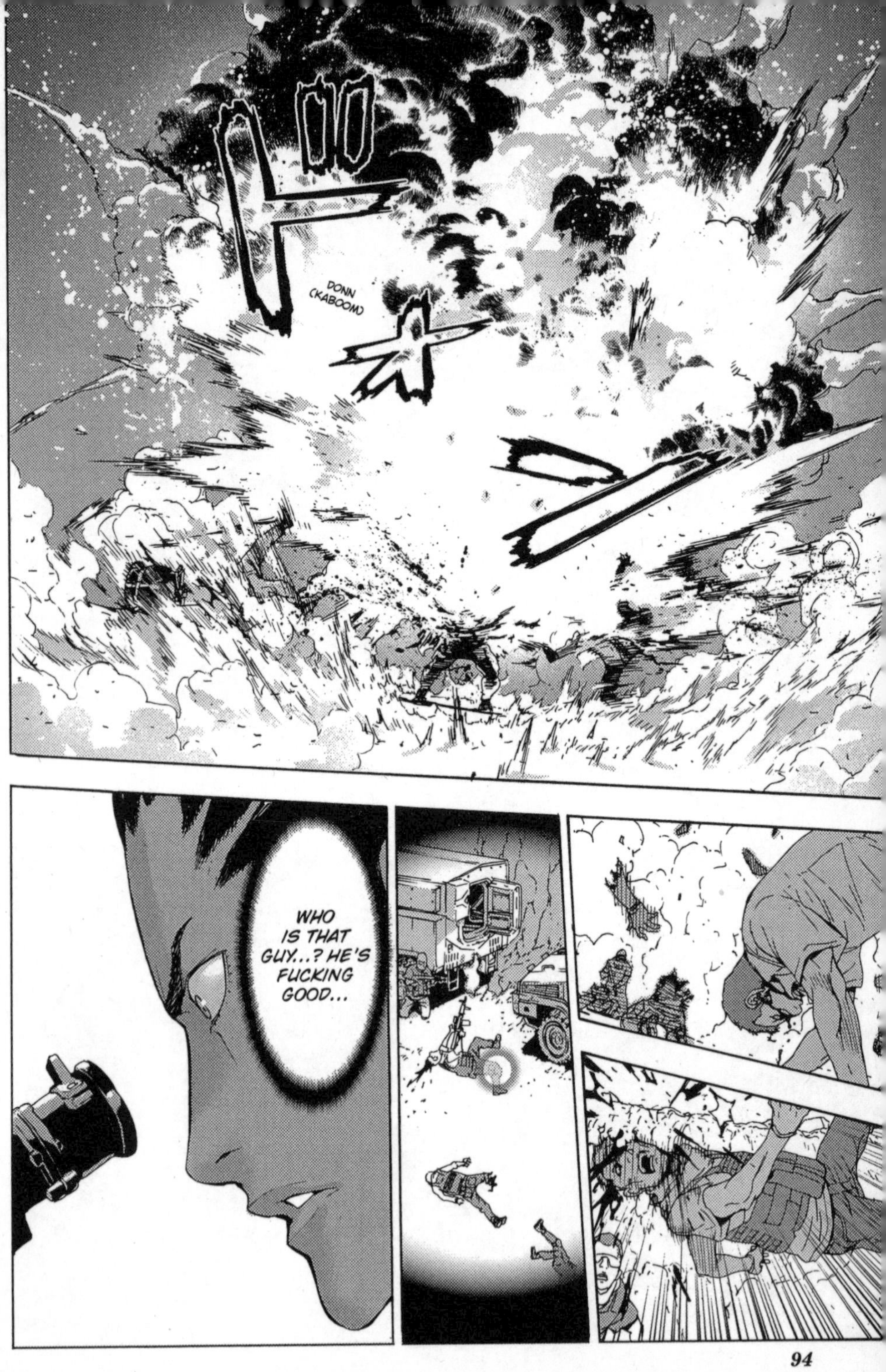
DONN
(KABOOM)
WHO IS THAT GUY...? HE'S FUCKING GOOD...

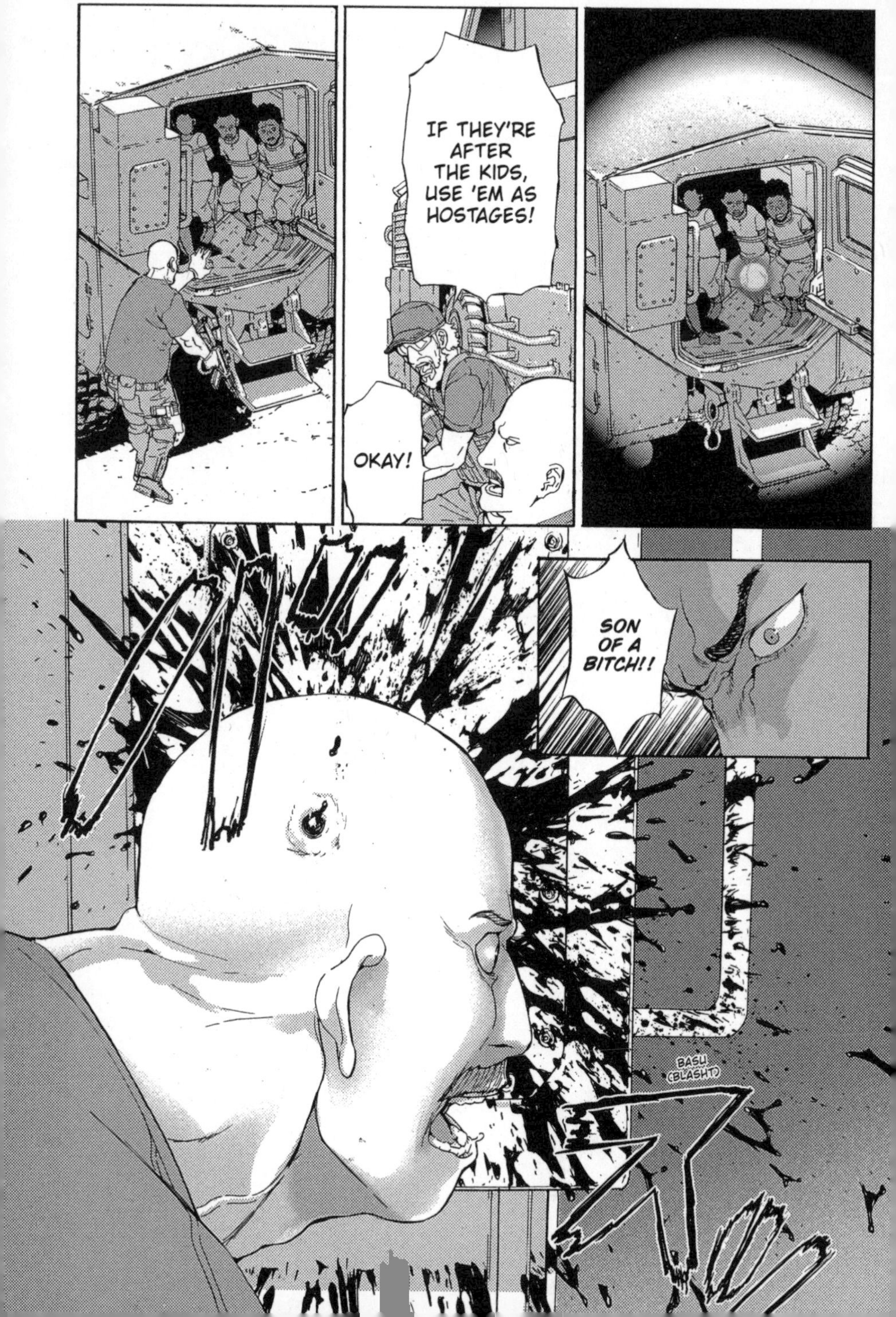
IF THEY'RE AFTER THE KIDS, USE 'EM AS HOSTAGES!
OKAY!
SON OF A BITCH!!
BASU (BLASHT)

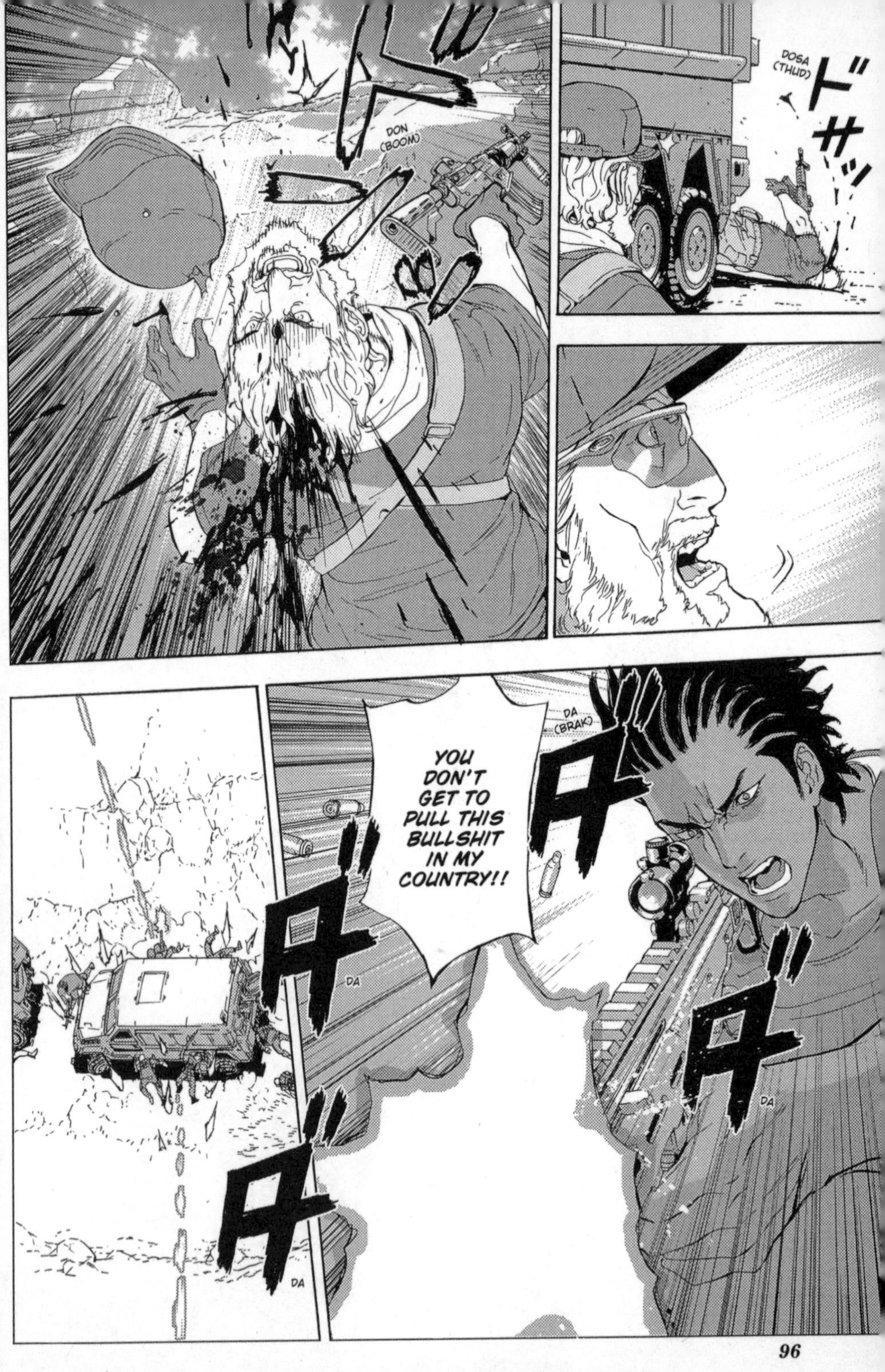
DOSA (THUD)
ドサッ
DON (BOOM)
DA (BRAK)
YOU DON'T GET TO PULL THIS BULLSHIT IN MY COUNTRY!!
DA
DA
DA

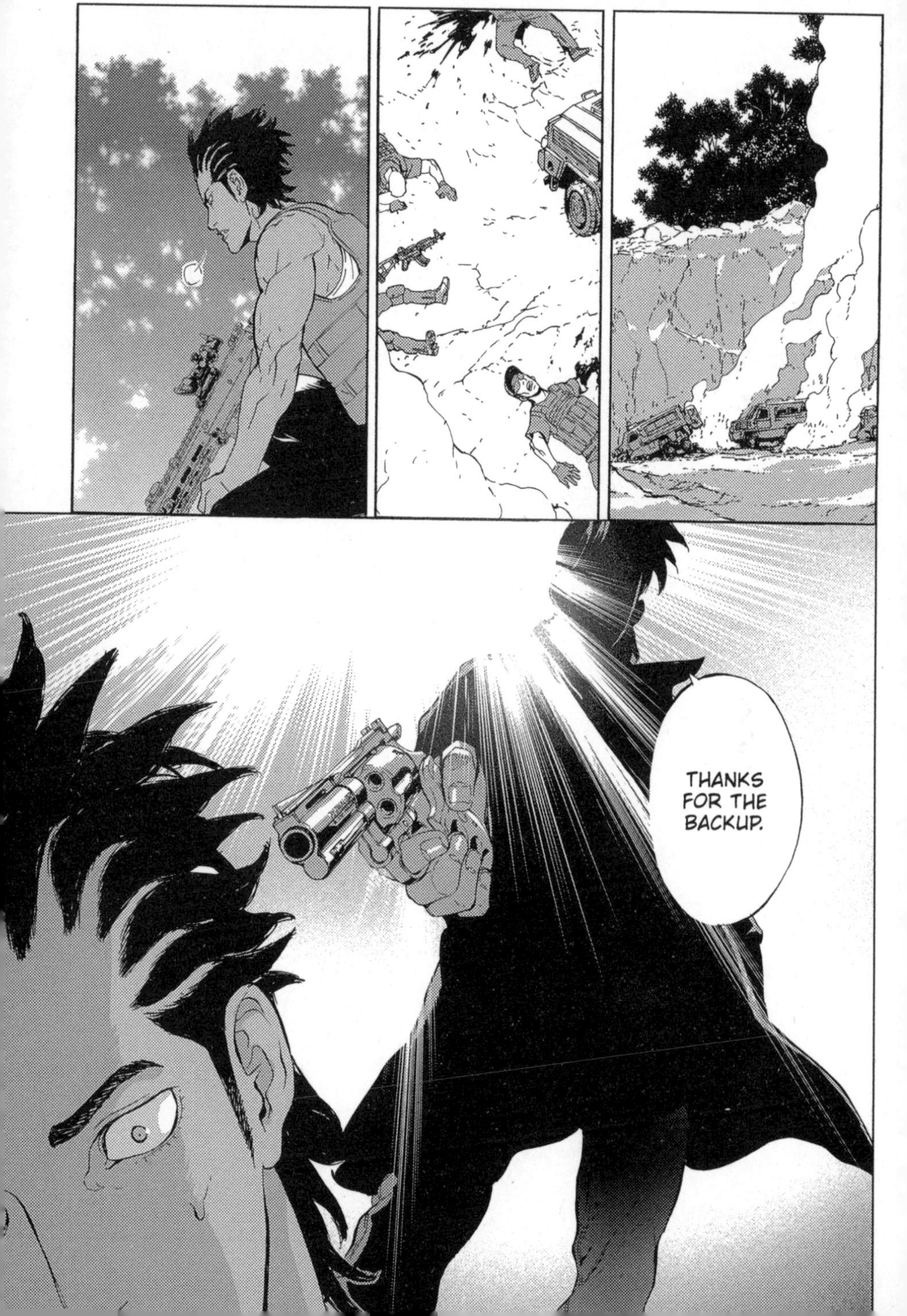
THANKS FOR THE BACKUP.

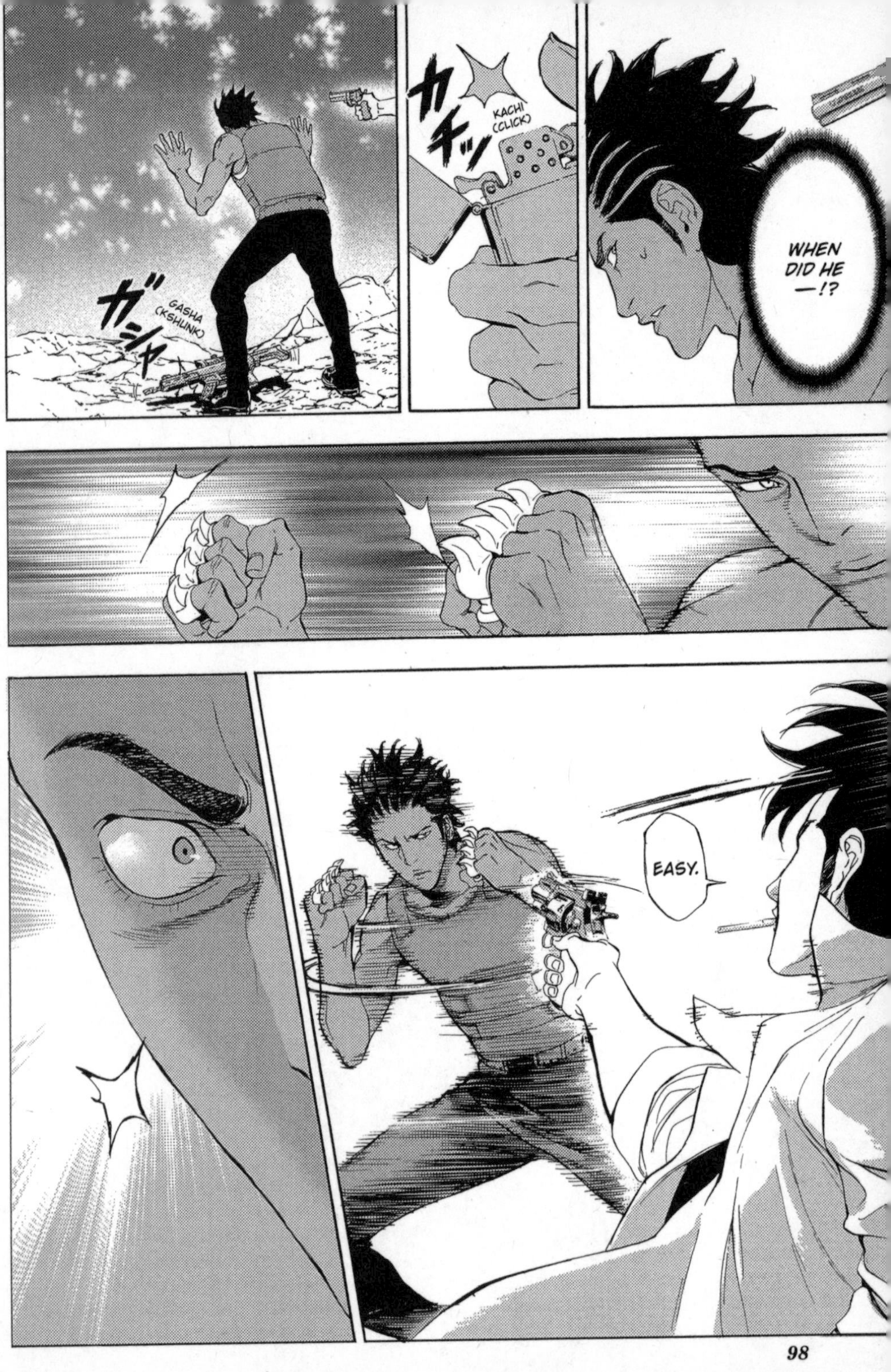
WHEN DID HE —!?
カチッ
KACHI (CLICK)
ガシャ
GASHA (KSHLINK)
EASY.

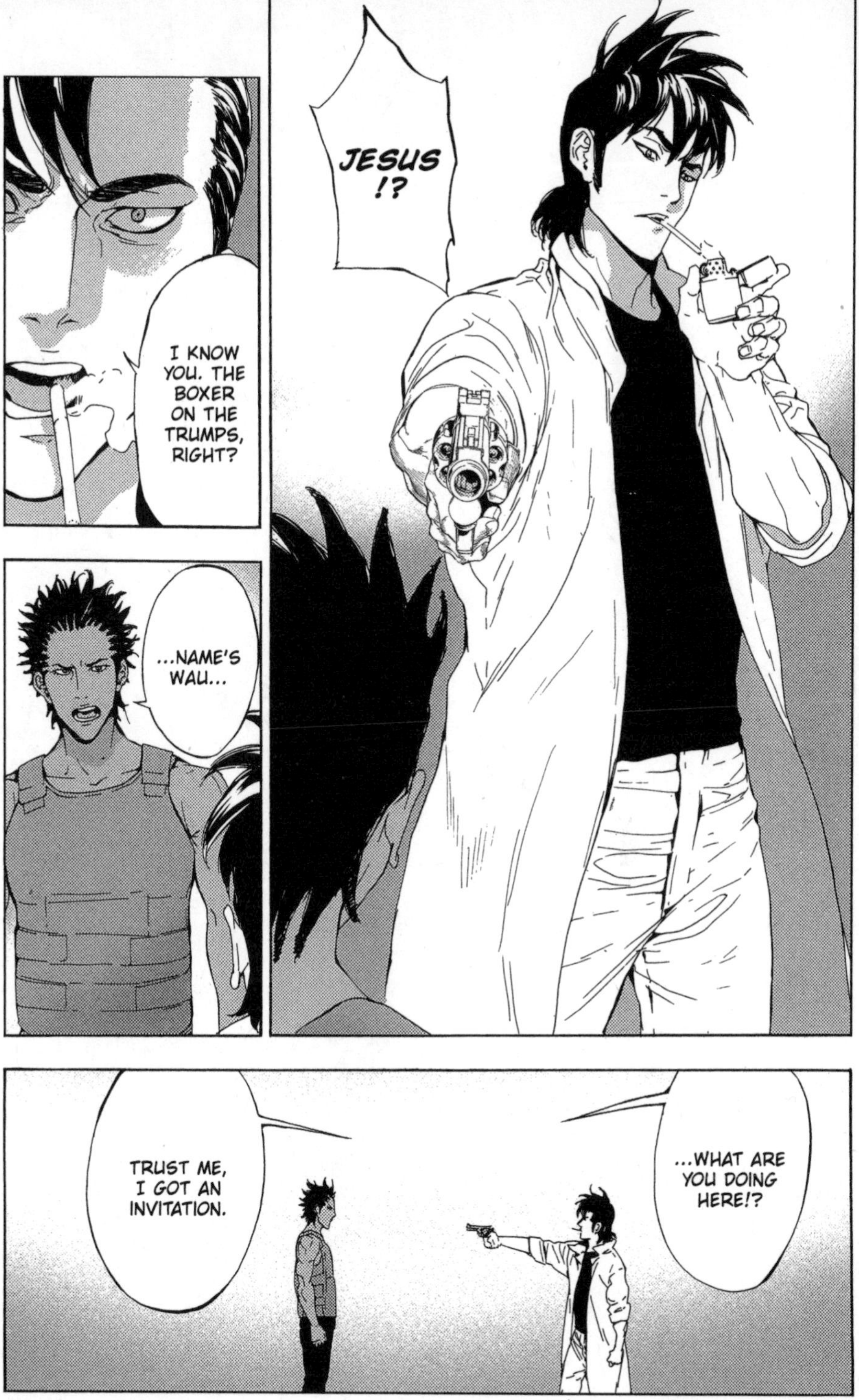
JESUS !?
I KNOW YOU. THE BOXER ON THE TRUMPS, RIGHT?
...NAME'S WAU...
...WHAT ARE YOU DOING HERE!?
TRUST ME, I GOT AN INVITATION.

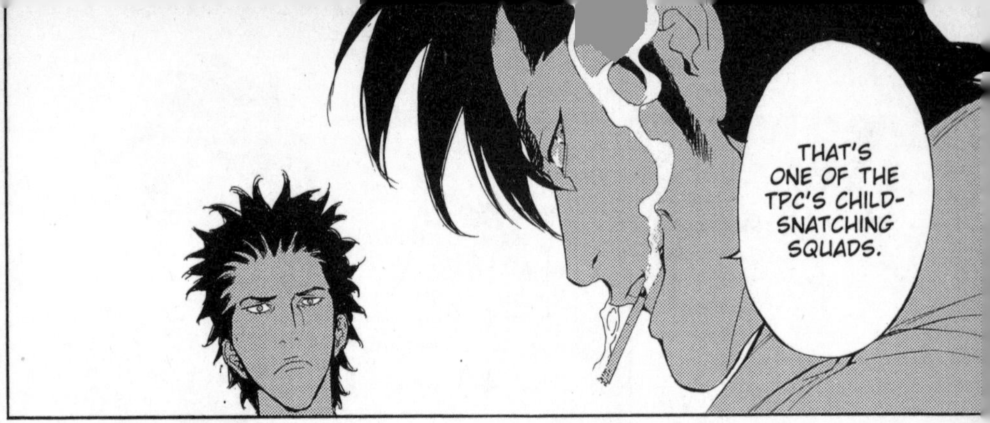
THAT'S ONE OF THE TPC'S CHILD-SNATCHING SQUADS.
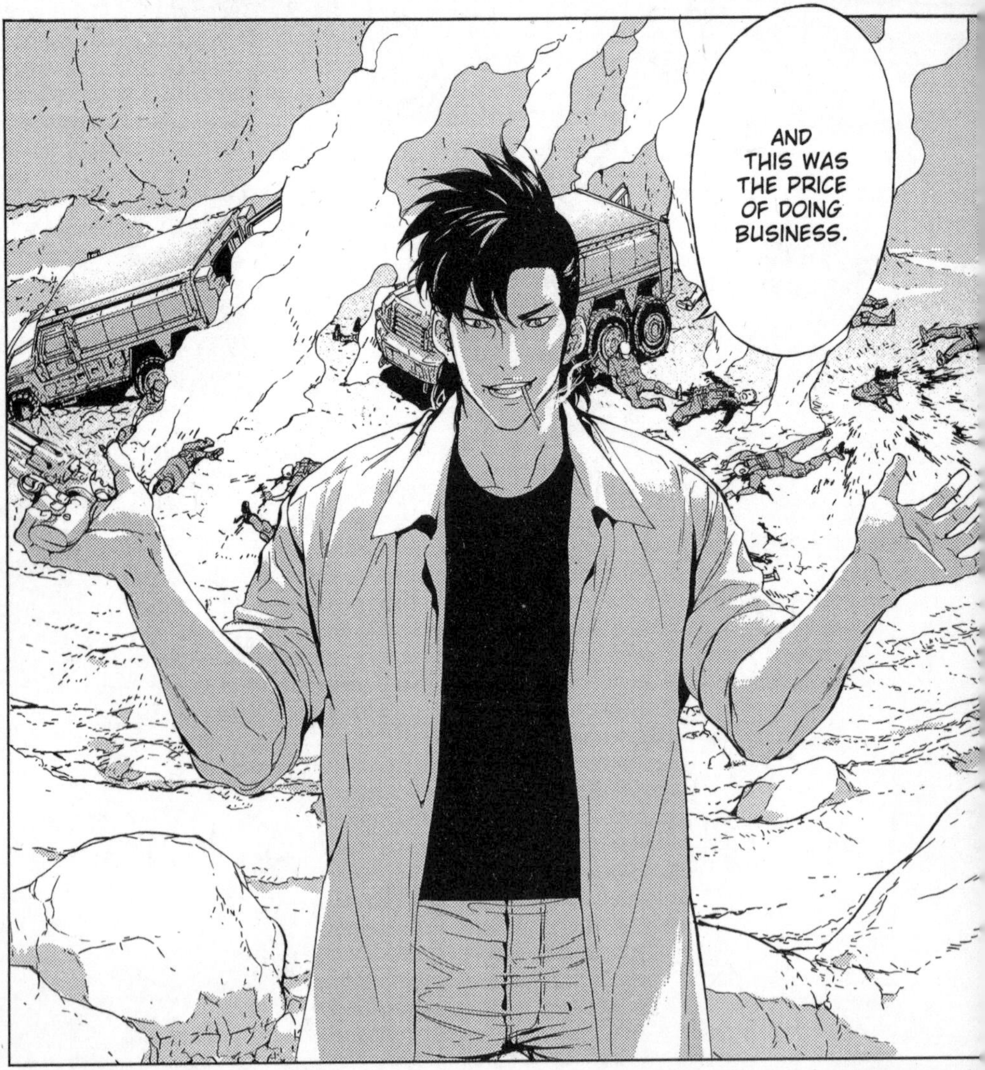
AND THIS WAS THE PRICE OF DOING BUSINESS.

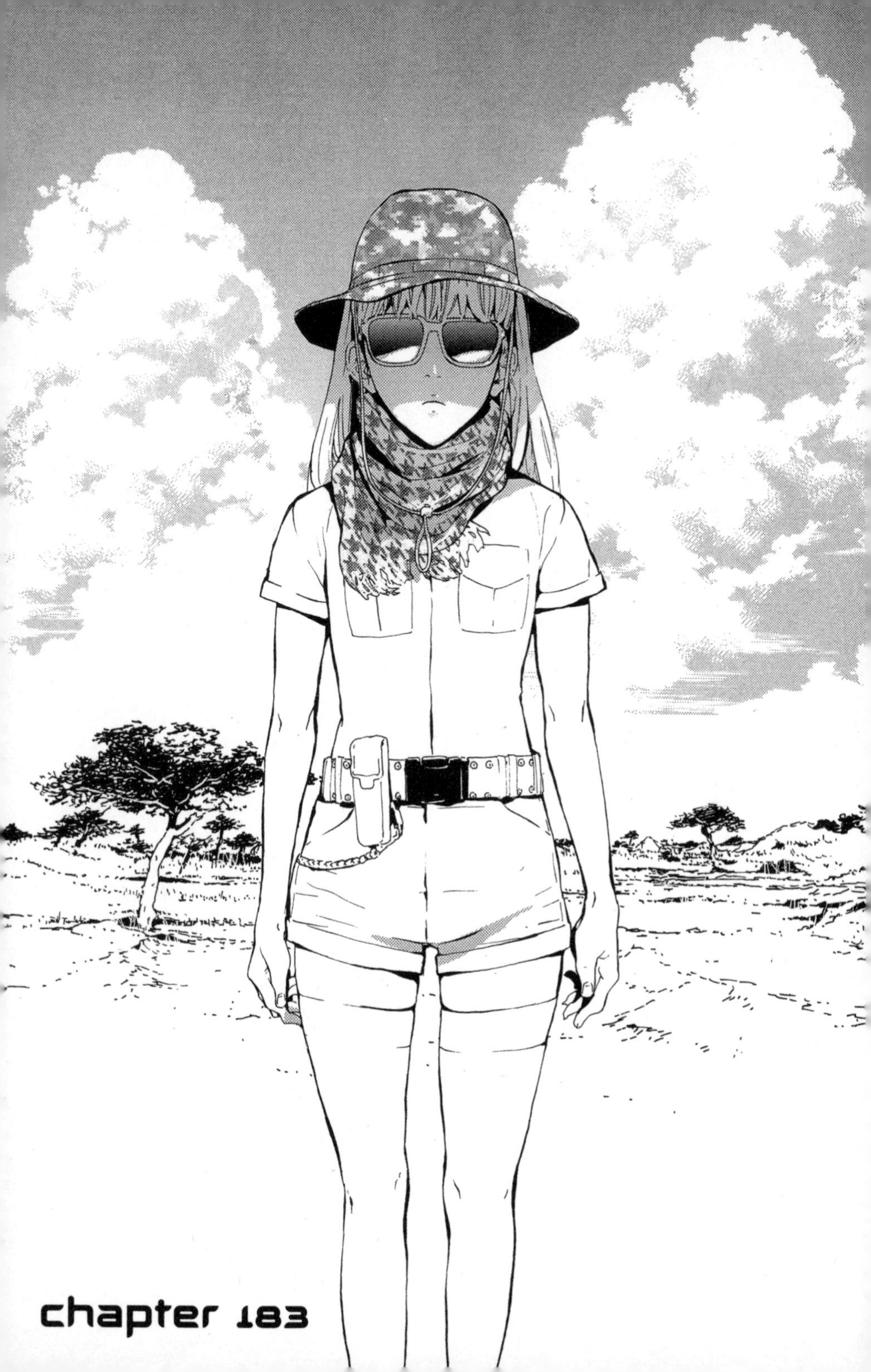

chapter 183

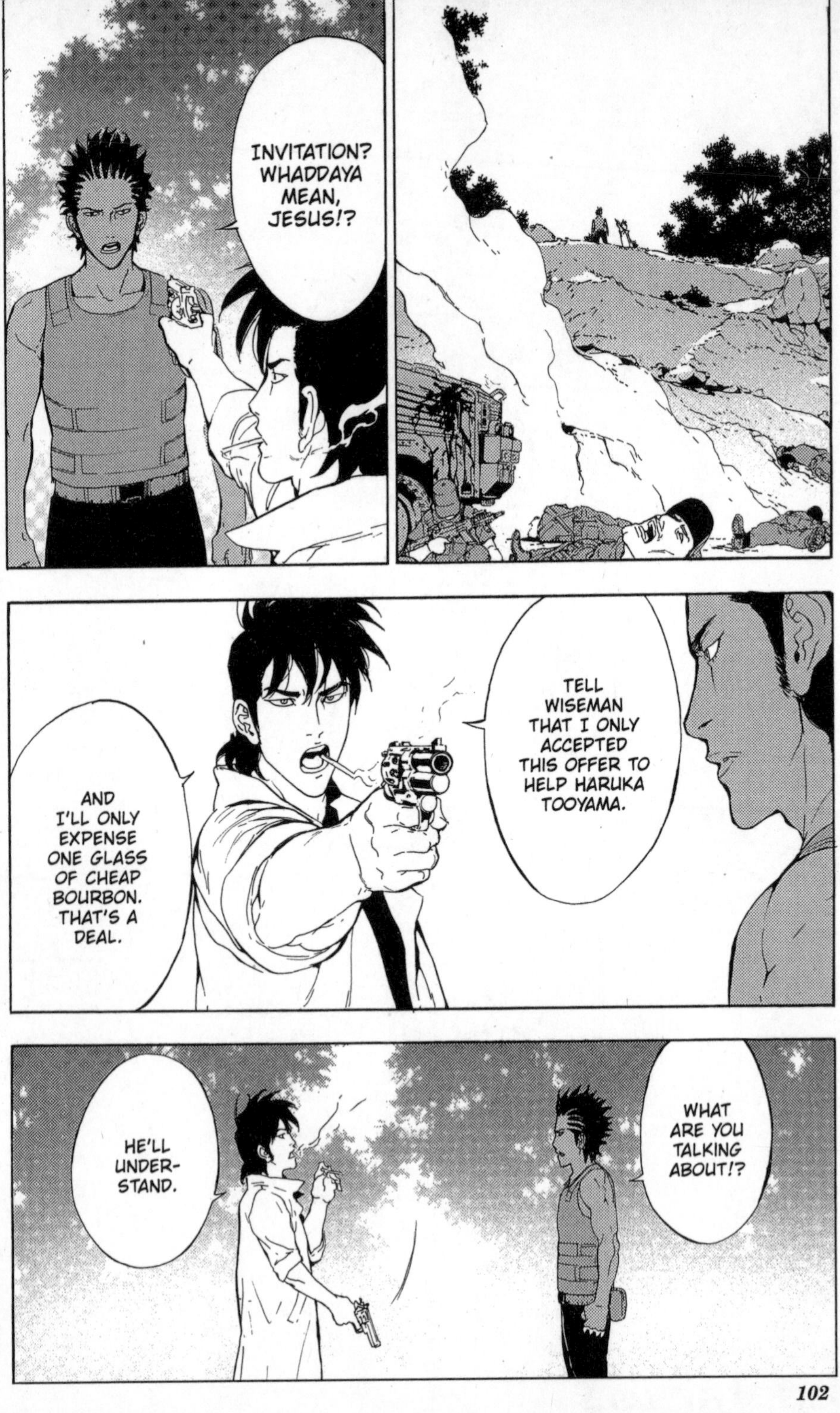
INVITATION? WHADDAYA MEAN, JESUS!?
TELL WISEMAN THAT I ONLY ACCEPTED THIS OFFER TO HELP HARUKA TOOYAMA.
AND I'LL ONLY EXPENSE ONE GLASS OF CHEAP BOURBON. THAT'S A DEAL.
WHAT ARE YOU TALKING ABOUT!?
HE'LL UNDER-STAND.

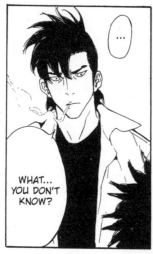

WHY WOULD THE TRANSPLANT CONNECTION DO THIS STUFF WITHIN DUHANA ANYWAY!?
WASN'T DANTE 313 JUST A PLAN TO CREATE AN ORGAN-MANUFACTURING PLANT!?
...
WHAT... YOU DON'T KNOW?
JUST BUILDING A "FACTORY" DOESN'T COVER THE ACTUAL SUPPLY GOING IN, RIGHT?
AND THAT LABEL IS JUST FOR SHOW. IN REALITY, IT'S A FACILITY FOR IMPREGNATING SLAVE WOMEN AND RAISING THE CHILDREN TO AN APPROPRIATE SIZE.
EVENTUALLY, ONCE THE CLONING INDUSTRY GETS IN FULL SWING, THEY'LL SWITCH OVER TO A NICE CLEAN BUSINESS, BUT I'M NOT GOING TO WAIT AROUND FOR THAT.
THEY SAY THERE'S MASSIVE FUNDING GOING INTO THIS PLACE TO BUILD AN EVENTUAL CLONING FACILITY.
THIS IS THE GROUP'S MAKE-OR-BREAK GAMBLE, SO IF I CAN RAZE THEIR ATTEMPT TO THE GROUND, IT'LL DEAL A FATAL BLOW TO THE TPC.

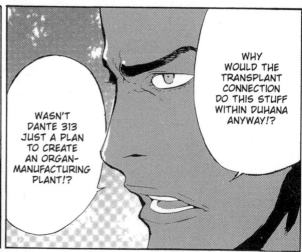

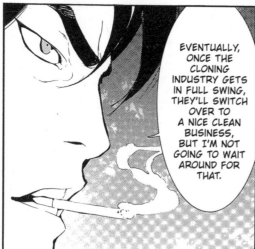

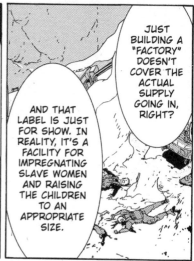

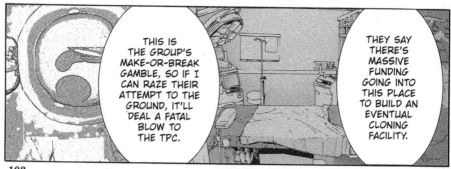

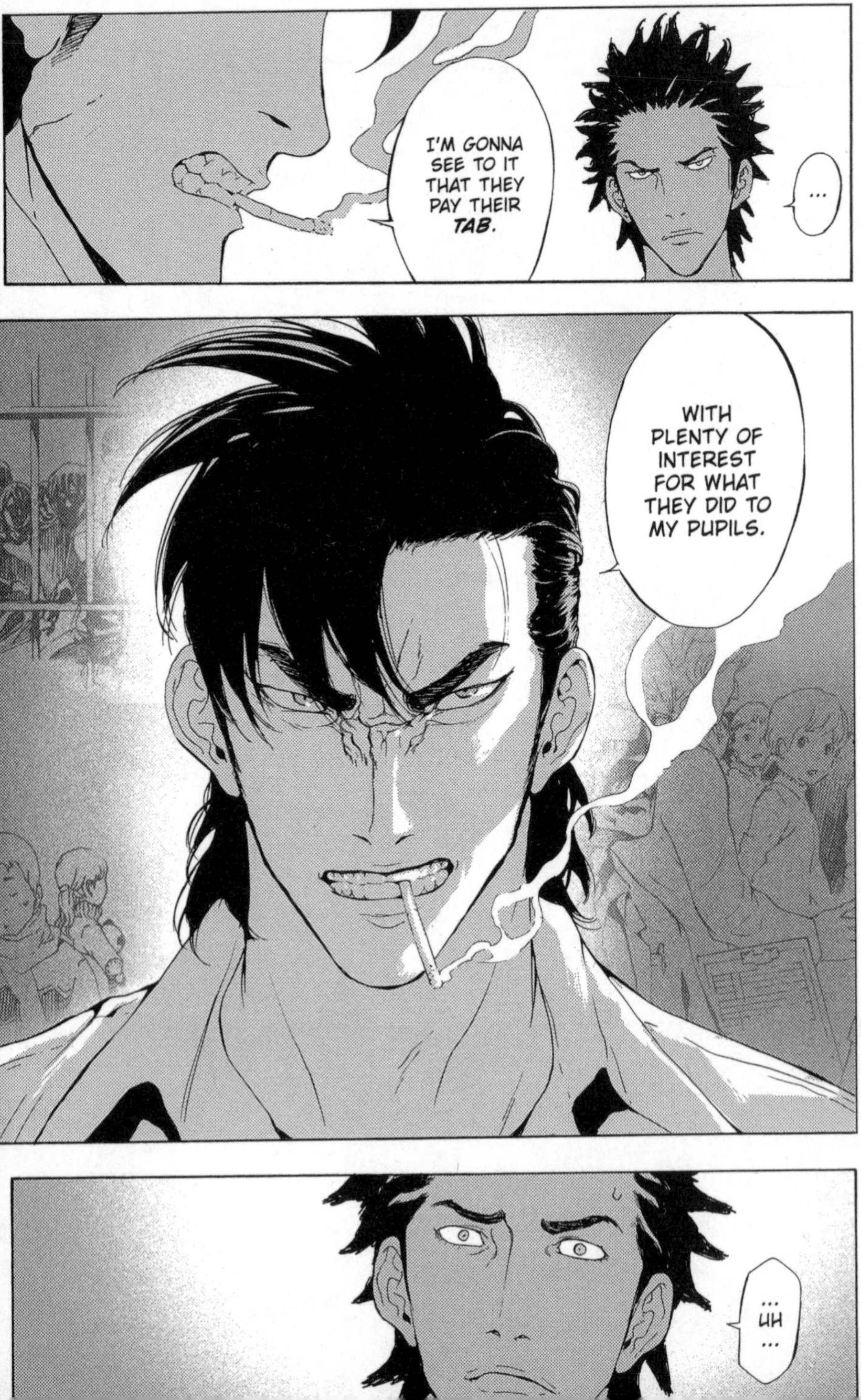
I'M GONNA SEE TO IT THAT THEY PAY THEIR *TAB*.
...
WITH PLENTY OF INTEREST FOR WHAT THEY DID TO MY PUPILS.
...UH...

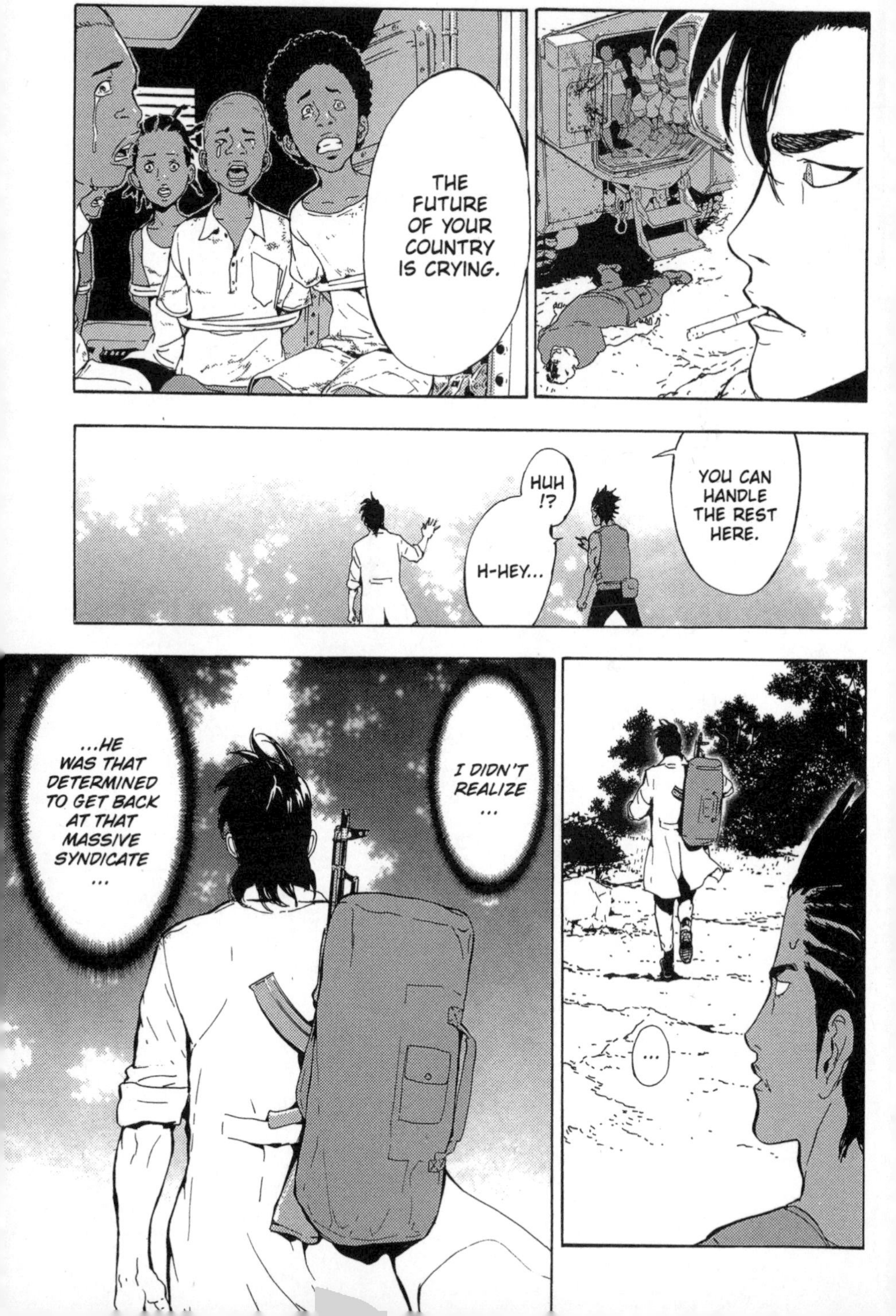
THE FUTURE OF YOUR COUNTRY IS CRYING.
YOU CAN HANDLE THE REST HERE.
HUH !?
H-HEY...
...
I DIDN'T REALIZE ...
...HE WAS THAT DETERMINED TO GET BACK AT THAT MASSIVE SYNDICATE ...

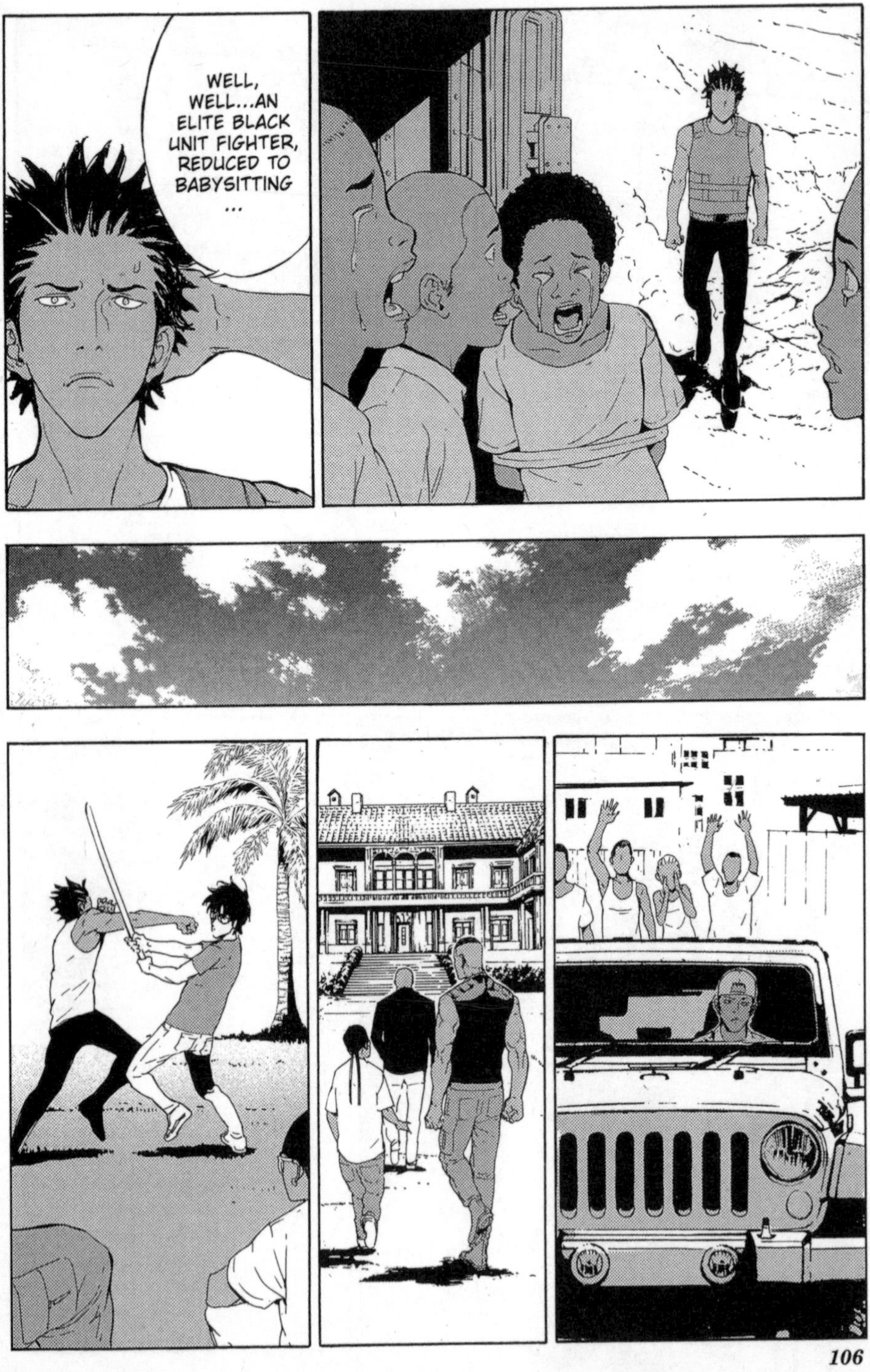
WELL, WELL...AN ELITE BLACK UNIT FIGHTER, REDUCED TO BABYSITTING ...

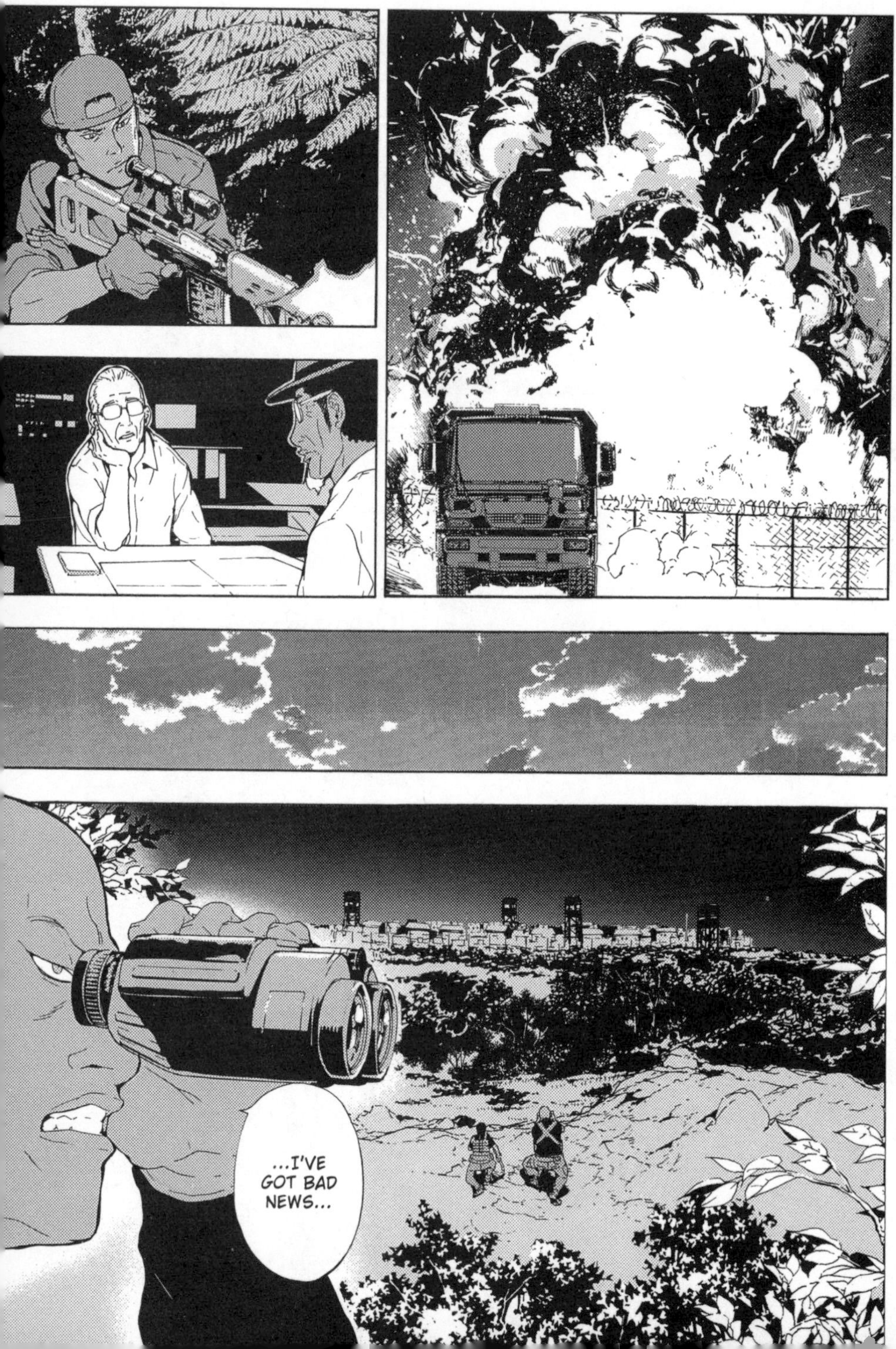
...I'VE GOT BAD NEWS...

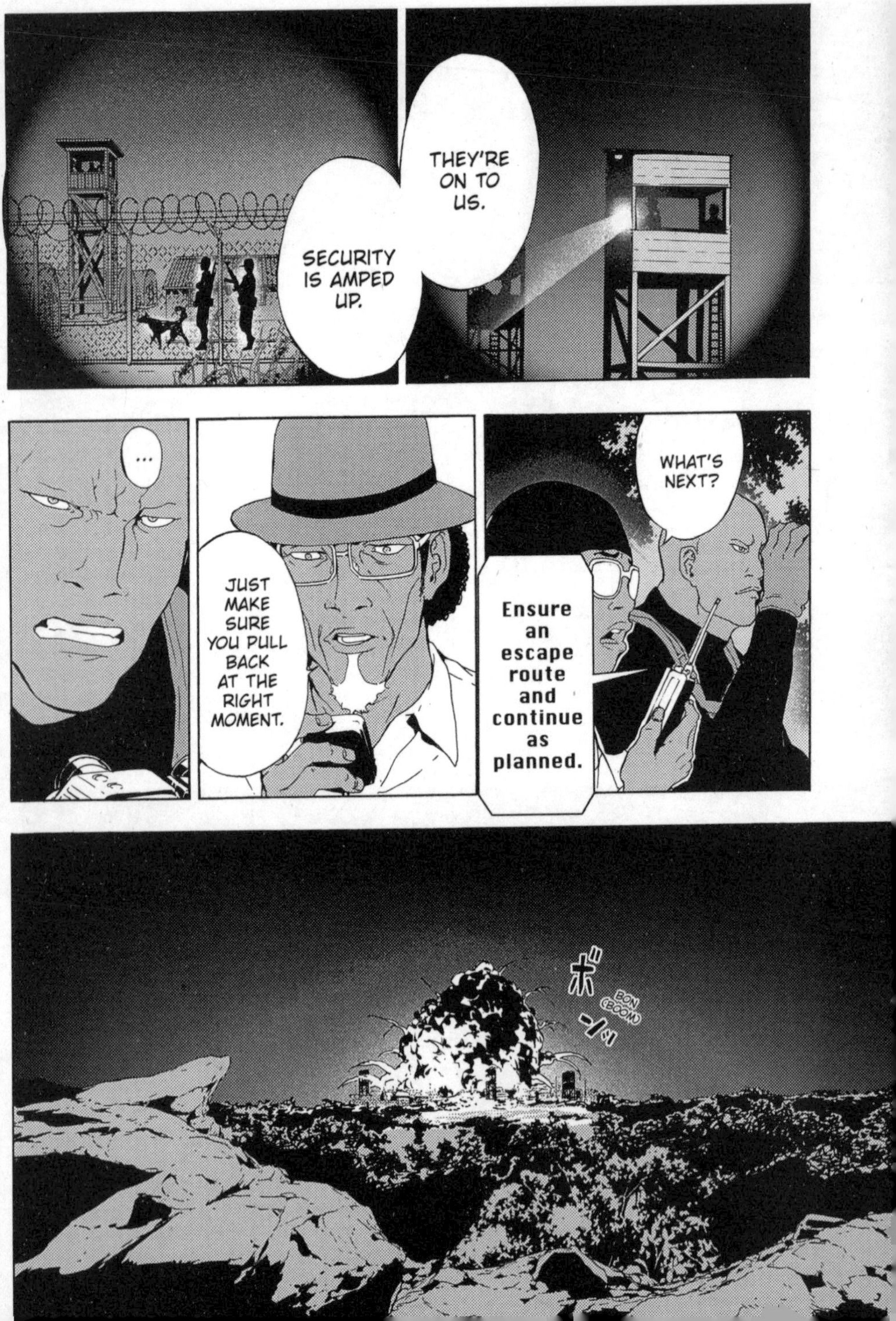
THEY'RE ON TO US.
SECURITY IS AMPED UP.
WHAT'S NEXT?
Ensure an escape route and continue as planned.
JUST MAKE SURE YOU PULL BACK AT THE RIGHT MOMENT.
...
ボーッ
BON (BOOM)

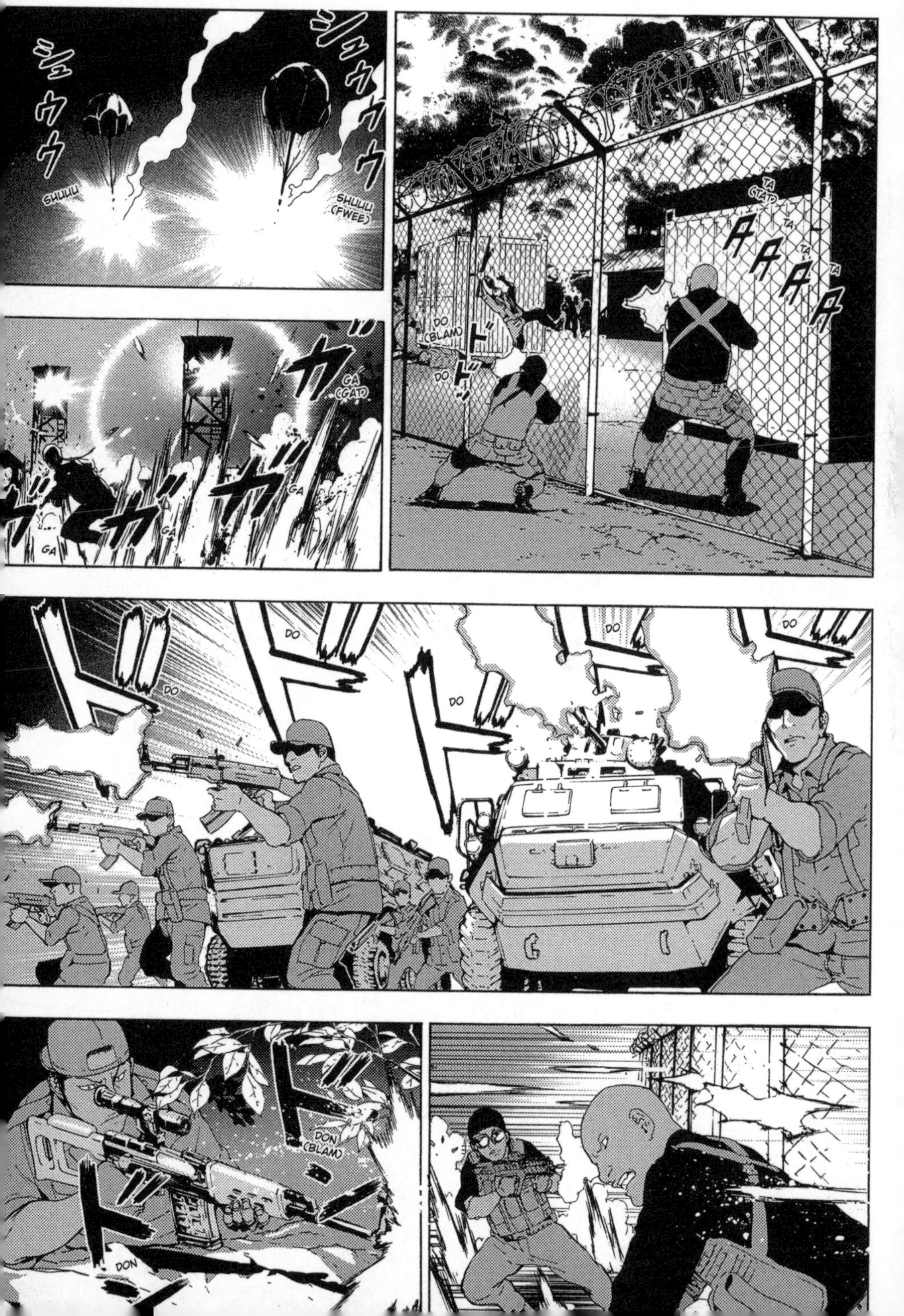
TA
(TAT)
TA
TA
TA
DO
(BLAM)
DO
シュウウウ
SHUUU
(FWEE)
シュウウ
SHUUU
GA
(GAT)
GA
GA
GA
DO
DO
DO
DO
DO
DON
(BLAM)
DON

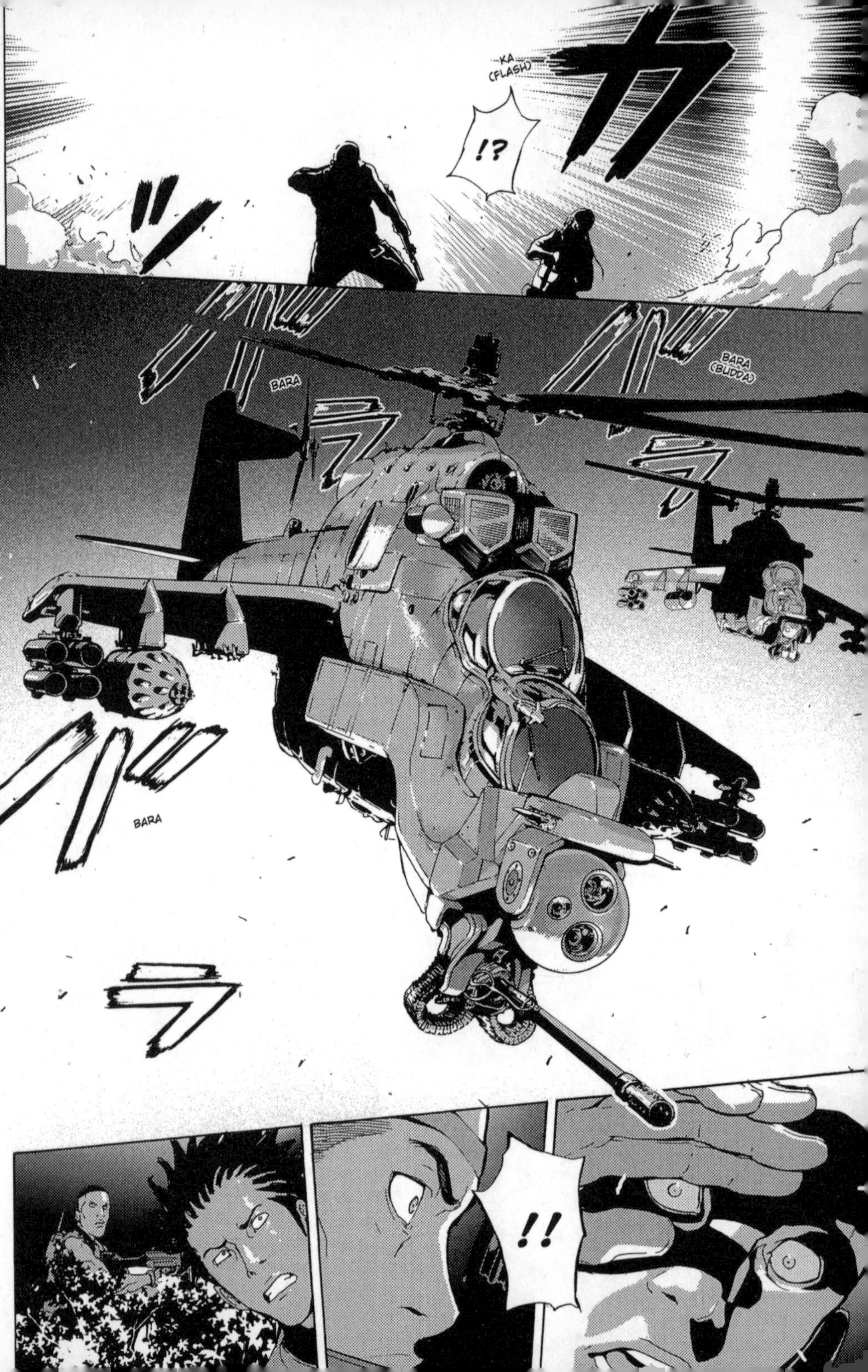
KA (FLASH)
!?
BARA (BUDDA)
BARA
BARA
!!

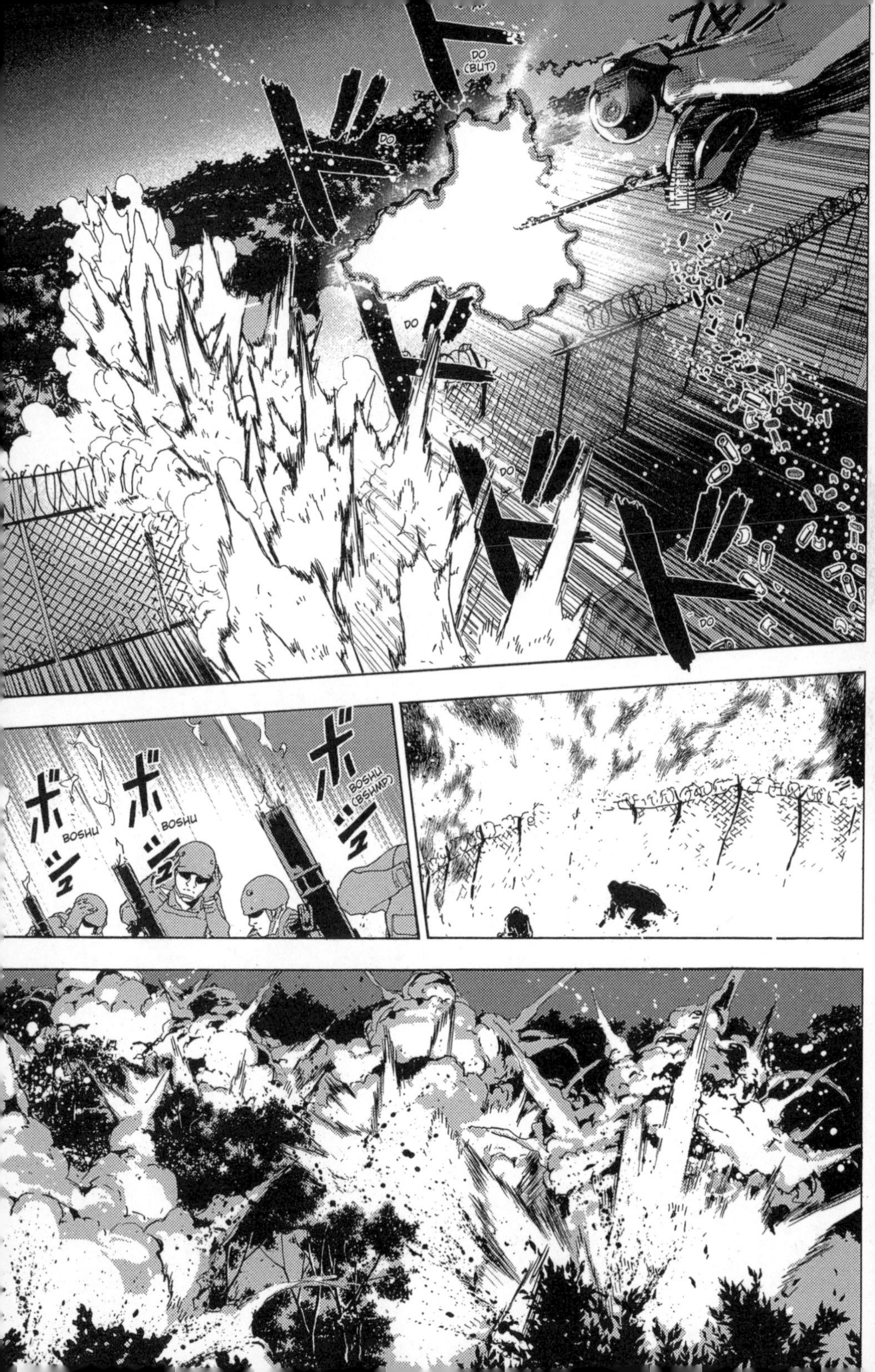
DO (BUT)
DO
DO
DO
DO
BOSHU (BSHMP)
BOSHU
BOSHU

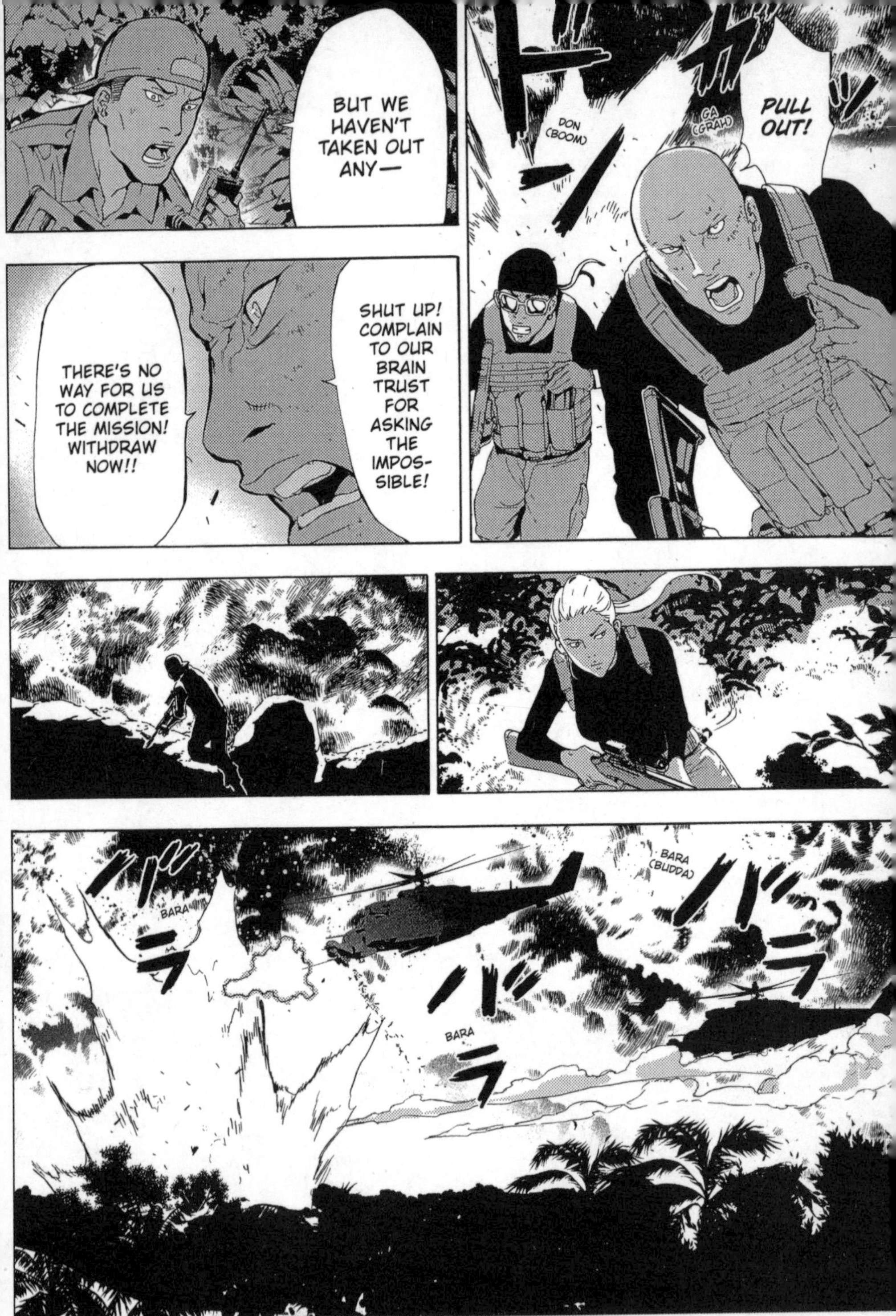
PULL OUT!
GA (GRAH)
DON (BOOM)
BUT WE HAVEN'T TAKEN OUT ANY—
SHUT UP! COMPLAIN TO OUR BRAIN TRUST FOR ASKING THE IMPOSSIBLE!
THERE'S NO WAY FOR US TO COMPLETE THE MISSION! WITHDRAW NOW!!
BARA (BUDDA)
BARA
BARA

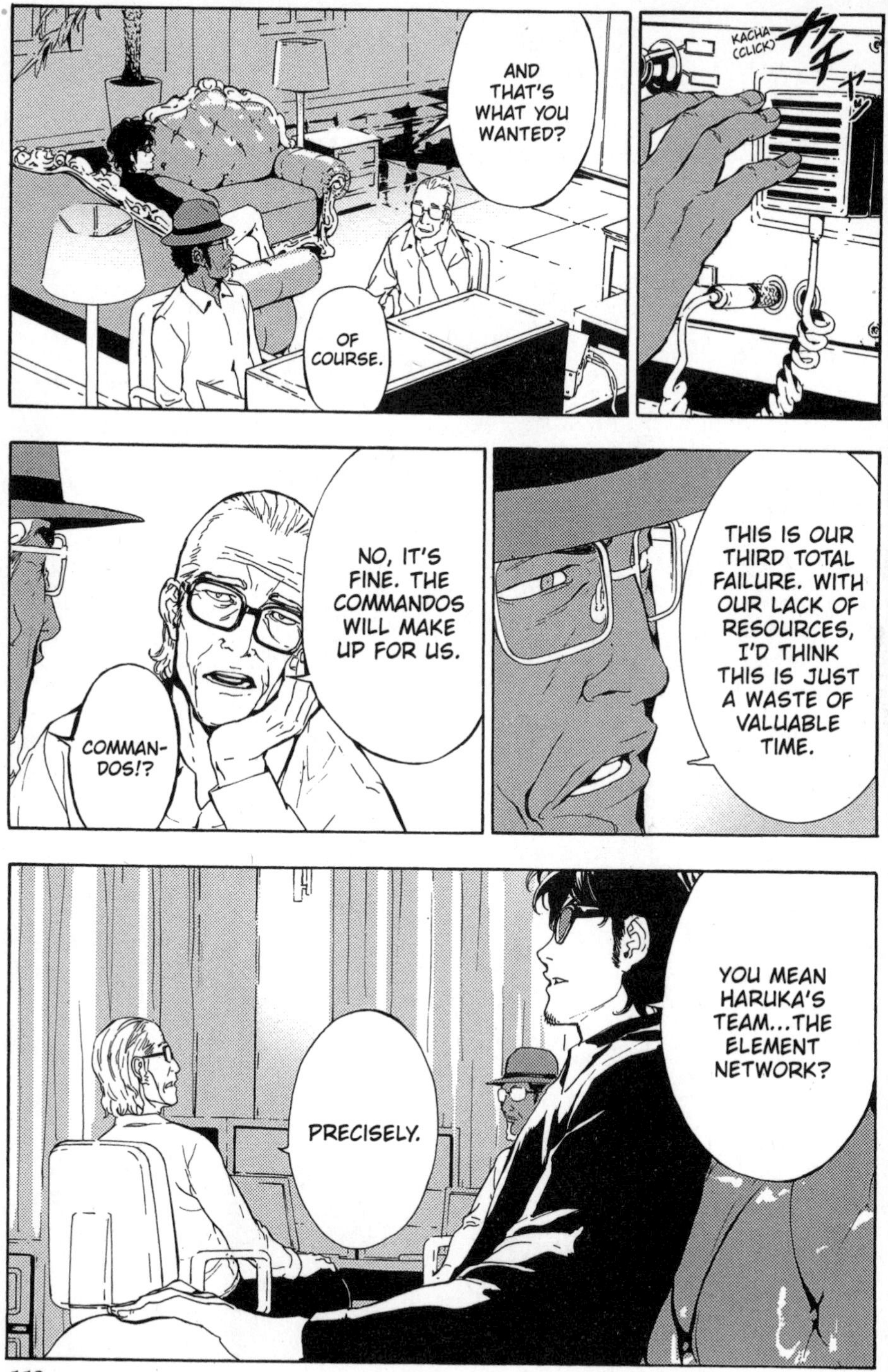
KACHA (CLICK)
AND THAT'S WHAT YOU WANTED?
OF COURSE.
THIS IS OUR THIRD TOTAL FAILURE. WITH OUR LACK OF RESOURCES, I'D THINK THIS IS JUST A WASTE OF VALUABLE TIME.
NO, IT'S FINE. THE COMMANDOS WILL MAKE UP FOR US.
COMMAN-DOS!?
YOU MEAN HARUKA'S TEAM...THE ELEMENT NETWORK?
PRECISELY.

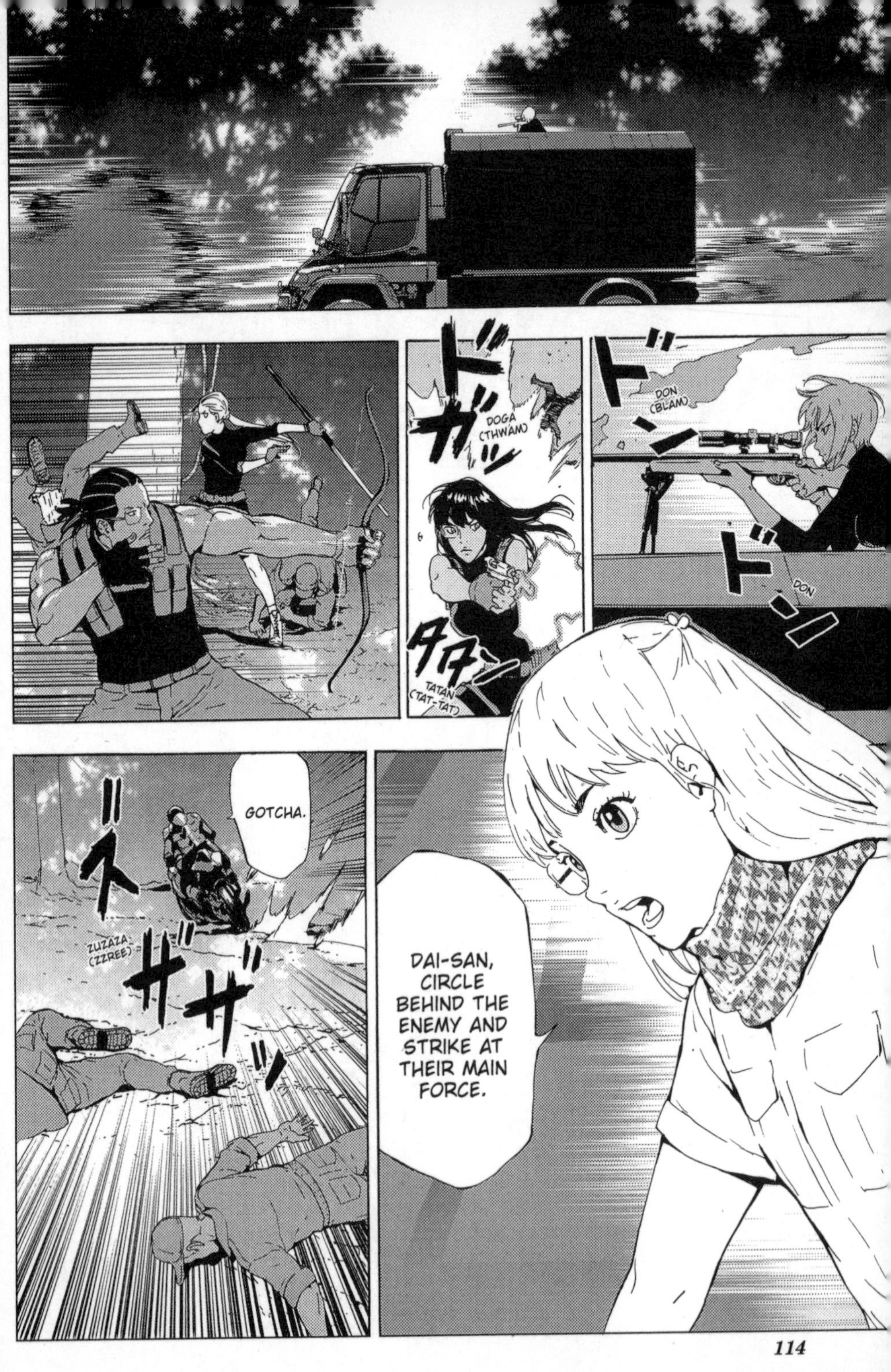
DON (BLAM)
DON
DOGA (THWAM)
TATAN (TAT-TAT)
DAI-SAN, CIRCLE BEHIND THE ENEMY AND STRIKE AT THEIR MAIN FORCE.
GOTCHA.
ZUZAZA (ZZREE)

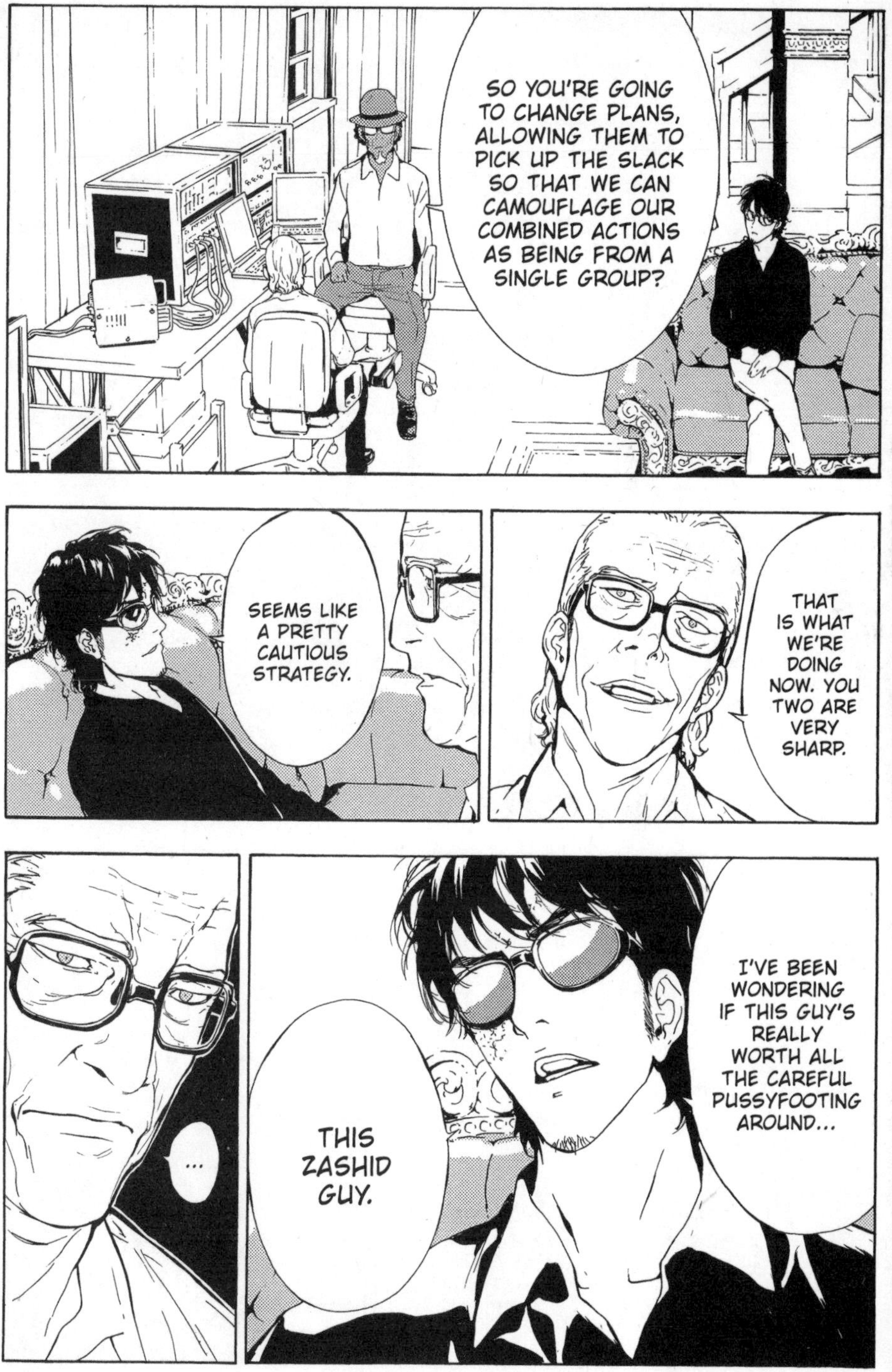
SO YOU'RE GOING TO CHANGE PLANS, ALLOWING THEM TO PICK UP THE SLACK SO THAT WE CAN CAMOUFLAGE OUR COMBINED ACTIONS AS BEING FROM A SINGLE GROUP?
THAT IS WHAT WE'RE DOING NOW. YOU TWO ARE VERY SHARP.
SEEMS LIKE A PRETTY CAUTIOUS STRATEGY.
I'VE BEEN WONDERING IF THIS GUY'S REALLY WORTH ALL THE CAREFUL PUSSYFOOTING AROUND...
THIS ZASHID GUY.
...

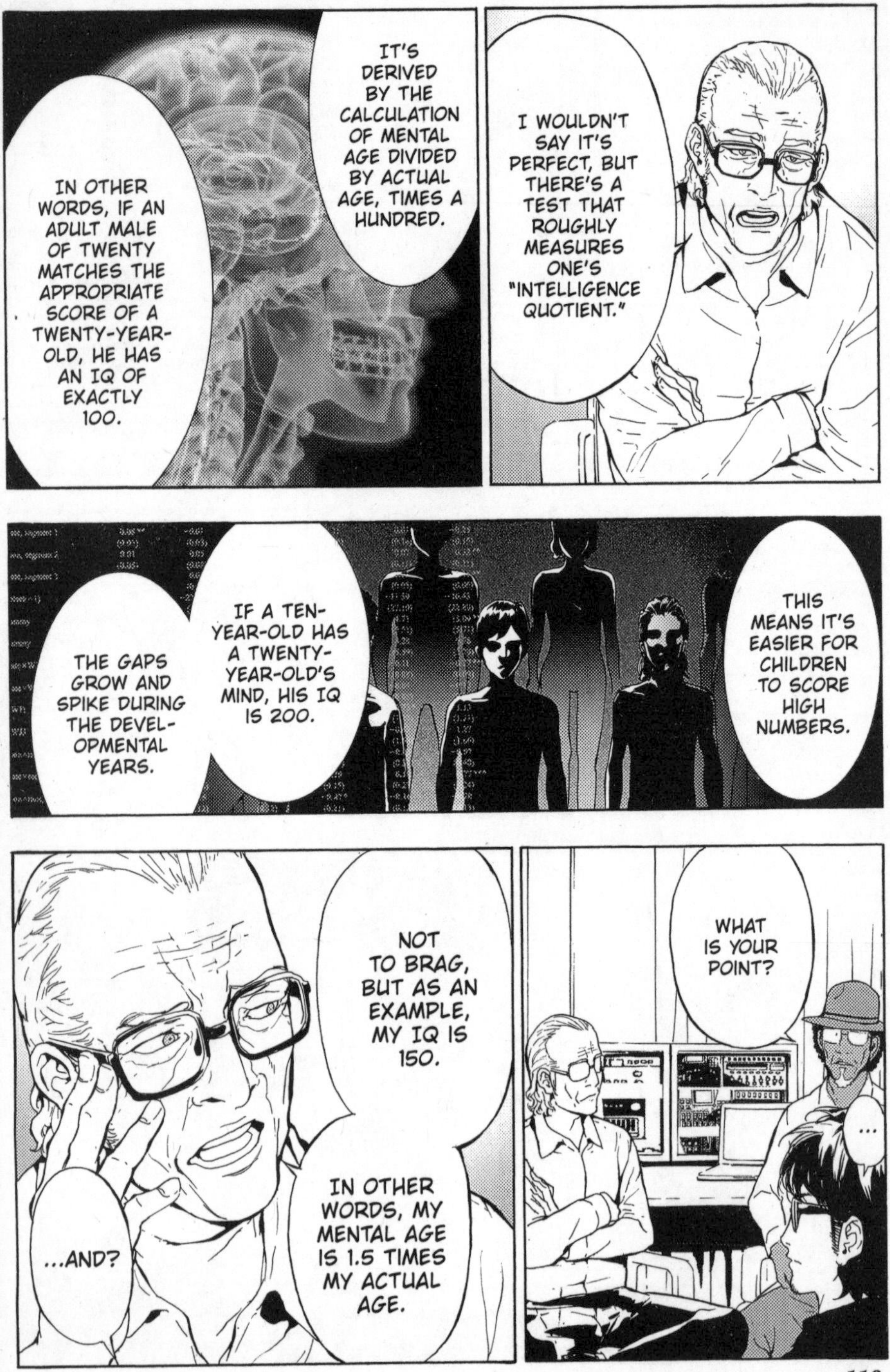
I WOULDN'T SAY IT'S PERFECT, BUT THERE'S A TEST THAT ROUGHLY MEASURES ONE'S "INTELLIGENCE QUOTIENT."
IT'S DERIVED BY THE CALCULATION OF MENTAL AGE DIVIDED BY ACTUAL AGE, TIMES A HUNDRED.
IN OTHER WORDS, IF AN ADULT MALE OF TWENTY MATCHES THE APPROPRIATE SCORE OF A TWENTY-YEAR-OLD, HE HAS AN IQ OF EXACTLY 100.
THIS MEANS IT'S EASIER FOR CHILDREN TO SCORE HIGH NUMBERS.
IF A TEN-YEAR-OLD HAS A TWENTY-YEAR-OLD'S MIND, HIS IQ IS 200.
THE GAPS GROW AND SPIKE DURING THE DEVEL-OPMENTAL YEARS.
WHAT IS YOUR POINT?
...
NOT TO BRAG, BUT AS AN EXAMPLE, MY IQ IS 150.
IN OTHER WORDS, MY MENTAL AGE IS 1.5 TIMES MY ACTUAL AGE.
...AND?

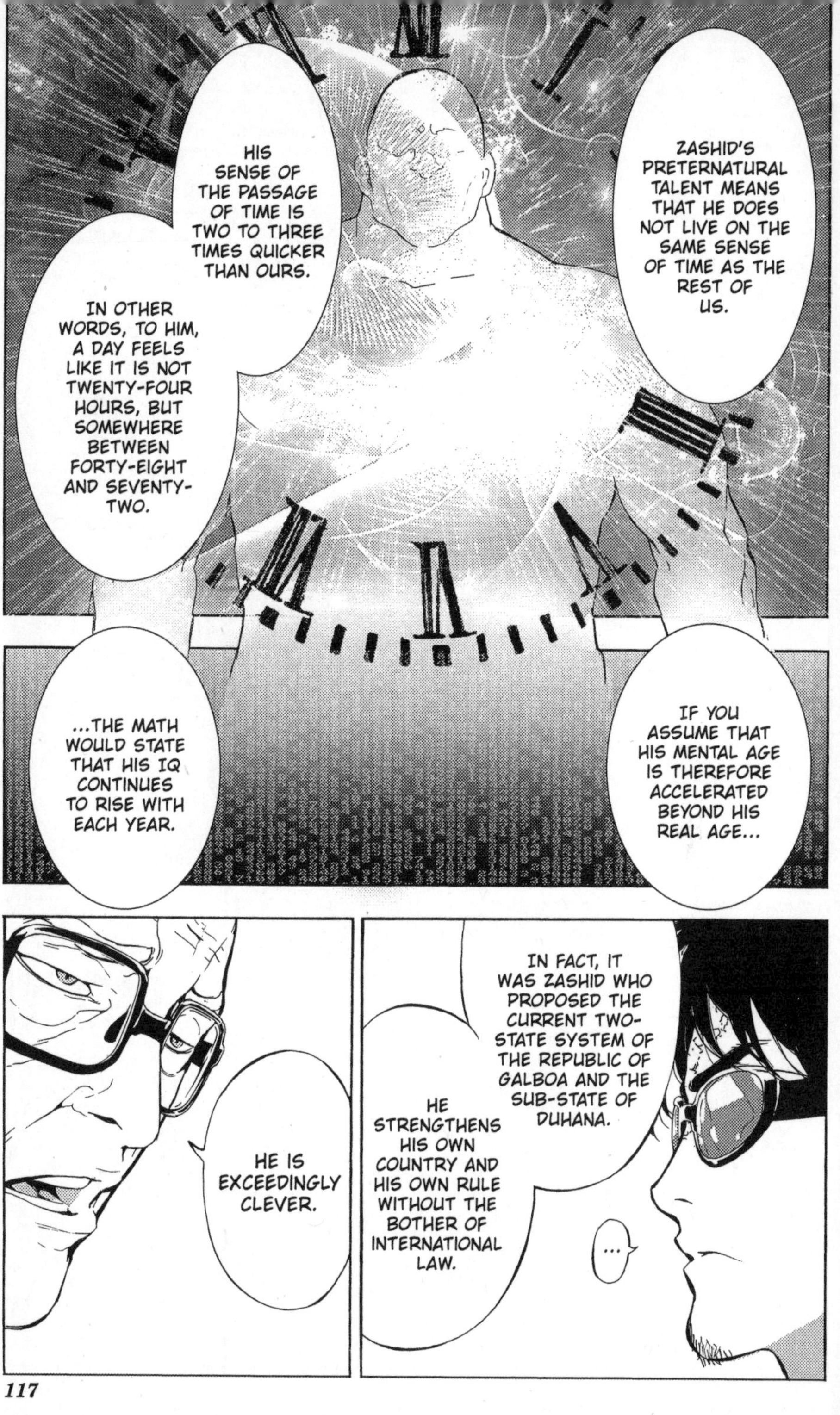
ZASHID'S PRETERNATURAL TALENT MEANS THAT HE DOES NOT LIVE ON THE SAME SENSE OF TIME AS THE REST OF US.
HIS SENSE OF THE PASSAGE OF TIME IS TWO TO THREE TIMES QUICKER THAN OURS.
IN OTHER WORDS, TO HIM, A DAY FEELS LIKE IT IS NOT TWENTY-FOUR HOURS, BUT SOMEWHERE BETWEEN FORTY-EIGHT AND SEVENTY-TWO.
IF YOU ASSUME THAT HIS MENTAL AGE IS THEREFORE ACCELERATED BEYOND HIS REAL AGE...
...THE MATH WOULD STATE THAT HIS IQ CONTINUES TO RISE WITH EACH YEAR.
IN FACT, IT WAS ZASHID WHO PROPOSED THE CURRENT TWO-STATE SYSTEM OF THE REPUBLIC OF GALBOA AND THE SUB-STATE OF DUHANA.
HE STRENGTHENS HIS OWN COUNTRY AND HIS OWN RULE WITHOUT THE BOTHER OF INTERNATIONAL LAW.
...
HE IS EXCEEDINGLY CLEVER.

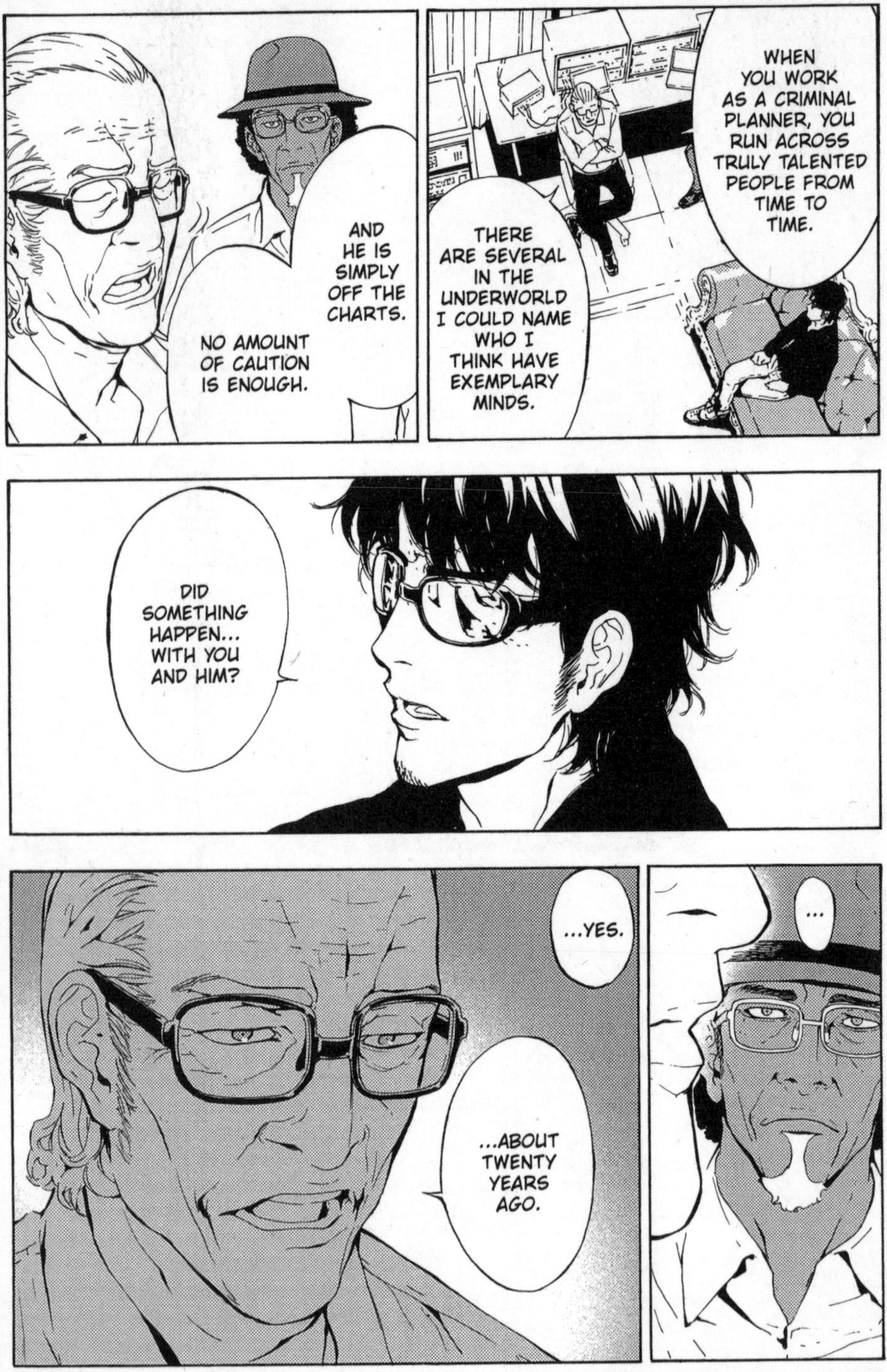
WHEN YOU WORK AS A CRIMINAL PLANNER, YOU RUN ACROSS TRULY TALENTED PEOPLE FROM TIME TO TIME.
THERE ARE SEVERAL IN THE UNDERWORLD I COULD NAME WHO I THINK HAVE EXEMPLARY MINDS.
AND HE IS SIMPLY OFF THE CHARTS.
NO AMOUNT OF CAUTION IS ENOUGH.
DID SOMETHING HAPPEN... WITH YOU AND HIM?
...
...YES.
...ABOUT TWENTY YEARS AGO.

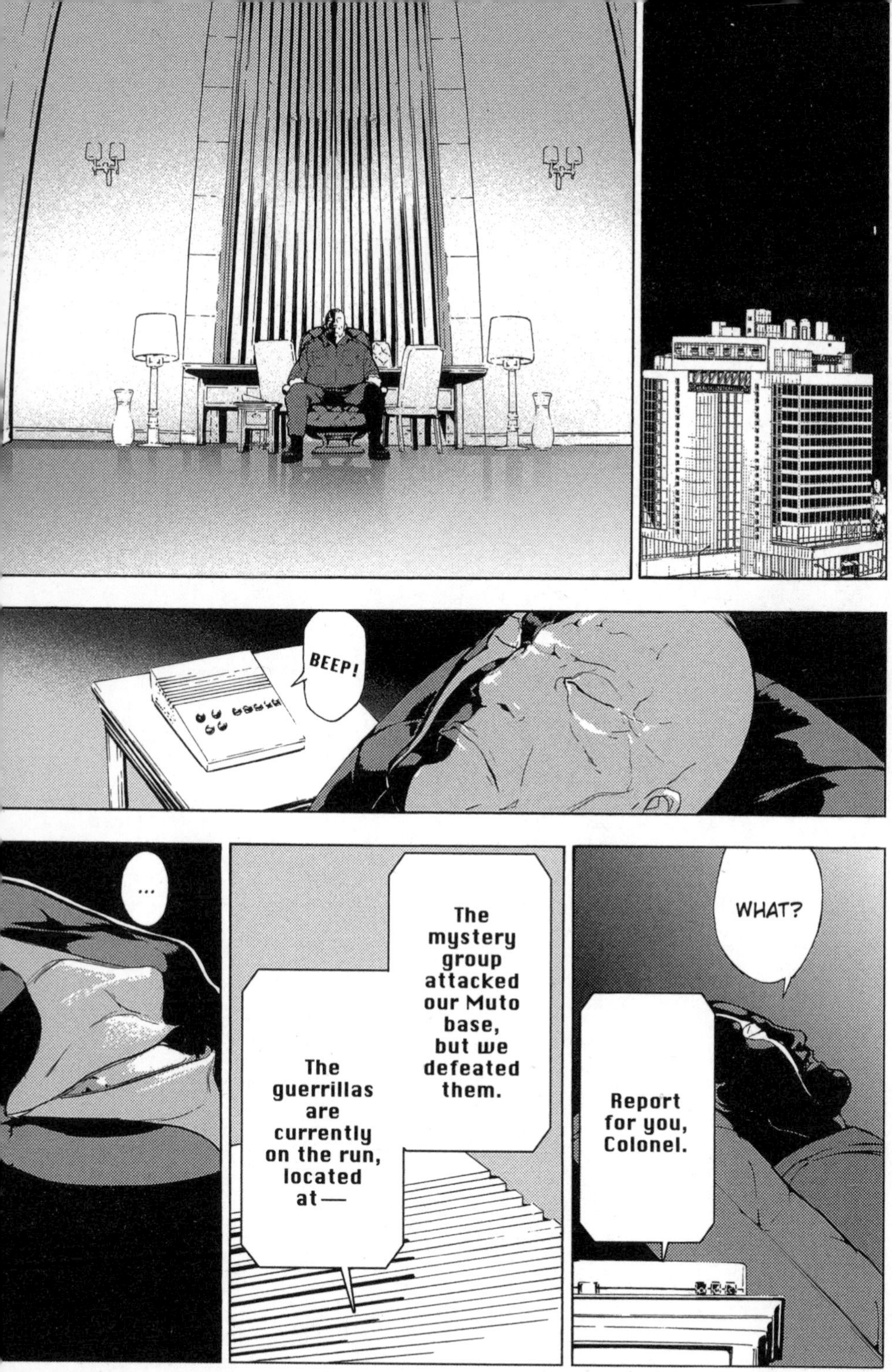
BEEP!
WHAT?
Report for you, Colonel.
The mystery group attacked our Muto base, but we defeated them.
The guerrillas are currently on the run, located at—
...

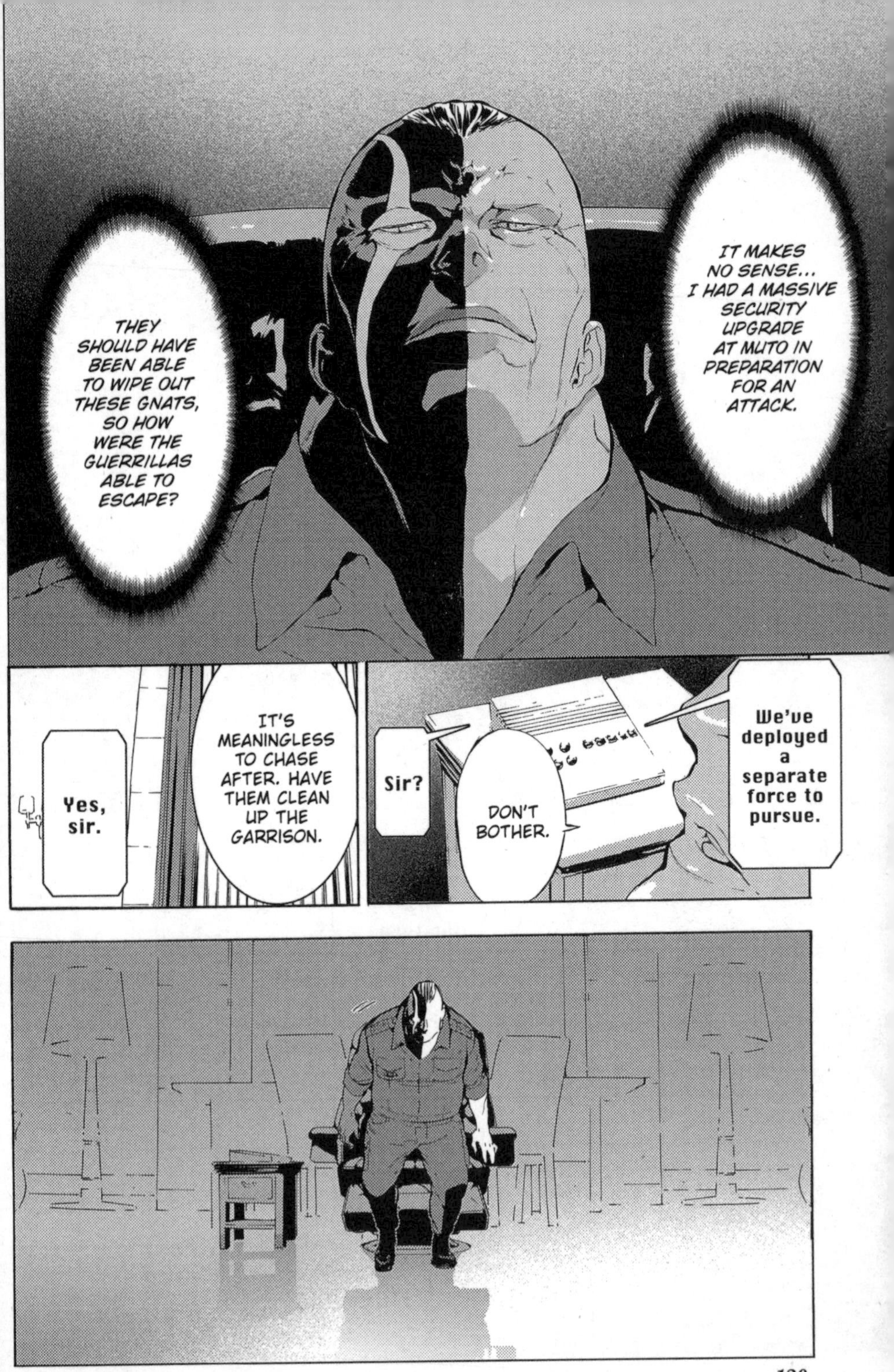
IT MAKES NO SENSE... I HAD A MASSIVE SECURITY UPGRADE AT MUTO IN PREPARATION FOR AN ATTACK.
THEY SHOULD HAVE BEEN ABLE TO WIPE OUT THESE GNATS, SO HOW WERE THE GUERRILLAS ABLE TO ESCAPE?
We've deployed a separate force to pursue.
DON'T BOTHER.
Sir?
IT'S MEANINGLESS TO CHASE AFTER. HAVE THEM CLEAN UP THE GARRISON.
Yes, sir.

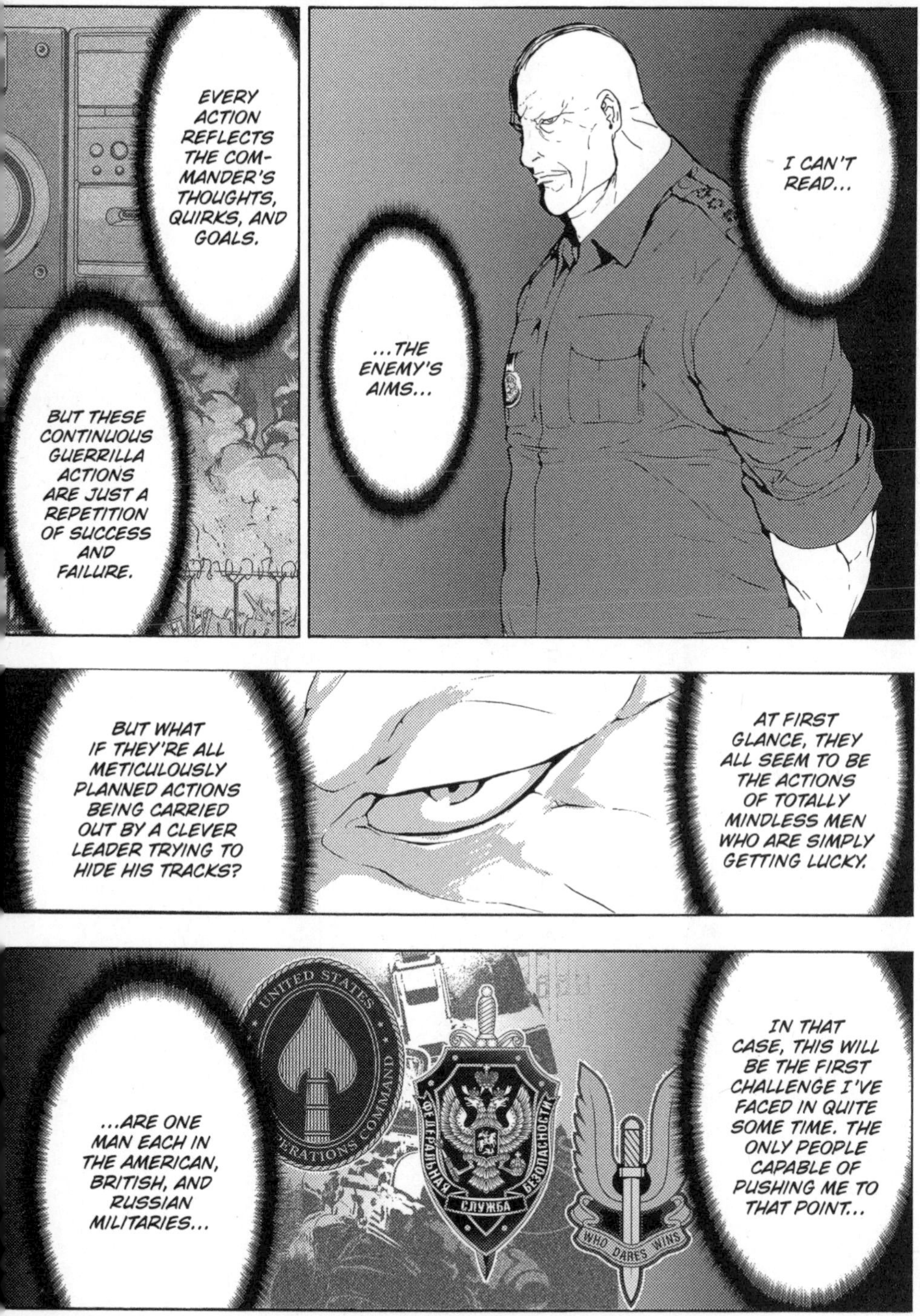
I CAN'T READ...
...THE ENEMY'S AIMS...
EVERY ACTION REFLECTS THE COM-MANDER'S THOUGHTS, QUIRKS, AND GOALS.
BUT THESE CONTINUOUS GUERRILLA ACTIONS ARE JUST A REPETITION OF SUCCESS AND FAILURE.
AT FIRST GLANCE, THEY ALL SEEM TO BE THE ACTIONS OF TOTALLY MINDLESS MEN WHO ARE SIMPLY GETTING LUCKY.
BUT WHAT IF THEY'RE ALL METICULOUSLY PLANNED ACTIONS BEING CARRIED OUT BY A CLEVER LEADER TRYING TO HIDE HIS TRACKS?
IN THAT CASE, THIS WILL BE THE FIRST CHALLENGE I'VE FACED IN QUITE SOME TIME. THE ONLY PEOPLE CAPABLE OF PUSHING ME TO THAT POINT...
...ARE ONE MAN EACH IN THE AMERICAN, BRITISH, AND RUSSIAN MILITARIES...
UNITED STATES
ERATIONS COMMAND
ФЕДЕРАЛЬНАЯ
СЛУЖБА
БЕЗОПАСНОСТИ
WHO DARES WINS

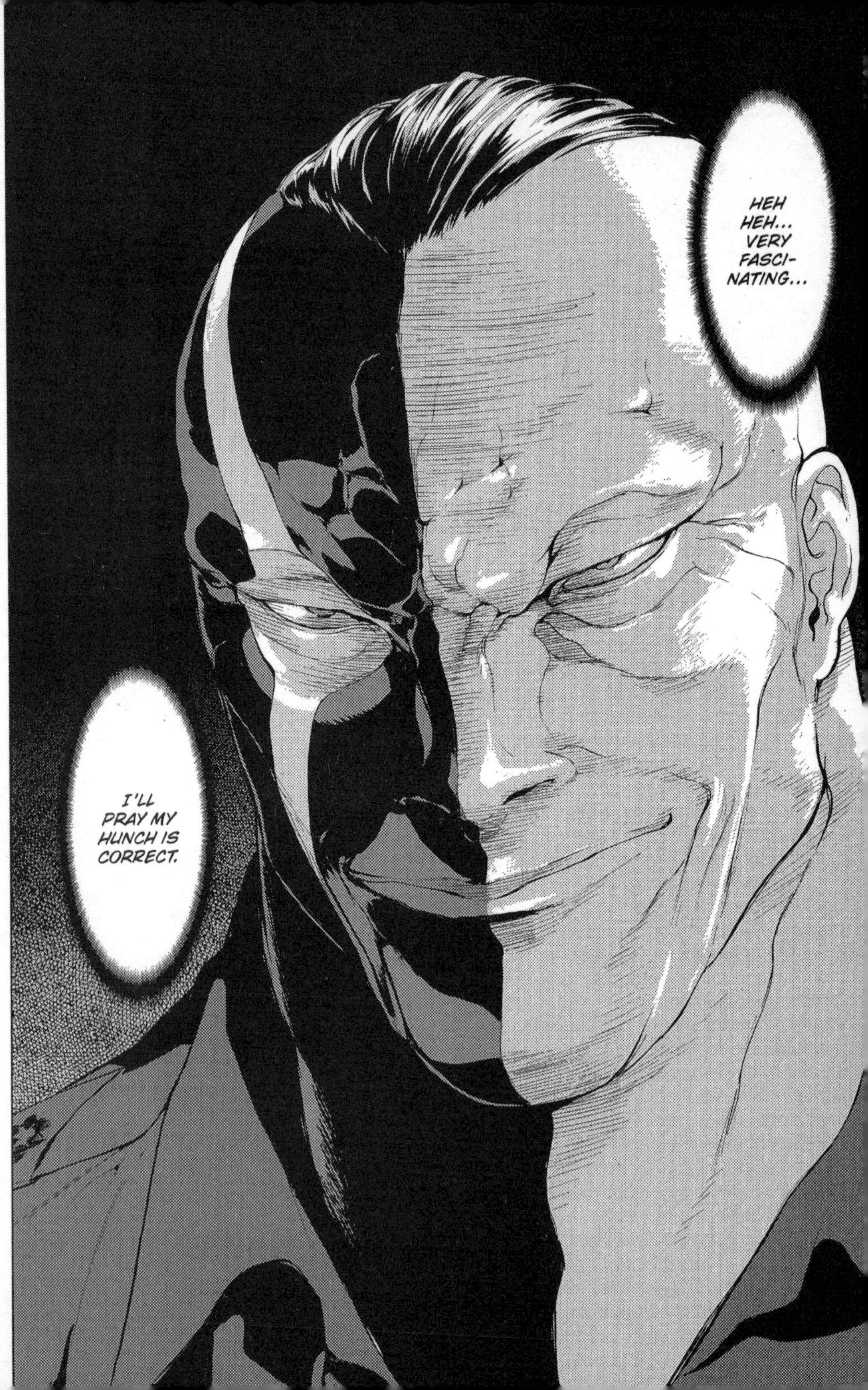
HEH HEH... VERY FASCI-NATING...
I'LL PRAY MY HUNCH IS CORRECT.

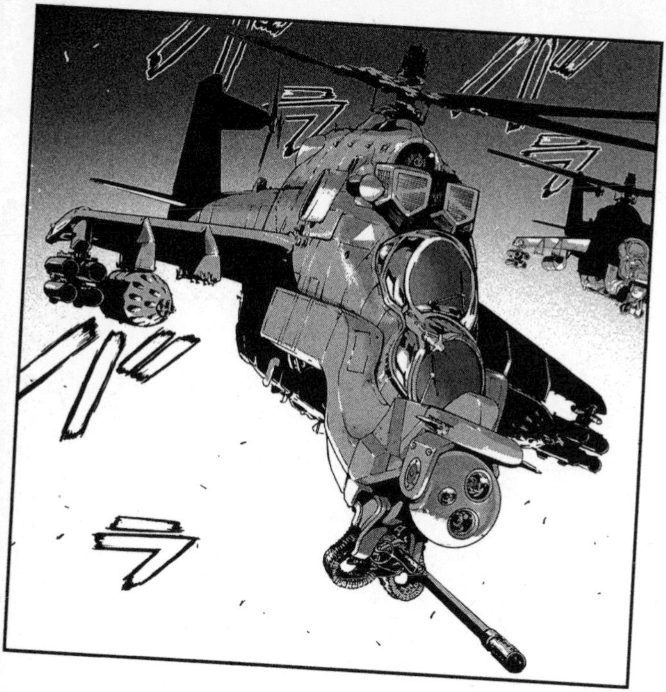
バラ
バラ
バラ

Until Death do us Part

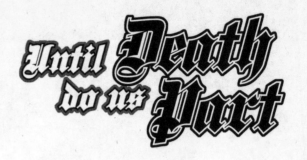

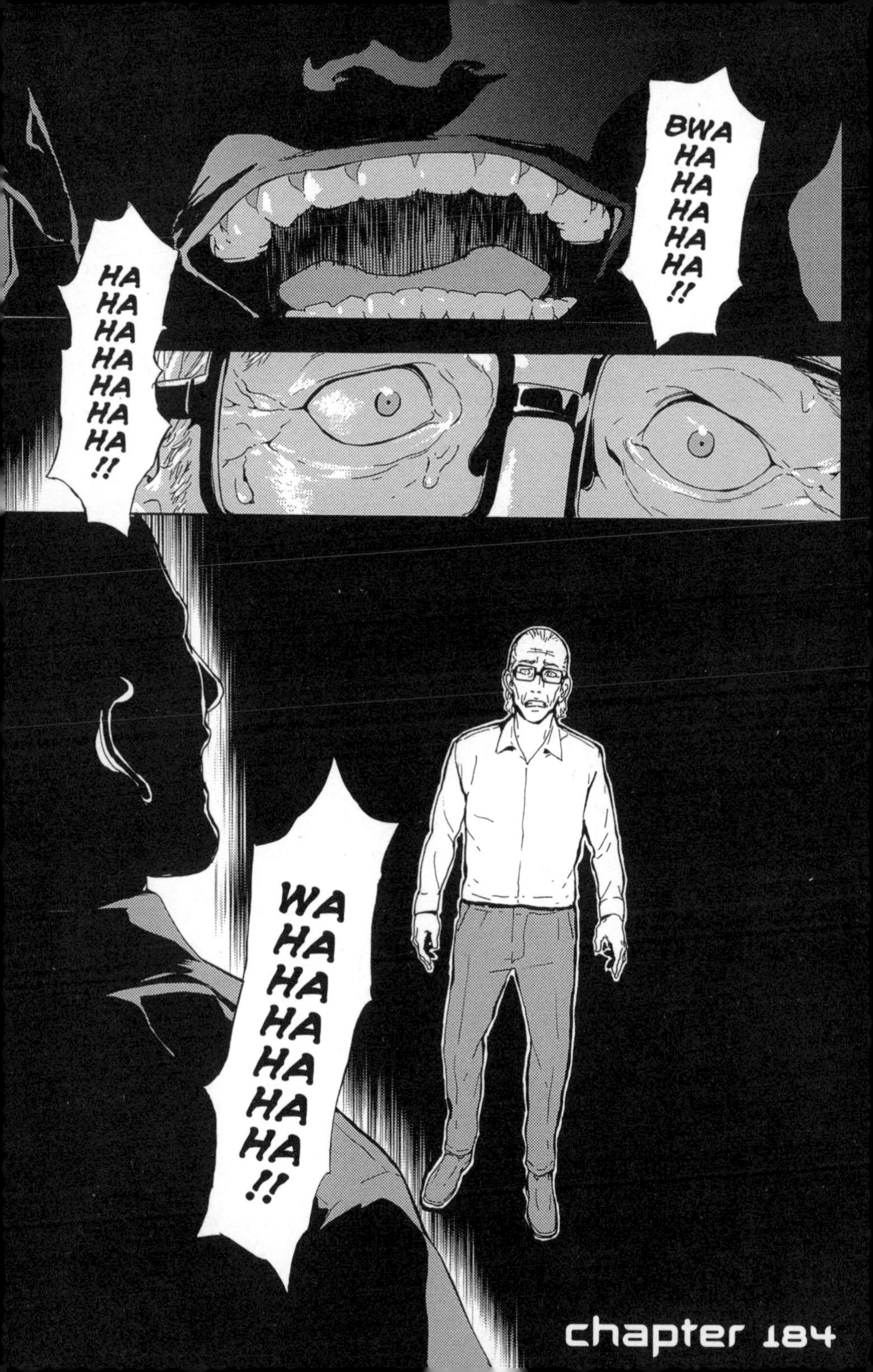
BWA HA HA HA HA HA!!
HA HA HA HA HA HA HA!!
WA HA HA HA HA HA HA HA HA!!
chapter 184

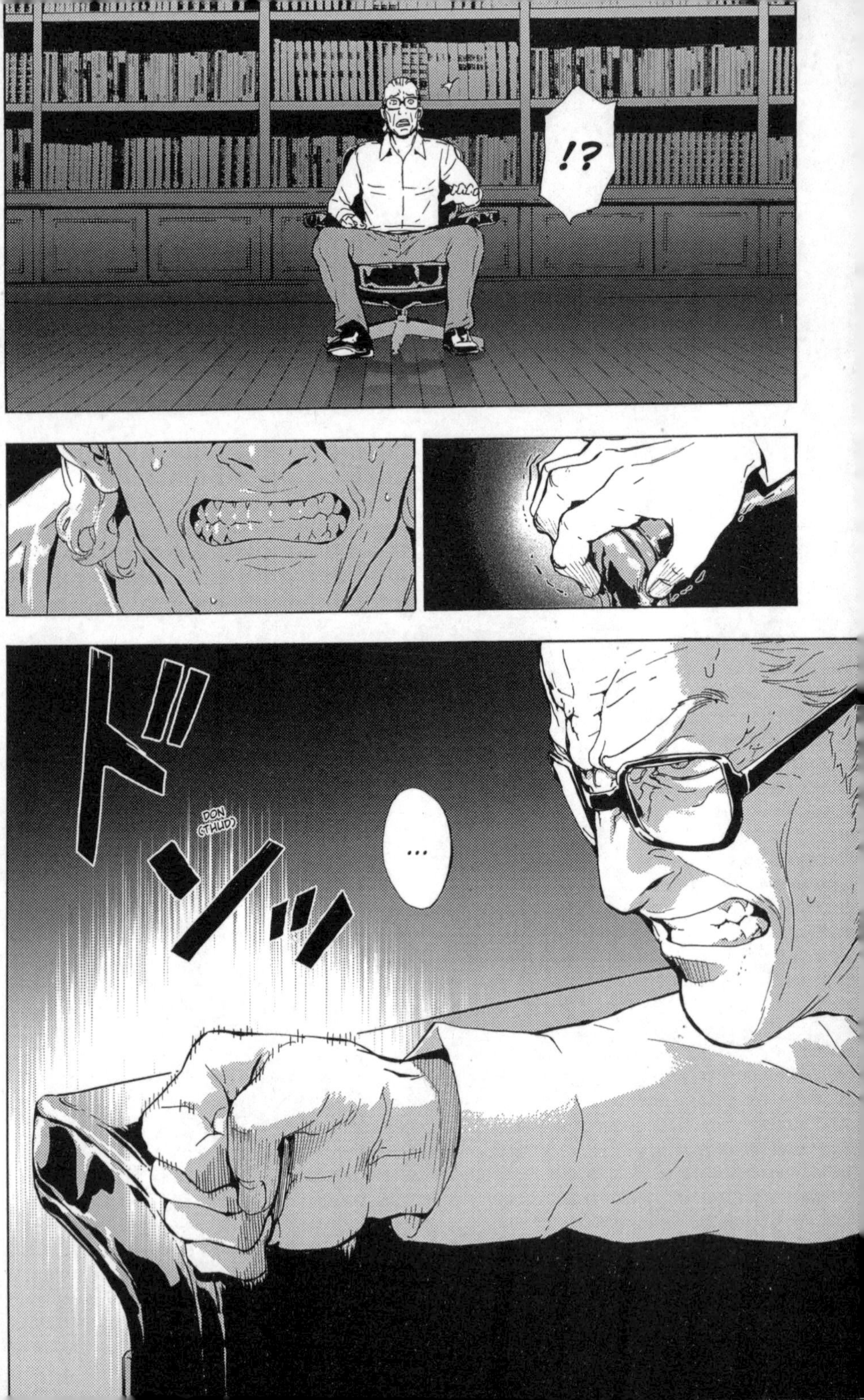
!?
...
ドンッ
DON (THUD)

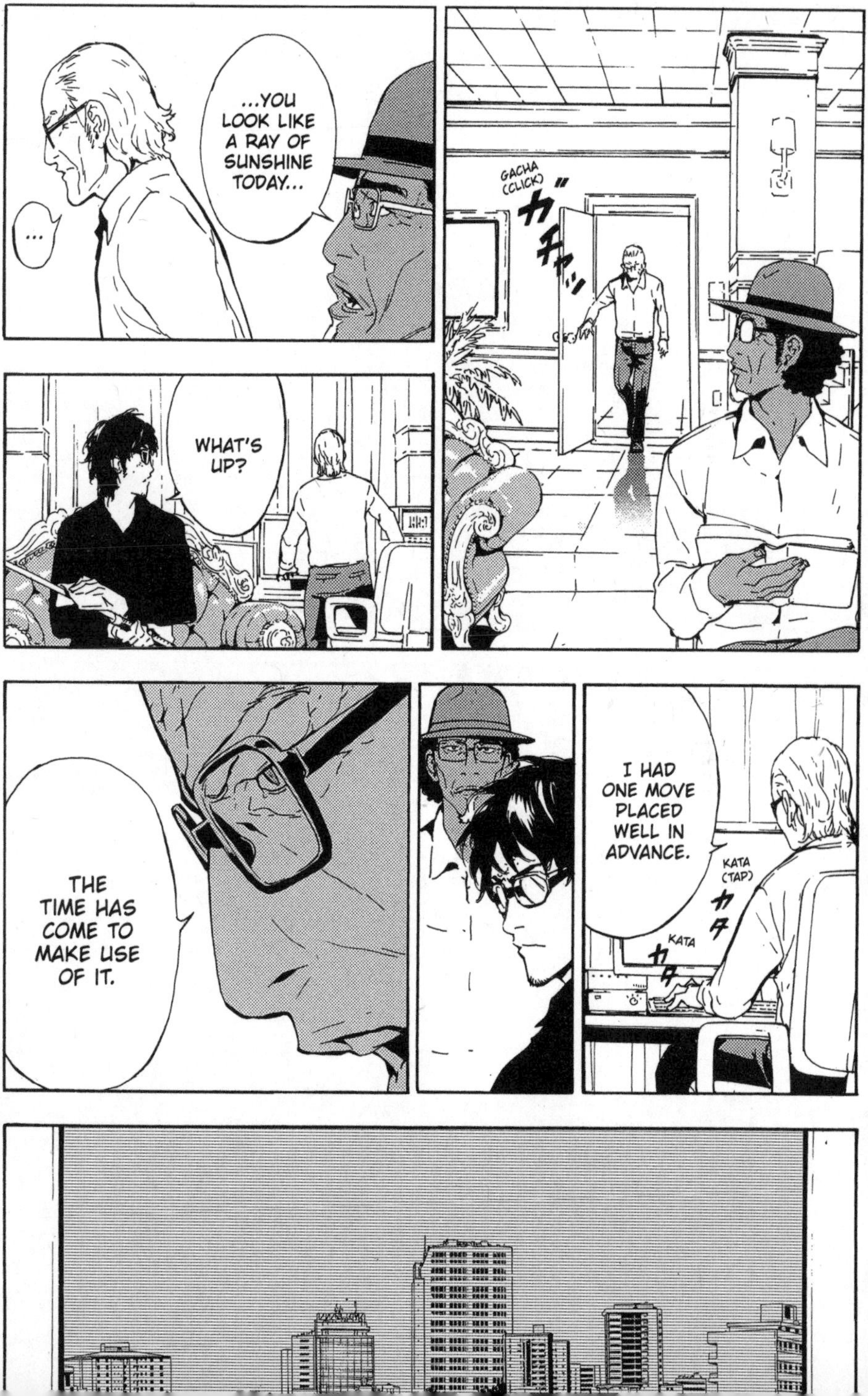
GACHA (CLICK)
...YOU LOOK LIKE A RAY OF SUNSHINE TODAY...
...
WHAT'S UP?
I HAD ONE MOVE PLACED WELL IN ADVANCE.
KATA (TAP)
KATA
THE TIME HAS COME TO MAKE USE OF IT.

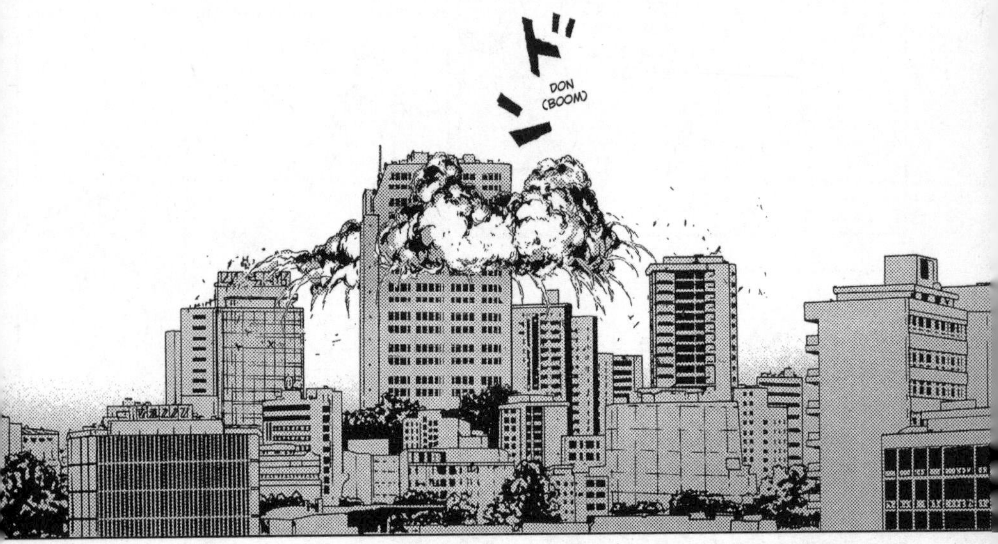
DON
(BOOM)
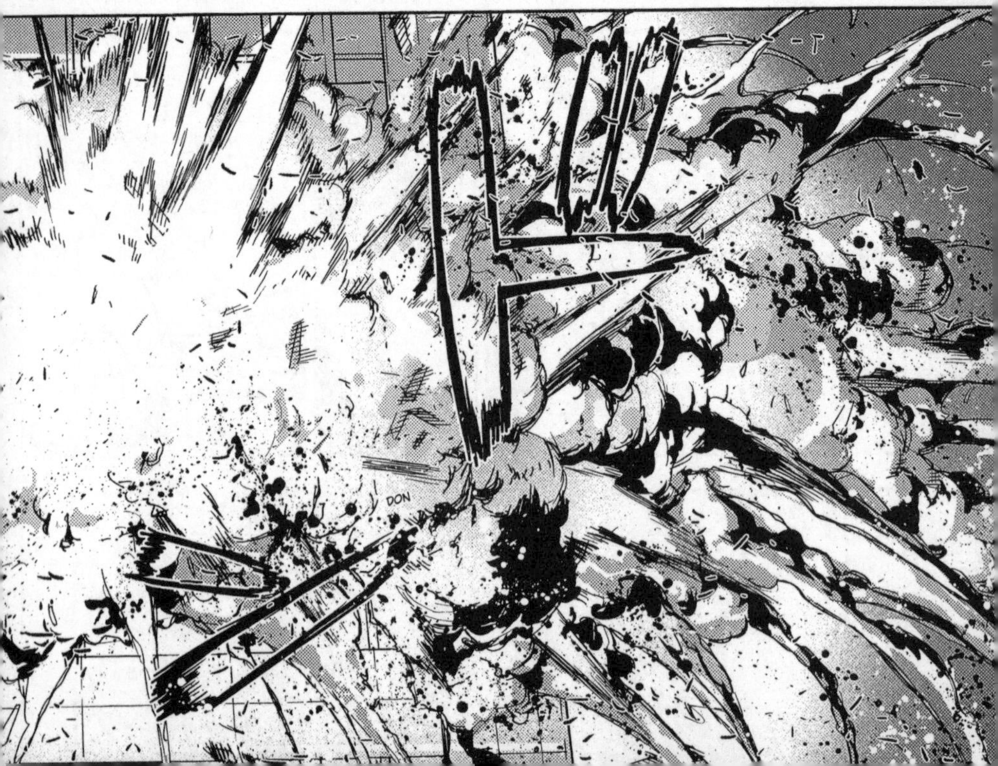
DON

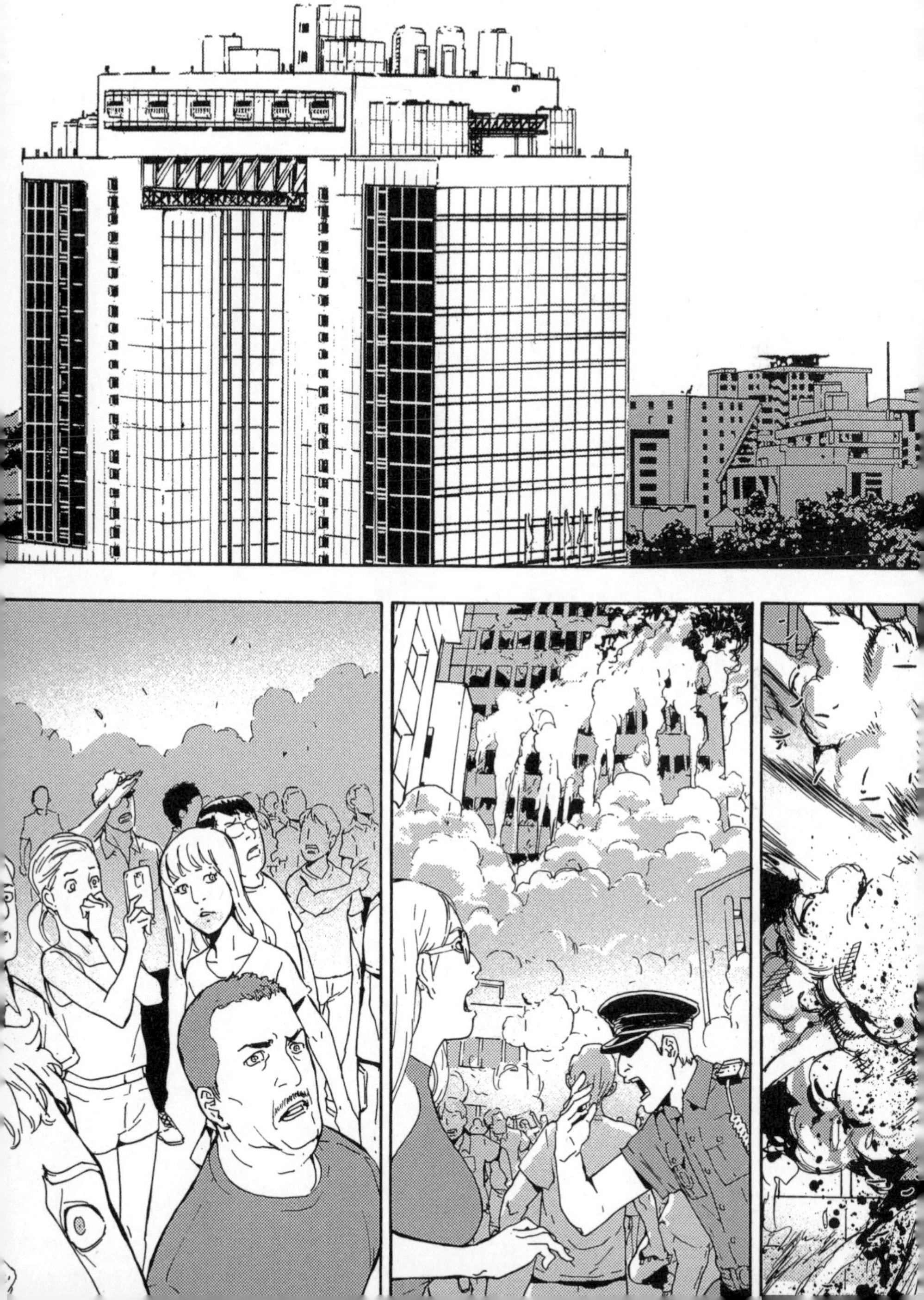

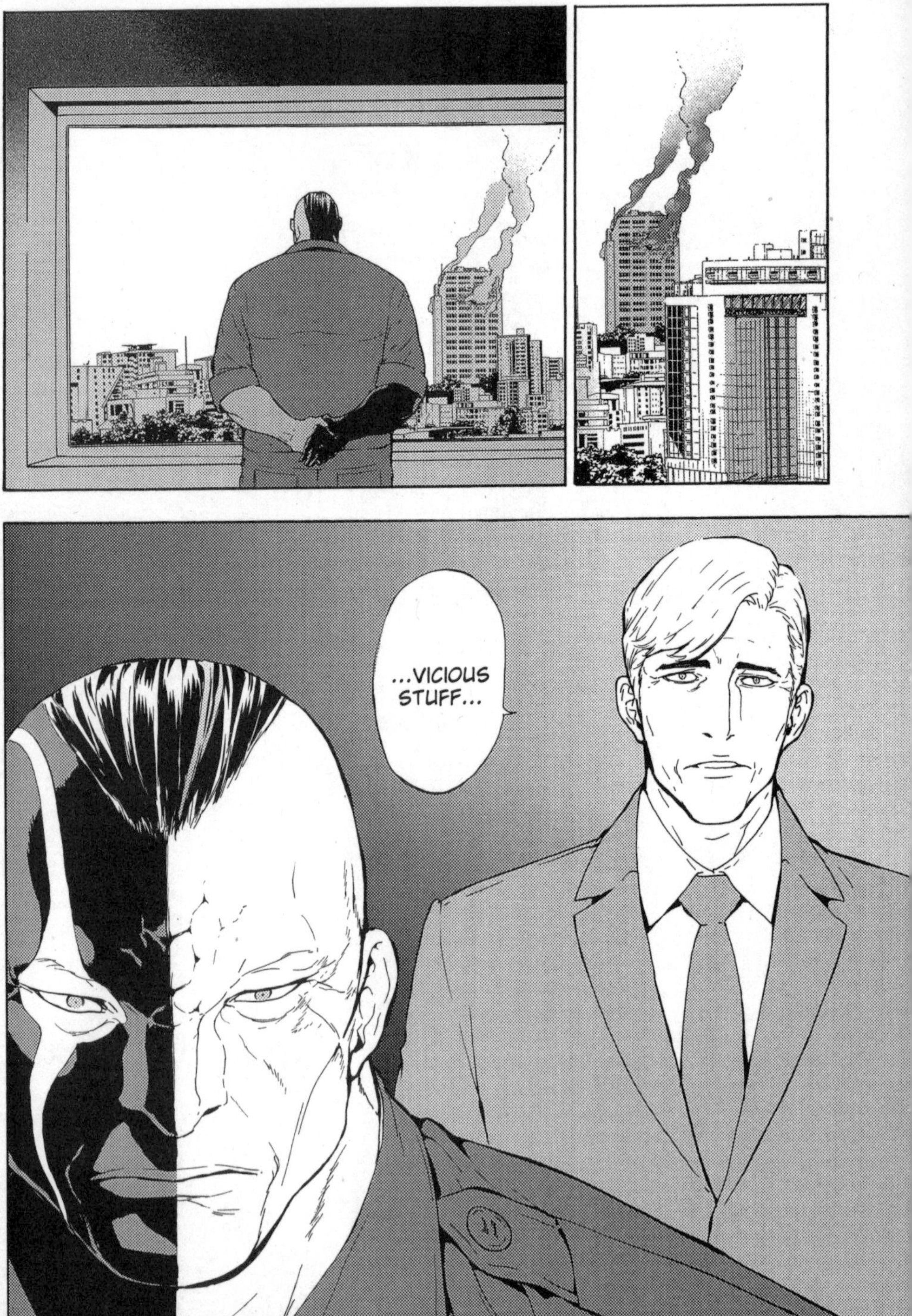
...VICIOUS STUFF...

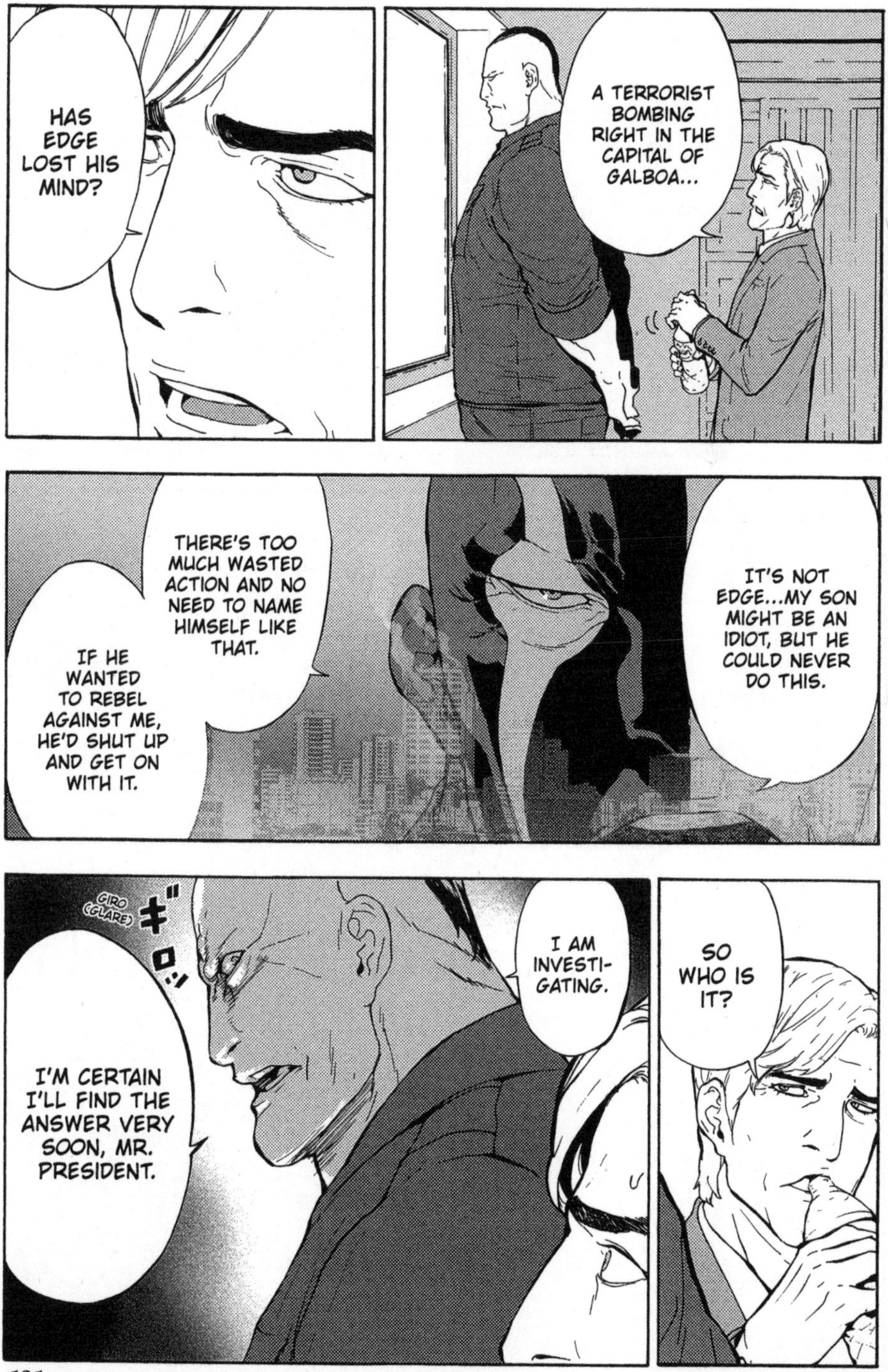
A TERRORIST BOMBING RIGHT IN THE CAPITAL OF GALBOA...
HAS EDGE LOST HIS MIND?
IT'S NOT EDGE...MY SON MIGHT BE AN IDIOT, BUT HE COULD NEVER DO THIS.
THERE'S TOO MUCH WASTED ACTION AND NO NEED TO NAME HIMSELF LIKE THAT.
IF HE WANTED TO REBEL AGAINST ME, HE'D SHUT UP AND GET ON WITH IT.
SO WHO IS IT?
I AM INVESTI-GATING.
ギロッ
GIRO (GLARE)
I'M CERTAIN I'LL FIND THE ANSWER VERY SOON, MR. PRESIDENT.

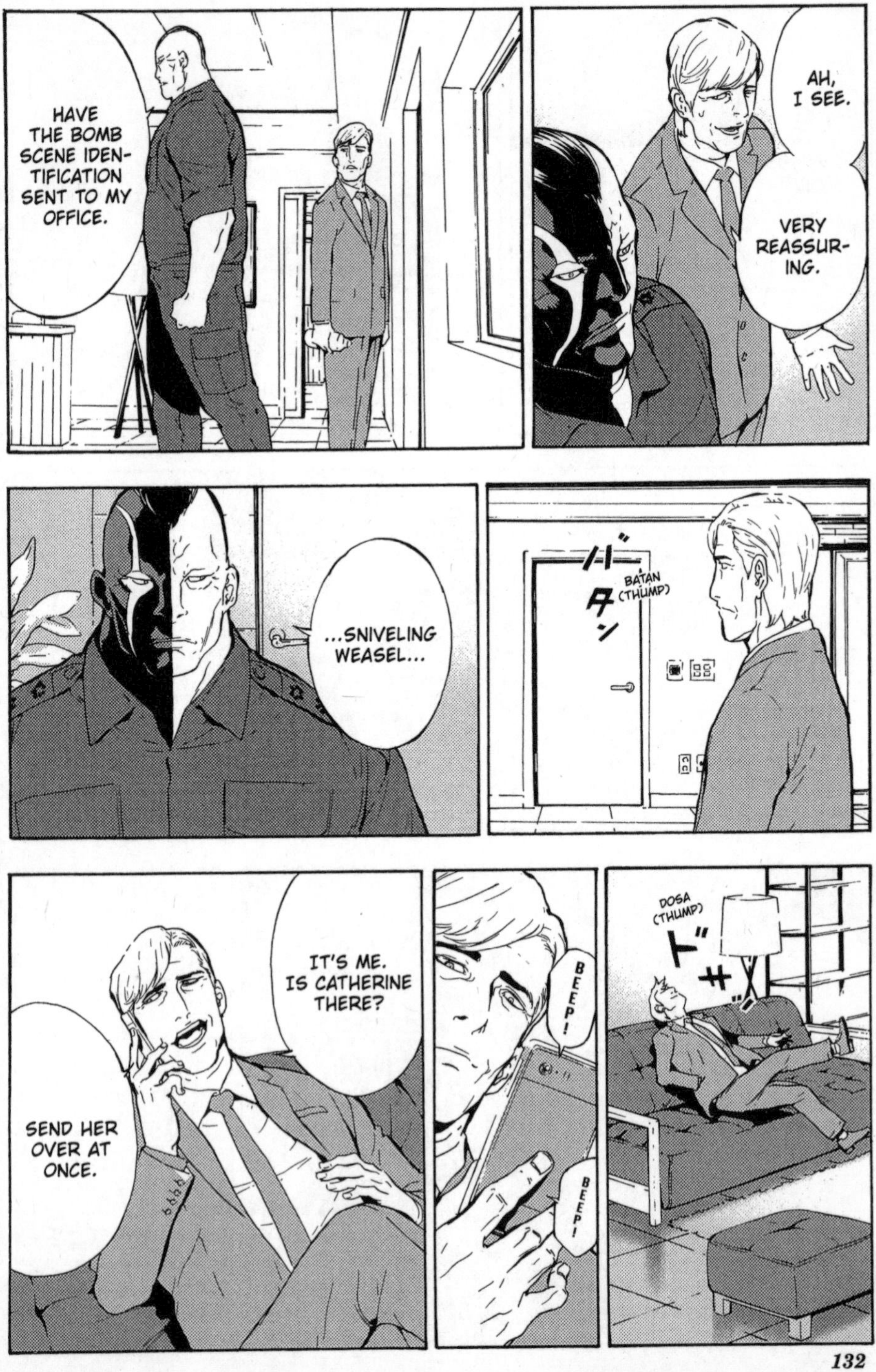
AH, I SEE.
VERY REASSURING.
HAVE THE BOMB SCENE IDENTIFICATION SENT TO MY OFFICE.
バタン
BATAN (THUMP)
...SNIVELING WEASEL...
ドサ
DOSA (THUMP)
BEEP!
BEEP!
IT'S ME. IS CATHERINE THERE?
SEND HER OVER AT ONCE.

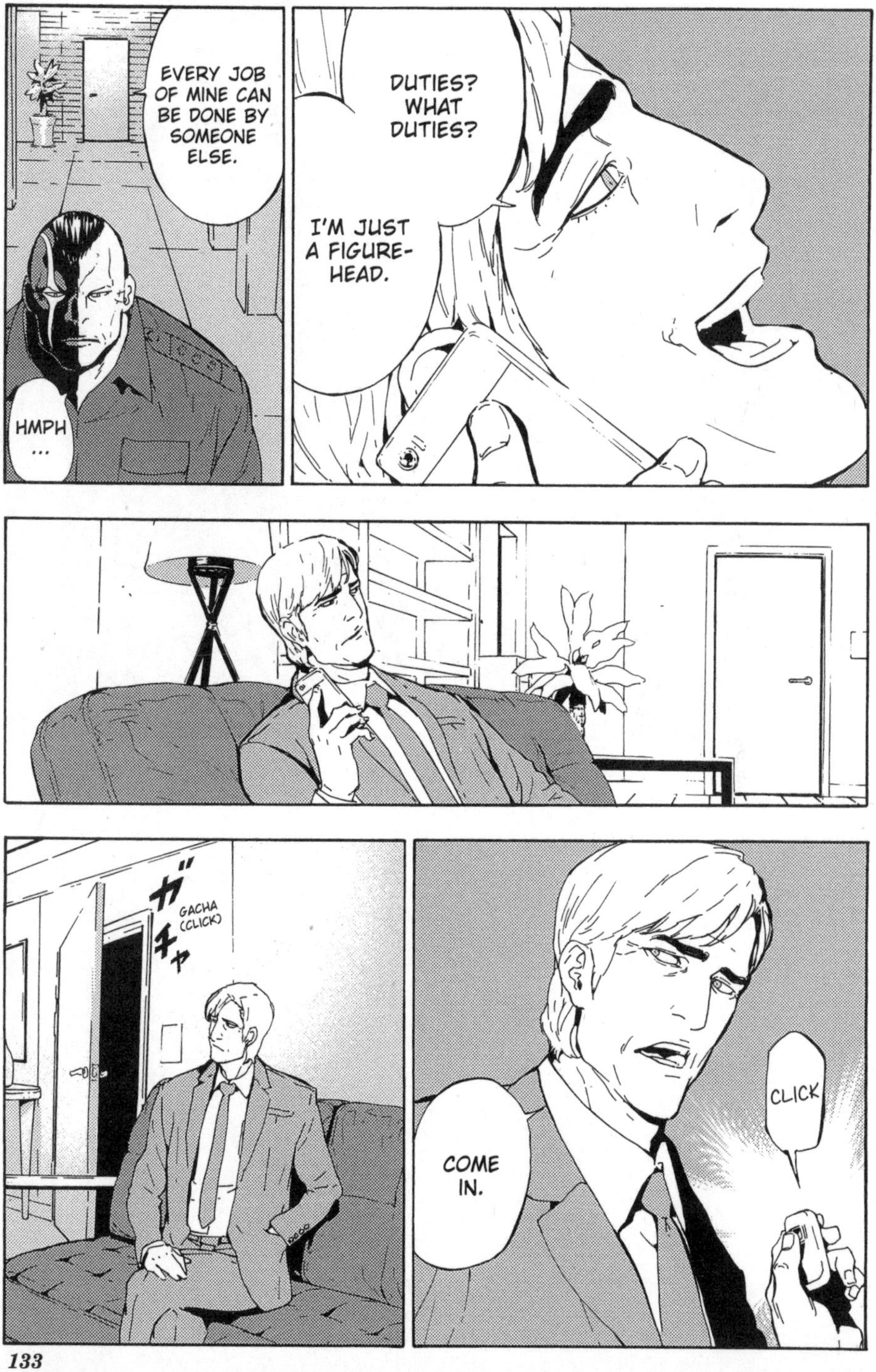
DUTIES? WHAT DUTIES?
I'M JUST A FIGURE-HEAD.
EVERY JOB OF MINE CAN BE DONE BY SOMEONE ELSE.
HMPH ...
CLICK
COME IN.
ガチャ
GACHA (CLICK)

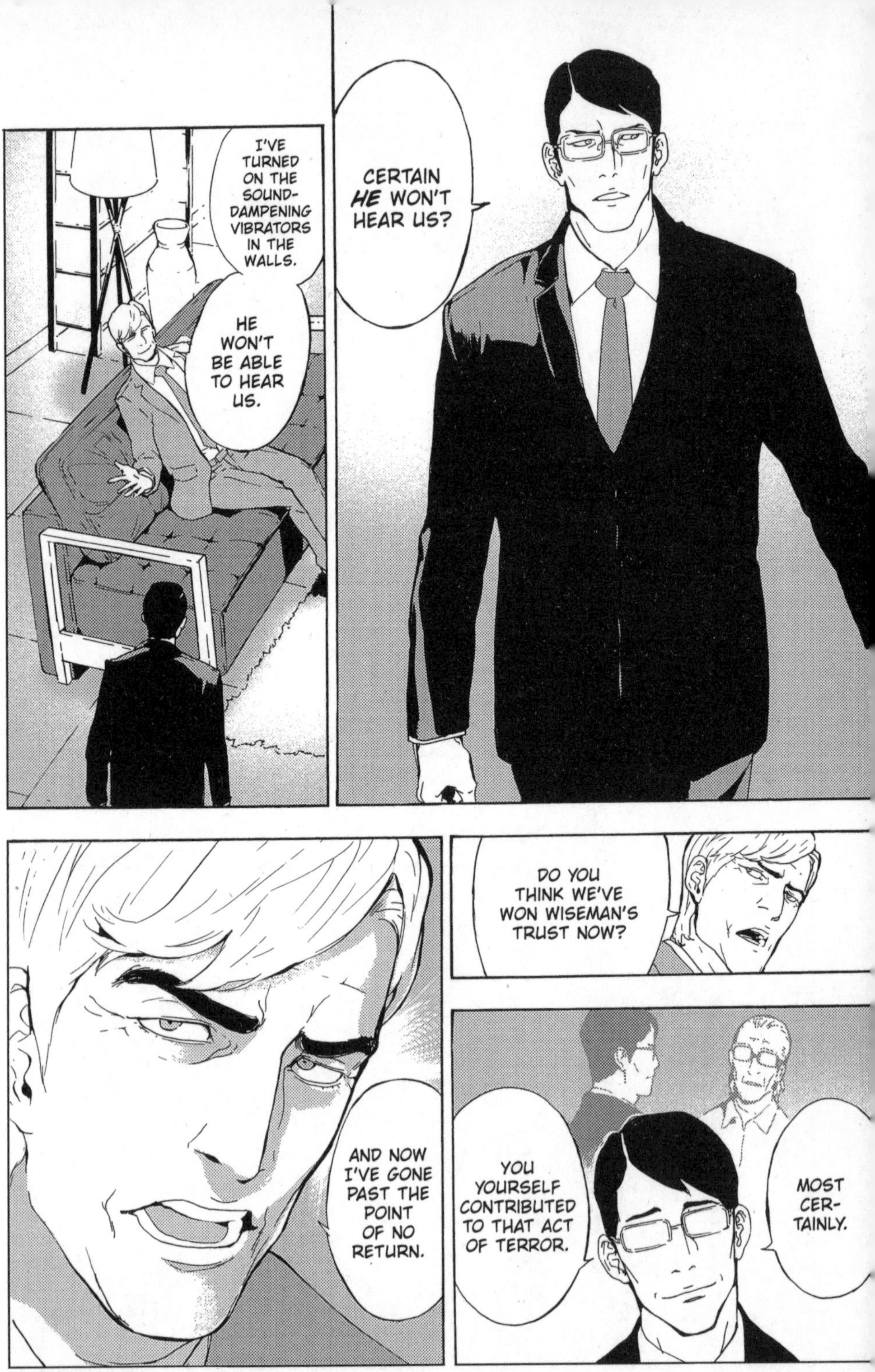
CERTAIN *HE* WON'T HEAR US?
I'VE TURNED ON THE SOUND-DAMPENING VIBRATORS IN THE WALLS.
HE WON'T BE ABLE TO HEAR US.
DO YOU THINK WE'VE WON WISEMAN'S TRUST NOW?
MOST CER-TAINLY.
YOU YOURSELF CONTRIBUTED TO THAT ACT OF TERROR.
AND NOW I'VE GONE PAST THE POINT OF NO RETURN.

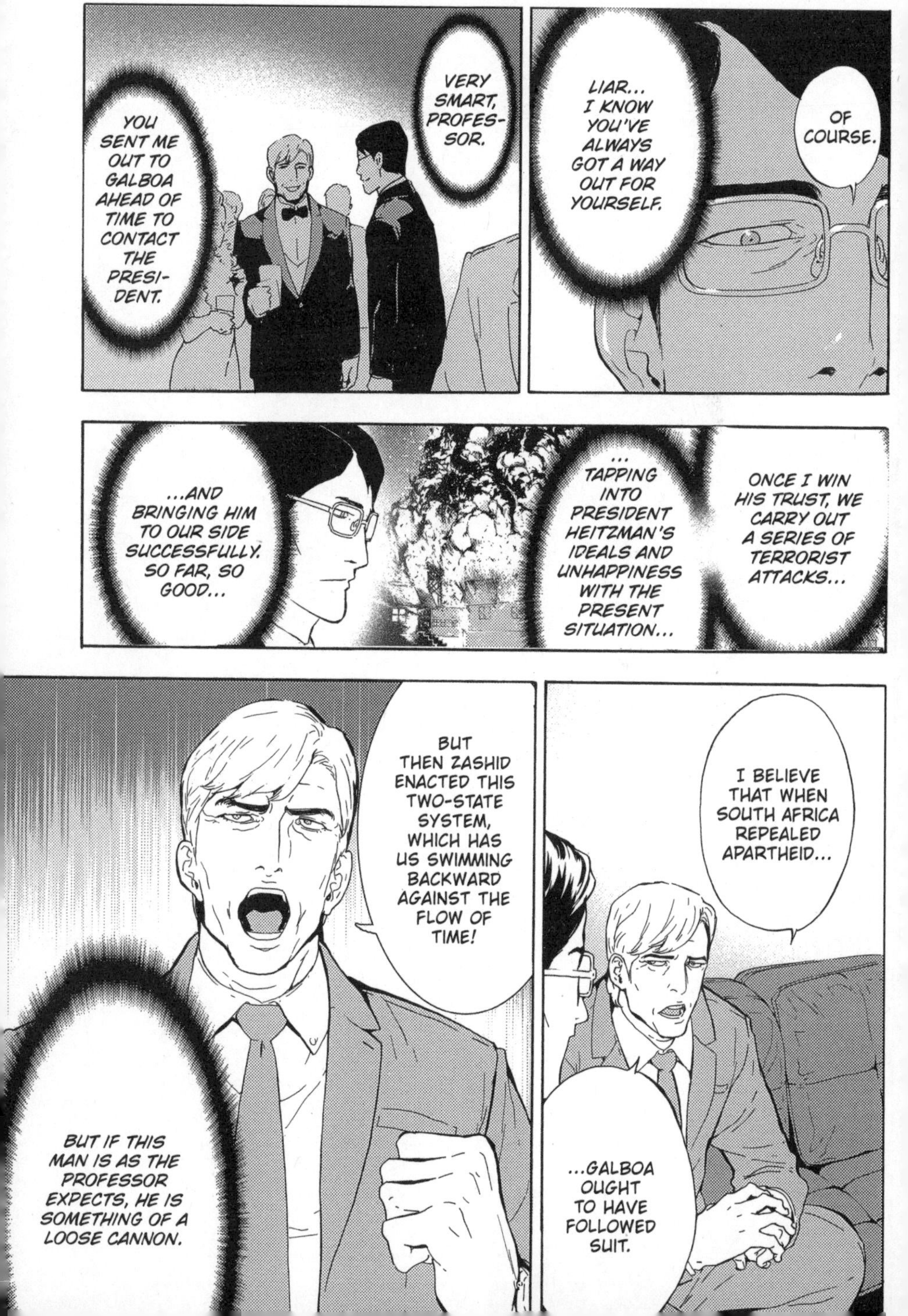
LIAR... I KNOW YOU'VE ALWAYS GOT A WAY OUT FOR YOURSELF.
OF COURSE.
VERY SMART, PROFES-SOR.
YOU SENT ME OUT TO GALBOA AHEAD OF TIME TO CONTACT THE PRESI-DENT.
ONCE I WIN HIS TRUST, WE CARRY OUT A SERIES OF TERRORIST ATTACKS...
...TAPPING INTO PRESIDENT HEITZMAN'S IDEALS AND UNHAPPINESS WITH THE PRESENT SITUATION...
...AND BRINGING HIM TO OUR SIDE SUCCESSFULLY. SO FAR, SO GOOD...
I BELIEVE THAT WHEN SOUTH AFRICA REPEALED APARTHEID...
...GALBOA OUGHT TO HAVE FOLLOWED SUIT.
BUT THEN ZASHID ENACTED THIS TWO-STATE SYSTEM, WHICH HAS US SWIMMING BACKWARD AGAINST THE FLOW OF TIME!
BUT IF THIS MAN IS AS THE PROFESSOR EXPECTS, HE IS SOMETHING OF A LOOSE CANNON.

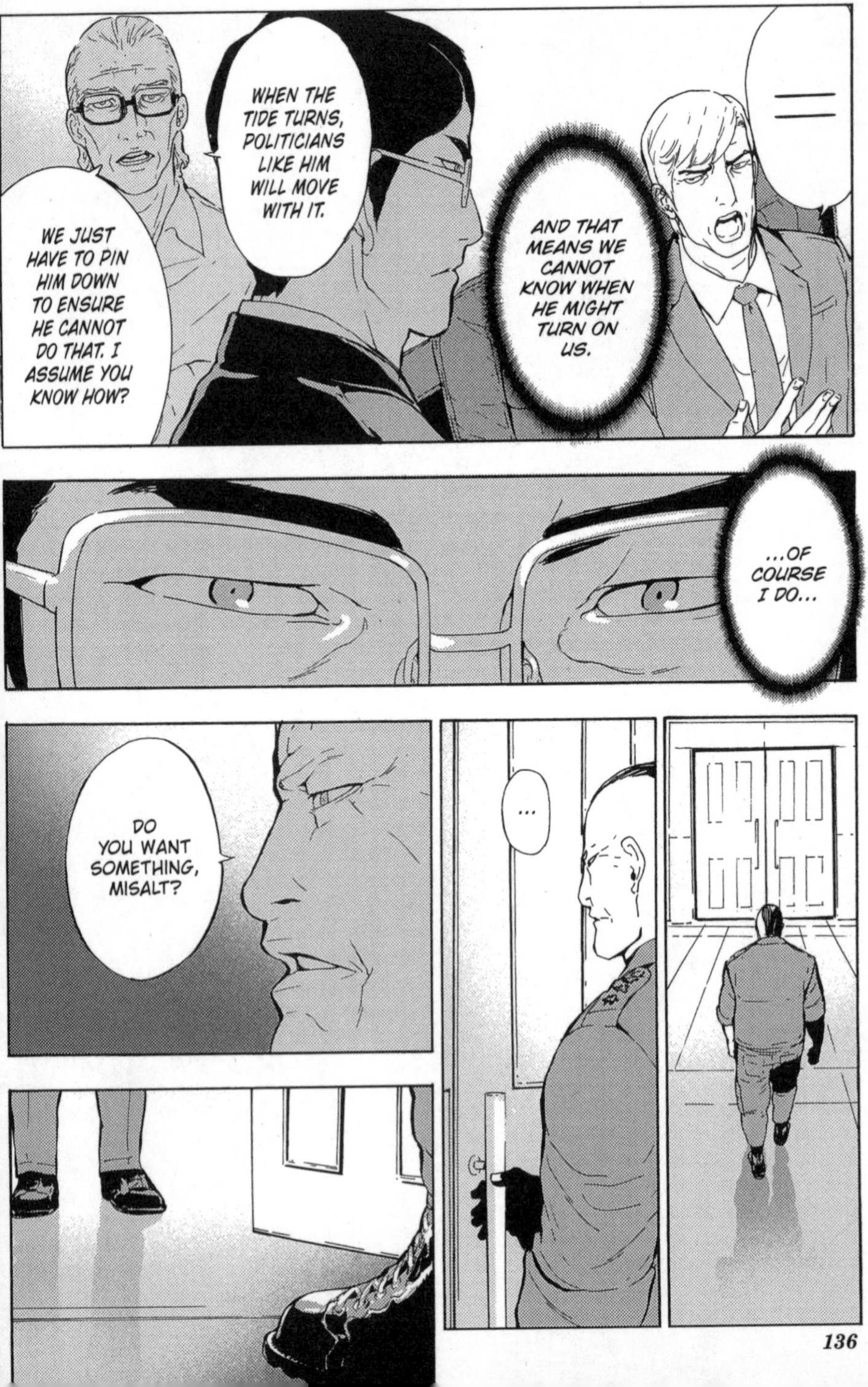
—
WHEN THE TIDE TURNS, POLITICIANS LIKE HIM WILL MOVE WITH IT.
AND THAT MEANS WE CANNOT KNOW WHEN HE MIGHT TURN ON US.
WE JUST HAVE TO PIN HIM DOWN TO ENSURE HE CANNOT DO THAT. I ASSUME YOU KNOW HOW?
...OF COURSE I DO...
...
DO YOU WANT SOMETHING, MISALT?

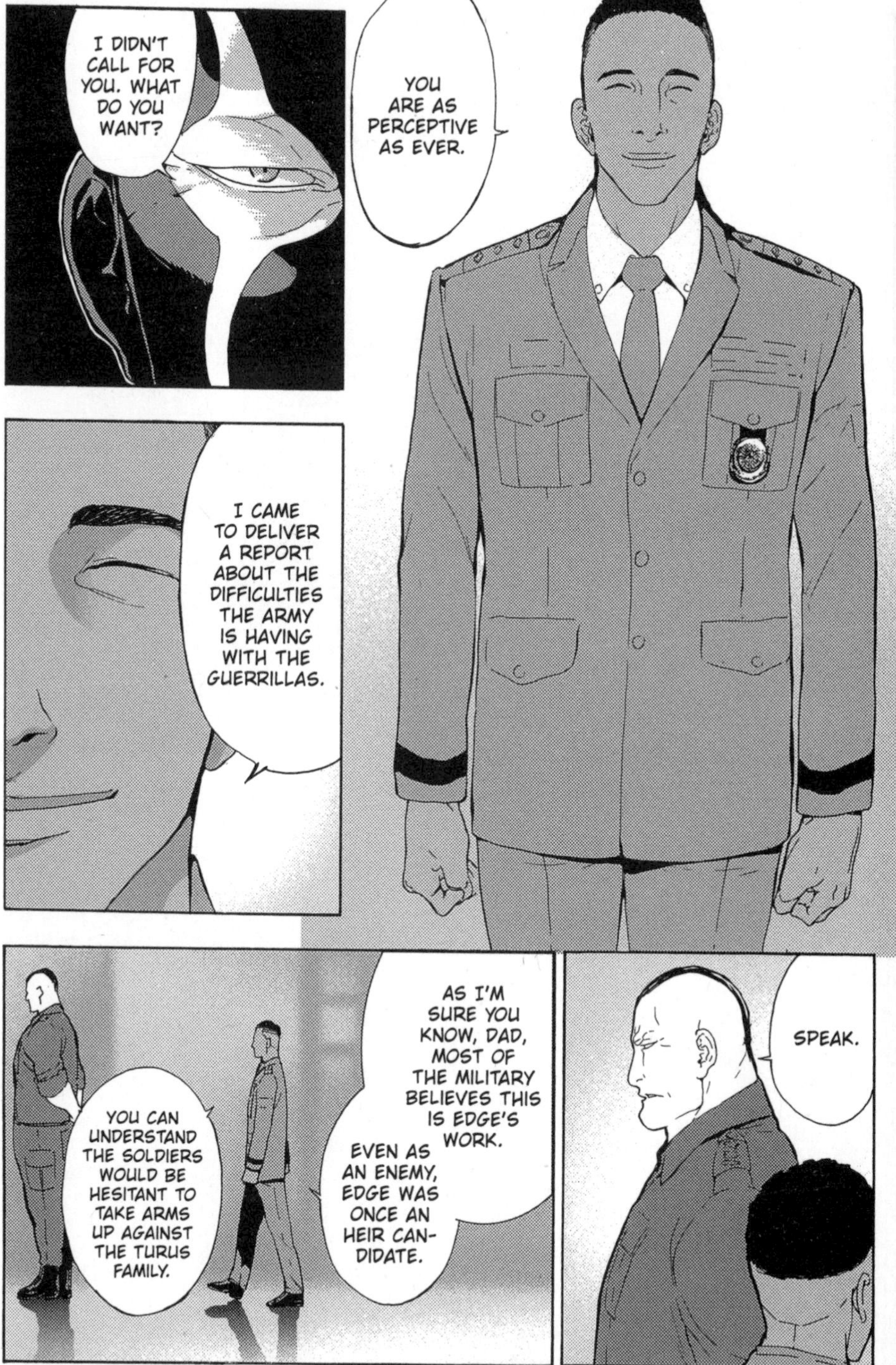
YOU ARE AS PERCEPTIVE AS EVER.
I DIDN'T CALL FOR YOU. WHAT DO YOU WANT?
I CAME TO DELIVER A REPORT ABOUT THE DIFFICULTIES THE ARMY IS HAVING WITH THE GUERRILLAS.
SPEAK.
AS I'M SURE YOU KNOW, DAD, MOST OF THE MILITARY BELIEVES THIS IS EDGE'S WORK.
EVEN AS AN ENEMY, EDGE WAS ONCE AN HEIR CAN-DIDATE.
YOU CAN UNDERSTAND THE SOLDIERS WOULD BE HESITANT TO TAKE ARMS UP AGAINST THE TURUS FAMILY.

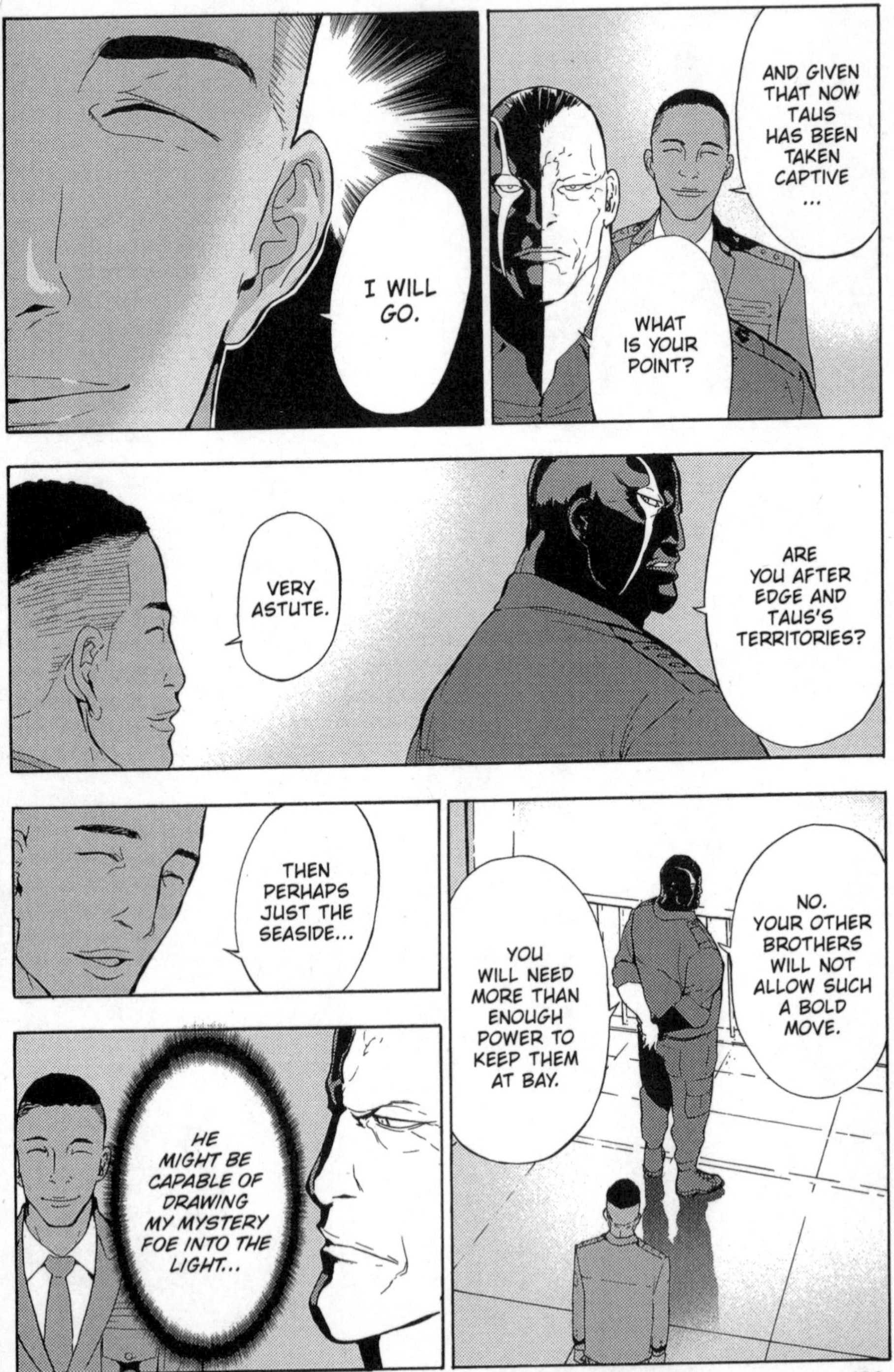
AND GIVEN THAT NOW TAUS HAS BEEN TAKEN CAPTIVE ...
WHAT IS YOUR POINT?
I WILL GO.
ARE YOU AFTER EDGE AND TAUS'S TERRITORIES?
VERY ASTUTE.
NO. YOUR OTHER BROTHERS WILL NOT ALLOW SUCH A BOLD MOVE.
YOU WILL NEED MORE THAN ENOUGH POWER TO KEEP THEM AT BAY.
THEN PERHAPS JUST THE SEASIDE...
HE MIGHT BE CAPABLE OF DRAWING MY MYSTERY FOE INTO THE LIGHT...

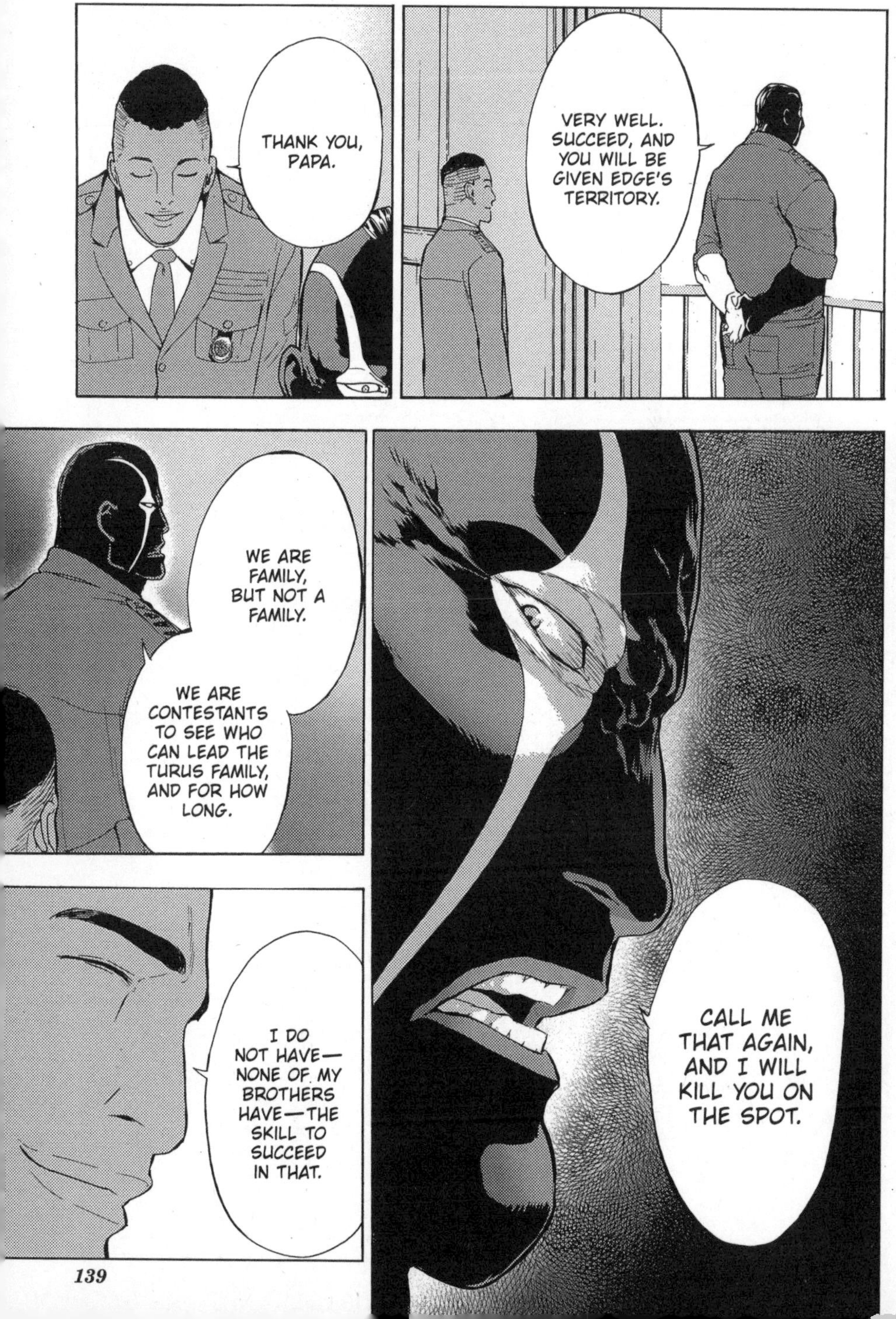
VERY WELL. SUCCEED, AND YOU WILL BE GIVEN EDGE'S TERRITORY.
THANK YOU, PAPA.
CALL ME THAT AGAIN, AND I WILL KILL YOU ON THE SPOT.
WE ARE FAMILY, BUT NOT A FAMILY.
WE ARE CONTESTANTS TO SEE WHO CAN LEAD THE TURUS FAMILY, AND FOR HOW LONG.
I DO NOT HAVE—NONE OF MY BROTHERS HAVE—THE SKILL TO SUCCEED IN THAT.

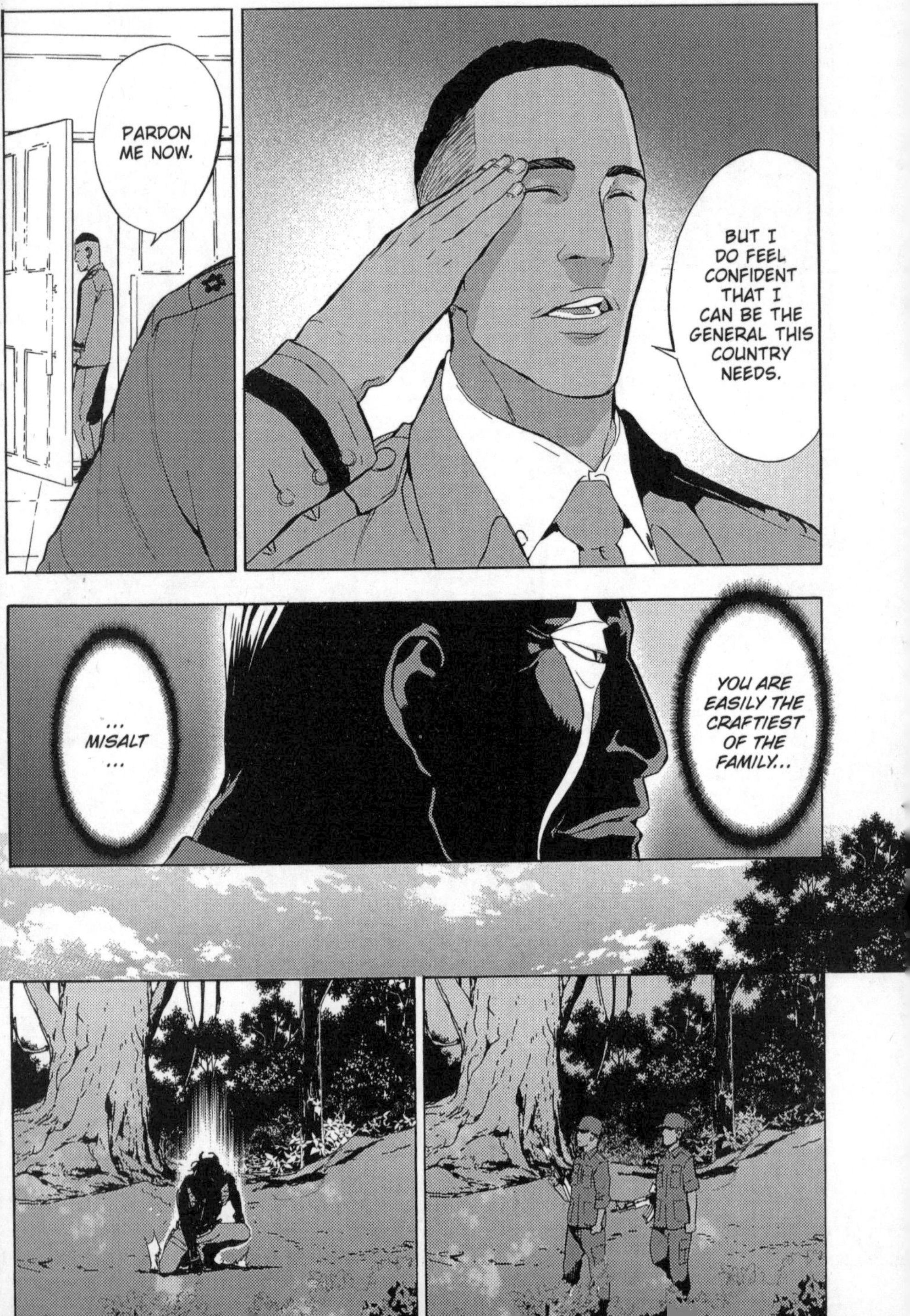
BUT I DO FEEL CONFIDENT THAT I CAN BE THE GENERAL THIS COUNTRY NEEDS.
PARDON ME NOW.
YOU ARE EASILY THE CRAFTIEST OF THE FAMILY...
... MISALT ...

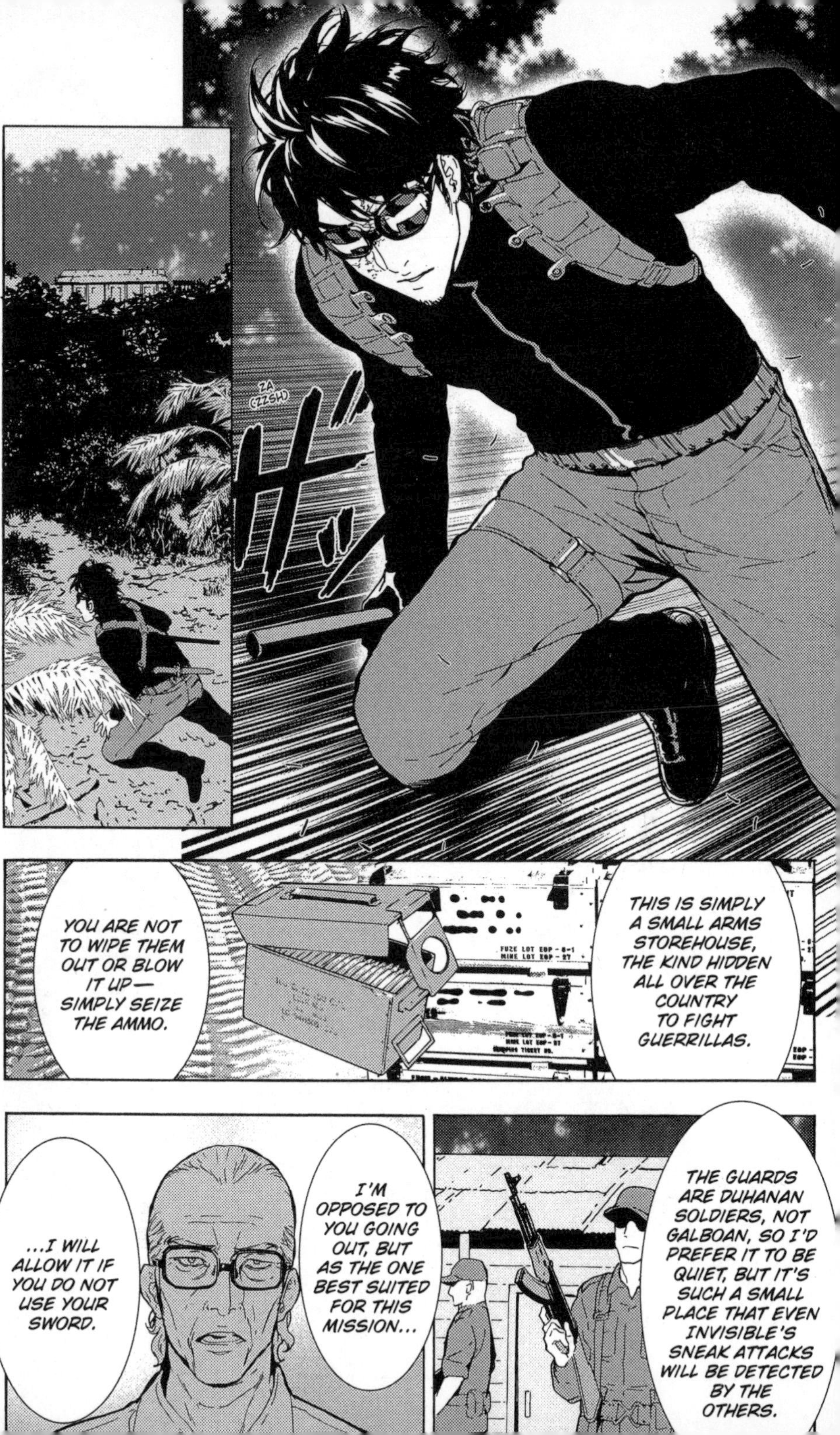
ZA (ZZSH)
THIS IS SIMPLY A SMALL ARMS STOREHOUSE, THE KIND HIDDEN ALL OVER THE COUNTRY TO FIGHT GUERRILLAS.
YOU ARE NOT TO WIPE THEM OUT OR BLOW IT UP— SIMPLY SEIZE THE AMMO.
THE GUARDS ARE DUHANAN SOLDIERS, NOT GALBOAN, SO I'D PREFER IT TO BE QUIET, BUT IT'S SUCH A SMALL PLACE THAT EVEN INVISIBLE'S SNEAK ATTACKS WILL BE DETECTED BY THE OTHERS.
I'M OPPOSED TO YOU GOING OUT, BUT AS THE ONE BEST SUITED FOR THIS MISSION...
...I WILL ALLOW IT IF YOU DO NOT USE YOUR SWORD.

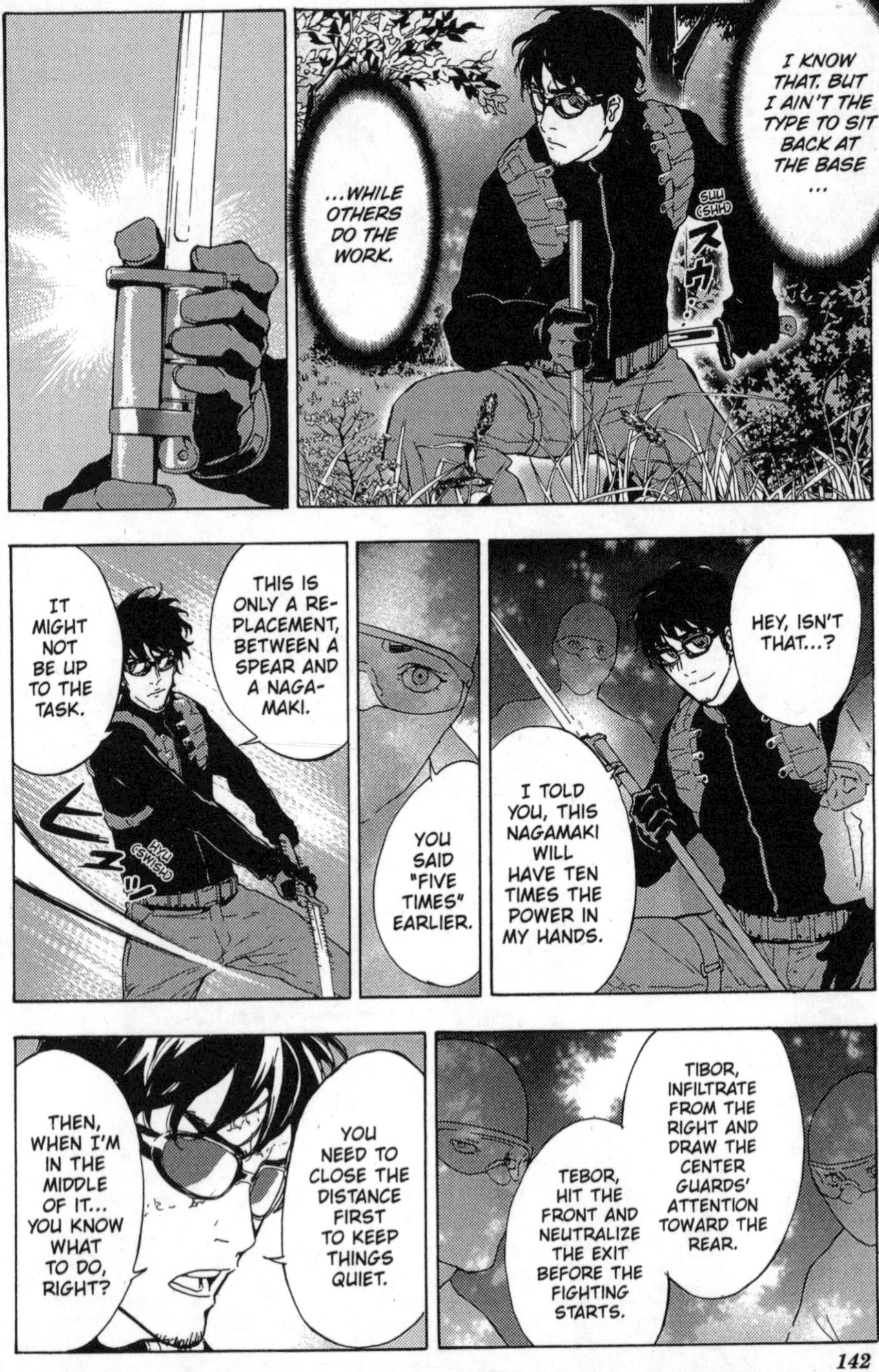
I KNOW THAT. BUT I AIN'T THE TYPE TO SIT BACK AT THE BASE ...
SUU (SWHD)
...WHILE OTHERS DO THE WORK.
HEY, ISN'T THAT...?
I TOLD YOU, THIS NAGAMAKI WILL HAVE TEN TIMES THE POWER IN MY HANDS.
YOU SAID "FIVE TIMES" EARLIER.
THIS IS ONLY A RE-PLACEMENT, BETWEEN A SPEAR AND A NAGA-MAKI.
IT MIGHT NOT BE UP TO THE TASK.
HYU (SWISH)
TIBOR, INFILTRATE FROM THE RIGHT AND DRAW THE CENTER GUARDS' ATTENTION TOWARD THE REAR.
TEBOR, HIT THE FRONT AND NEUTRALIZE THE EXIT BEFORE THE FIGHTING STARTS.
YOU NEED TO CLOSE THE DISTANCE FIRST TO KEEP THINGS QUIET.
THEN, WHEN I'M IN THE MIDDLE OF IT... YOU KNOW WHAT TO DO, RIGHT?

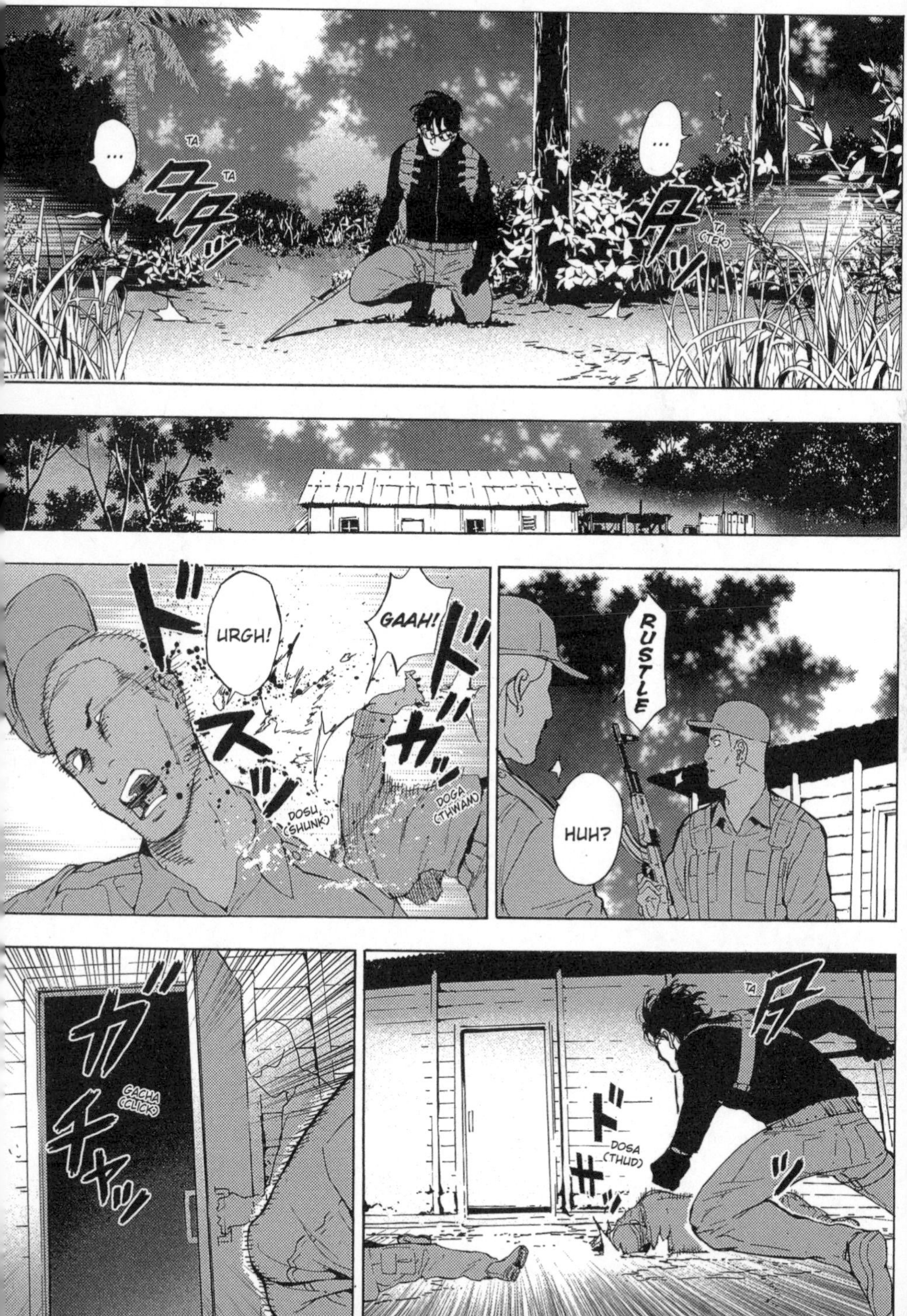
...
TA (TEK)
...
TA
TA
RUSTLE
HUH?
GAAH!
DOGA (THWAM)
URGH!
DOSU (SHUNK)
TA
DOSA (THUD)
GACHA (CLICK)

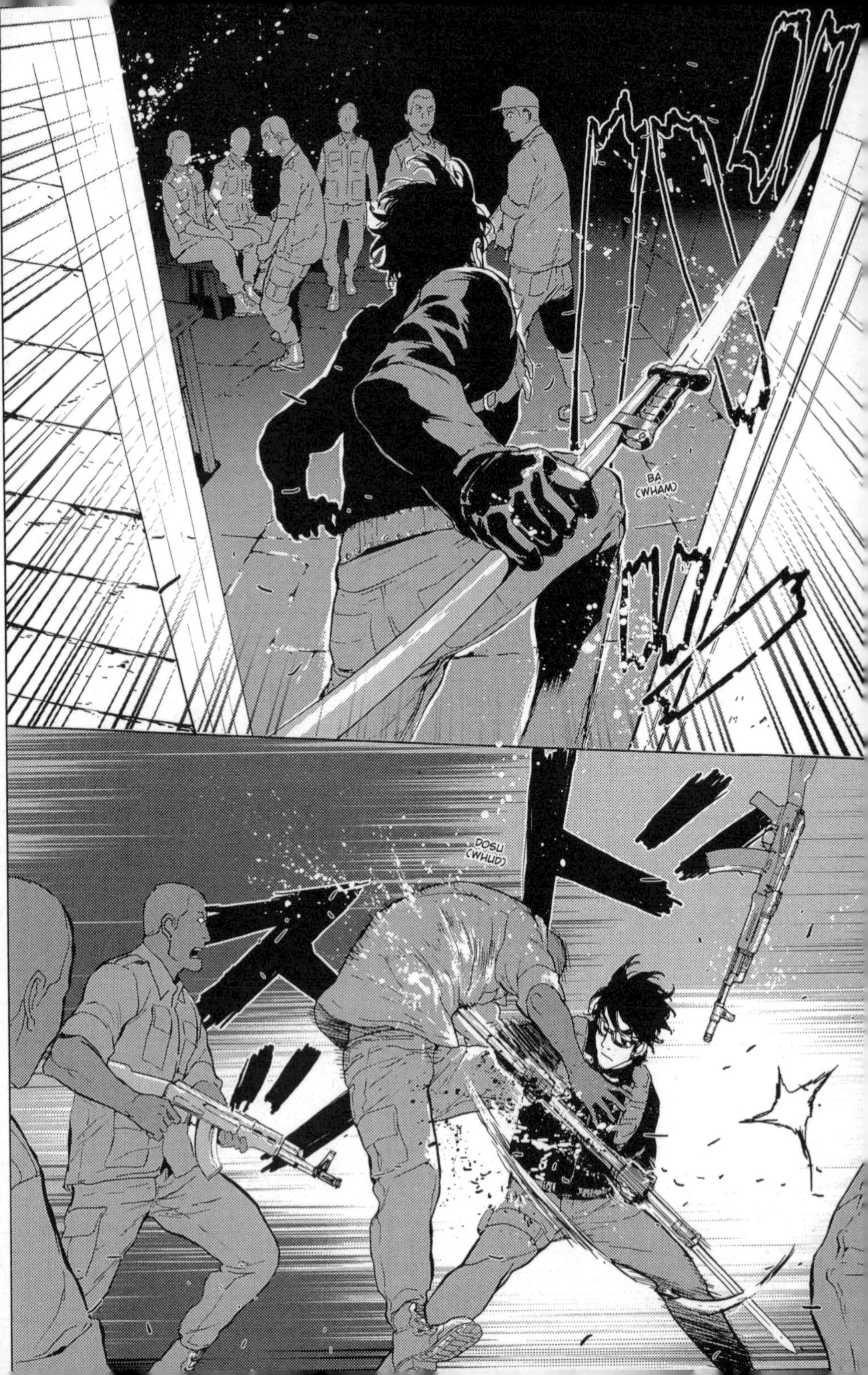
BA (WHAM)
DOSU (WHUD)

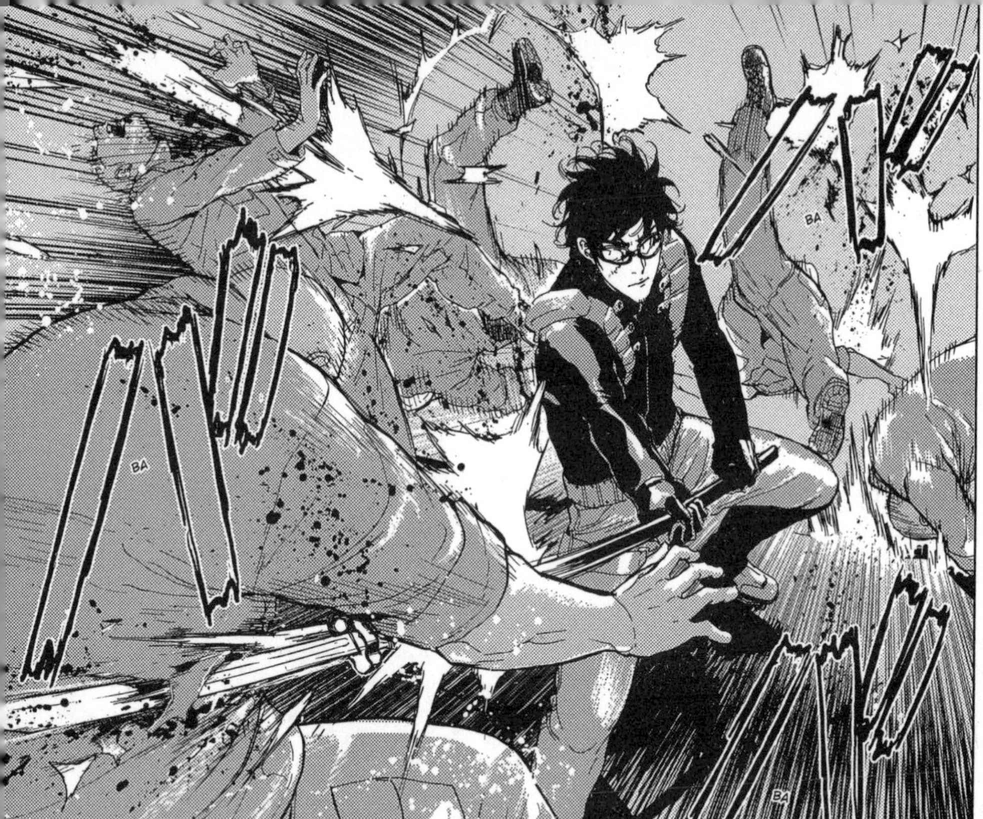
BA
BA
BA
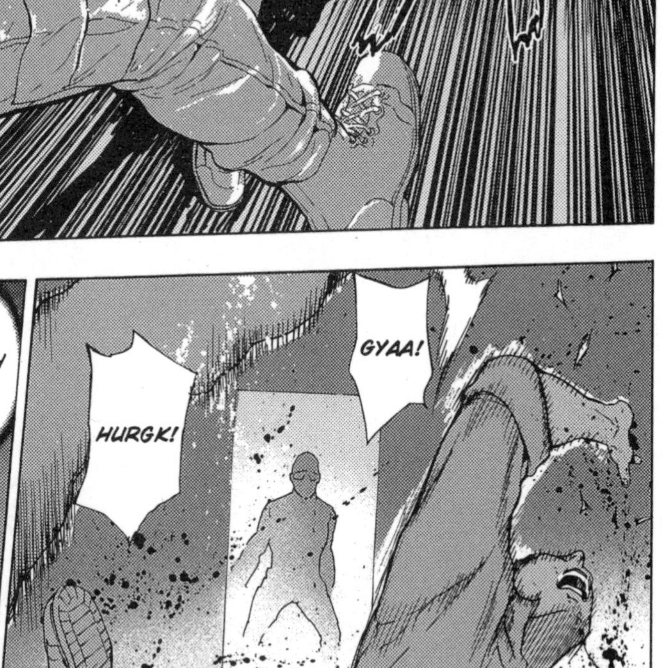
GYAA!
HURGK!
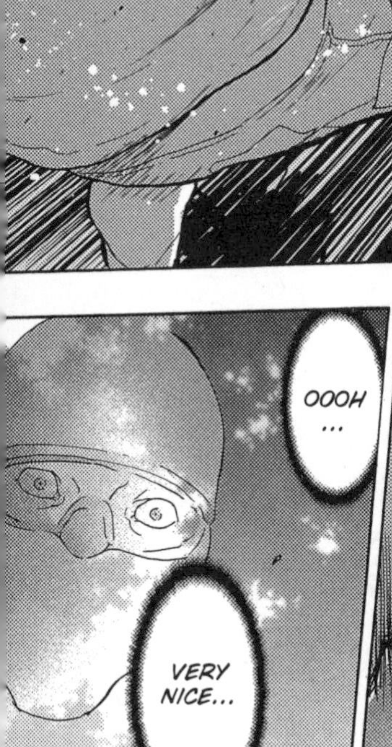
OOOH ...
VERY NICE...

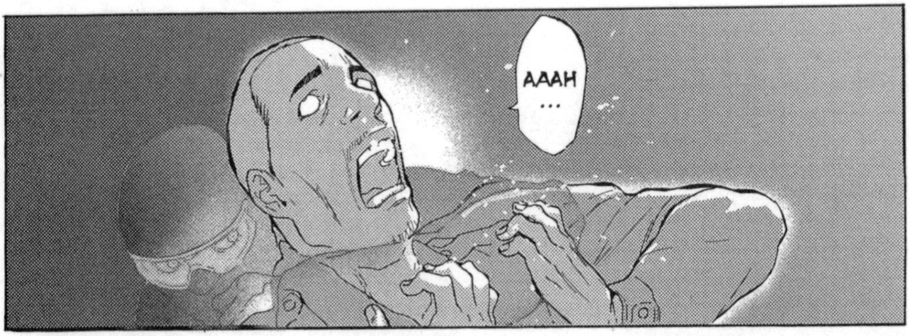
AAAH
...
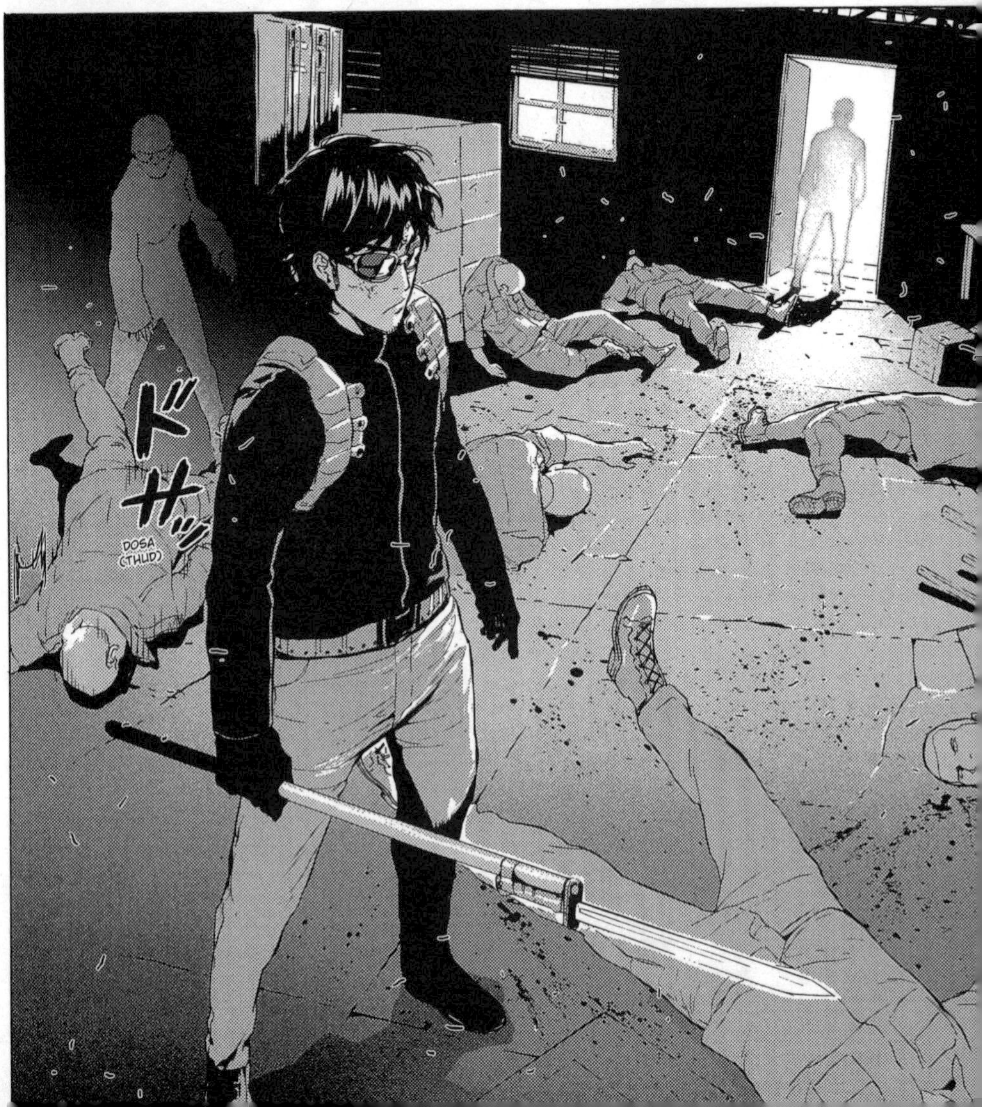
ドサッ
DOSA
(THUD)

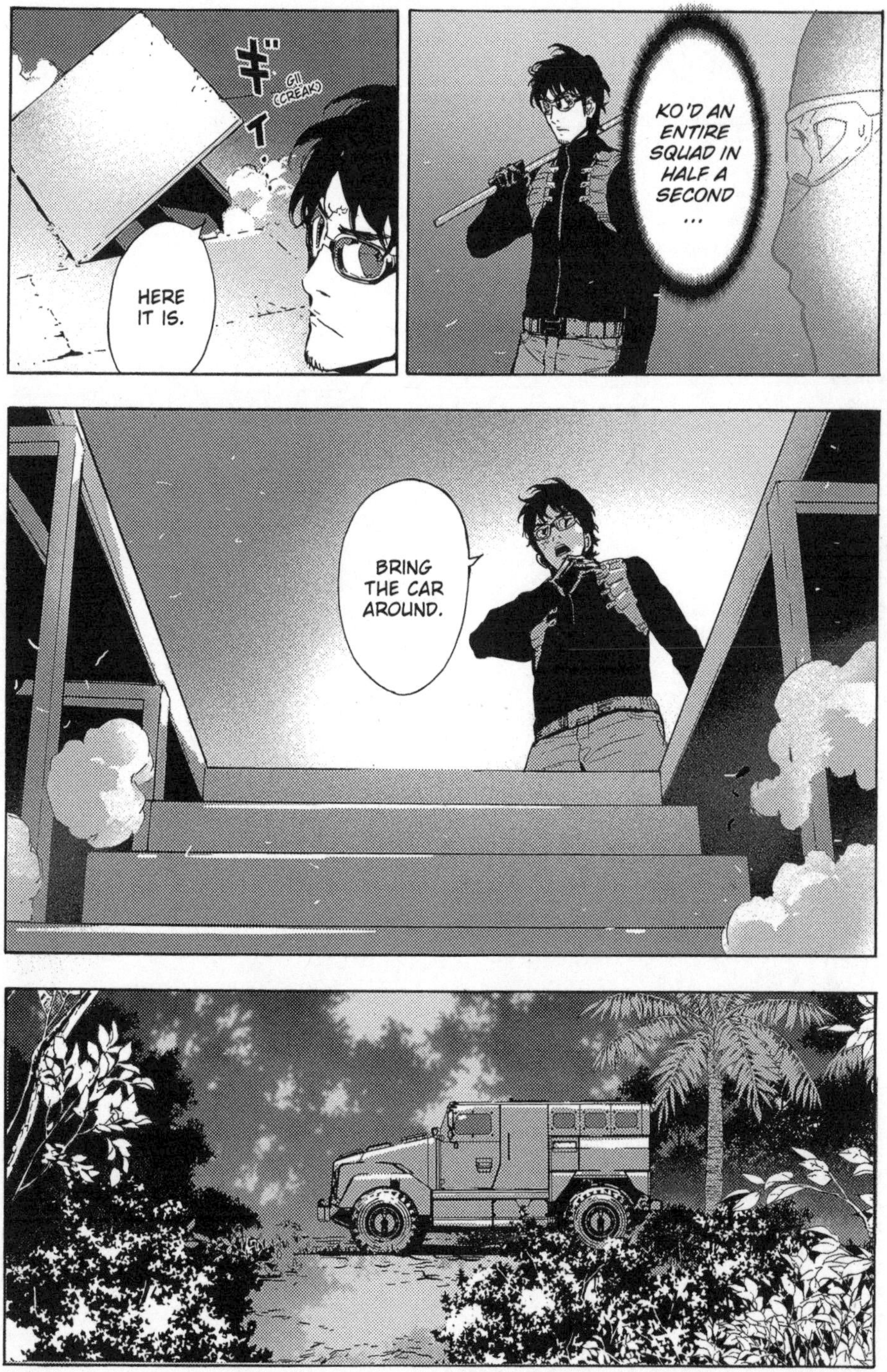
KO'D AN ENTIRE SQUAD IN HALF A SECOND ...
ギイ
GII (CREAK)
HERE IT IS.
BRING THE CAR AROUND.

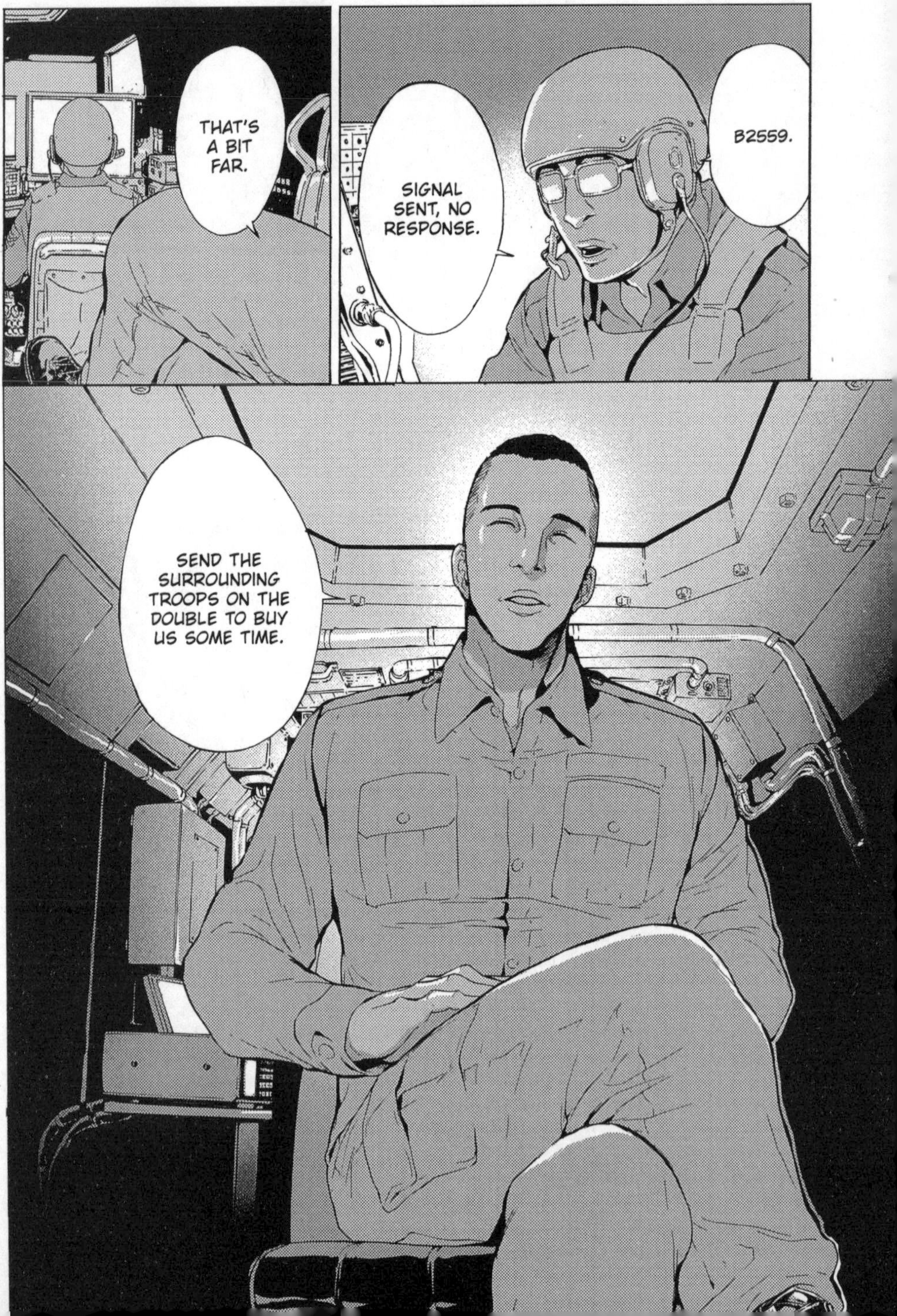
B2559.
SIGNAL SENT, NO RESPONSE.
THAT'S A BIT FAR.
SEND THE SURROUNDING TROOPS ON THE DOUBLE TO BUY US SOME TIME.

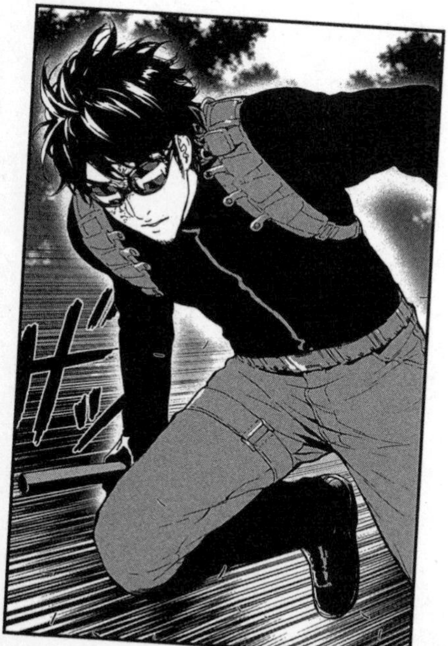
ザッ

Until Death do us Part

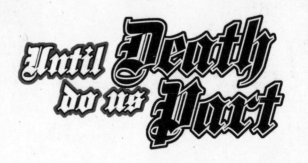

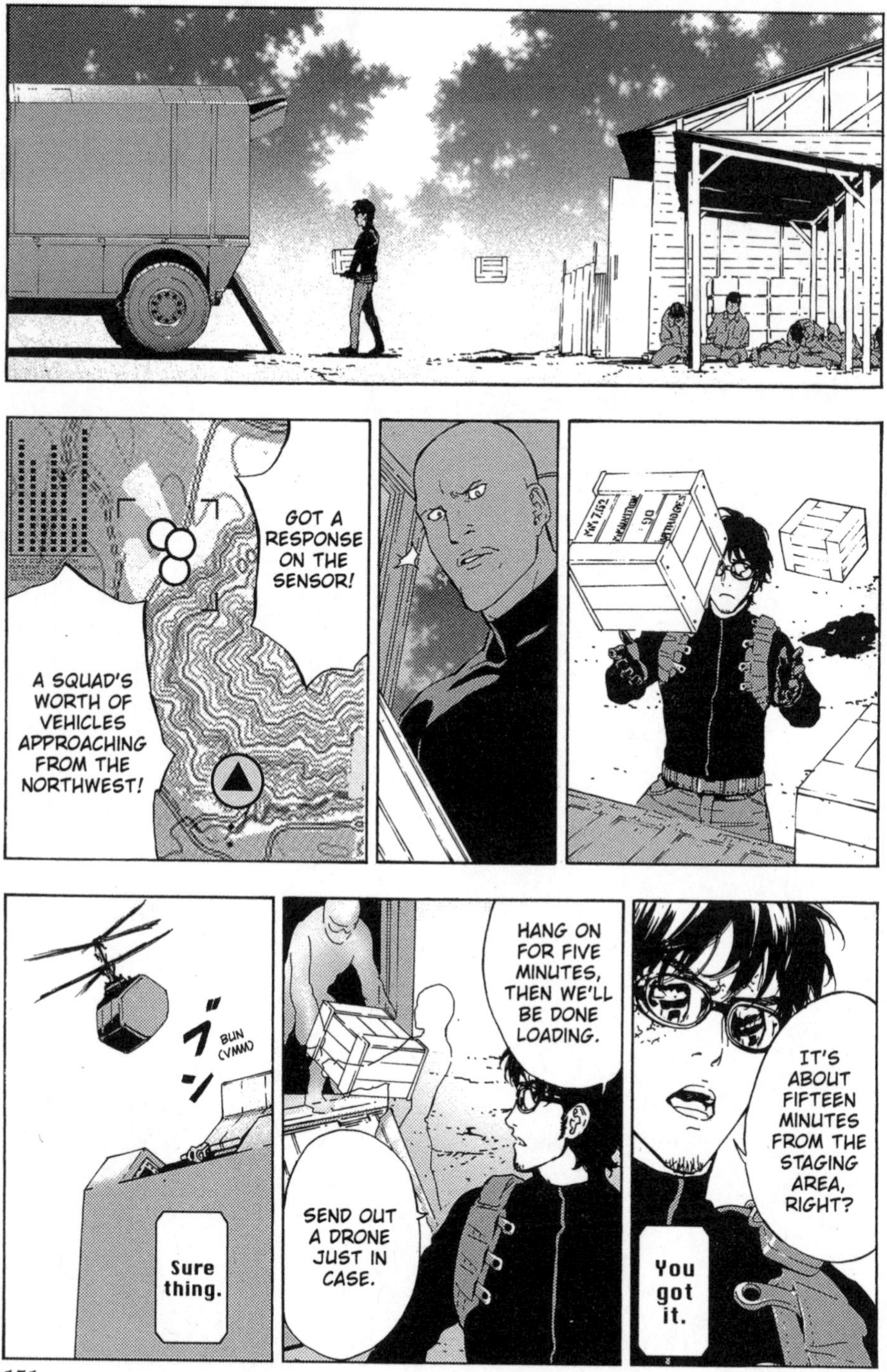
GOT A RESPONSE ON THE SENSOR!
A SQUAD'S WORTH OF VEHICLES APPROACHING FROM THE NORTHWEST!
IT'S ABOUT FIFTEEN MINUTES FROM THE STAGING AREA, RIGHT?
You got it.
HANG ON FOR FIVE MINUTES, THEN WE'LL BE DONE LOADING.
SEND OUT A DRONE JUST IN CASE.
BUN (VMM)
Sure thing.

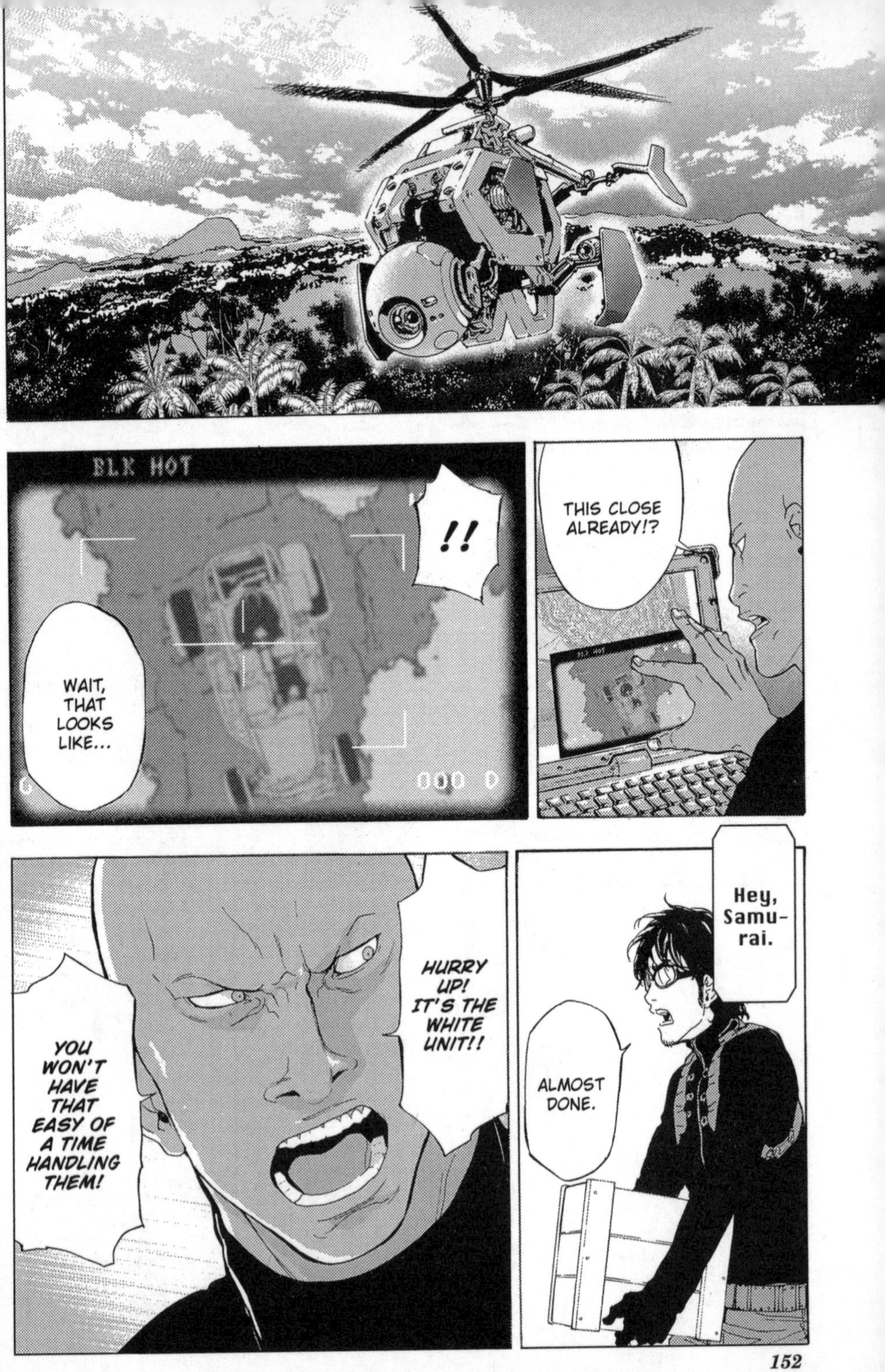
THIS CLOSE ALREADY!?
BLK HOT
!!
WAIT, THAT LOOKS LIKE...
Hey, Samu-rai.
ALMOST DONE.
HURRY UP! IT'S THE WHITE UNIT!!
YOU WON'T HAVE THAT EASY OF A TIME HANDLING THEM!

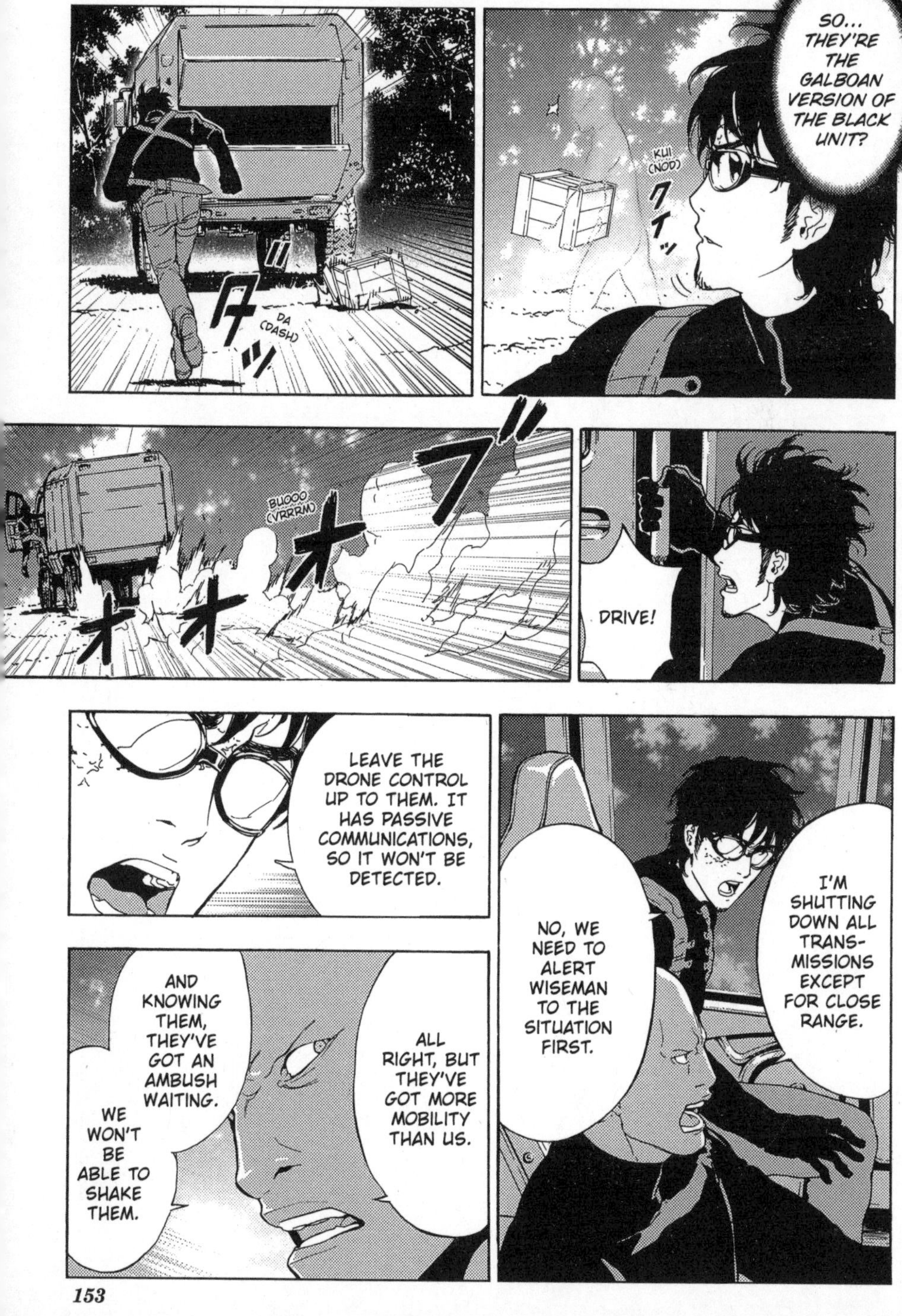
SO... THEY'RE THE GALBOAN VERSION OF THE BLACK UNIT?
KUI (NOD)
クイッ
DA (DASH)
タッ
DRIVE!
BUOOO (VRRRM)
ブオオオ
I'M SHUTTING DOWN ALL TRANS-MISSIONS EXCEPT FOR CLOSE RANGE.
NO, WE NEED TO ALERT WISEMAN TO THE SITUATION FIRST.
LEAVE THE DRONE CONTROL UP TO THEM. IT HAS PASSIVE COMMUNICATIONS, SO IT WON'T BE DETECTED.
ALL RIGHT, BUT THEY'VE GOT MORE MOBILITY THAN US.
AND KNOWING THEM, THEY'VE GOT AN AMBUSH WAITING.
WE WON'T BE ABLE TO SHAKE THEM.

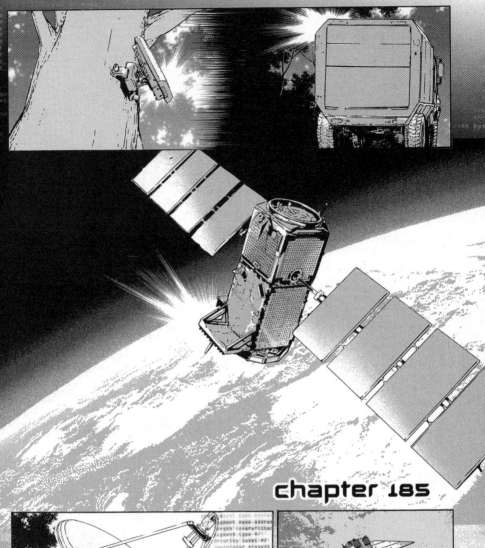

chapter 185

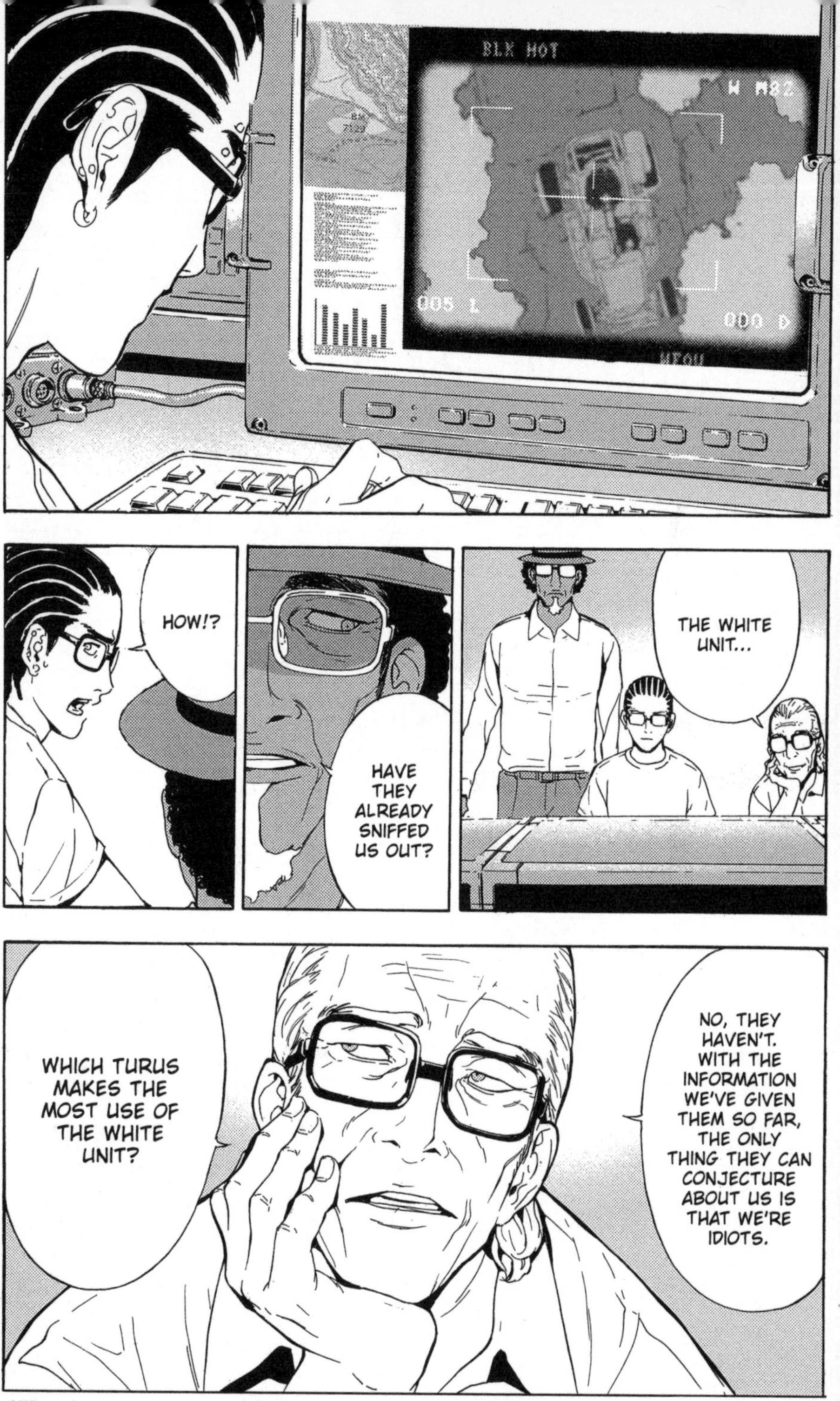
BLK HOT
W M82
005 1
000 D
THE WHITE UNIT...
HAVE THEY ALREADY SNIFFED US OUT?
HOW!?
NO, THEY HAVEN'T. WITH THE INFORMATION WE'VE GIVEN THEM SO FAR, THE ONLY THING THEY CAN CONJECTURE ABOUT US IS THAT WE'RE IDIOTS.
WHICH TURUS MAKES THE MOST USE OF THE WHITE UNIT?

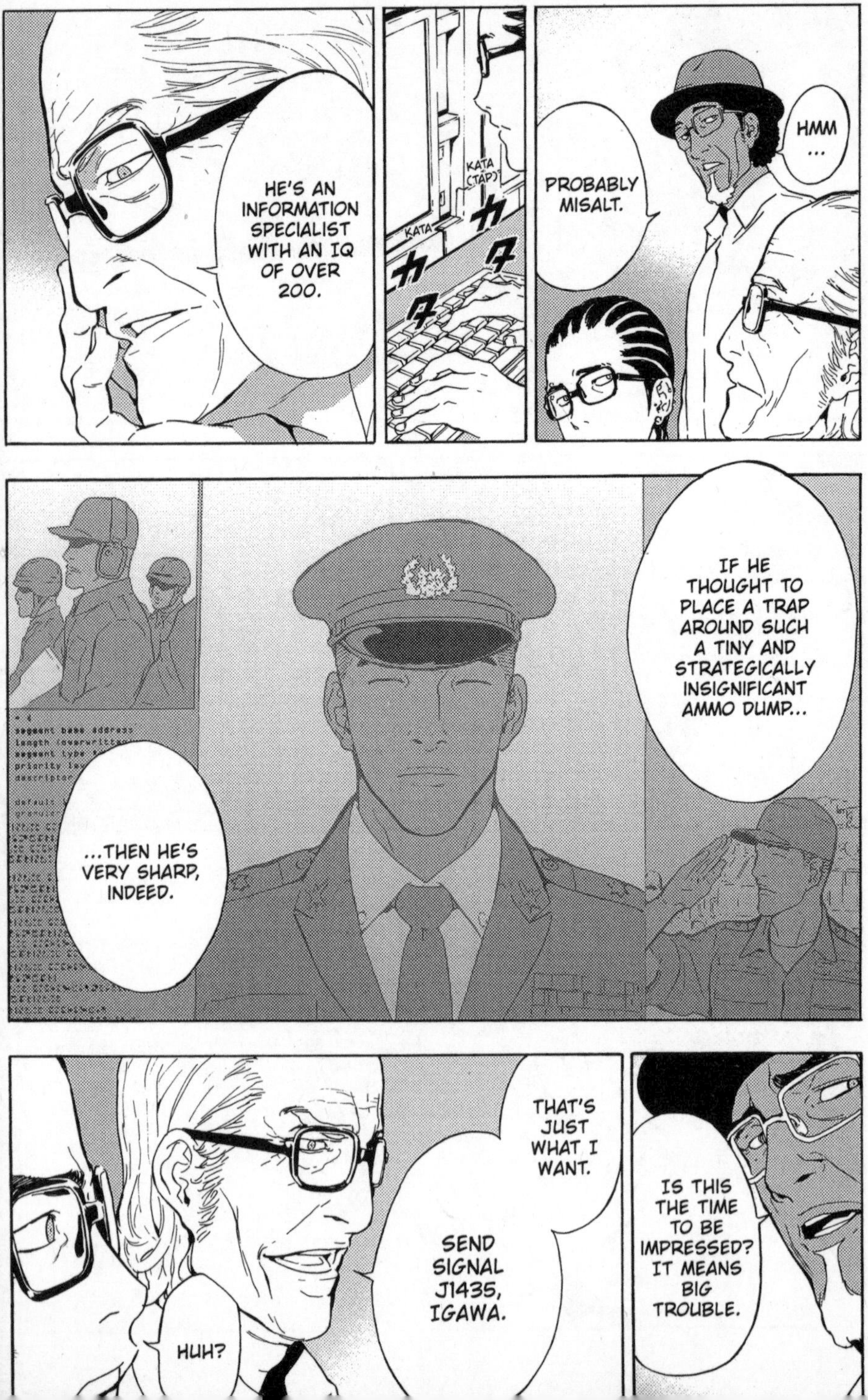
HMM ...
PROBABLY MISALT.
KATA (TAP)
KATA
HE'S AN INFORMATION SPECIALIST WITH AN IQ OF OVER 200.
IF HE THOUGHT TO PLACE A TRAP AROUND SUCH A TINY AND STRATEGICALLY INSIGNIFICANT AMMO DUMP...
...THEN HE'S VERY SHARP, INDEED.
IS THIS THE TIME TO BE IMPRESSED? IT MEANS BIG TROUBLE.
THAT'S JUST WHAT I WANT.
SEND SIGNAL J1435, IGAWA.
HUH?

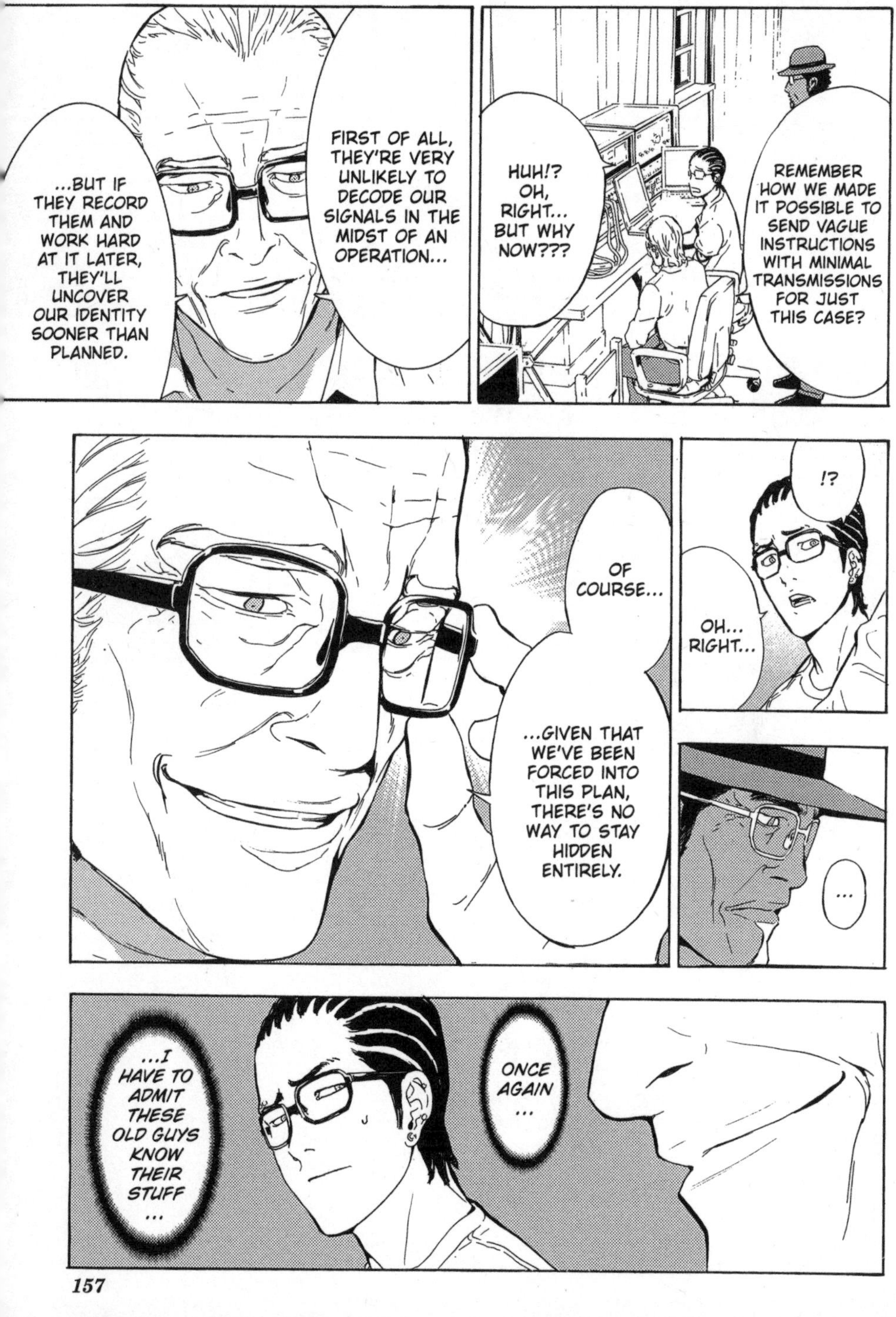
REMEMBER HOW WE MADE IT POSSIBLE TO SEND VAGUE INSTRUCTIONS WITH MINIMAL TRANSMISSIONS FOR JUST THIS CASE?
HUH!? OH, RIGHT... BUT WHY NOW???
FIRST OF ALL, THEY'RE VERY UNLIKELY TO DECODE OUR SIGNALS IN THE MIDST OF AN OPERATION...
...BUT IF THEY RECORD THEM AND WORK HARD AT IT LATER, THEY'LL UNCOVER OUR IDENTITY SOONER THAN PLANNED.
!?
OH... RIGHT...
...
OF COURSE...
...GIVEN THAT WE'VE BEEN FORCED INTO THIS PLAN, THERE'S NO WAY TO STAY HIDDEN ENTIRELY.
ONCE AGAIN ...
...I HAVE TO ADMIT THESE OLD GUYS KNOW THEIR STUFF ...

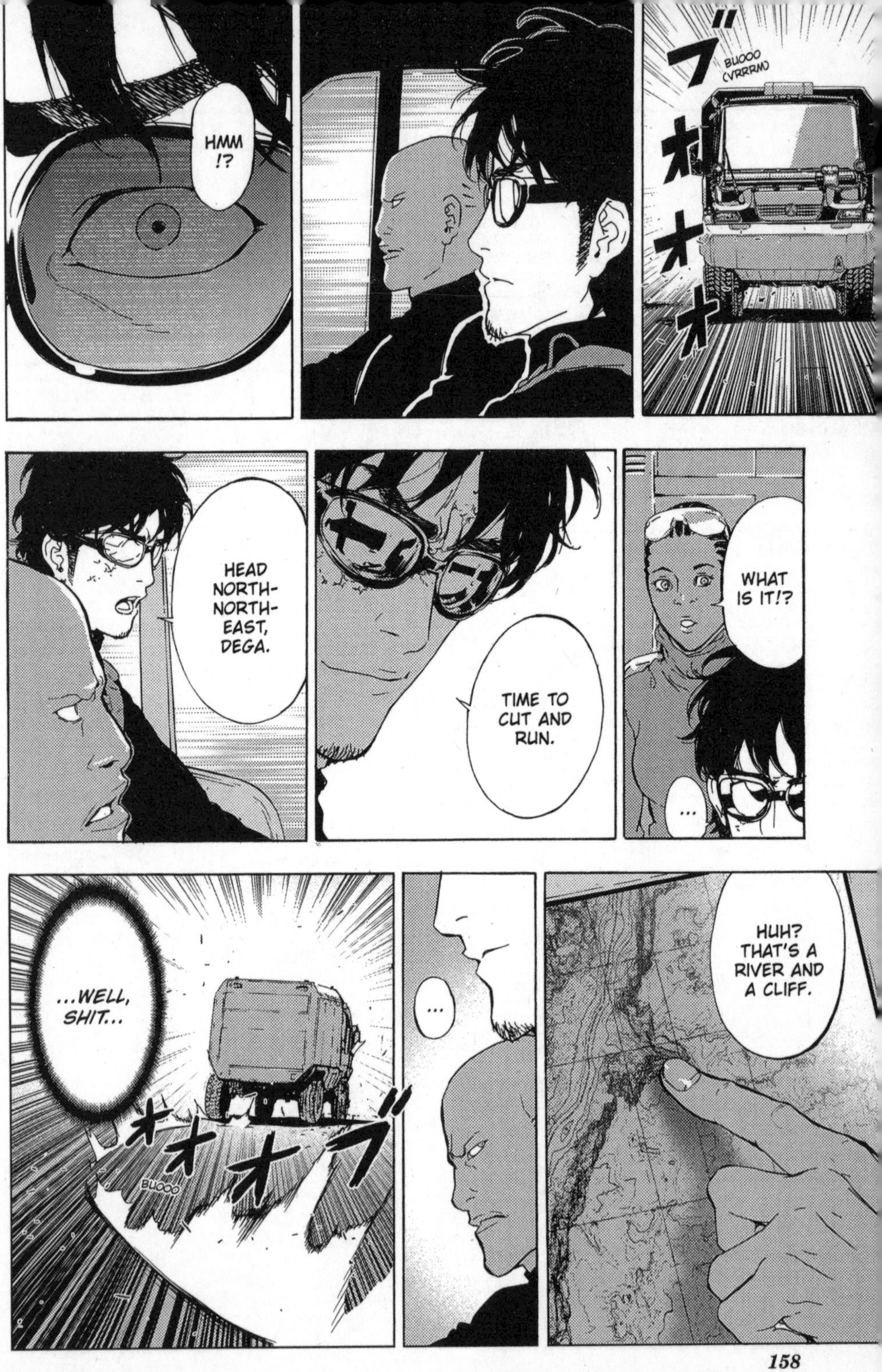
BUOOO (VRRRM)
HMM !?
WHAT IS IT!?
...
TIME TO CUT AND RUN.
HEAD NORTH-NORTHEAST, DEGA.
HUH? THAT'S A RIVER AND A CLIFF.
...
...WELL, SHIT...
BUOOO

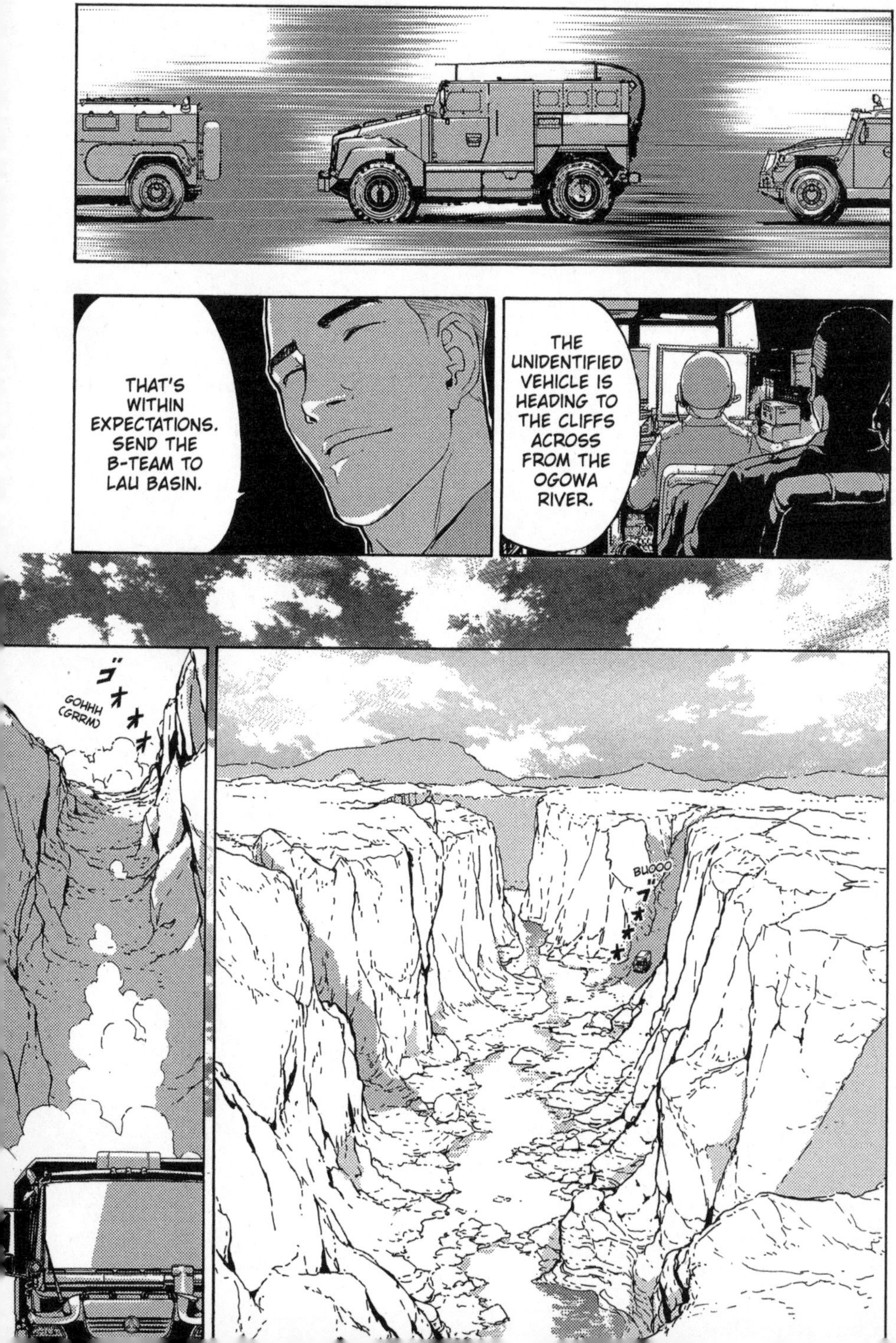
THE UNIDENTIFIED VEHICLE IS HEADING TO THE CLIFFS ACROSS FROM THE OGOWA RIVER.
THAT'S WITHIN EXPECTATIONS. SEND THE B-TEAM TO LAU BASIN.
ブオオオ
BUOOO
ゴオオオ
GOHHH (GRRM)

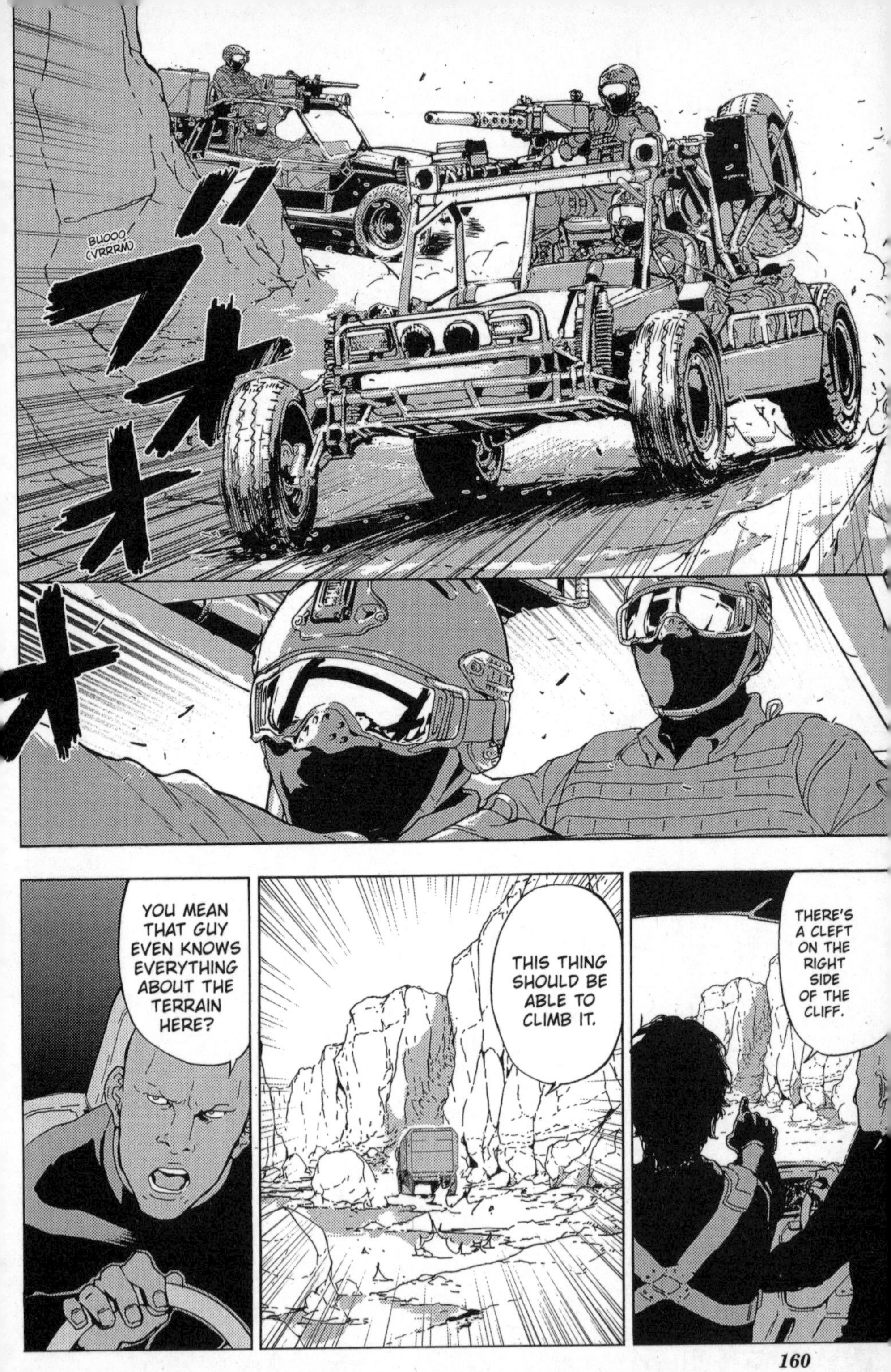
BUOOO (VRRRM)
THERE'S A CLEFT ON THE RIGHT SIDE OF THE CLIFF.
THIS THING SHOULD BE ABLE TO CLIMB IT.
YOU MEAN THAT GUY EVEN KNOWS EVERYTHING ABOUT THE TERRAIN HERE?

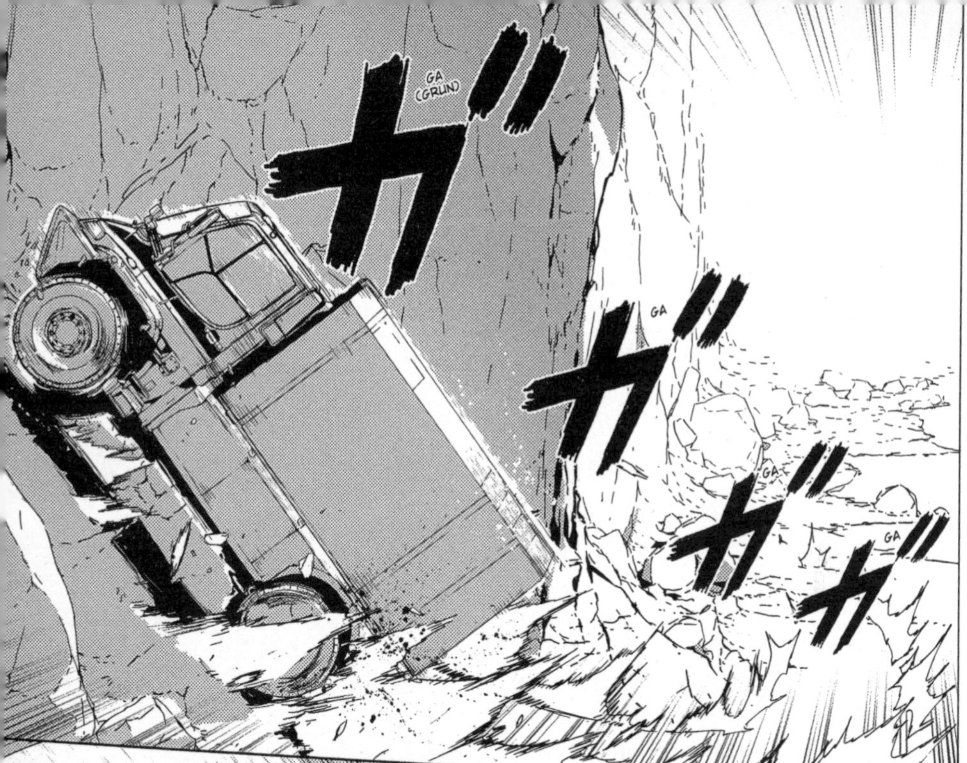
GA (GRUN)
GA
GA
GA
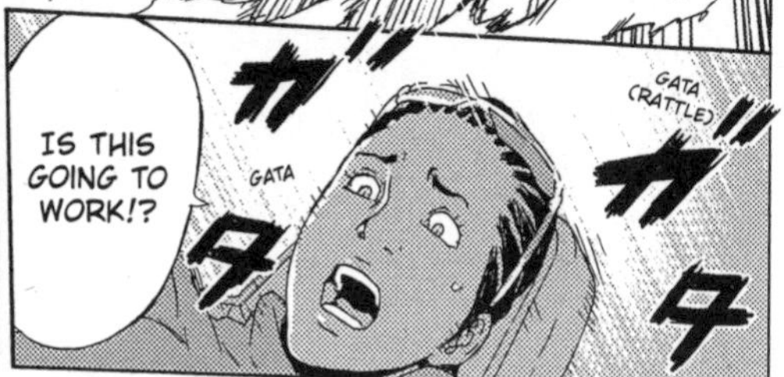
GATA (RATTLE)
GATA
IS THIS GOING TO WORK!?
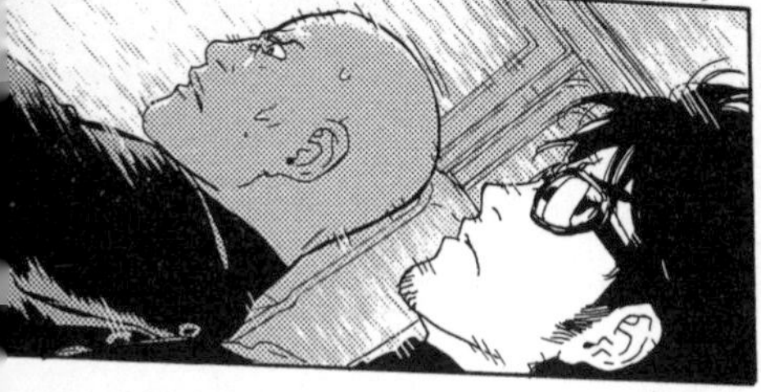
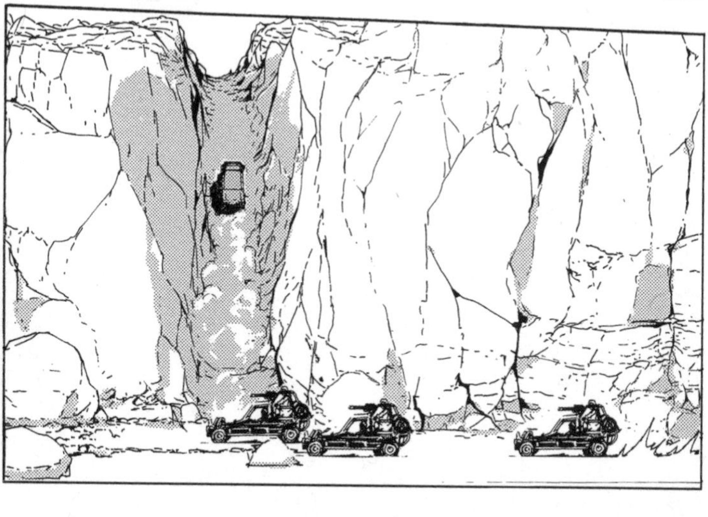
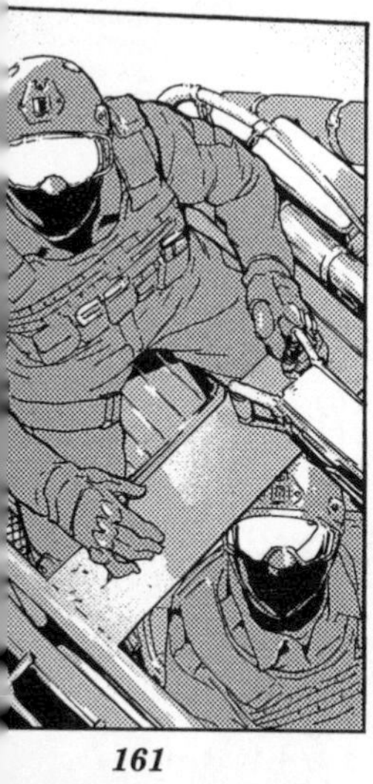

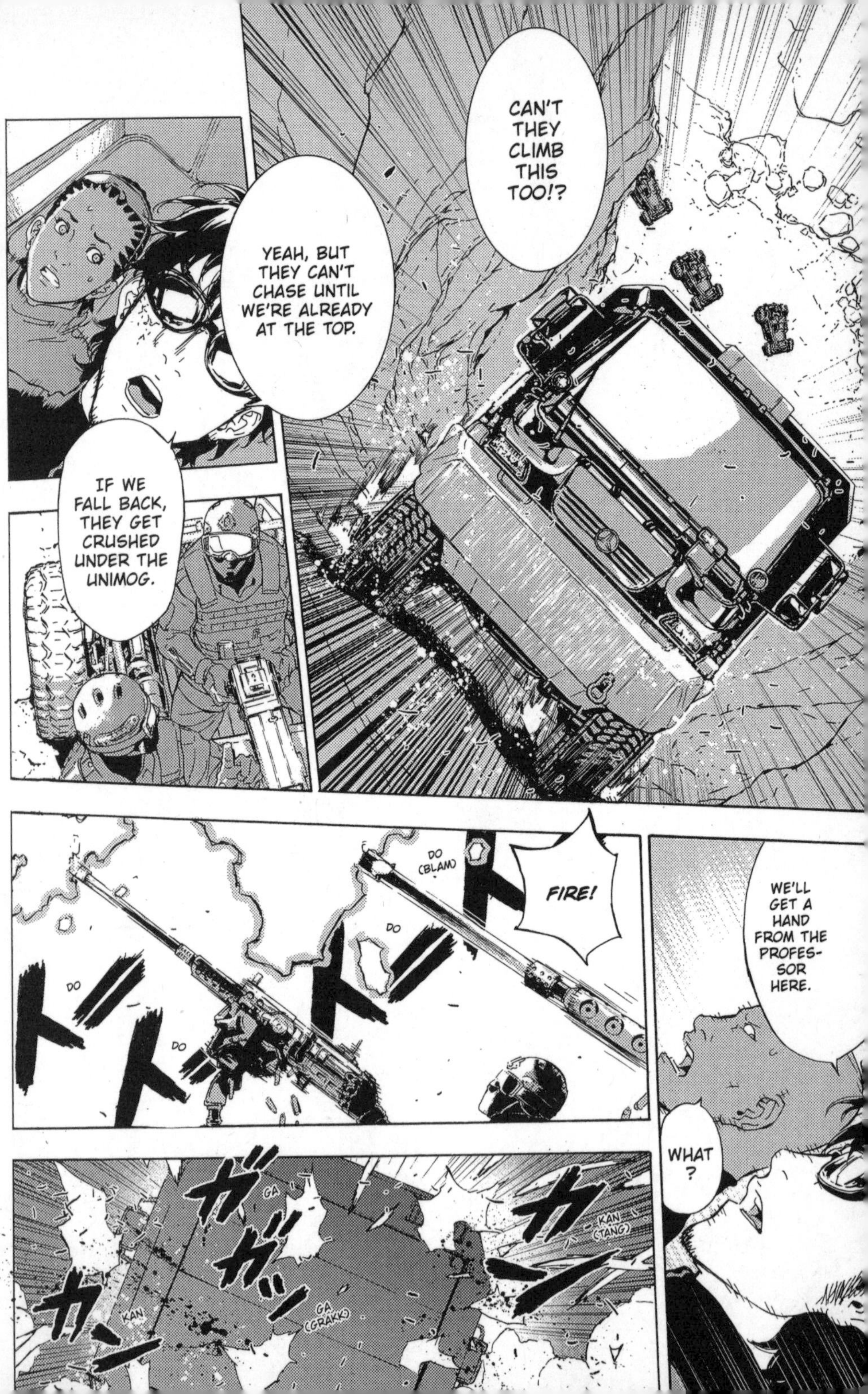
CAN'T THEY CLIMB THIS TOO!?
YEAH, BUT THEY CAN'T CHASE UNTIL WE'RE ALREADY AT THE TOP.
IF WE FALL BACK, THEY GET CRUSHED UNDER THE UNIMOG.
WE'LL GET A HAND FROM THE PROFES-SOR HERE.
WHAT?
FIRE!
DO (BLAM)
DO
DO
DO
KAN (TANG)
GA
GA (GRAKK)
KAN

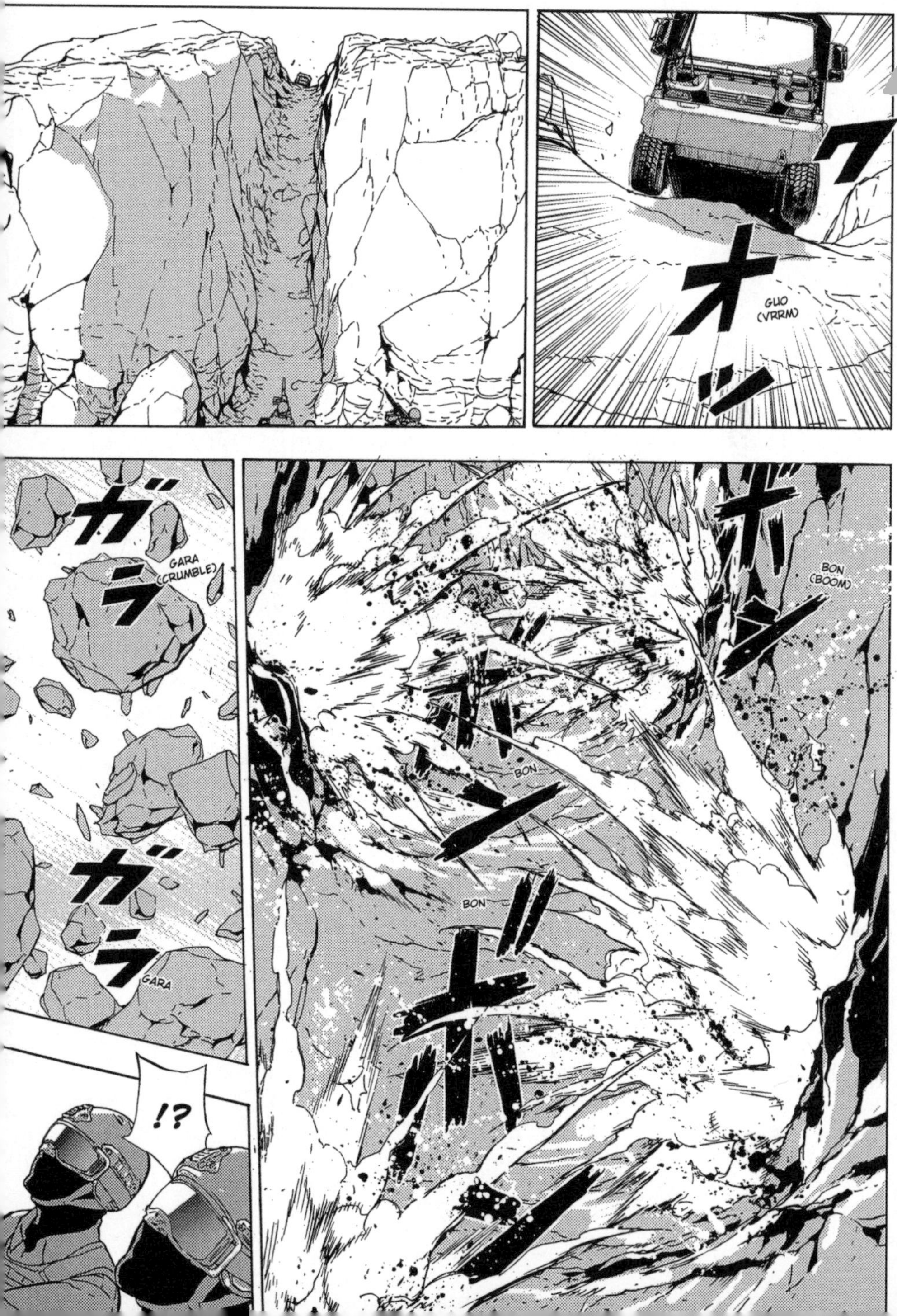
グオッ
GUO (VRRM)
ボン
BON (BOOM)
ボン
BON
ボン
BON
ガラ
GARA (CRUMBLE)
ガラ
GARA
!?

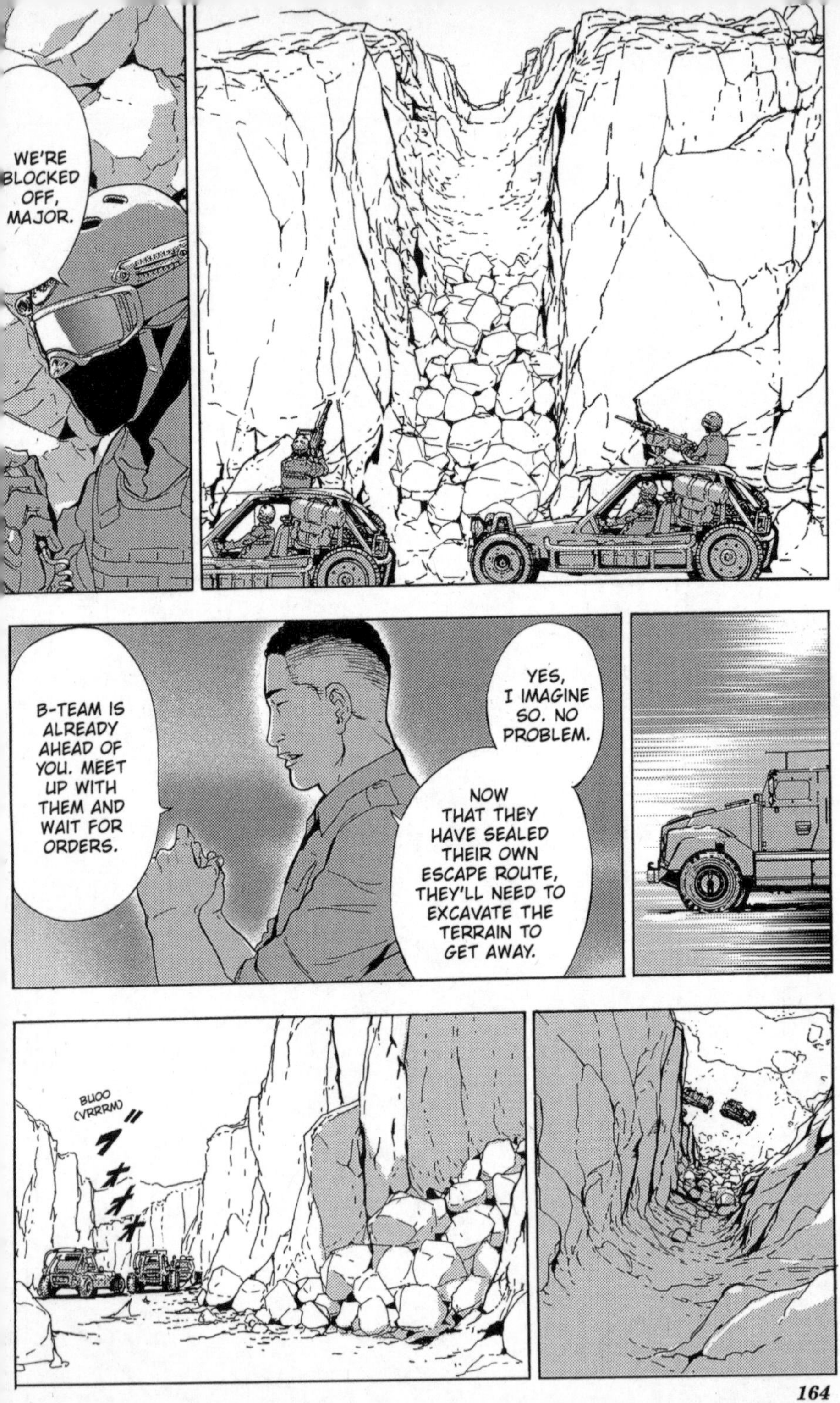
WE'RE BLOCKED OFF, MAJOR.
YES, I IMAGINE SO. NO PROBLEM.
NOW THAT THEY HAVE SEALED THEIR OWN ESCAPE ROUTE, THEY'LL NEED TO EXCAVATE THE TERRAIN TO GET AWAY.
B-TEAM IS ALREADY AHEAD OF YOU. MEET UP WITH THEM AND WAIT FOR ORDERS.
BUOO (VRRRM)

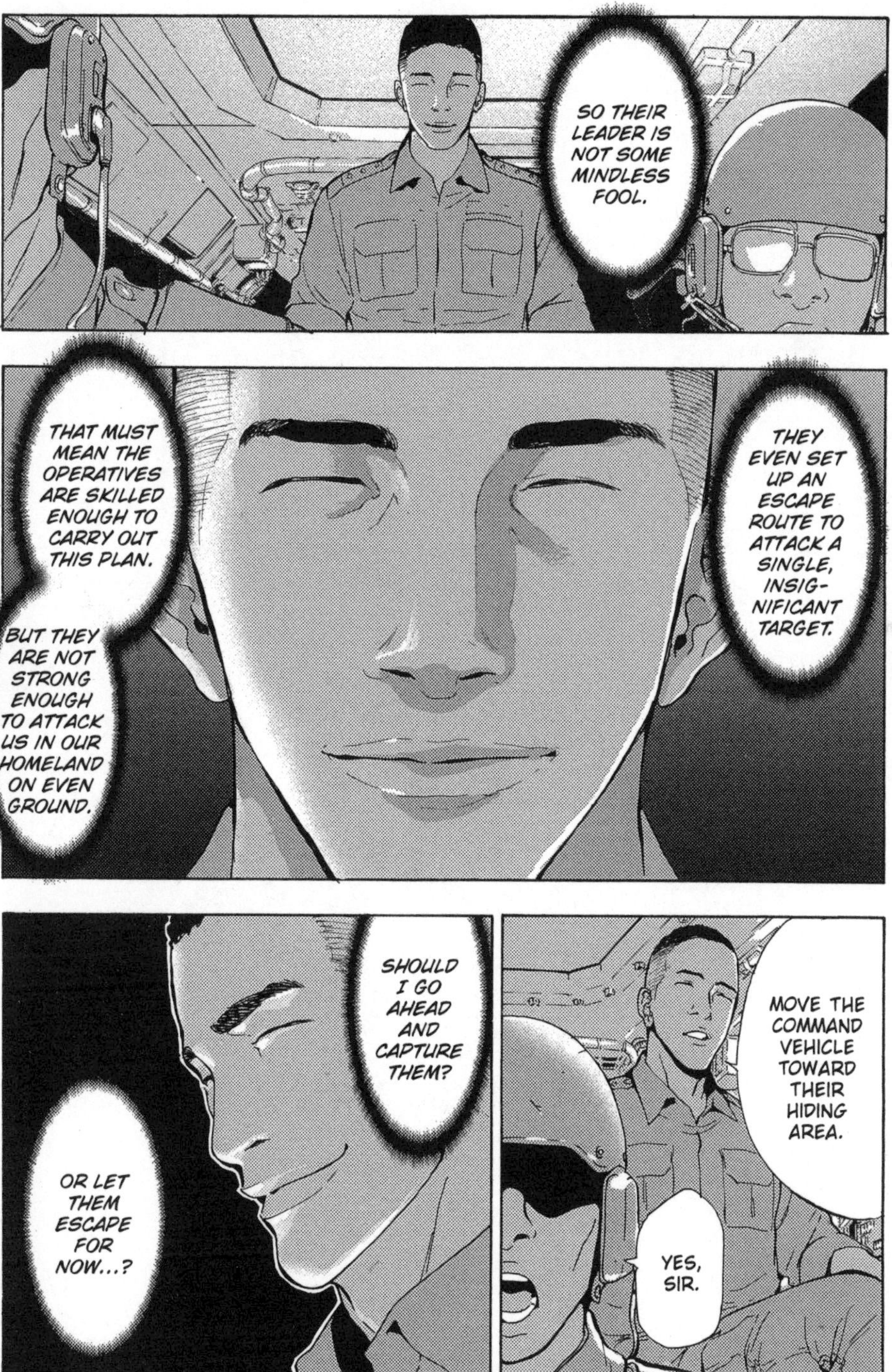
SO THEIR LEADER IS NOT SOME MINDLESS FOOL.
THEY EVEN SET UP AN ESCAPE ROUTE TO ATTACK A SINGLE, INSIG-NIFICANT TARGET.
THAT MUST MEAN THE OPERATIVES ARE SKILLED ENOUGH TO CARRY OUT THIS PLAN.
BUT THEY ARE NOT STRONG ENOUGH TO ATTACK US IN OUR HOMELAND ON EVEN GROUND.
MOVE THE COMMAND VEHICLE TOWARD THEIR HIDING AREA.
YES, SIR.
SHOULD I GO AHEAD AND CAPTURE THEM?
OR LET THEM ESCAPE FOR NOW...?

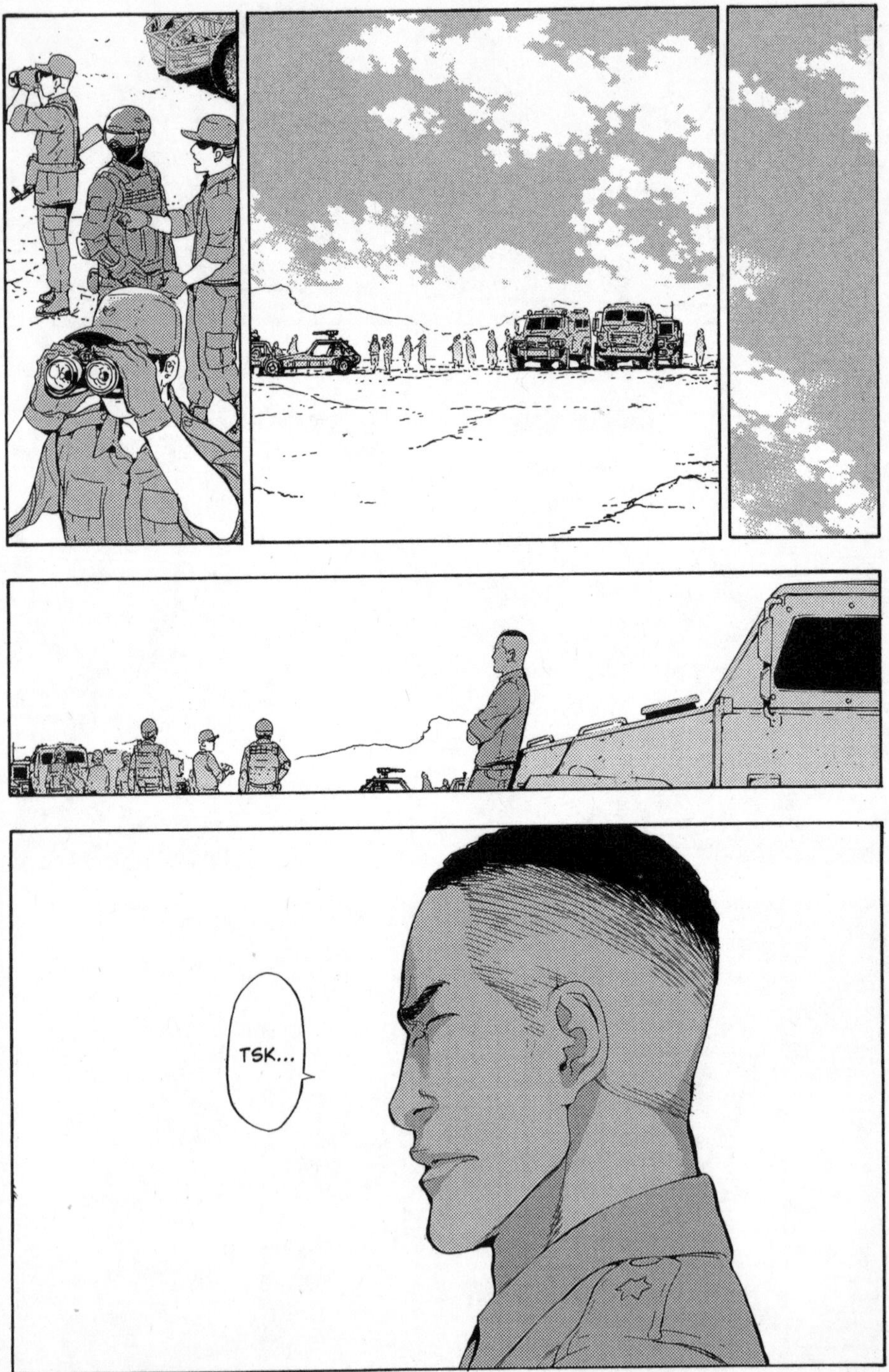
TSK...

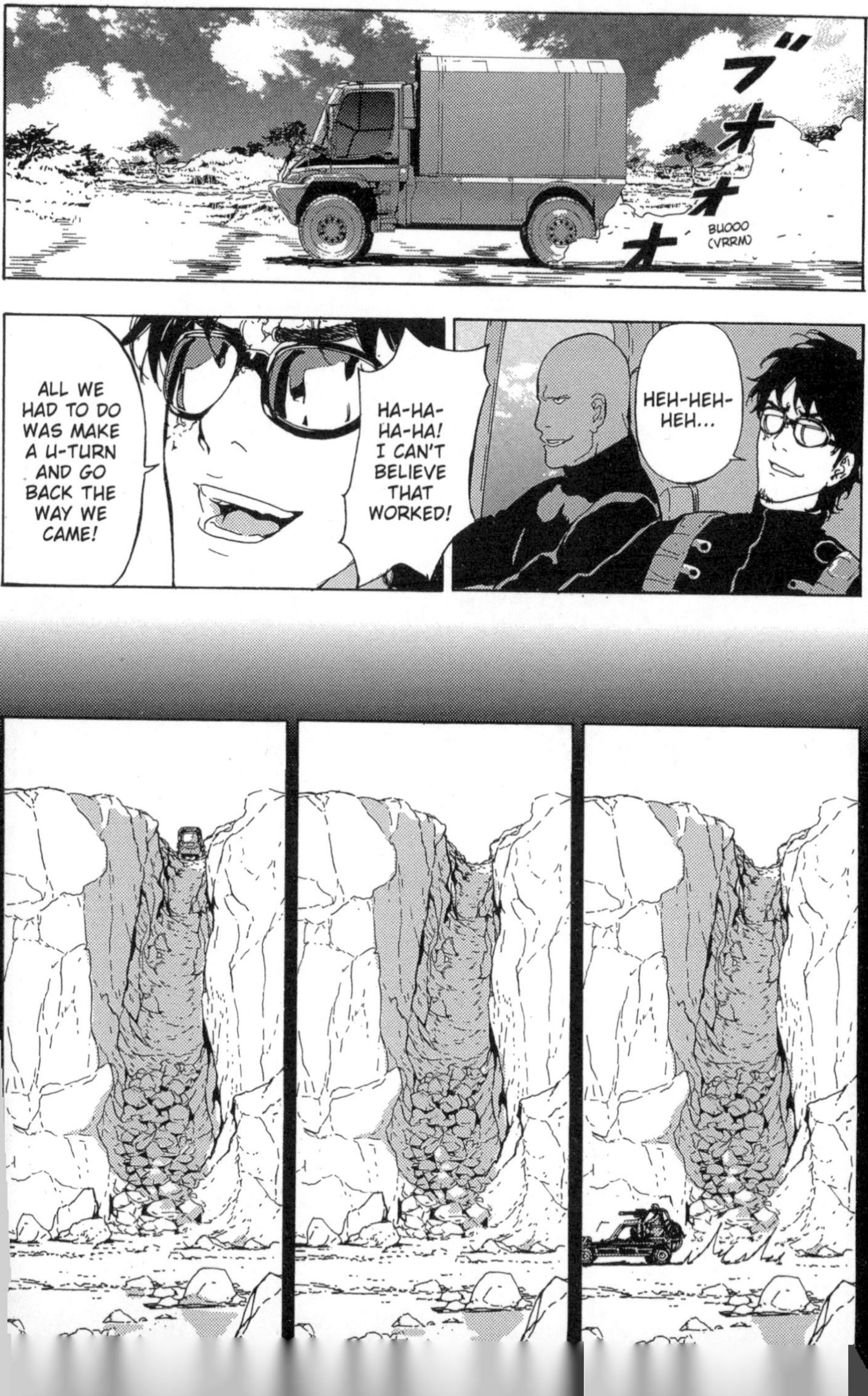
ブオオオ
BUOOO (VRRM)
HEH-HEH-HEH...
HA-HA-HA-HA! I CAN'T BELIEVE THAT WORKED!
ALL WE HAD TO DO WAS MAKE A U-TURN AND GO BACK THE WAY WE CAME!

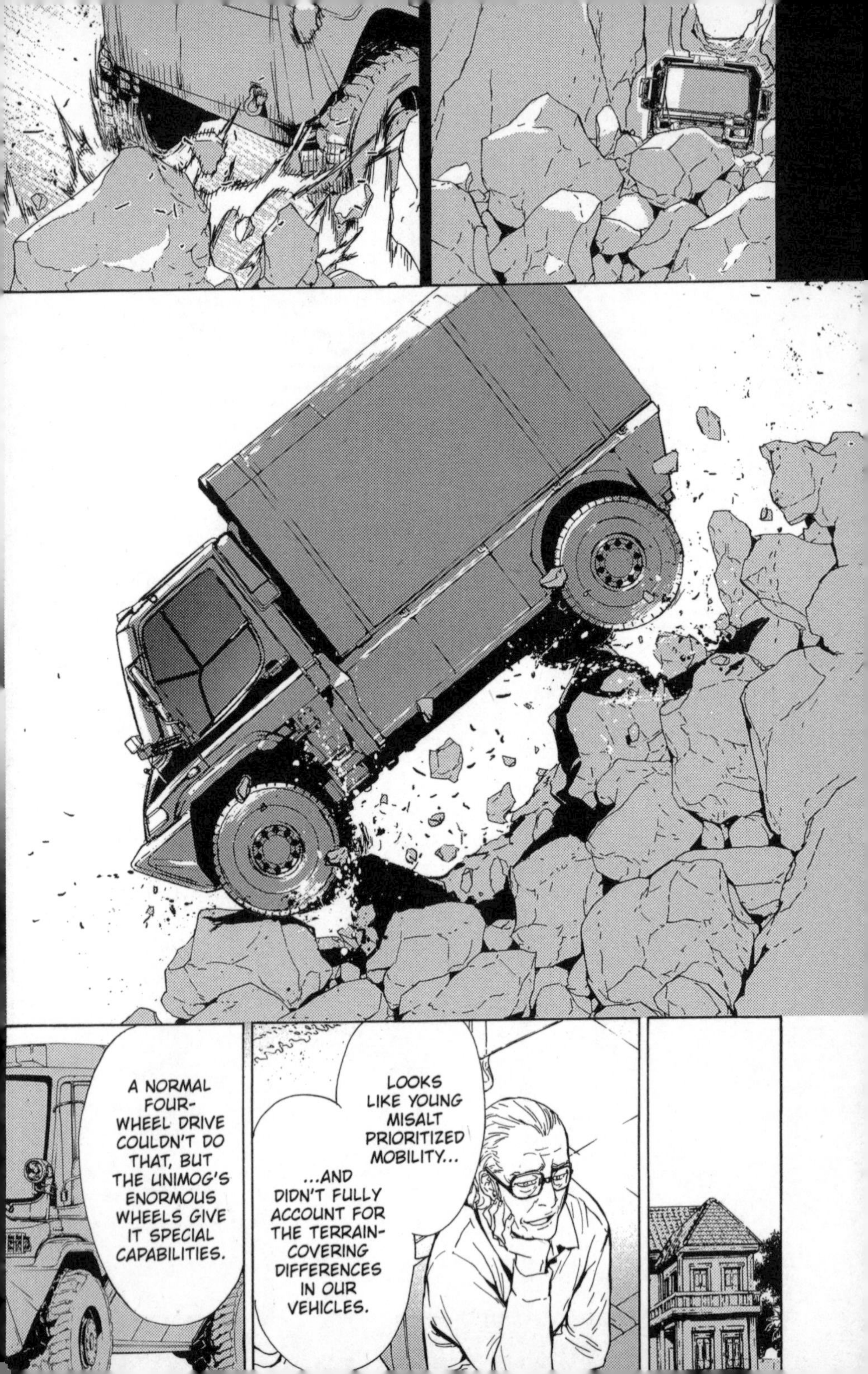
LOOKS LIKE YOUNG MISALT PRIORITIZED MOBILITY...
...AND DIDN'T FULLY ACCOUNT FOR THE TERRAIN-COVERING DIFFERENCES IN OUR VEHICLES.
A NORMAL FOUR-WHEEL DRIVE COULDN'T DO THAT, BUT THE UNIMOG'S ENORMOUS WHEELS GIVE IT SPECIAL CAPABILITIES.

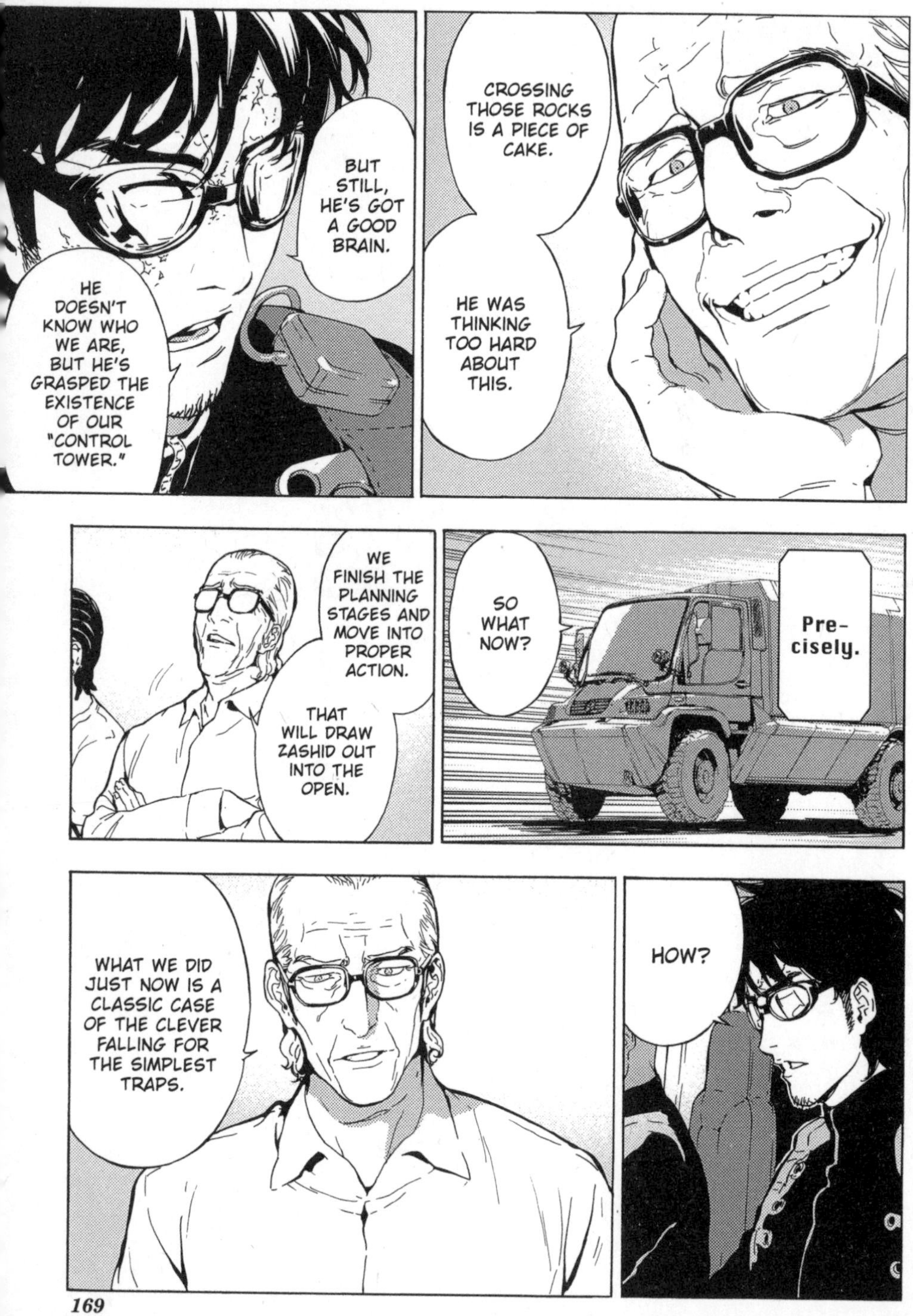
CROSSING THOSE ROCKS IS A PIECE OF CAKE.
HE WAS THINKING TOO HARD ABOUT THIS.
BUT STILL, HE'S GOT A GOOD BRAIN.
HE DOESN'T KNOW WHO WE ARE, BUT HE'S GRASPED THE EXISTENCE OF OUR "CONTROL TOWER."
Pre-cisely.
SO WHAT NOW?
WE FINISH THE PLANNING STAGES AND MOVE INTO PROPER ACTION.
THAT WILL DRAW ZASHID OUT INTO THE OPEN.
HOW?
WHAT WE DID JUST NOW IS A CLASSIC CASE OF THE CLEVER FALLING FOR THE SIMPLEST TRAPS.

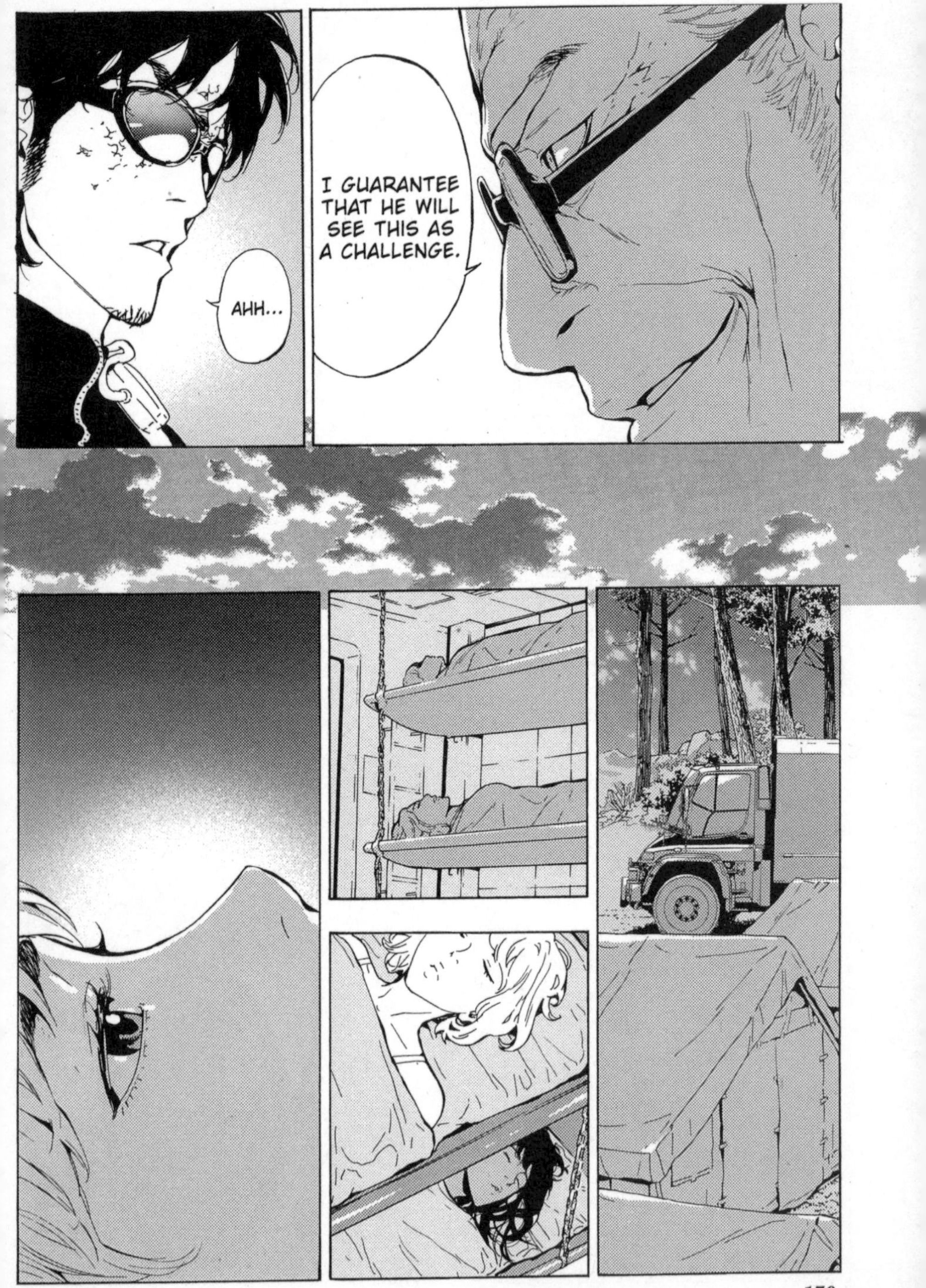
I GUARANTEE THAT HE WILL SEE THIS AS A CHALLENGE.
AHH...

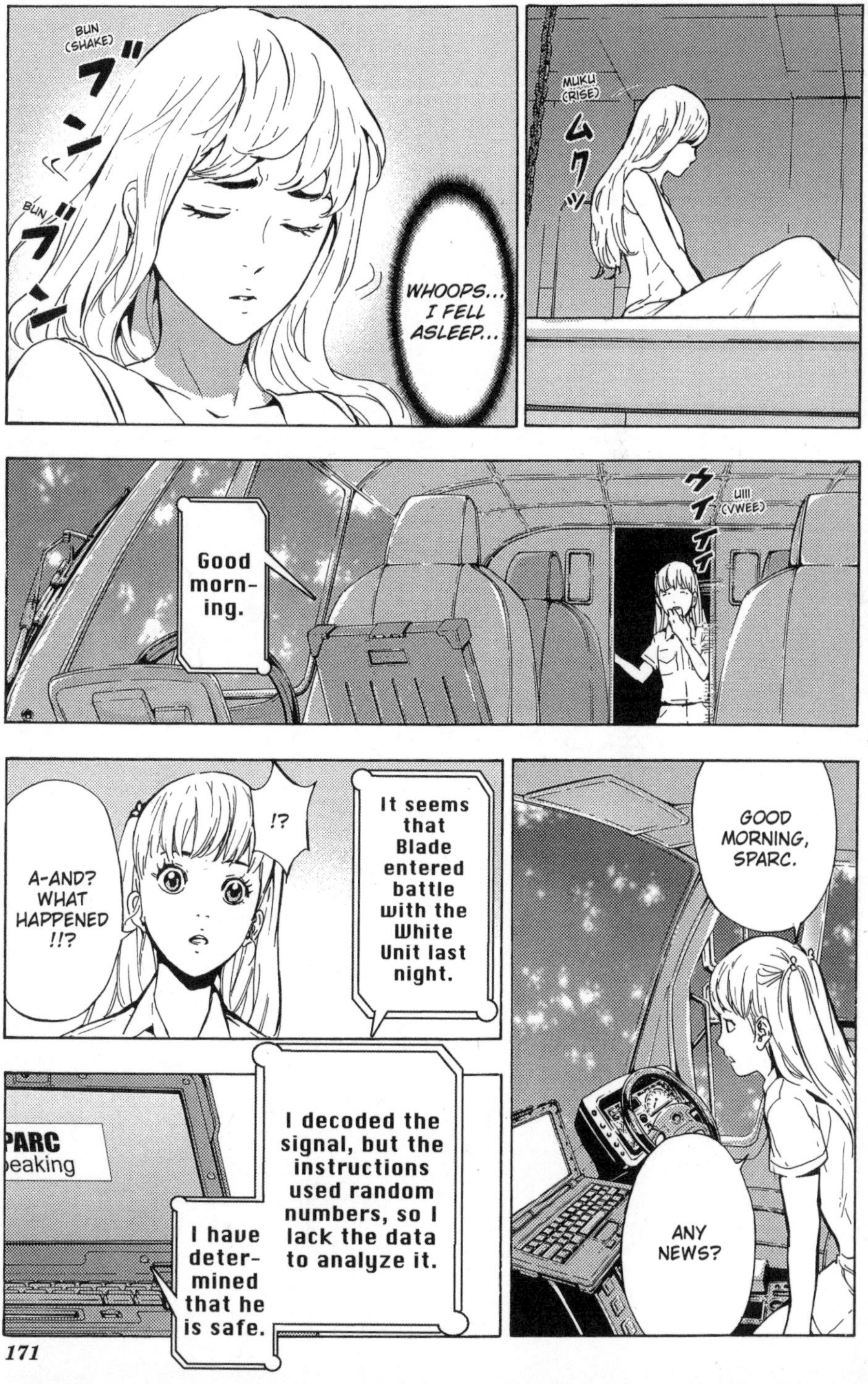
MUKU (RISE)
ムクッ
BUN (SHAKE)
ブン
BUN
ブン
WHOOPS... I FELL ASLEEP...
UIII (VWEE)
ウイィィ
Good morning.
GOOD MORNING, SPARC.
ANY NEWS?
It seems that Blade entered battle with the White Unit last night.
!?
A-AND? WHAT HAPPENED!!?
I decoded the signal, but the instructions used random numbers, so I lack the data to analyze it.
I have determined that he is safe.
PARC
eaking

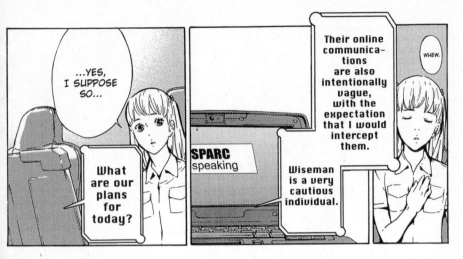

WHEW.
Their online communications are also intentionally vague, with the expectation that I would intercept them.
Wiseman is a very cautious individual.
SPARC speaking
...YES, I SUPPOSE SO...
What are our plans for today?
...
WE'RE GOING TO NEUTRALIZE GIDO TURUS.
Yes, Miss Haruka.
SPARC speaking

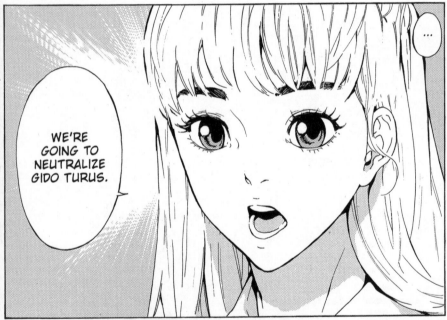

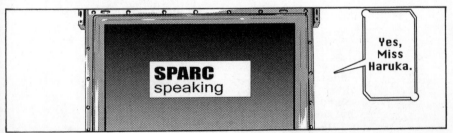

Until Death do us Part

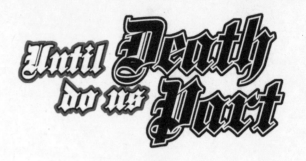

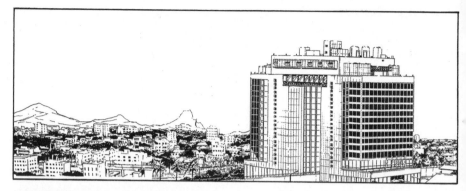

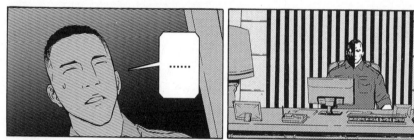

...I SEE...

WELL DONE.

...you aren't going to punish me?

Um...

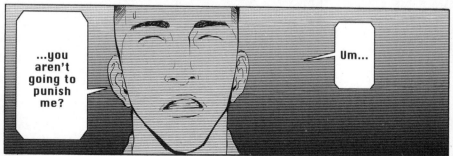

175

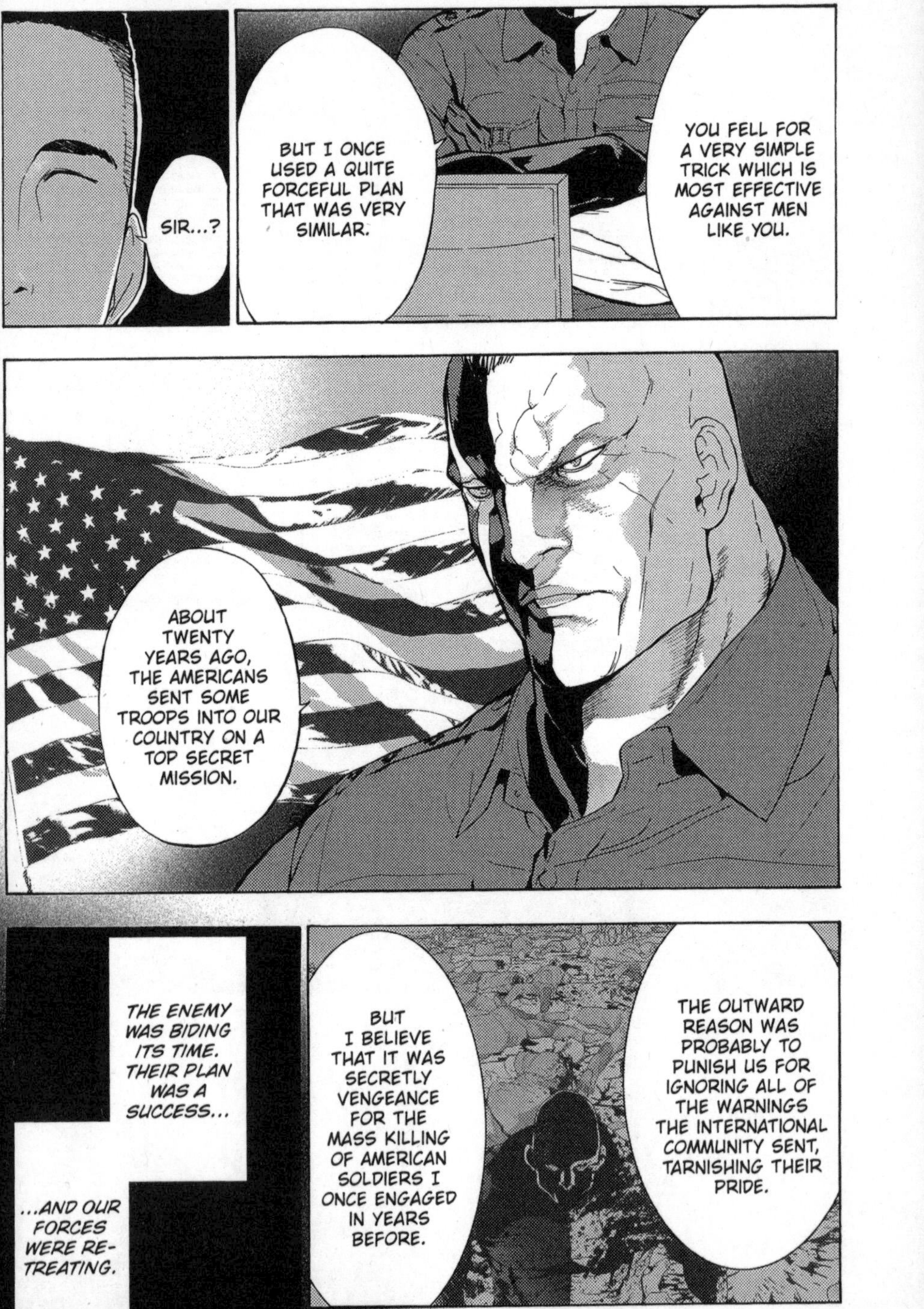
YOU FELL FOR A VERY SIMPLE TRICK WHICH IS MOST EFFECTIVE AGAINST MEN LIKE YOU.
BUT I ONCE USED A QUITE FORCEFUL PLAN THAT WAS VERY SIMILAR.
SIR...?
ABOUT TWENTY YEARS AGO, THE AMERICANS SENT SOME TROOPS INTO OUR COUNTRY ON A TOP SECRET MISSION.
THE OUTWARD REASON WAS PROBABLY TO PUNISH US FOR IGNORING ALL OF THE WARNINGS THE INTERNATIONAL COMMUNITY SENT, TARNISHING THEIR PRIDE.
BUT I BELIEVE THAT IT WAS SECRETLY VENGEANCE FOR THE MASS KILLING OF AMERICAN SOLDIERS I ONCE ENGAGED IN YEARS BEFORE.
THE ENEMY WAS BIDING ITS TIME. THEIR PLAN WAS A SUCCESS...
...AND OUR FORCES WERE RE-TREATING.

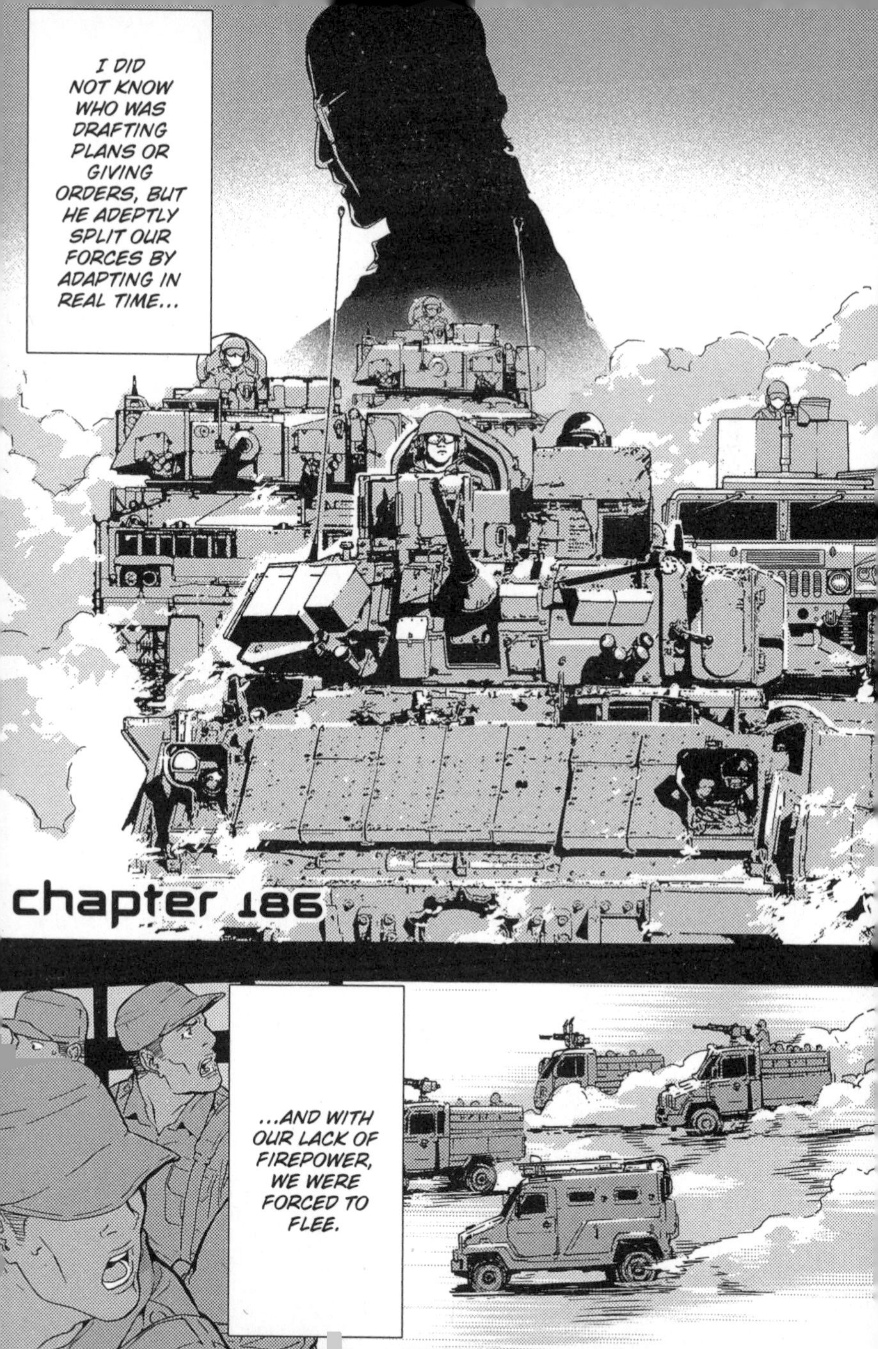
I DID NOT KNOW WHO WAS DRAFTING PLANS OR GIVING ORDERS, BUT HE ADEPTLY SPLIT OUR FORCES BY ADAPTING IN REAL TIME...
chapter 186
...AND WITH OUR LACK OF FIREPOWER, WE WERE FORCED TO FLEE.

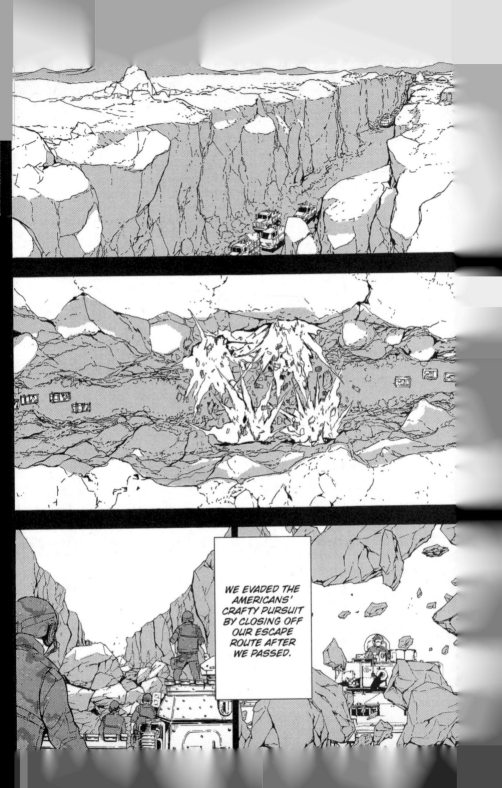

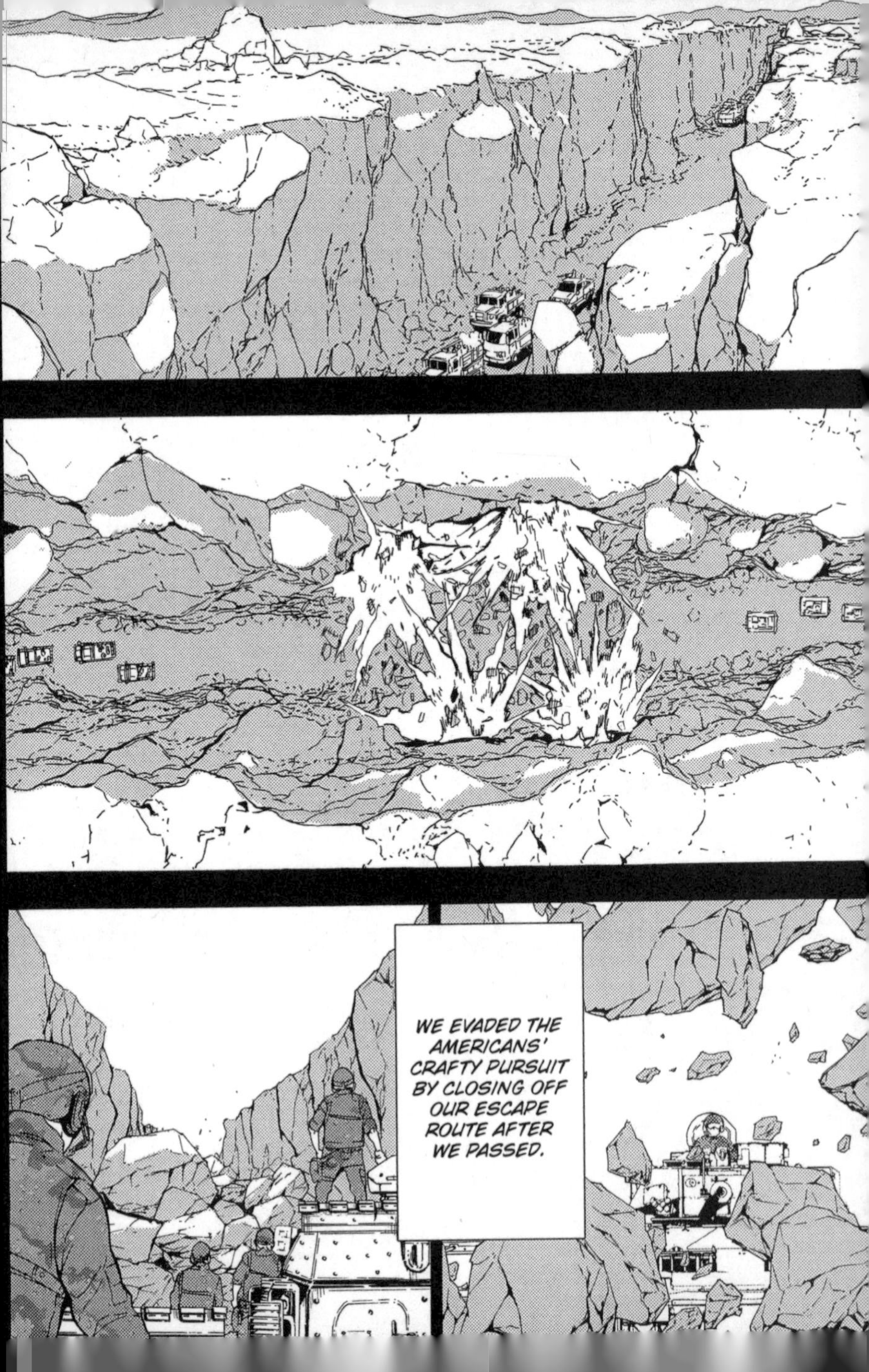
WE EVADED THE AMERICANS' CRAFTY PURSUIT BY CLOSING OFF OUR ESCAPE ROUTE AFTER WE PASSED.

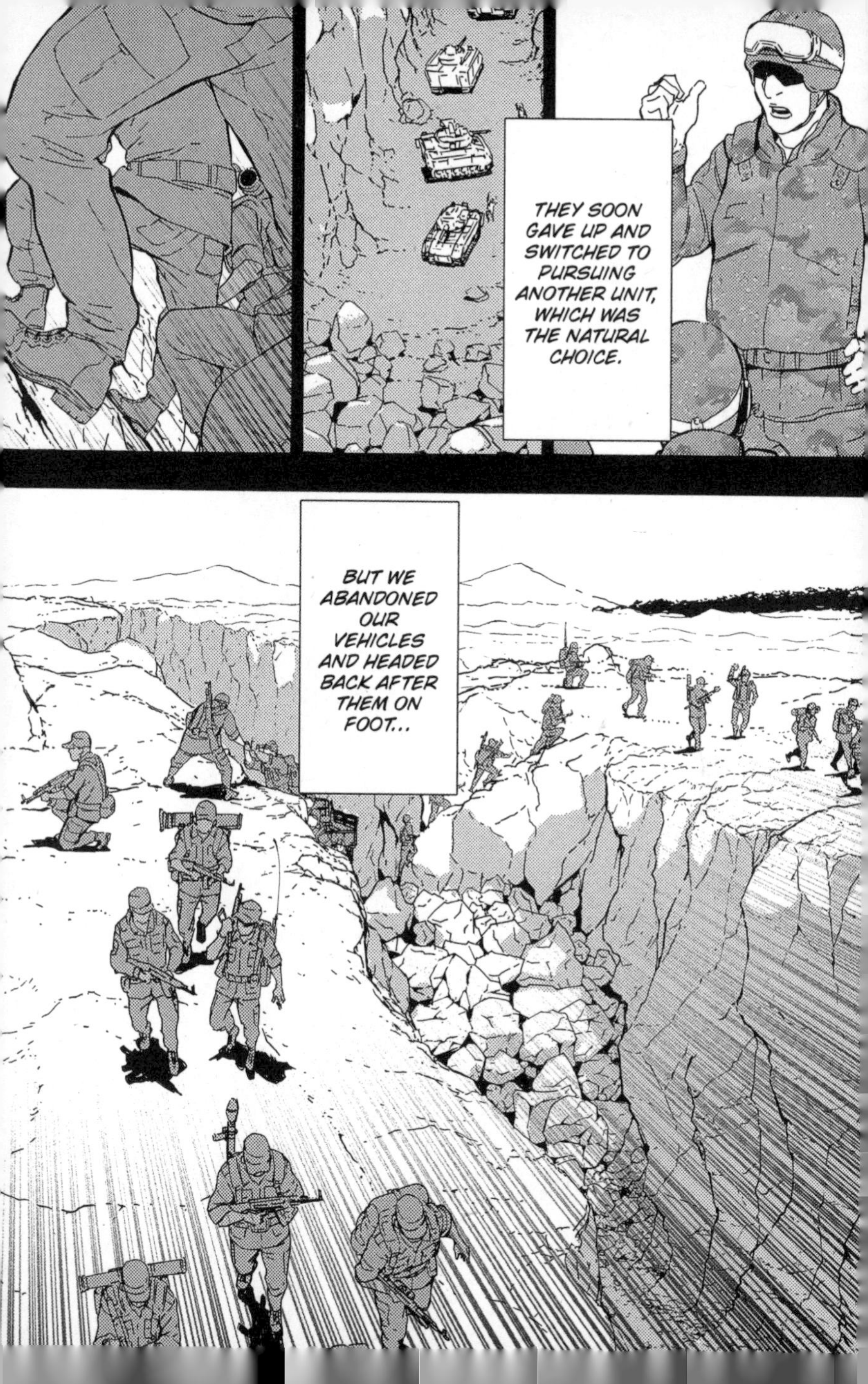
THEY SOON GAVE UP AND SWITCHED TO PURSUING ANOTHER UNIT, WHICH WAS THE NATURAL CHOICE.
BUT WE ABANDONED OUR VEHICLES AND HEADED BACK AFTER THEM ON FOOT...

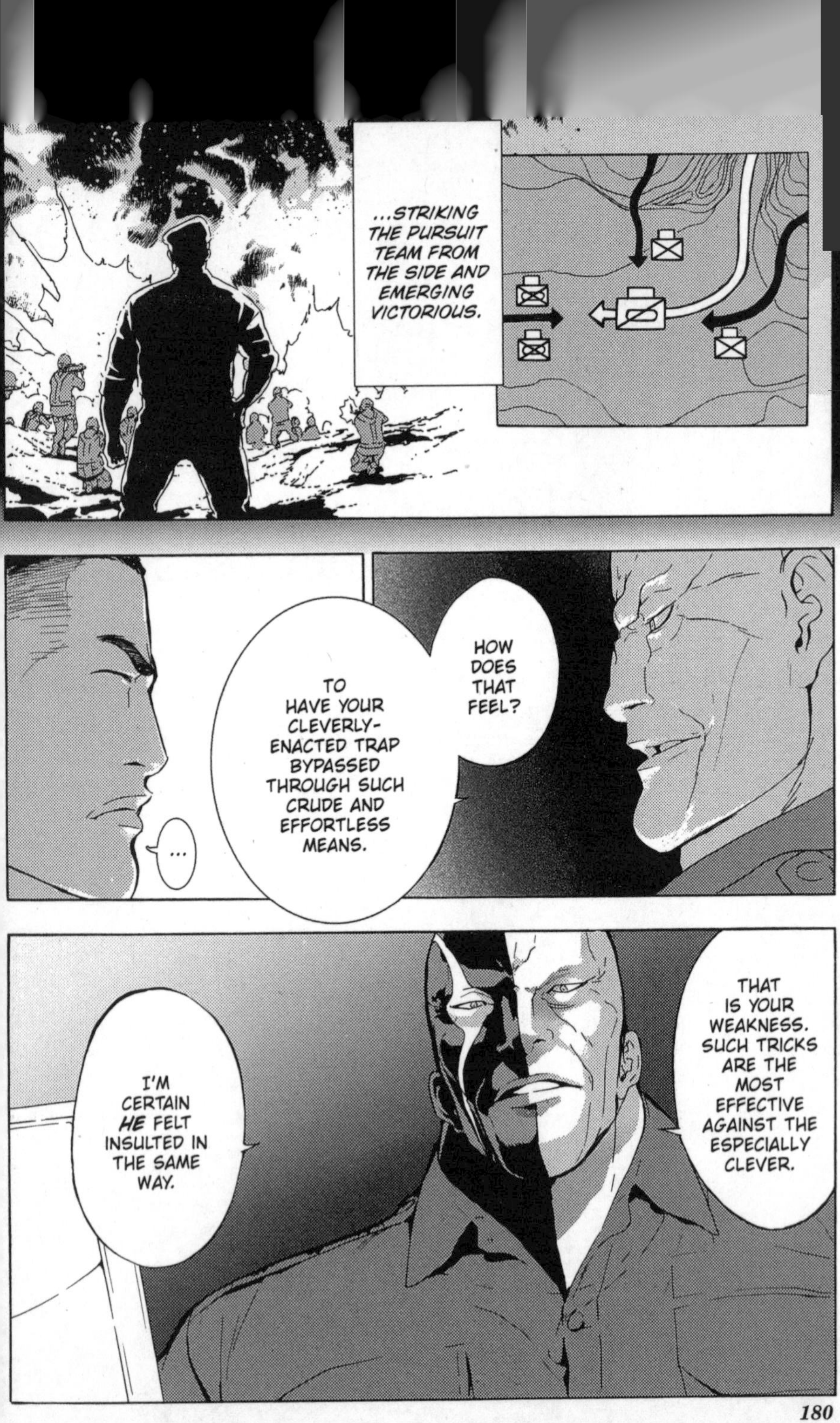
...STRIKING THE PURSUIT TEAM FROM THE SIDE AND EMERGING VICTORIOUS.
HOW DOES THAT FEEL?
TO HAVE YOUR CLEVERLY-ENACTED TRAP BYPASSED THROUGH SUCH CRUDE AND EFFORTLESS MEANS.
...
THAT IS YOUR WEAKNESS. SUCH TRICKS ARE THE MOST EFFECTIVE AGAINST THE ESPECIALLY CLEVER.
I'M CERTAIN *HE* FELT INSULTED IN THE SAME WAY.

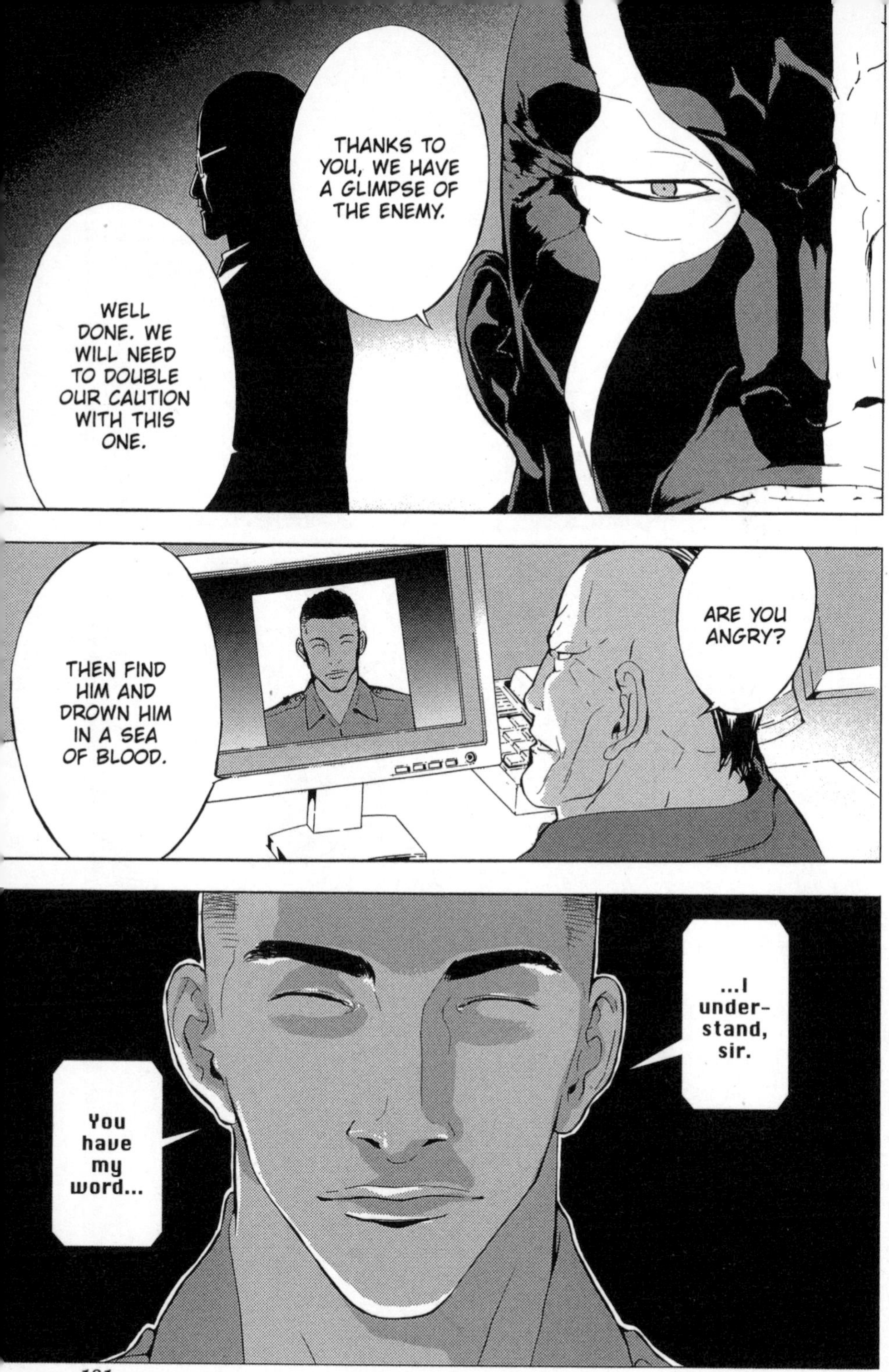
THANKS TO YOU, WE HAVE A GLIMPSE OF THE ENEMY.
WELL DONE. WE WILL NEED TO DOUBLE OUR CAUTION WITH THIS ONE.
ARE YOU ANGRY?
THEN FIND HIM AND DROWN HIM IN A SEA OF BLOOD.
...I under-stand, sir.
You have my word...

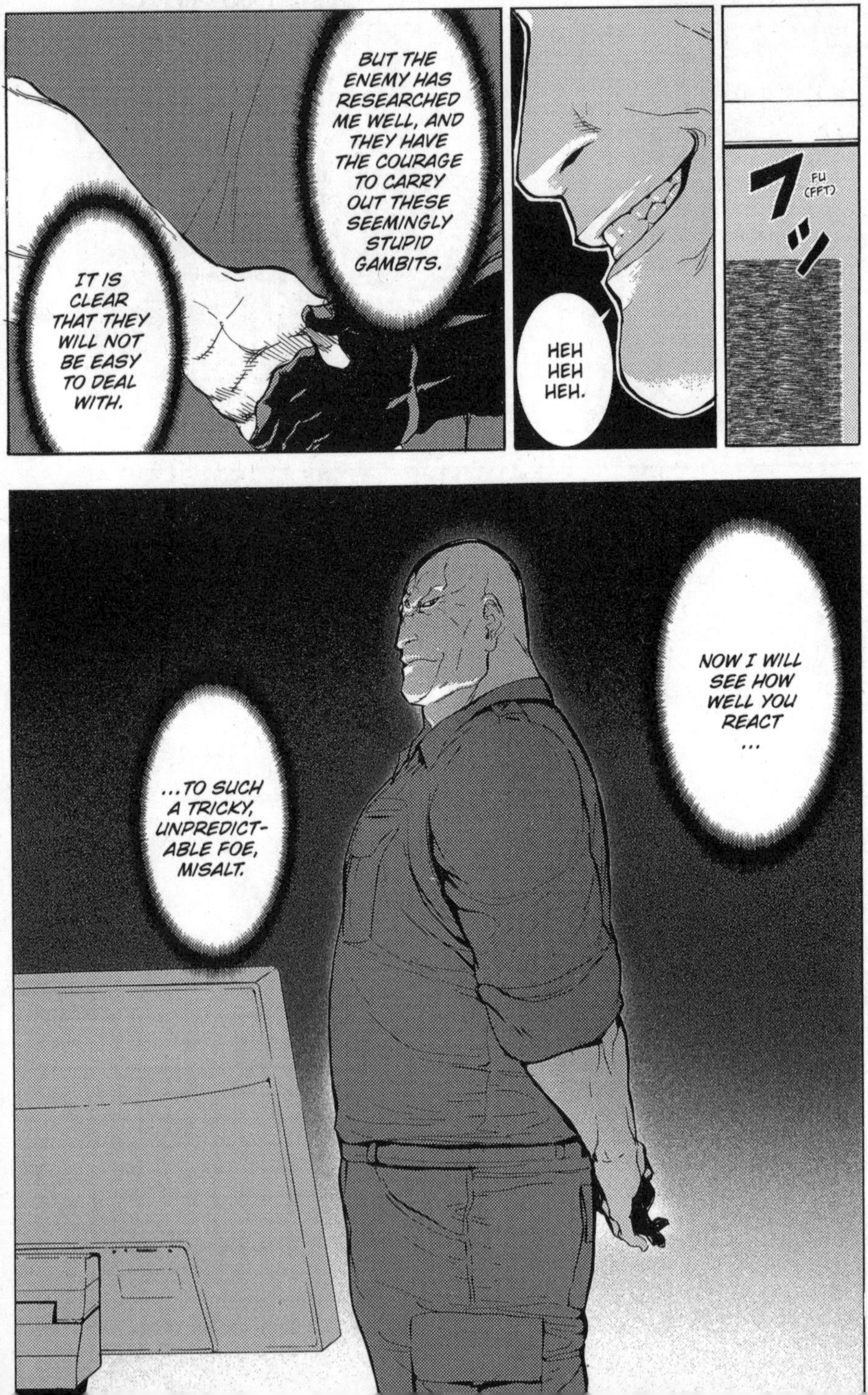
フッ
FU (FFT)
HEH HEH HEH.
BUT THE ENEMY HAS RESEARCHED ME WELL, AND THEY HAVE THE COURAGE TO CARRY OUT THESE SEEMINGLY STUPID GAMBITS.
IT IS CLEAR THAT THEY WILL NOT BE EASY TO DEAL WITH.
NOW I WILL SEE HOW WELL YOU REACT ...
...TO SUCH A TRICKY, UNPREDICTABLE FOE, MISALT.

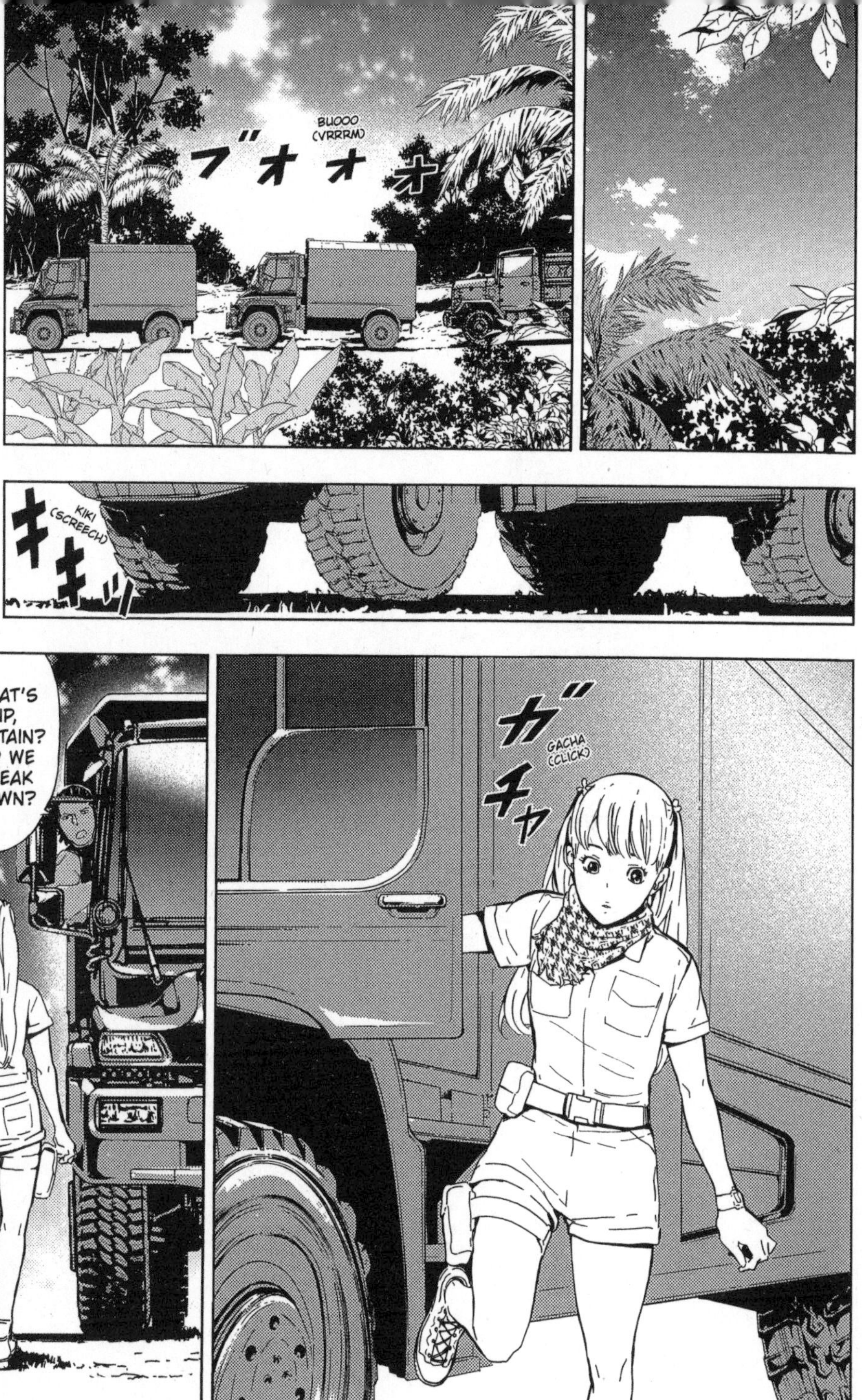
BUOOO (VRRRM)
ブオオオ
KIKI (SCREECH)
キキッ
GACHA (CLICK)
ガチャ
WHAT'S UP, CAPTAIN? DID WE BREAK DOWN?

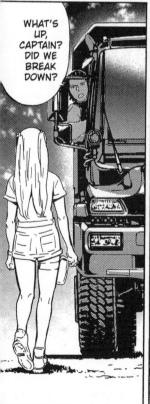

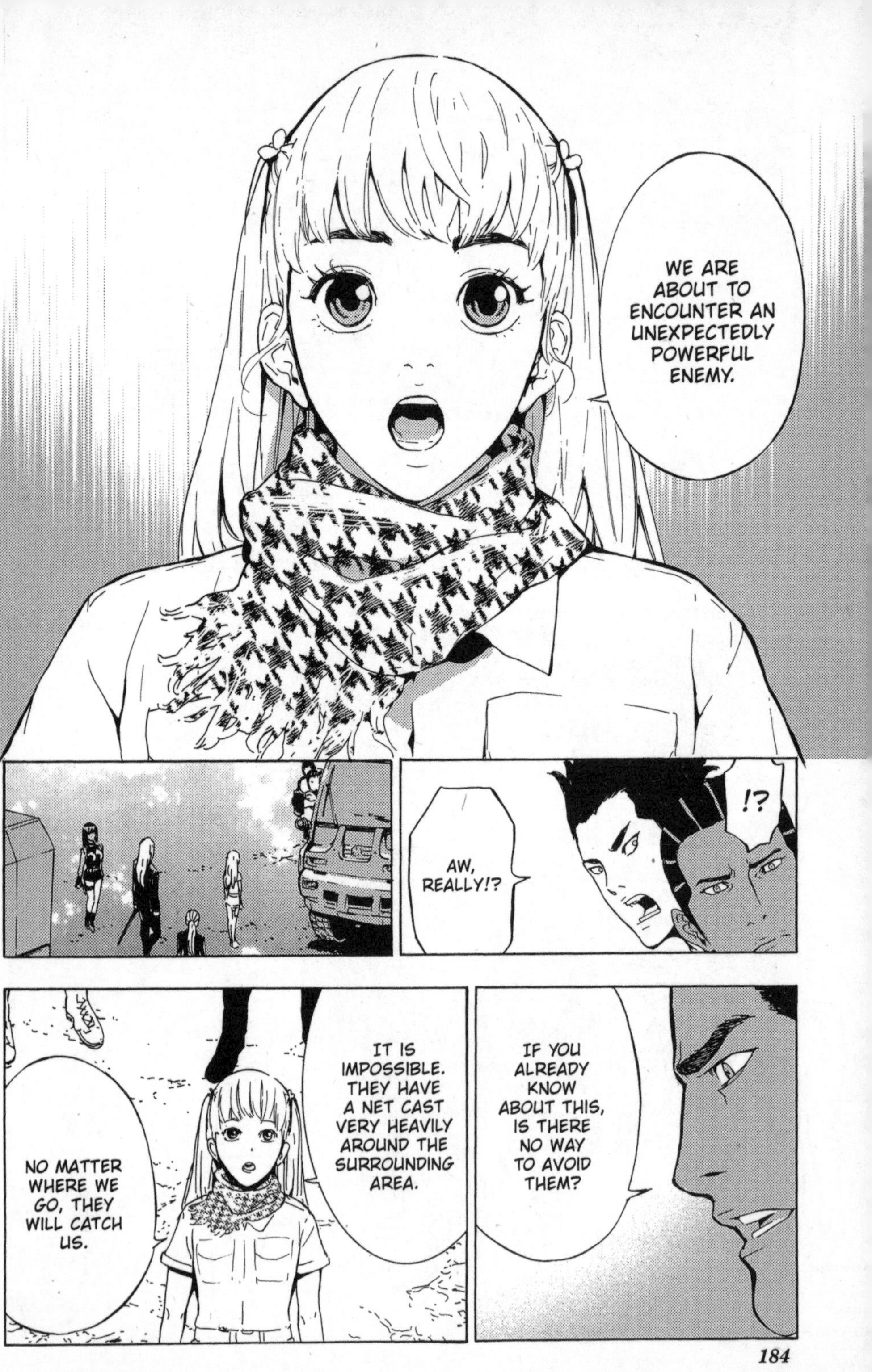
WE ARE ABOUT TO ENCOUNTER AN UNEXPECTEDLY POWERFUL ENEMY.
!?
AW, REALLY!?
IF YOU ALREADY KNOW ABOUT THIS, IS THERE NO WAY TO AVOID THEM?
IT IS IMPOSSIBLE. THEY HAVE A NET CAST VERY HEAVILY AROUND THE SURROUNDING AREA.
NO MATTER WHERE WE GO, THEY WILL CATCH US.

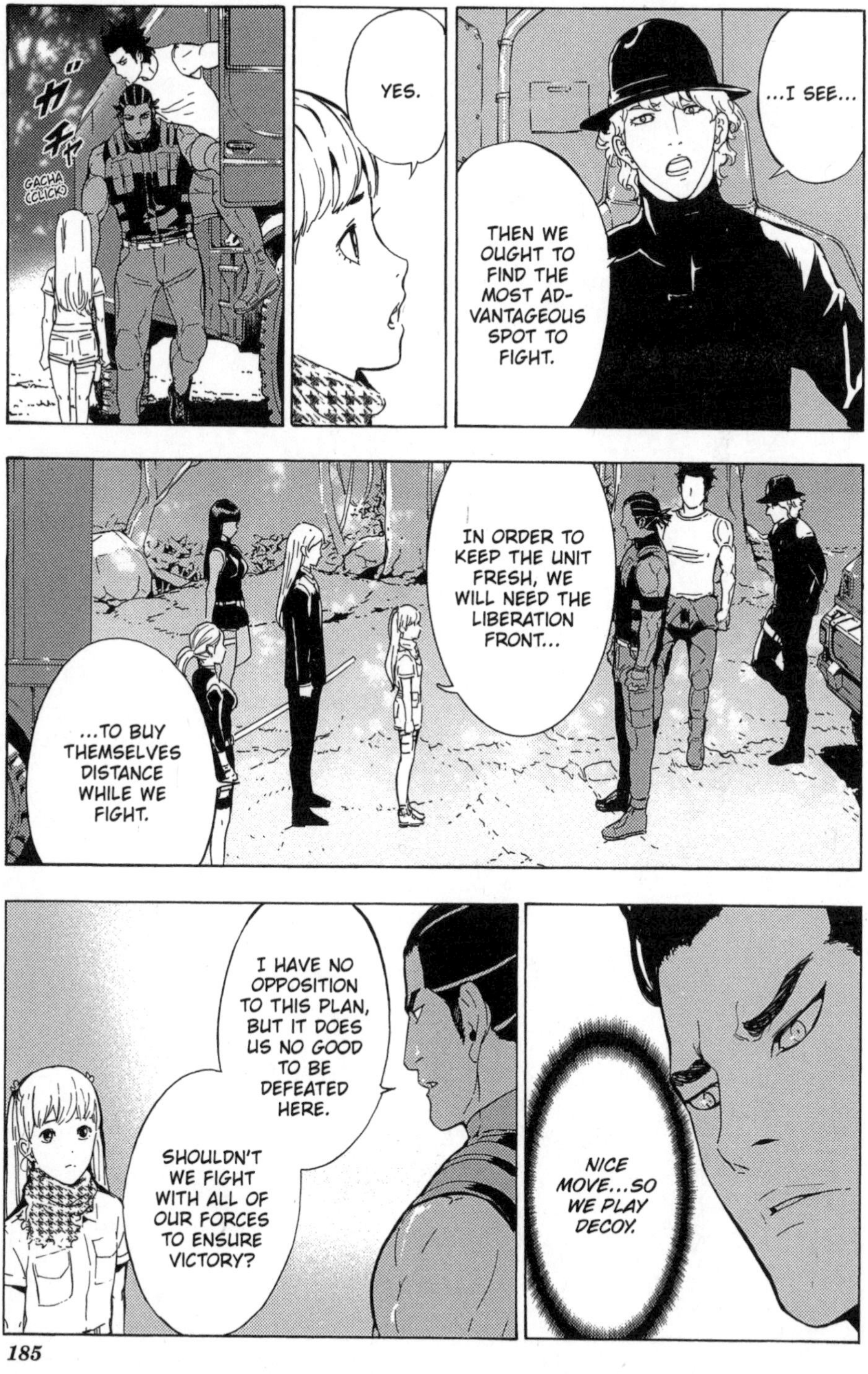
...I SEE...
THEN WE OUGHT TO FIND THE MOST ADVANTAGEOUS SPOT TO FIGHT.
YES.
ガチャ
GACHA (CLICK)
IN ORDER TO KEEP THE UNIT FRESH, WE WILL NEED THE LIBERATION FRONT...
...TO BUY THEMSELVES DISTANCE WHILE WE FIGHT.
NICE MOVE...SO WE PLAY DECOY.
I HAVE NO OPPOSITION TO THIS PLAN, BUT IT DOES US NO GOOD TO BE DEFEATED HERE.
SHOULDN'T WE FIGHT WITH ALL OF OUR FORCES TO ENSURE VICTORY?

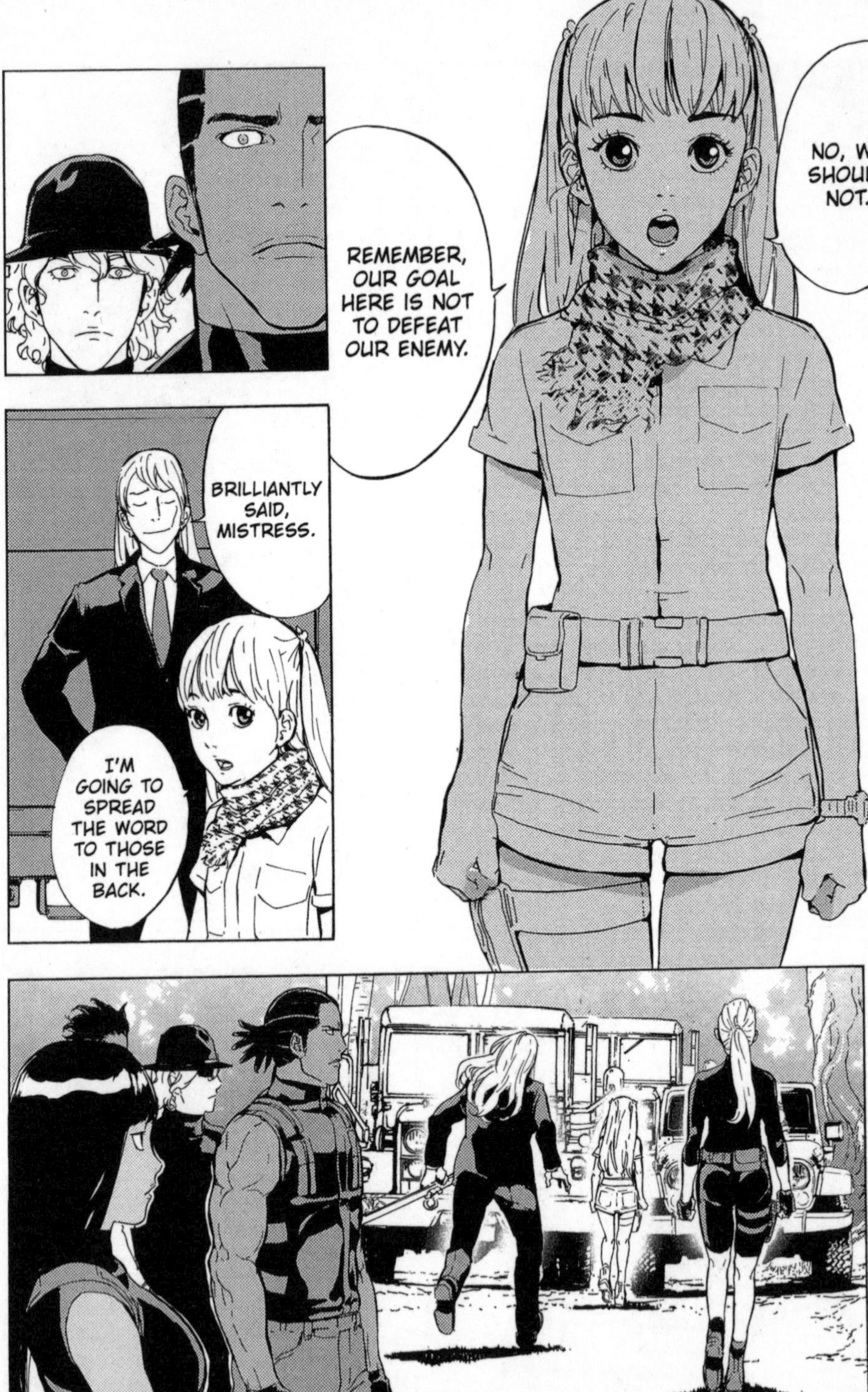
NO, WE SHOULD NOT.
REMEMBER, OUR GOAL HERE IS NOT TO DEFEAT OUR ENEMY.
BRILLIANTLY SAID, MISTRESS.
I'M GOING TO SPREAD THE WORD TO THOSE IN THE BACK.

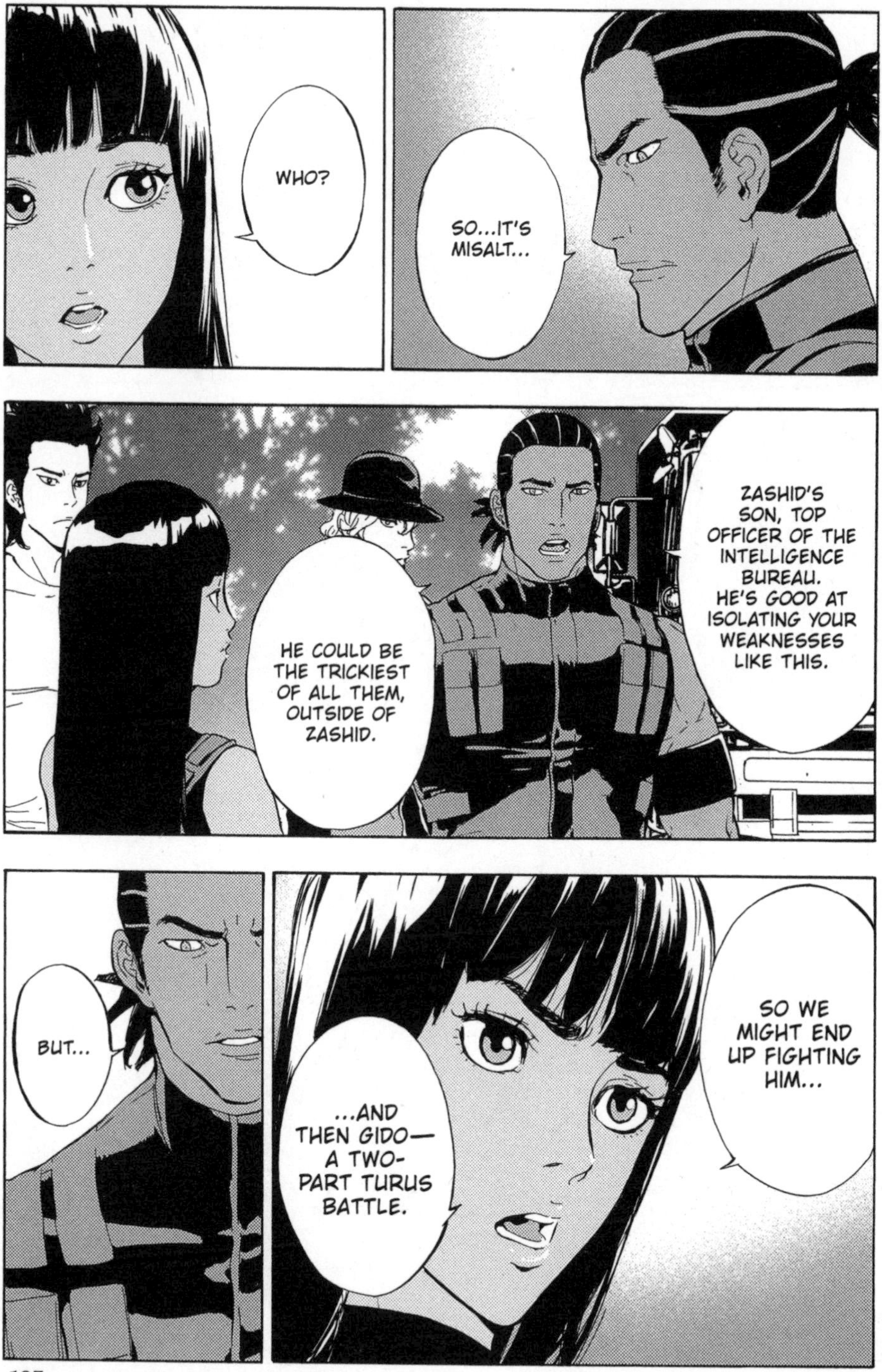
SO...IT'S MISALT...
WHO?
ZASHID'S SON, TOP OFFICER OF THE INTELLIGENCE BUREAU. HE'S GOOD AT ISOLATING YOUR WEAKNESSES LIKE THIS.
HE COULD BE THE TRICKIEST OF ALL THEM, OUTSIDE OF ZASHID.
SO WE MIGHT END UP FIGHTING HIM...
...AND THEN GIDO— A TWO-PART TURUS BATTLE.
BUT...

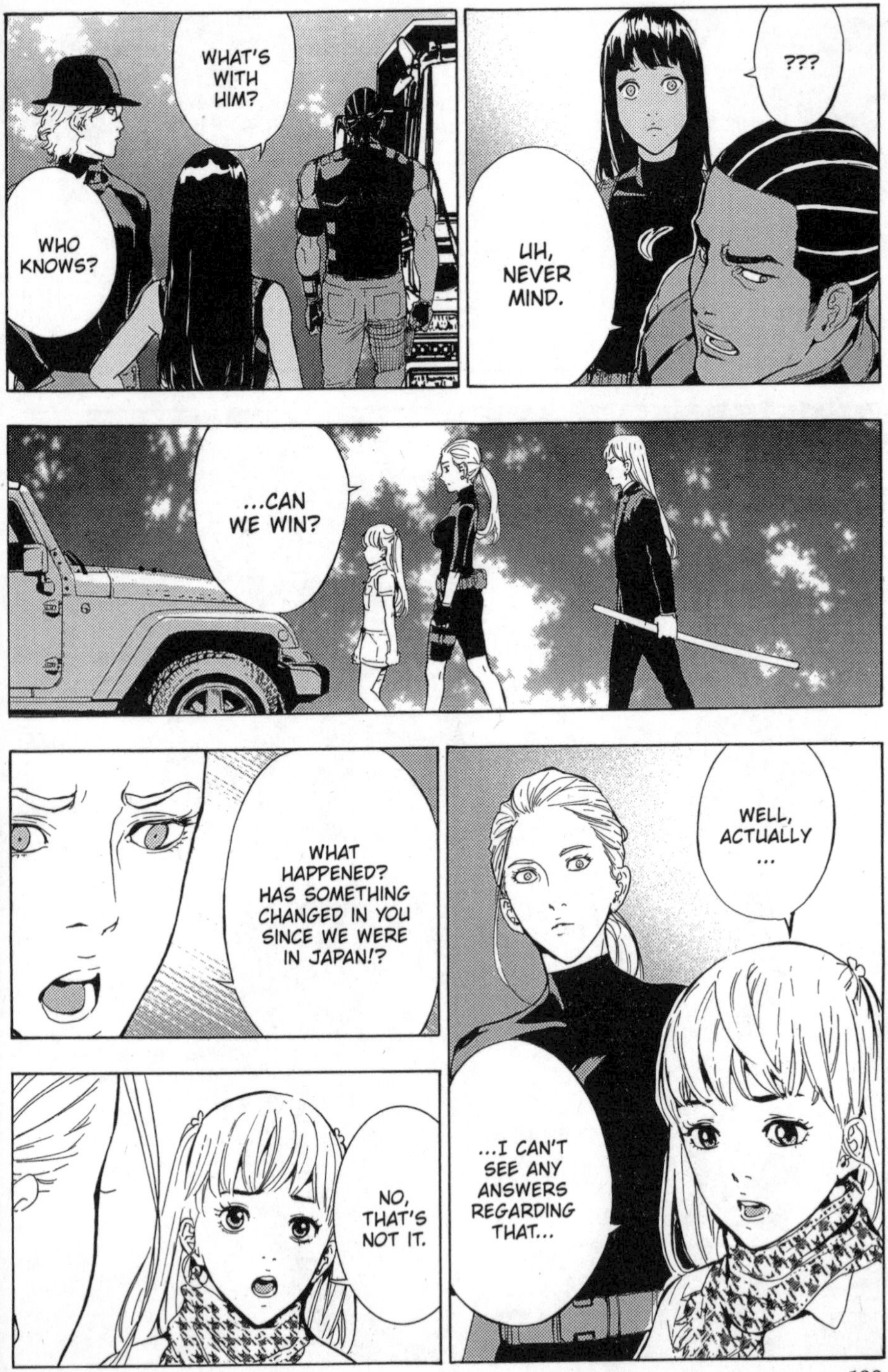
???
UH, NEVER MIND.
WHAT'S WITH HIM?
WHO KNOWS?
...CAN WE WIN?
WELL, ACTUALLY ...
...I CAN'T SEE ANY ANSWERS REGARDING THAT...
WHAT HAPPENED? HAS SOMETHING CHANGED IN YOU SINCE WE WERE IN JAPAN!?
NO, THAT'S NOT IT.

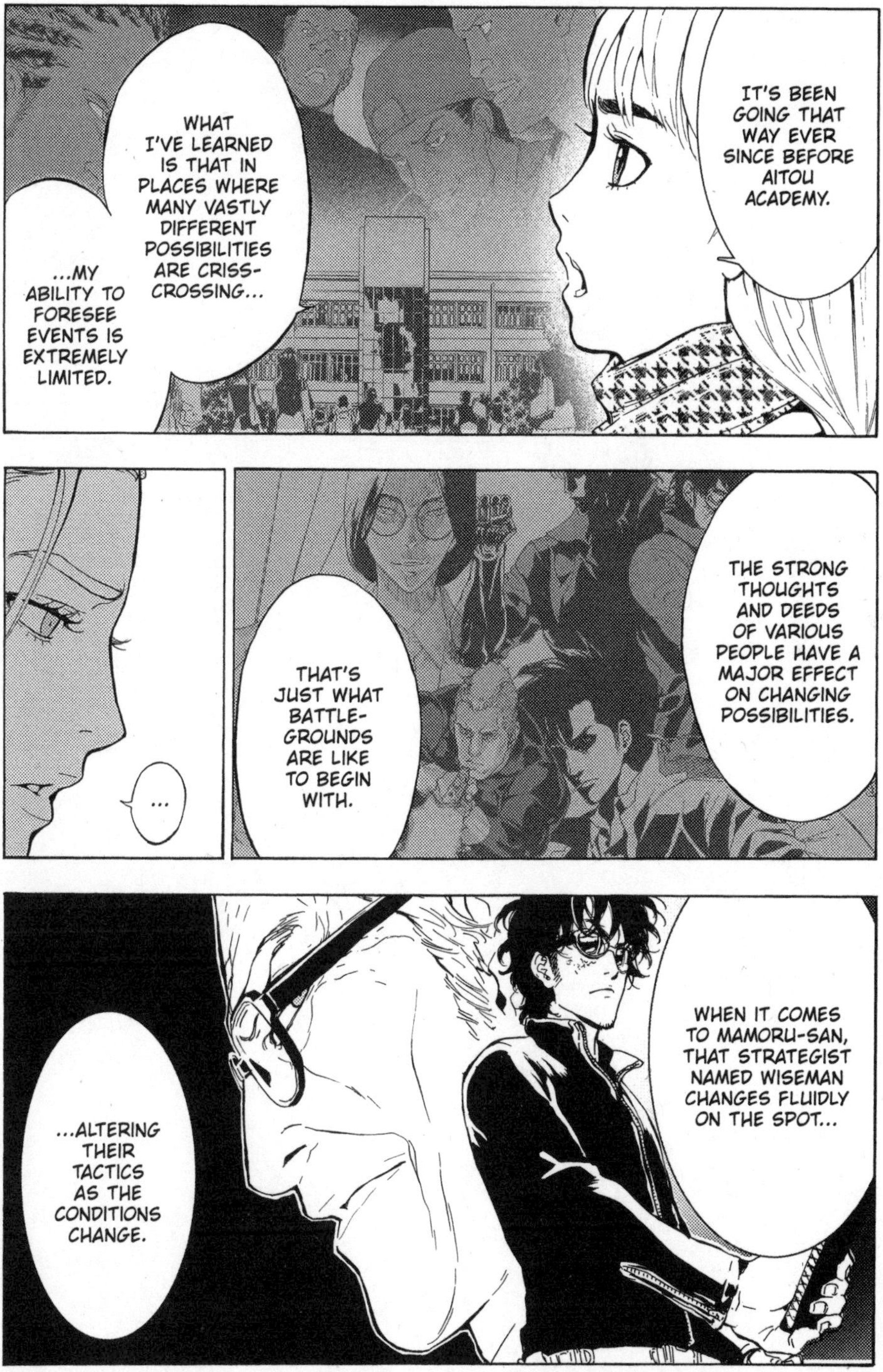
IT'S BEEN GOING THAT WAY EVER SINCE BEFORE AITOU ACADEMY.
WHAT I'VE LEARNED IS THAT IN PLACES WHERE MANY VASTLY DIFFERENT POSSIBILITIES ARE CRISS-CROSSING...
...MY ABILITY TO FORESEE EVENTS IS EXTREMELY LIMITED.
THE STRONG THOUGHTS AND DEEDS OF VARIOUS PEOPLE HAVE A MAJOR EFFECT ON CHANGING POSSIBILITIES.
THAT'S JUST WHAT BATTLE-GROUNDS ARE LIKE TO BEGIN WITH.
...
WHEN IT COMES TO MAMORU-SAN, THAT STRATEGIST NAMED WISEMAN CHANGES FLUIDLY ON THE SPOT...
...ALTERING THEIR TACTICS AS THE CONDITIONS CHANGE.

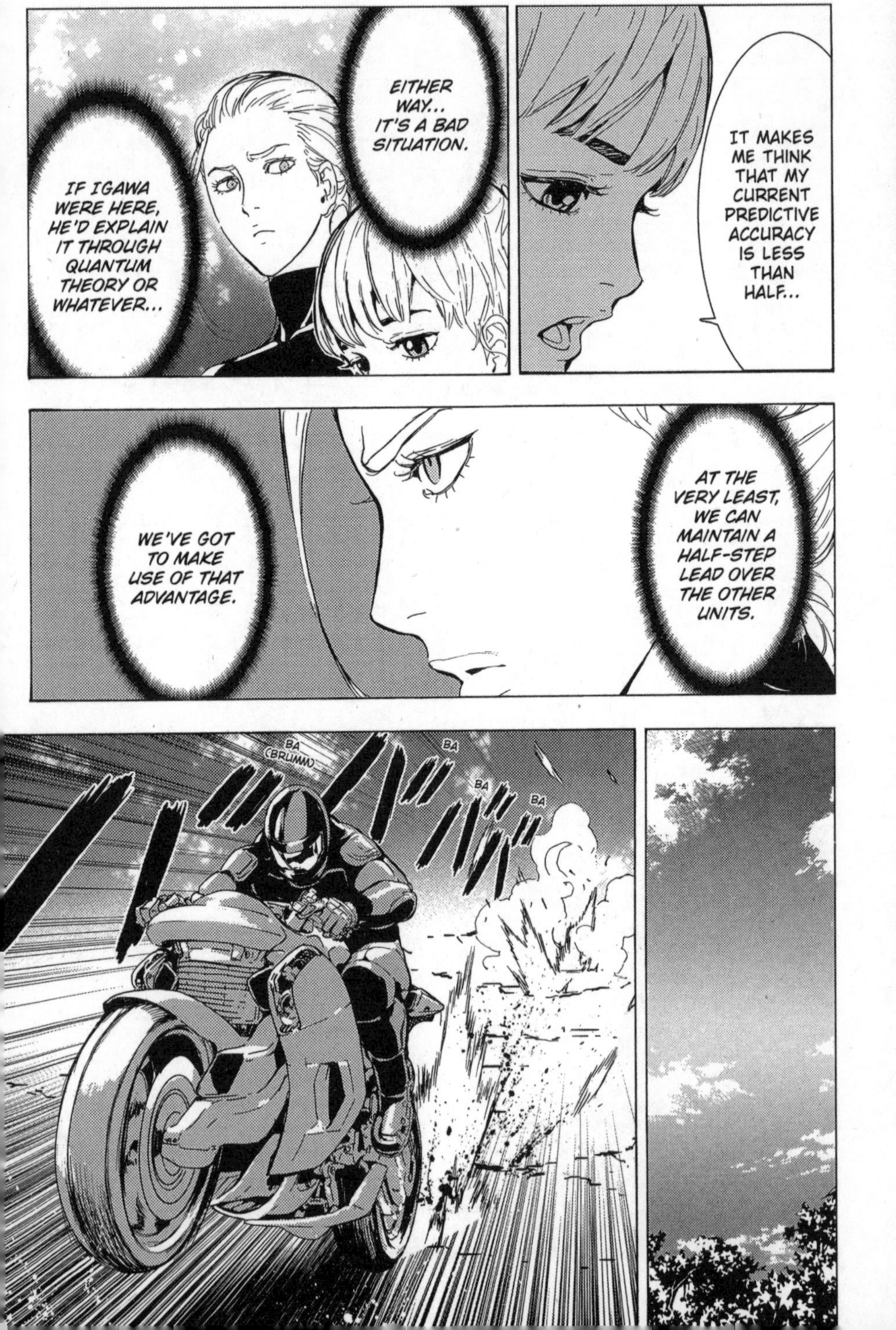
IT MAKES ME THINK THAT MY CURRENT PREDICTIVE ACCURACY IS LESS THAN HALF...
EITHER WAY... IT'S A BAD SITUATION.
IF IGAWA WERE HERE, HE'D EXPLAIN IT THROUGH QUANTUM THEORY OR WHATEVER...
AT THE VERY LEAST, WE CAN MAINTAIN A HALF-STEP LEAD OVER THE OTHER UNITS.
WE'VE GOT TO MAKE USE OF THAT ADVANTAGE.
BA (BRUMM)
BA
BA
BA

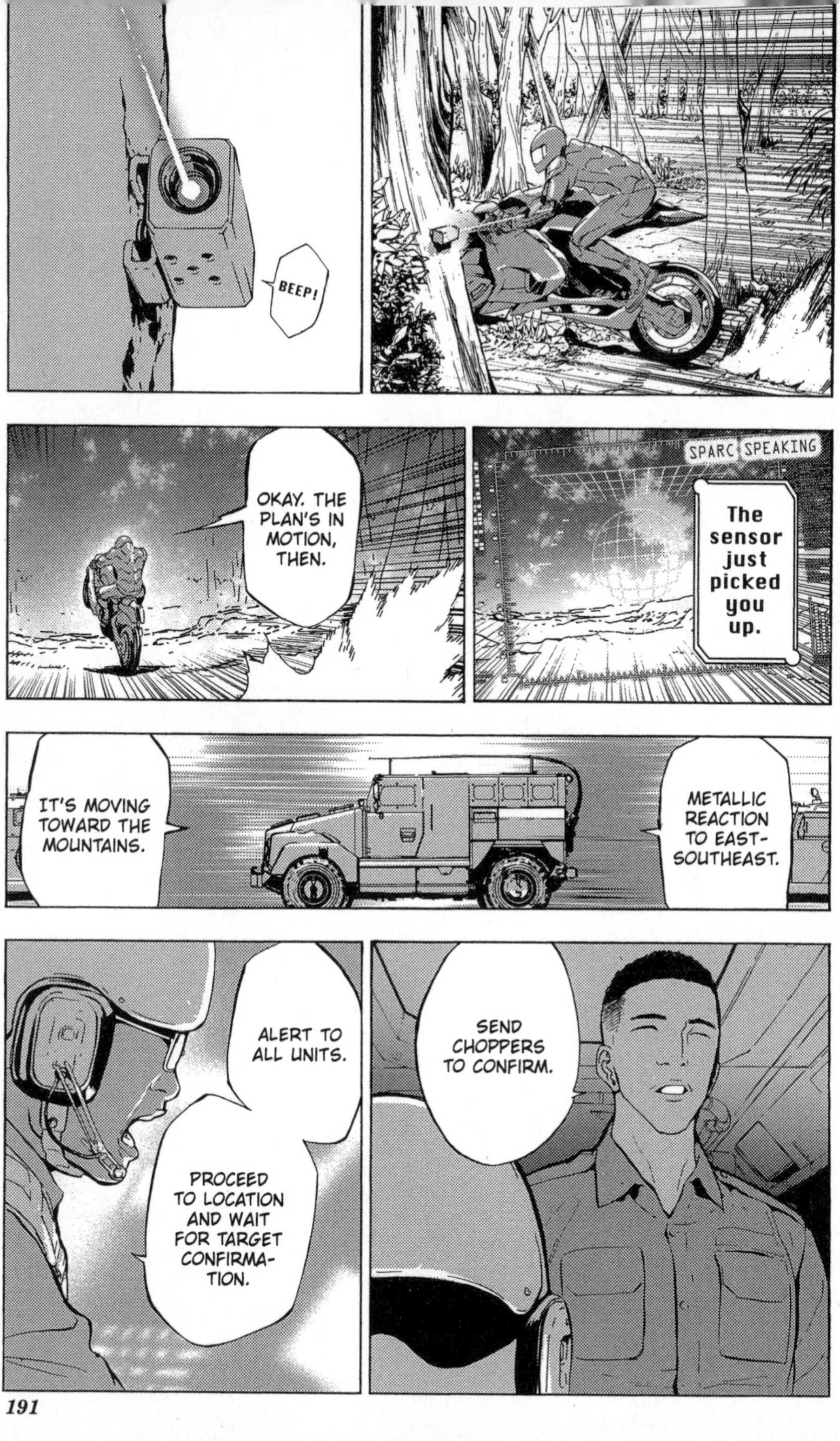
BEEP!
SPARC SPEAKING
The sensor just picked you up.
OKAY. THE PLAN'S IN MOTION, THEN.
METALLIC REACTION TO EAST-SOUTHEAST.
IT'S MOVING TOWARD THE MOUNTAINS.
SEND CHOPPERS TO CONFIRM.
ALERT TO ALL UNITS.
PROCEED TO LOCATION AND WAIT FOR TARGET CONFIRMATION.

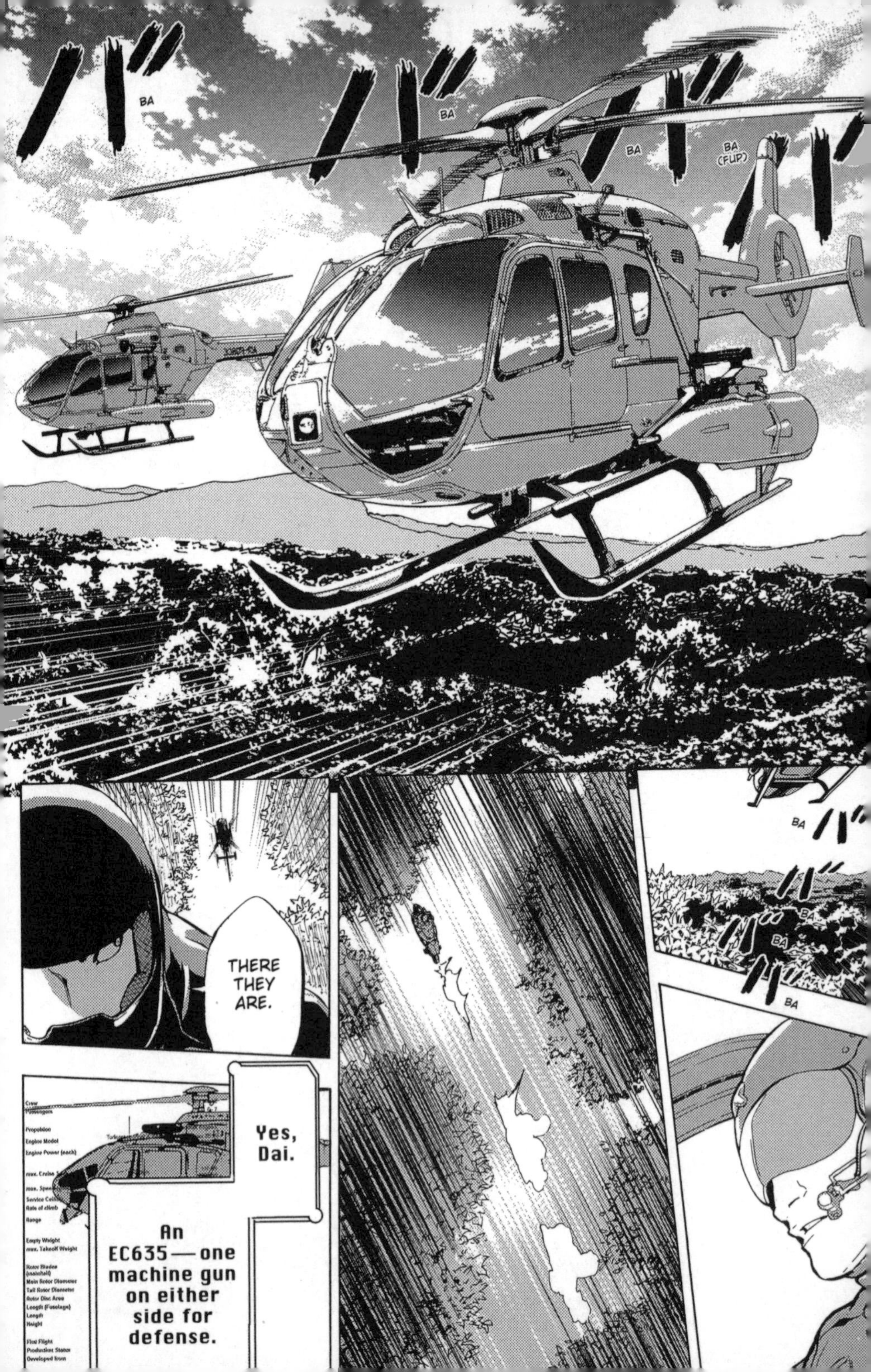
BA
(FLIP)
BA
BA
BA
BA
BA
BA
BA
THERE THEY ARE.
Yes, Dai.
An EC635—one machine gun on either side for defense.

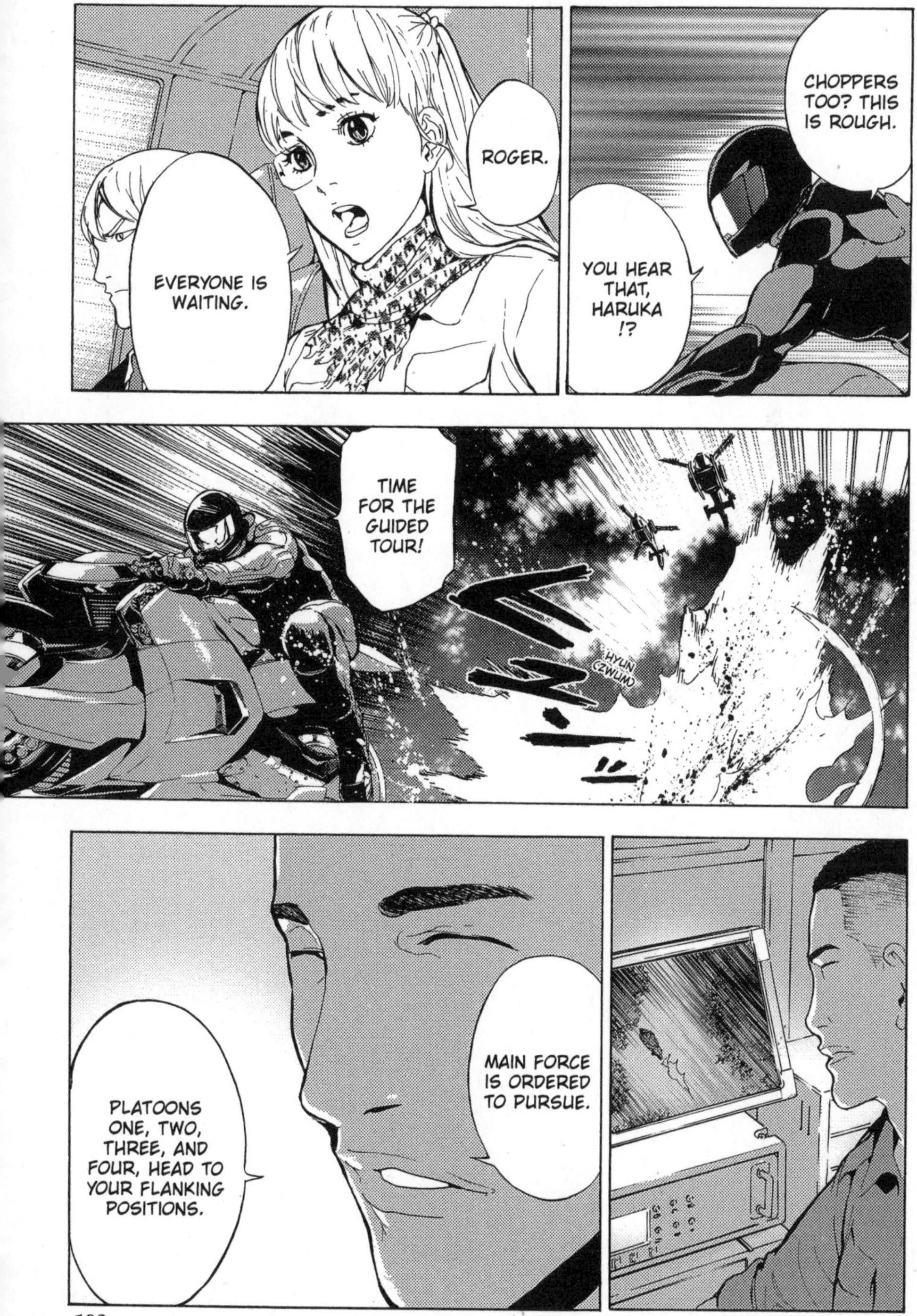
CHOPPERS TOO? THIS IS ROUGH.
YOU HEAR THAT, HARUKA!?
ROGER.
EVERYONE IS WAITING.
TIME FOR THE GUIDED TOUR!
HYUN (ZWUM)
MAIN FORCE IS ORDERED TO PURSUE.
PLATOONS ONE, TWO, THREE, AND FOUR, HEAD TO YOUR FLANKING POSITIONS.

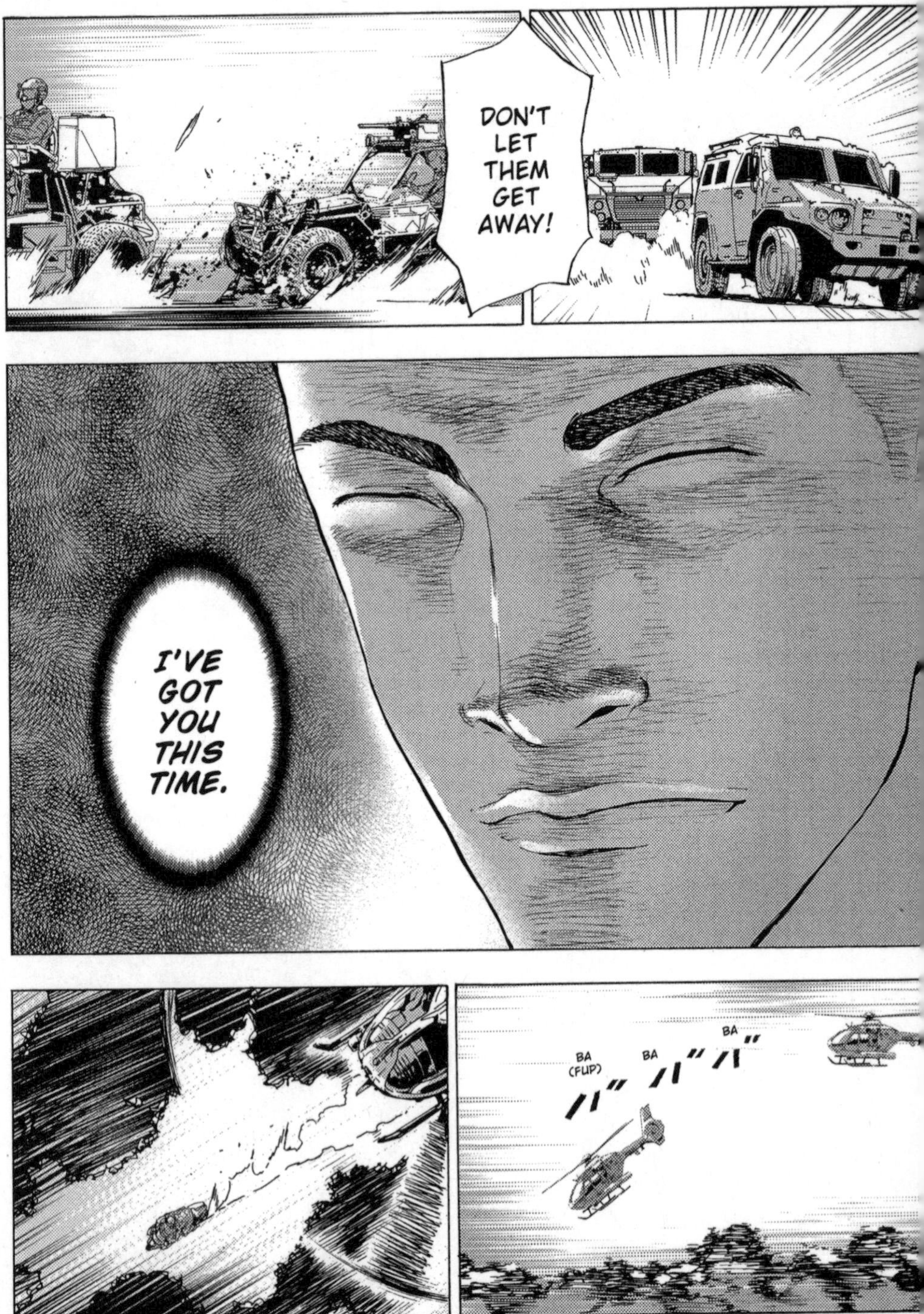
DON'T LET THEM GET AWAY!
I'VE GOT YOU THIS TIME.
BA (FUP)
BA
BA

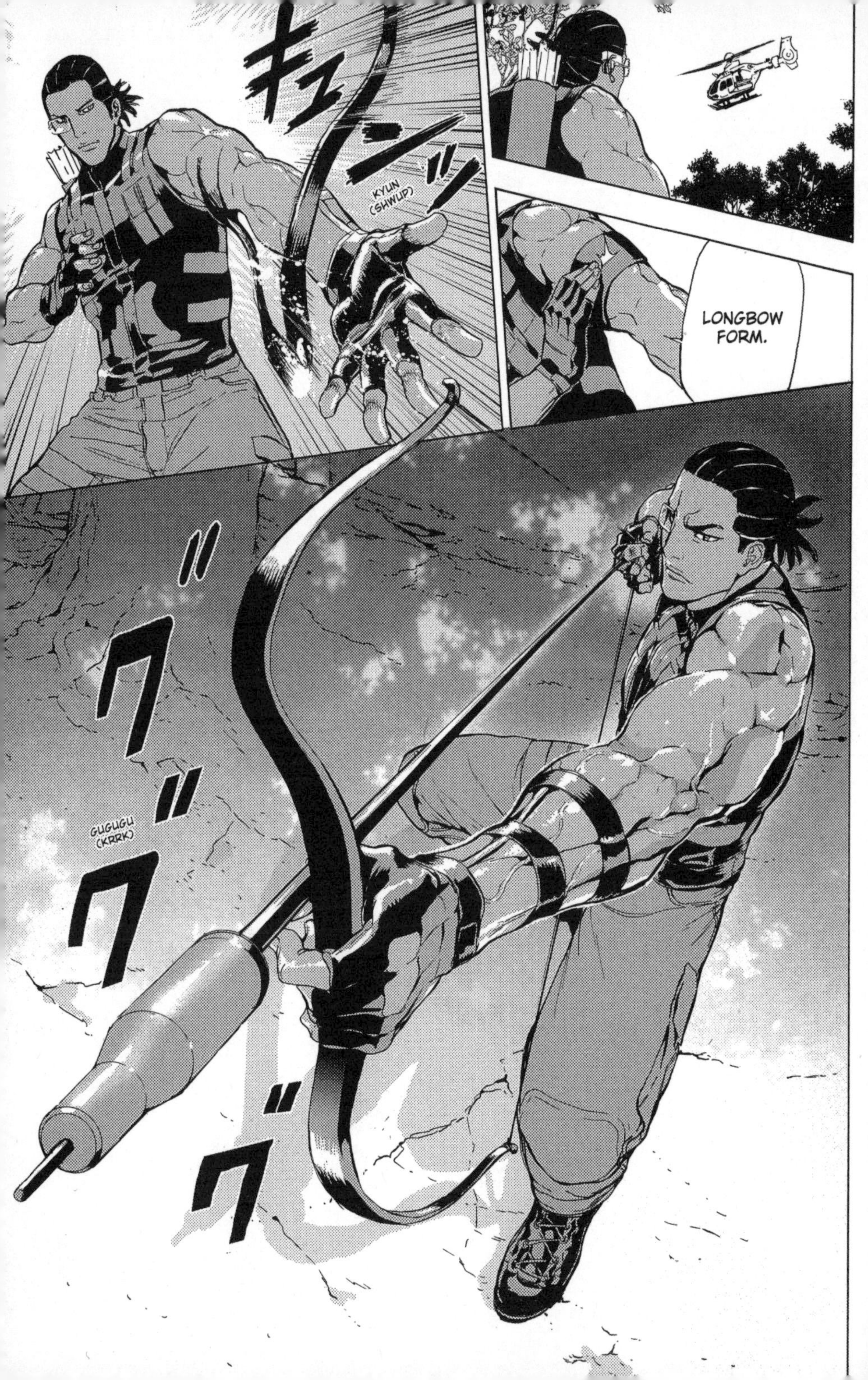
LONGBOW FORM.
KYUN (SHWUP)
GUGUGU (KRRK)

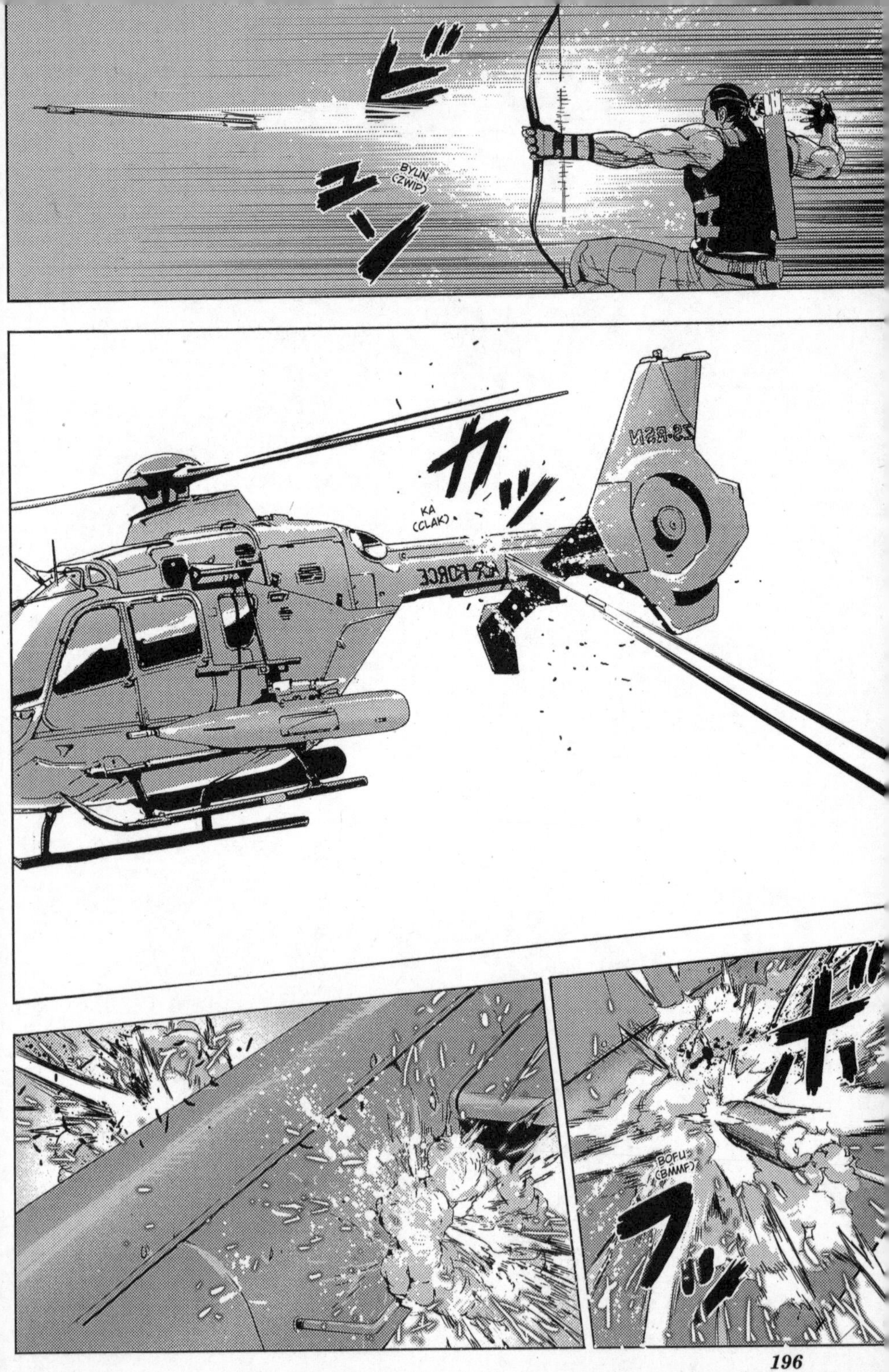
BYUN
(ZWIP)
KA
(CLAK)
BOFU
(BMMF)

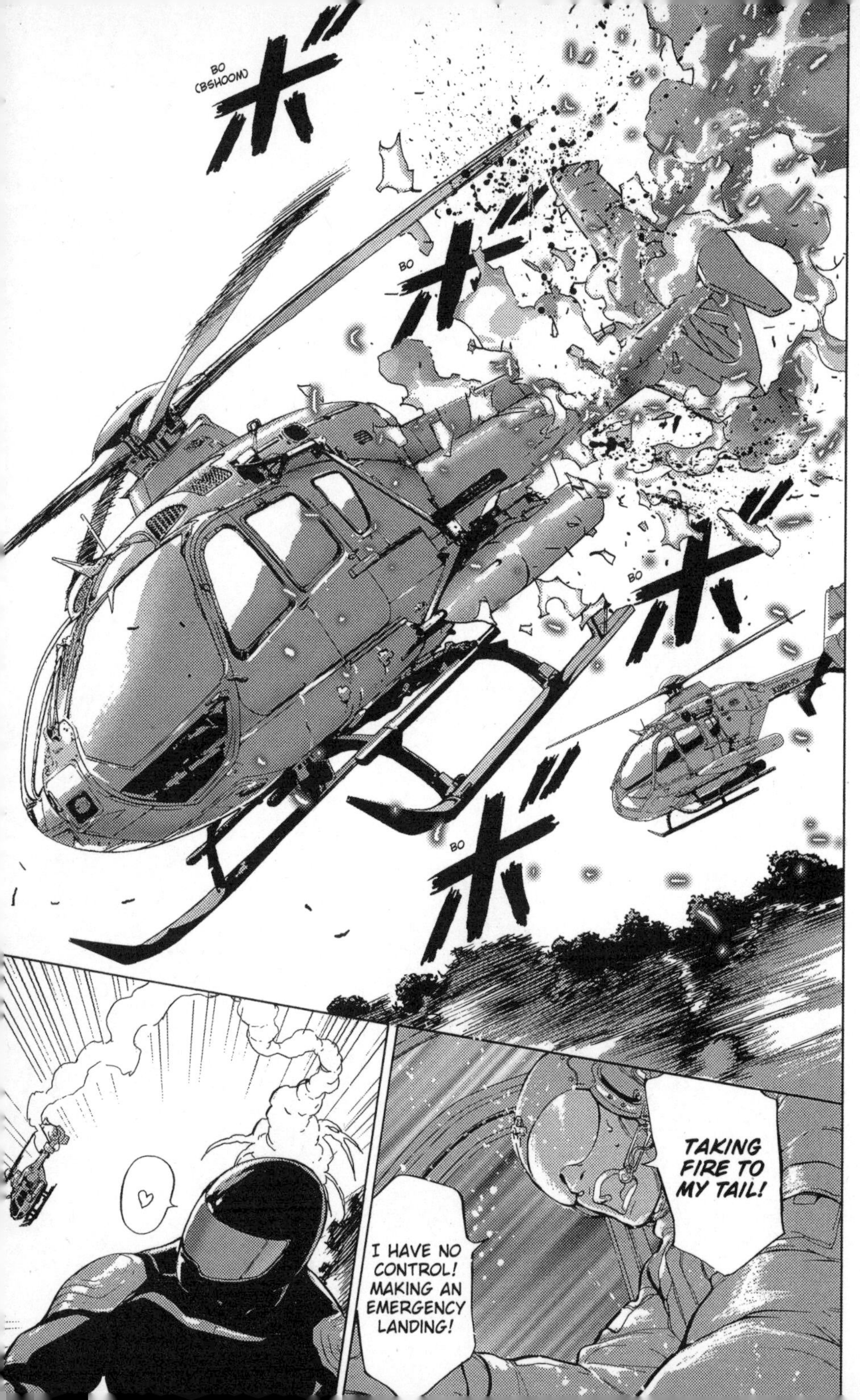
ボ
BO
(BSHOOM)
ボ
BO
ボ
BO
ボ
BO
TAKING FIRE TO MY TAIL!
I HAVE NO CONTROL! MAKING AN EMERGENCY LANDING!

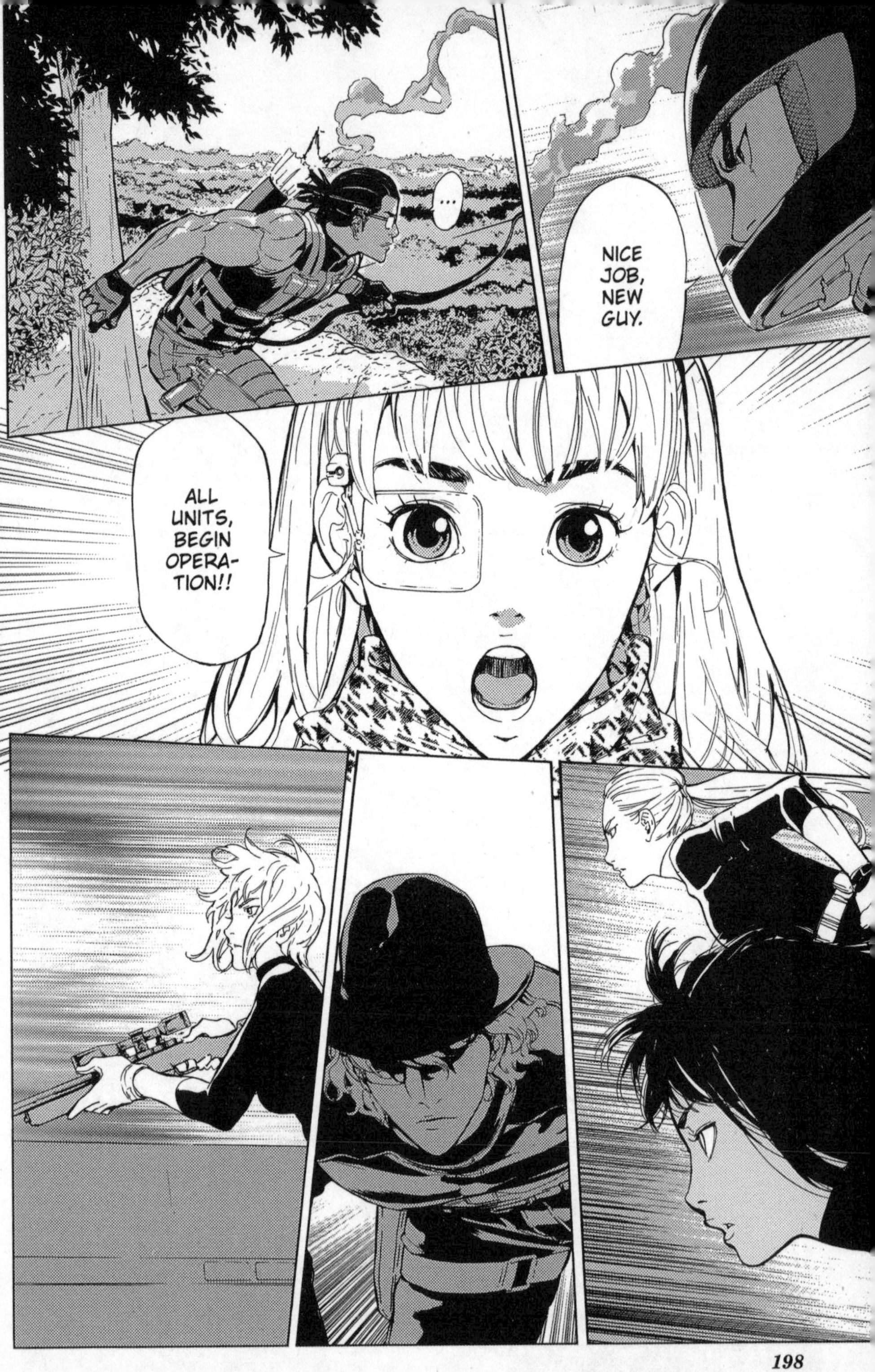
NICE JOB, NEW GUY.
...
ALL UNITS, BEGIN OPERATION!!

Until Death do us Part

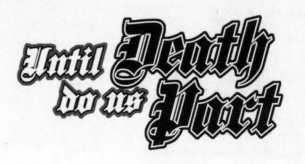

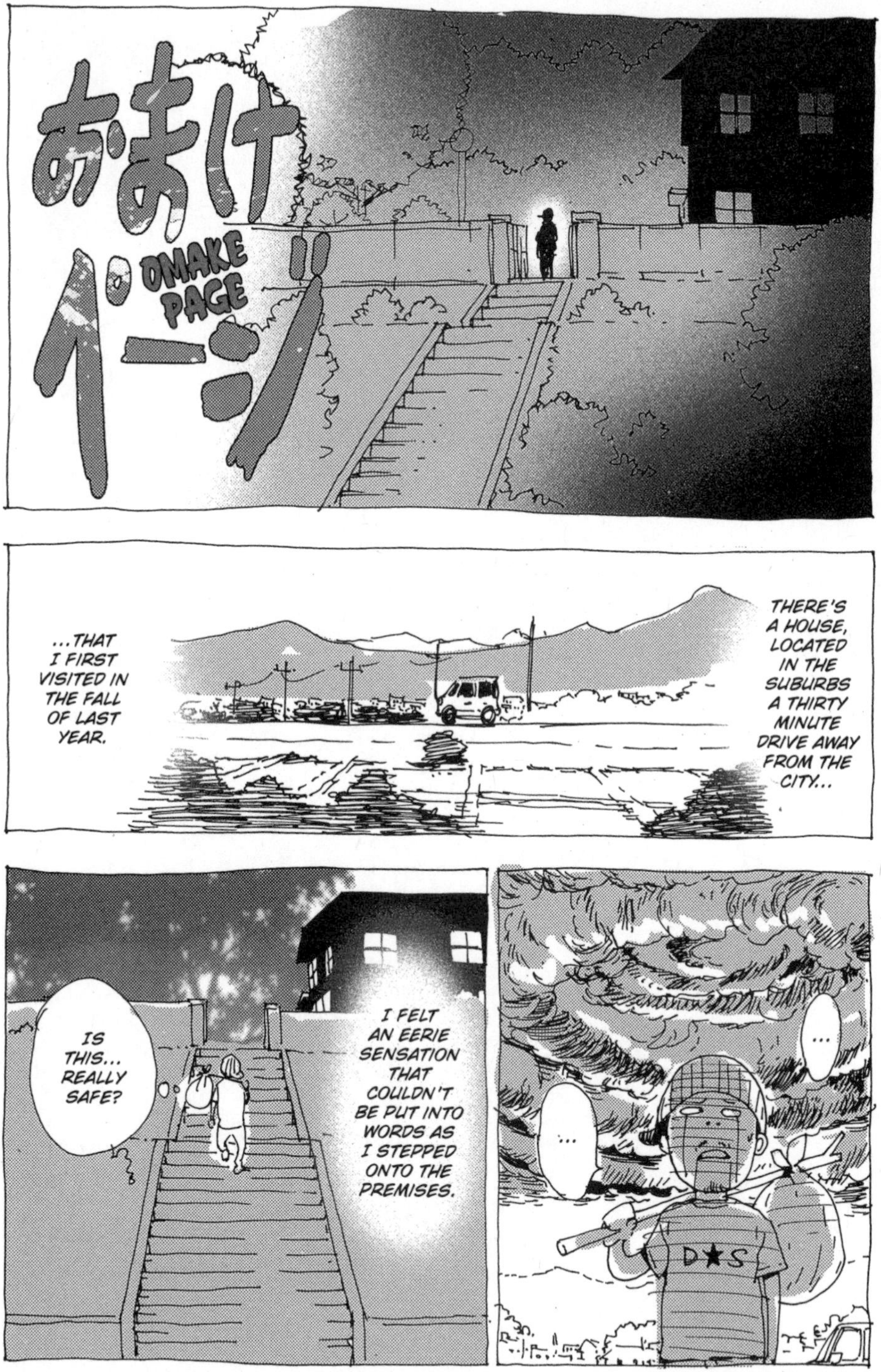
おまけページ
OMAKE PAGE
THERE'S A HOUSE, LOCATED IN THE SUBURBS A THIRTY MINUTE DRIVE AWAY FROM THE CITY...
...THAT I FIRST VISITED IN THE FALL OF LAST YEAR.
...
...
D★S
I FELT AN EERIE SENSATION THAT COULDN'T BE PUT INTO WORDS AS I STEPPED ONTO THE PREMISES.
IS THIS... REALLY SAFE?

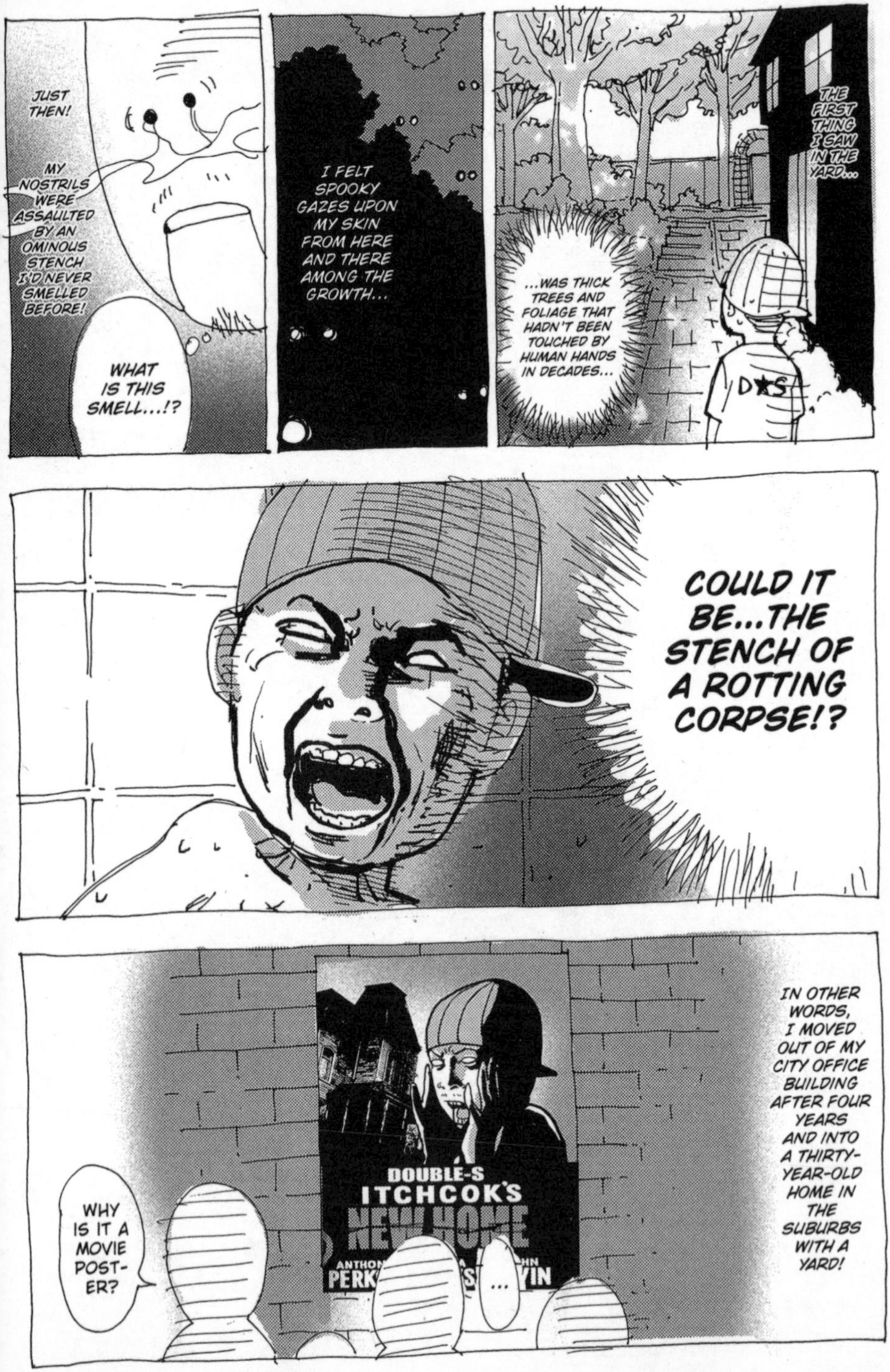
THE FIRST THING I SAW IN THE YARD...
...WAS THICK TREES AND FOLIAGE THAT HADN'T BEEN TOUCHED BY HUMAN HANDS IN DECADES...
I FELT SPOOKY GAZES UPON MY SKIN FROM HERE AND THERE AMONG THE GROWTH...
JUST THEN!
MY NOSTRILS WERE ASSAULTED BY AN OMINOUS STENCH I'D NEVER SMELLED BEFORE!
WHAT IS THIS SMELL...!?
COULD IT BE...THE STENCH OF A ROTTING CORPSE!?
IN OTHER WORDS, I MOVED OUT OF MY CITY OFFICE BUILDING AFTER FOUR YEARS AND INTO A THIRTY-YEAR-OLD HOME IN THE SUBURBS WITH A YARD!
DOUBLE-S
ITCHCOK'S
...
WHY IS IT A MOVIE POSTER?

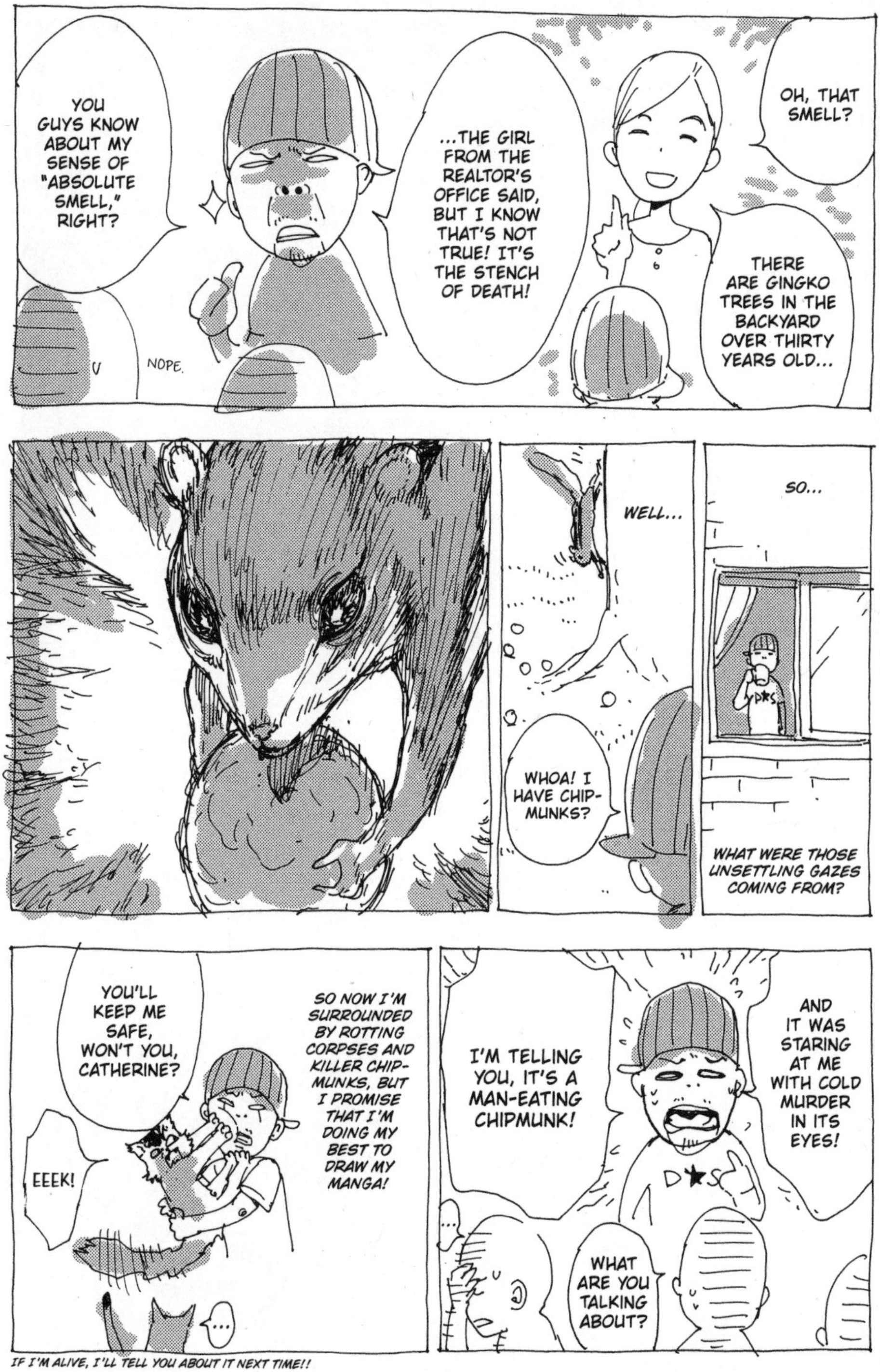
OH, THAT SMELL?
THERE ARE GINGKO TREES IN THE BACKYARD OVER THIRTY YEARS OLD...
...THE GIRL FROM THE REALTOR'S OFFICE SAID, BUT I KNOW THAT'S NOT TRUE! IT'S THE STENCH OF DEATH!
YOU GUYS KNOW ABOUT MY SENSE OF "ABSOLUTE SMELL," RIGHT?
NOPE.
SO...
WHAT WERE THOSE UNSETTLING GAZES COMING FROM?
WELL...
WHOA! I HAVE CHIPMUNKS?
AND IT WAS STARING AT ME WITH COLD MURDER IN ITS EYES!
I'M TELLING YOU, IT'S A MAN-EATING CHIPMUNK!
WHAT ARE YOU TALKING ABOUT?
...
SO NOW I'M SURROUNDED BY ROTTING CORPSES AND KILLER CHIPMUNKS, BUT I PROMISE THAT I'M DOING MY BEST TO DRAW MY MANGA!
YOU'LL KEEP ME SAFE, WON'T YOU, CATHERINE?
EEEK!
...

IF I'M ALIVE, I'LL TELL YOU ABOUT IT NEXT TIME!!

THE CONTINUING(?) ADVENTURES OF POLICE CAT CATHERINE

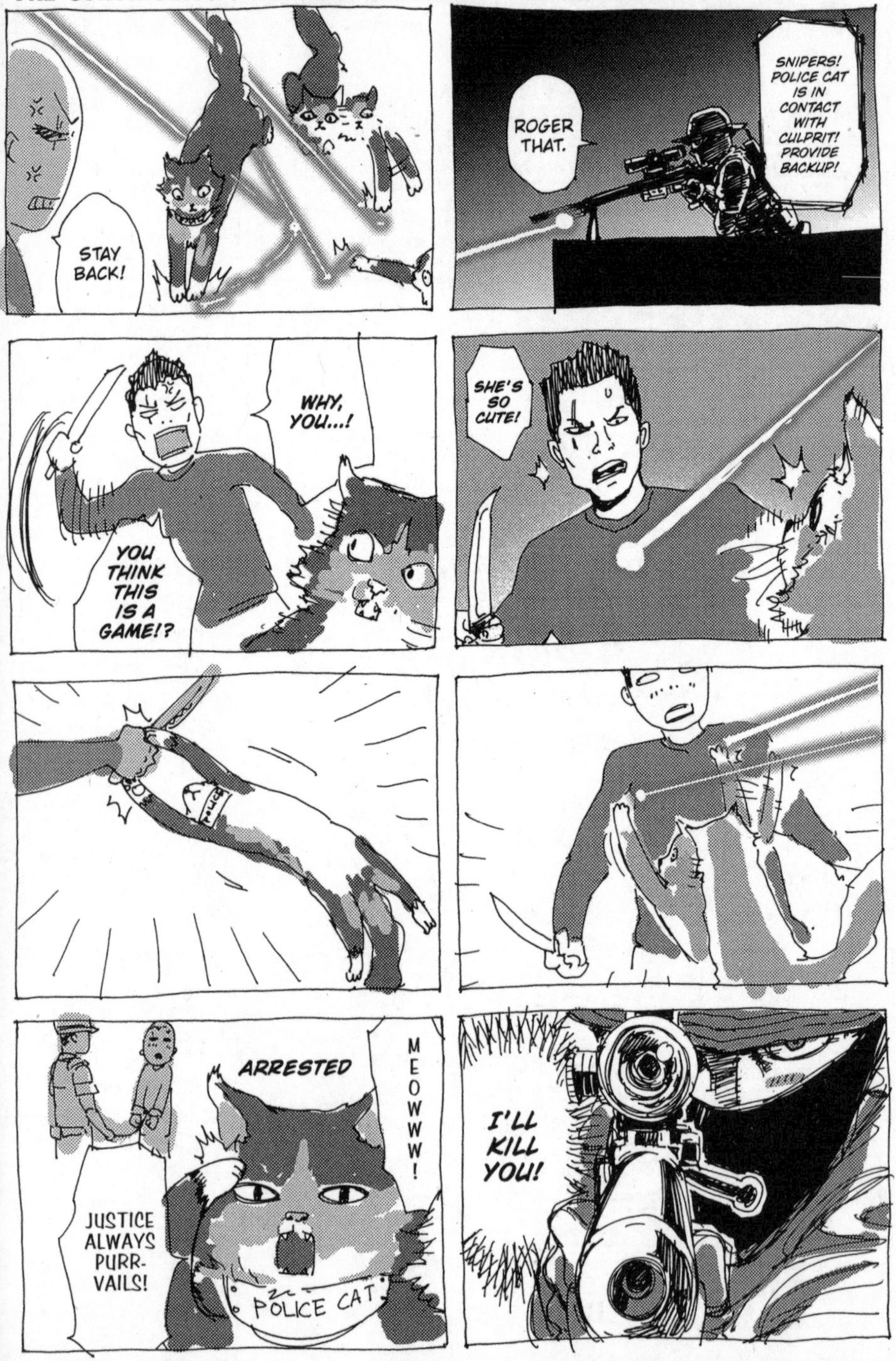

SNIPERS! POLICE CAT IS IN CONTACT WITH CULPRIT! PROVIDE BACKUP!
ROGER THAT.
STAY BACK!
SHE'S SO CUTE!
WHY, YOU...!
YOU THINK THIS IS A GAME!?
I'LL KILL YOU!
MEOWWW!
ARRESTED
JUSTICE ALWAYS PURR-VAILS!
POLICE CAT

Art Staff
hansil ♀: Background Art/Screentone
noeri ♀: Background Art/Screentone

Military Advisor
Lee Hyun Seok (warmania)

Special Thanks
Shingo Takano

Crossover Planning
JESUS—Sajin Kouro, Yami no Aegis, Akatsuki no Aegis
Written by Kyouichi Nanatsuki, Art by Yoshihide Fujiwara
(Shogakukan)

Design Assistance
Hitoshi Fukuchi

Until Death do us Part

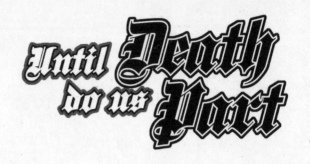

chapter 187

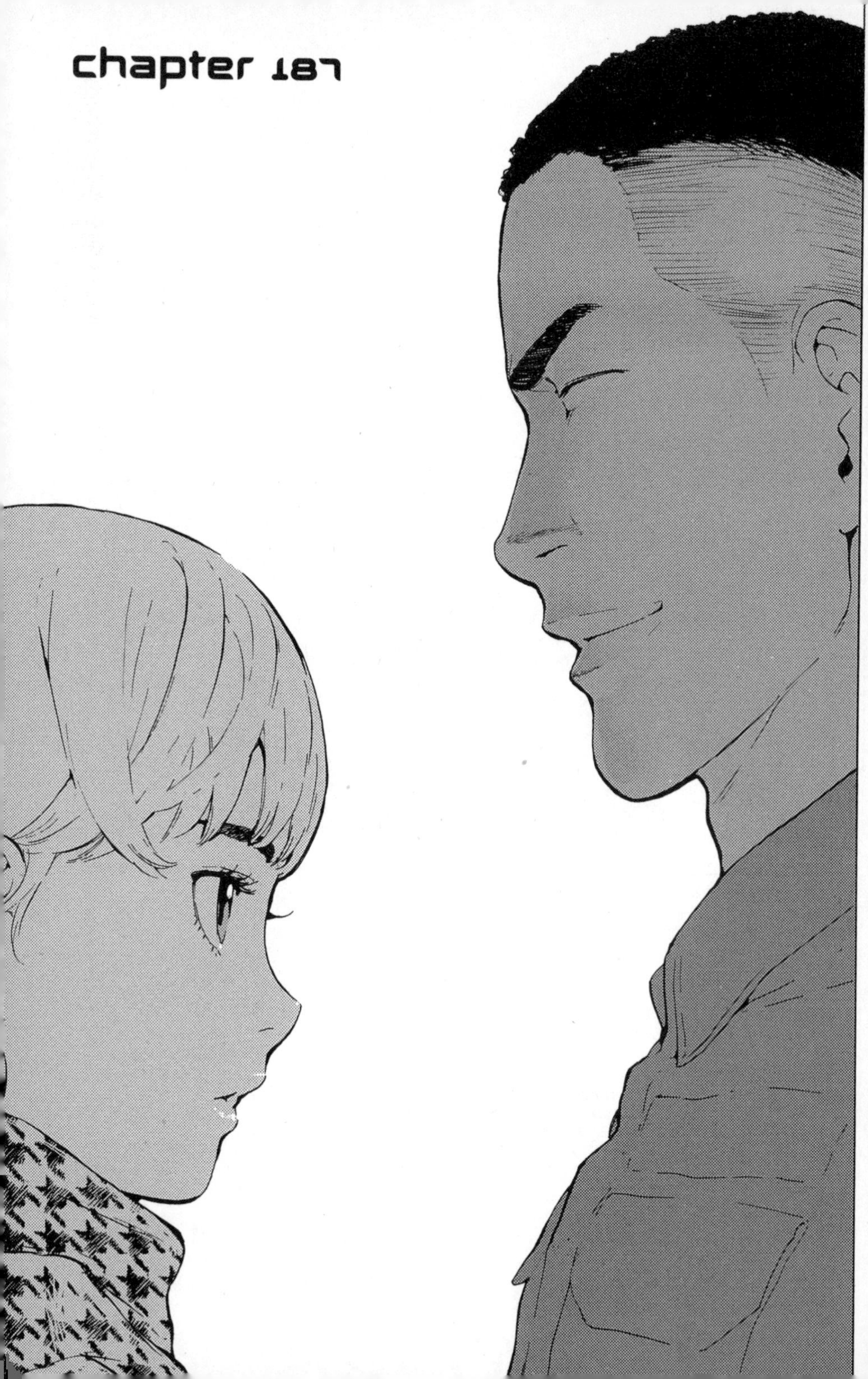

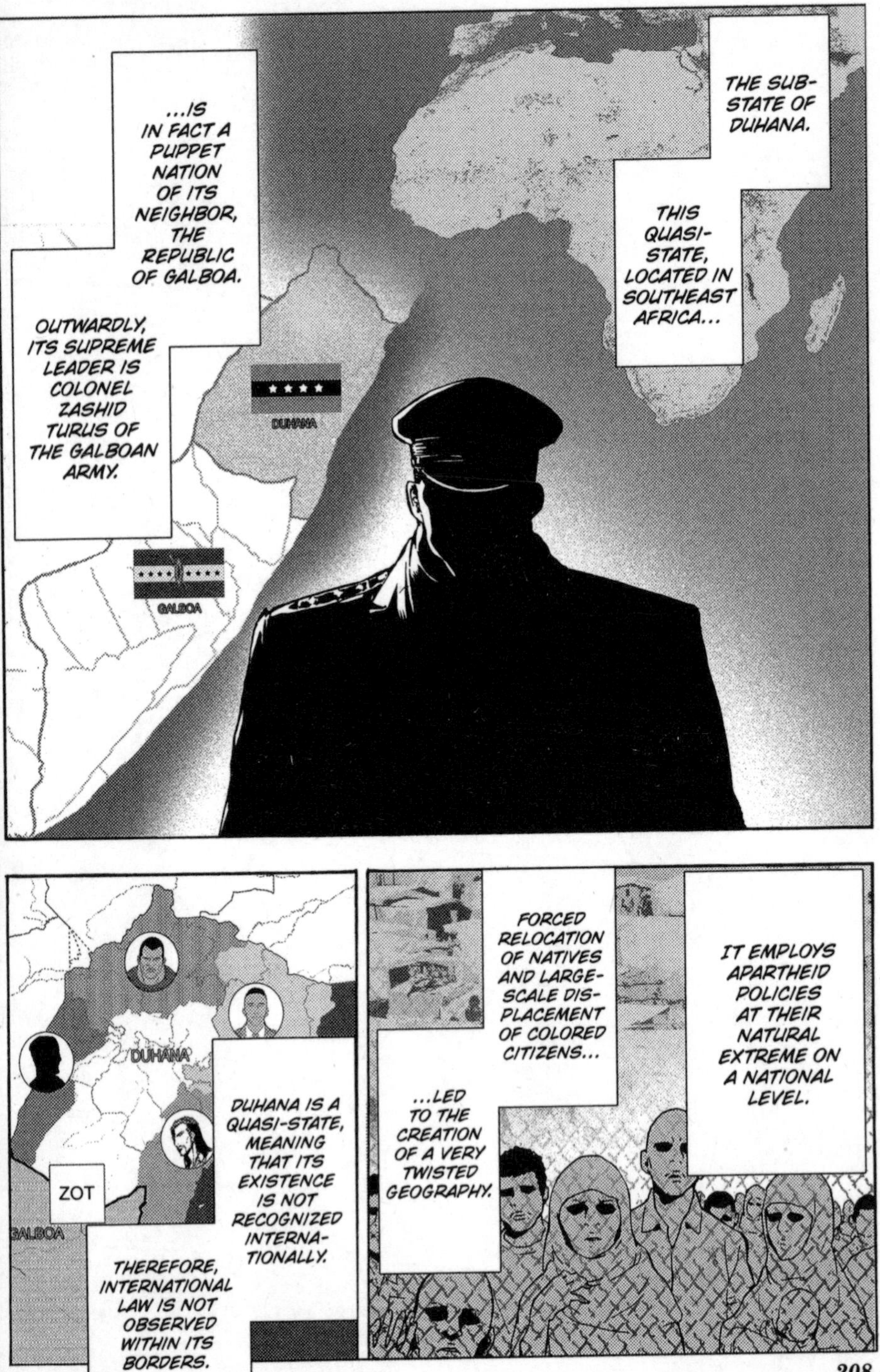
THE SUB-STATE OF DUHANA.
THIS QUASI-STATE, LOCATED IN SOUTHEAST AFRICA...
...IS IN FACT A PUPPET NATION OF ITS NEIGHBOR, THE REPUBLIC OF GALBOA.
OUTWARDLY, ITS SUPREME LEADER IS COLONEL ZASHID TURUS OF THE GALBOAN ARMY.
DUHANA
GALBOA
IT EMPLOYS APARTHEID POLICIES AT THEIR NATURAL EXTREME ON A NATIONAL LEVEL.
FORCED RELOCATION OF NATIVES AND LARGE-SCALE DISPLACEMENT OF COLORED CITIZENS...
...LED TO THE CREATION OF A VERY TWISTED GEOGRAPHY.
DUHANA
ZOT
GALBOA
DUHANA IS A QUASI-STATE, MEANING THAT ITS EXISTENCE IS NOT RECOGNIZED INTERNATIONALLY.
THEREFORE, INTERNATIONAL LAW IS NOT OBSERVED WITHIN ITS BORDERS.

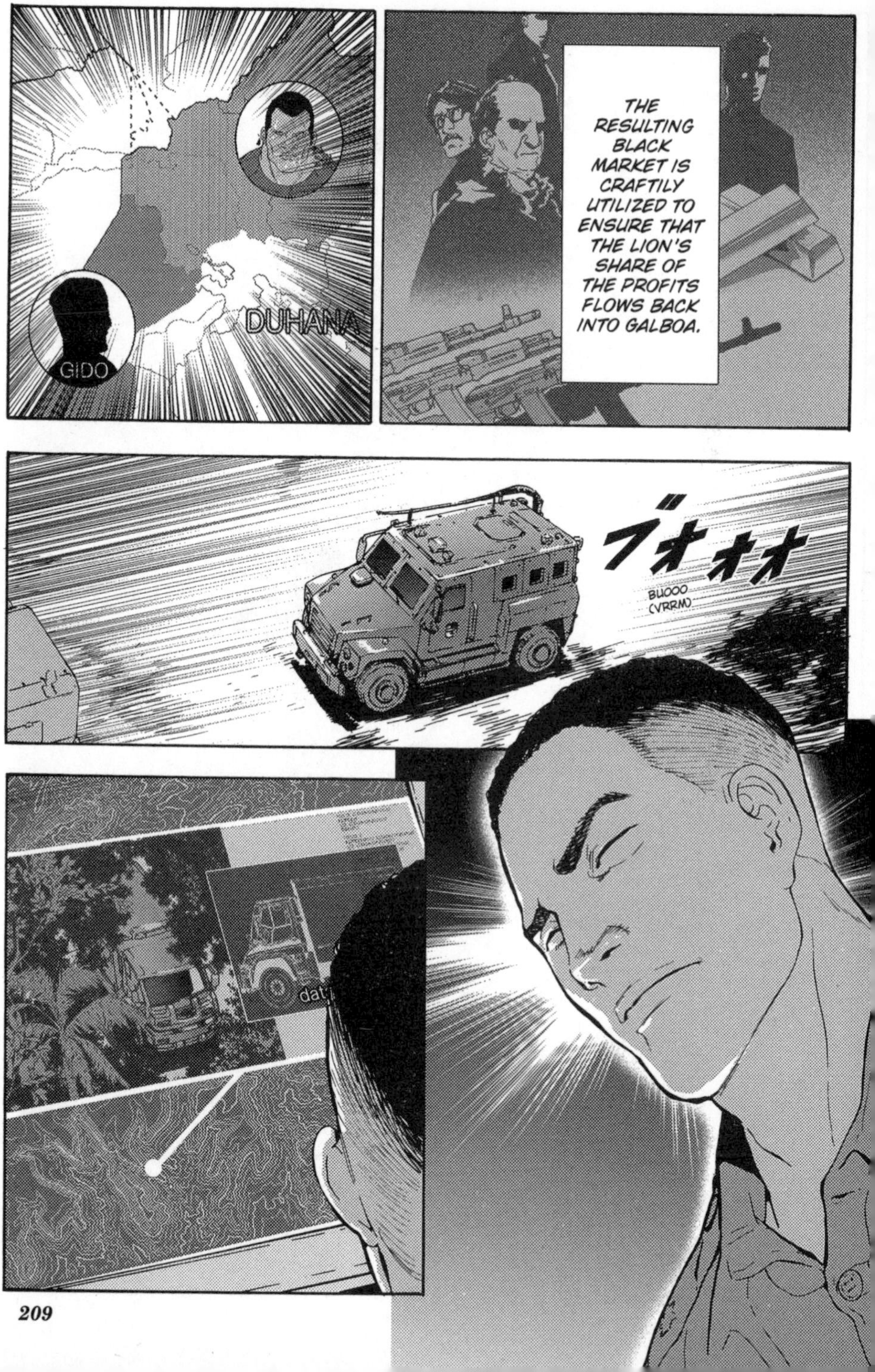
THE RESULTING BLACK MARKET IS CRAFTILY UTILIZED TO ENSURE THAT THE LION'S SHARE OF THE PROFITS FLOWS BACK INTO GALBOA.
DUHANA
GIDO
ブォォォ
BUOOO (VRRM)

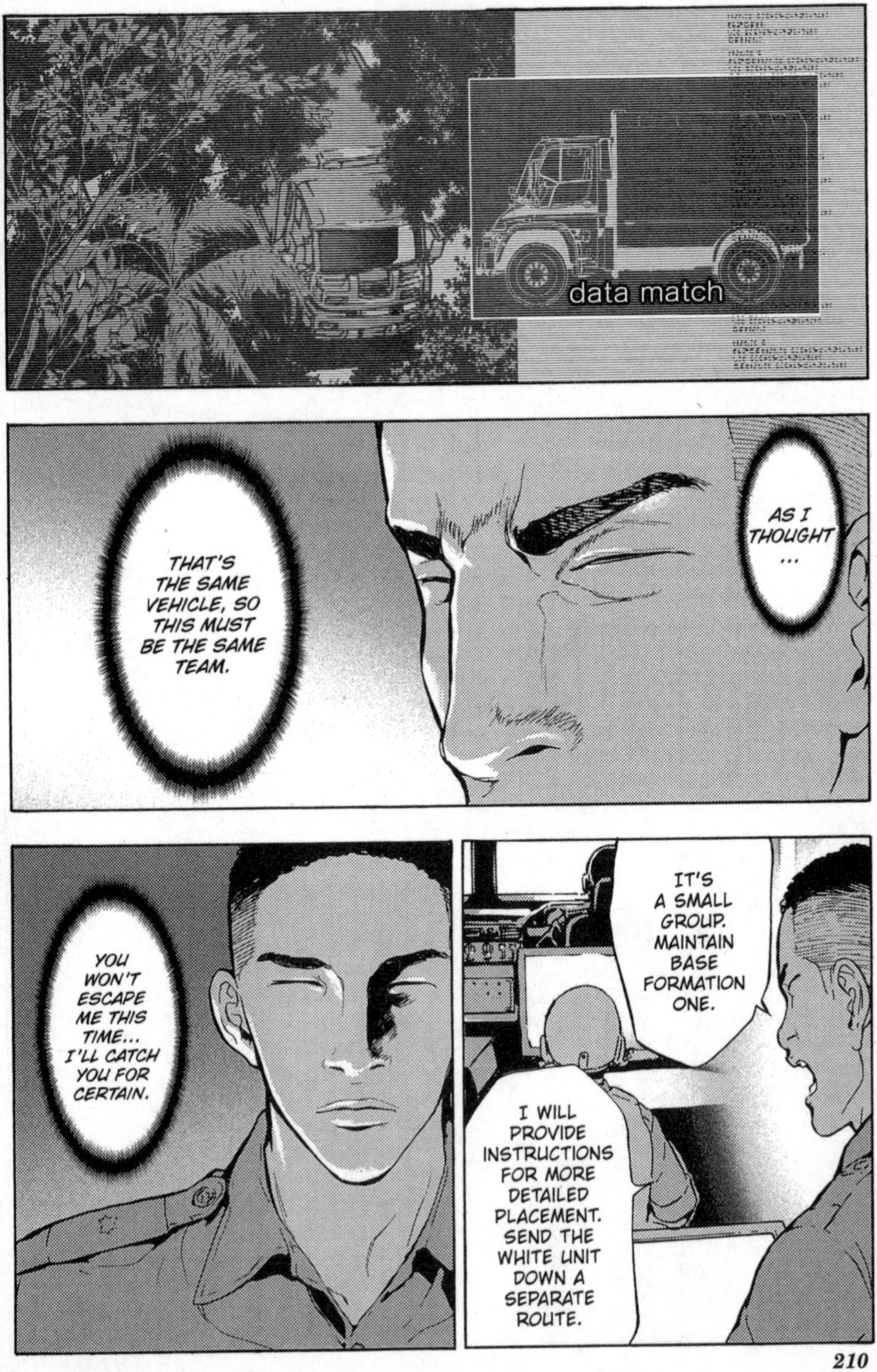
data match
AS I THOUGHT...
THAT'S THE SAME VEHICLE, SO THIS MUST BE THE SAME TEAM.
IT'S A SMALL GROUP. MAINTAIN BASE FORMATION ONE.
I WILL PROVIDE INSTRUCTIONS FOR MORE DETAILED PLACEMENT. SEND THE WHITE UNIT DOWN A SEPARATE ROUTE.
YOU WON'T ESCAPE ME THIS TIME... I'LL CATCH YOU FOR CERTAIN.

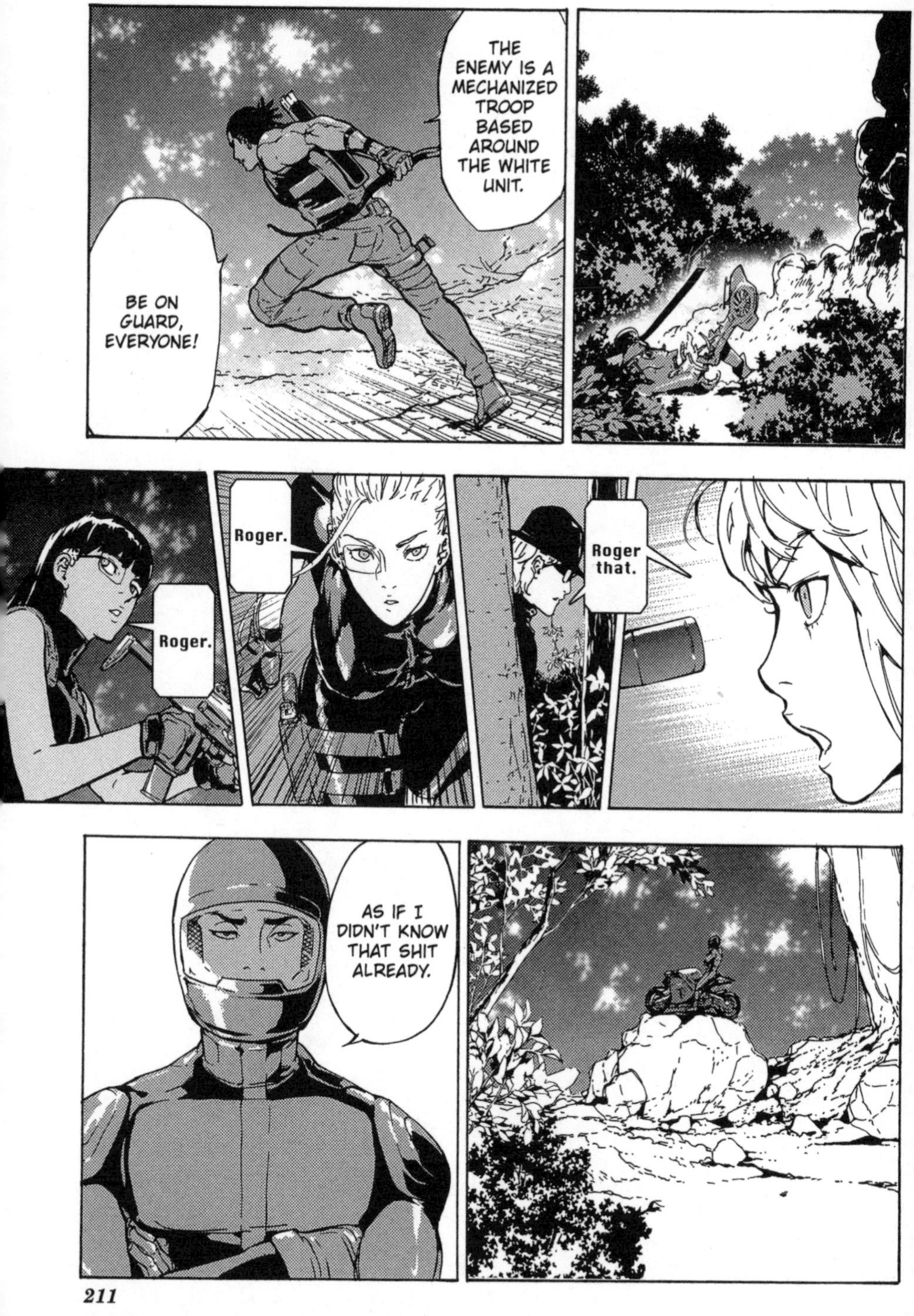
THE ENEMY IS A MECHANIZED TROOP BASED AROUND THE WHITE UNIT.
BE ON GUARD, EVERYONE!
Roger that.
Roger.
Roger.
AS IF I DIDN'T KNOW THAT SHIT ALREADY.

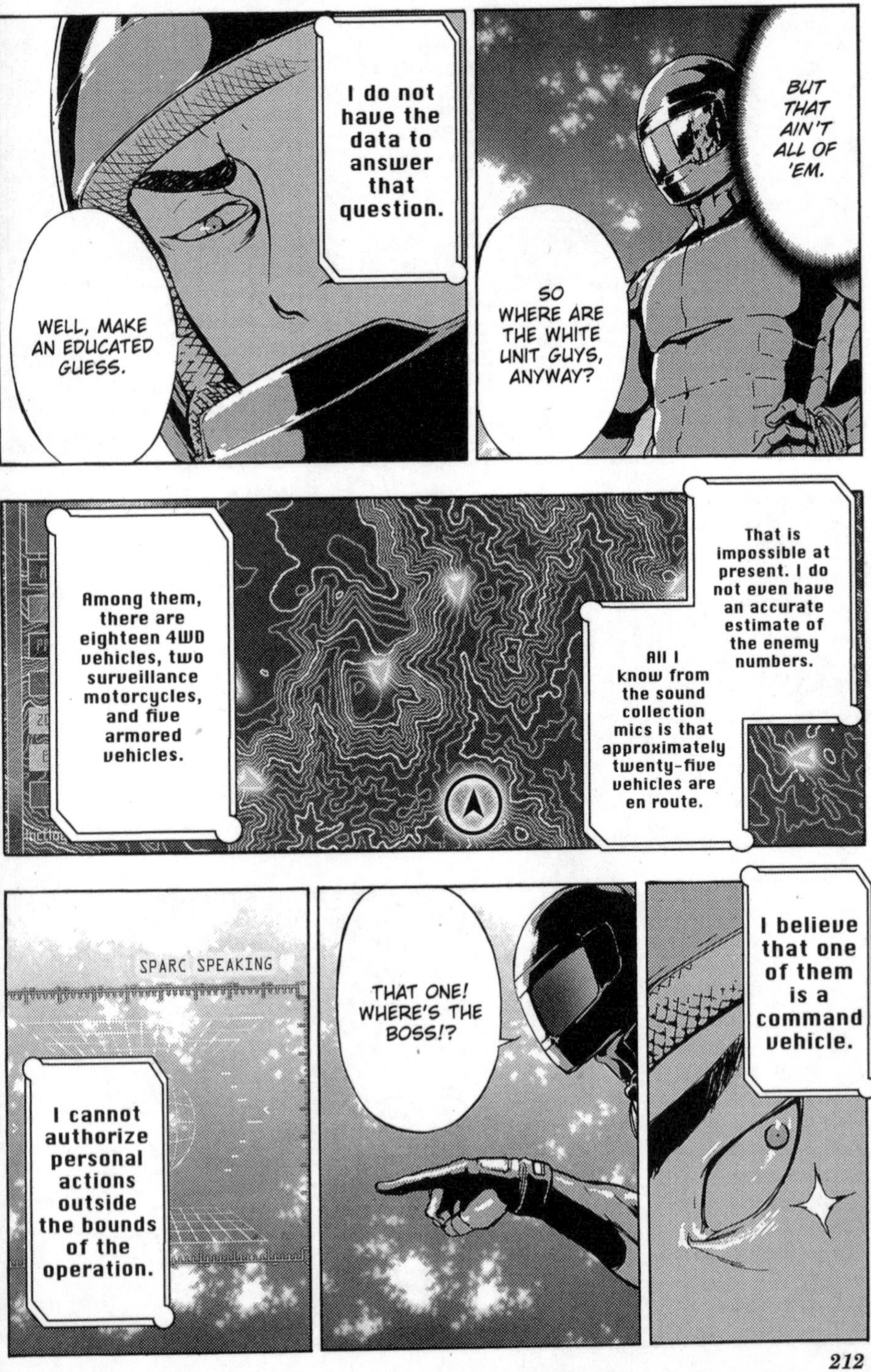
BUT THAT AIN'T ALL OF 'EM.
SO WHERE ARE THE WHITE UNIT GUYS, ANYWAY?
I do not have the data to answer that question.
WELL, MAKE AN EDUCATED GUESS.
That is impossible at present. I do not even have an accurate estimate of the enemy numbers.
All I know from the sound collection mics is that approximately twenty-five vehicles are en route.
Among them, there are eighteen 4WD vehicles, two surveillance motorcycles, and five armored vehicles.
I believe that one of them is a command vehicle.
THAT ONE! WHERE'S THE BOSS!?
SPARC SPEAKING
I cannot authorize personal actions outside the bounds of the operation.

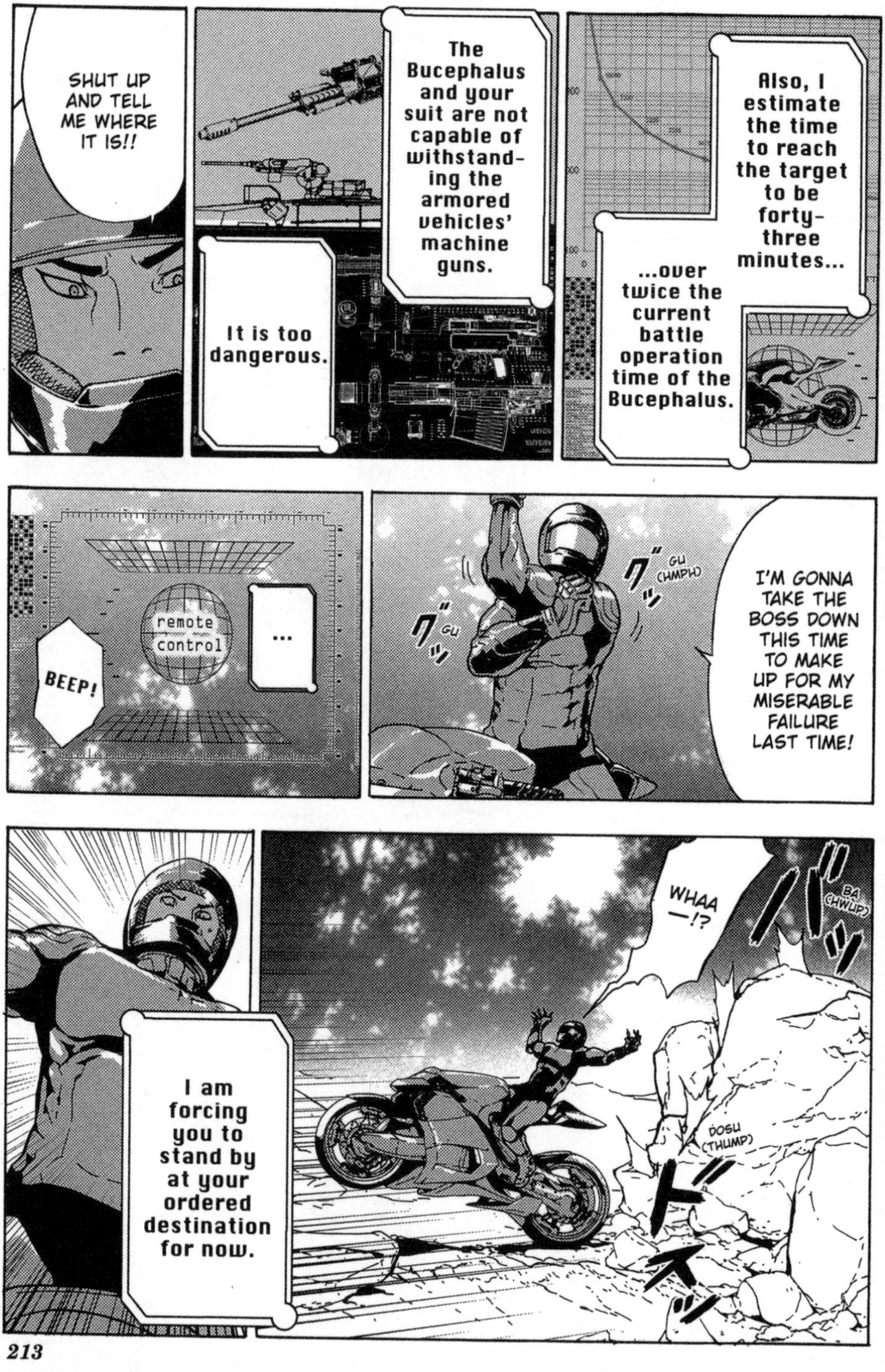
Also, I estimate the time to reach the target to be forty-three minutes...
...over twice the current battle operation time of the Bucephalus.
The Bucephalus and your suit are not capable of withstanding the armored vehicles' machine guns.
It is too dangerous.
SHUT UP AND TELL ME WHERE IT IS!!
I'M GONNA TAKE THE BOSS DOWN THIS TIME TO MAKE UP FOR MY MISERABLE FAILURE LAST TIME!
GU (HMPH)
GU
remote control
...
BEEP!
WHAA—!?
BA (HWUP)
DOSU (THUMP)
I am forcing you to stand by at your ordered destination for now.

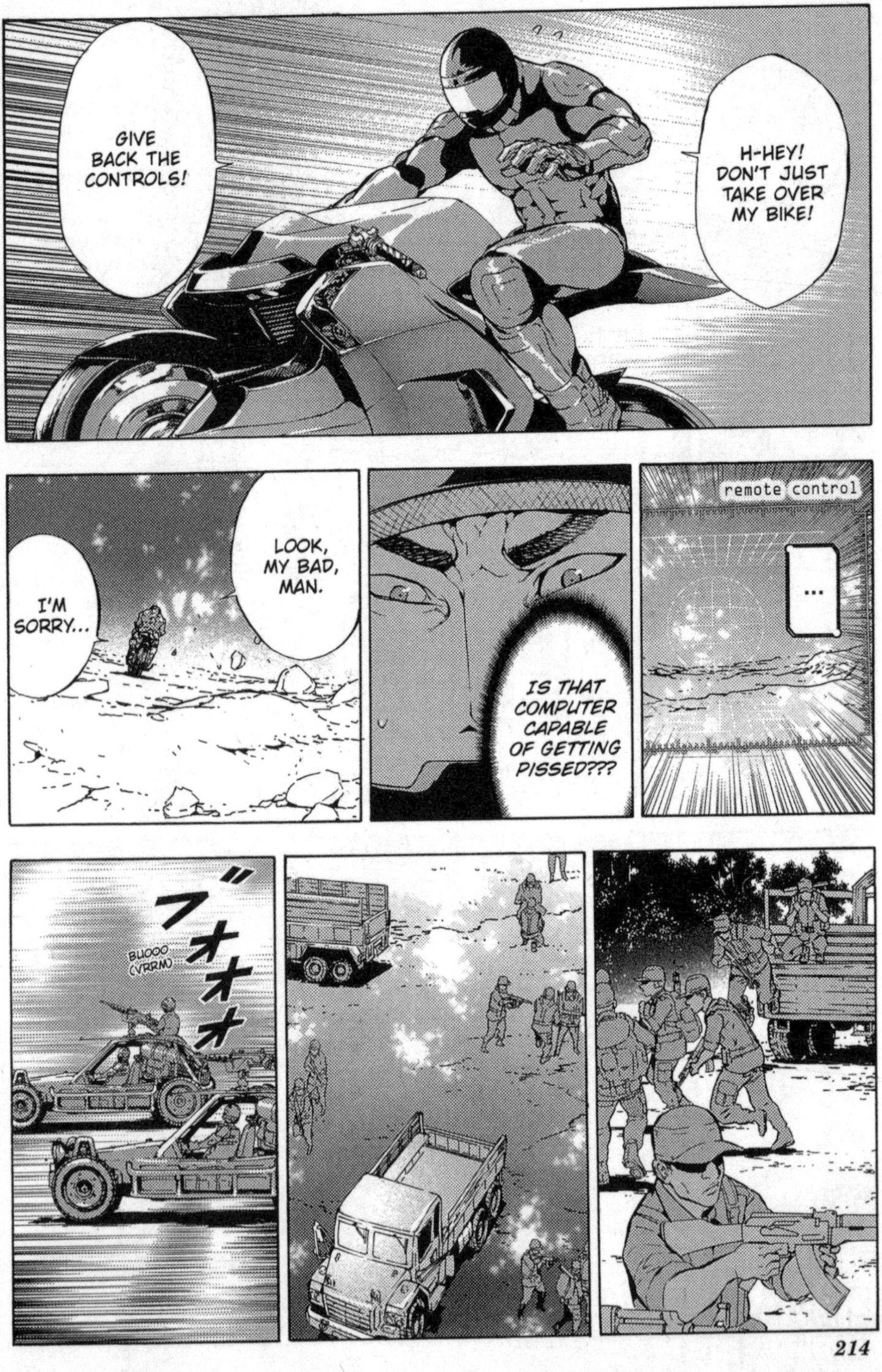
H-HEY! DON'T JUST TAKE OVER MY BIKE!
GIVE BACK THE CONTROLS!
remote control
...
IS THAT COMPUTER CAPABLE OF GETTING PISSED???
LOOK, MY BAD, MAN.
I'M SORRY...
ブオオオ
BUOOO (VRRM)

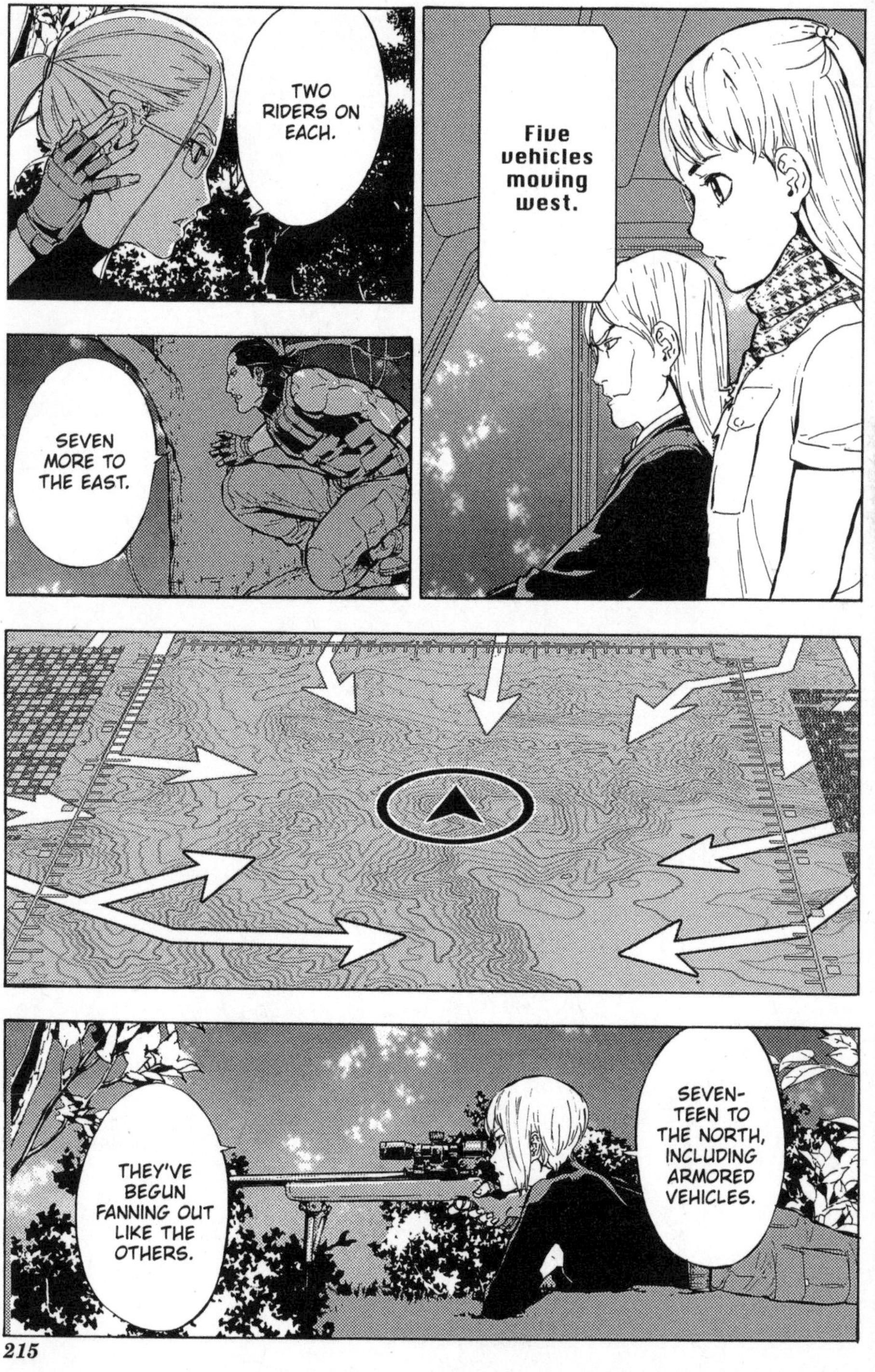
Five vehicles moving west.
TWO RIDERS ON EACH.
SEVEN MORE TO THE EAST.
SEVEN-TEEN TO THE NORTH, INCLUDING ARMORED VEHICLES.
THEY'VE BEGUN FANNING OUT LIKE THE OTHERS.

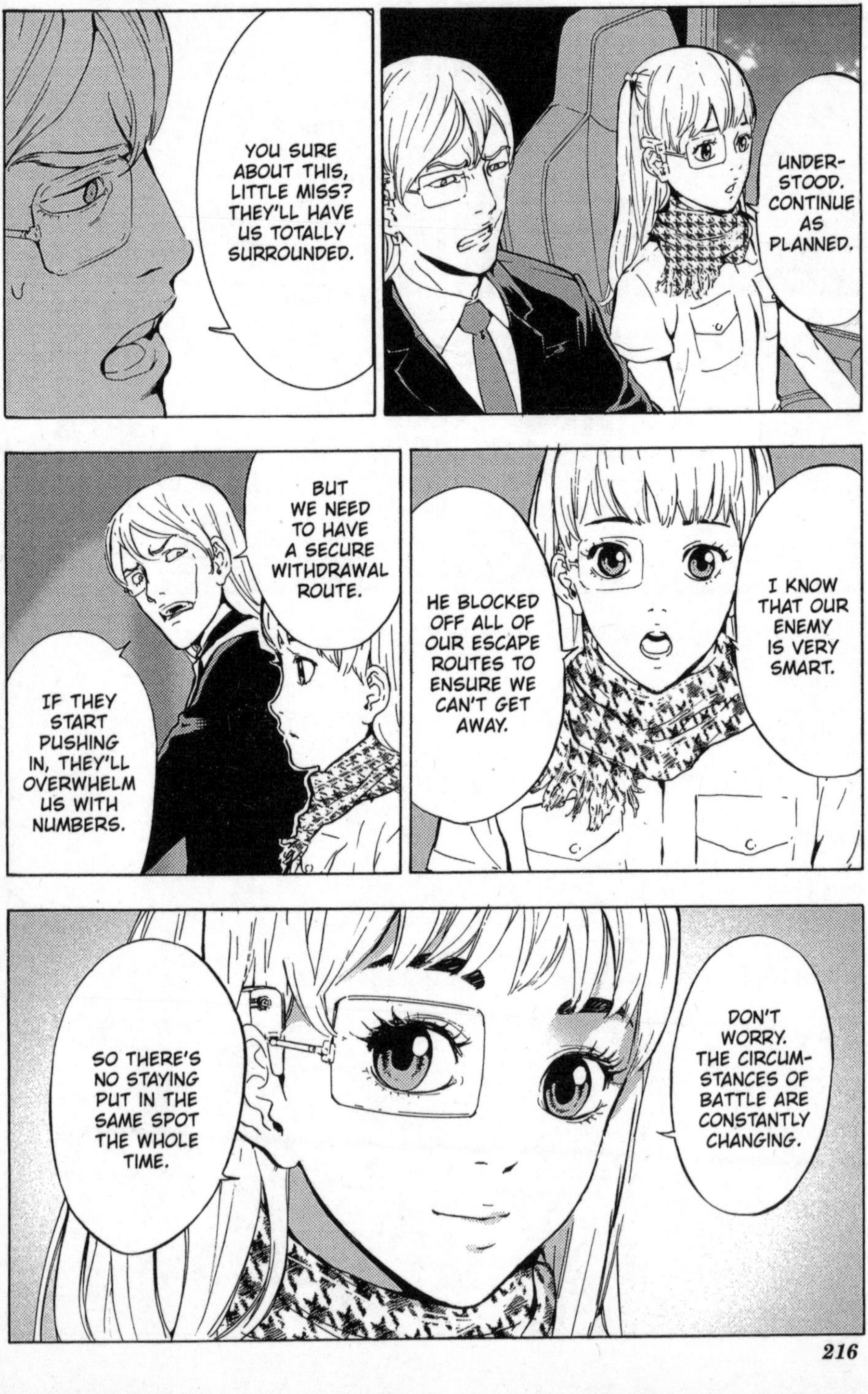
UNDER-STOOD. CONTINUE AS PLANNED.
YOU SURE ABOUT THIS, LITTLE MISS? THEY'LL HAVE US TOTALLY SURROUNDED.
I KNOW THAT OUR ENEMY IS VERY SMART.
HE BLOCKED OFF ALL OF OUR ESCAPE ROUTES TO ENSURE WE CAN'T GET AWAY.
BUT WE NEED TO HAVE A SECURE WITHDRAWAL ROUTE.
IF THEY START PUSHING IN, THEY'LL OVERWHELM US WITH NUMBERS.
DON'T WORRY. THE CIRCUM-STANCES OF BATTLE ARE CONSTANTLY CHANGING.
SO THERE'S NO STAYING PUT IN THE SAME SPOT THE WHOLE TIME.

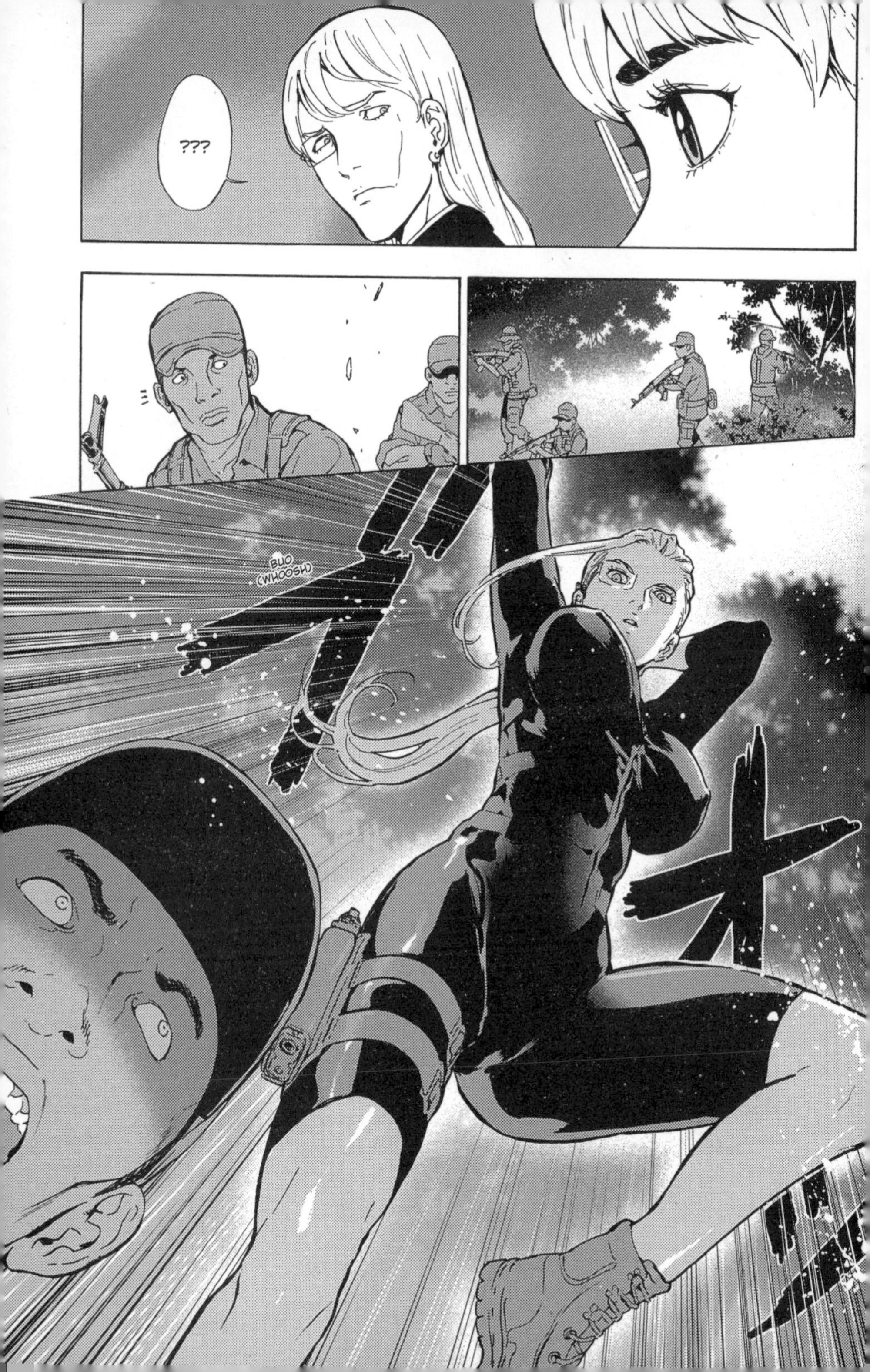
???
BUO (WHOOSH)

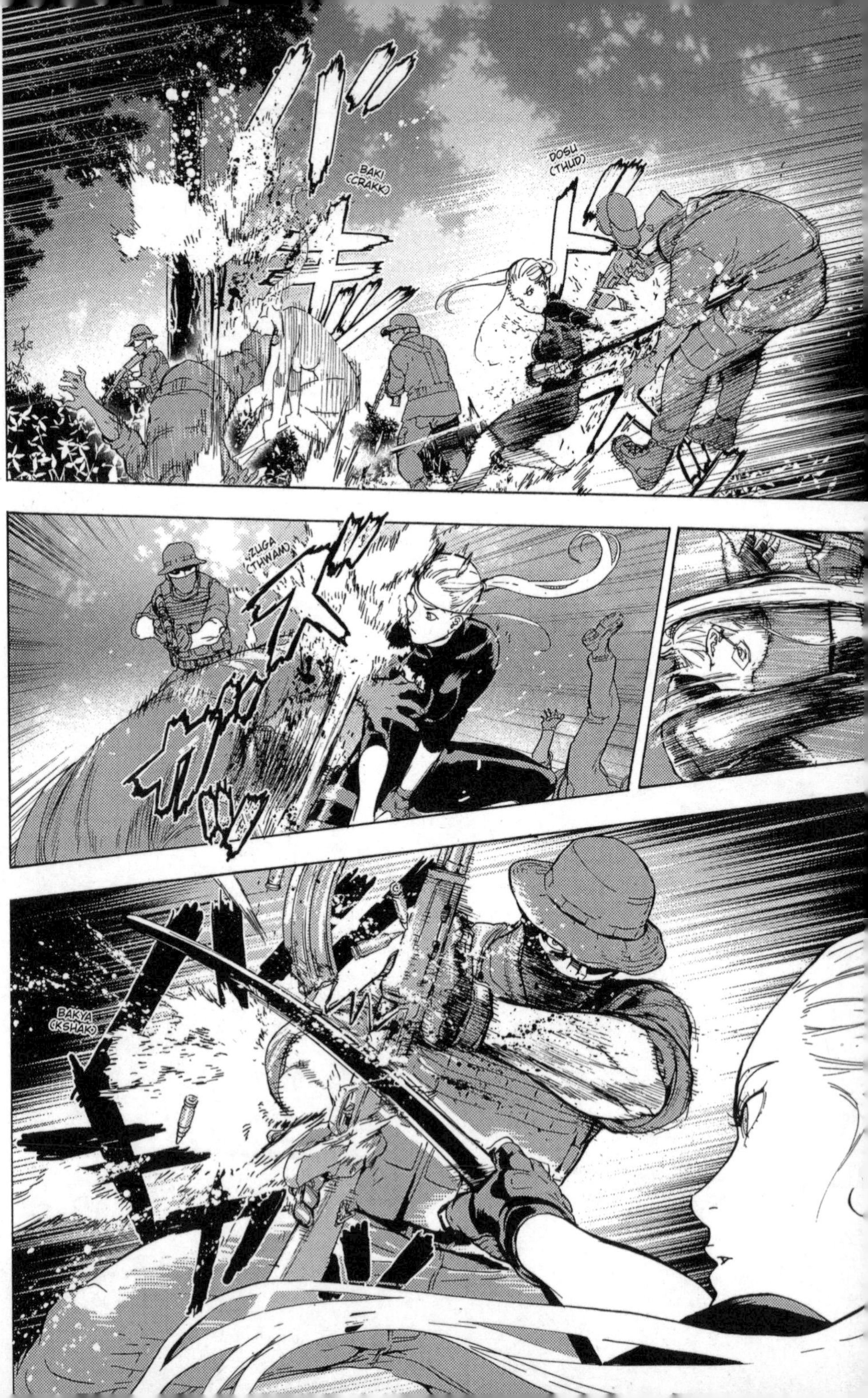
DOSU (THUD)
BAKI (CRAKK)
ZUGA (THWAM)
BAKYA (KSHAK)

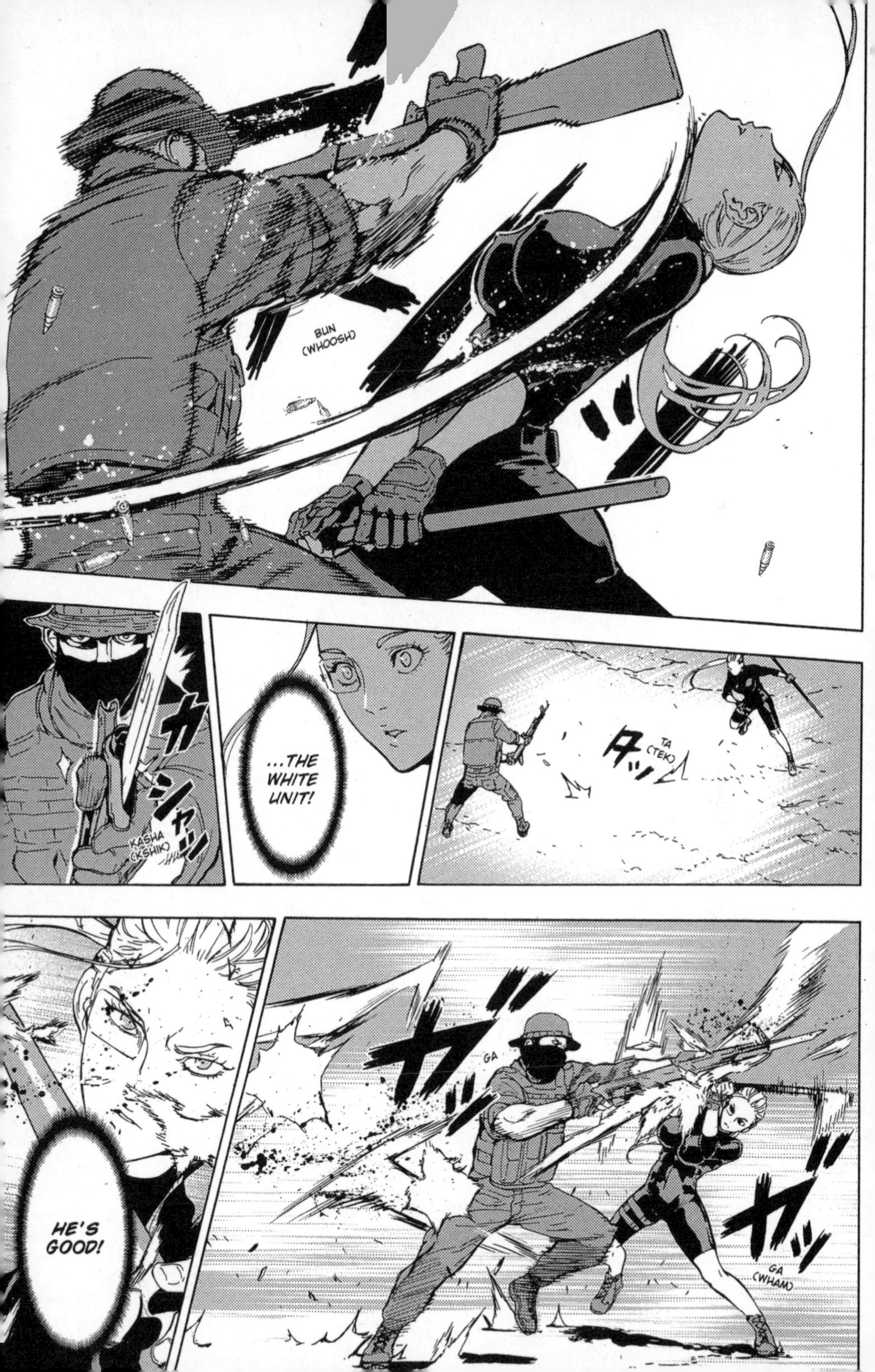
BUN (WHOOSH)
TA (TEK)
...THE WHITE UNIT!
KASHA (KSHIK)
GA
GA (WHAM)
HE'S GOOD!

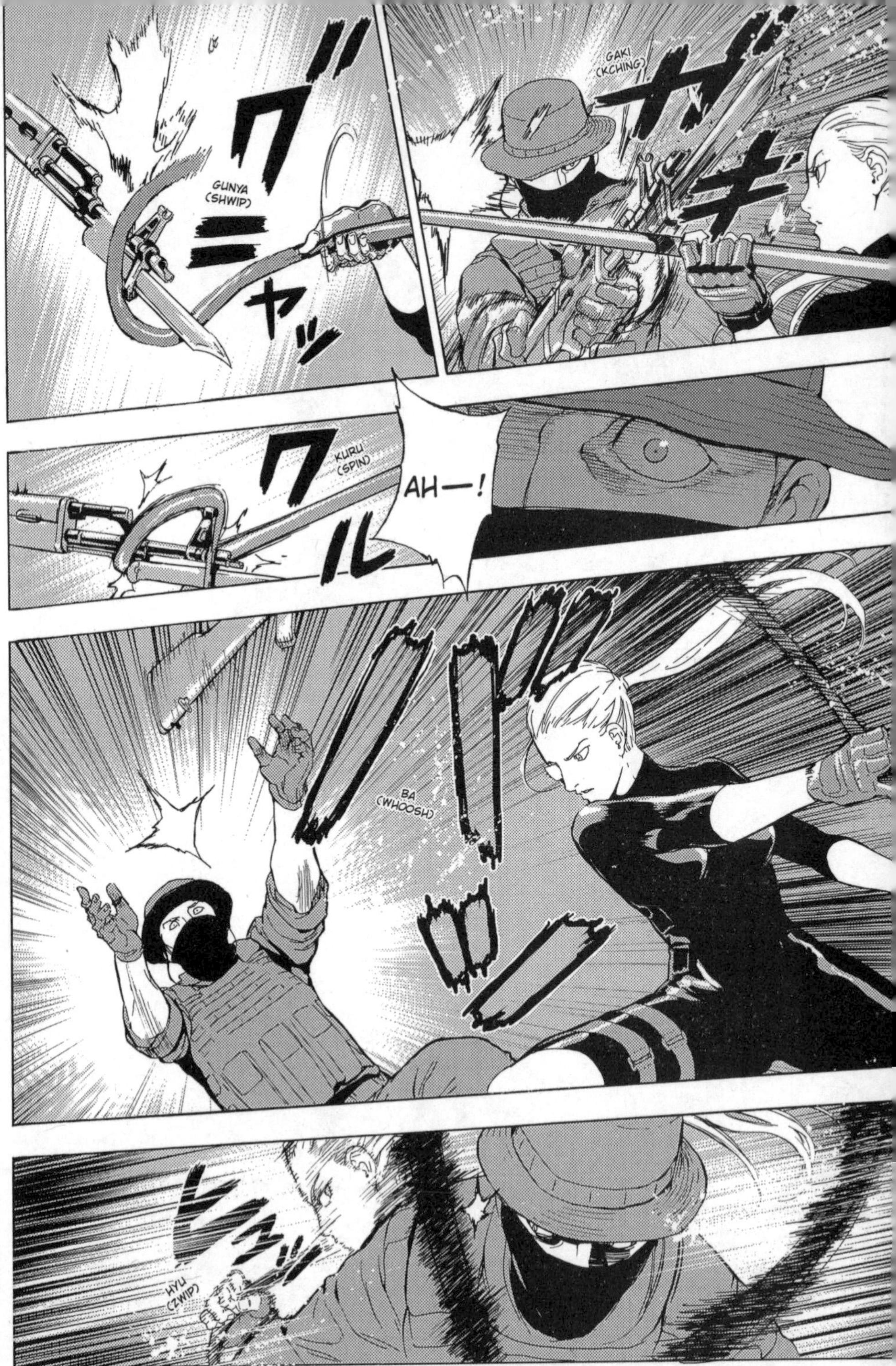
GAKI
(KCHING)
GUNYA
(SHWIP)
AH—!
KURU
(SPIN)
BA
(WHOOSH)
HYU
(ZWIP)

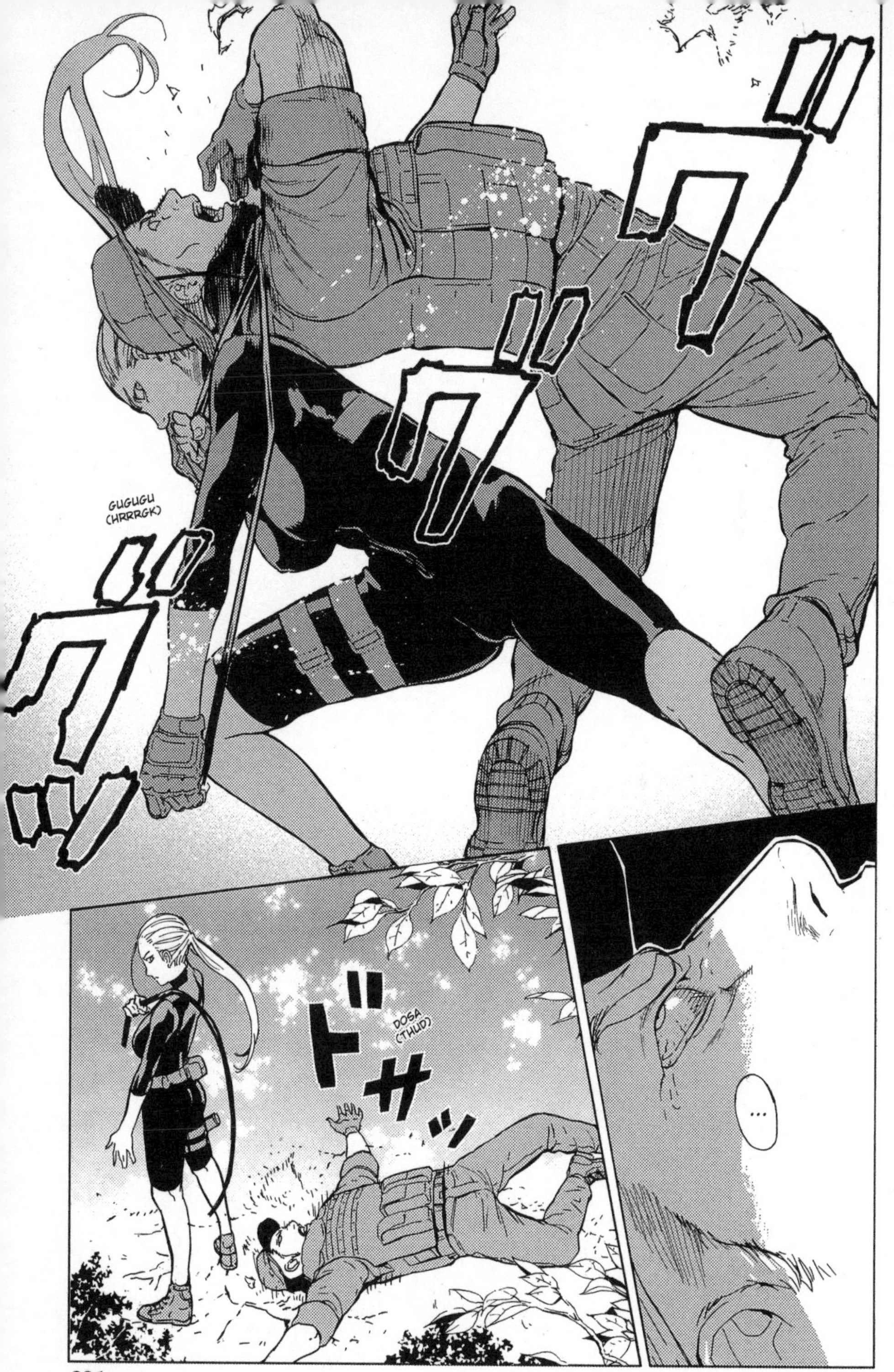
GUGUGU
(HRRRGK)
...
DOSA
(THUD)

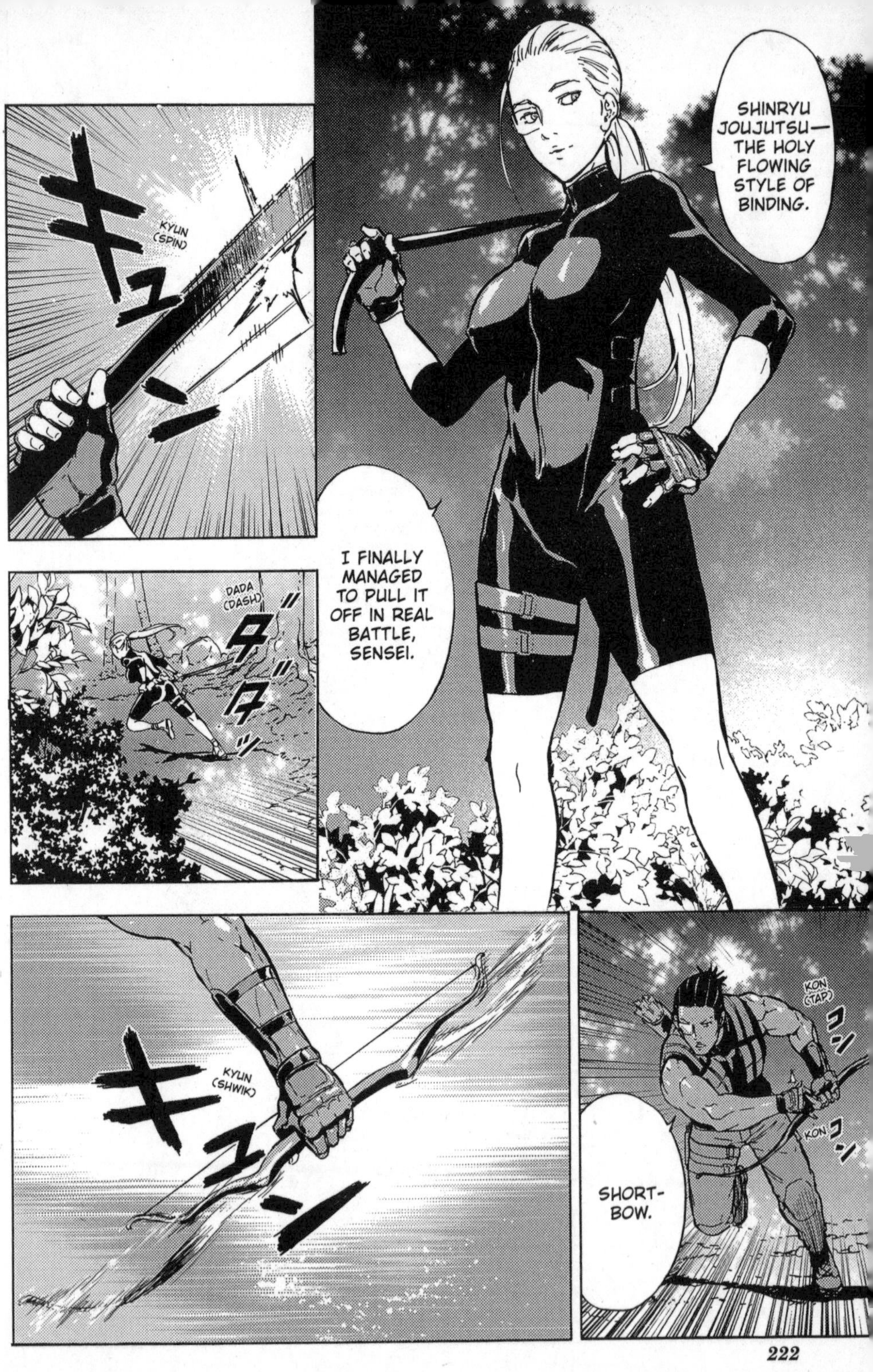
SHINRYU JOUJUTSU— THE HOLY FLOWING STYLE OF BINDING.
I FINALLY MANAGED TO PULL IT OFF IN REAL BATTLE, SENSEI.
KYUN (SPIN)
DADA (DASH)
KON (TAP)
KON
SHORT-BOW.
KYUN (SHWIK)

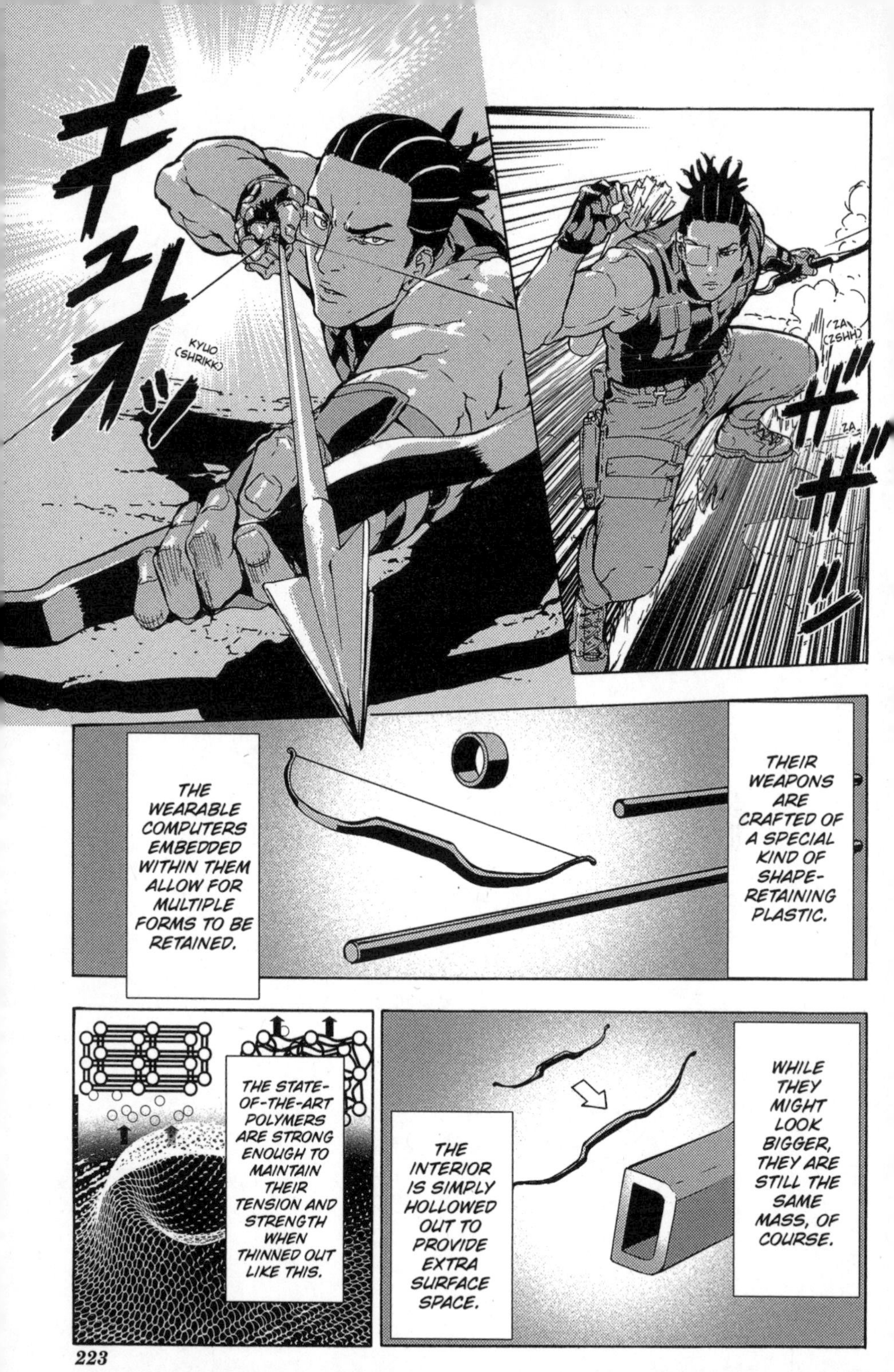
ZA (ZSHH)
ZA
KYUO (SHRIKK)
THEIR WEAPONS ARE CRAFTED OF A SPECIAL KIND OF SHAPE-RETAINING PLASTIC.
THE WEARABLE COMPUTERS EMBEDDED WITHIN THEM ALLOW FOR MULTIPLE FORMS TO BE RETAINED.
WHILE THEY MIGHT LOOK BIGGER, THEY ARE STILL THE SAME MASS, OF COURSE.
THE INTERIOR IS SIMPLY HOLLOWED OUT TO PROVIDE EXTRA SURFACE SPACE.
THE STATE-OF-THE-ART POLYMERS ARE STRONG ENOUGH TO MAINTAIN THEIR TENSION AND STRENGTH WHEN THINNED OUT LIKE THIS.

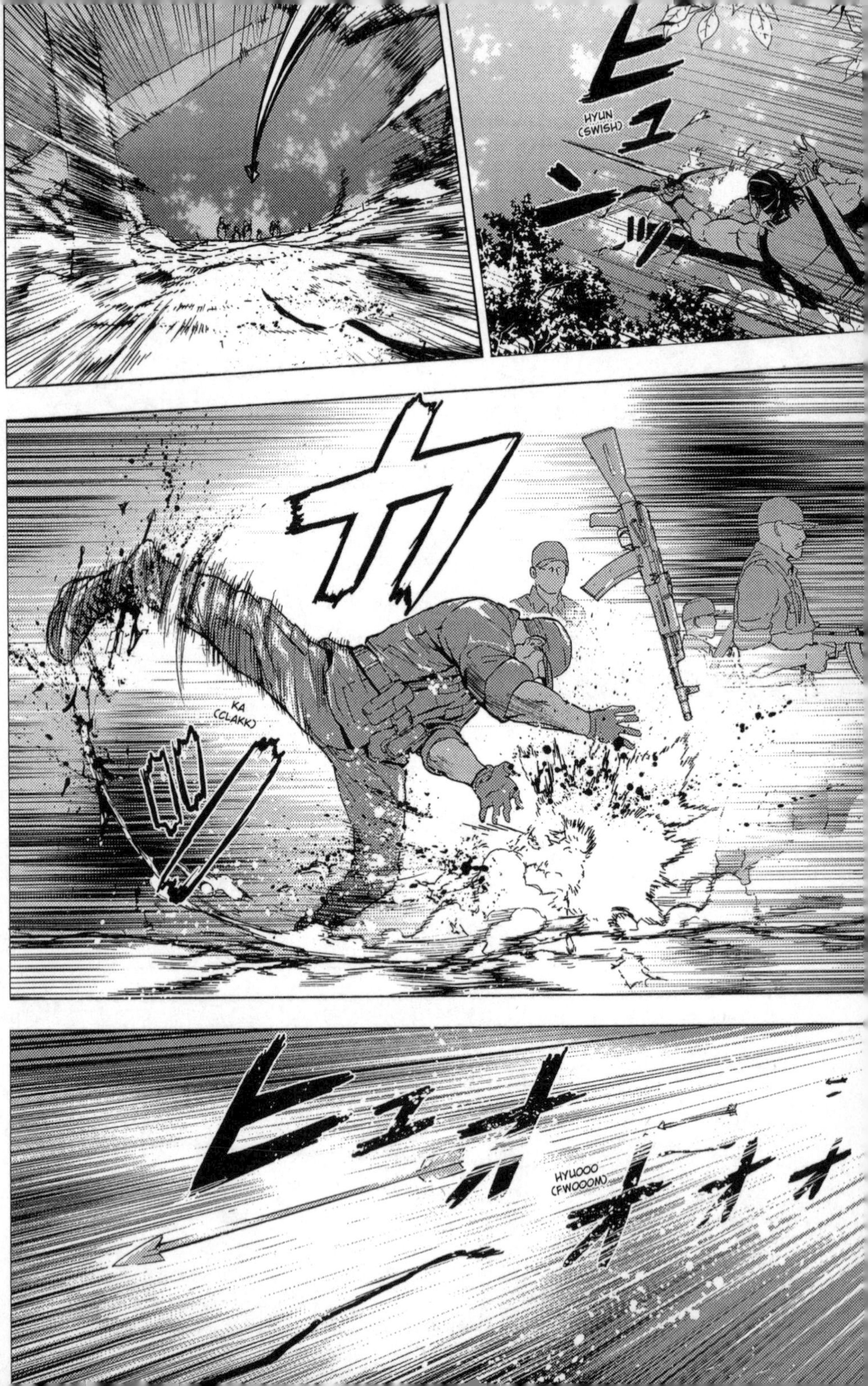
HYUN
(SWISH)
KA
(CLAKK)
HYUOOO
(FWOOOM)

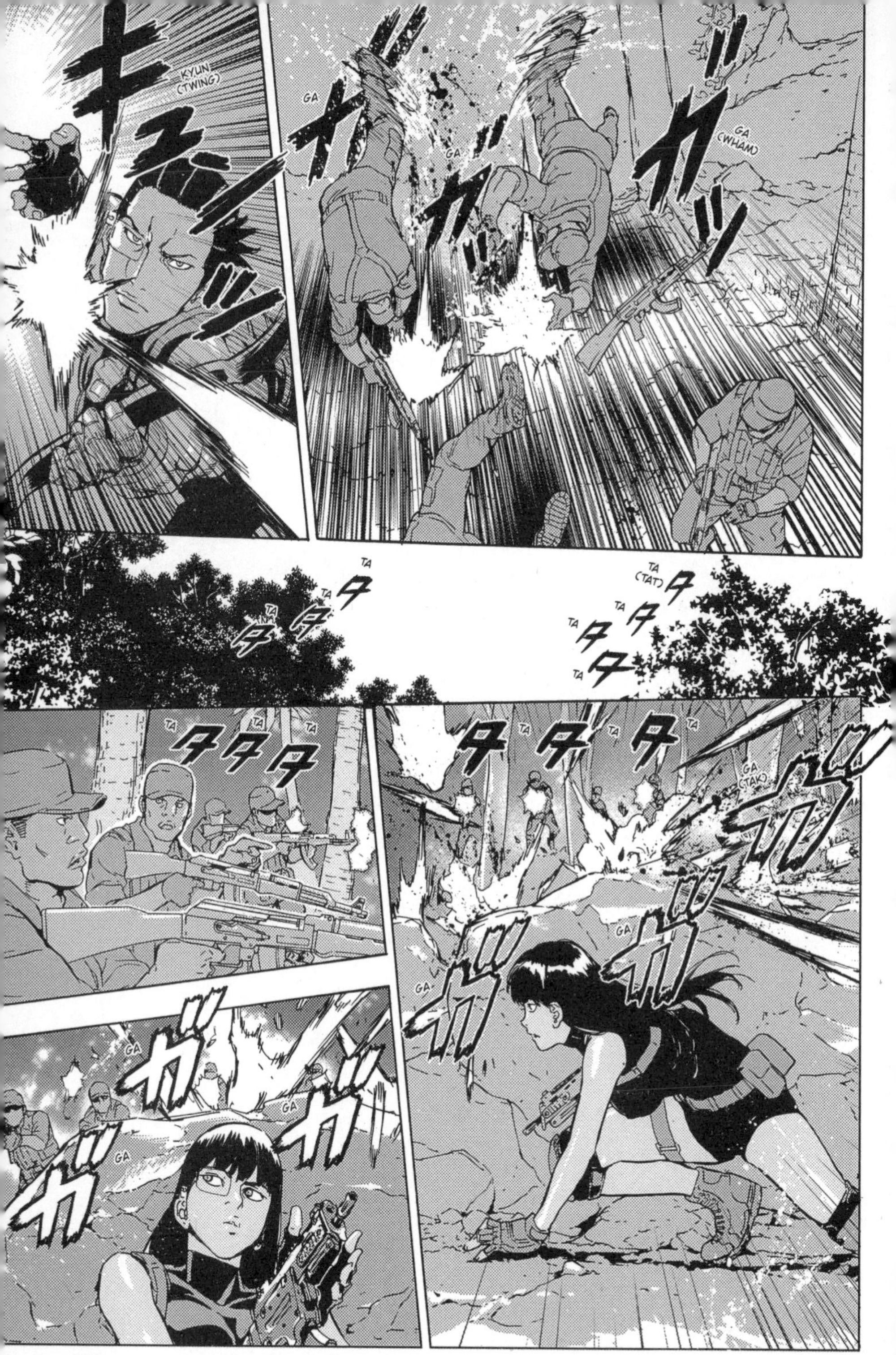
GA
(WHAM)
GA
GA
KYUN
(TWING)
TA
(TAT)
TA
TA
TA
TA
TA
TA
TA
TA
TA
GA
(TAK)
GA
GA
TA
TA
TA
GA
GA
GA

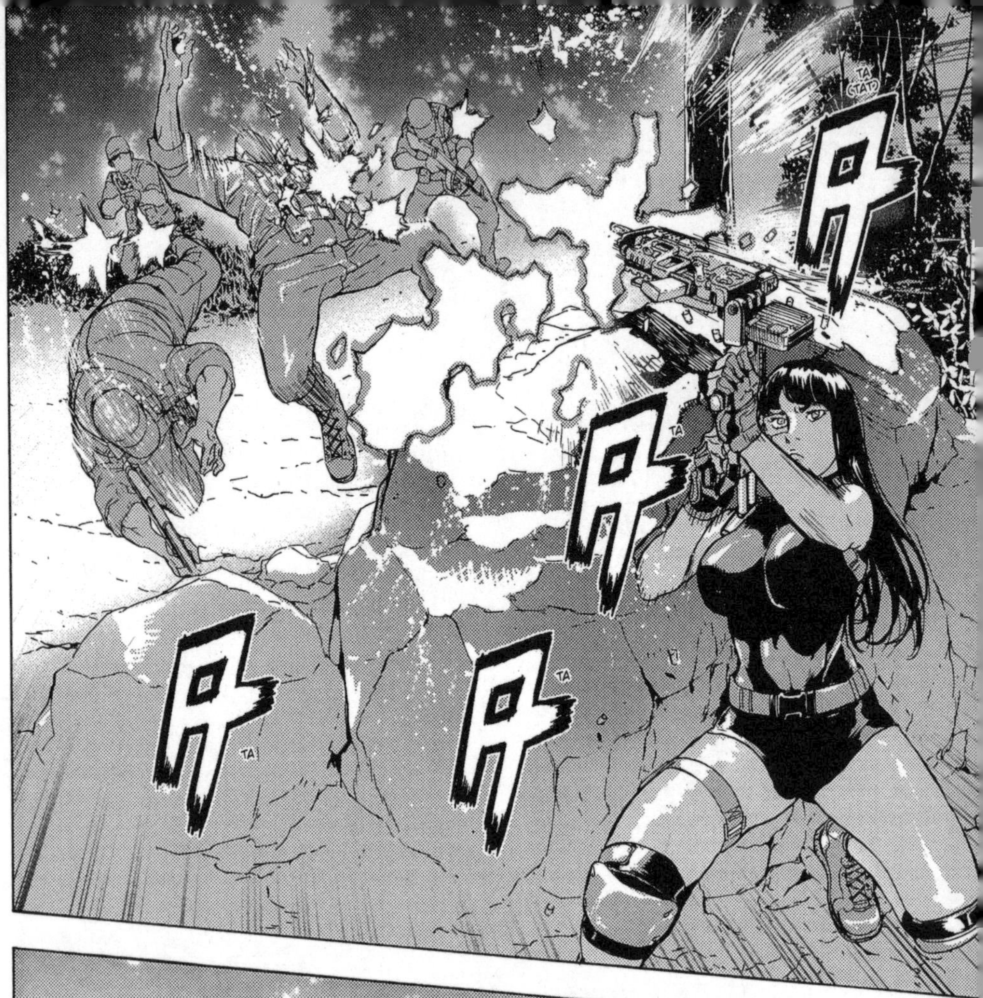
タ
TA
(TAT)
タ
TA
タ
TA
タ
TA
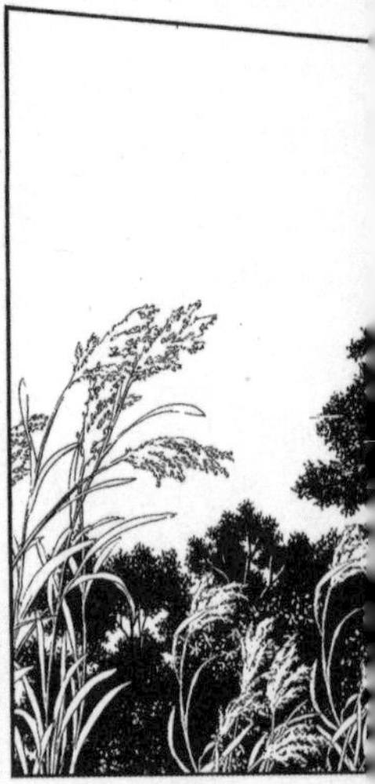
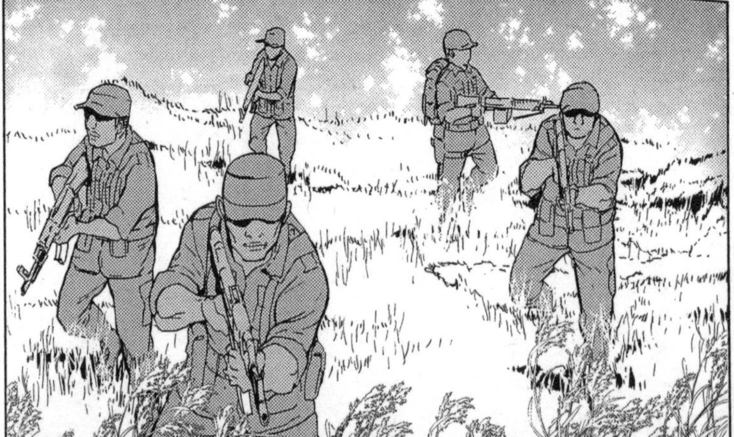

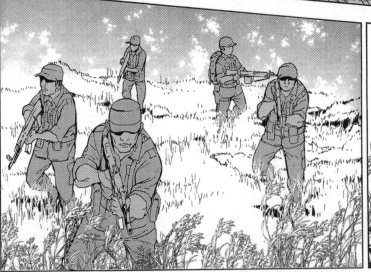

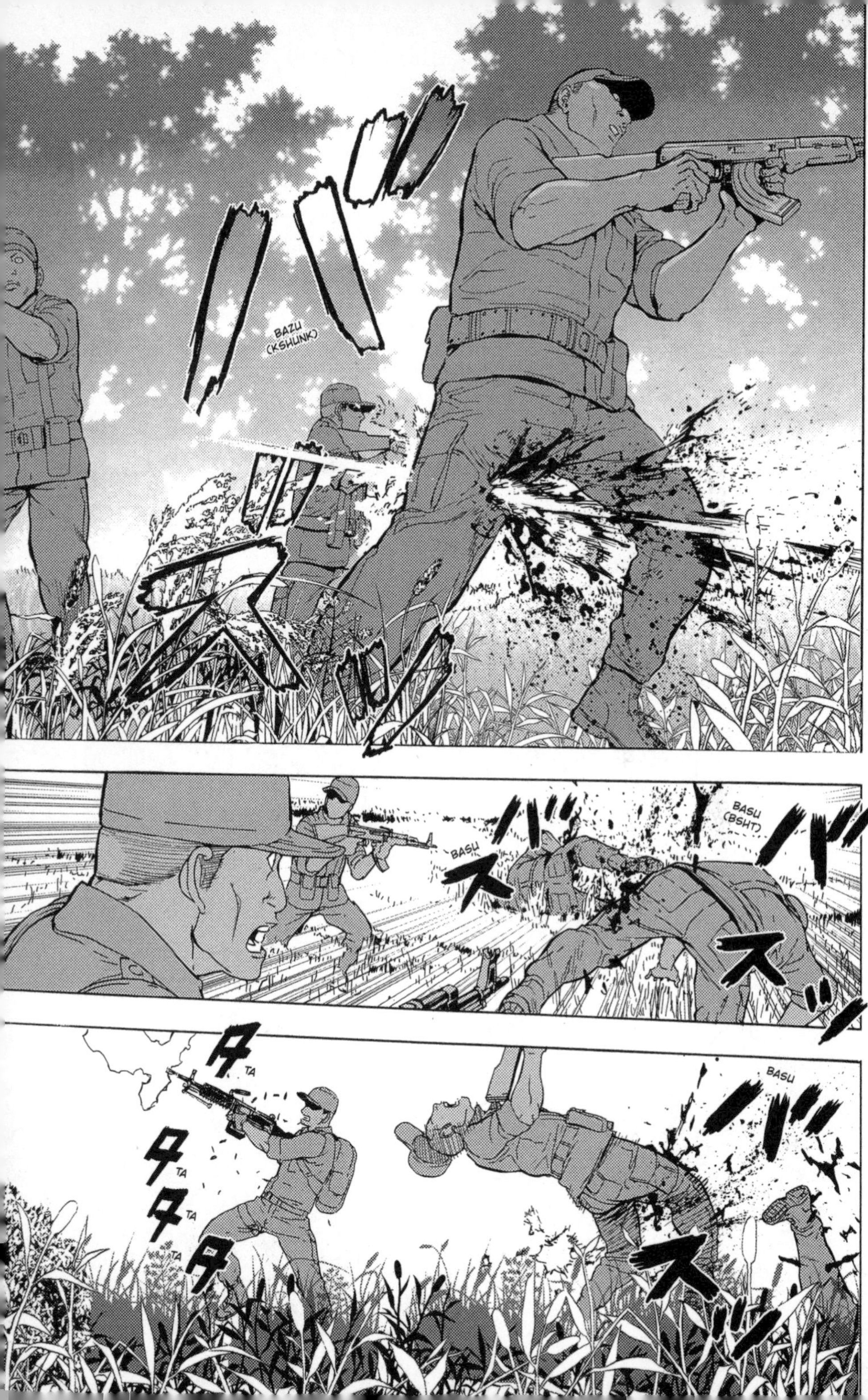
BAZU
(KSHUNK)
BASU
(BSHT)
BASU
BASU
TA
TA
TA
TA

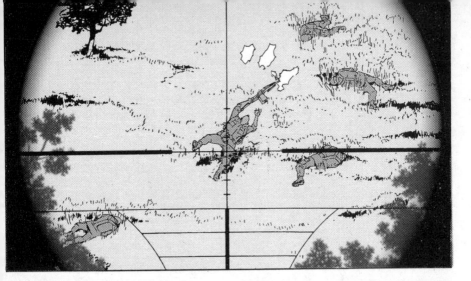

INCRED-IBLE... IT'S SO EASY.

WITH TOOYAMA'S POWERS, THERE'S NO FOE A SNIPER CAN'T HIT.

IT'S ALMOST TOO EASY...

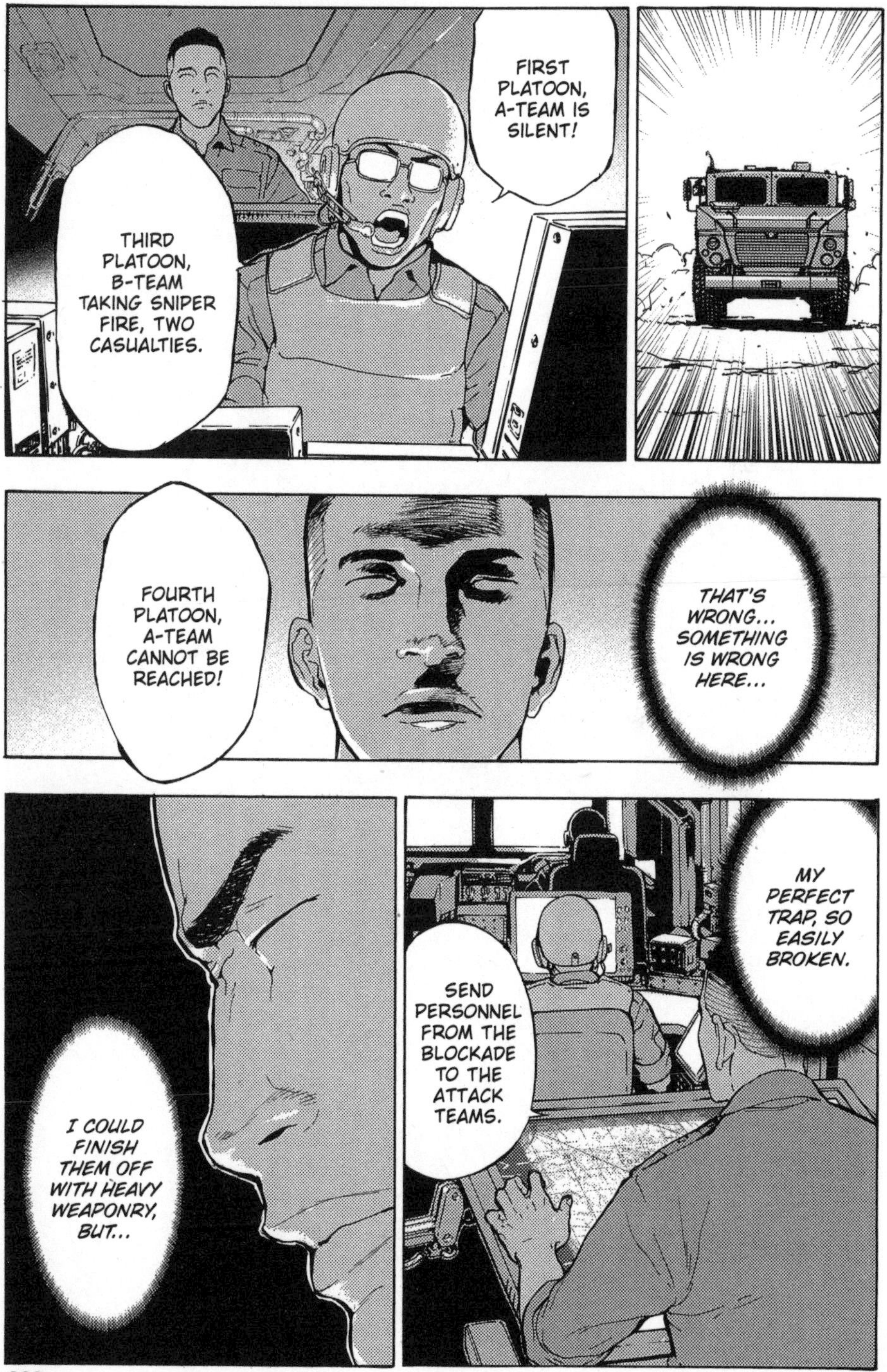
FIRST PLATOON, A-TEAM IS SILENT!
THIRD PLATOON, B-TEAM TAKING SNIPER FIRE, TWO CASUALTIES.
THAT'S WRONG... SOMETHING IS WRONG HERE...
FOURTH PLATOON, A-TEAM CANNOT BE REACHED!
MY PERFECT TRAP, SO EASILY BROKEN.
SEND PERSONNEL FROM THE BLOCKADE TO THE ATTACK TEAMS.
I COULD FINISH THEM OFF WITH HEAVY WEAPONRY, BUT...

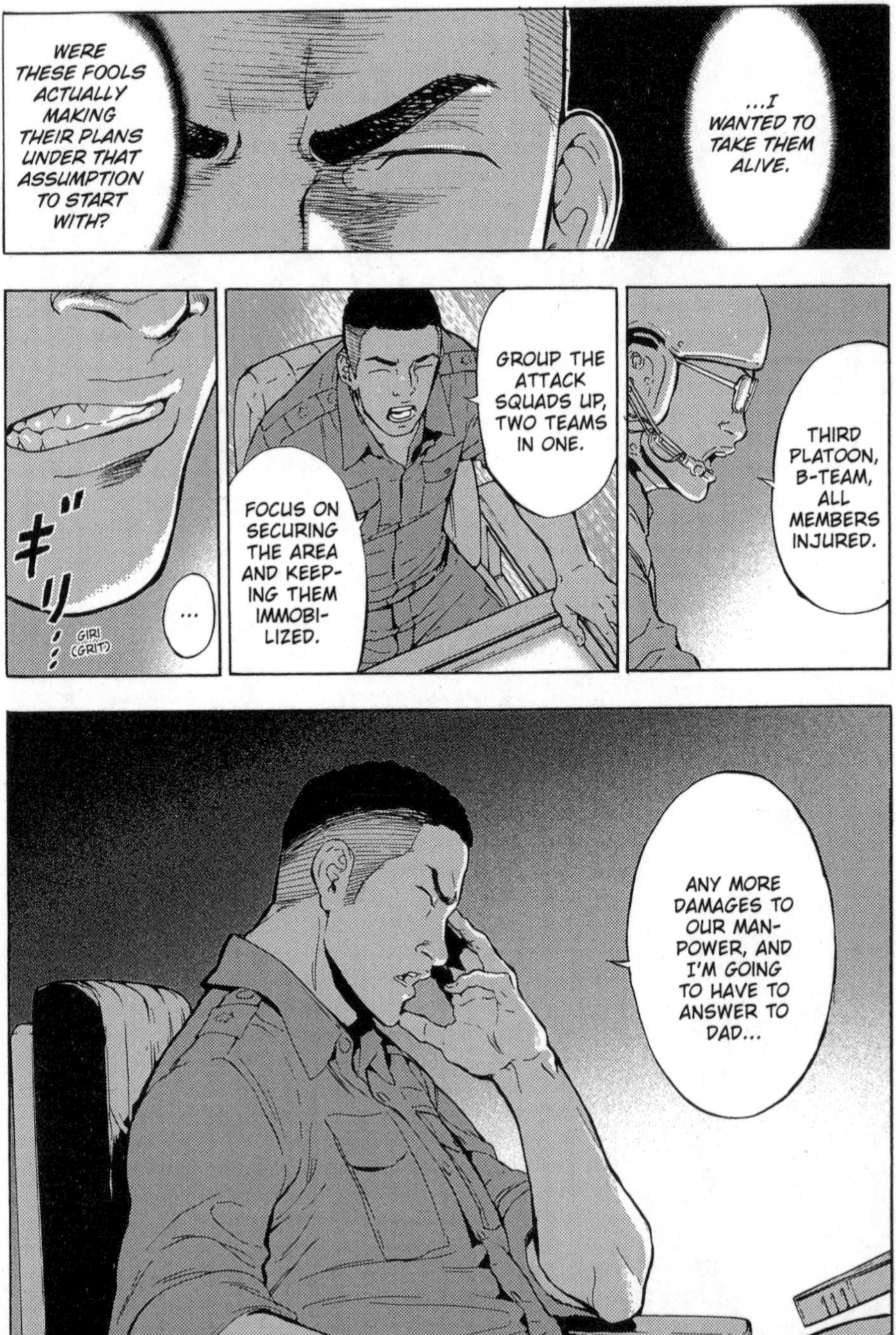
...I WANTED TO TAKE THEM ALIVE.
WERE THESE FOOLS ACTUALLY MAKING THEIR PLANS UNDER THAT ASSUMPTION TO START WITH?
THIRD PLATOON, B-TEAM, ALL MEMBERS INJURED.
GROUP THE ATTACK SQUADS UP, TWO TEAMS IN ONE.
FOCUS ON SECURING THE AREA AND KEEP-ING THEM IMMOBI-LIZED.
...
ギリ
GIRI (GRIT)
ANY MORE DAMAGES TO OUR MAN-POWER, AND I'M GOING TO HAVE TO ANSWER TO DAD...

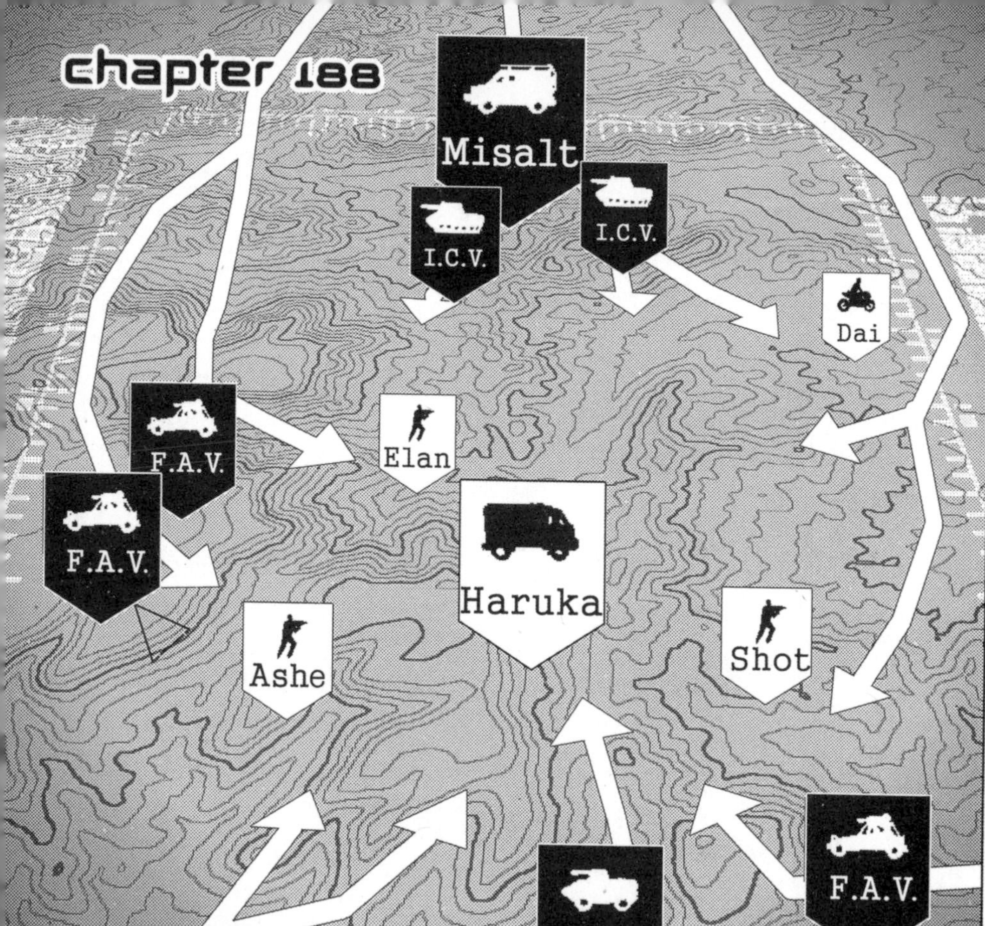
chapter 188
Misalt
I.C.V.
I.C.V.
Dai
Elan
F.A.V.
F.A.V.
Haruka
Shot
Ashe
F.A.V.
I.C.V.
I.C.V.

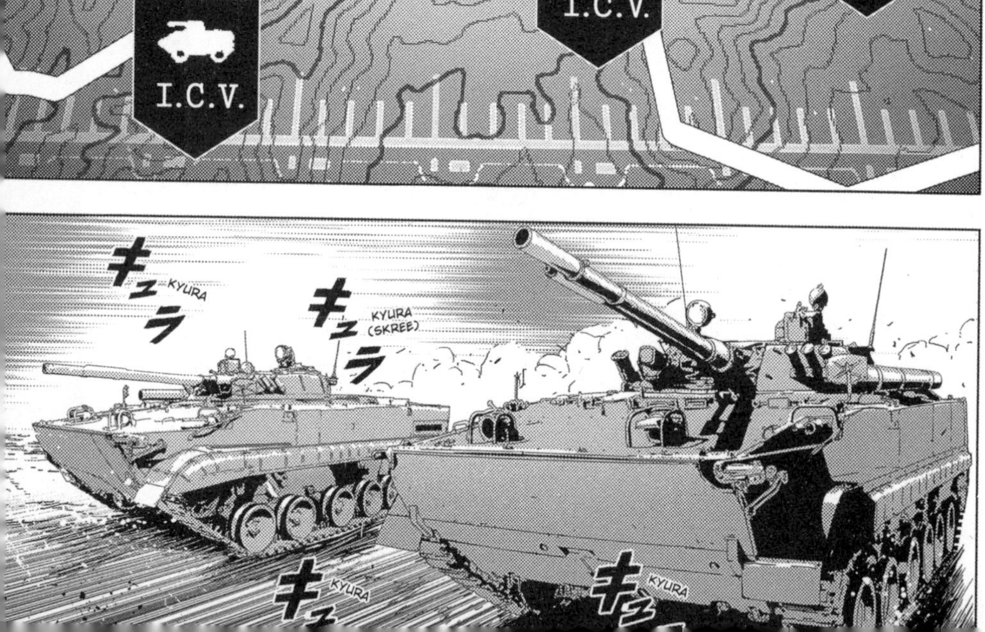
キュラ
KYURA (SKREE)
キュラ
KYURA
キュ
KYURA
キュ
KYURA

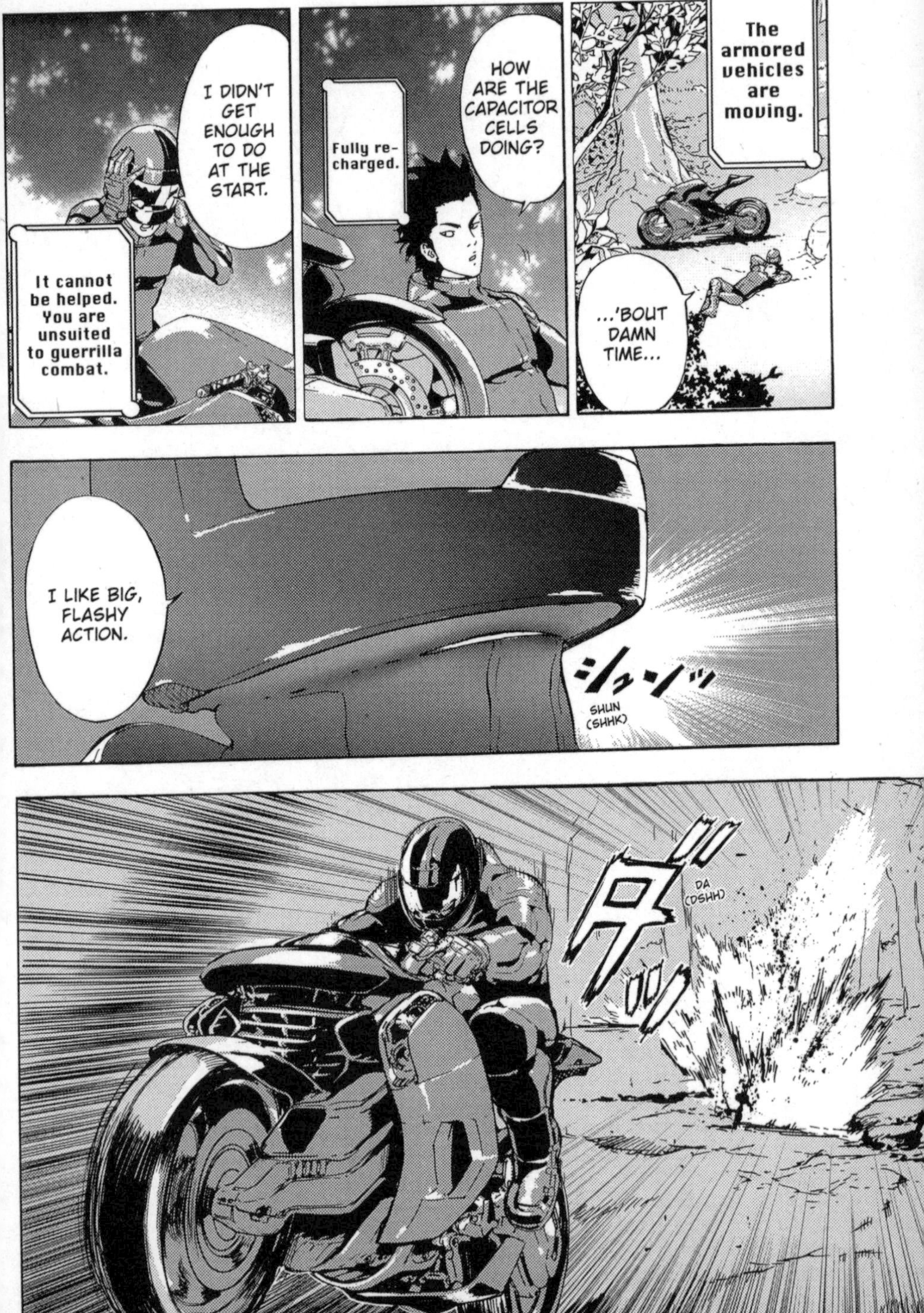
The armored vehicles are moving.
...'BOUT DAMN TIME...
HOW ARE THE CAPACITOR CELLS DOING?
Fully re-charged.
I DIDN'T GET ENOUGH TO DO AT THE START.
It cannot be helped. You are unsuited to guerrilla combat.
I LIKE BIG, FLASHY ACTION.
SHUN (SHHK)
DA (DSHH)

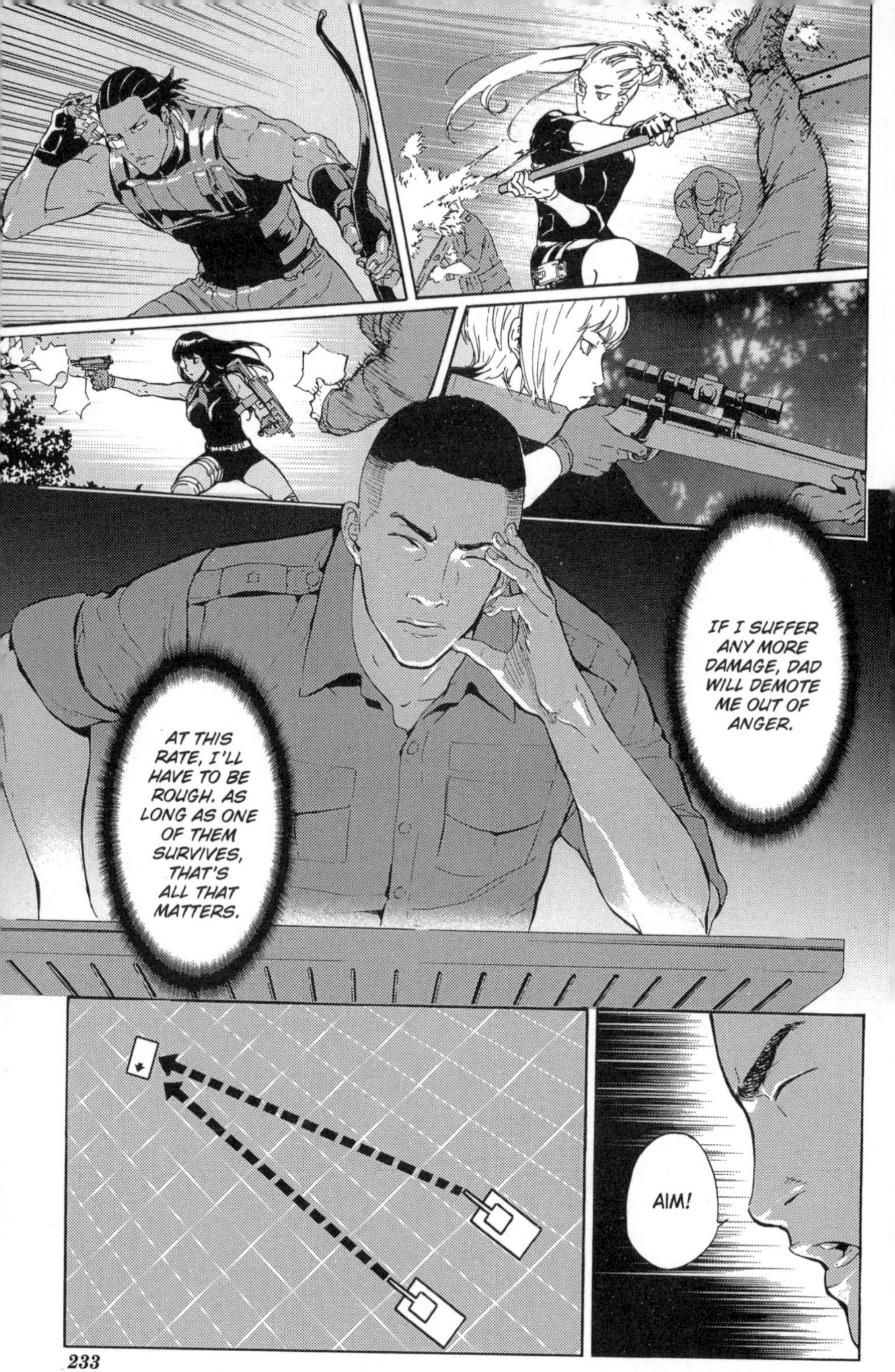
IF I SUFFER ANY MORE DAMAGE, DAD WILL DEMOTE ME OUT OF ANGER.
AT THIS RATE, I'LL HAVE TO BE ROUGH. AS LONG AS ONE OF THEM SURVIVES, THAT'S ALL THAT MATTERS.
AIM!

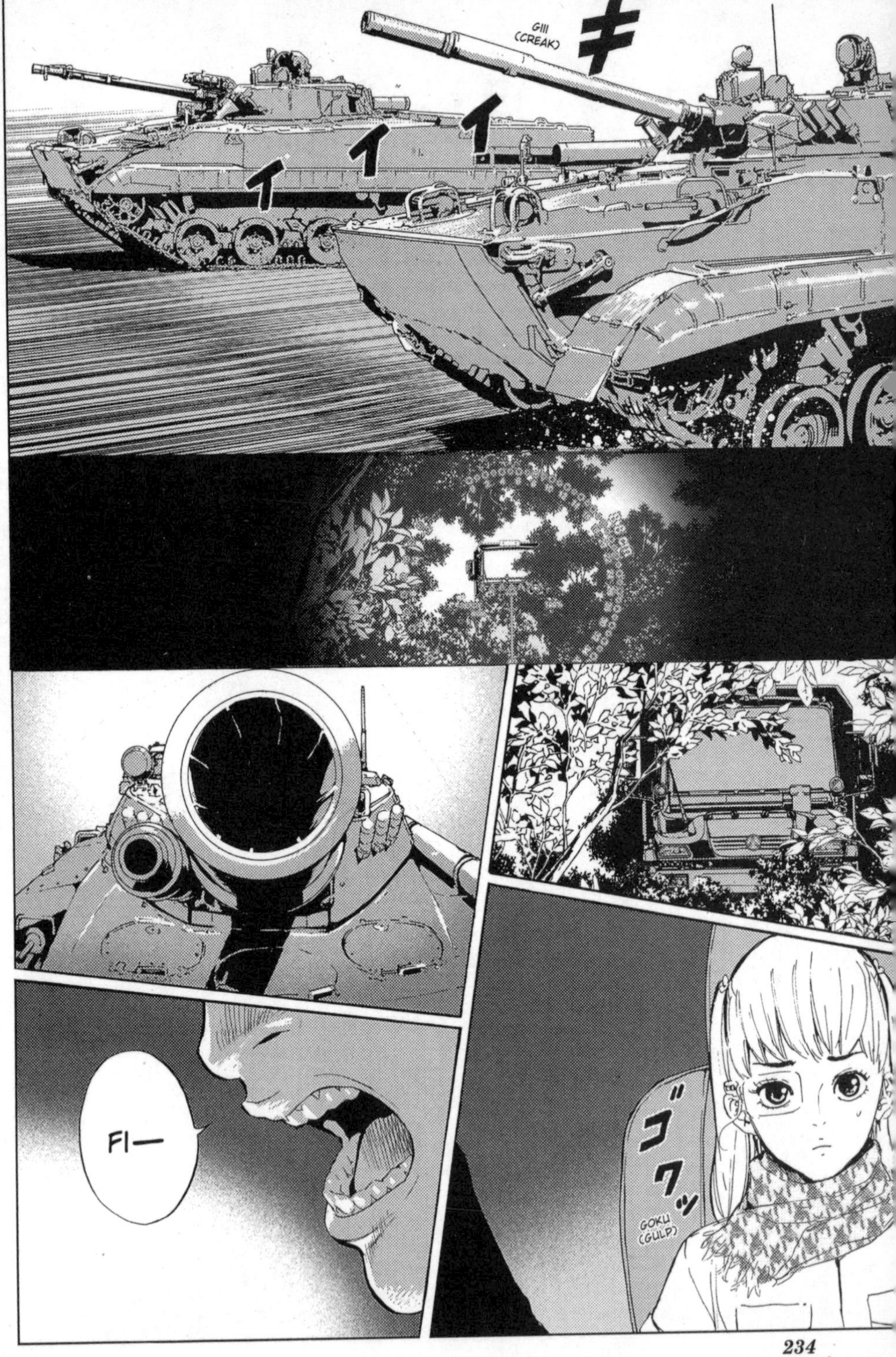
ギ
GIII (CREAK)
イイイ
ゴクッ
GOKU (GULP)
FI—

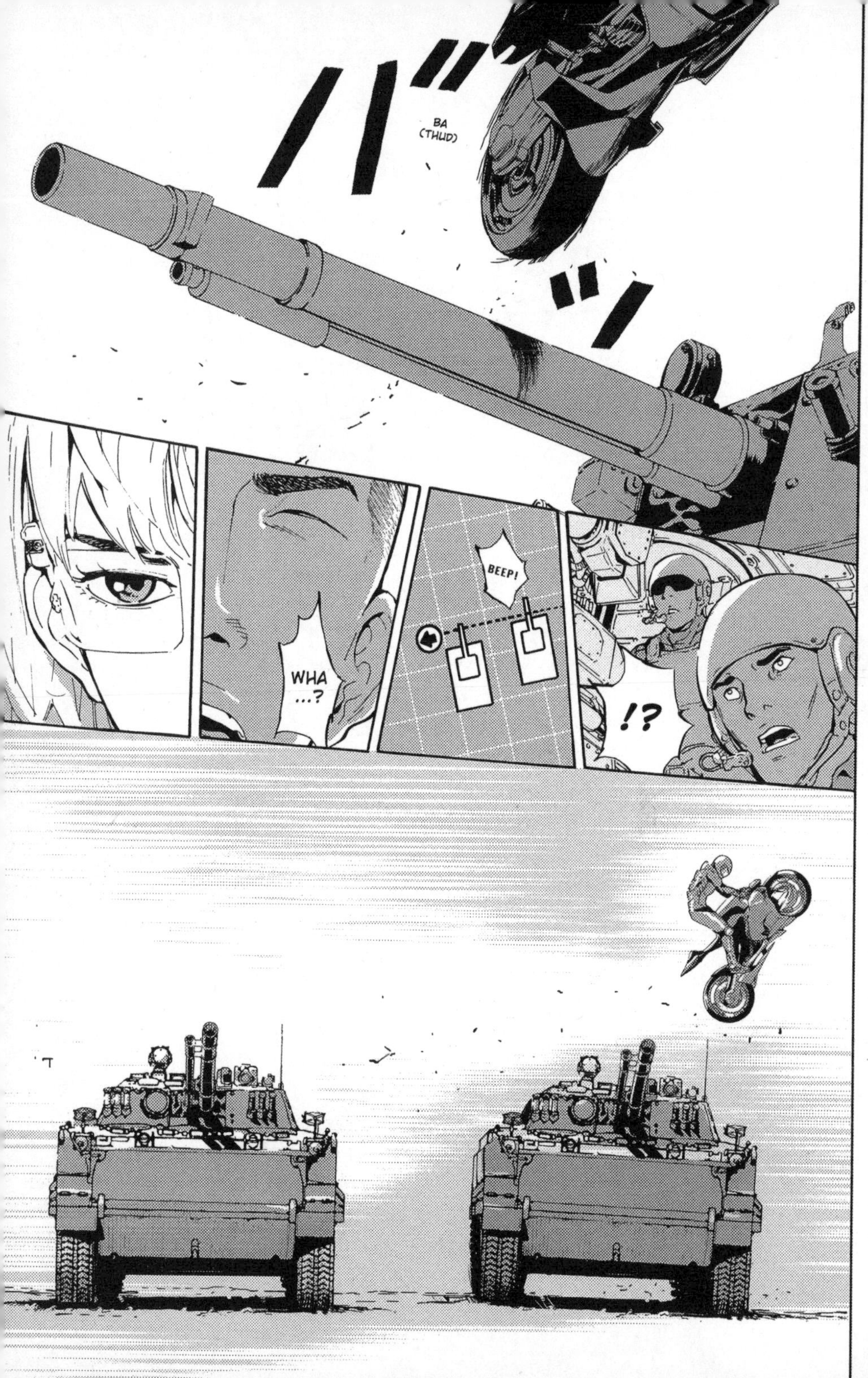
BA (THUD)
!?
BEEP!
WHA ...?

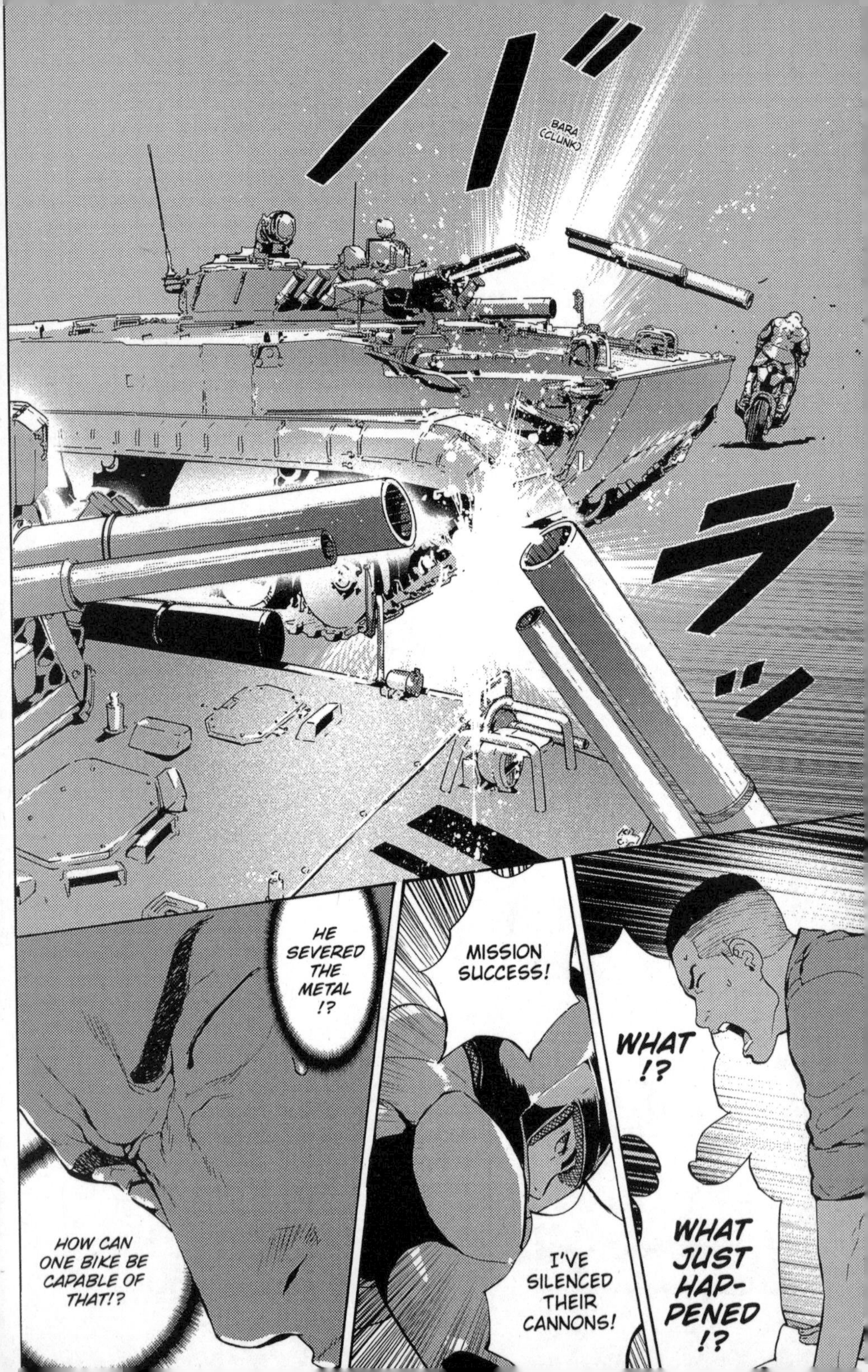
BARA (CLUNK)
WHAT!?
WHAT JUST HAP-PENED!?
MISSION SUCCESS!
I'VE SILENCED THEIR CANNONS!
HE SEVERED THE METAL!?
HOW CAN ONE BIKE BE CAPABLE OF THAT!?

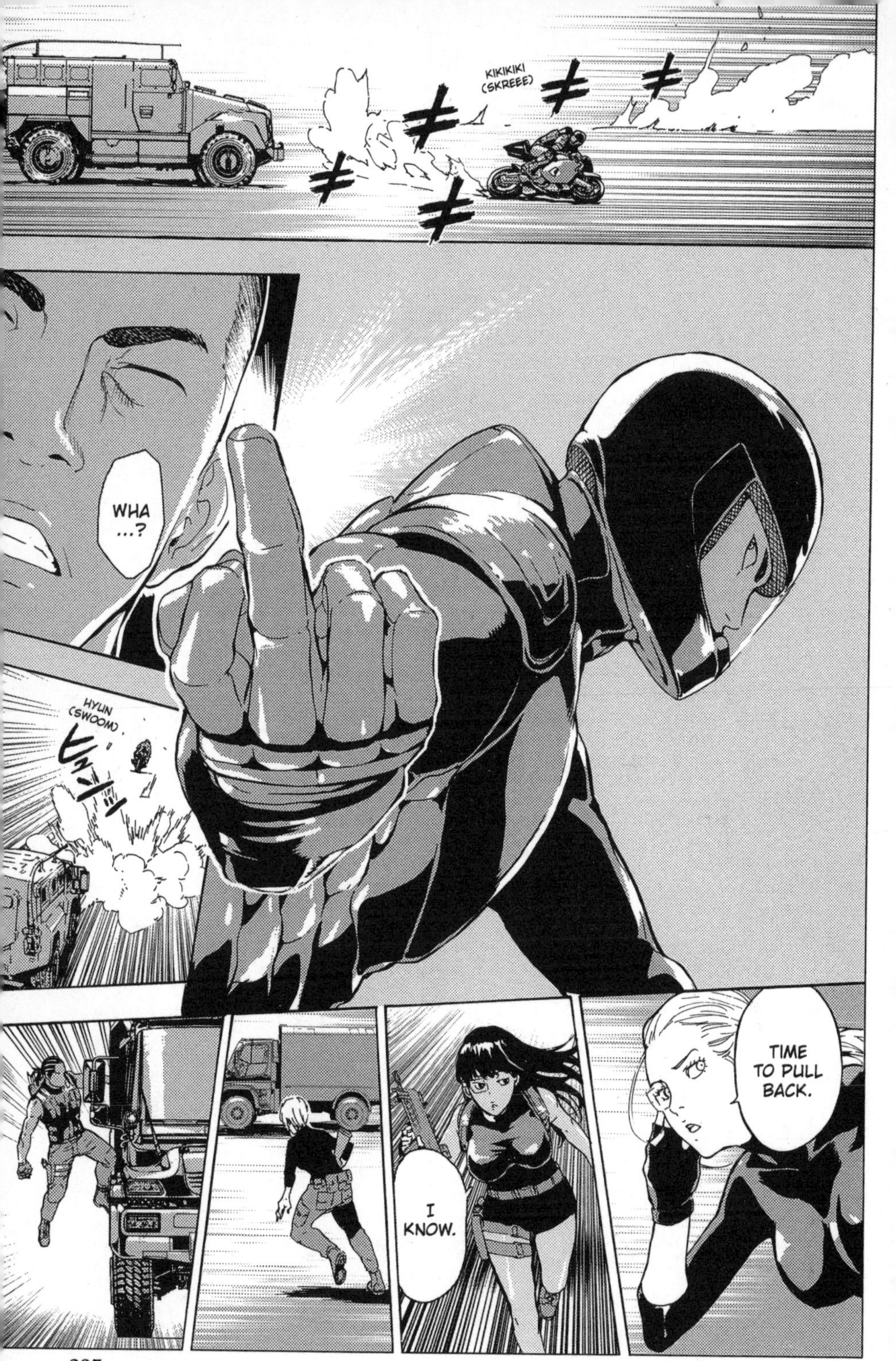
KIKIKIKI (SKREEE)
WHA ...?
HYUN (SWOOM)
TIME TO PULL BACK.
I KNOW.

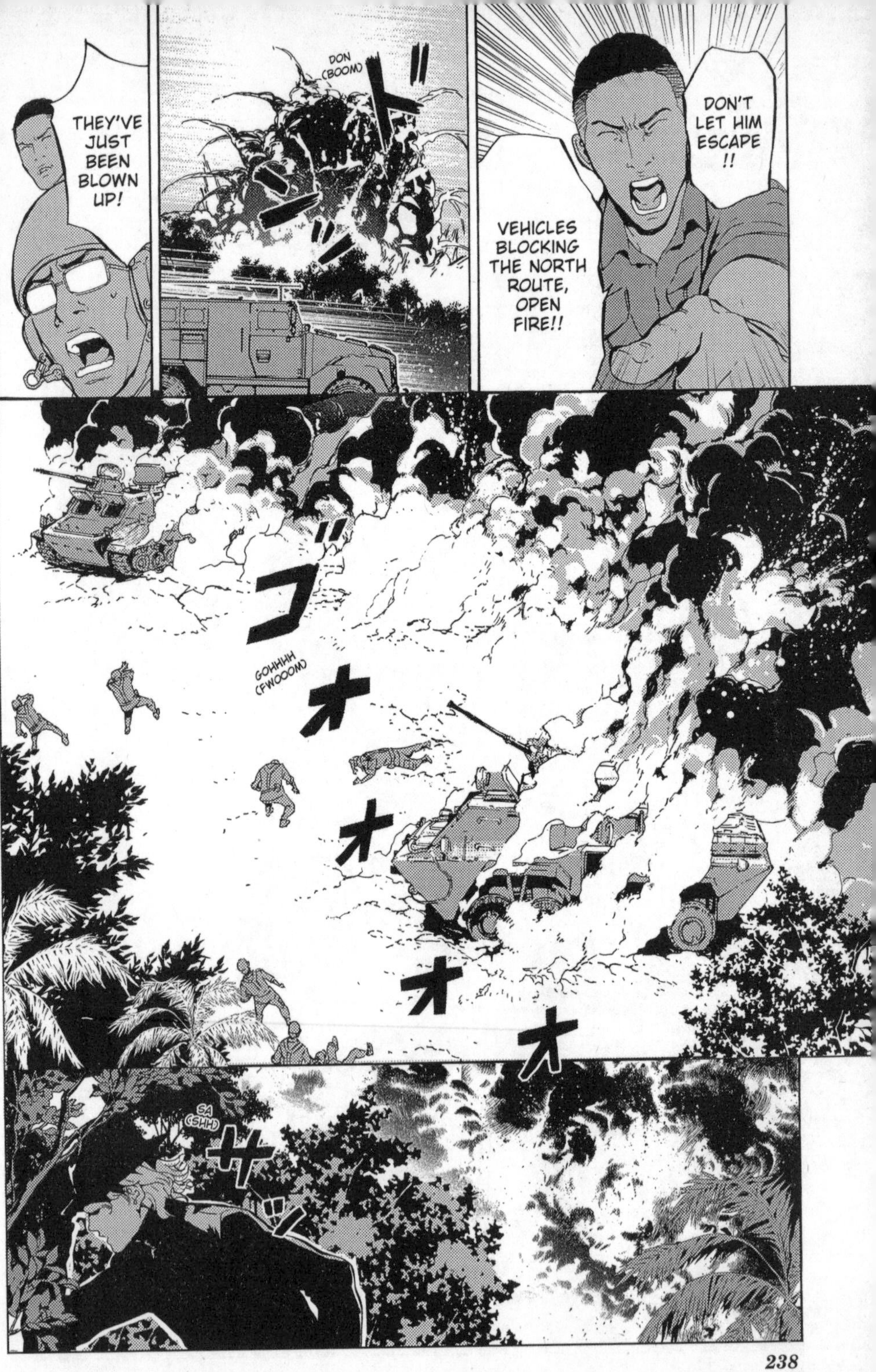
DON'T LET HIM ESCAPE !!
VEHICLES BLOCKING THE NORTH ROUTE, OPEN FIRE!!
DON (BOOM)
THEY'VE JUST BEEN BLOWN UP!
GOHHHH (FWOOOM)
SA (SHH)

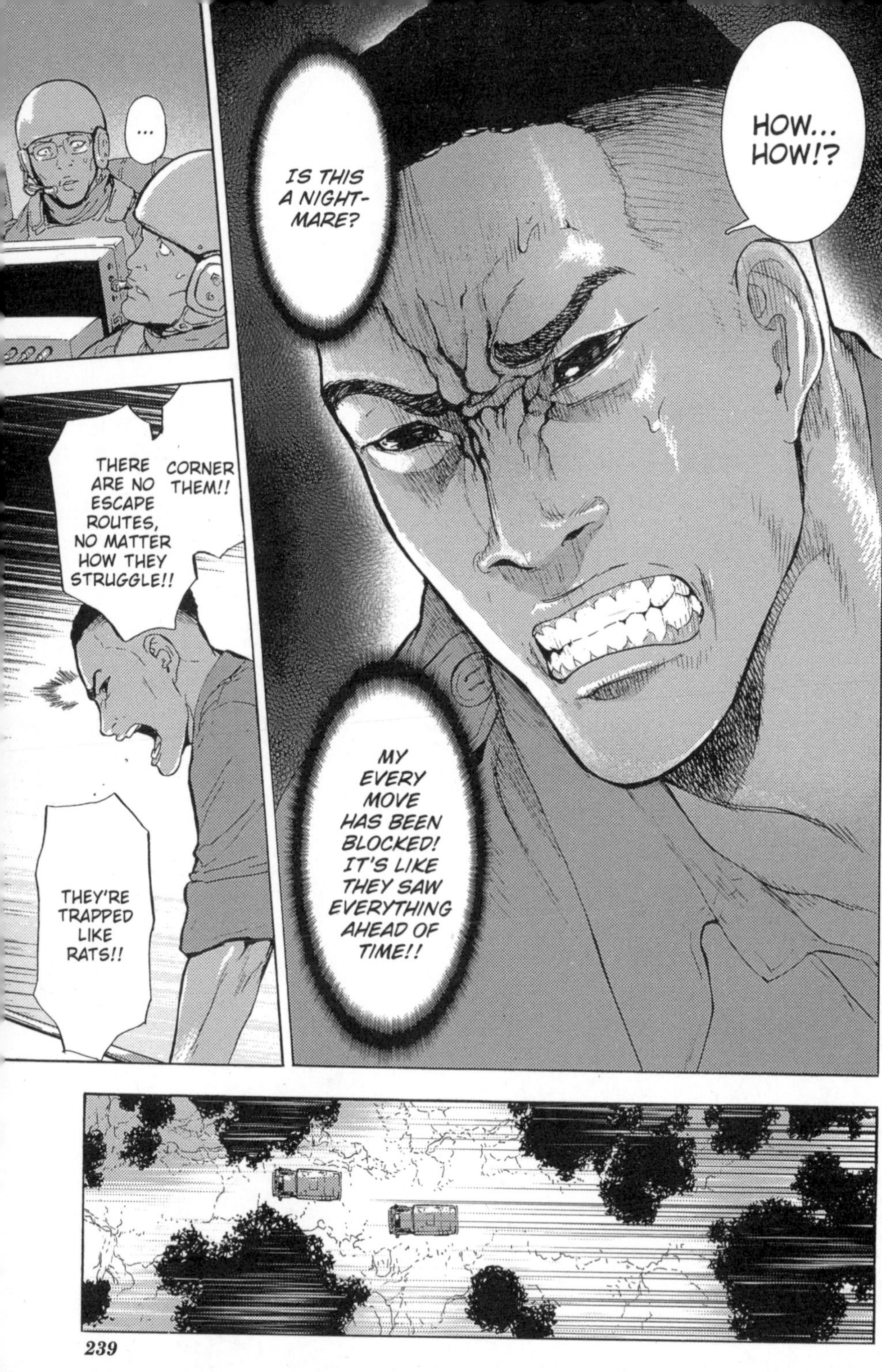
HOW... HOW!?
IS THIS A NIGHT-MARE?
MY EVERY MOVE HAS BEEN BLOCKED! IT'S LIKE THEY SAW EVERYTHING AHEAD OF TIME!!
...
CORNER THEM!!
THERE ARE NO ESCAPE ROUTES, NO MATTER HOW THEY STRUGGLE!!
THEY'RE TRAPPED LIKE RATS!!

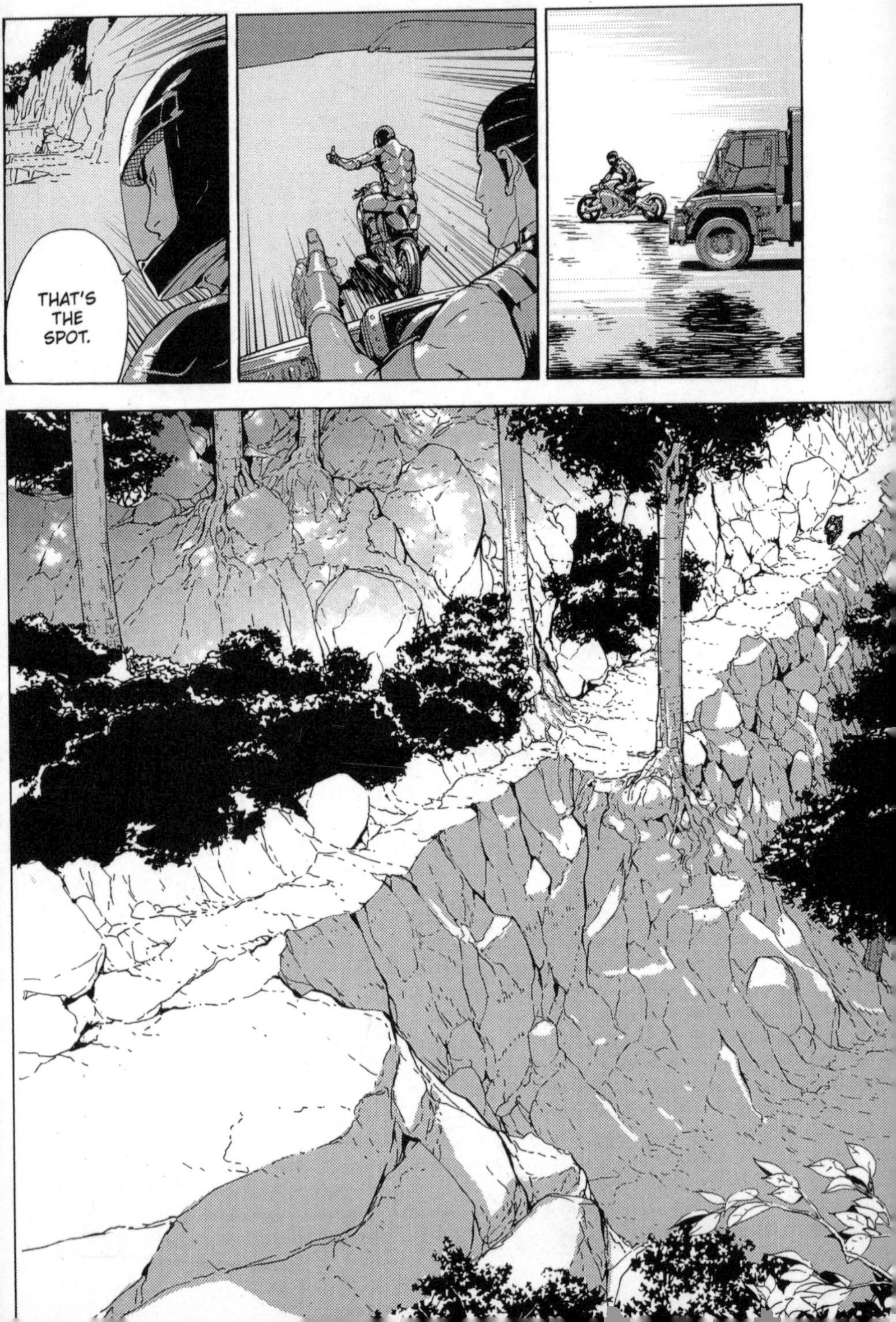
THAT'S THE SPOT.

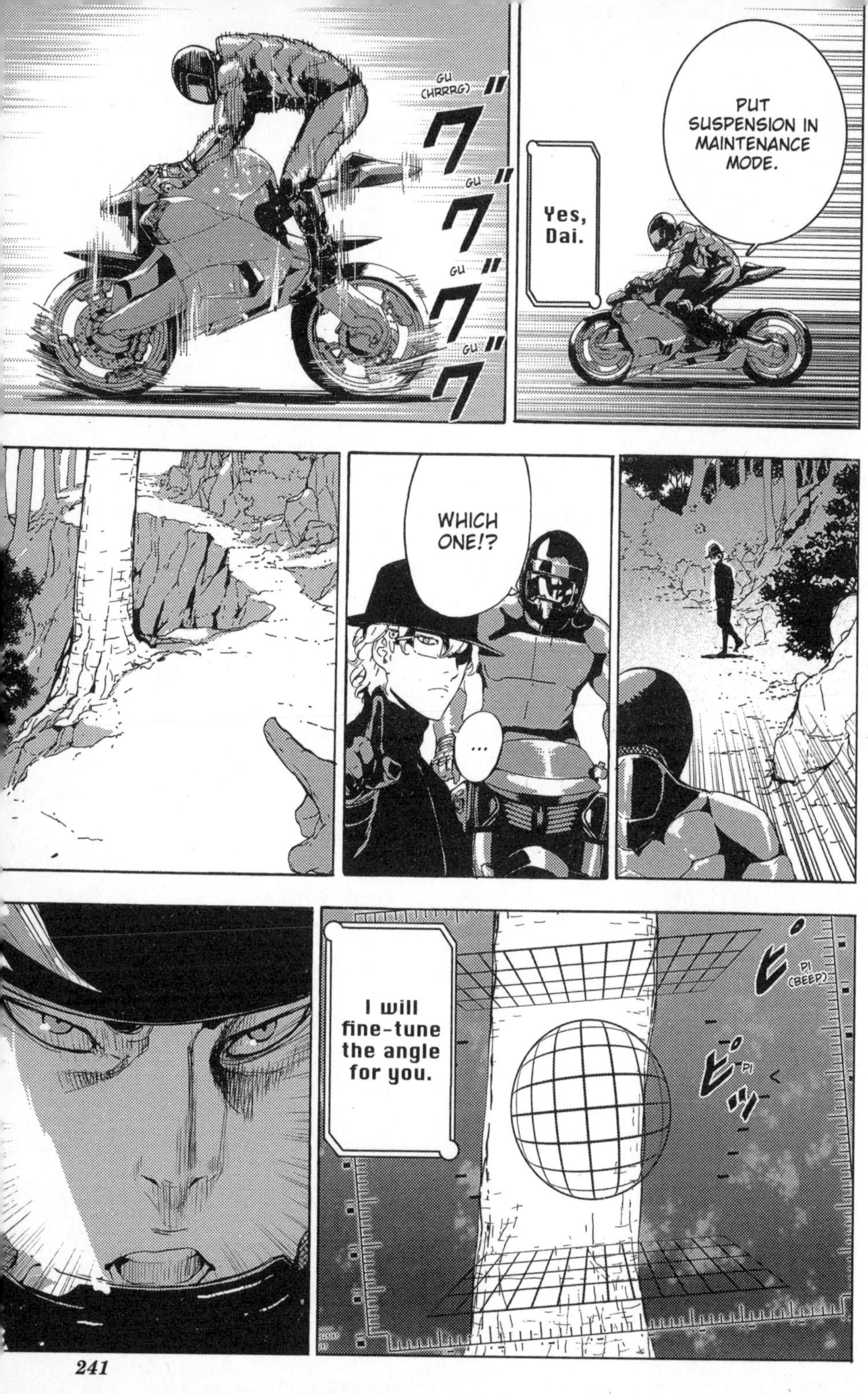
PUT SUSPENSION IN MAINTENANCE MODE.
Yes, Dai.
GU (HRRRG)
GU
GU
GU
WHICH ONE!?
...
PI (BEEP)
PI
I will fine-tune the angle for you.

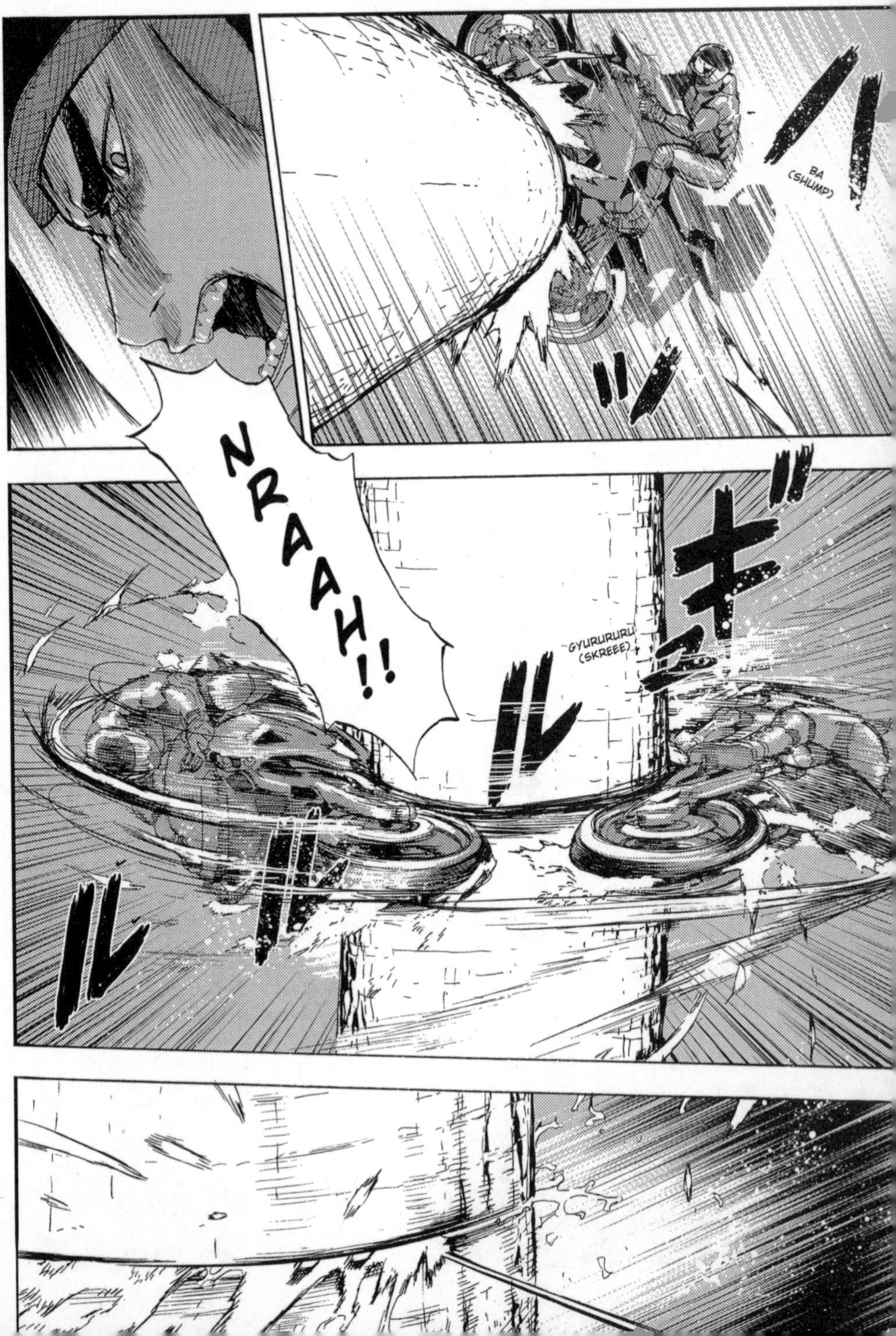
BA
(SHUMP)
NRAAH!!
GYURURURU
(SKREEE)

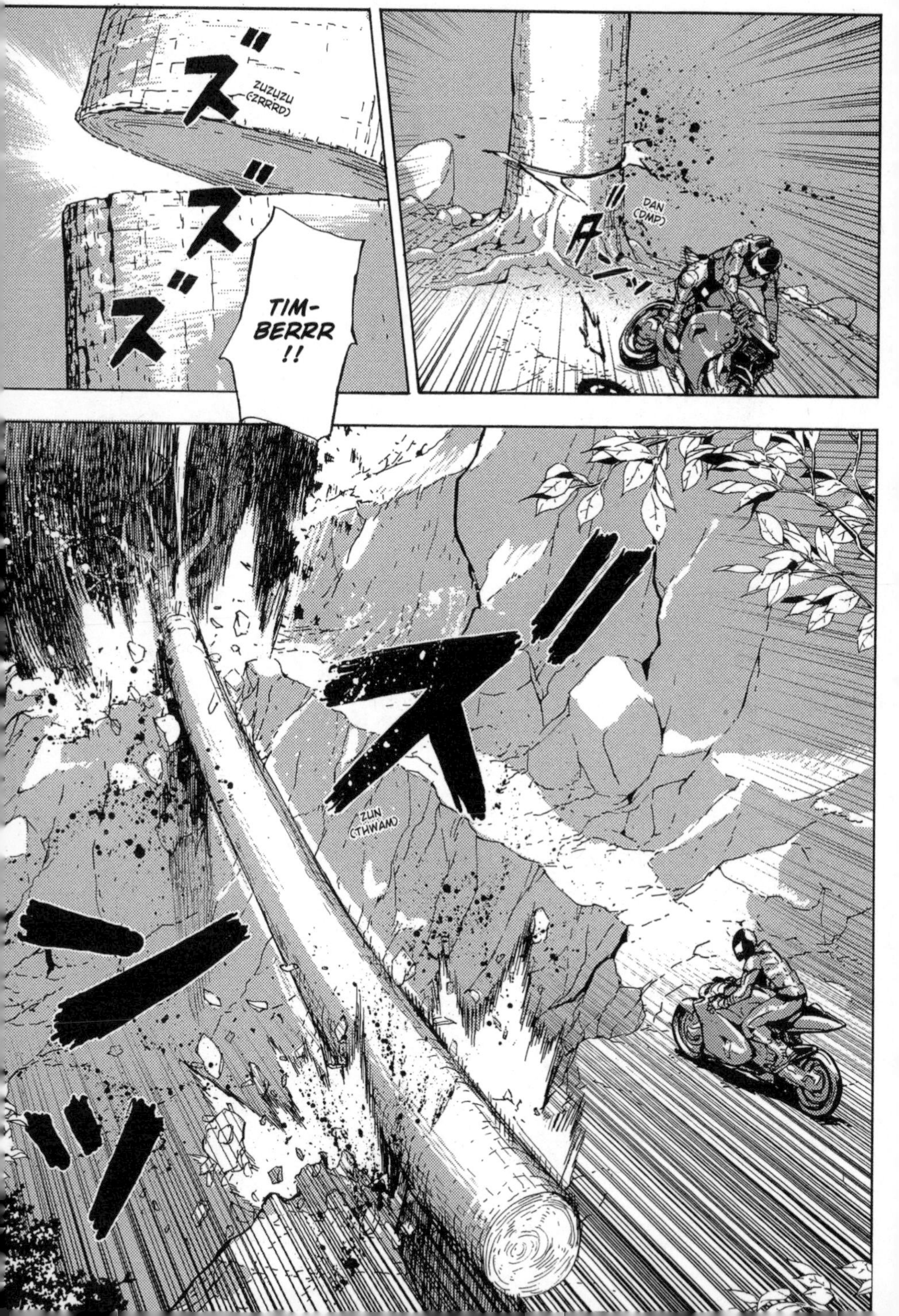
DAN
(DMP)
ZUZUZU
(ZRRRD)
TIM-
BERRR
!!
ZUN
(THWAM)

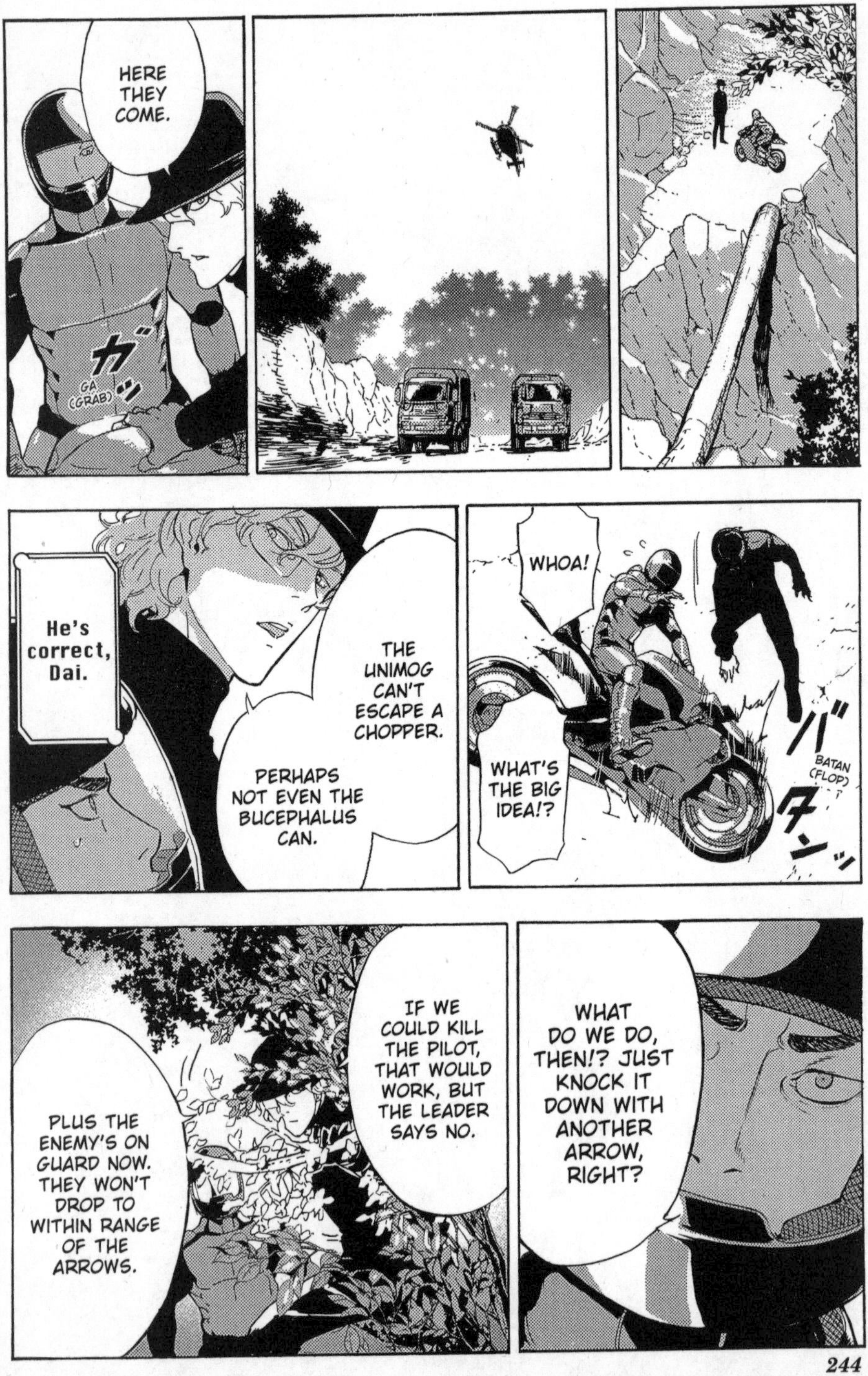
HERE THEY COME.
GA (GRAB)
WHOA!
WHAT'S THE BIG IDEA!?
BATAN (FLOP)
THE UNIMOG CAN'T ESCAPE A CHOPPER.
PERHAPS NOT EVEN THE BUCEPHALUS CAN.
He's correct, Dai.
WHAT DO WE DO, THEN!? JUST KNOCK IT DOWN WITH ANOTHER ARROW, RIGHT?
IF WE COULD KILL THE PILOT, THAT WOULD WORK, BUT THE LEADER SAYS NO.
PLUS THE ENEMY'S ON GUARD NOW. THEY WON'T DROP TO WITHIN RANGE OF THE ARROWS.

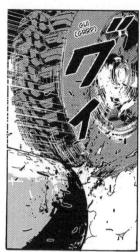

GUI
(GRRP)

THAT'S IT,
HUH!?

GATAN
(THUMP)

GOTO
(KTHUNK)

GOTO

GOTO

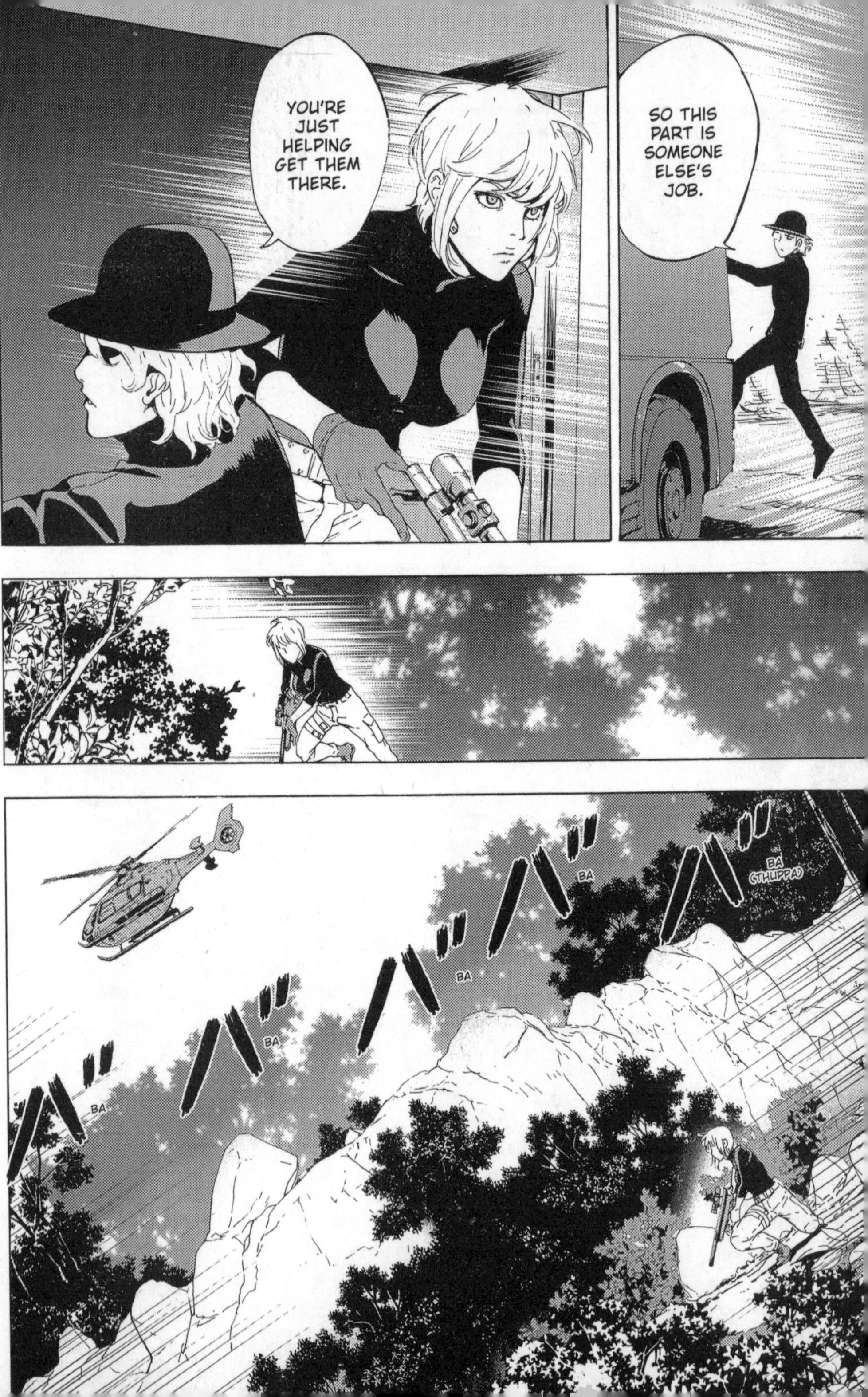
SO THIS PART IS SOMEONE ELSE'S JOB.
YOU'RE JUST HELPING GET THEM THERE.
BA (THUPPA)
BA
BA
BA
BA

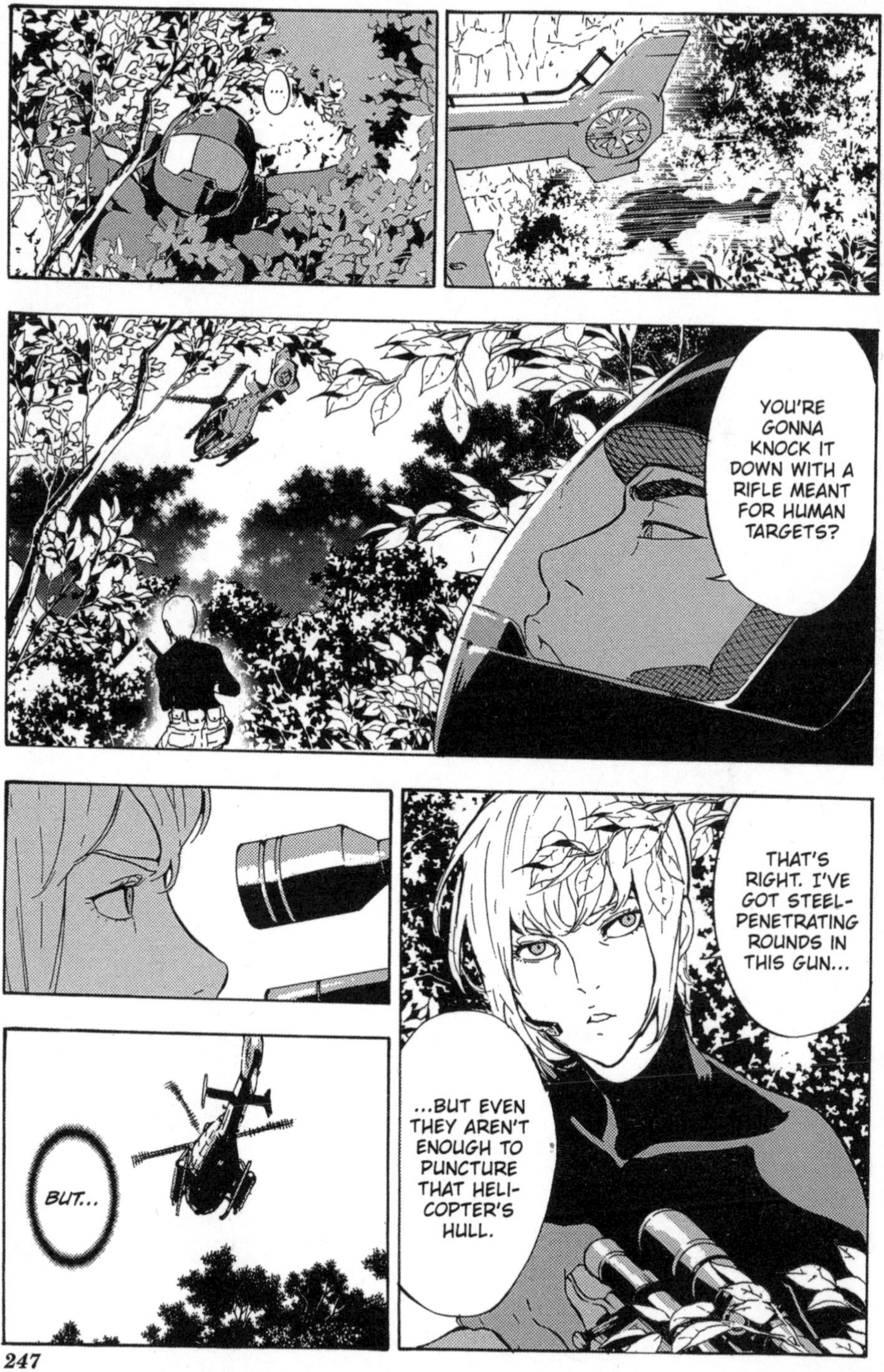
...
YOU'RE GONNA KNOCK IT DOWN WITH A RIFLE MEANT FOR HUMAN TARGETS?
THAT'S RIGHT. I'VE GOT STEEL-PENETRATING ROUNDS IN THIS GUN...
...BUT EVEN THEY AREN'T ENOUGH TO PUNCTURE THAT HELI-COPTER'S HULL.
BUT...

THOSE SINGLE-ROTOR HELIS ALL HAVE ONE FATAL WEAKNESS.

IF YOU CAN HIT THE FANTAIL IN THE RIGHT SPOT...

FUU
(HUFF)

DON
(BLAM)

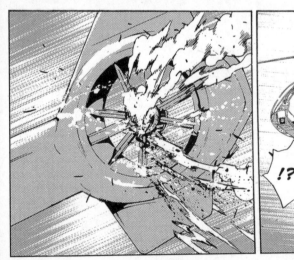

BAKIN
(KRAKK)

!?

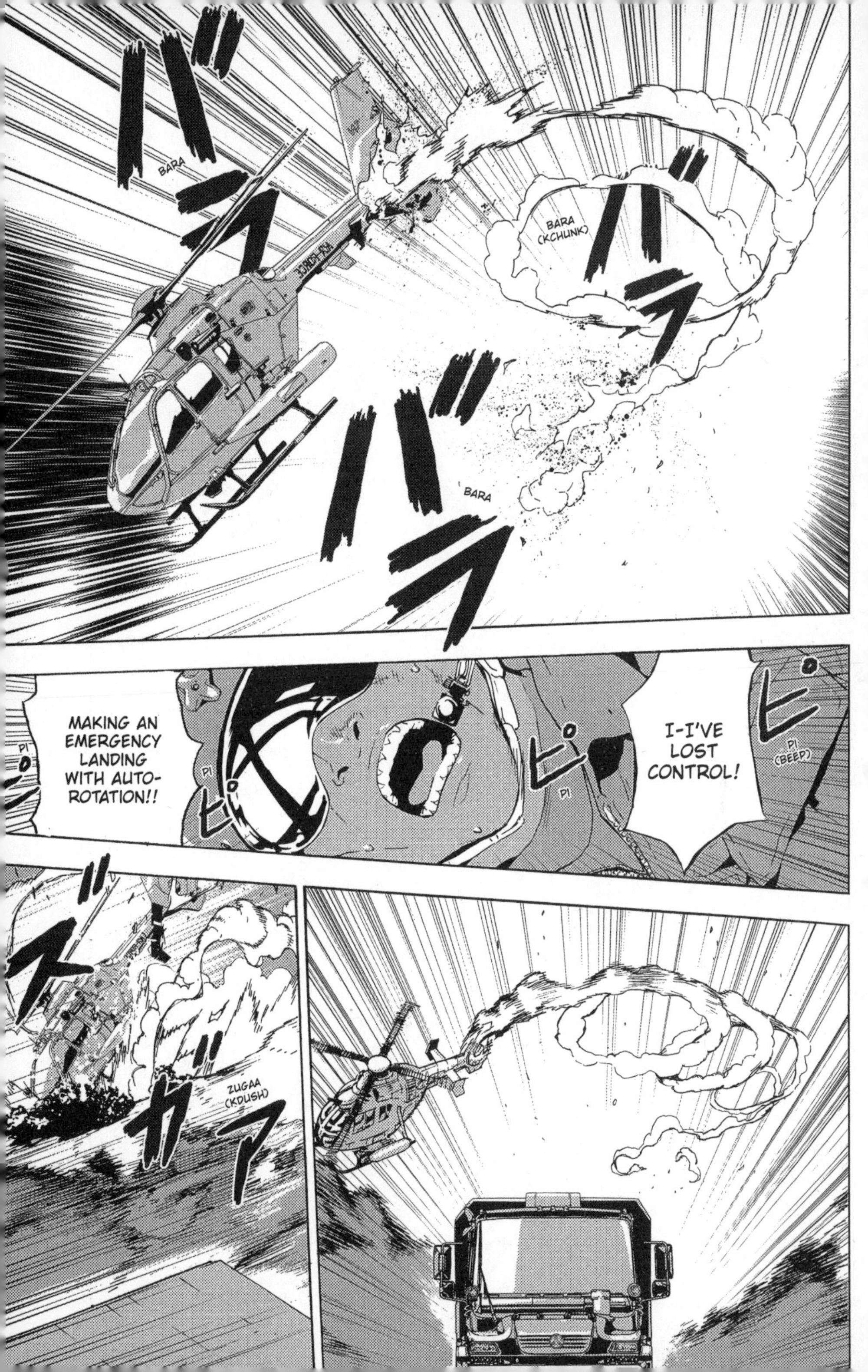
BARA (KCHUNK)
BARA
BARA
PI (BEEP)
I-I'VE LOST CONTROL!
PI
PI
MAKING AN EMERGENCY LANDING WITH AUTO-ROTATION!!
PI
ZUGAA (KDUSH)

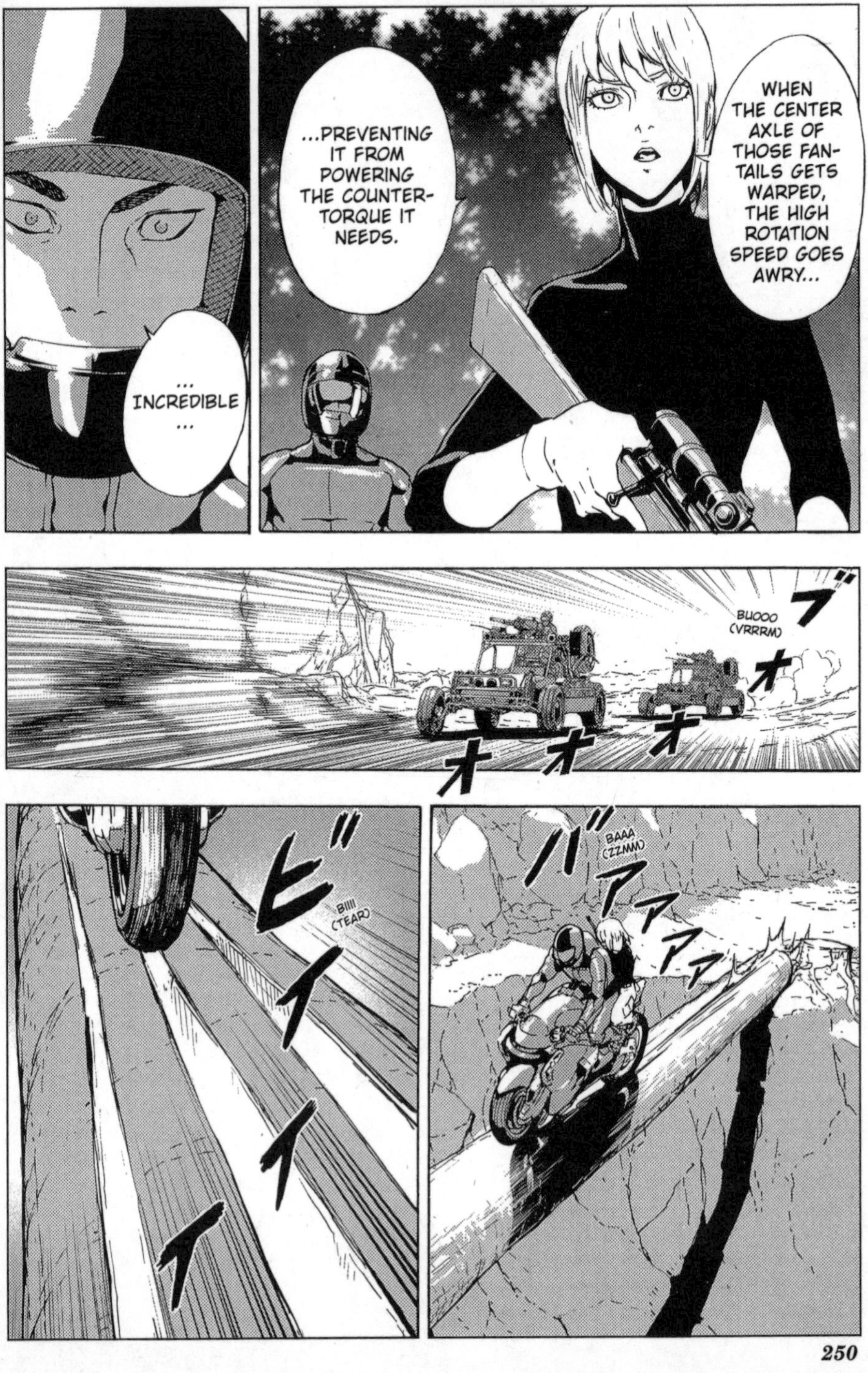
WHEN THE CENTER AXLE OF THOSE FAN-TAILS GETS WARPED, THE HIGH ROTATION SPEED GOES AWRY...
...PREVENTING IT FROM POWERING THE COUNTER-TORQUE IT NEEDS.
... INCREDIBLE ...
BUOOO (VRRRM)
BAAA (ZZMM)
BIIII (TEAR)

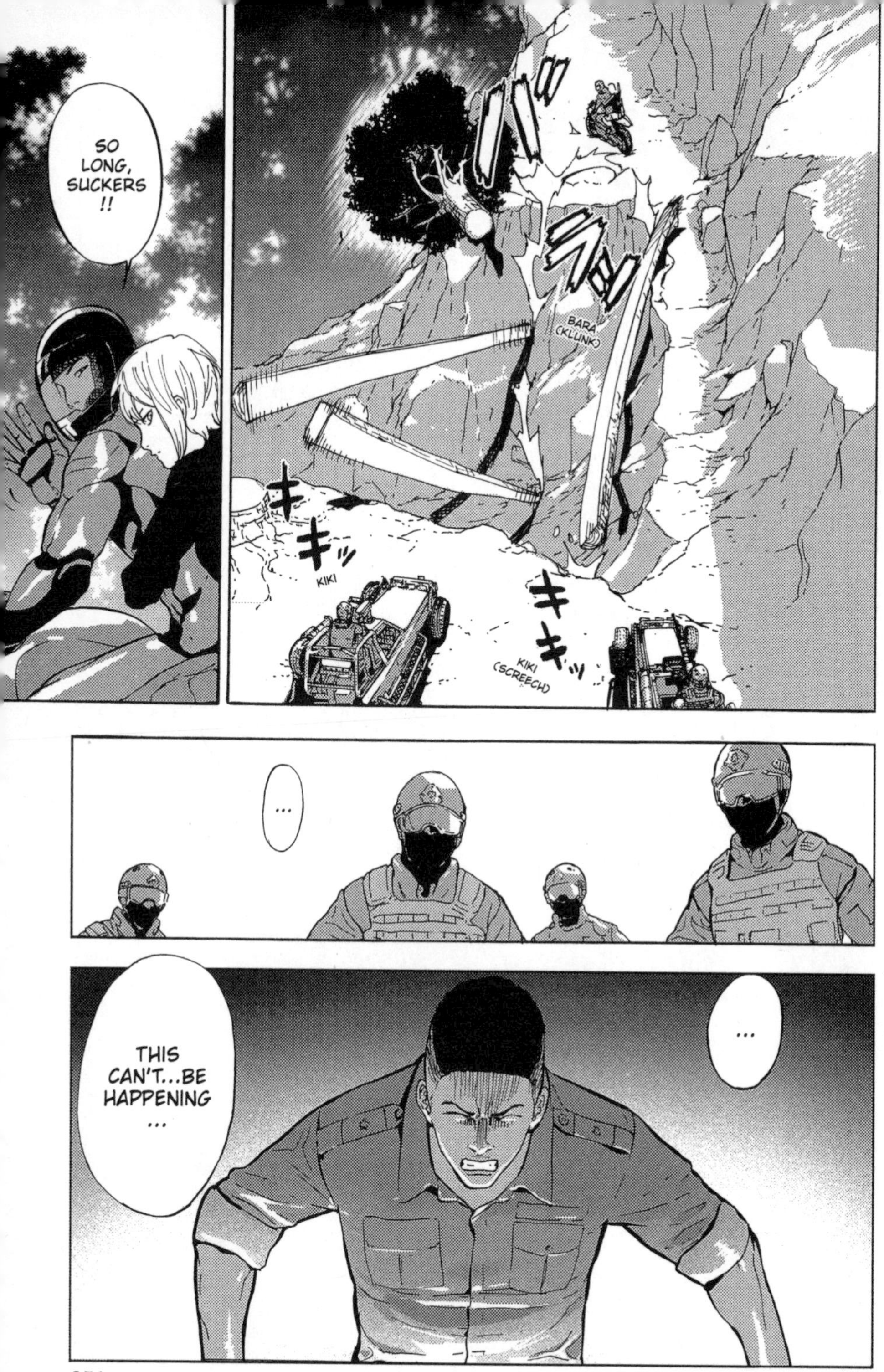
BARA (KLUNK)
KIKI
KIKI (SCREECH)
SO LONG, SUCKERS!!
...
...
THIS CAN'T...BE HAPPENING...

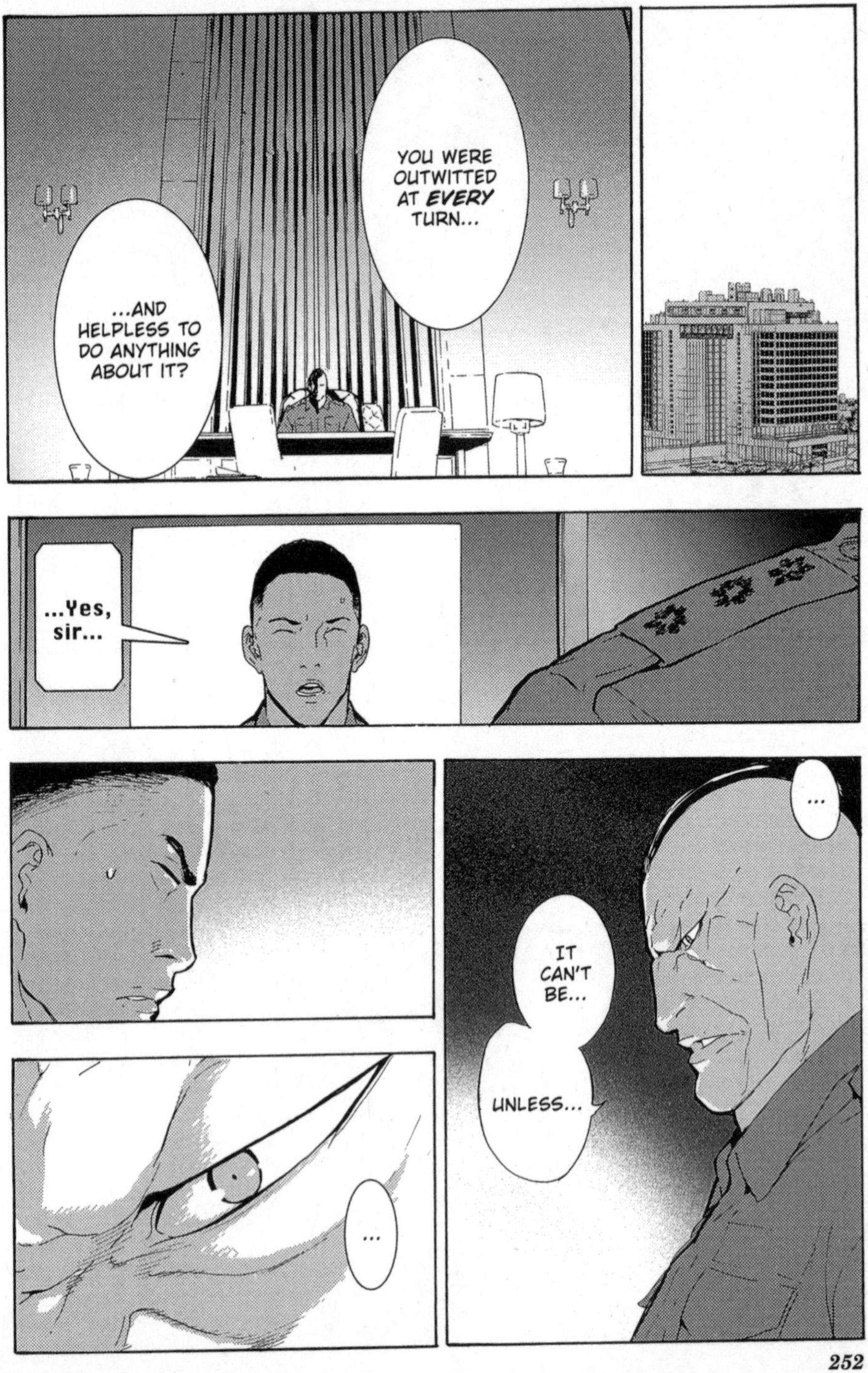
YOU WERE OUTWITTED AT EVERY TURN...
...AND HELPLESS TO DO ANYTHING ABOUT IT?
...Yes, sir...
...
IT CAN'T BE...
UNLESS...
...

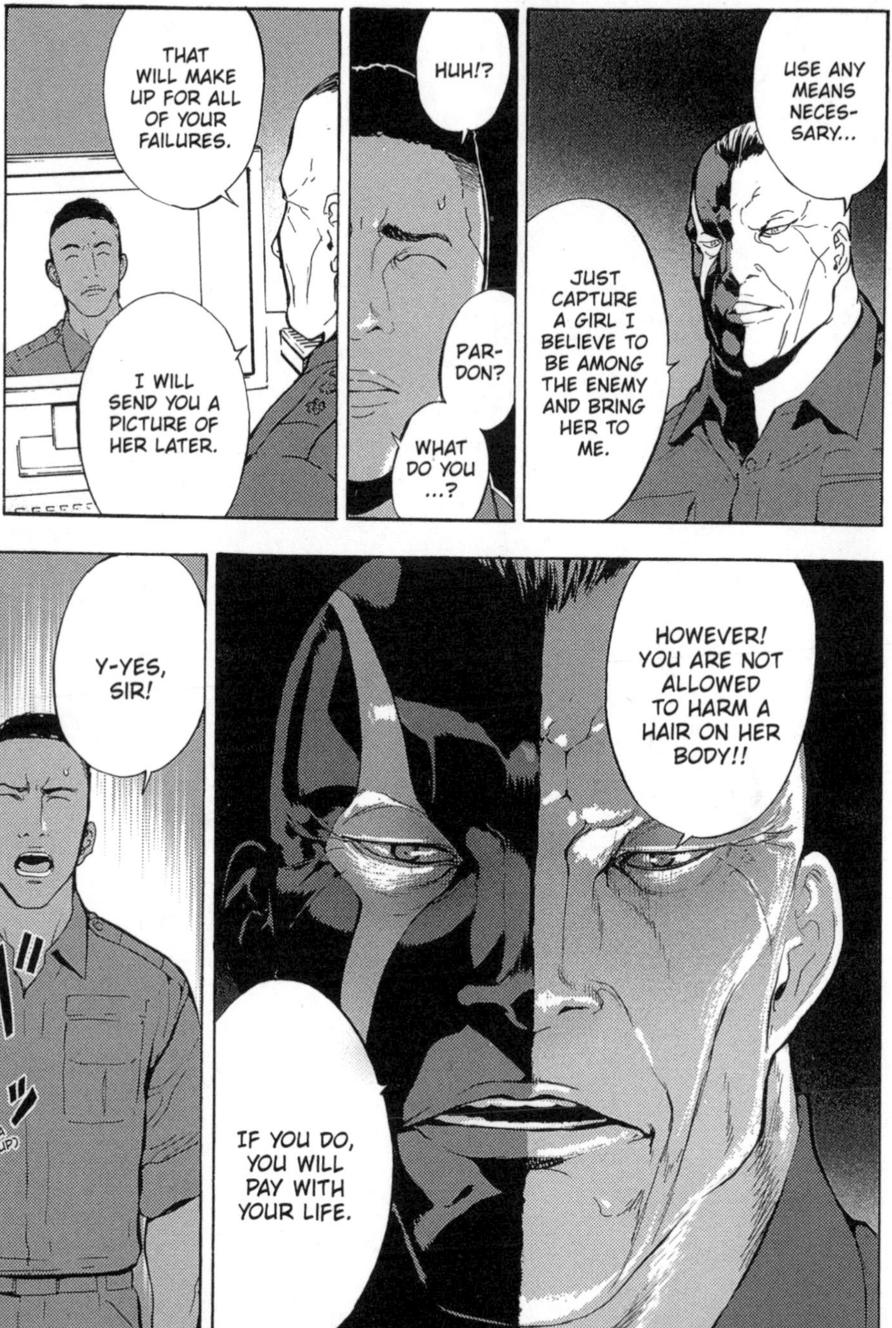
USE ANY MEANS NECES- SARY...
JUST CAPTURE A GIRL I BELIEVE TO BE AMONG THE ENEMY AND BRING HER TO ME.
HUH!?
PAR- DON?
WHAT DO YOU ...?
THAT WILL MAKE UP FOR ALL OF YOUR FAILURES.
I WILL SEND YOU A PICTURE OF HER LATER.
HOWEVER! YOU ARE NOT ALLOWED TO HARM A HAIR ON HER BODY!!
IF YOU DO, YOU WILL PAY WITH YOUR LIFE.
Y-YES, SIR!
BA (HUP)

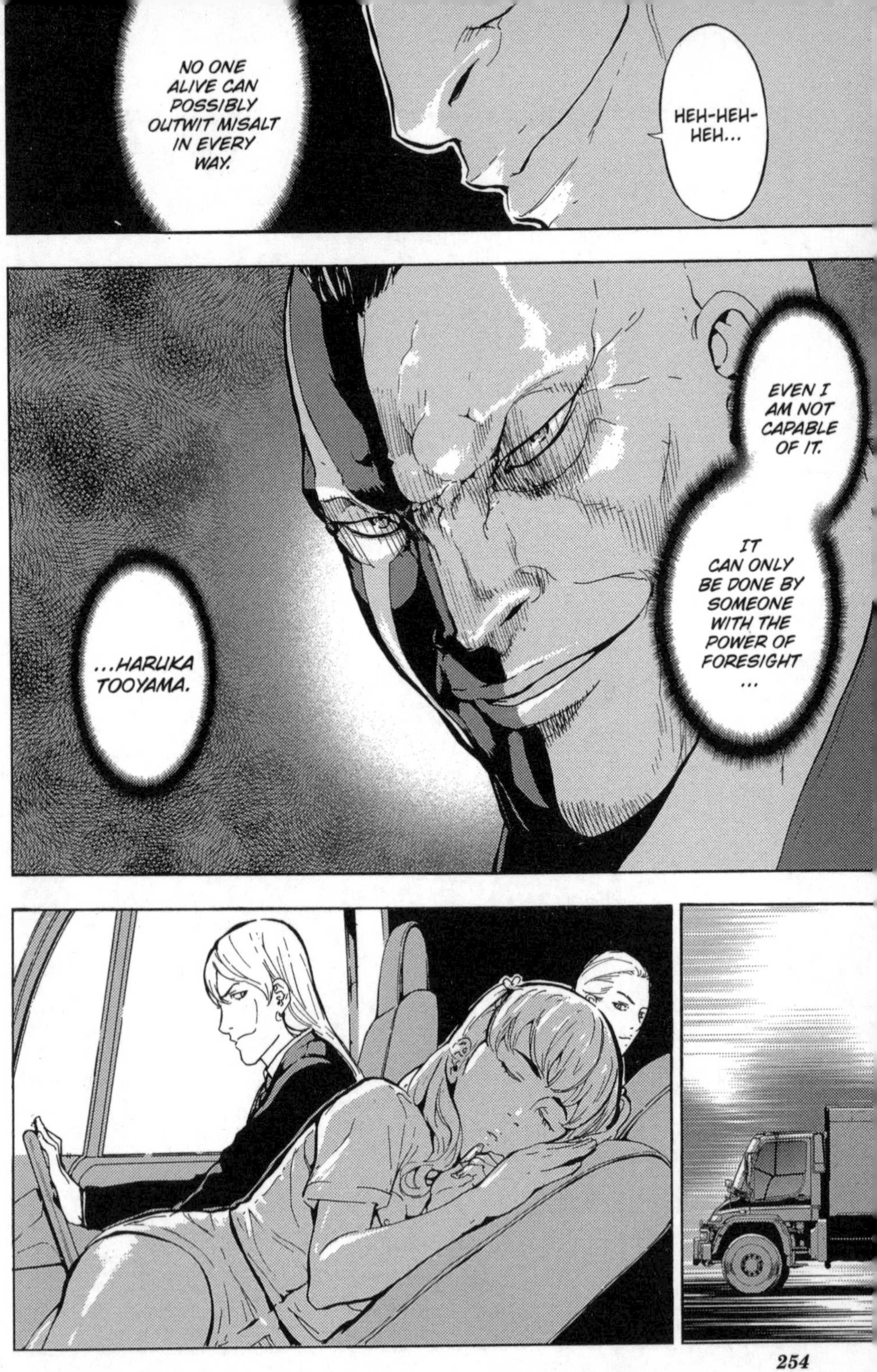
HEH-HEH-HEH...
NO ONE ALIVE CAN POSSIBLY OUTWIT MISALT IN EVERY WAY.
EVEN I AM NOT CAPABLE OF IT.
IT CAN ONLY BE DONE BY SOMEONE WITH THE POWER OF FORESIGHT ...
...HARUKA TOOYAMA.

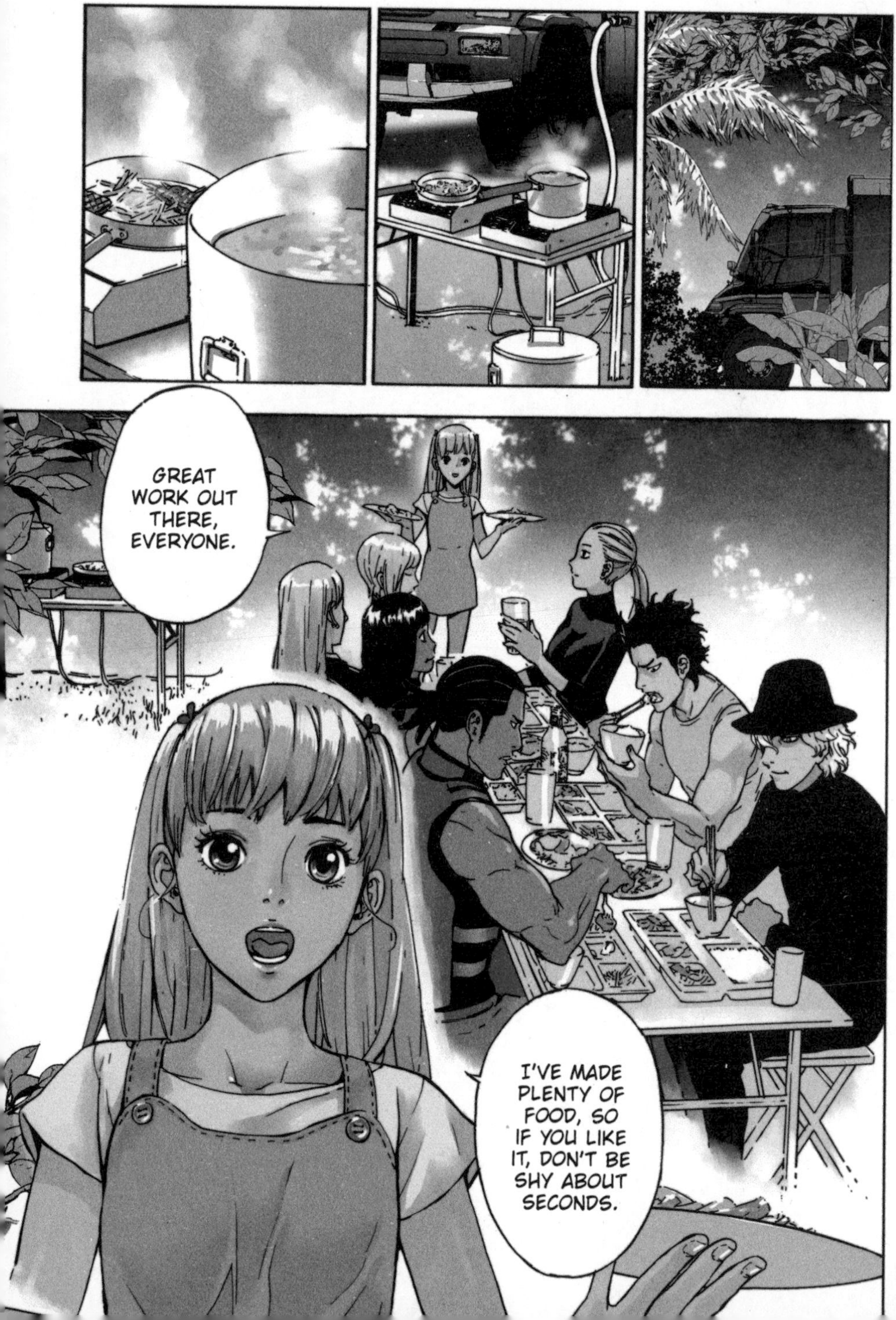
GREAT WORK OUT THERE, EVERYONE.
I'VE MADE PLENTY OF FOOD, SO IF YOU LIKE IT, DON'T BE SHY ABOUT SECONDS.

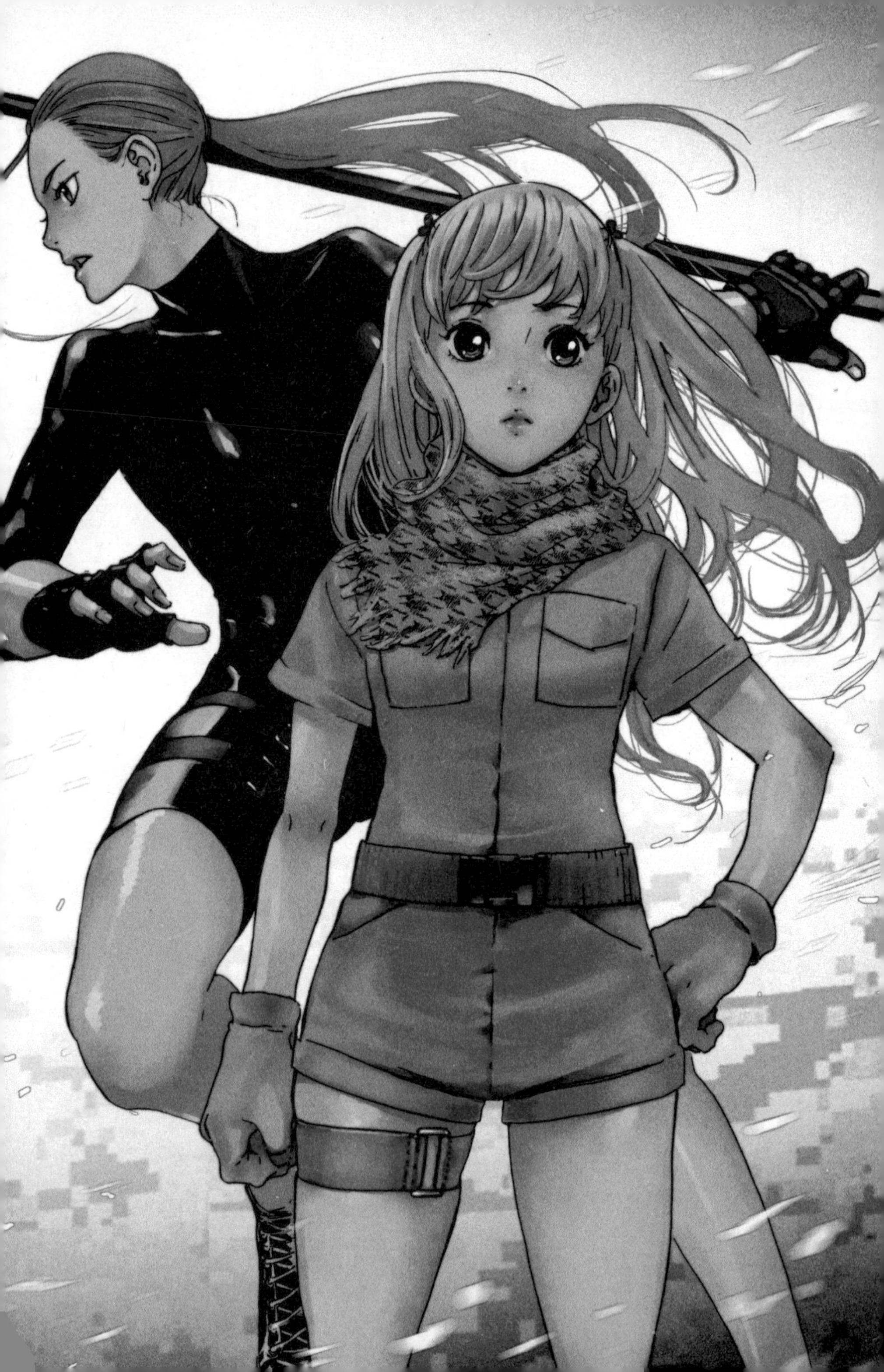

chapter 189

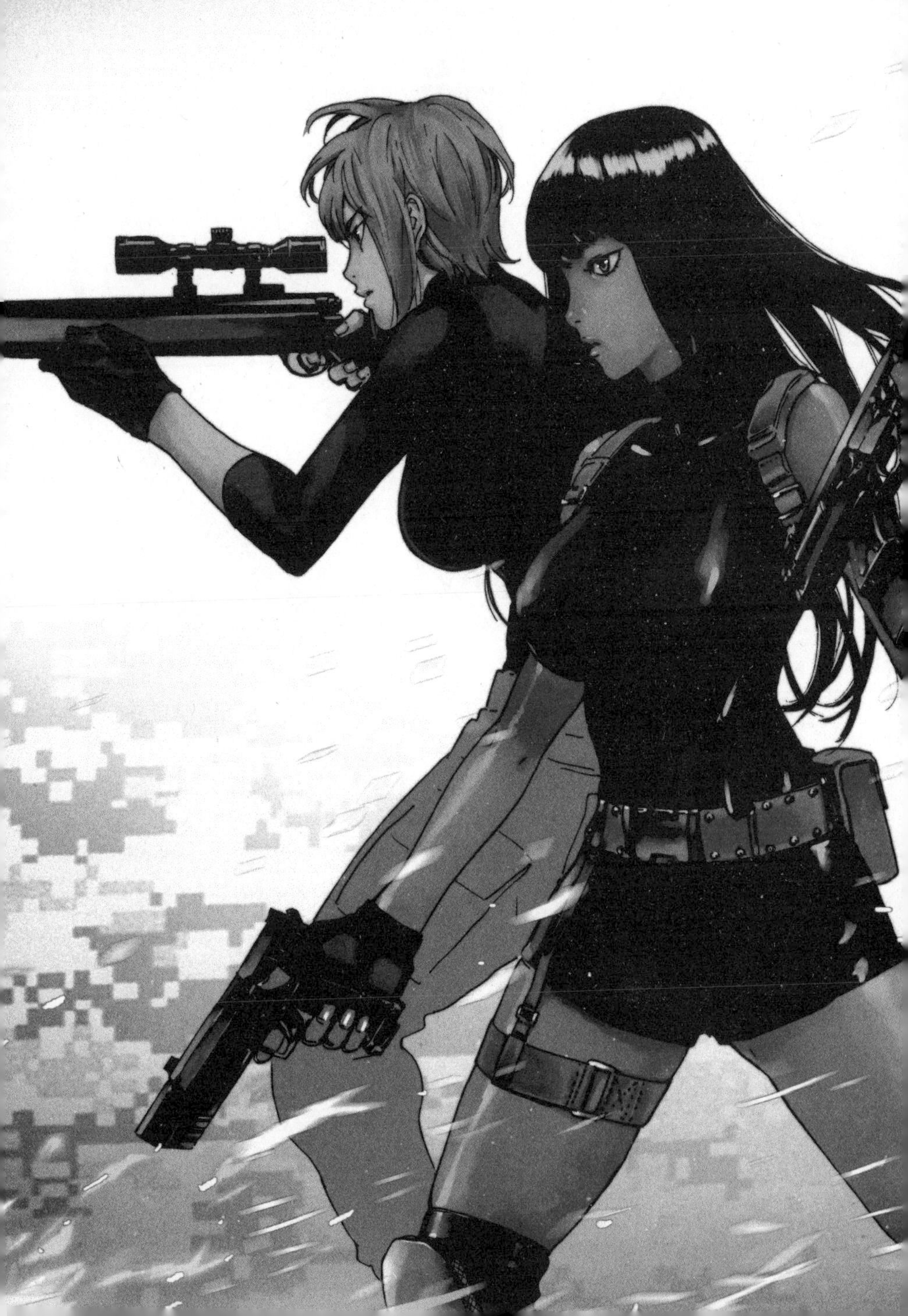

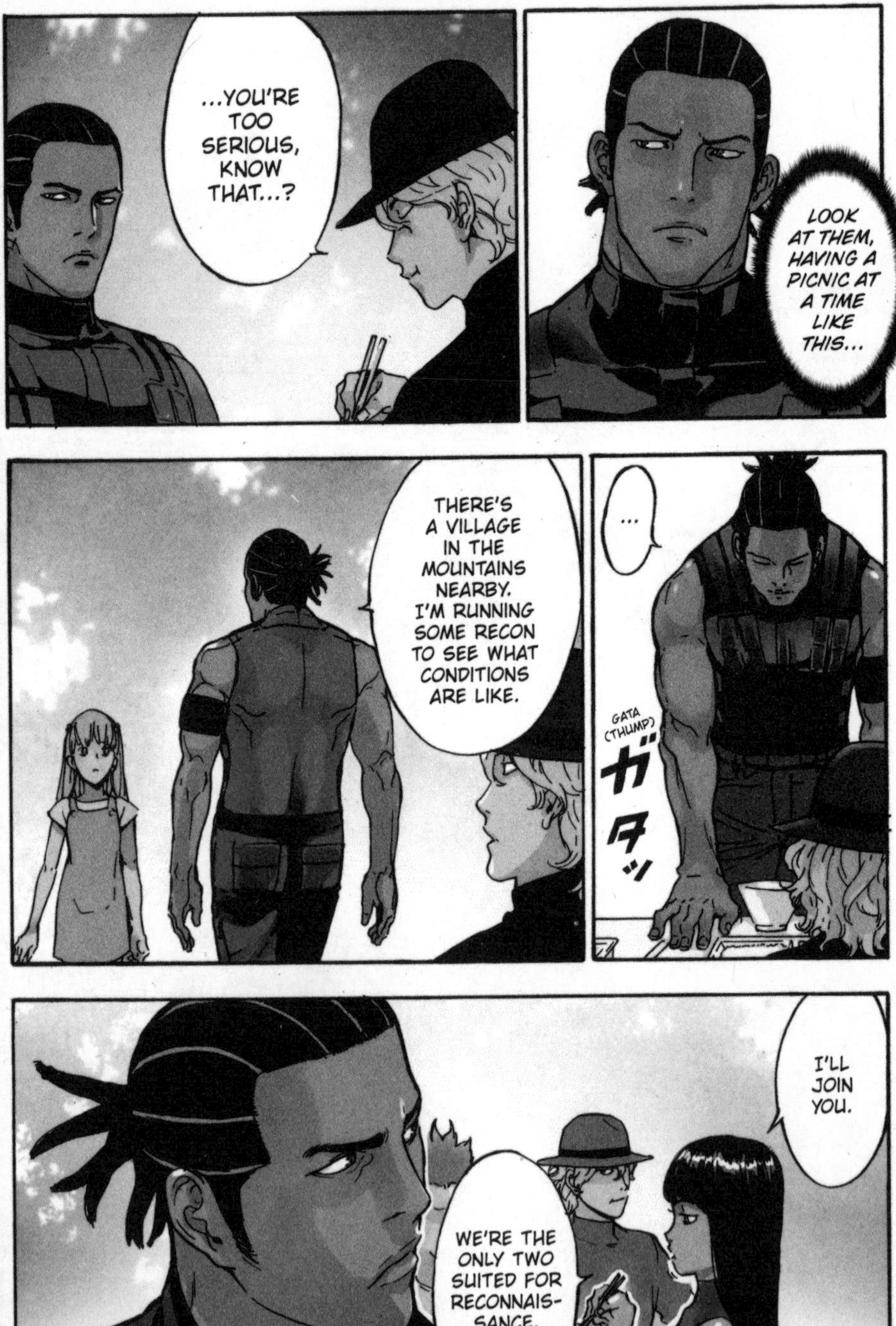
LOOK AT THEM, HAVING A PICNIC AT A TIME LIKE THIS...
...YOU'RE TOO SERIOUS, KNOW THAT...?
...
GATA (THUMP)
ガタッ
THERE'S A VILLAGE IN THE MOUNTAINS NEARBY. I'M RUNNING SOME RECON TO SEE WHAT CONDITIONS ARE LIKE.
I'LL JOIN YOU.
WE'RE THE ONLY TWO SUITED FOR RECONNAIS-SANCE.

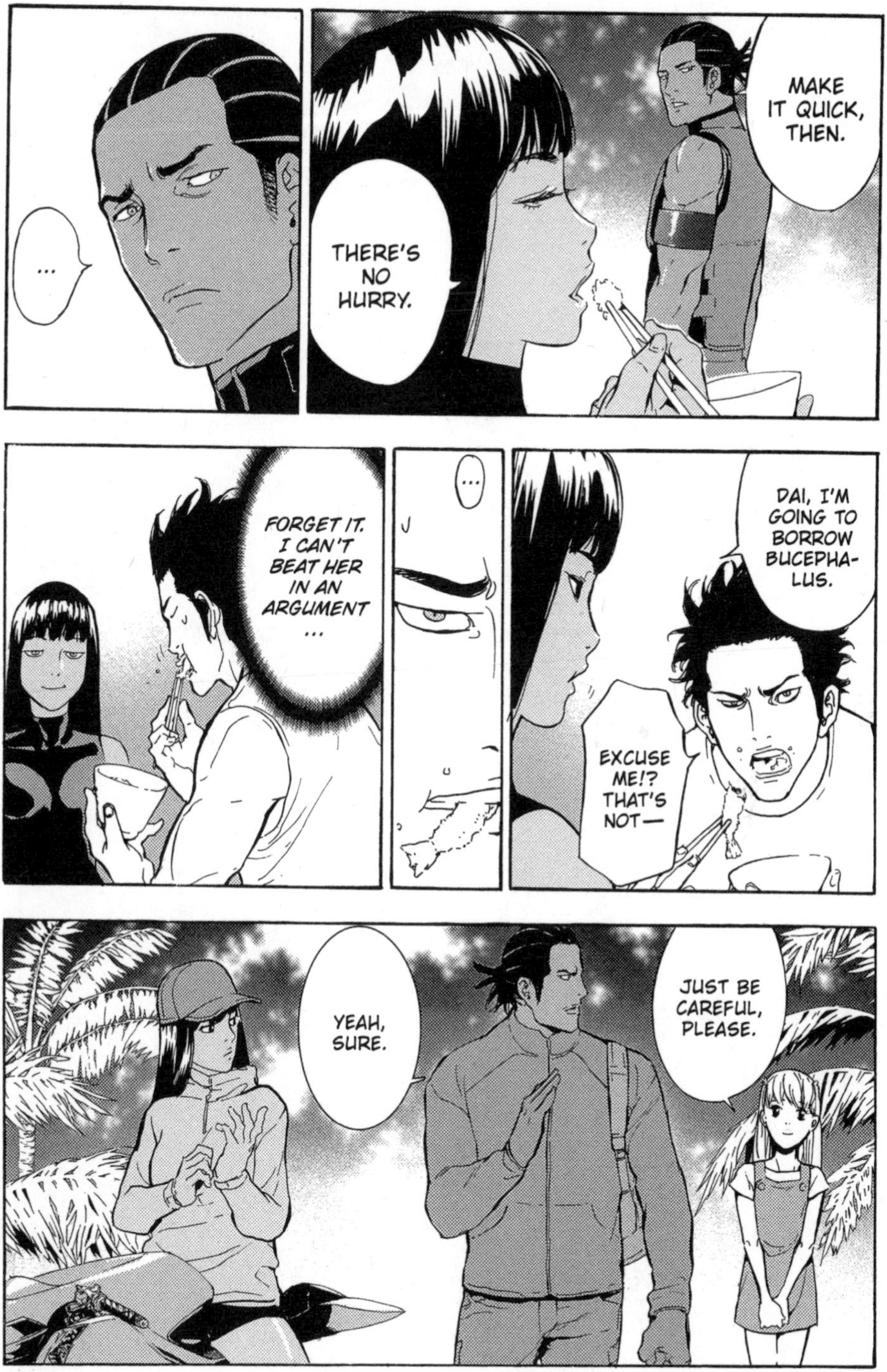
MAKE IT QUICK, THEN.
THERE'S NO HURRY.
...
DAI, I'M GOING TO BORROW BUCEPHA-LUS.
EXCUSE ME!? THAT'S NOT—
...
FORGET IT. I CAN'T BEAT HER IN AN ARGUMENT ...
JUST BE CAREFUL, PLEASE.
YEAH, SURE.

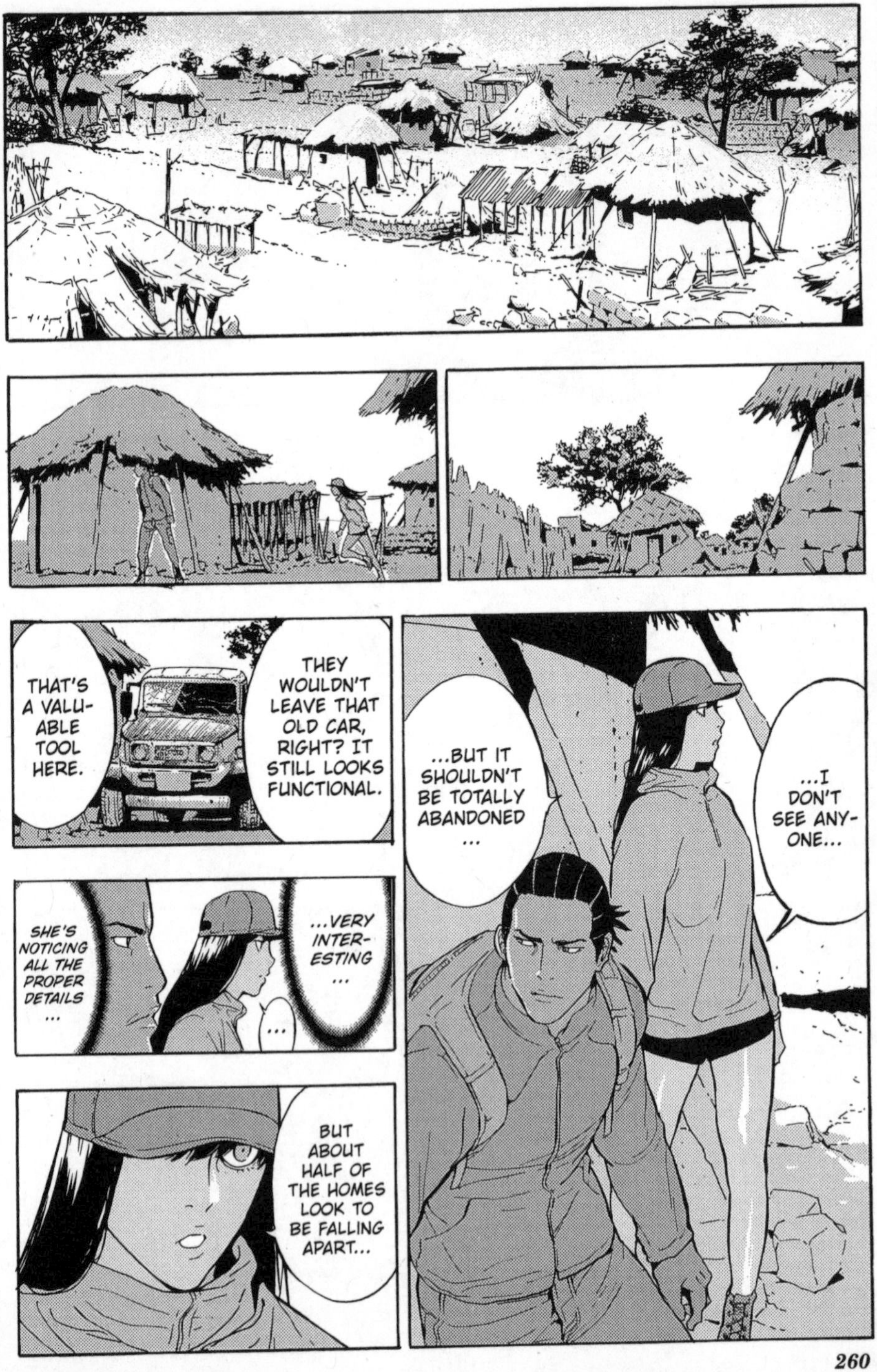
...I DON'T SEE ANYONE...
...BUT IT SHOULDN'T BE TOTALLY ABANDONED...
THEY WOULDN'T LEAVE THAT OLD CAR, RIGHT? IT STILL LOOKS FUNCTIONAL.
THAT'S A VALUABLE TOOL HERE.
...VERY INTERESTING...
...
SHE'S NOTICING ALL THE PROPER DETAILS...
BUT ABOUT HALF OF THE HOMES LOOK TO BE FALLING APART...

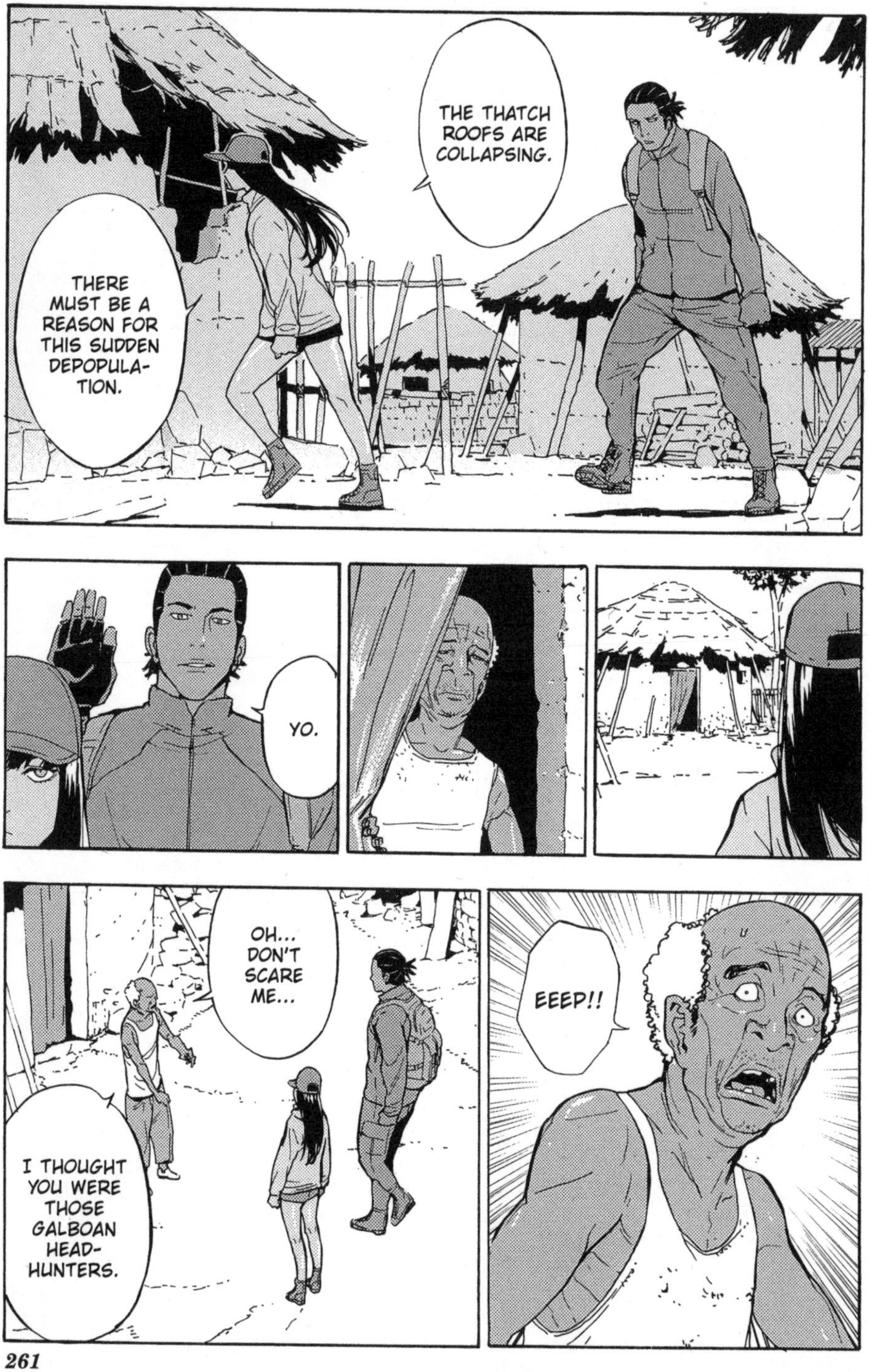
THE THATCH ROOFS ARE COLLAPSING.
THERE MUST BE A REASON FOR THIS SUDDEN DEPOPULA-TION.
YO.
EEEP!!
OH... DON'T SCARE ME...
I THOUGHT YOU WERE THOSE GALBOAN HEAD-HUNTERS.

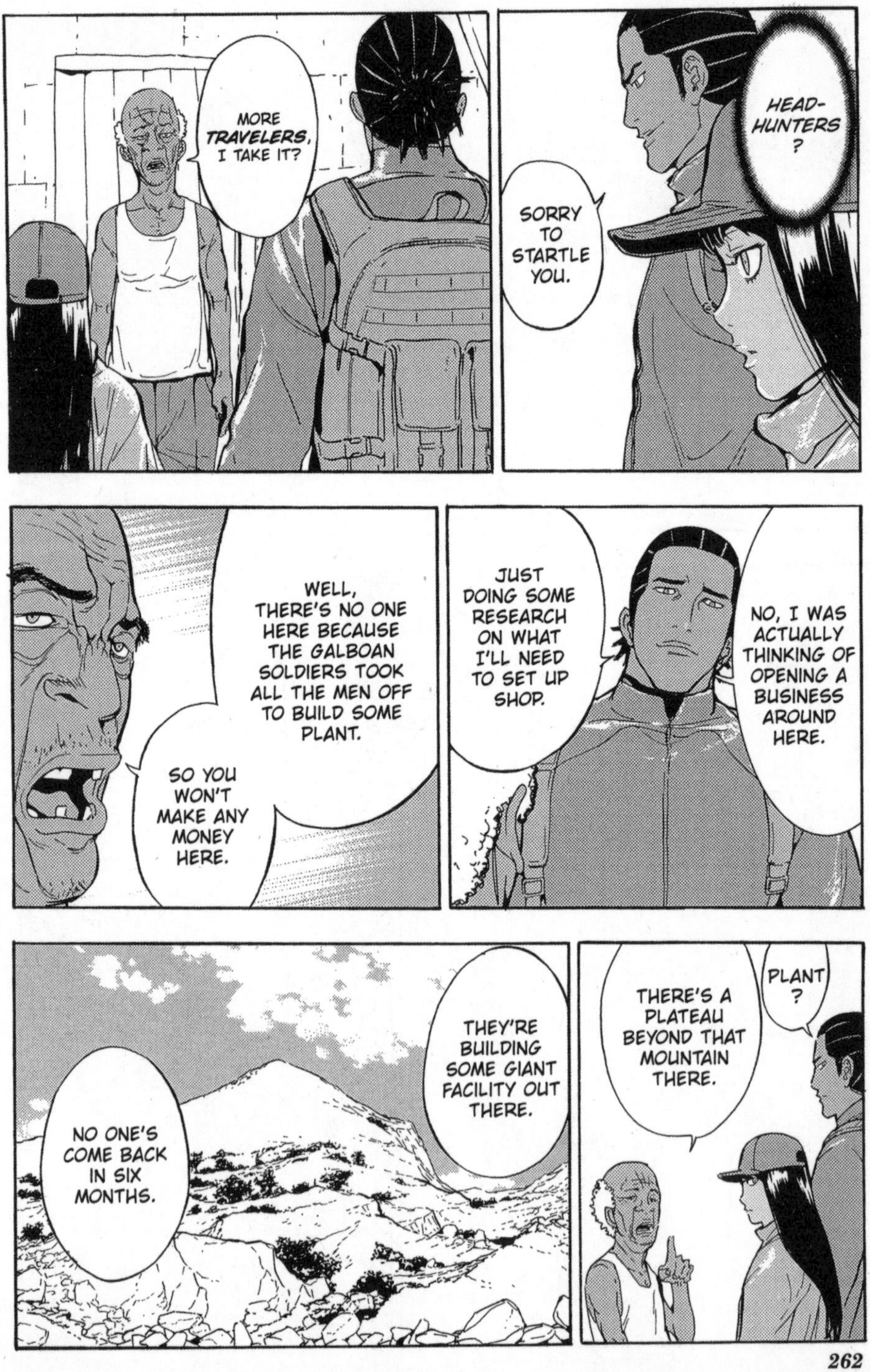
HEAD-HUNTERS?
SORRY TO STARTLE YOU.
MORE *TRAVELERS*, I TAKE IT?
NO, I WAS ACTUALLY THINKING OF OPENING A BUSINESS AROUND HERE.
JUST DOING SOME RESEARCH ON WHAT I'LL NEED TO SET UP SHOP.
WELL, THERE'S NO ONE HERE BECAUSE THE GALBOAN SOLDIERS TOOK ALL THE MEN OFF TO BUILD SOME PLANT.
SO YOU WON'T MAKE ANY MONEY HERE.
PLANT?
THERE'S A PLATEAU BEYOND THAT MOUNTAIN THERE.
THEY'RE BUILDING SOME GIANT FACILITY OUT THERE.
NO ONE'S COME BACK IN SIX MONTHS.

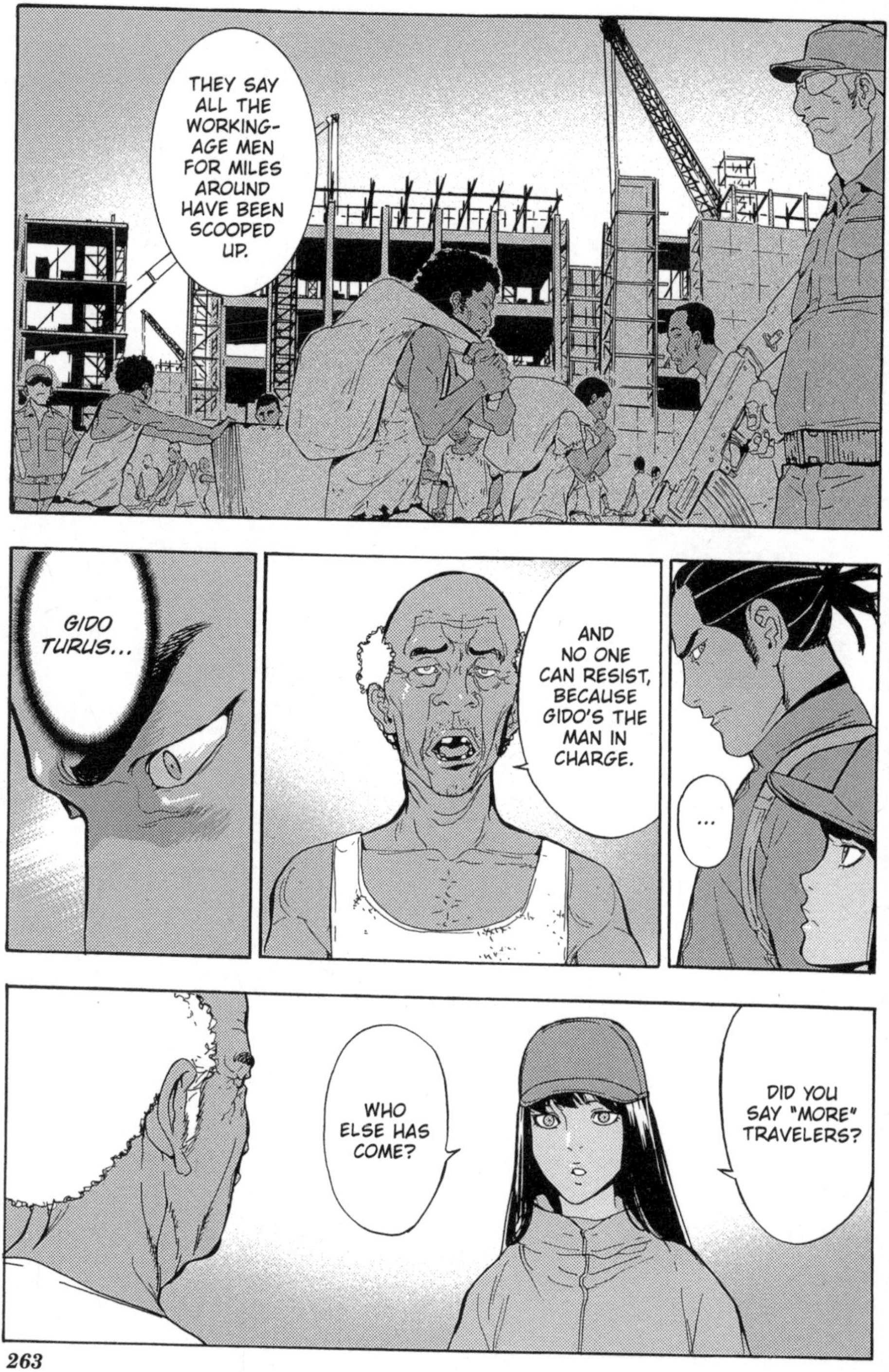
THEY SAY ALL THE WORKING-AGE MEN FOR MILES AROUND HAVE BEEN SCOOPED UP.
...
AND NO ONE CAN RESIST, BECAUSE GIDO'S THE MAN IN CHARGE.
GIDO TURUS...
DID YOU SAY "MORE" TRAVELERS?
WHO ELSE HAS COME?

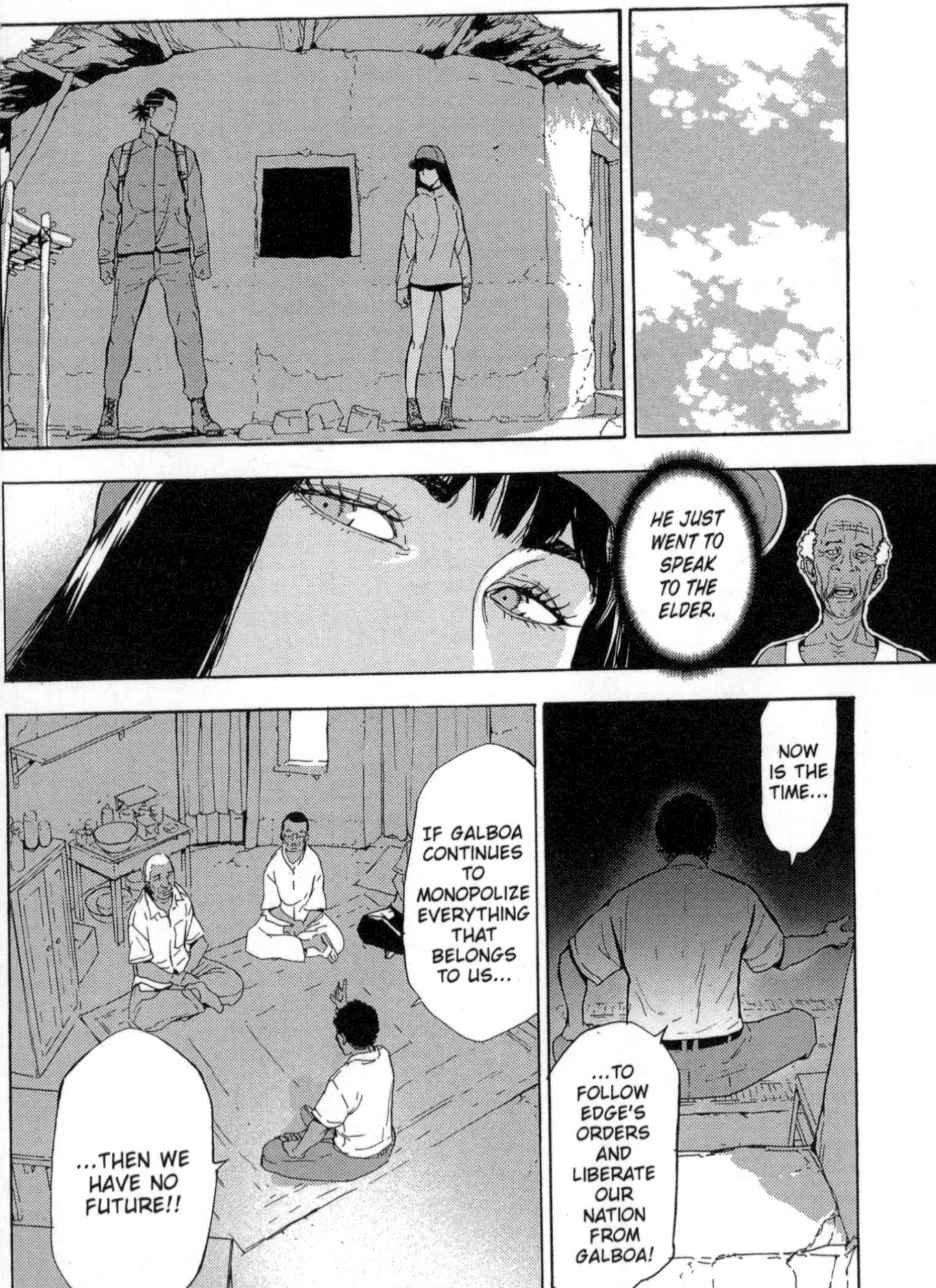
HE JUST WENT TO SPEAK TO THE ELDER.
NOW IS THE TIME...
...TO FOLLOW EDGE'S ORDERS AND LIBERATE OUR NATION FROM GALBOA!
IF GALBOA CONTINUES TO MONOPOLIZE EVERYTHING THAT BELONGS TO US...
...THEN WE HAVE NO FUTURE!!

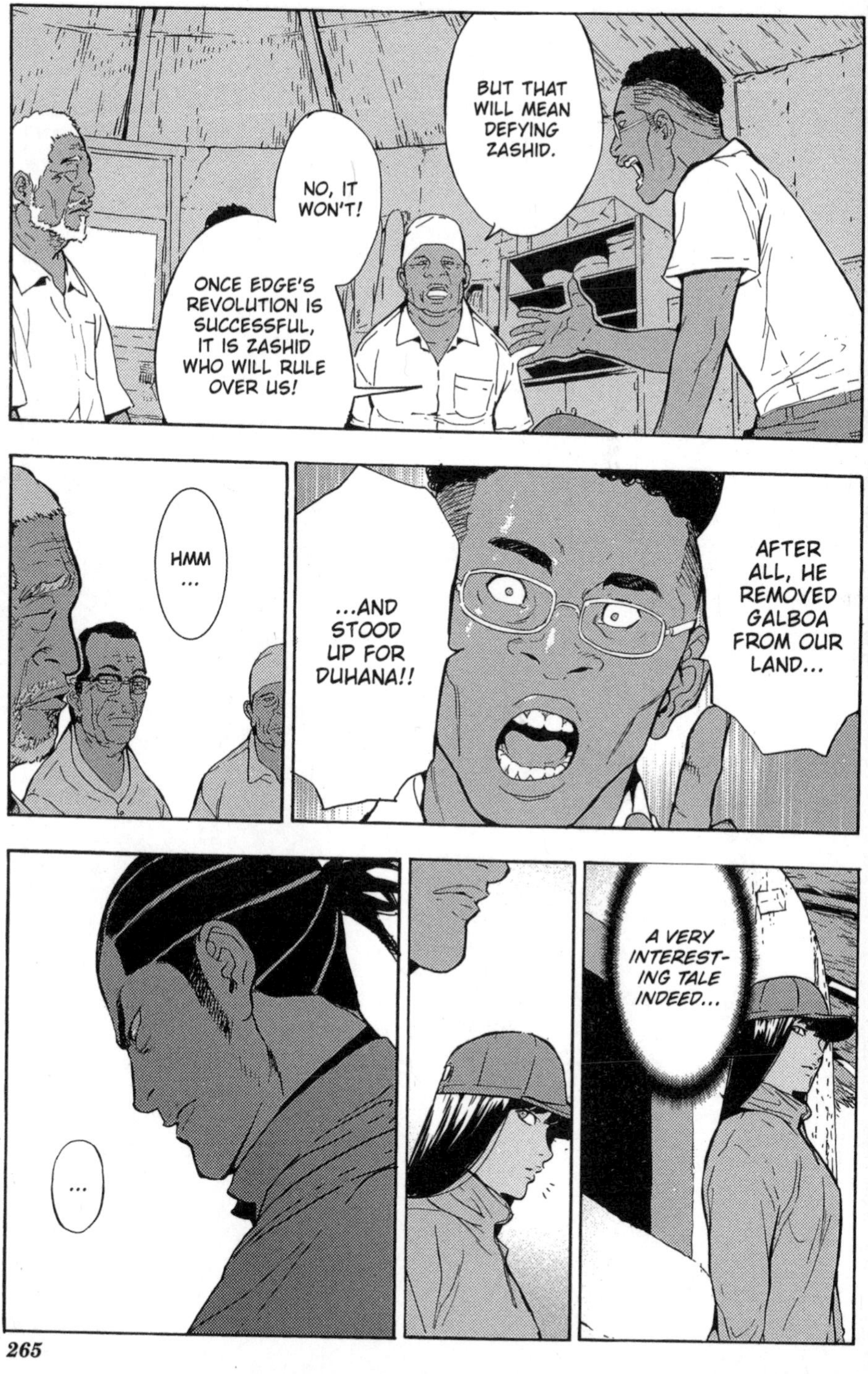
BUT THAT WILL MEAN DEFYING ZASHID.
NO, IT WON'T!
ONCE EDGE'S REVOLUTION IS SUCCESSFUL, IT IS ZASHID WHO WILL RULE OVER US!
AFTER ALL, HE REMOVED GALBOA FROM OUR LAND...
...AND STOOD UP FOR DUHANA!!
HMM ...
A VERY INTEREST-ING TALE INDEED...
...

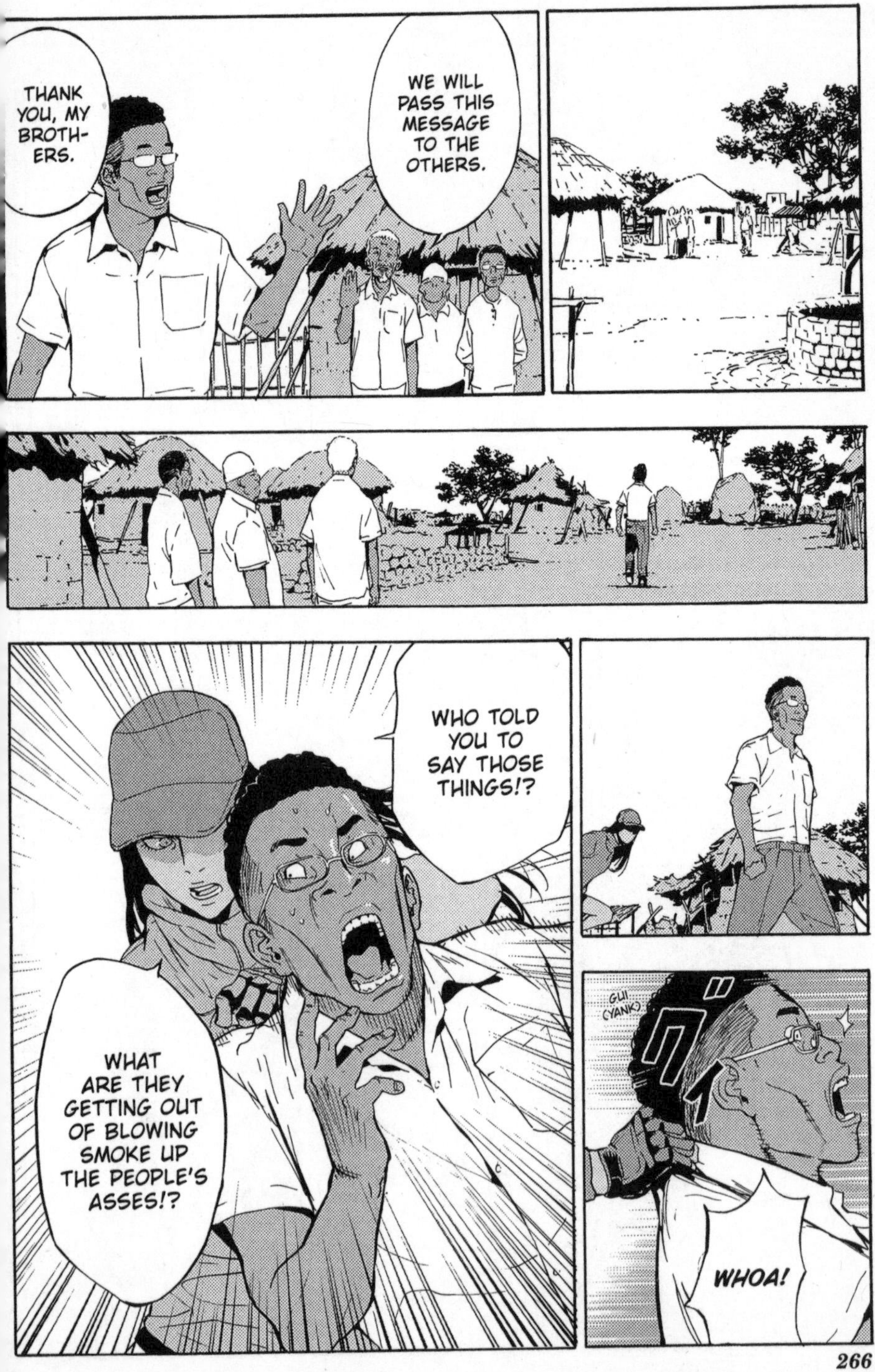
WE WILL PASS THIS MESSAGE TO THE OTHERS.
THANK YOU, MY BROTH-ERS.
GUI (YANK)
WHOA!
WHO TOLD YOU TO SAY THOSE THINGS!?
WHAT ARE THEY GETTING OUT OF BLOWING SMOKE UP THE PEOPLE'S ASSES!?

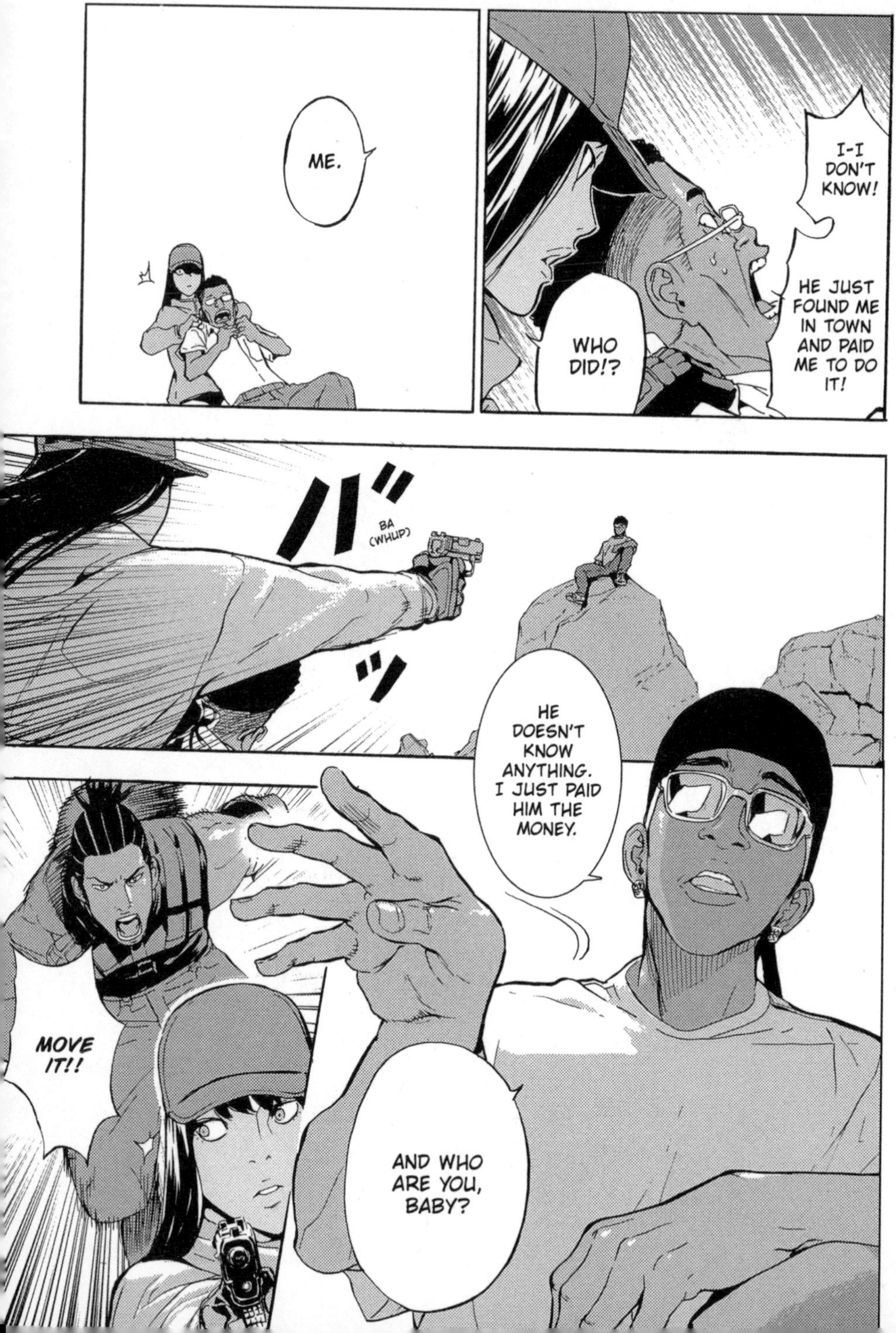
I-I DON'T KNOW!
HE JUST FOUND ME IN TOWN AND PAID ME TO DO IT!
WHO DID!?
ME.
バッ
BA (WHUP)
HE DOESN'T KNOW ANYTHING. I JUST PAID HIM THE MONEY.
MOVE IT!!
AND WHO ARE YOU, BABY?

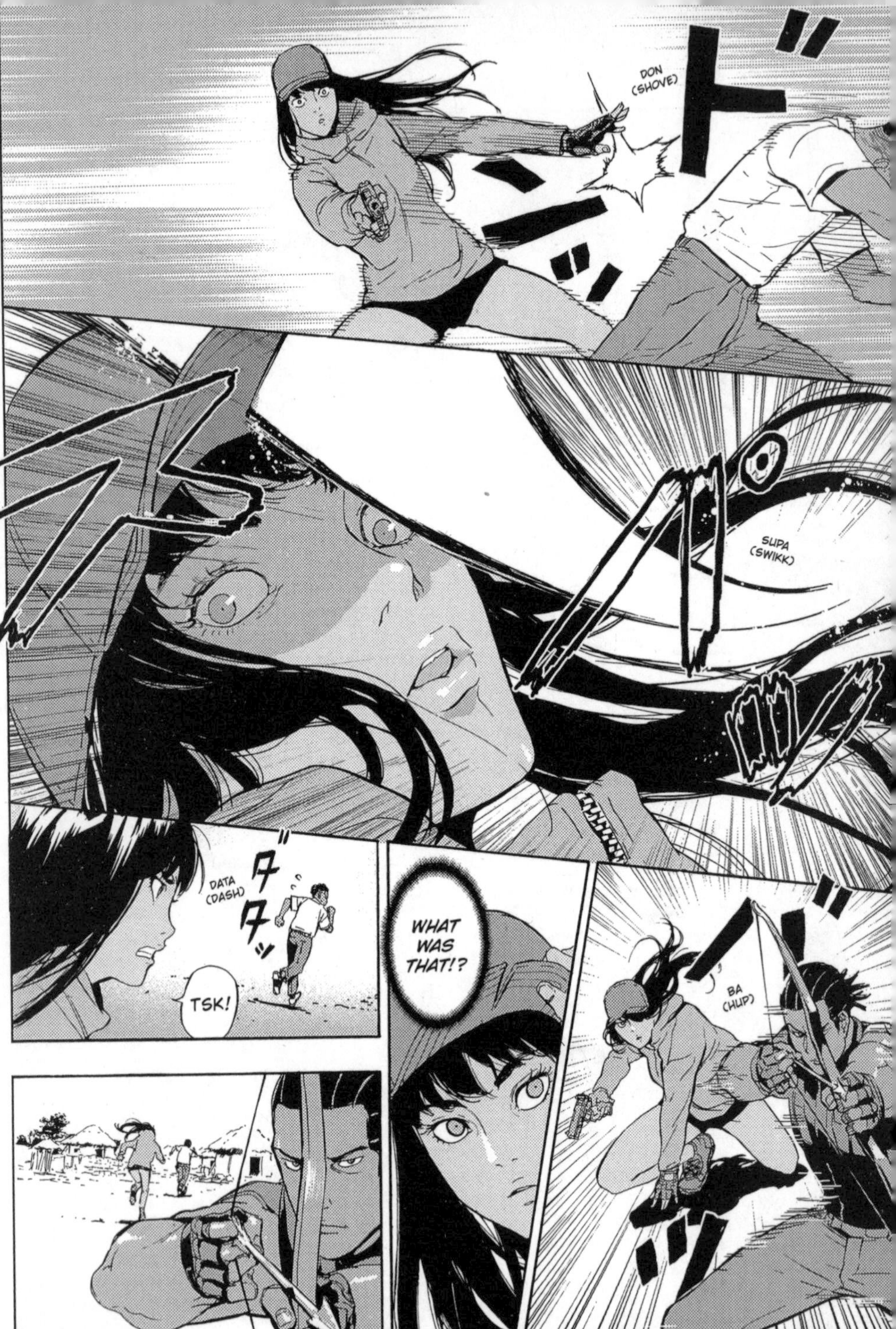
DON
(SHOVE)
SUPA
(SWIKK)
BA
(HUP)
WHAT WAS THAT!?
DATA
(DASH)
TSK!

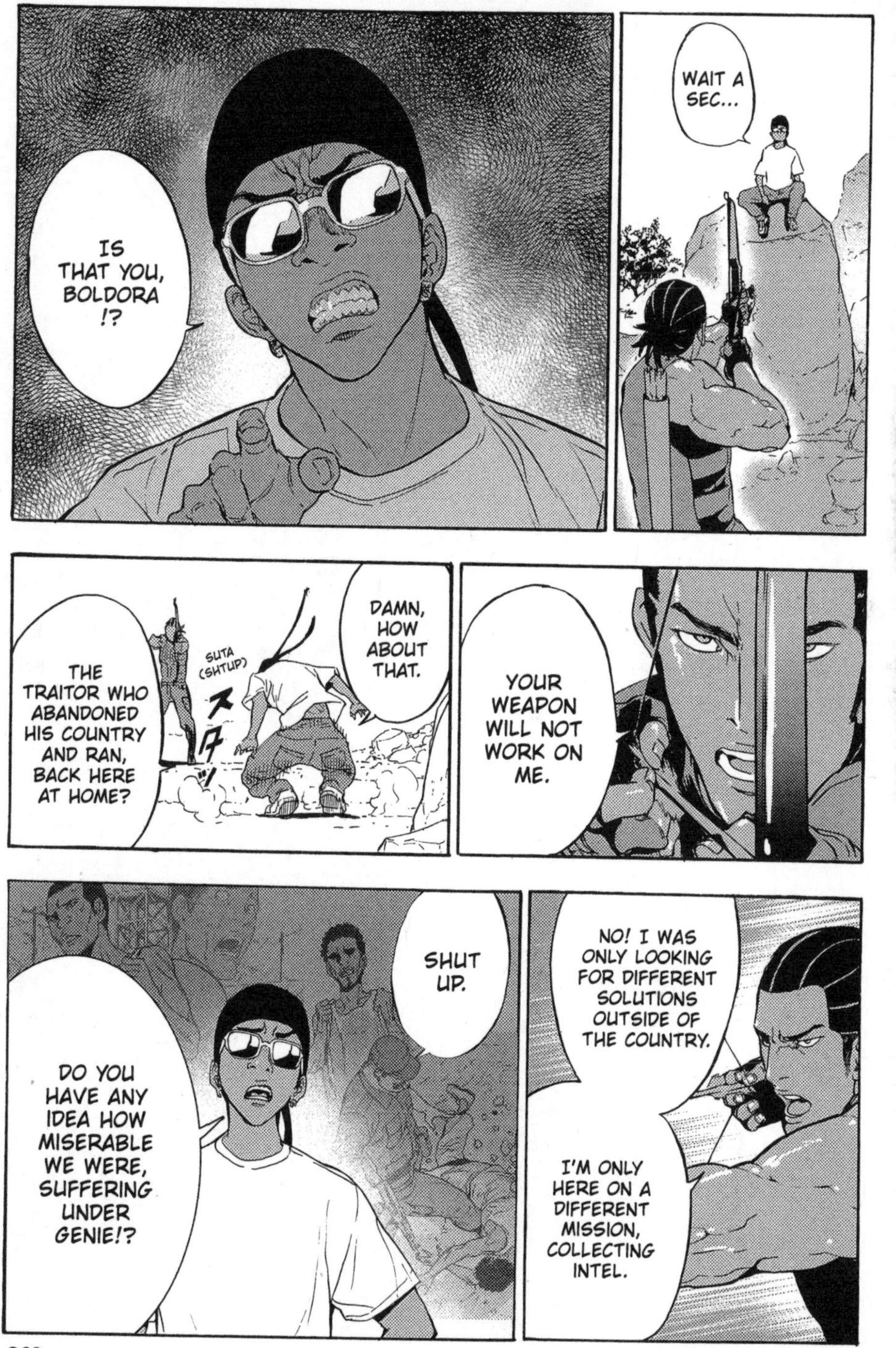
WAIT A SEC...
IS THAT YOU, BOLDORA!?
YOUR WEAPON WILL NOT WORK ON ME.
DAMN, HOW ABOUT THAT.
SUTA (SHTUP)
スタッ
THE TRAITOR WHO ABANDONED HIS COUNTRY AND RAN, BACK HERE AT HOME?
NO! I WAS ONLY LOOKING FOR DIFFERENT SOLUTIONS OUTSIDE OF THE COUNTRY.
I'M ONLY HERE ON A DIFFERENT MISSION, COLLECTING INTEL.
SHUT UP.
DO YOU HAVE ANY IDEA HOW MISERABLE WE WERE, SUFFERING UNDER GENIE!?

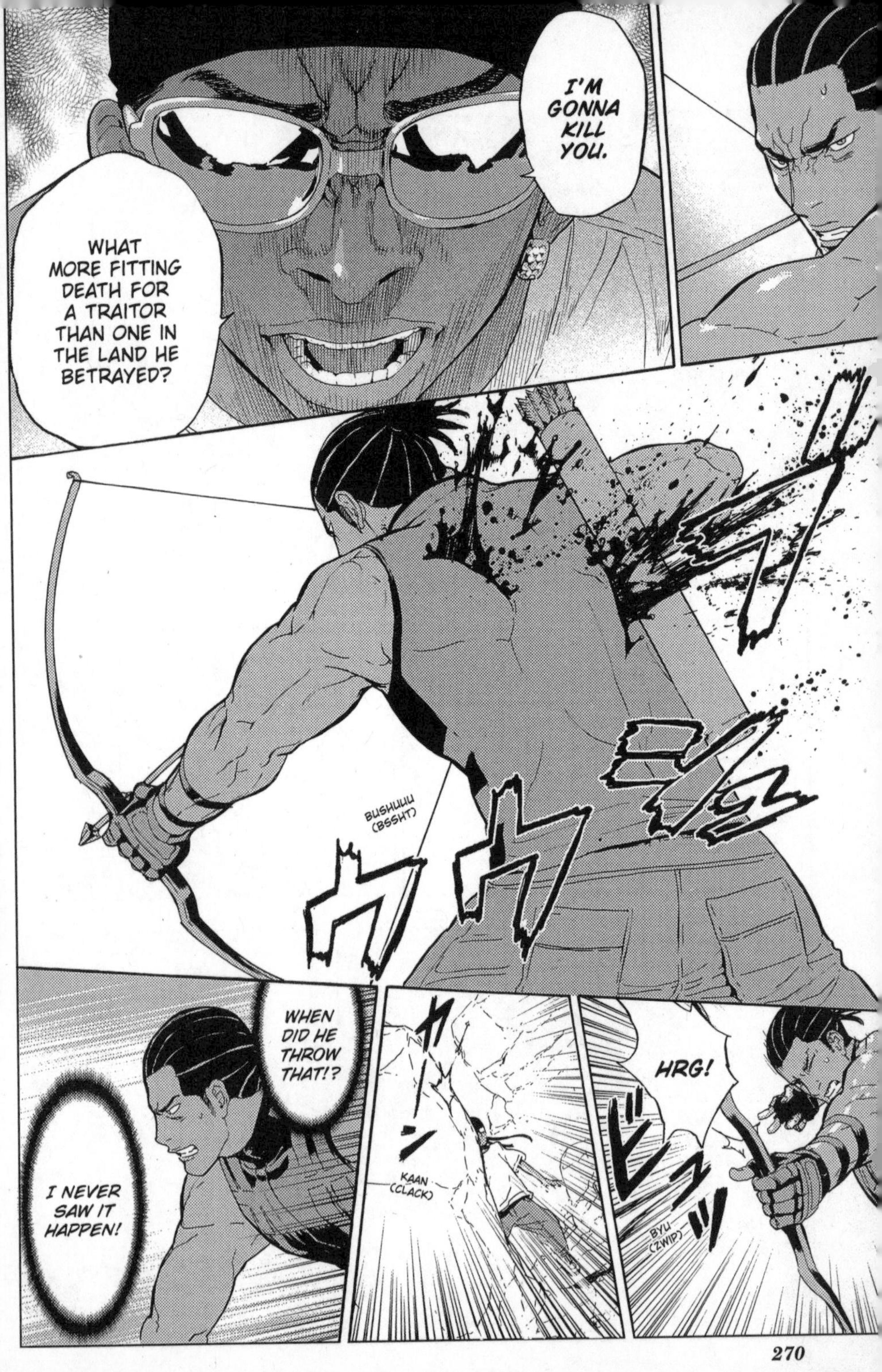
I'M GONNA KILL YOU.
WHAT MORE FITTING DEATH FOR A TRAITOR THAN ONE IN THE LAND HE BETRAYED?
BUSHUUU (BSSHT)
HRG!
BYU (ZWIP)
KAAN (CLACK)
WHEN DID HE THROW THAT!?
I NEVER SAW IT HAPPEN!

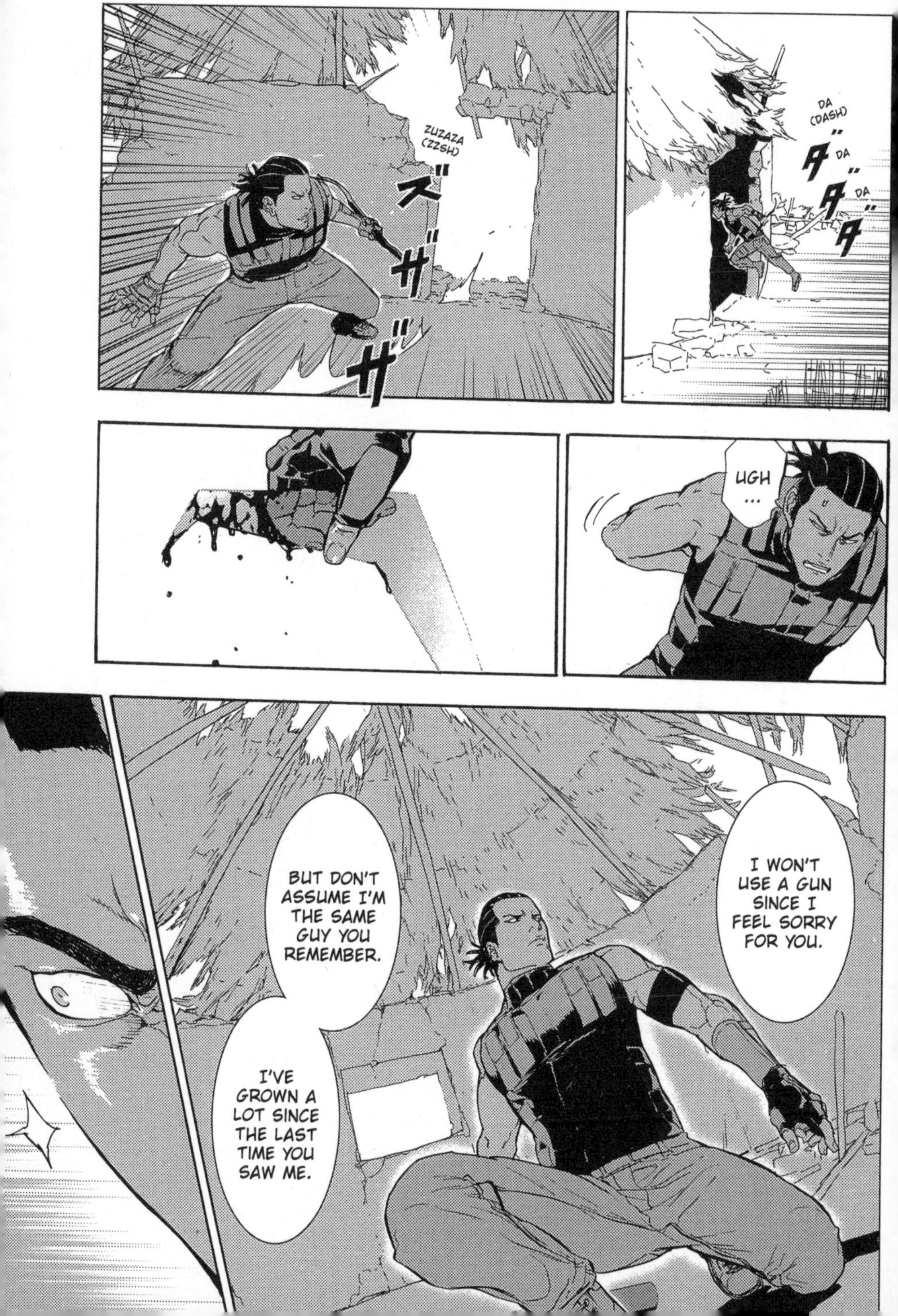
DA (DASH)
DA
DA
ZUZAZA (ZZSH)
UGH ...
I WON'T USE A GUN SINCE I FEEL SORRY FOR YOU.
BUT DON'T ASSUME I'M THE SAME GUY YOU REMEMBER.
I'VE GROWN A LOT SINCE THE LAST TIME YOU SAW ME.

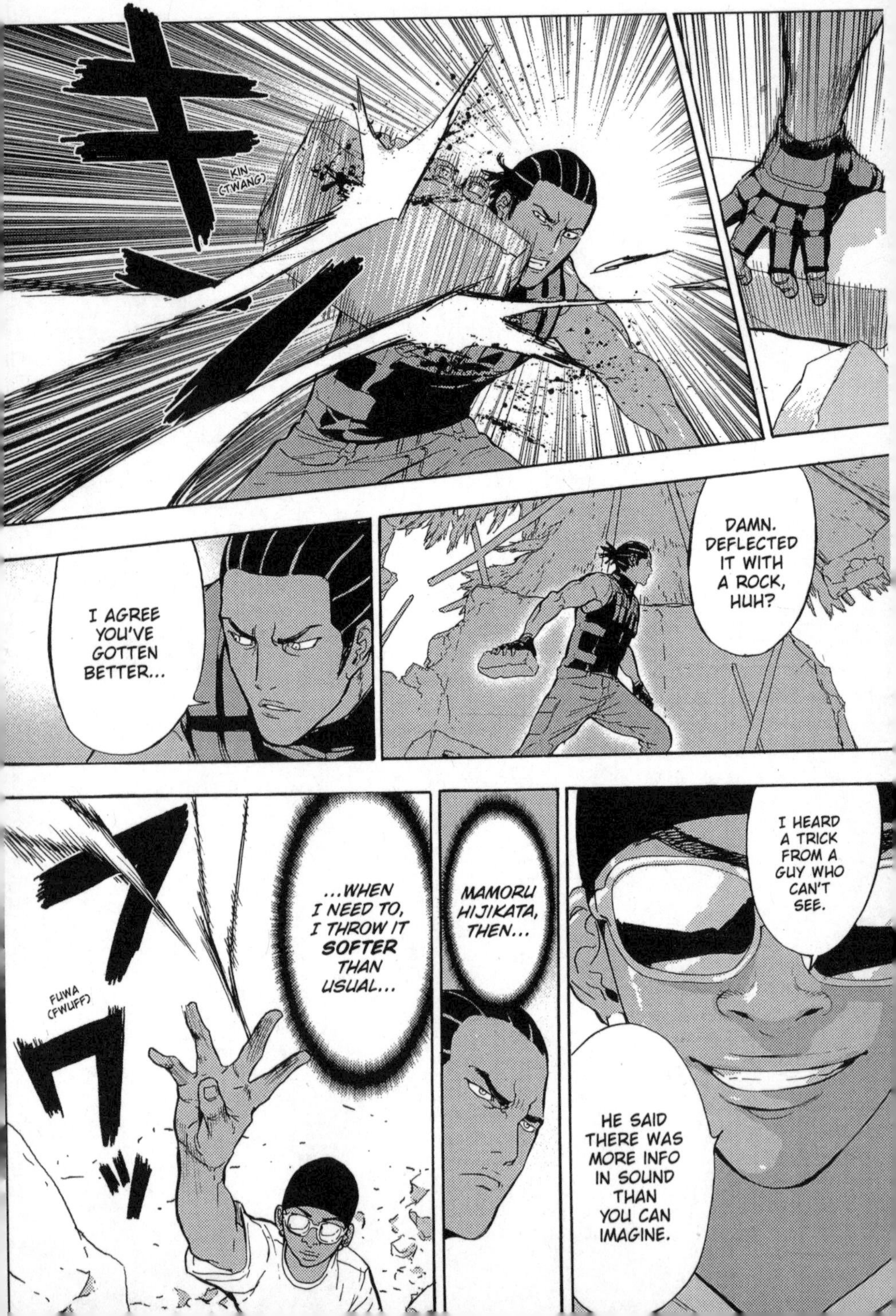
KIN (TWANG)
DAMN. DEFLECTED IT WITH A ROCK, HUH?
I AGREE YOU'VE GOTTEN BETTER...
I HEARD A TRICK FROM A GUY WHO CAN'T SEE.
HE SAID THERE WAS MORE INFO IN SOUND THAN YOU CAN IMAGINE.
MAMORU HIJIKATA, THEN...
...WHEN I NEED TO, I THROW IT SOFTER THAN USUAL...
FUWA (FWUFF)

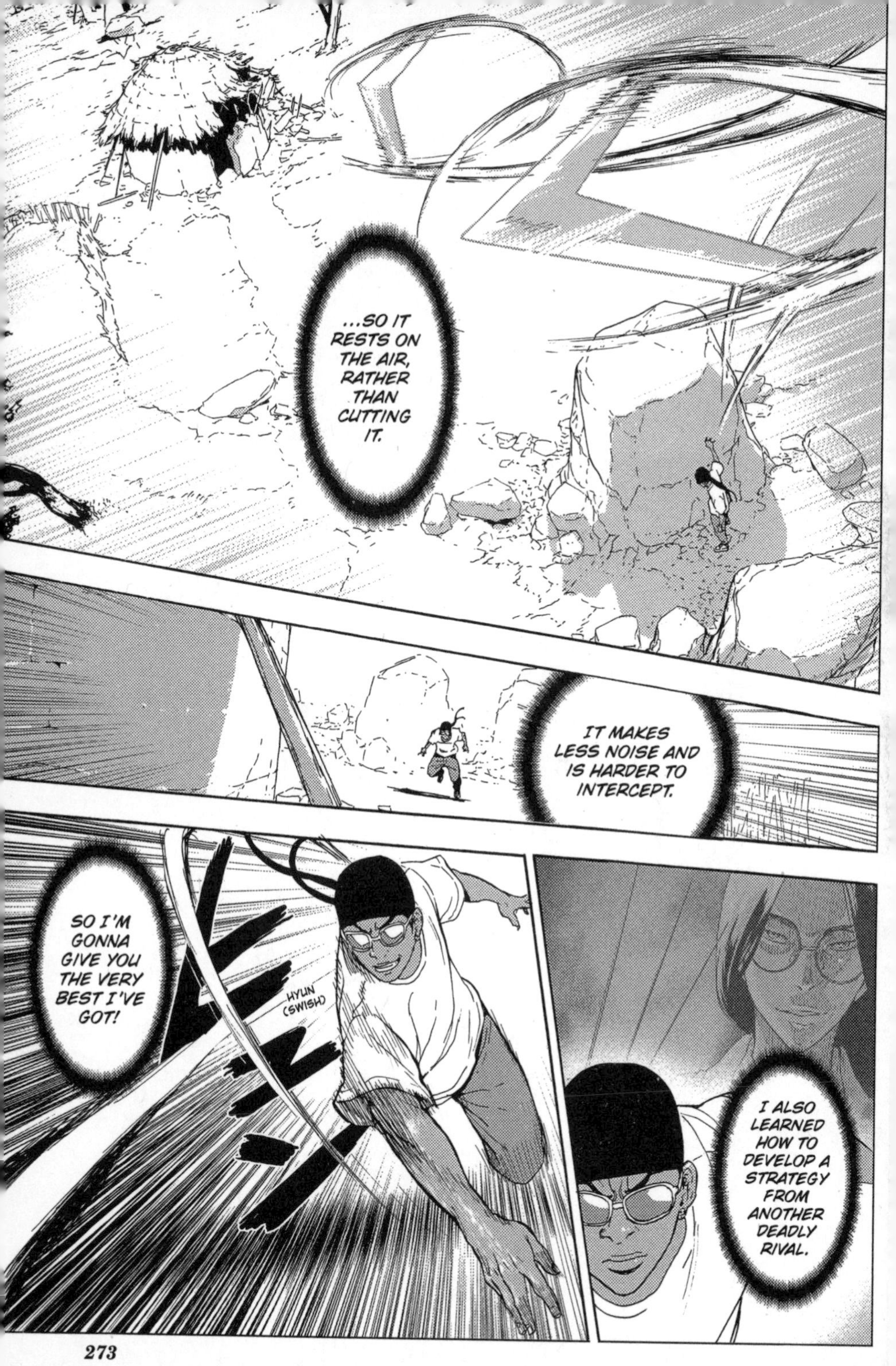
...SO IT RESTS ON THE AIR, RATHER THAN CUTTING IT.
IT MAKES LESS NOISE AND IS HARDER TO INTERCEPT.
I ALSO LEARNED HOW TO DEVELOP A STRATEGY FROM ANOTHER DEADLY RIVAL.
SO I'M GONNA GIVE YOU THE VERY BEST I'VE GOT!
HYUN (SWISH)

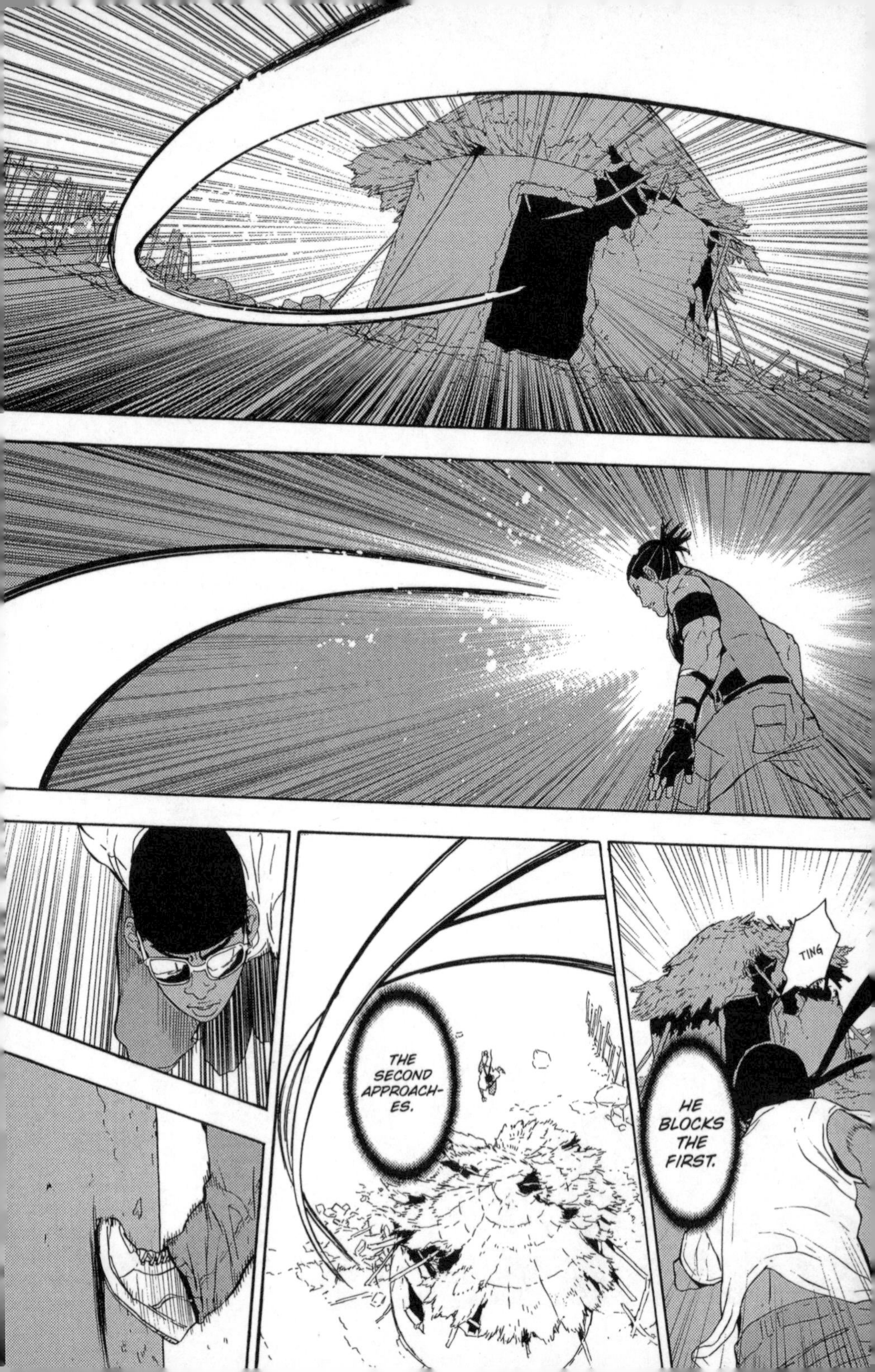
TING
HE BLOCKS THE FIRST.
THE SECOND APPROACH-ES.

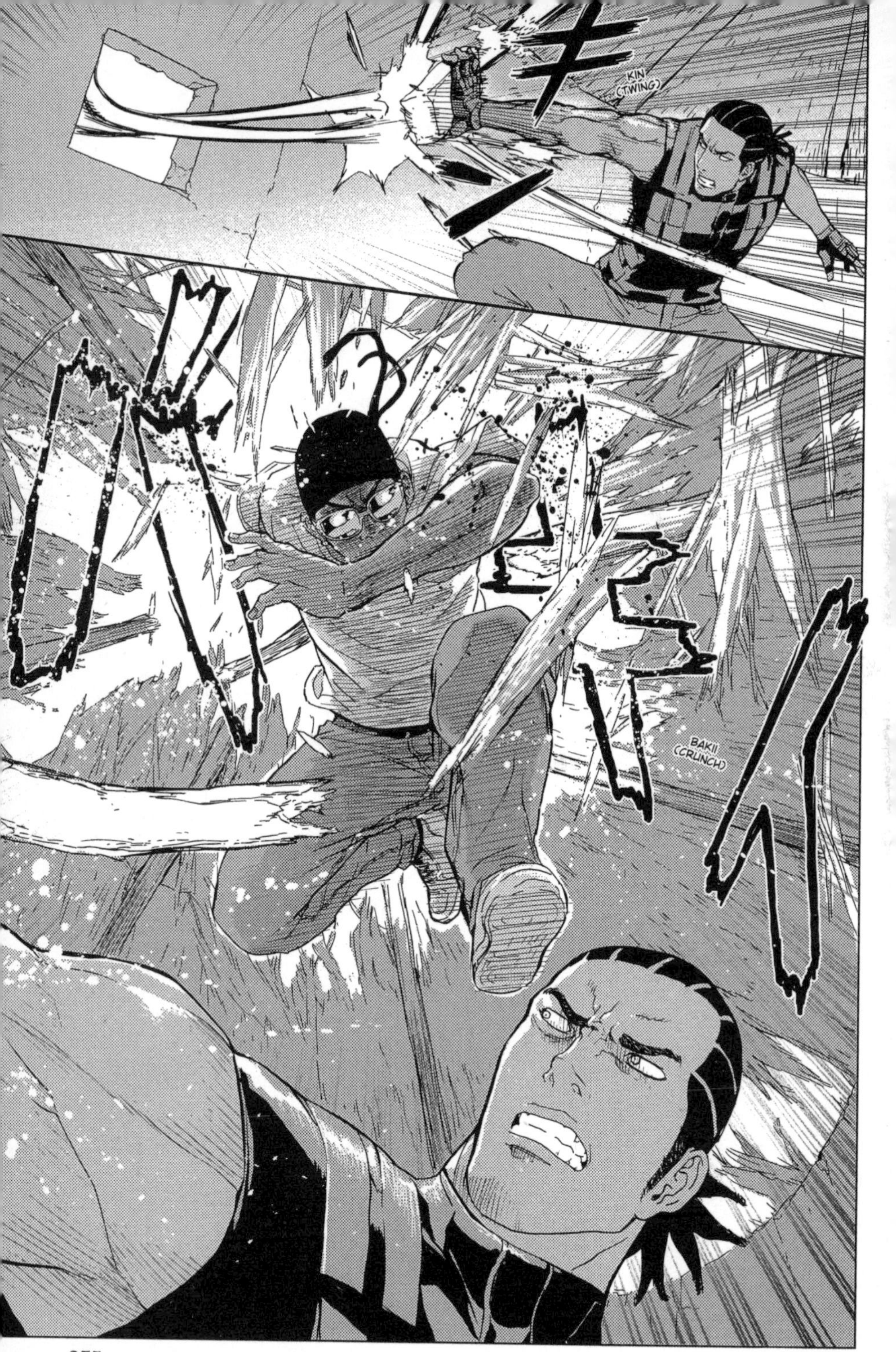
KIN
(TWING)
BAKII
(CRUNCH)

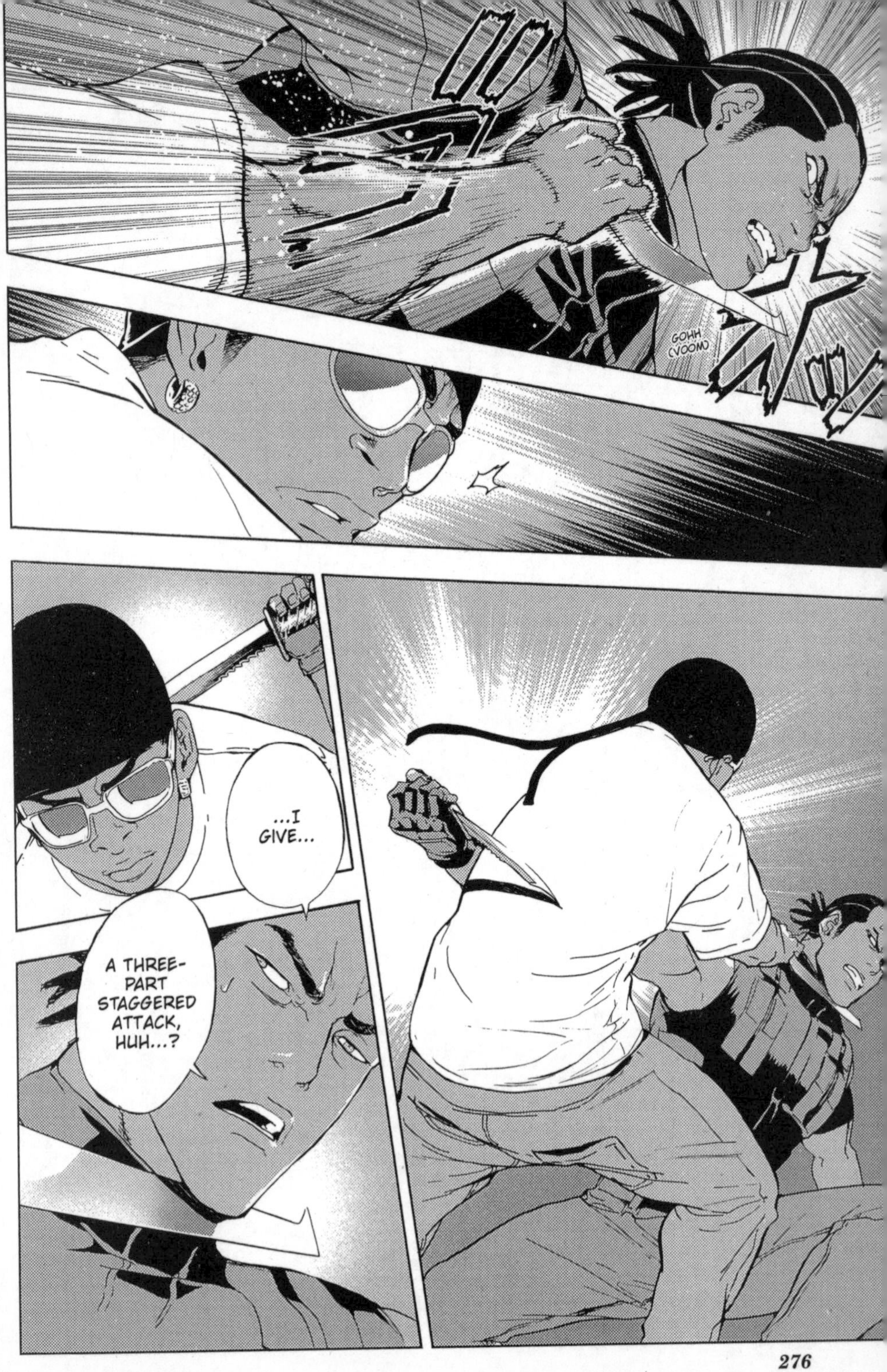
GOHH (VOOM)
...I GIVE...
A THREE-PART STAGGERED ATTACK, HUH...?

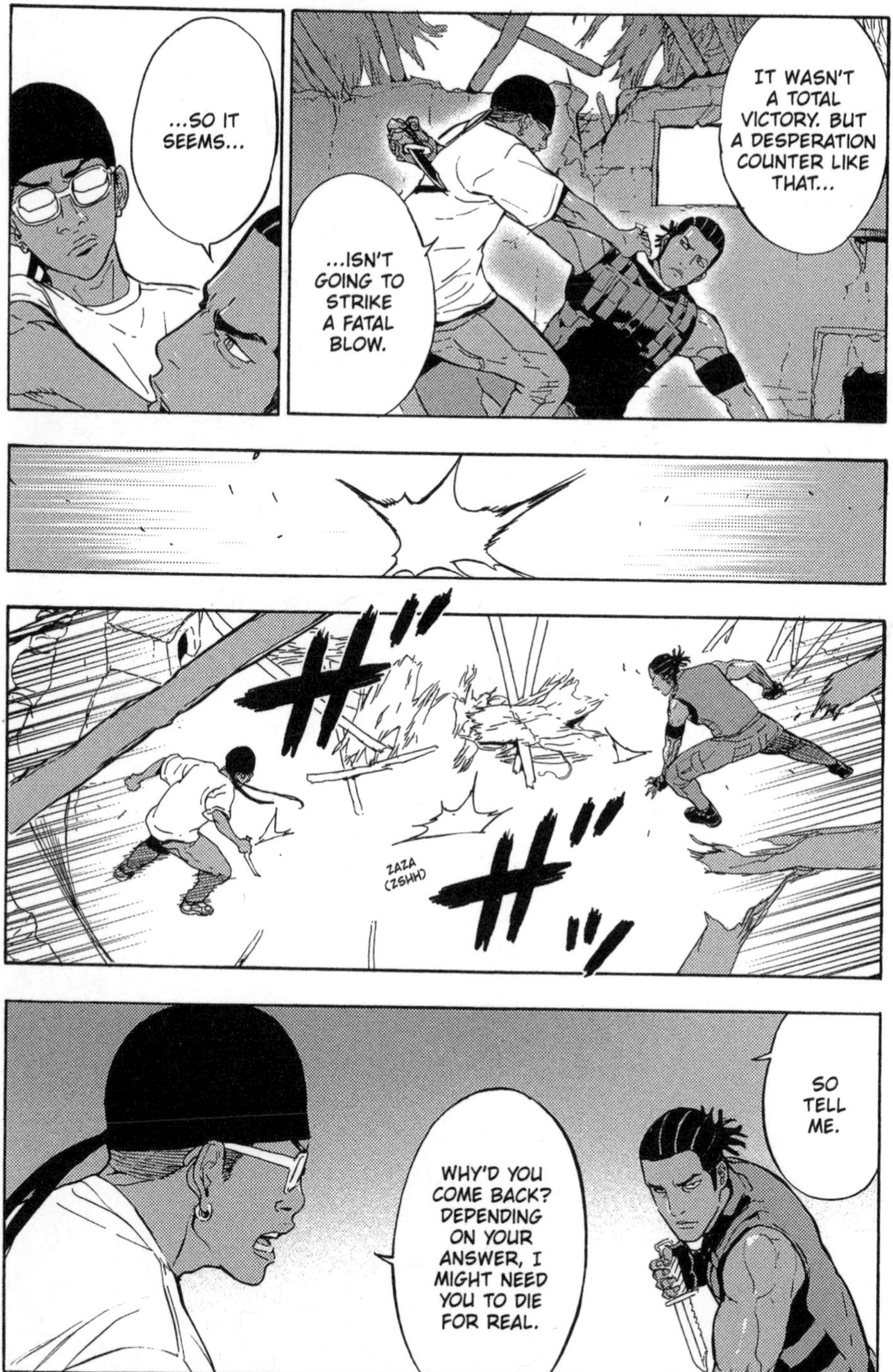
IT WASN'T A TOTAL VICTORY. BUT A DESPERATION COUNTER LIKE THAT...
...ISN'T GOING TO STRIKE A FATAL BLOW.
...SO IT SEEMS...
ZAZA (ZSHH)
SO TELL ME.
WHY'D YOU COME BACK? DEPENDING ON YOUR ANSWER, I MIGHT NEED YOU TO DIE FOR REAL.

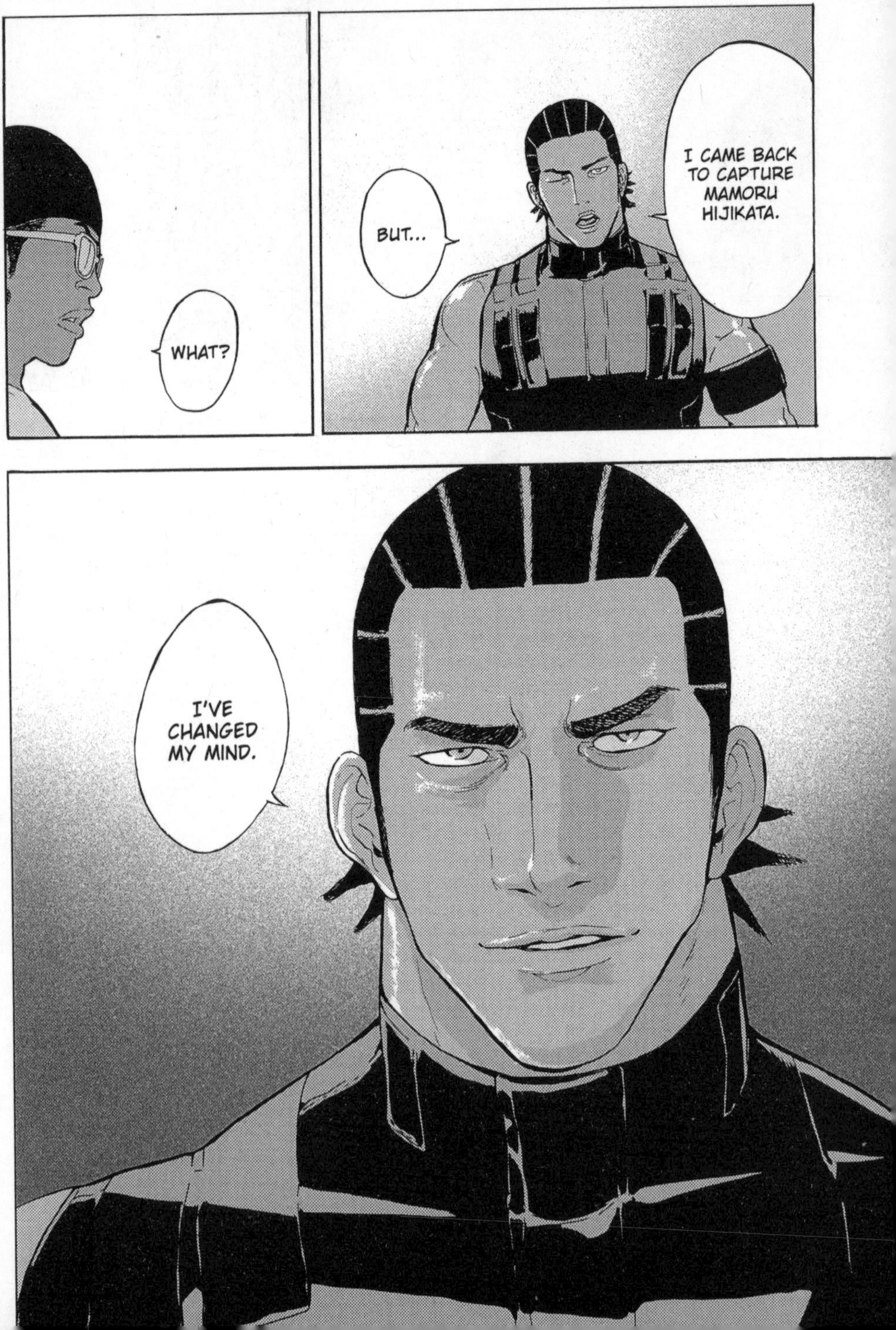
I CAME BACK TO CAPTURE MAMORU HIJIKATA.
BUT...
WHAT?
I'VE CHANGED MY MIND.

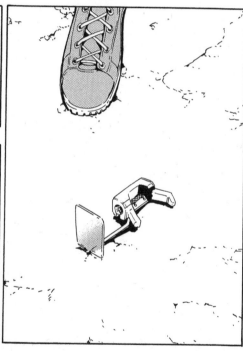

...

...WHERE DID HE...?

Until Death do us Part

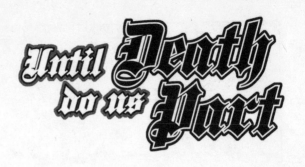

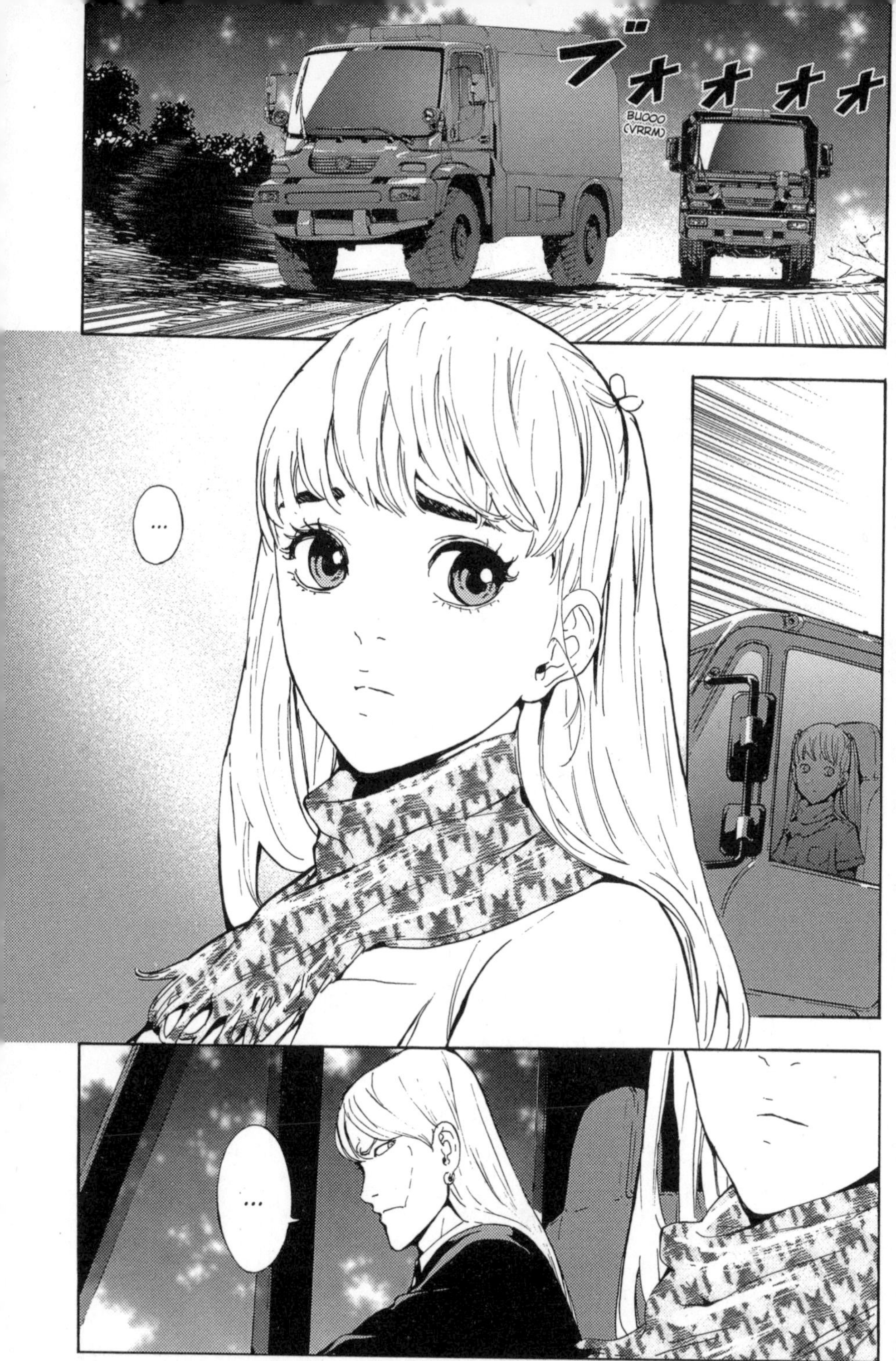
ブォォォォ
BUOOO (VRRM)
...
...

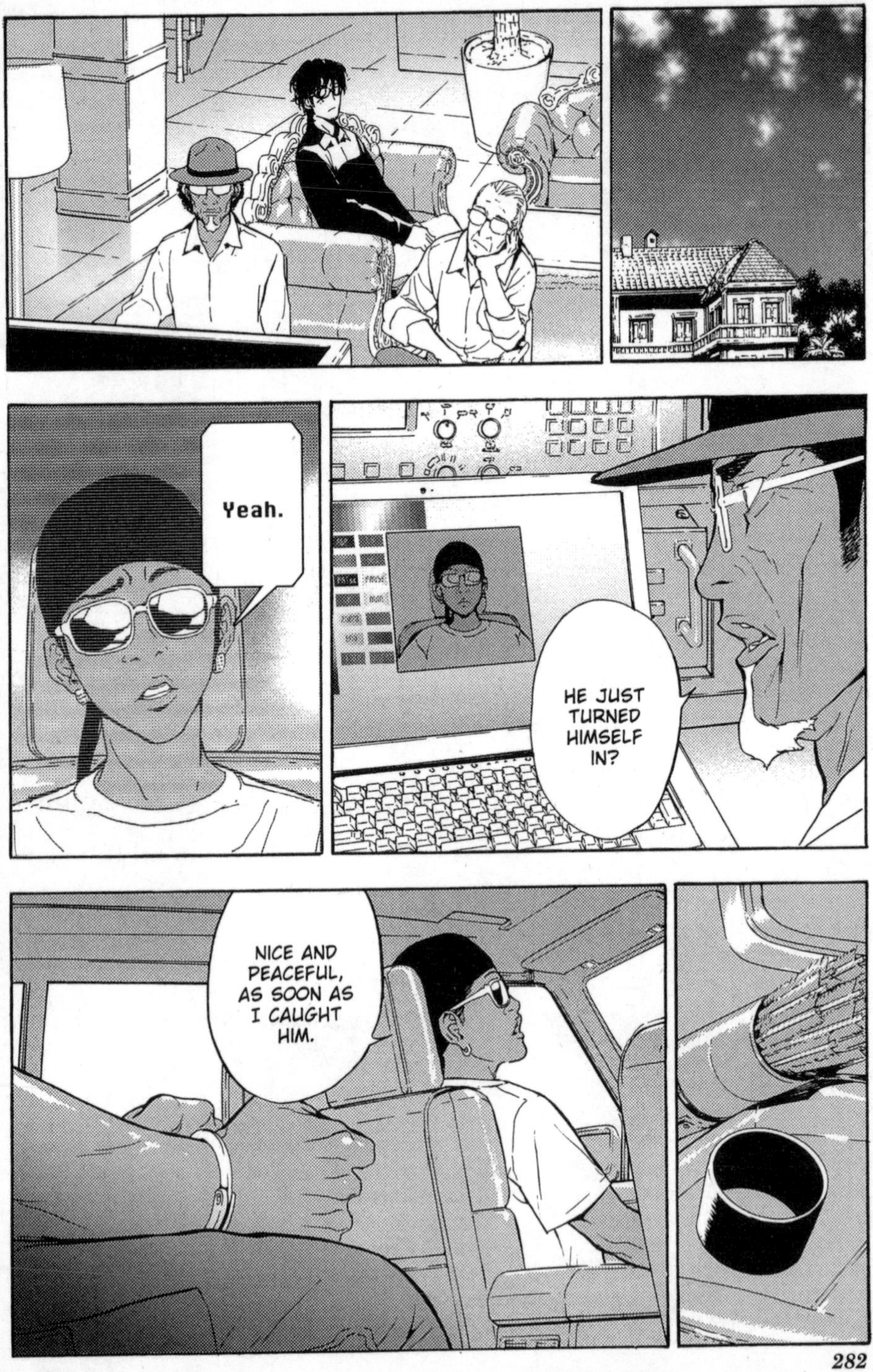
HE JUST TURNED HIMSELF IN?
Yeah.
NICE AND PEACEFUL, AS SOON AS I CAUGHT HIM.

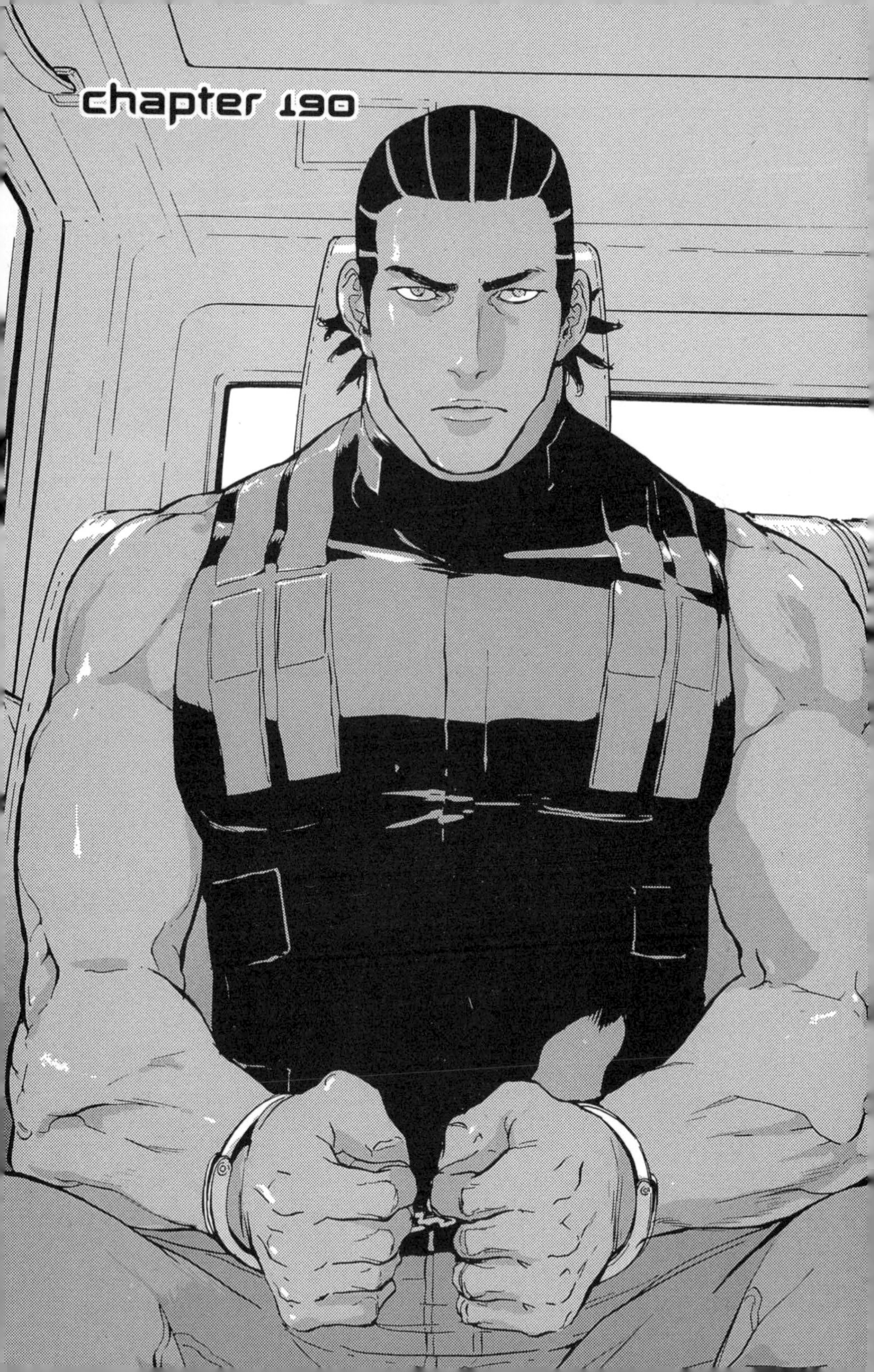
chapter 190

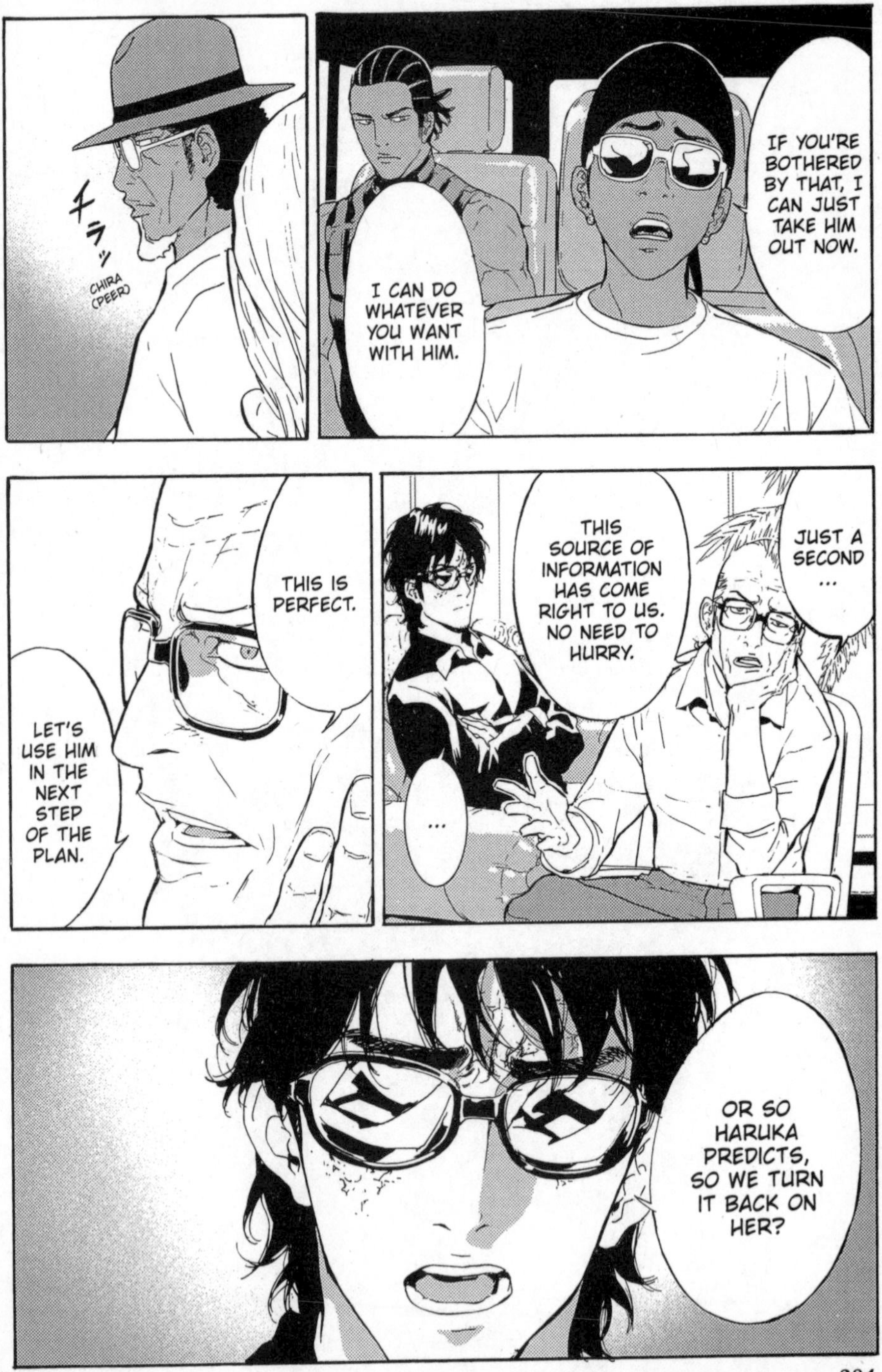
IF YOU'RE BOTHERED BY THAT, I CAN JUST TAKE HIM OUT NOW.
I CAN DO WHATEVER YOU WANT WITH HIM.
チラッ
CHIRA (PEER)
JUST A SECOND ...
THIS SOURCE OF INFORMATION HAS COME RIGHT TO US. NO NEED TO HURRY.
...
THIS IS PERFECT.
LET'S USE HIM IN THE NEXT STEP OF THE PLAN.
OR SO HARUKA PREDICTS, SO WE TURN IT BACK ON HER?

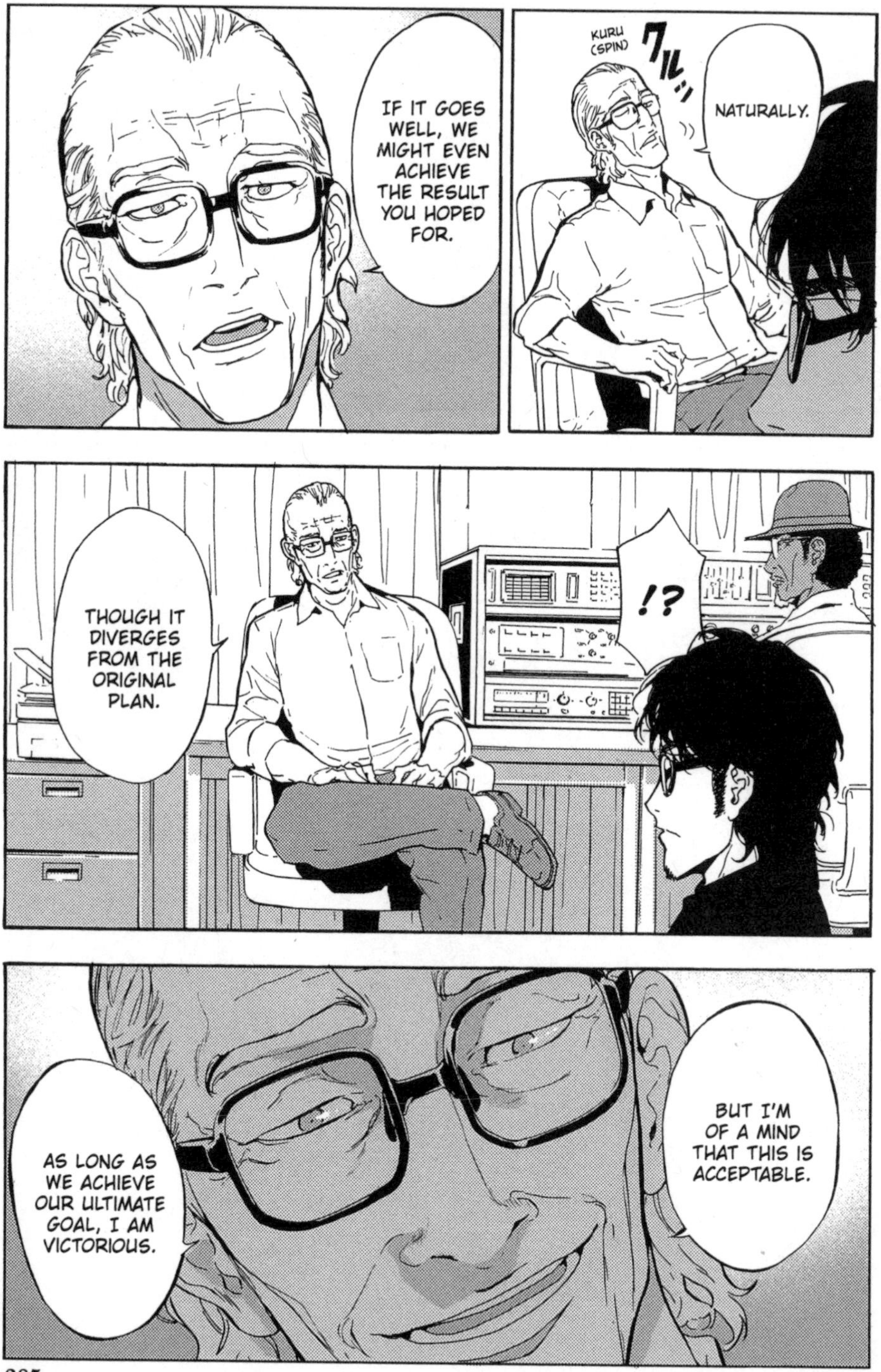
KURU (SPIN)
クル
NATURALLY.
IF IT GOES WELL, WE MIGHT EVEN ACHIEVE THE RESULT YOU HOPED FOR.
!?
THOUGH IT DIVERGES FROM THE ORIGINAL PLAN.
BUT I'M OF A MIND THAT THIS IS ACCEPTABLE.
AS LONG AS WE ACHIEVE OUR ULTIMATE GOAL, I AM VICTORIOUS.

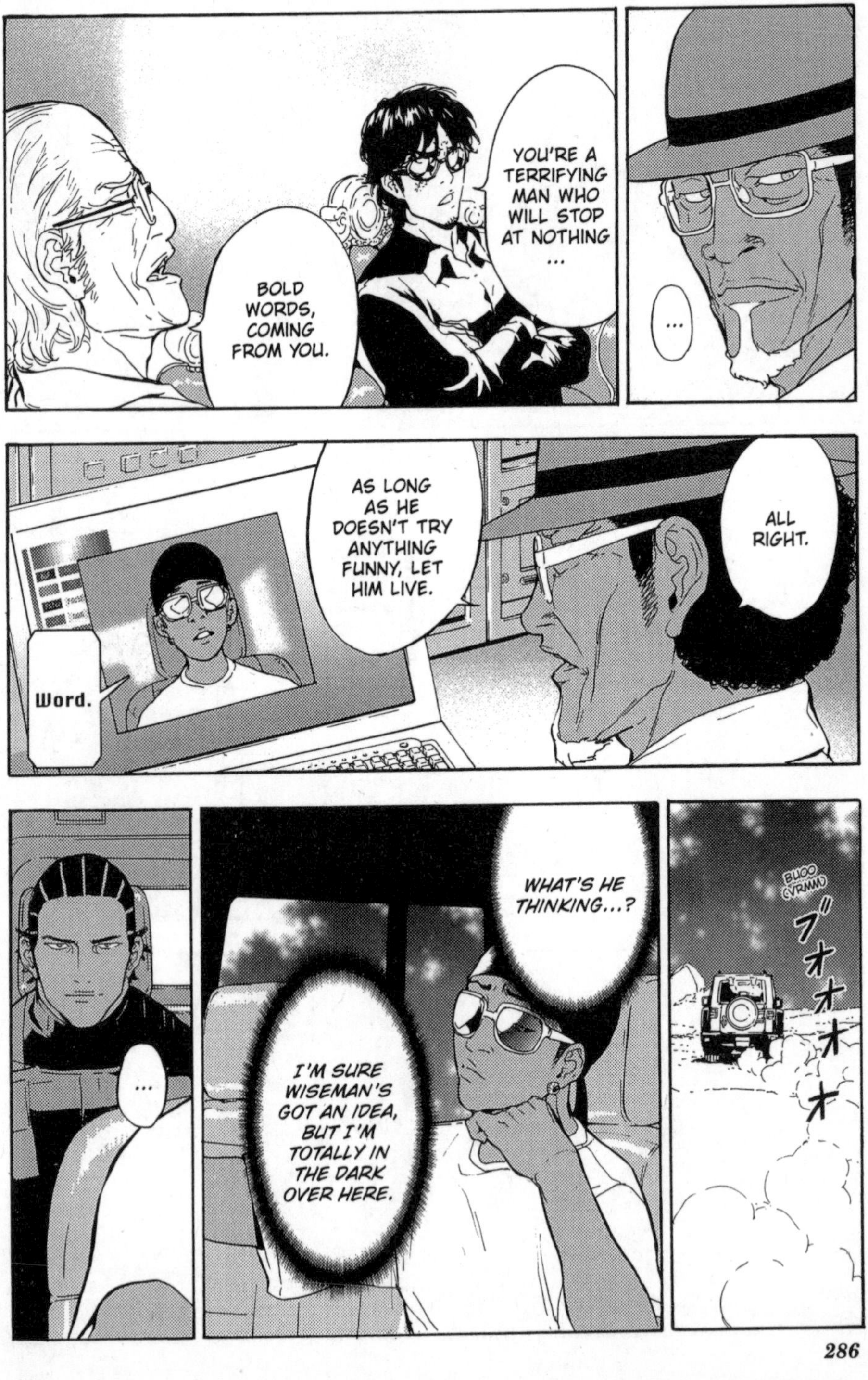
...
YOU'RE A TERRIFYING MAN WHO WILL STOP AT NOTHING ...
BOLD WORDS, COMING FROM YOU.
ALL RIGHT.
AS LONG AS HE DOESN'T TRY ANYTHING FUNNY, LET HIM LIVE.
Word.
BUOO (VRMM)
ブオオオオ
WHAT'S HE THINKING...?
I'M SURE WISEMAN'S GOT AN IDEA, BUT I'M TOTALLY IN THE DARK OVER HERE.
...

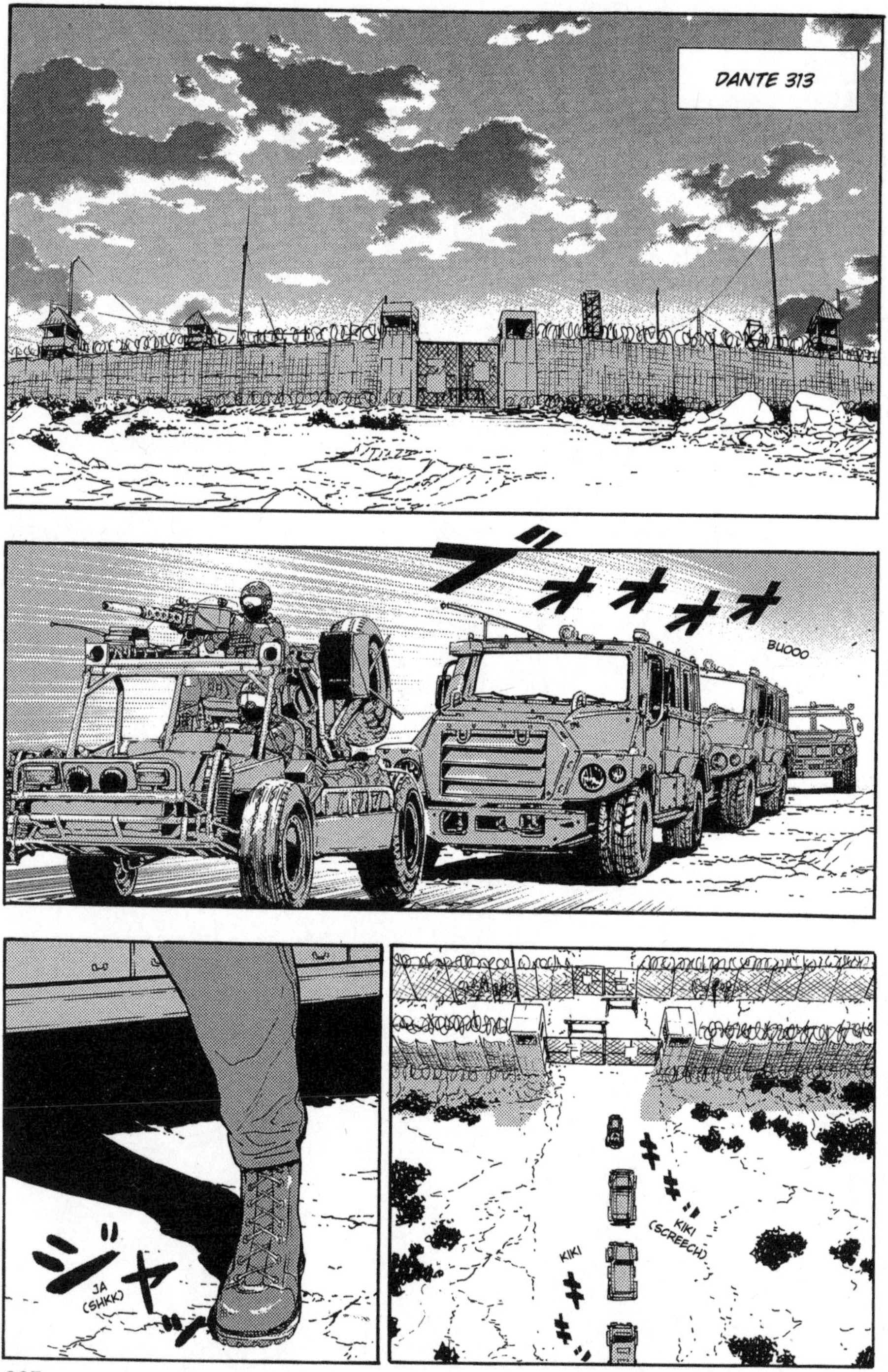
DANTE 313
ブオオオオ
BUOOO
キキッ
KIKI (SCREECH)
KIKI
キキッ
ジャッ
JA (SHKK)

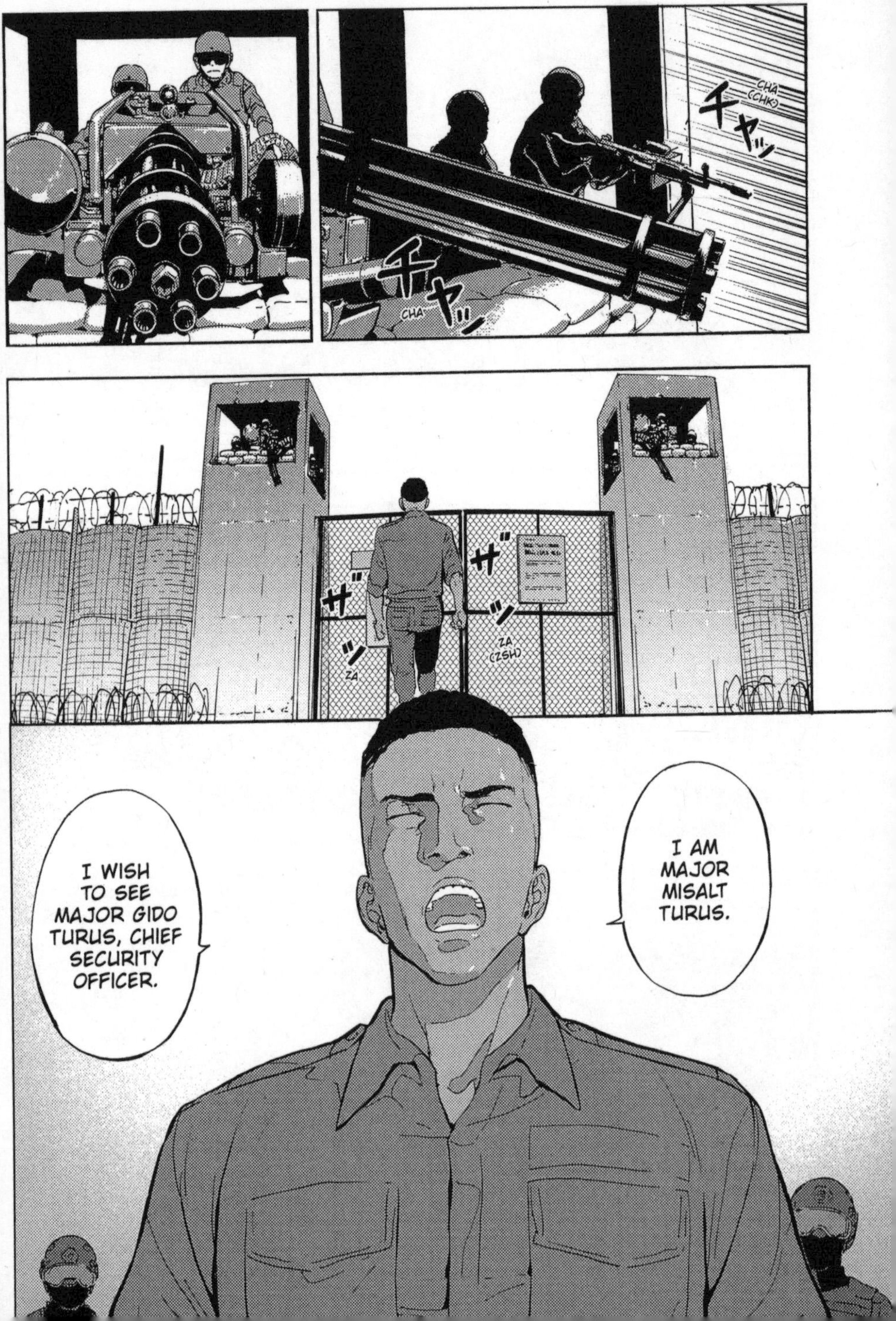
CHA (CHK)
チャッ
チャッ
CHA
ザッ
ZA (ZSH)
ザッ
ZA
I AM MAJOR MISALT TURUS.
I WISH TO SEE MAJOR GIDO TURUS, CHIEF SECURITY OFFICER.

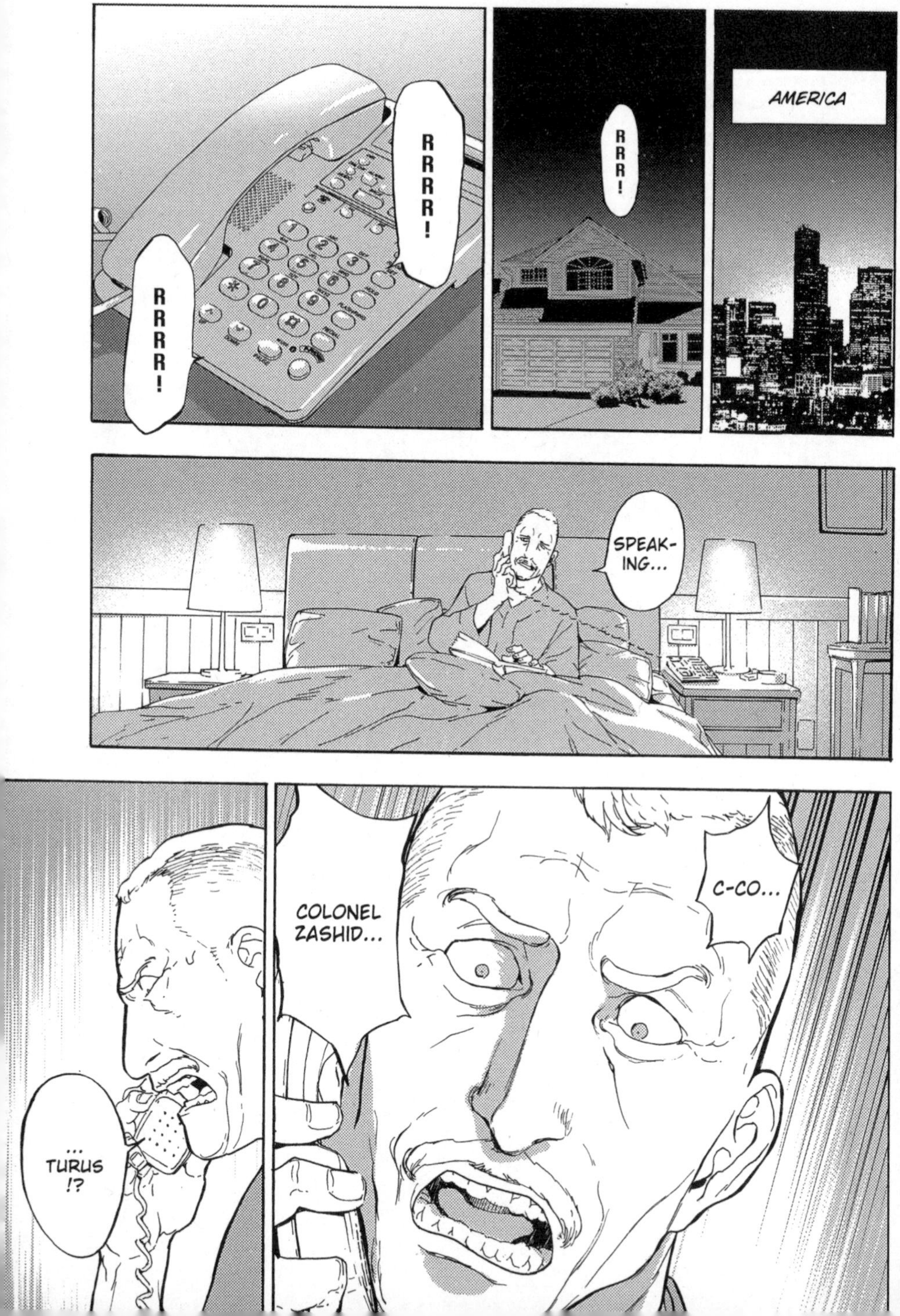
AMERICA
RRR!
RRRR!
RRRR!
SPEAK-ING...
C-CO...
COLONEL ZASHID...
...TURUS!?

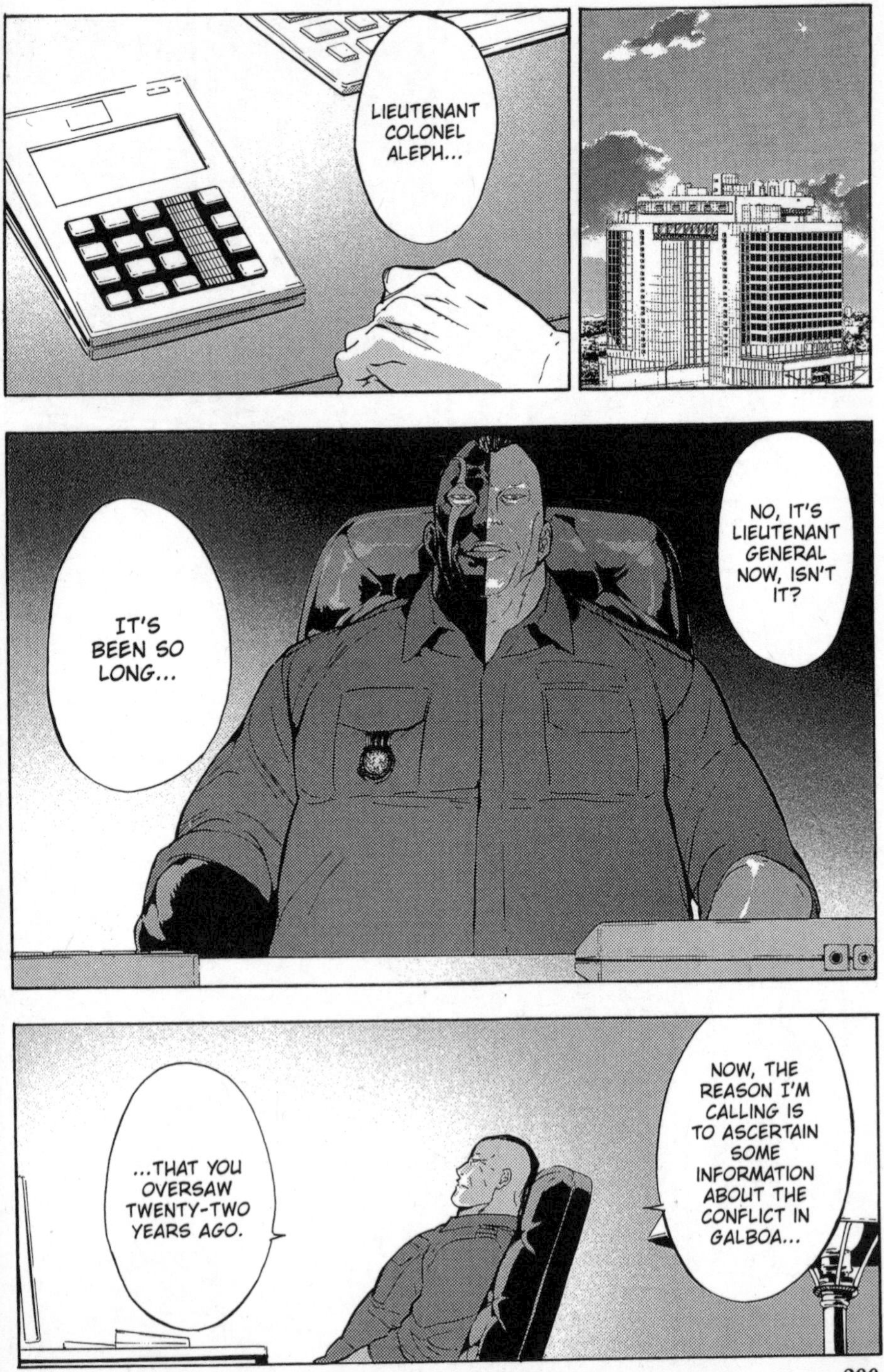
LIEUTENANT COLONEL ALEPH...
NO, IT'S LIEUTENANT GENERAL NOW, ISN'T IT?
IT'S BEEN SO LONG...
NOW, THE REASON I'M CALLING IS TO ASCERTAIN SOME INFORMATION ABOUT THE CONFLICT IN GALBOA...
...THAT YOU OVERSAW TWENTY-TWO YEARS AGO.

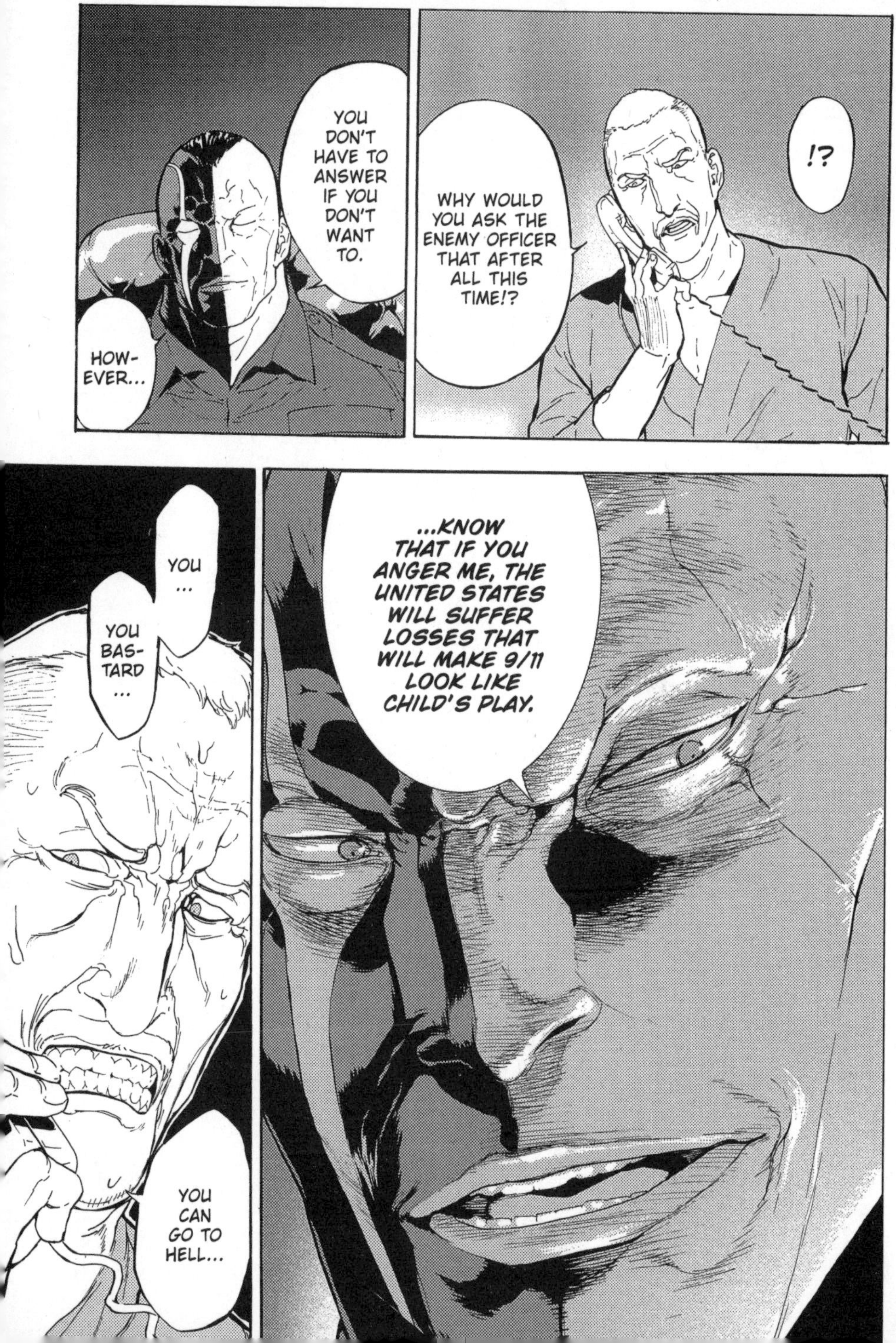
!?
WHY WOULD YOU ASK THE ENEMY OFFICER THAT AFTER ALL THIS TIME!?
YOU DON'T HAVE TO ANSWER IF YOU DON'T WANT TO.
HOW-EVER...
...KNOW THAT IF YOU ANGER ME, THE UNITED STATES WILL SUFFER LOSSES THAT WILL MAKE 9/11 LOOK LIKE CHILD'S PLAY.
YOU ...
YOU BAS-TARD ...
YOU CAN GO TO HELL...

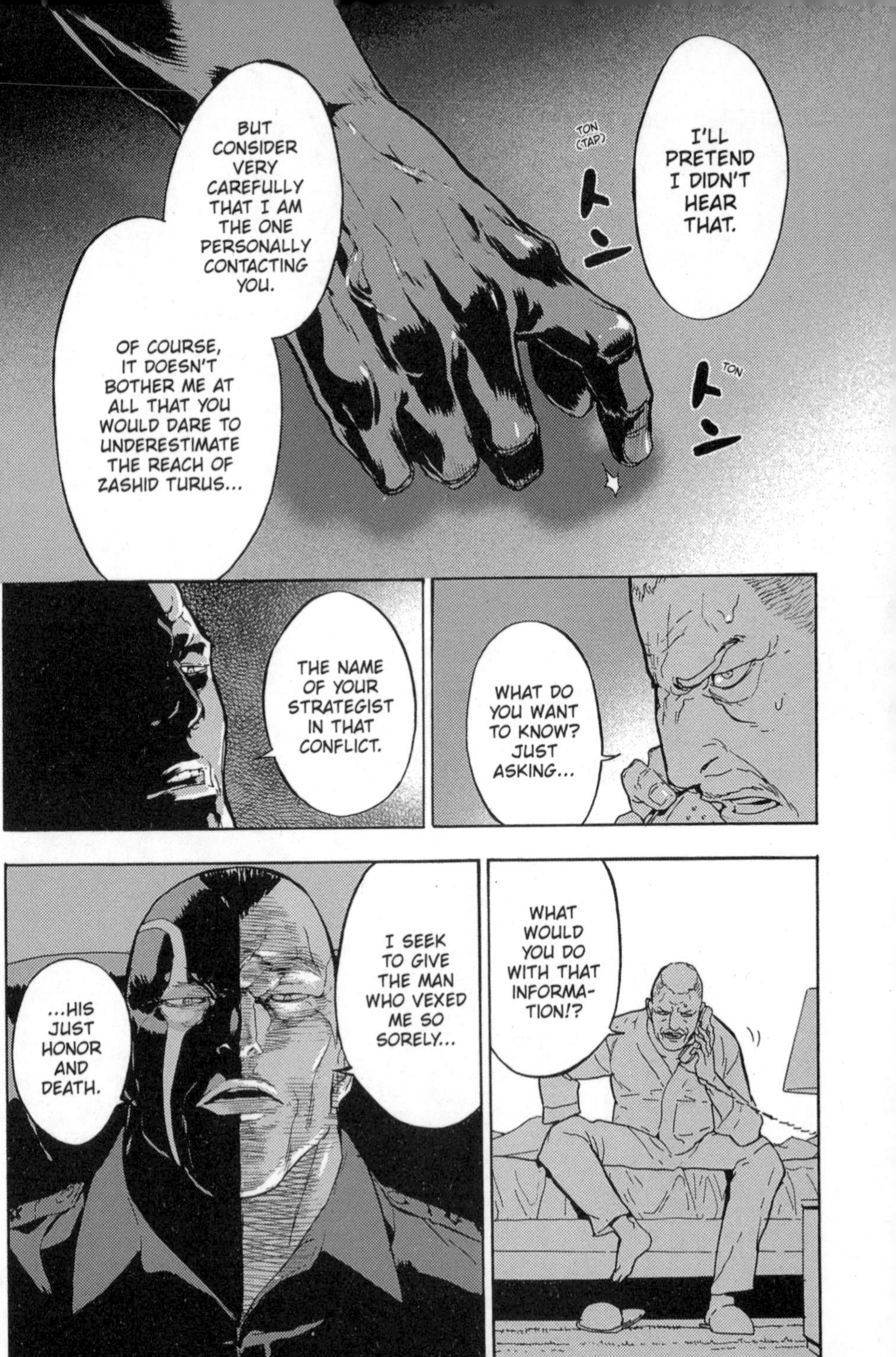
TON (TAP)
トン
I'LL PRETEND I DIDN'T HEAR THAT.
BUT CONSIDER VERY CAREFULLY THAT I AM THE ONE PERSONALLY CONTACTING YOU.
TON
トン
OF COURSE, IT DOESN'T BOTHER ME AT ALL THAT YOU WOULD DARE TO UNDERESTIMATE THE REACH OF ZASHID TURUS...
WHAT DO YOU WANT TO KNOW? JUST ASKING...
THE NAME OF YOUR STRATEGIST IN THAT CONFLICT.
WHAT WOULD YOU DO WITH THAT INFORMATION!?
I SEEK TO GIVE THE MAN WHO VEXED ME SO SORELY...
...HIS JUST HONOR AND DEATH.

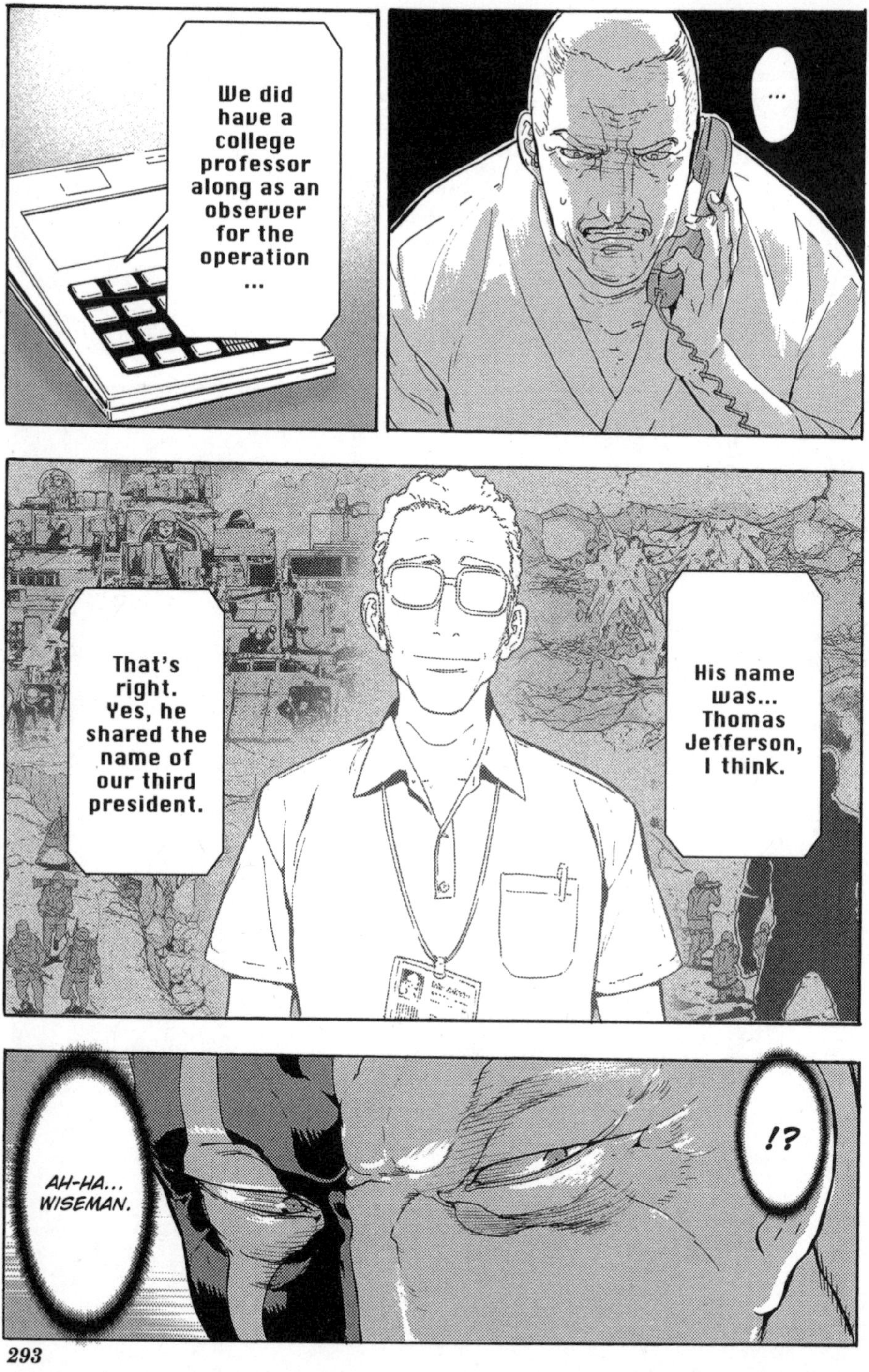
...
We did have a college professor along as an observer for the operation ...
His name was... Thomas Jefferson, I think.
That's right. Yes, he shared the name of our third president.
!?
AH-HA... WISEMAN.

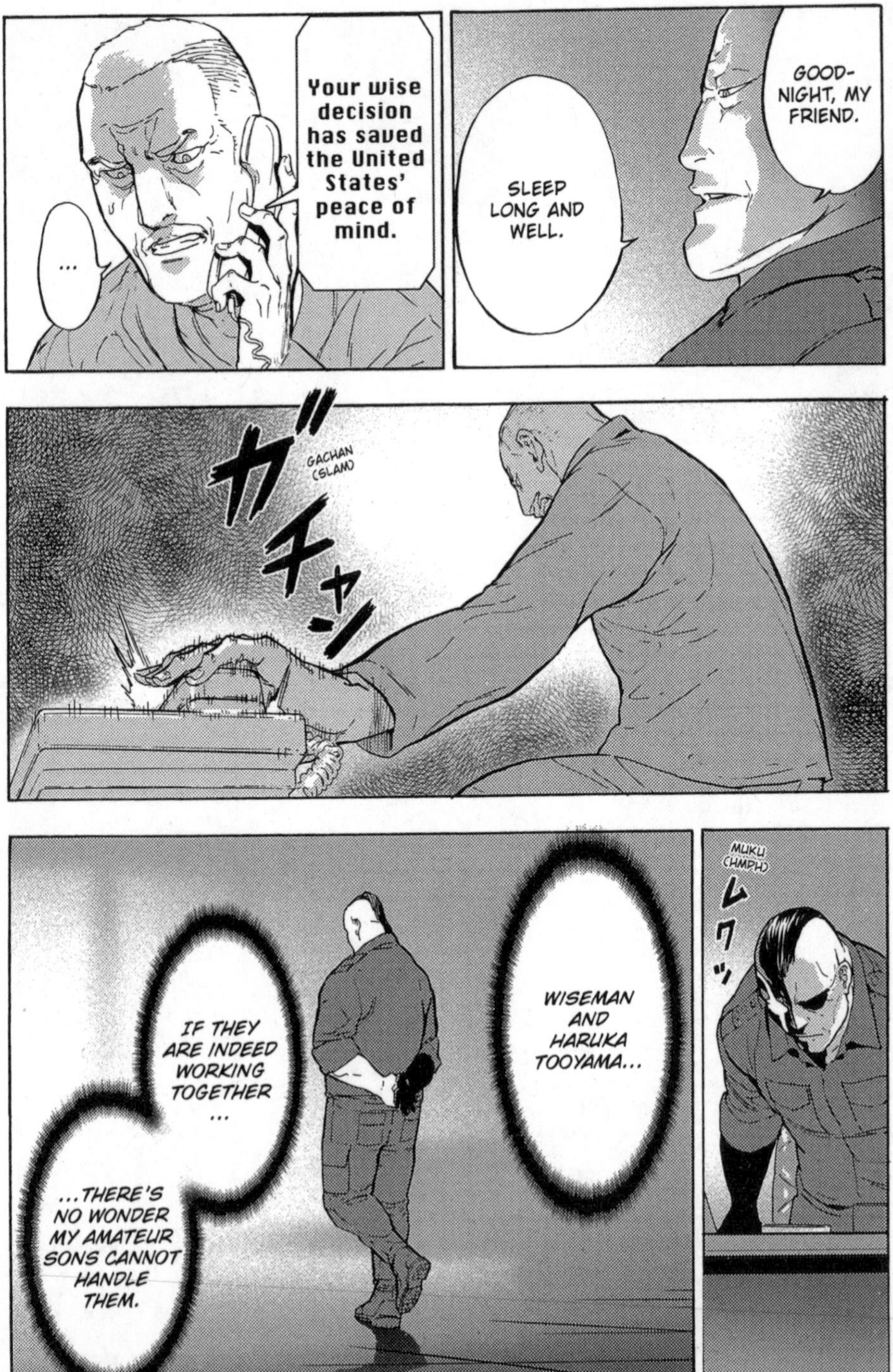
GOOD-NIGHT, MY FRIEND.
SLEEP LONG AND WELL.
Your wise decision has saved the United States' peace of mind.
...
GACHAN (SLAM)
ガチャン
MUKU (HMPH)
ムクッ
WISEMAN AND HARUKA TOOYAMA...
IF THEY ARE INDEED WORKING TOGETHER...
...THERE'S NO WONDER MY AMATEUR SONS CANNOT HANDLE THEM.

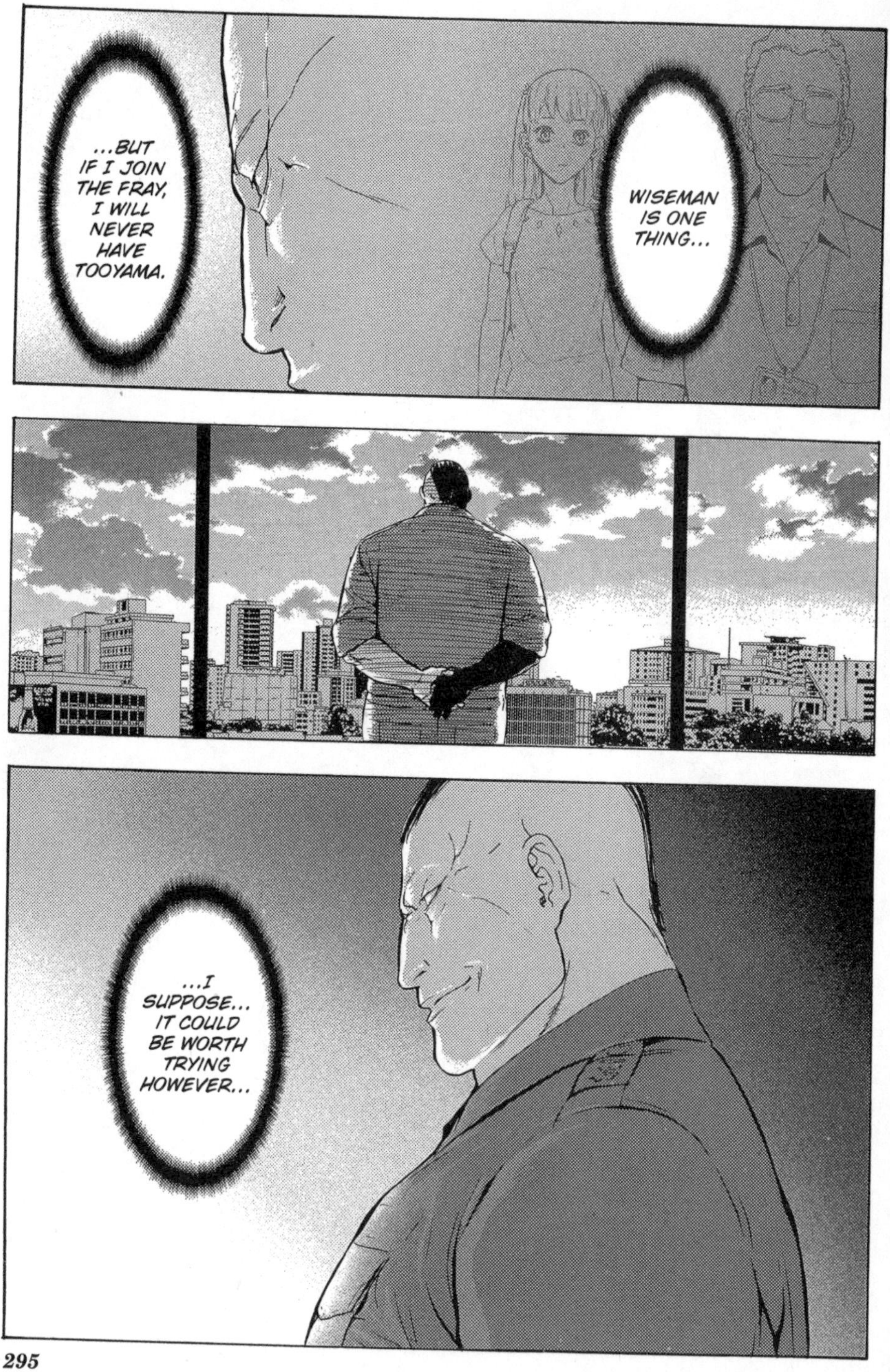
WISEMAN IS ONE THING...
...BUT IF I JOIN THE FRAY, I WILL NEVER HAVE TOOYAMA.
...I SUPPOSE... IT COULD BE WORTH TRYING HOWEVER...

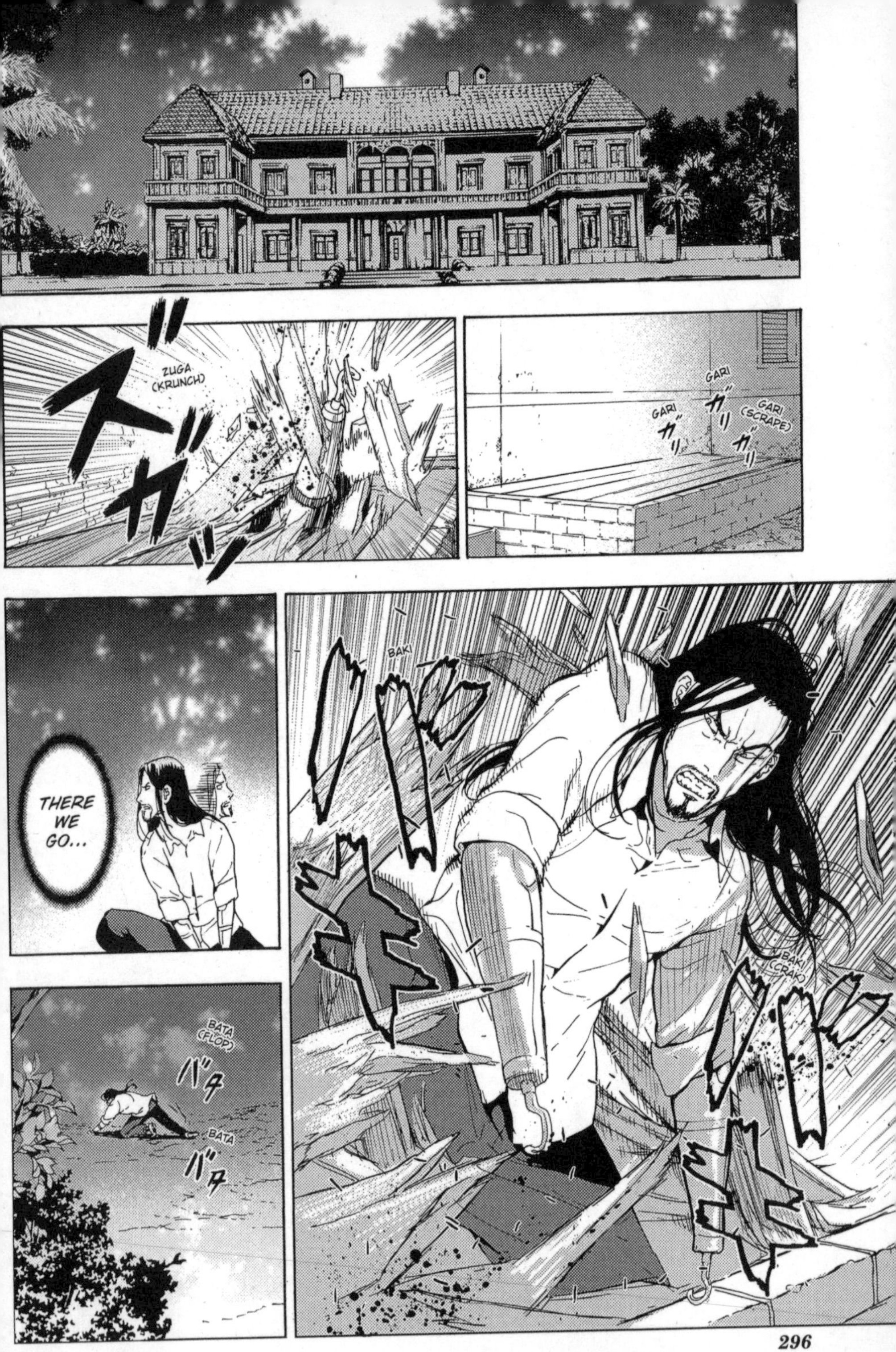
GARI
GARI
GARI (SCRAPE)
ZUGA (KRUNCH)
BAKI
BAKI (CRAK)
THERE WE GO...
BATA (FLOP)
BATA

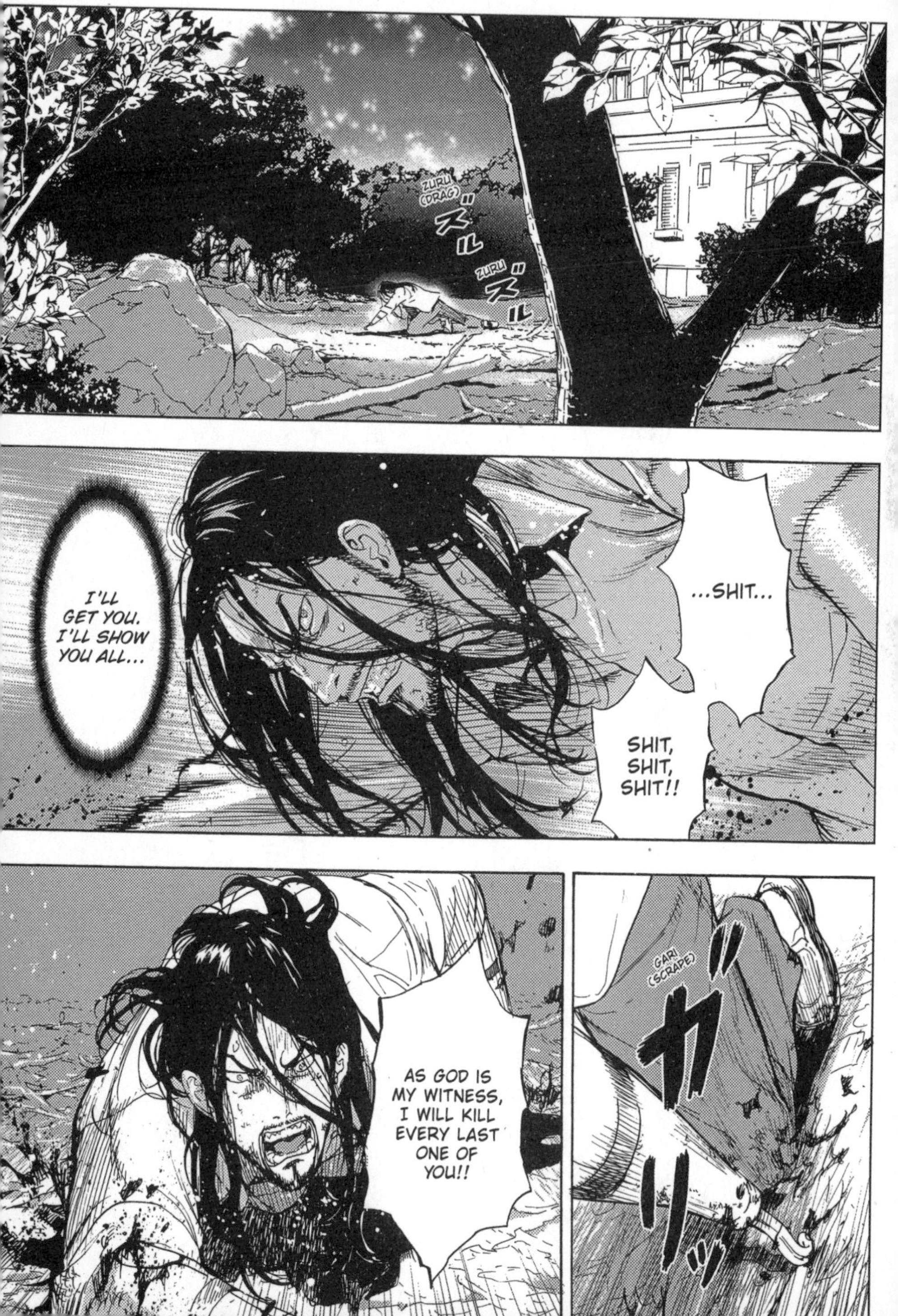
ZURU (DRAG)
ZURU
...SHIT...
SHIT, SHIT, SHIT!!
I'LL GET YOU. I'LL SHOW YOU ALL...
GARI (SCRAPE)
AS GOD IS MY WITNESS, I WILL KILL EVERY LAST ONE OF YOU!!

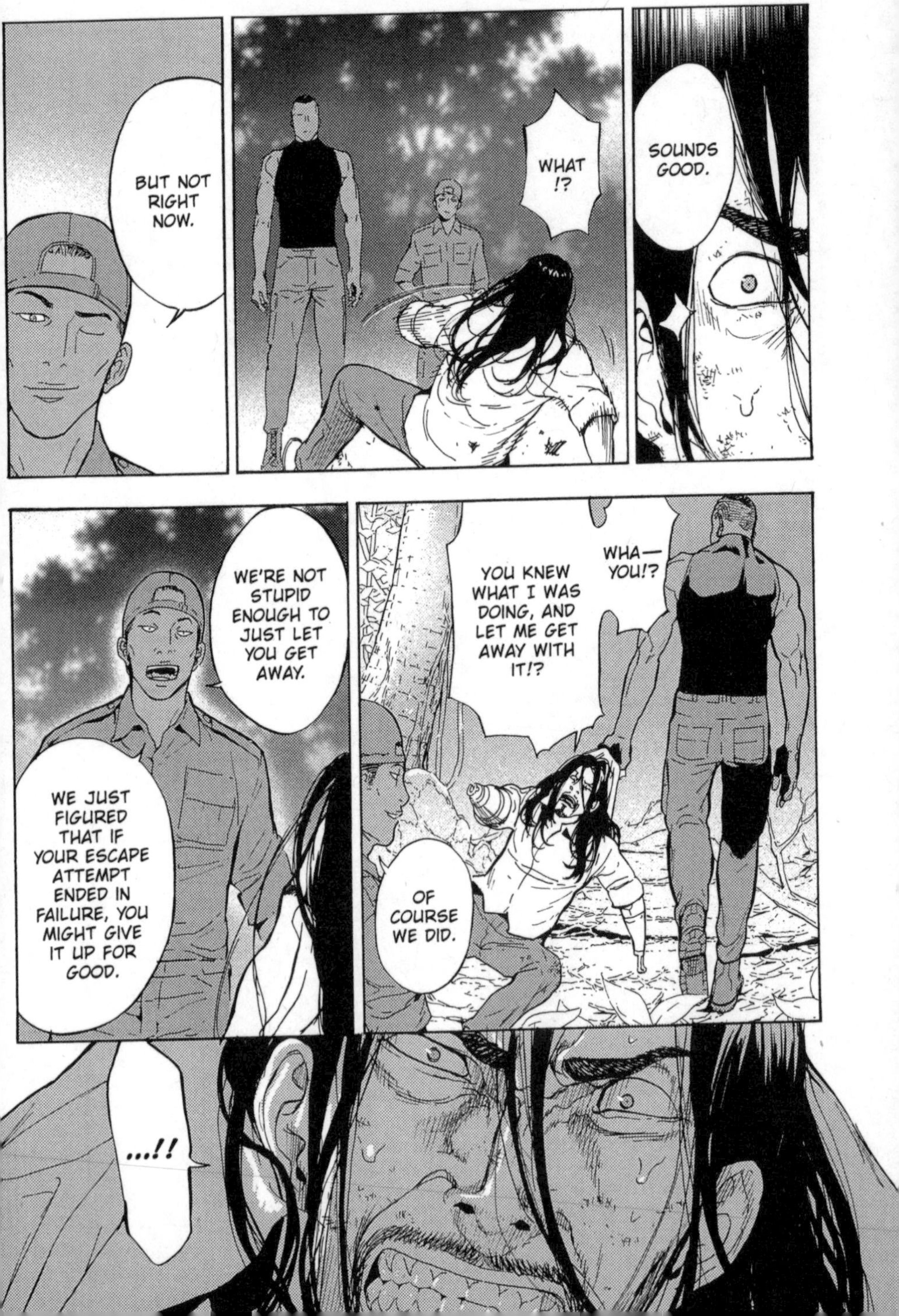
SOUNDS GOOD.
WHAT !?
BUT NOT RIGHT NOW.
WHA— YOU!?
YOU KNEW WHAT I WAS DOING, AND LET ME GET AWAY WITH IT!?
OF COURSE WE DID.
WE'RE NOT STUPID ENOUGH TO JUST LET YOU GET AWAY.
WE JUST FIGURED THAT IF YOUR ESCAPE ATTEMPT ENDED IN FAILURE, YOU MIGHT GIVE IT UP FOR GOOD.
...!!

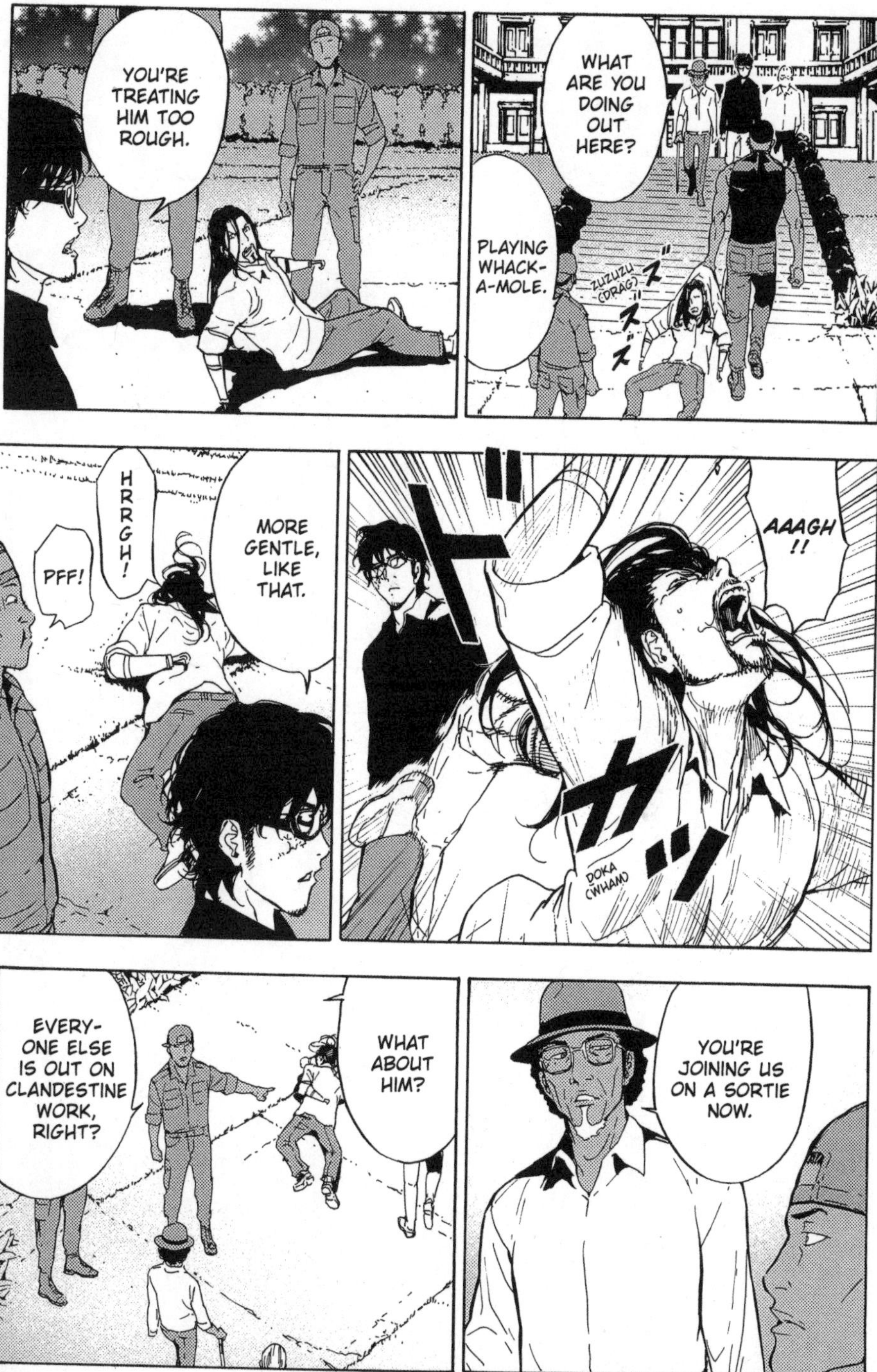
WHAT ARE YOU DOING OUT HERE?
PLAYING WHACK-A-MOLE.
ズズズ
ZUZUZU (DRAG)
YOU'RE TREATING HIM TOO ROUGH.
AAAGH!!
ドカッ
DOKA (WHAM)
MORE GENTLE, LIKE THAT.
HRRGH!
PFF!
YOU'RE JOINING US ON A SORTIE NOW.
WHAT ABOUT HIM?
EVERY-ONE ELSE IS OUT ON CLANDESTINE WORK, RIGHT?

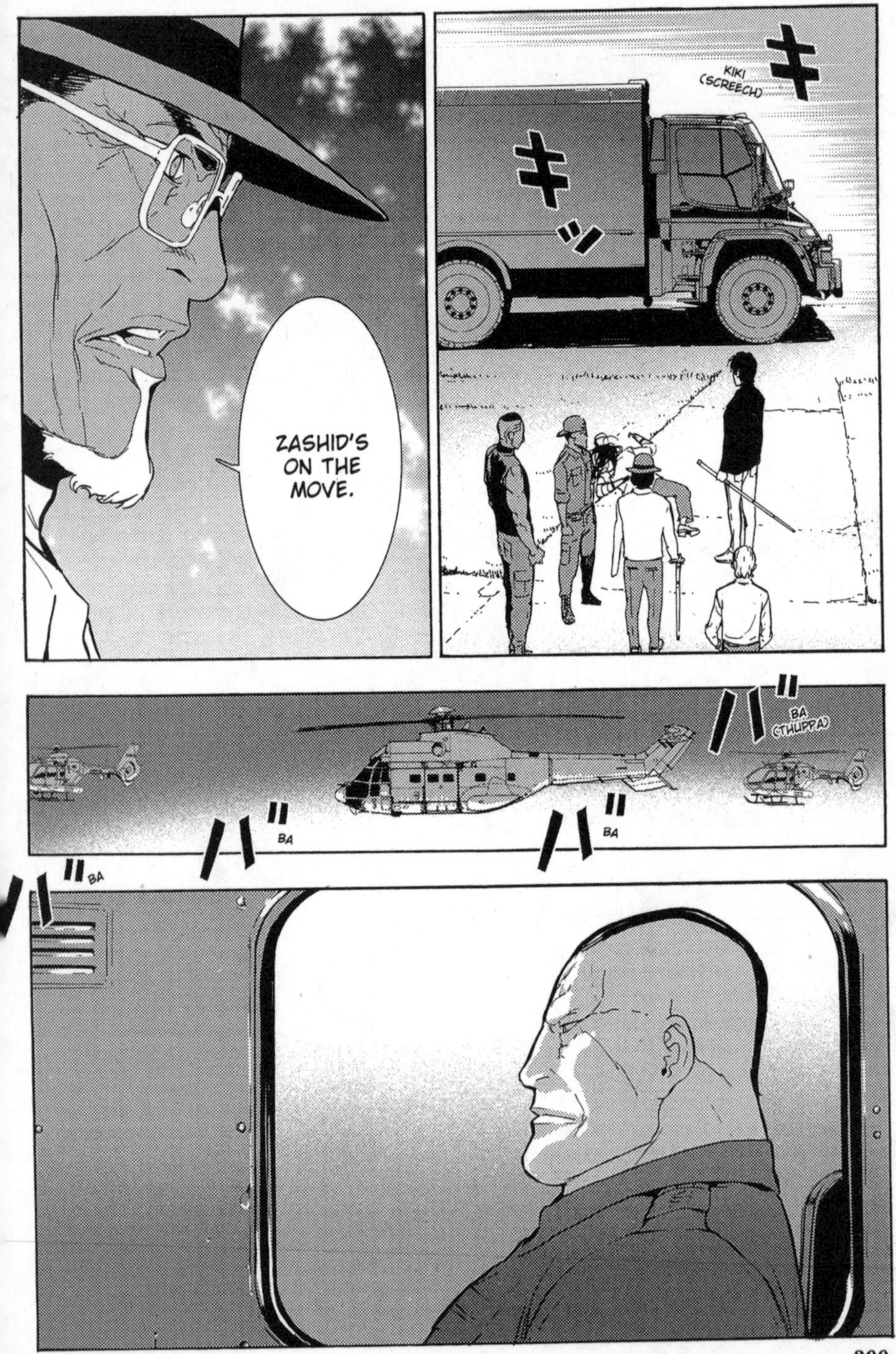

KIKI (SCREECH)
ZASHID'S ON THE MOVE.
BA (THUPPA)
BA
BA
BA

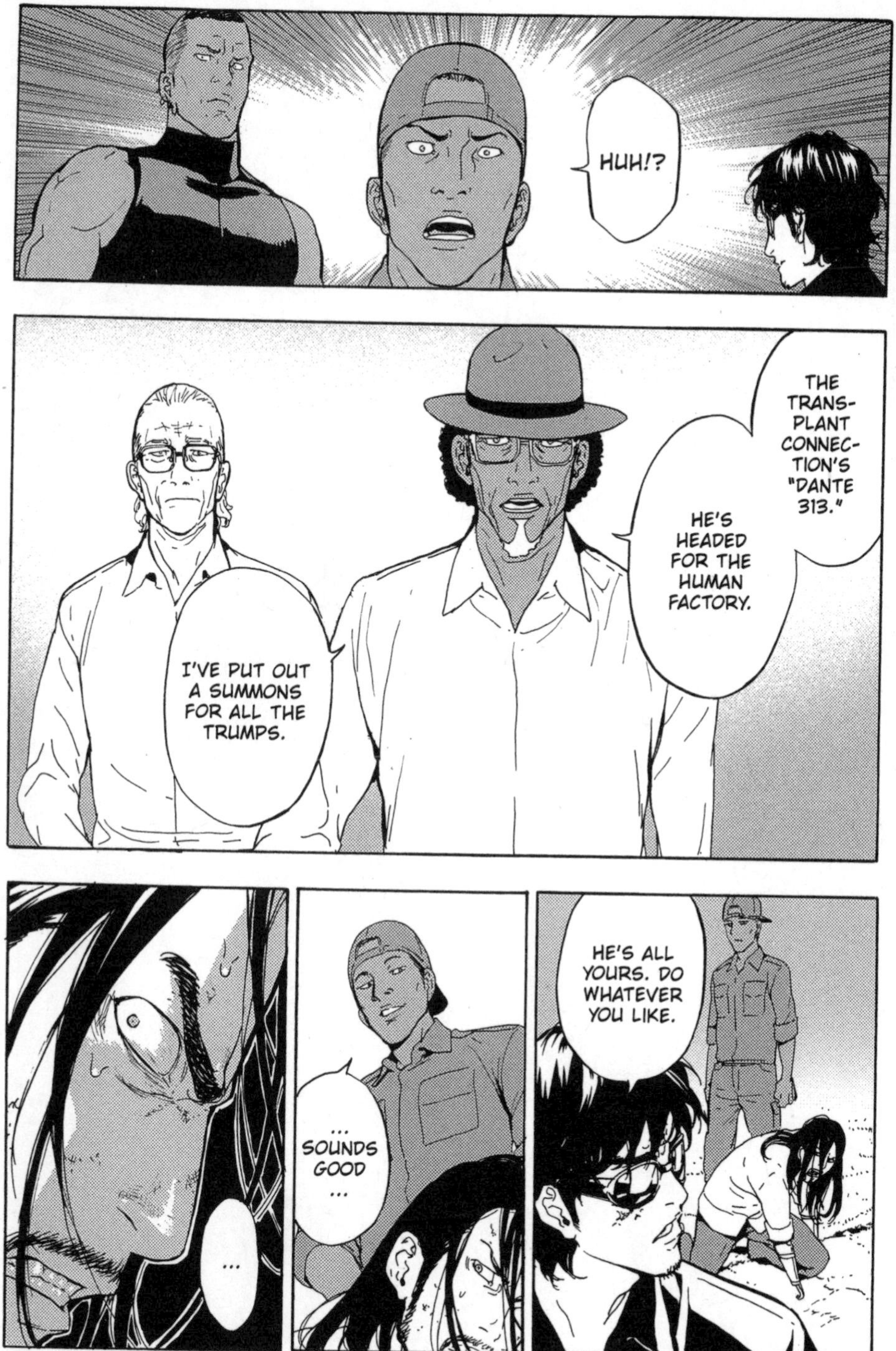
HUH!?
THE TRANS-PLANT CONNEC-TION'S "DANTE 313."
HE'S HEADED FOR THE HUMAN FACTORY.
I'VE PUT OUT A SUMMONS FOR ALL THE TRUMPS.
HE'S ALL YOURS. DO WHATEVER YOU LIKE.
... SOUNDS GOOD ...
...

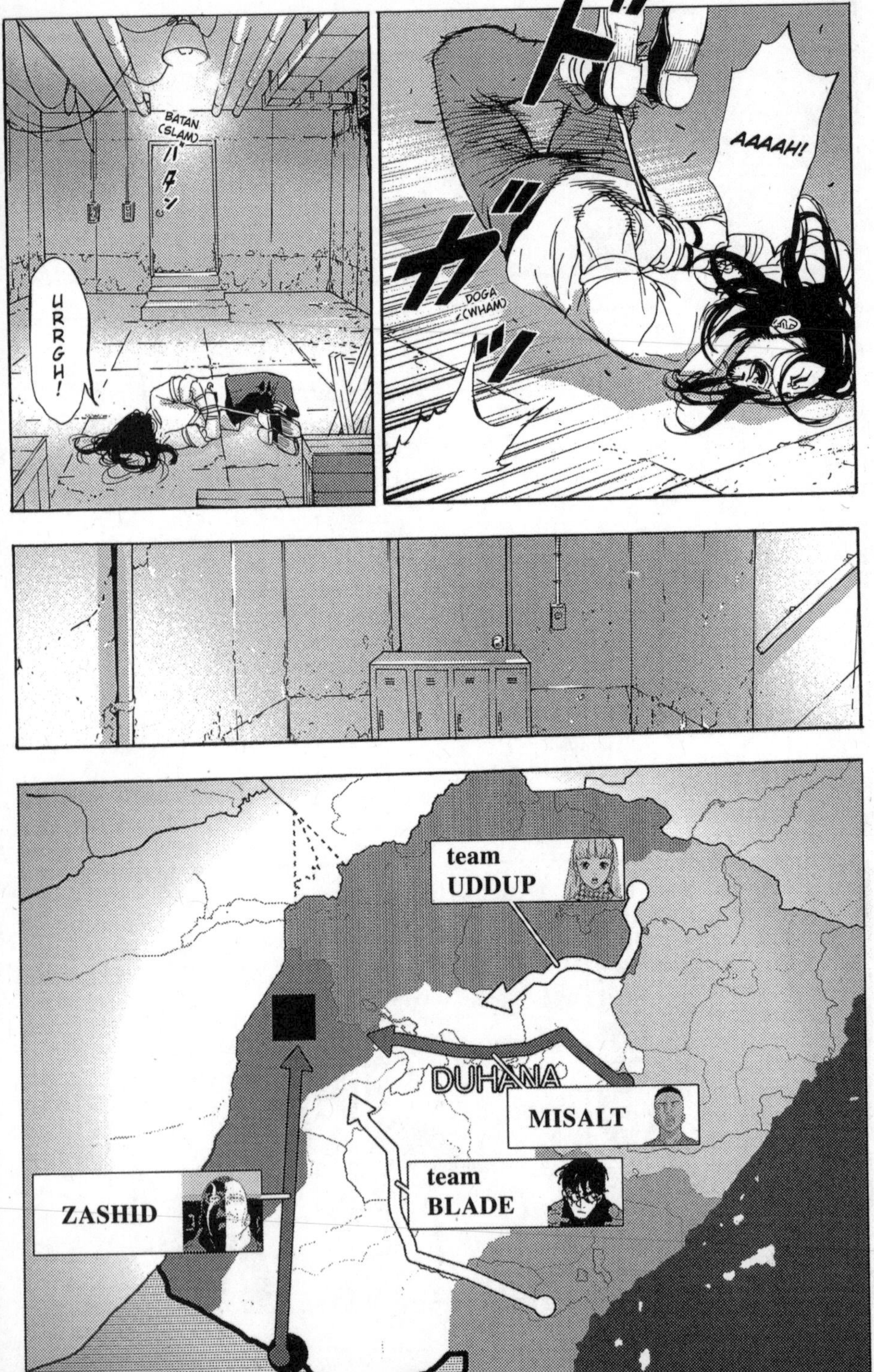
AAAAH!
DOGA
(WHAM)
BATAN
(SLAM)
バタン
URRGH!
team
UDDUP
DUHANA
MISALT
team
BLADE
ZASHID

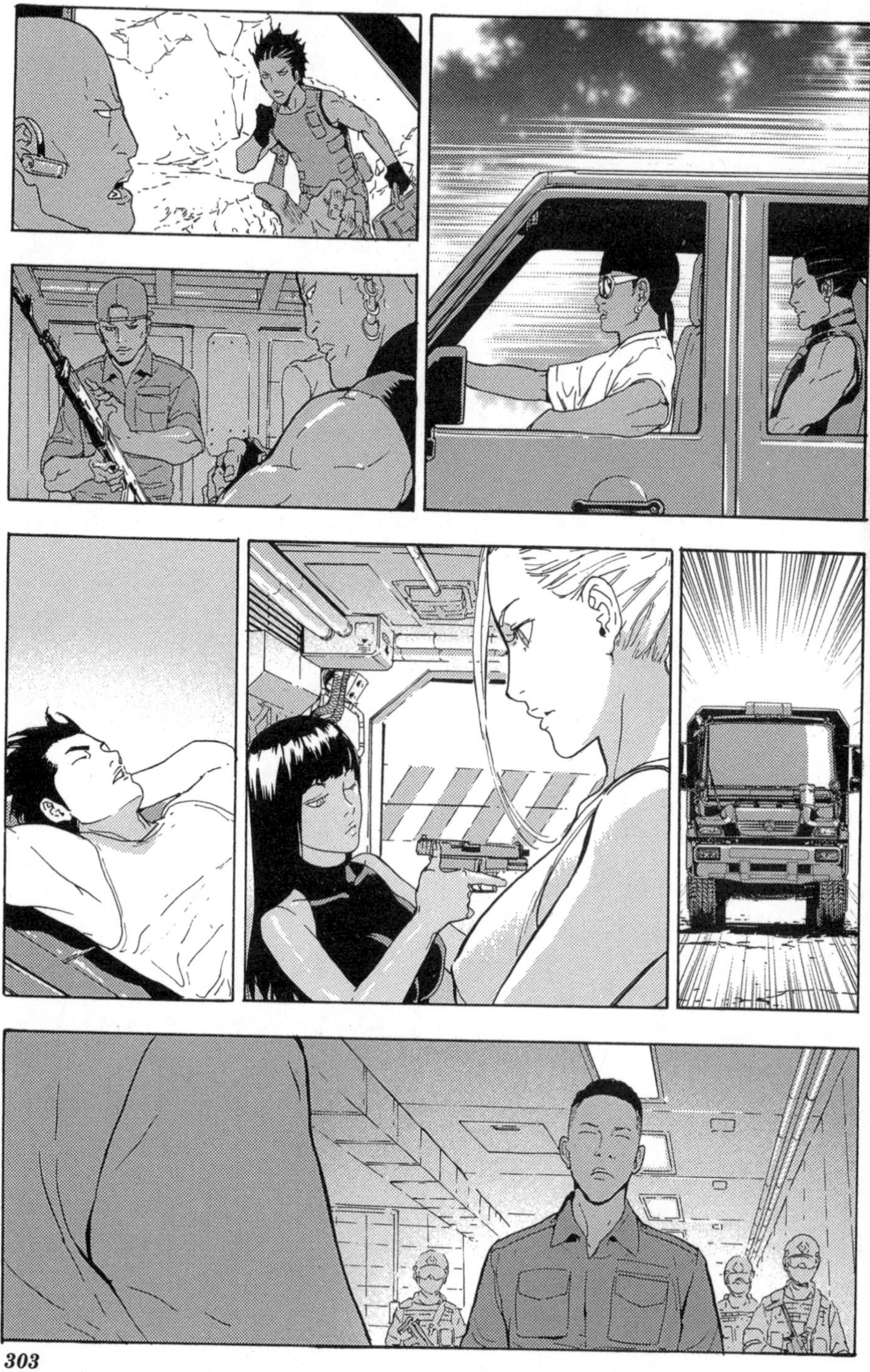

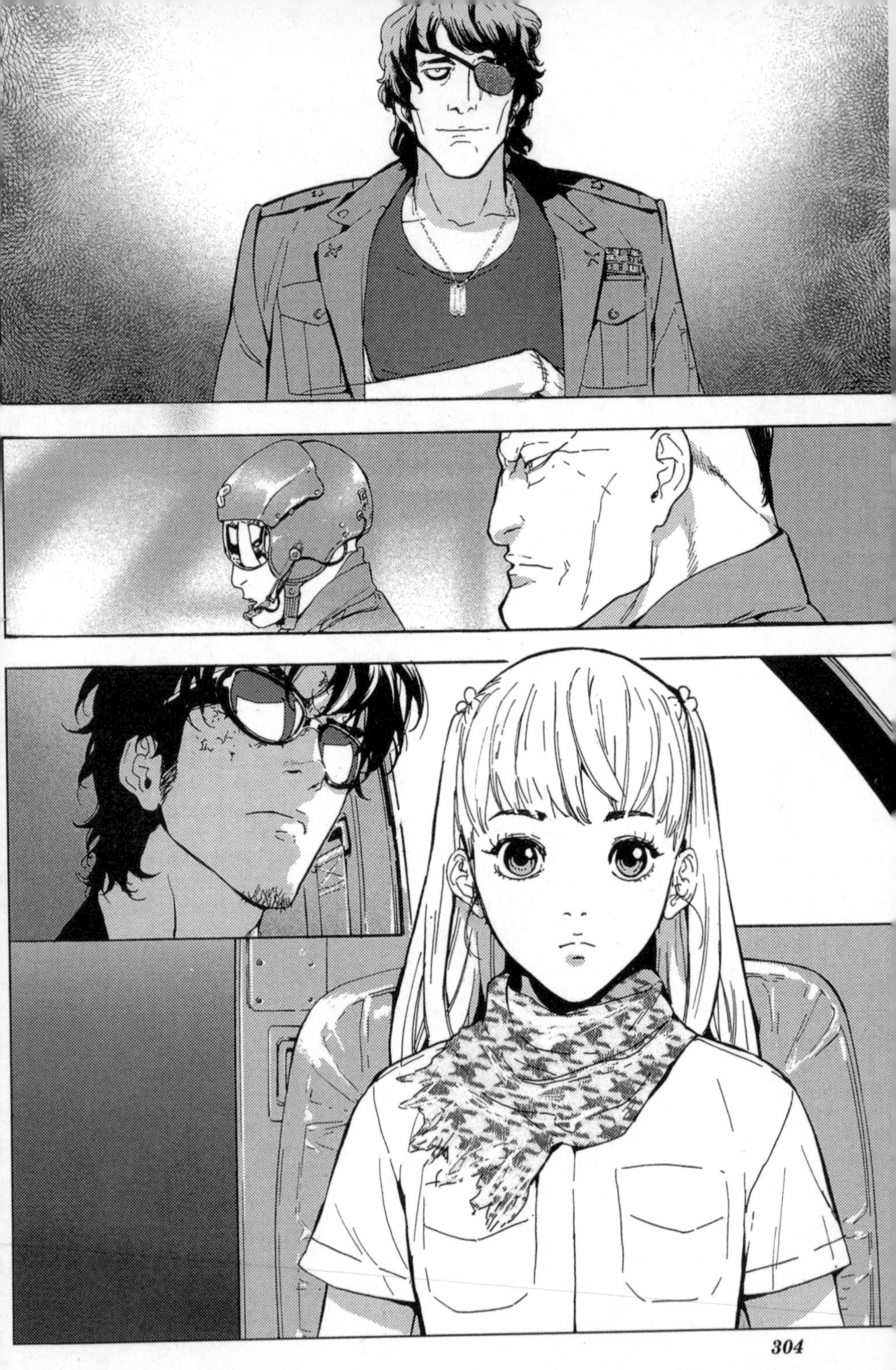

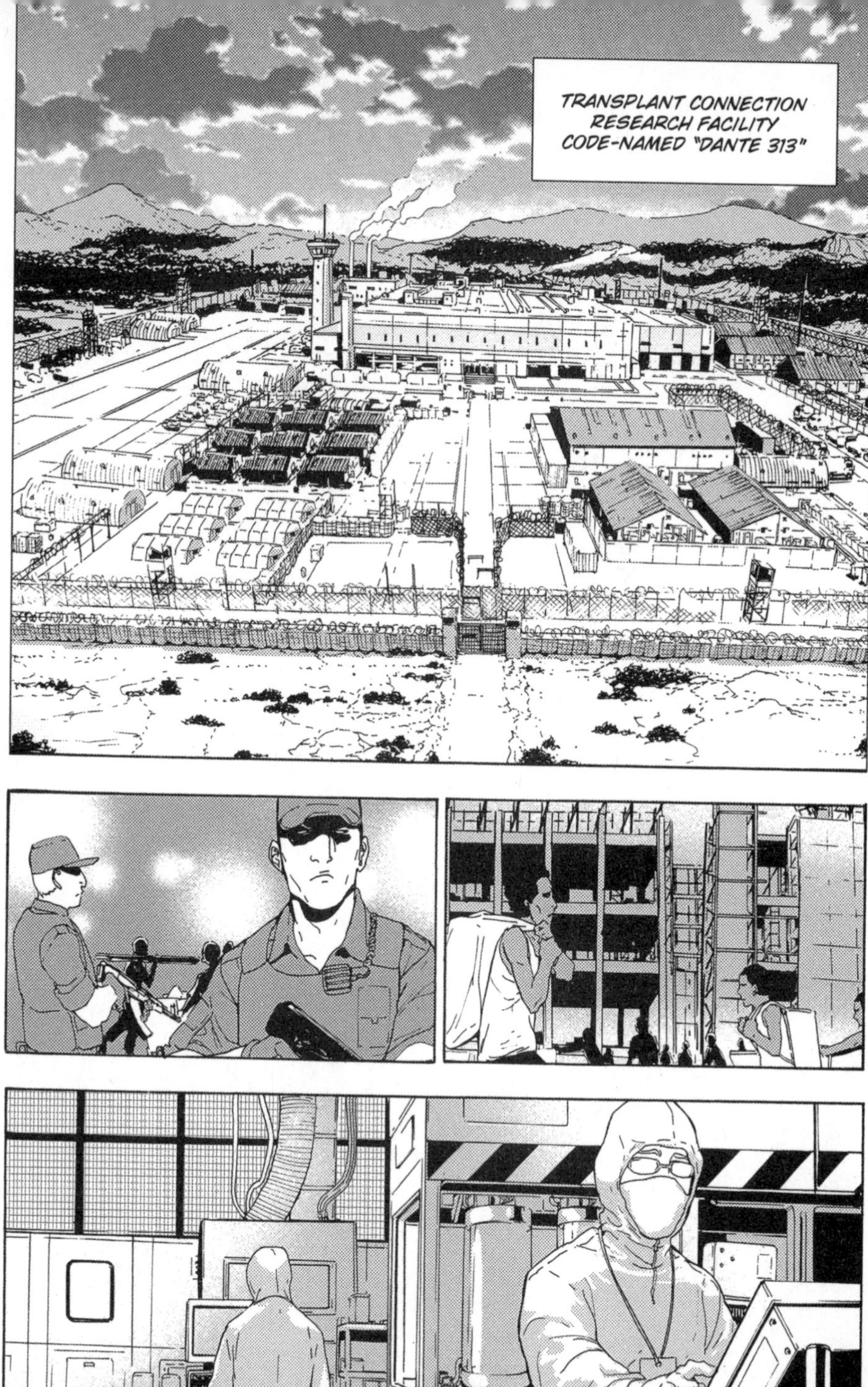
TRANSPLANT CONNECTION RESEARCH FACILITY CODE-NAMED "DANTE 313"

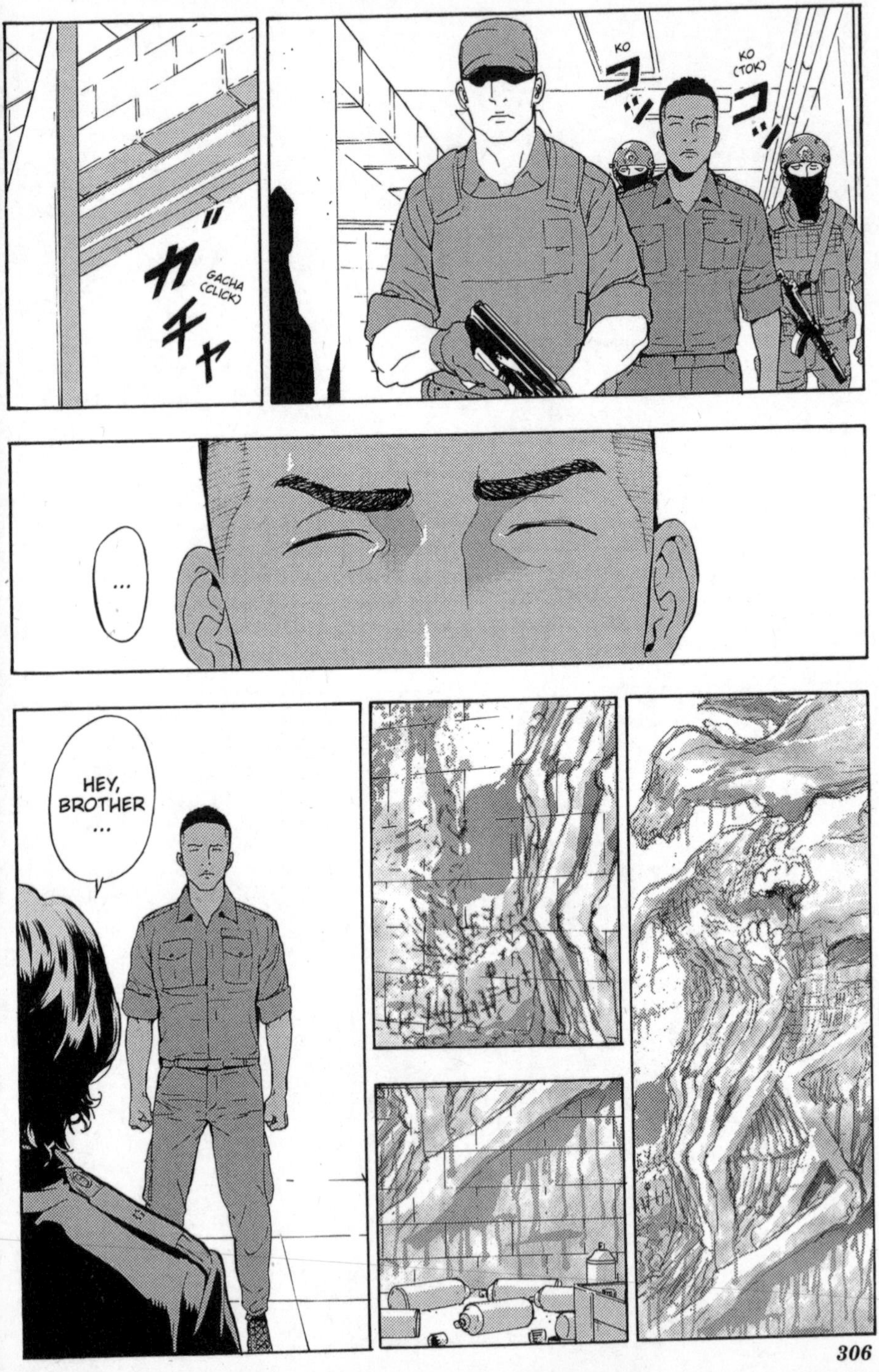
コッ
KO
コッ
KO (TOK)
ガチャ
GACHA (CLICK)
...
HEY, BROTHER ...

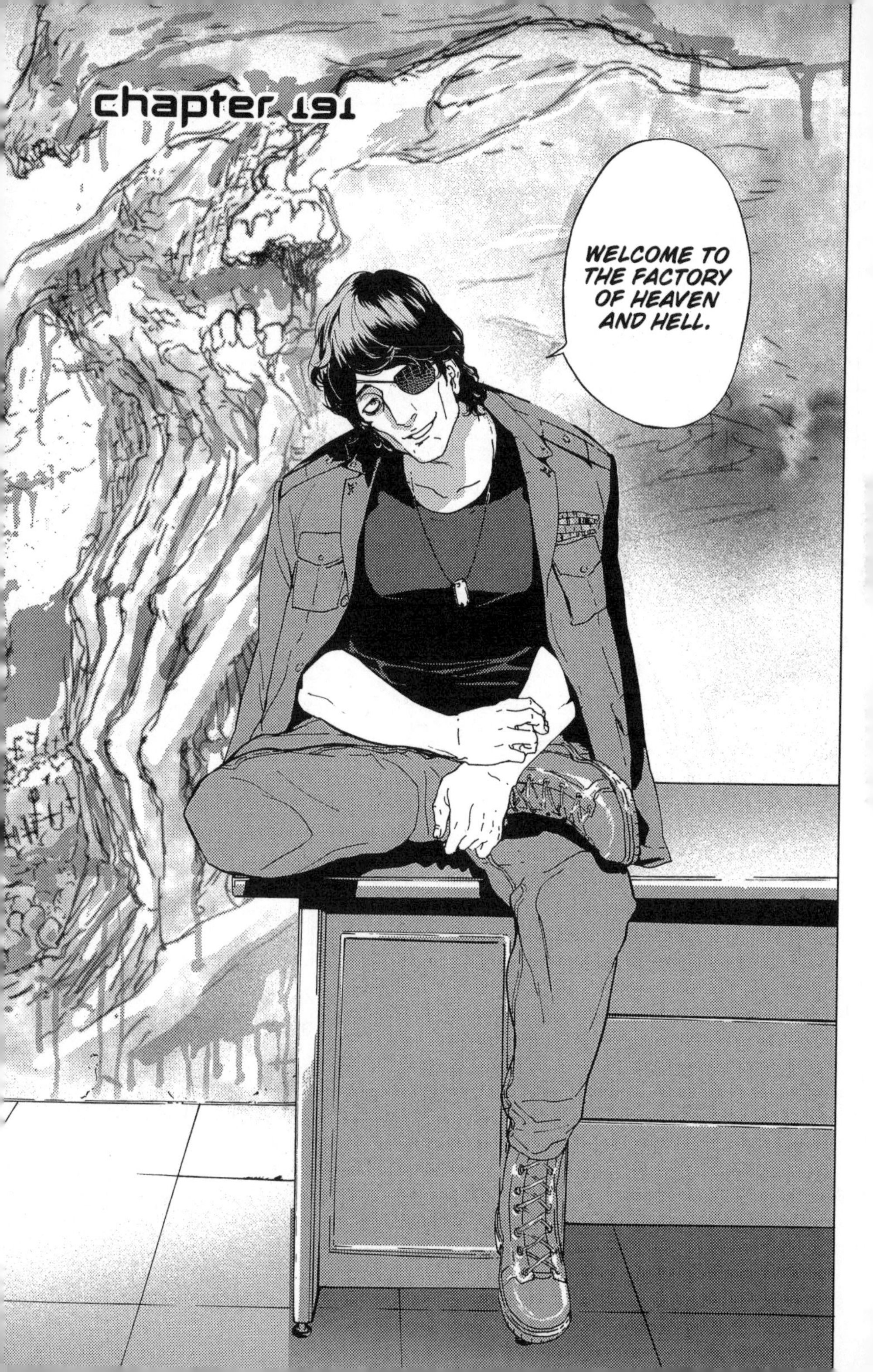
chapter 191
WELCOME TO THE FACTORY OF HEAVEN AND HELL.

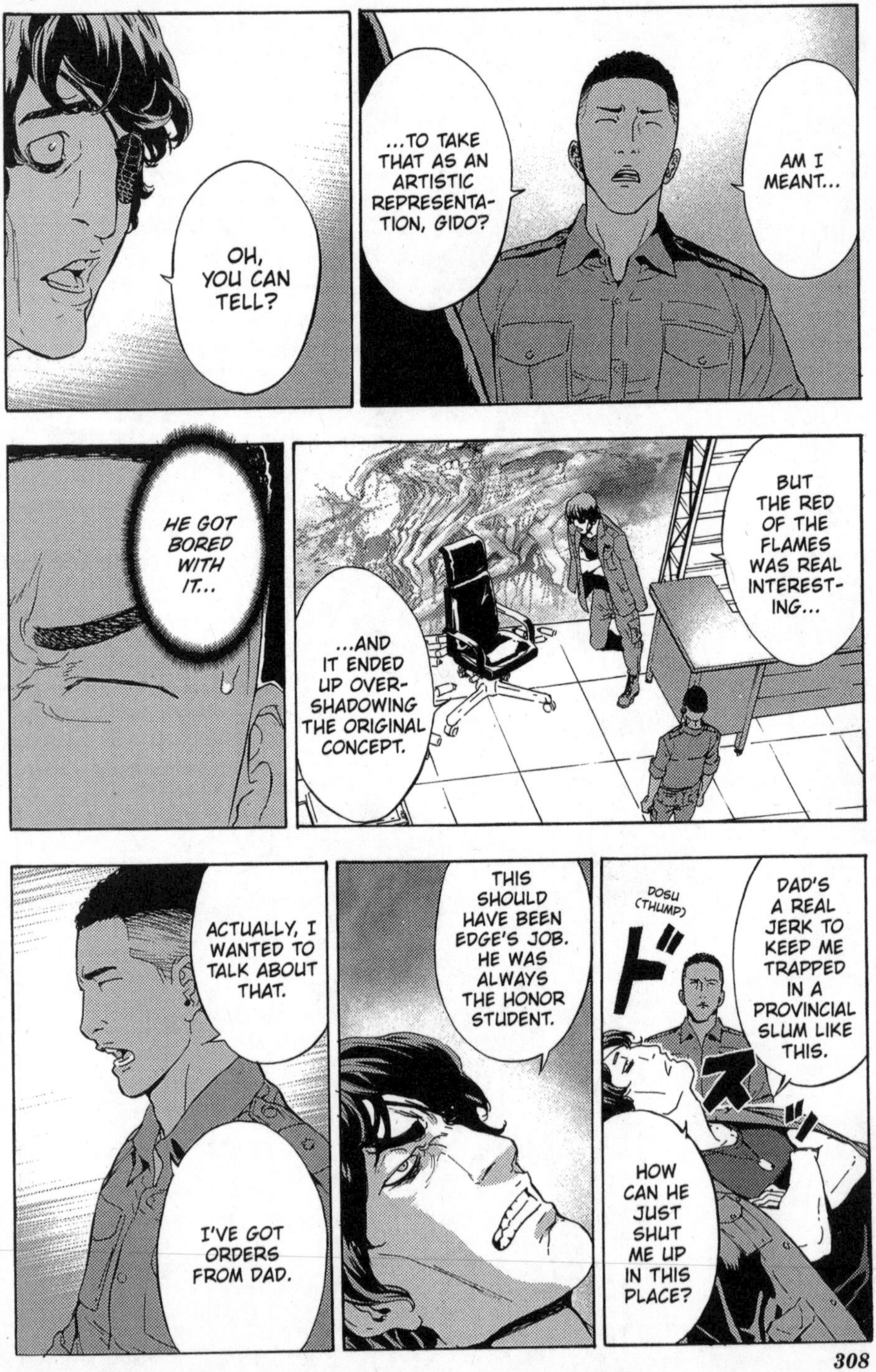
AM I MEANT...
...TO TAKE THAT AS AN ARTISTIC REPRESENTATION, GIDO?
OH, YOU CAN TELL?
BUT THE RED OF THE FLAMES WAS REAL INTERESTING...
...AND IT ENDED UP OVERSHADOWING THE ORIGINAL CONCEPT.
HE GOT BORED WITH IT...
DAD'S A REAL JERK TO KEEP ME TRAPPED IN A PROVINCIAL SLUM LIKE THIS.
DOSU (THUMP)
ドスッ
HOW CAN HE JUST SHUT ME UP IN THIS PLACE?
THIS SHOULD HAVE BEEN EDGE'S JOB. HE WAS ALWAYS THE HONOR STUDENT.
ACTUALLY, I WANTED TO TALK ABOUT THAT.
I'VE GOT ORDERS FROM DAD.

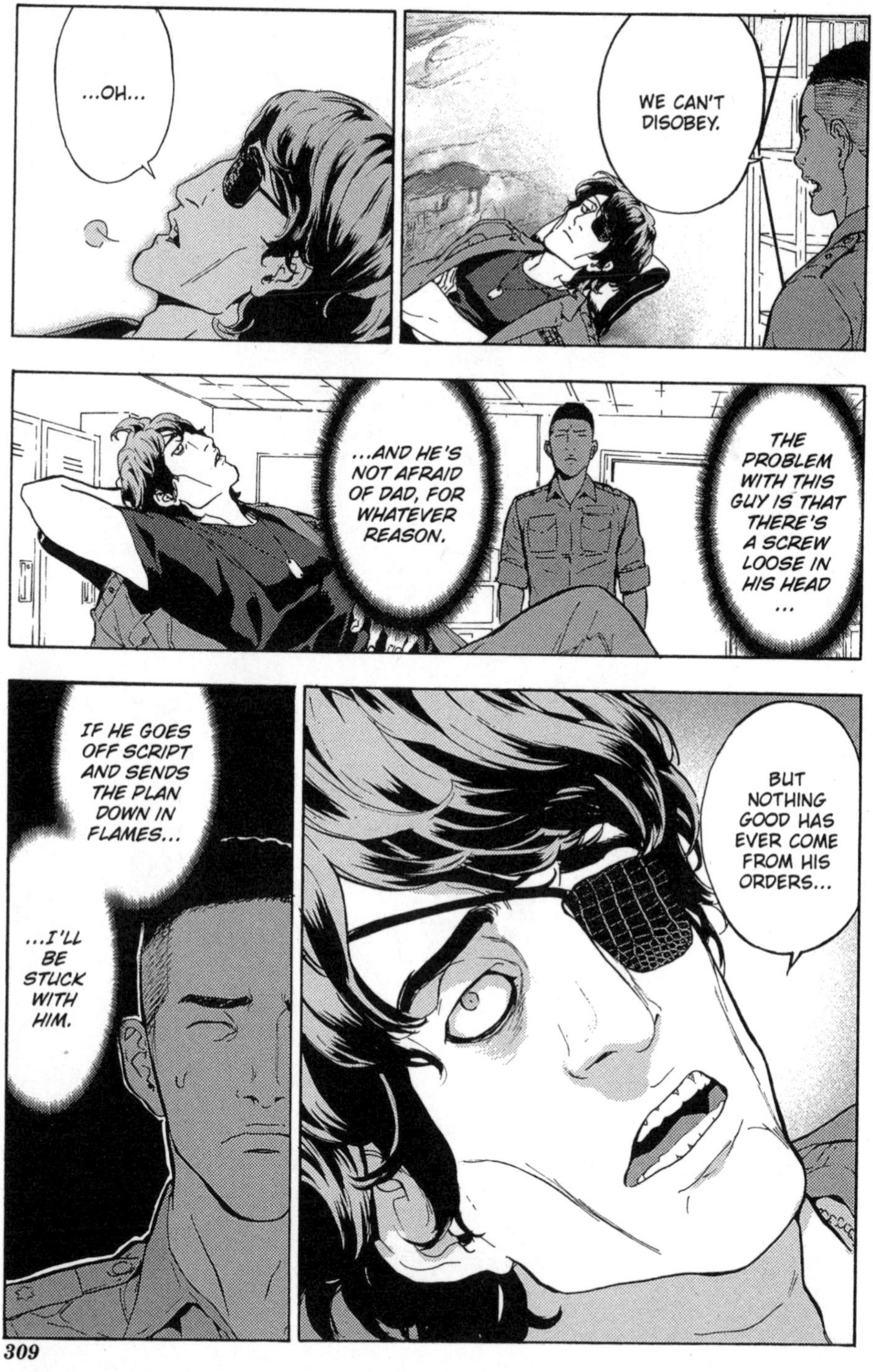
WE CAN'T DISOBEY.
...OH...
THE PROBLEM WITH THIS GUY IS THAT THERE'S A SCREW LOOSE IN HIS HEAD...
...AND HE'S NOT AFRAID OF DAD, FOR WHATEVER REASON.
BUT NOTHING GOOD HAS EVER COME FROM HIS ORDERS...
IF HE GOES OFF SCRIPT AND SENDS THE PLAN DOWN IN FLAMES...
...I'LL BE STUCK WITH HIM.

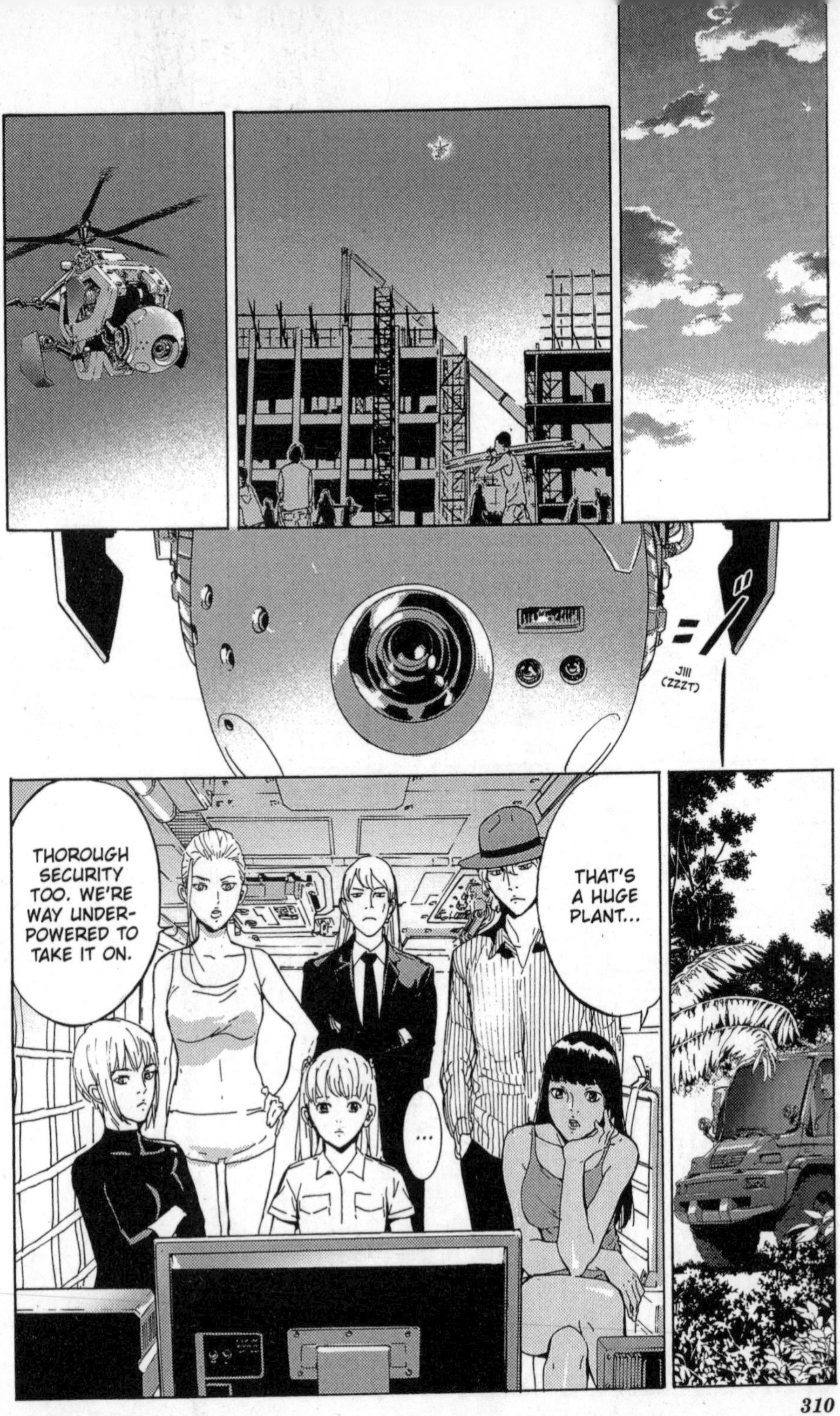
JIII
(ZZZT)
THAT'S A HUGE PLANT...
THOROUGH SECURITY TOO. WE'RE WAY UNDER-POWERED TO TAKE IT ON.
...

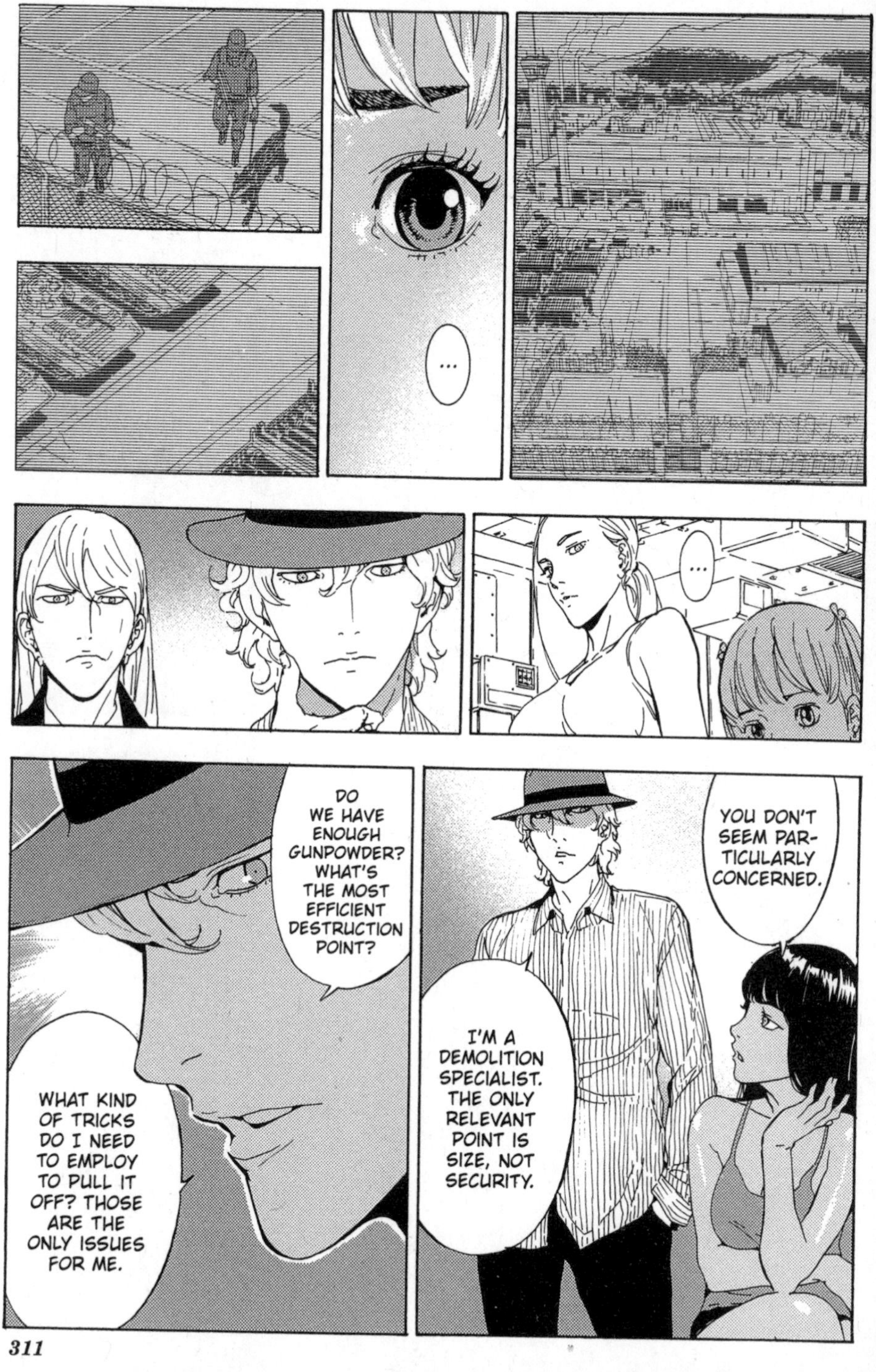
...
...
YOU DON'T SEEM PAR-TICULARLY CONCERNED.
I'M A DEMOLITION SPECIALIST. THE ONLY RELEVANT POINT IS SIZE, NOT SECURITY.
DO WE HAVE ENOUGH GUNPOWDER? WHAT'S THE MOST EFFICIENT DESTRUCTION POINT?
WHAT KIND OF TRICKS DO I NEED TO EMPLOY TO PULL IT OFF? THOSE ARE THE ONLY ISSUES FOR ME.

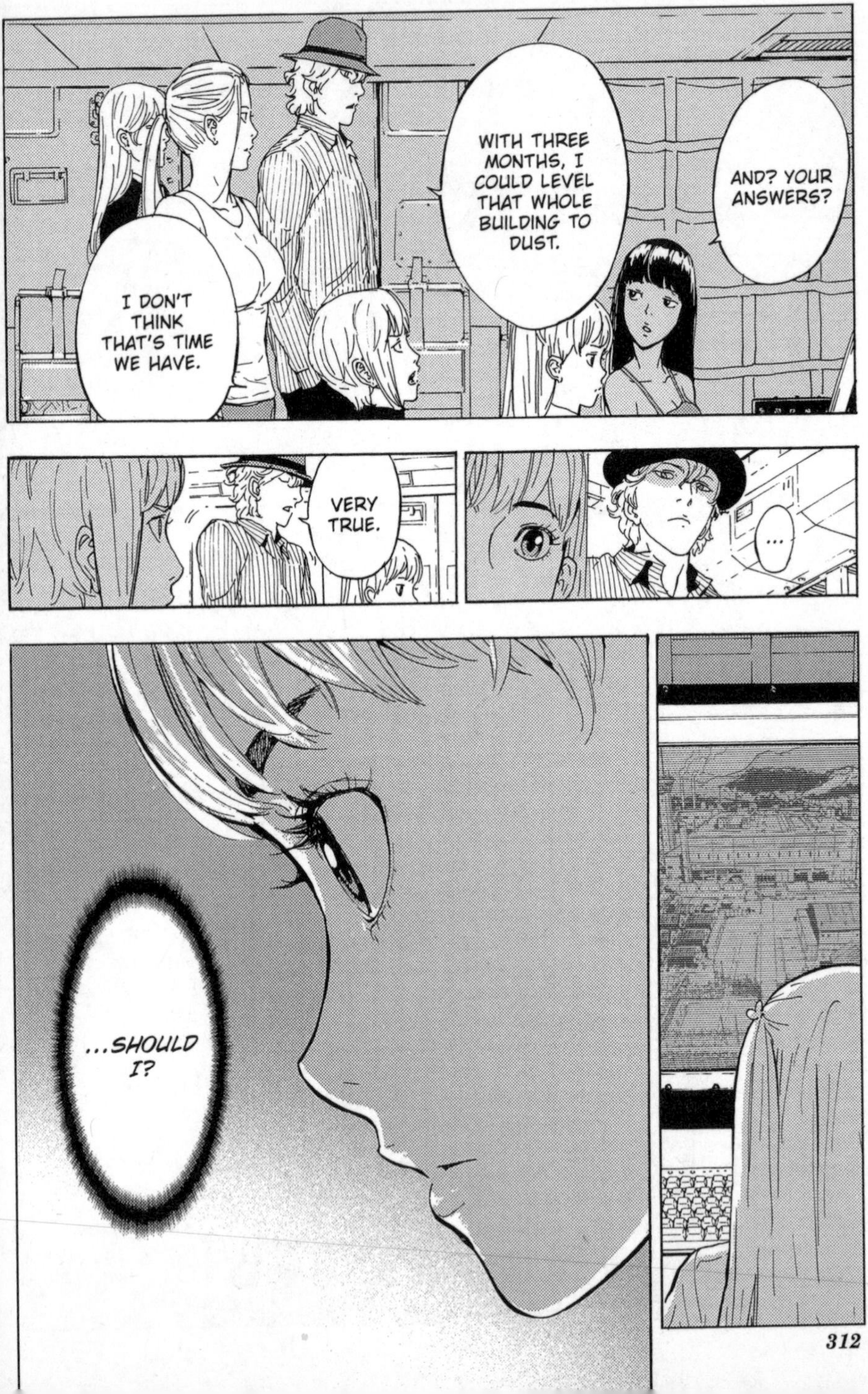
AND? YOUR ANSWERS?
WITH THREE MONTHS, I COULD LEVEL THAT WHOLE BUILDING TO DUST.
I DON'T THINK THAT'S TIME WE HAVE.
...
VERY TRUE.
...SHOULD I?

IF WE PROCEED WITH THIS, IT WILL EXPOSE EVERYONE TO DANGER.
BUT IF WE STOP HERE, IT WON'T JUST BE THEM.
THEN THE DANGER WILL EVEN EXTEND TO MAMORU-SAN...
WHAT IF I MAKE THE WRONG MOVE...?

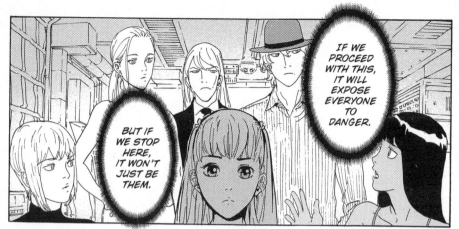

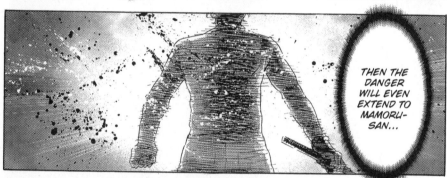

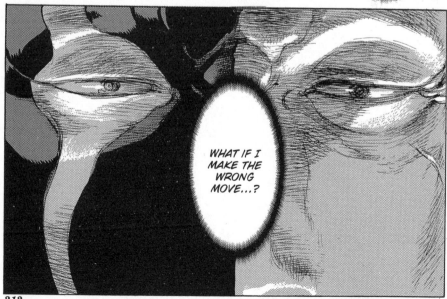

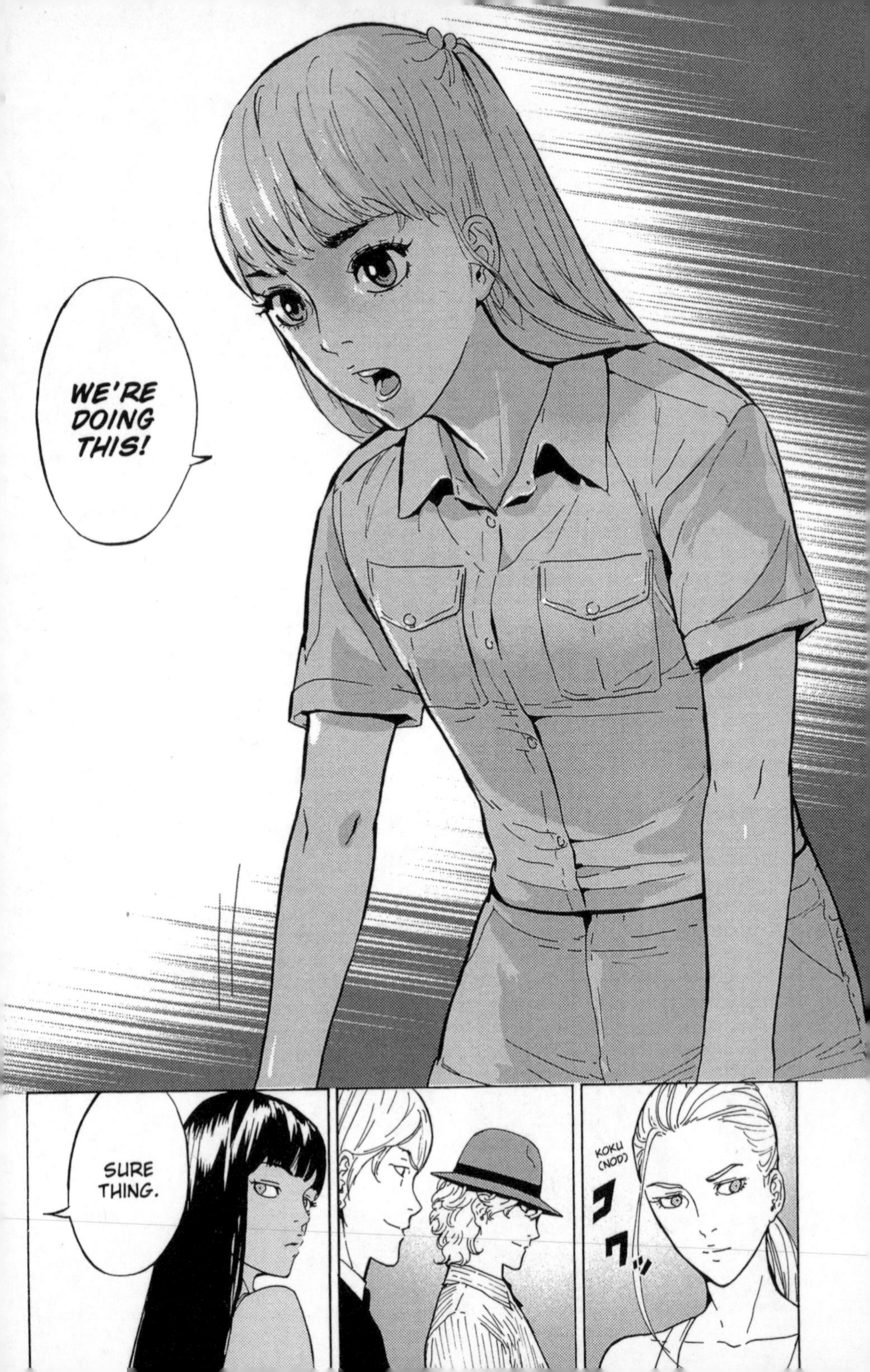
WE'RE DOING THIS!
KOKU (NOD)
SURE THING.

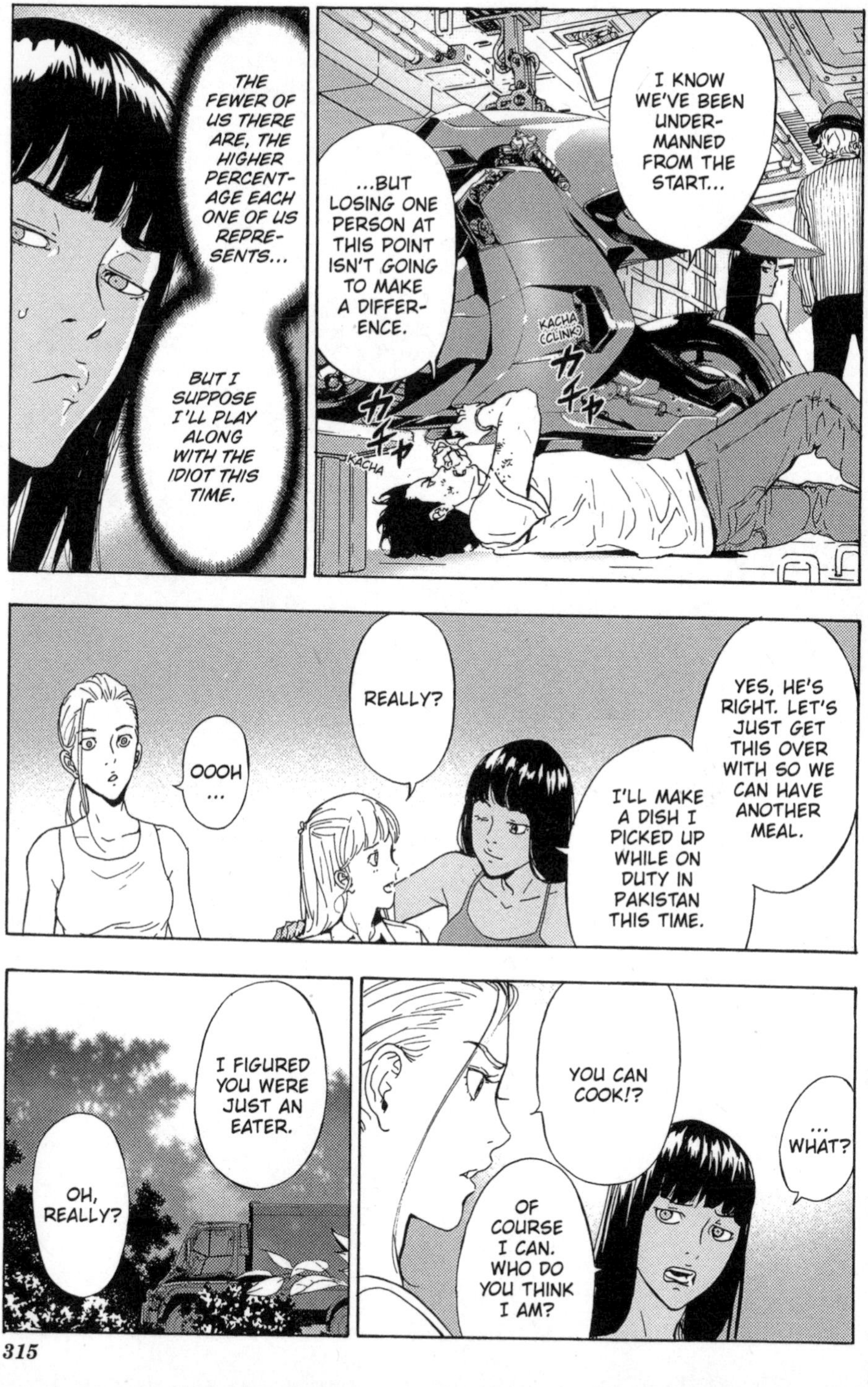
I KNOW WE'VE BEEN UNDER-MANNED FROM THE START...
...BUT LOSING ONE PERSON AT THIS POINT ISN'T GOING TO MAKE A DIFFER-ENCE.
KACHA (CLINK)
カチャ
カチャ
KACHA
THE FEWER OF US THERE ARE, THE HIGHER PERCENT-AGE EACH ONE OF US REPRE-SENTS...
BUT I SUPPOSE I'LL PLAY ALONG WITH THE IDIOT THIS TIME.
YES, HE'S RIGHT. LET'S JUST GET THIS OVER WITH SO WE CAN HAVE ANOTHER MEAL.
I'LL MAKE A DISH I PICKED UP WHILE ON DUTY IN PAKISTAN THIS TIME.
REALLY?
OOOH ...
YOU CAN COOK!?
... WHAT?
OF COURSE I CAN. WHO DO YOU THINK I AM?
I FIGURED YOU WERE JUST AN EATER.
OH, REALLY?

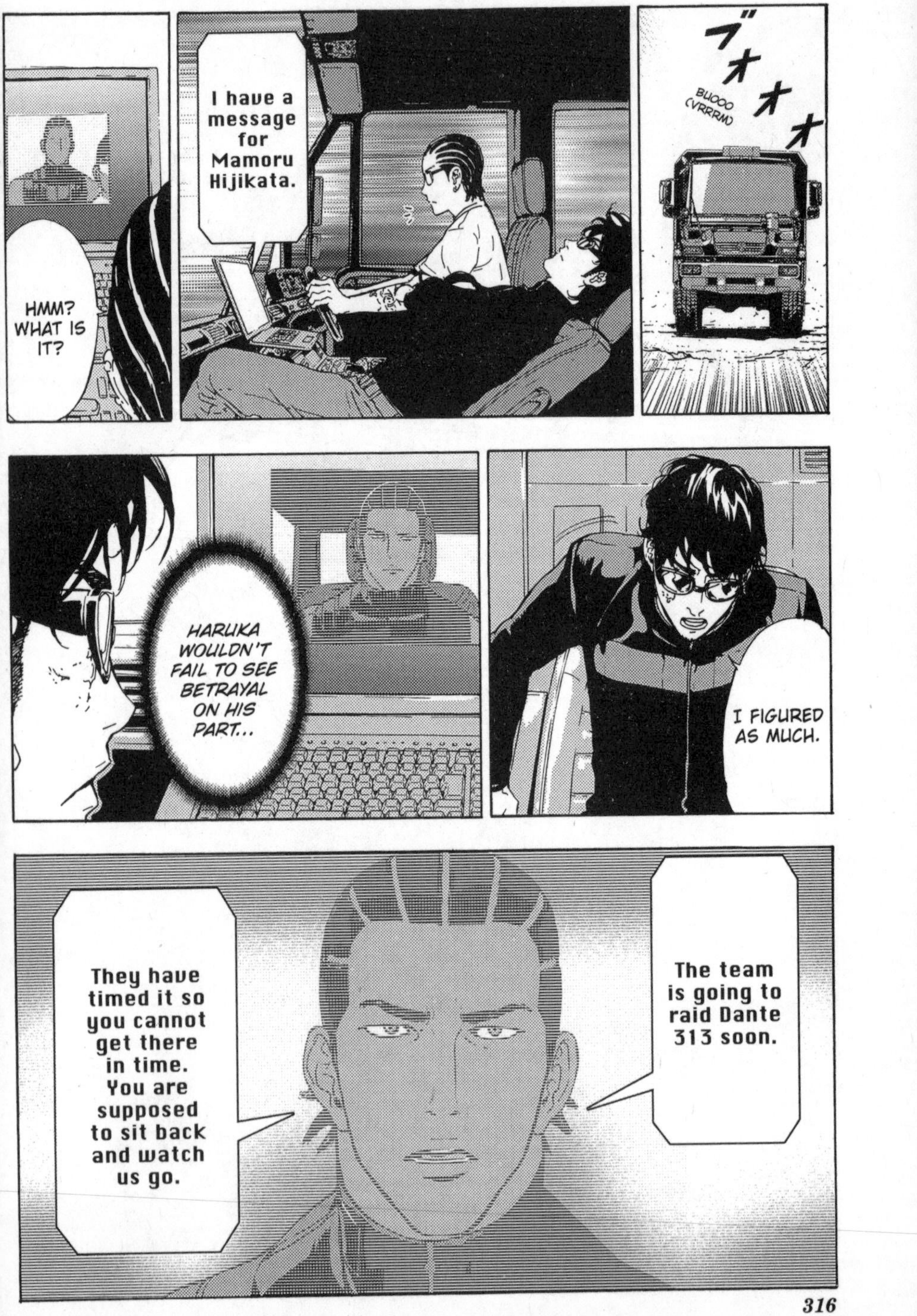
ブオオオオ
BUOOO (VRRRM)
I have a message for Mamoru Hijikata.
HMM? WHAT IS IT?
I FIGURED AS MUCH.
HARUKA WOULDN'T FAIL TO SEE BETRAYAL ON HIS PART...
The team is going to raid Dante 313 soon.
They have timed it so you cannot get there in time. You are supposed to sit back and watch us go.

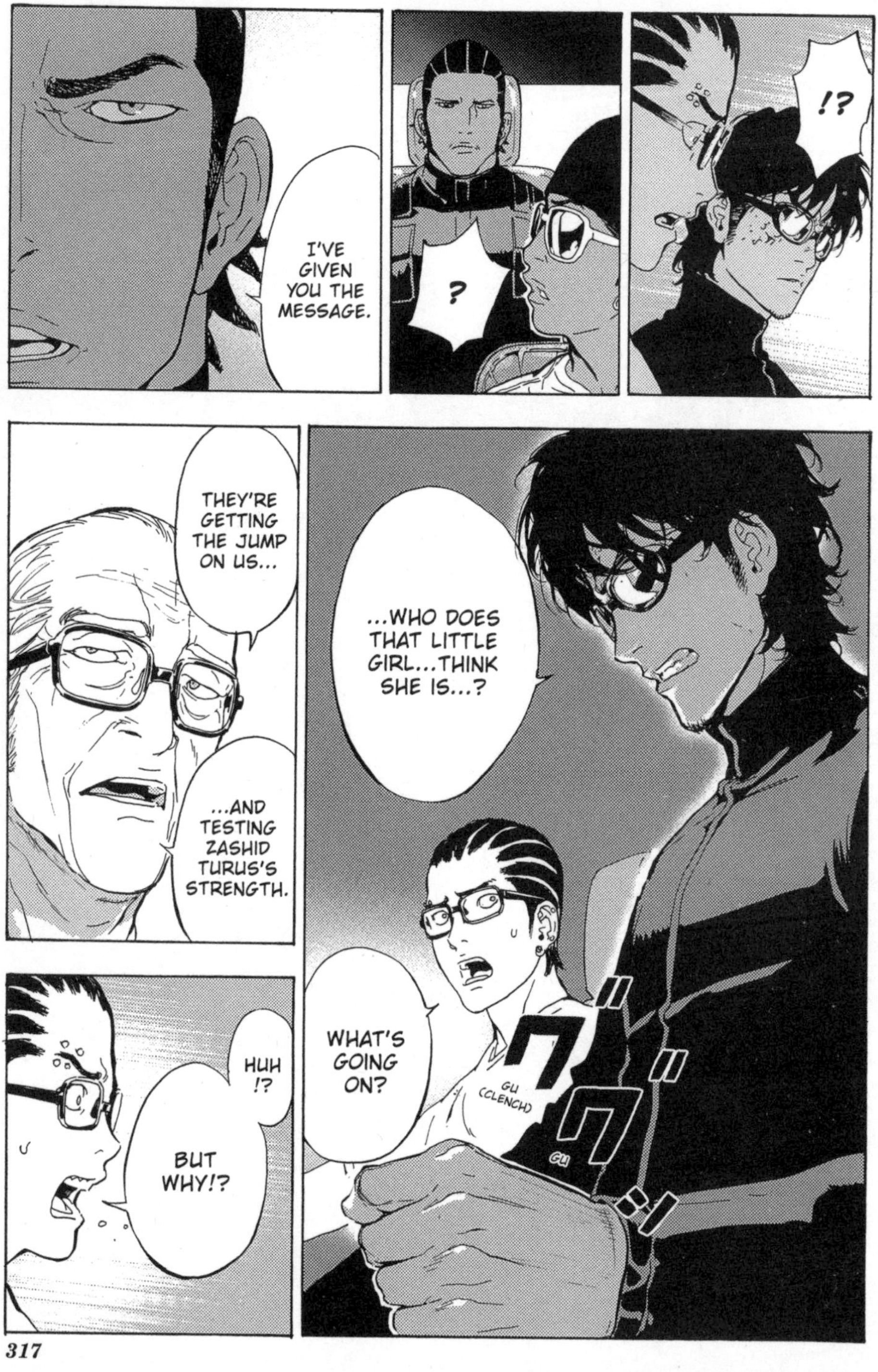
!?
?
I'VE GIVEN YOU THE MESSAGE.
...WHO DOES THAT LITTLE GIRL...THINK SHE IS...?
WHAT'S GOING ON?
GU (CLENCH)
GU
THEY'RE GETTING THE JUMP ON US...
...AND TESTING ZASHID TURUS'S STRENGTH.
HUH!?
BUT WHY!?

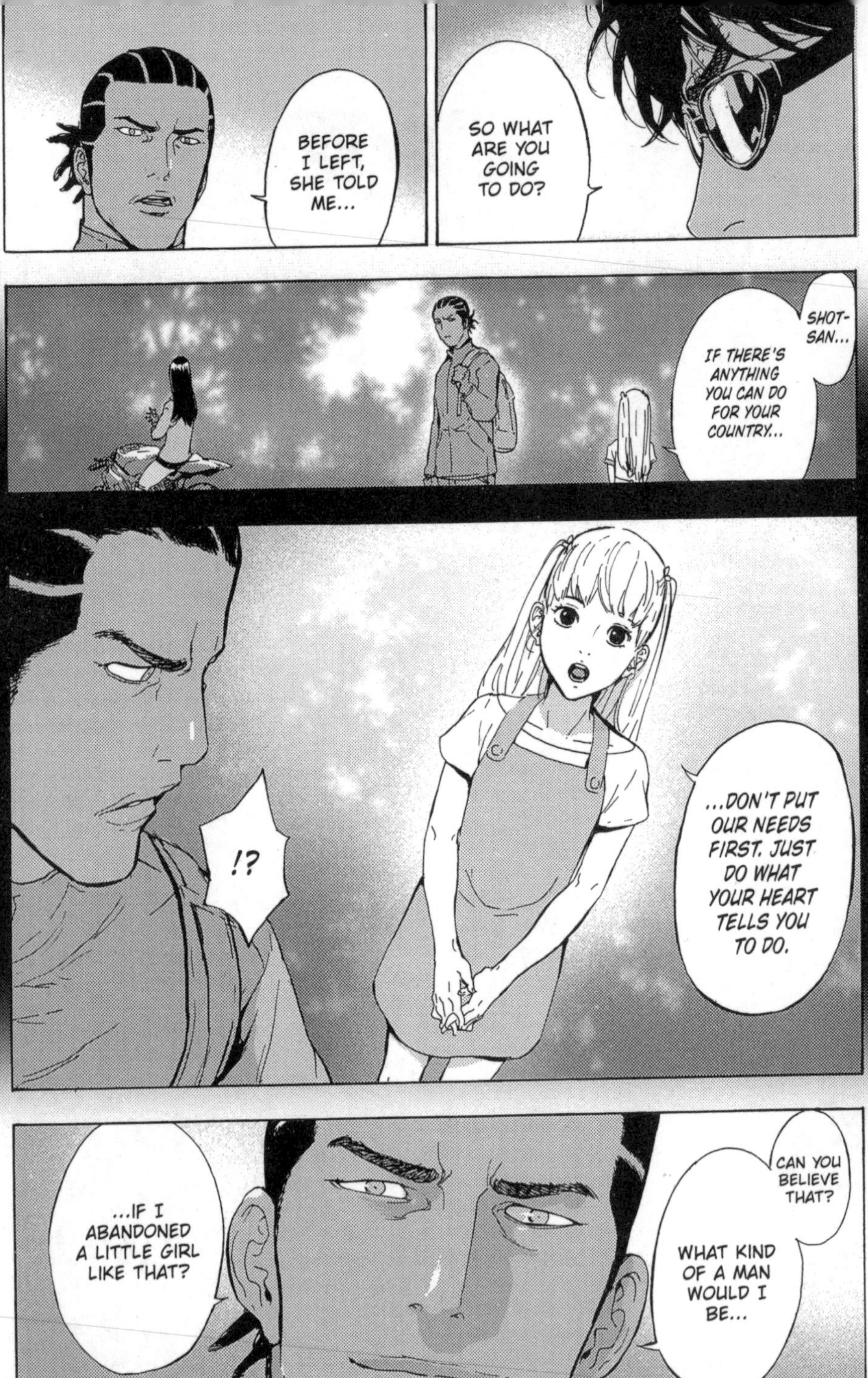
SO WHAT ARE YOU GOING TO DO?
BEFORE I LEFT, SHE TOLD ME...
SHOT-SAN...
IF THERE'S ANYTHING YOU CAN DO FOR YOUR COUNTRY...
...DON'T PUT OUR NEEDS FIRST. JUST DO WHAT YOUR HEART TELLS YOU TO DO.
!?
CAN YOU BELIEVE THAT?
WHAT KIND OF A MAN WOULD I BE...
...IF I ABANDONED A LITTLE GIRL LIKE THAT?

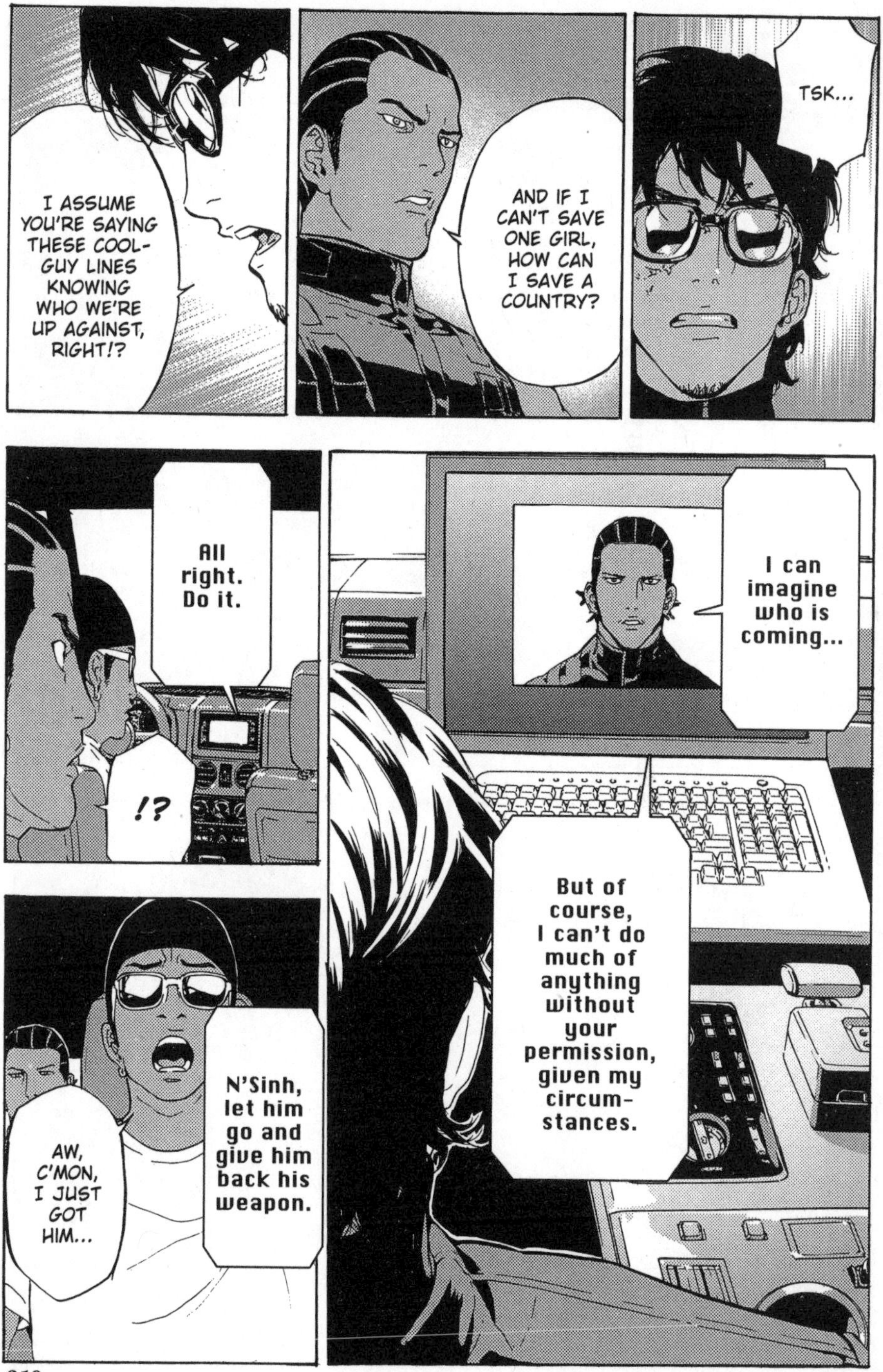
TSK...
AND IF I CAN'T SAVE ONE GIRL, HOW CAN I SAVE A COUNTRY?
I ASSUME YOU'RE SAYING THESE COOL-GUY LINES KNOWING WHO WE'RE UP AGAINST, RIGHT!?
I can imagine who is coming...
But of course, I can't do much of anything without your permission, given my circum-stances.
All right. Do it.
!?
N'Sinh, let him go and give him back his weapon.
AW, C'MON, I JUST GOT HIM...

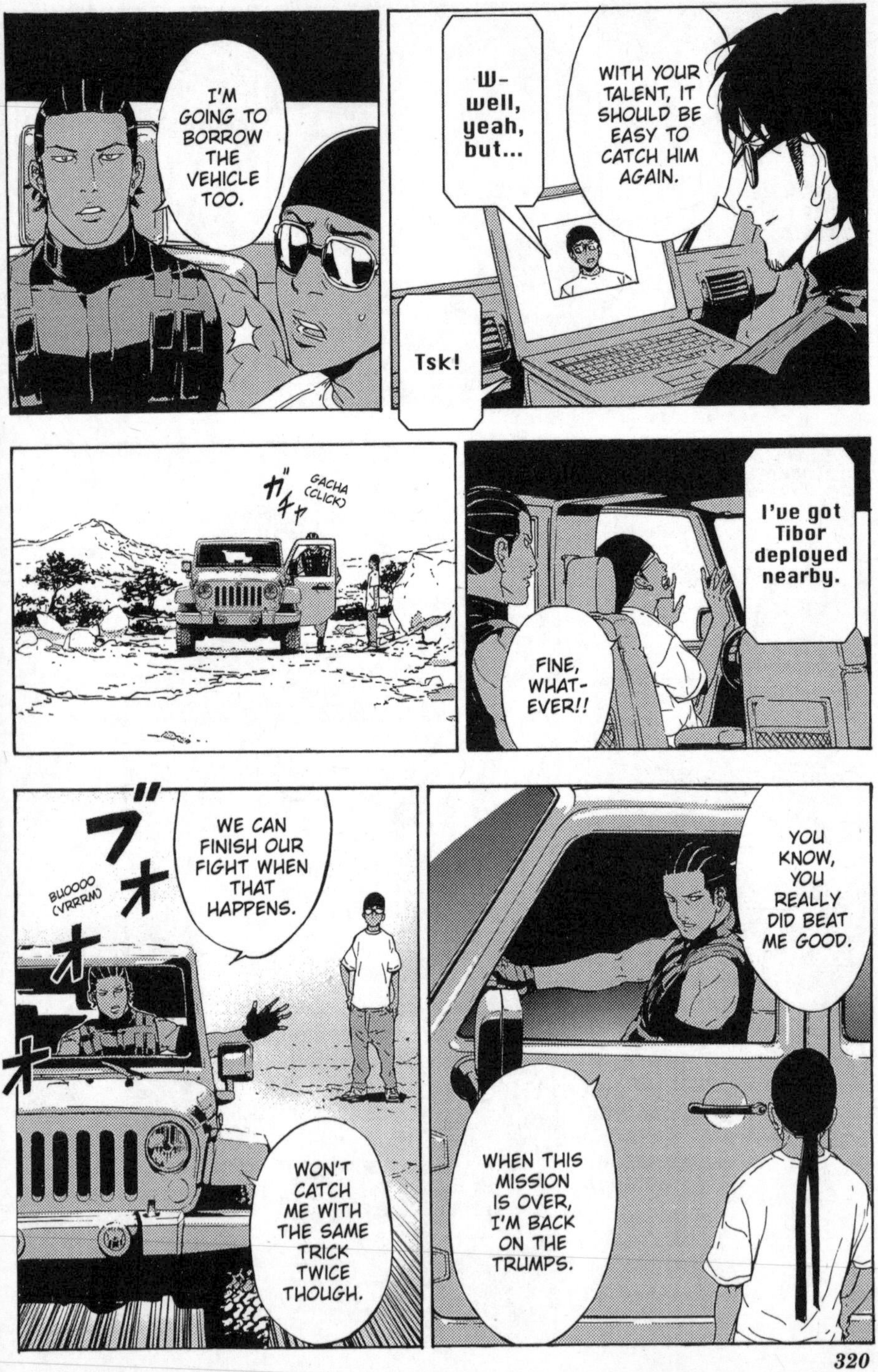
WITH YOUR TALENT, IT SHOULD BE EASY TO CATCH HIM AGAIN.
W-well, yeah, but...
Tsk!
I'M GOING TO BORROW THE VEHICLE TOO.
I've got Tibor deployed nearby.
FINE, WHAT-EVER!!
GACHA (CLICK)
YOU KNOW, YOU REALLY DID BEAT ME GOOD.
WHEN THIS MISSION IS OVER, I'M BACK ON THE TRUMPS.
WE CAN FINISH OUR FIGHT WHEN THAT HAPPENS.
BUOOOO (VRRRM)
WON'T CATCH ME WITH THE SAME TRICK TWICE THOUGH.

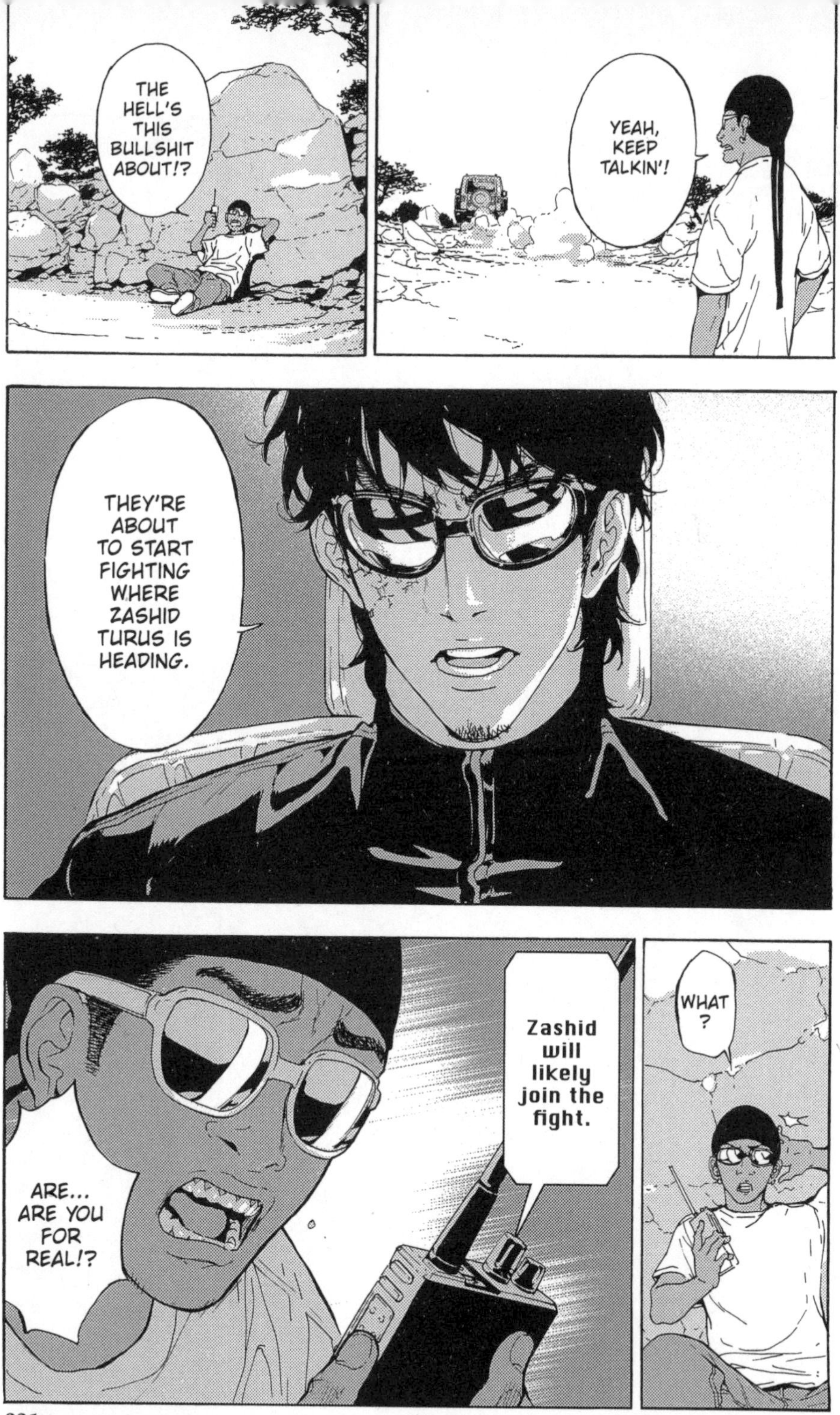
YEAH, KEEP TALKIN'!
THE HELL'S THIS BULLSHIT ABOUT!?
THEY'RE ABOUT TO START FIGHTING WHERE ZASHID TURUS IS HEADING.
WHAT?
Zashid will likely join the fight.
ARE... ARE YOU FOR REAL!?

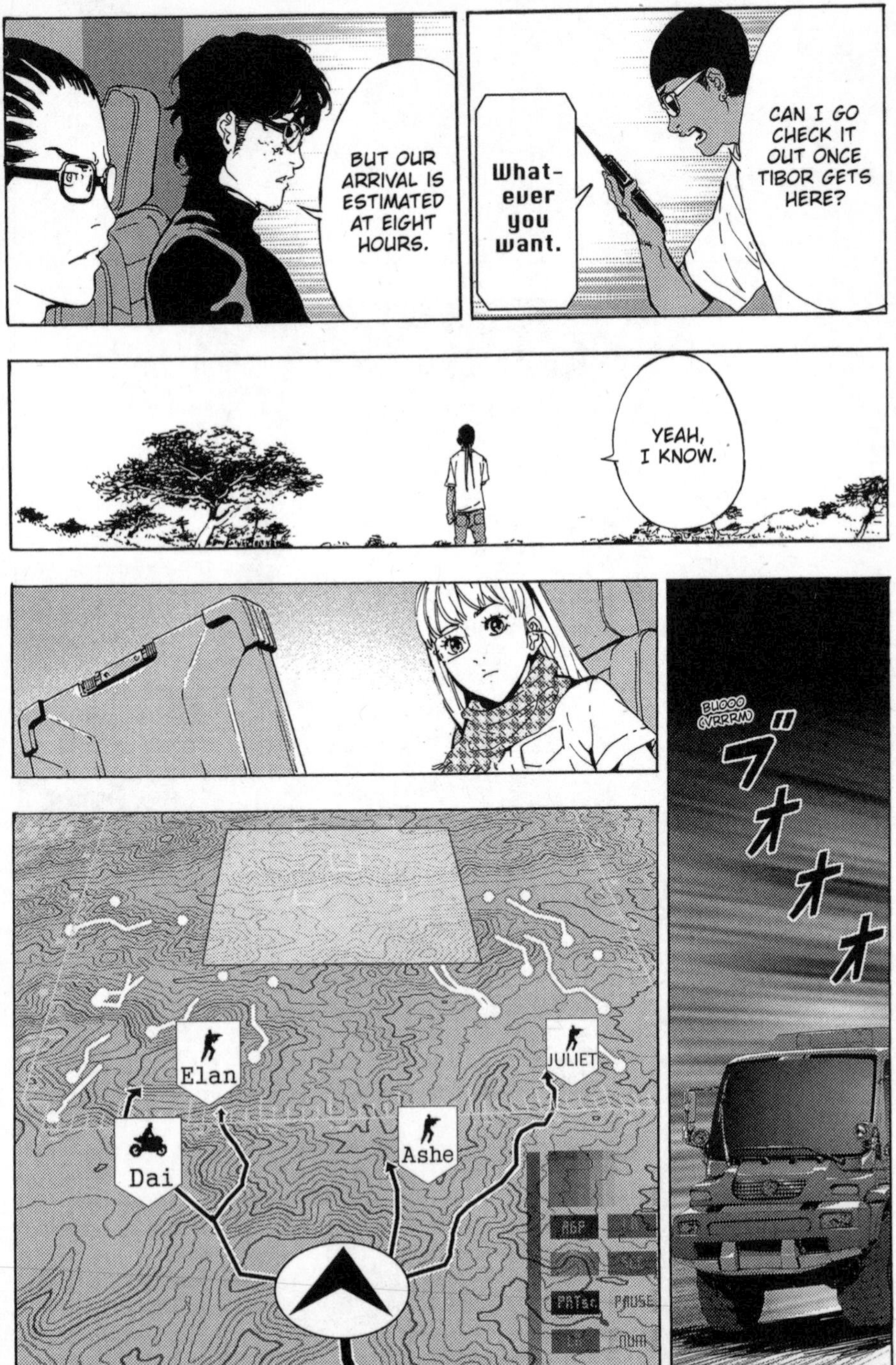
CAN I GO CHECK IT OUT ONCE TIBOR GETS HERE?
What-ever you want.
BUT OUR ARRIVAL IS ESTIMATED AT EIGHT HOURS.
YEAH, I KNOW.
BUOOO (VRRRM)
ブオオオ
JULIET
Elan
Ashe
Dai
PAUSE
NUM

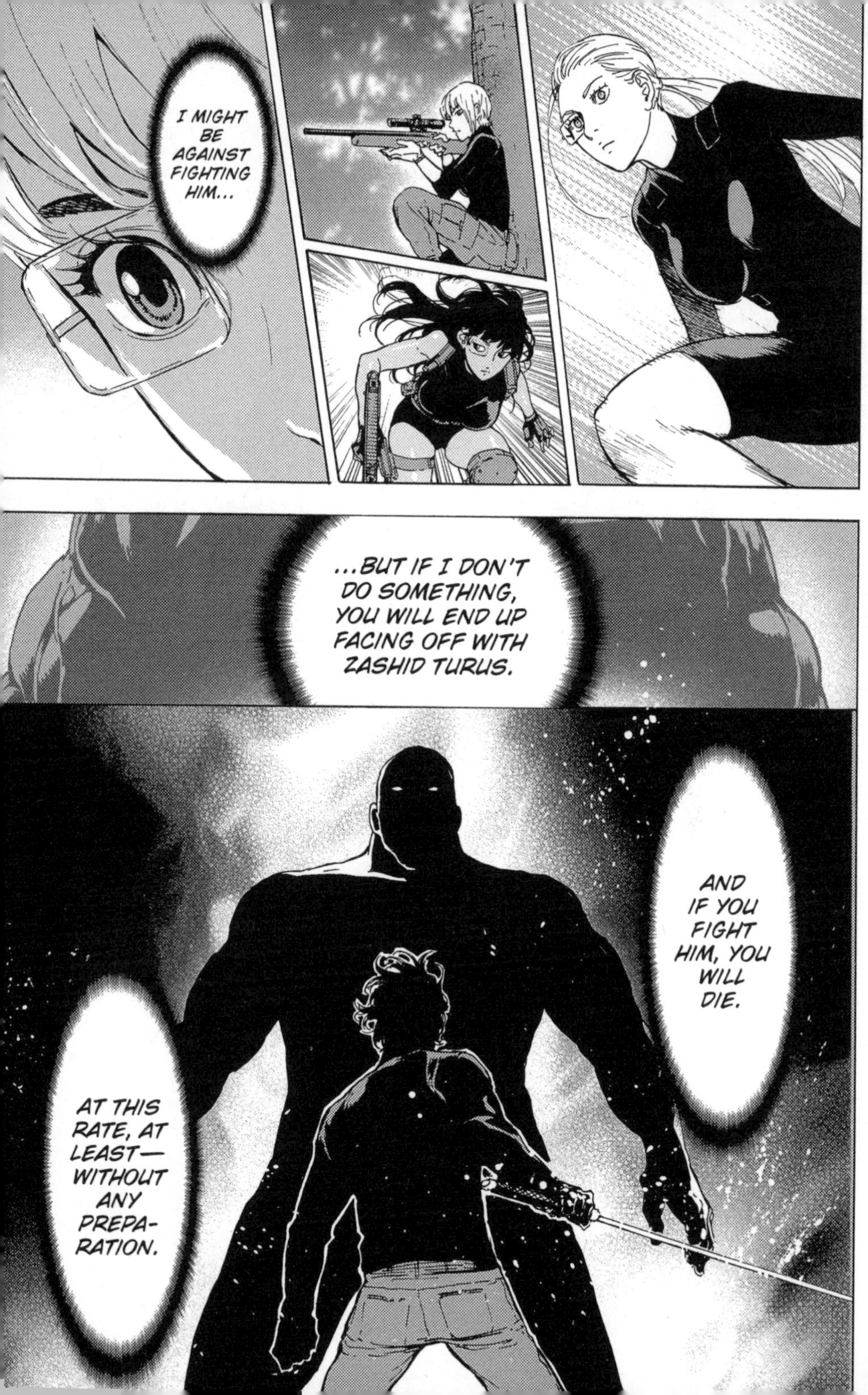
I MIGHT BE AGAINST FIGHTING HIM...
...BUT IF I DON'T DO SOMETHING, YOU WILL END UP FACING OFF WITH ZASHID TURUS.
AND IF YOU FIGHT HIM, YOU WILL DIE.
AT THIS RATE, AT LEAST— WITHOUT ANY PREPA- RATION.

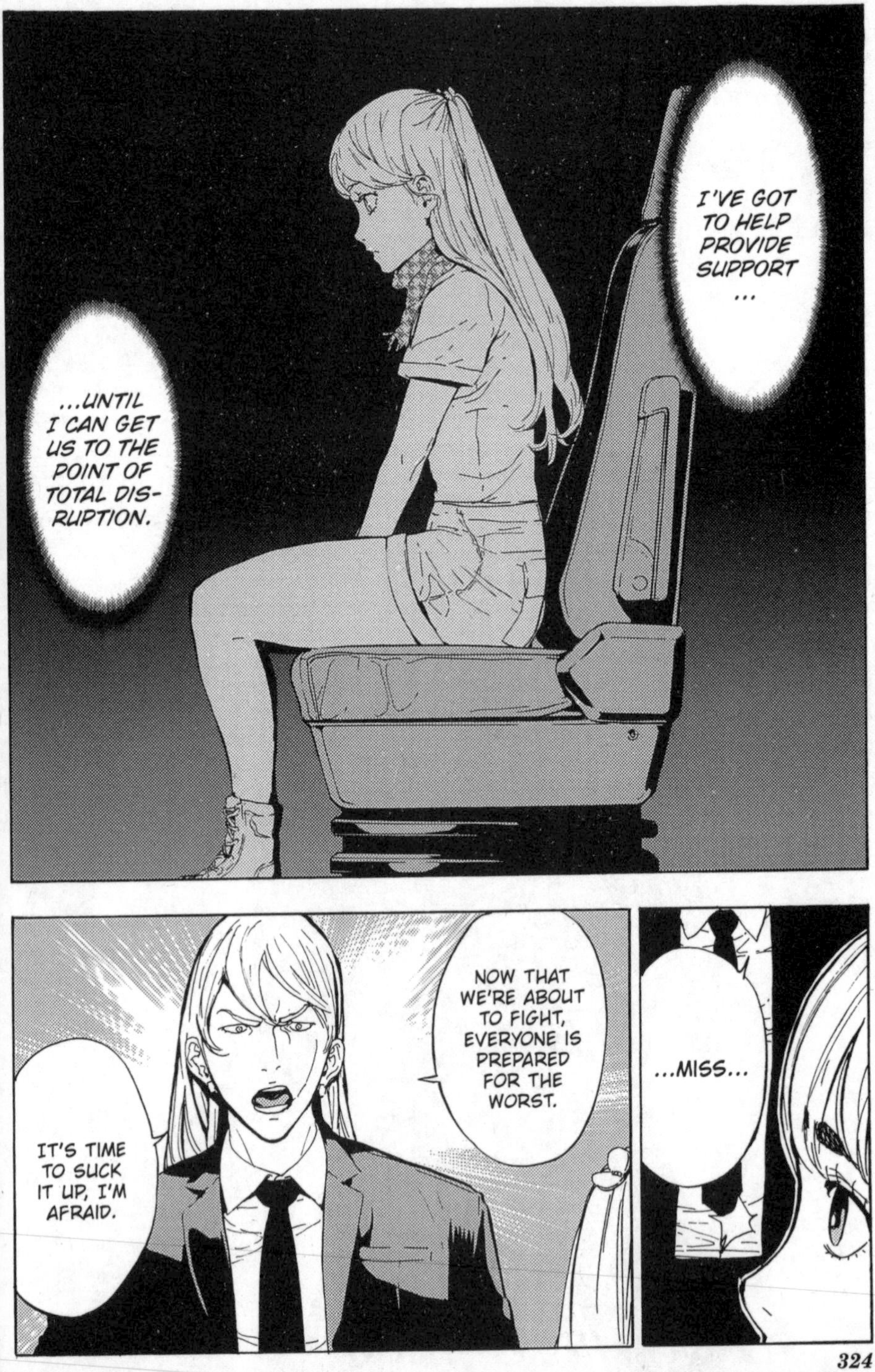
I'VE GOT TO HELP PROVIDE SUPPORT ...
...UNTIL I CAN GET US TO THE POINT OF TOTAL DIS-RUPTION.
...MISS...
NOW THAT WE'RE ABOUT TO FIGHT, EVERYONE IS PREPARED FOR THE WORST.
IT'S TIME TO SUCK IT UP, I'M AFRAID.

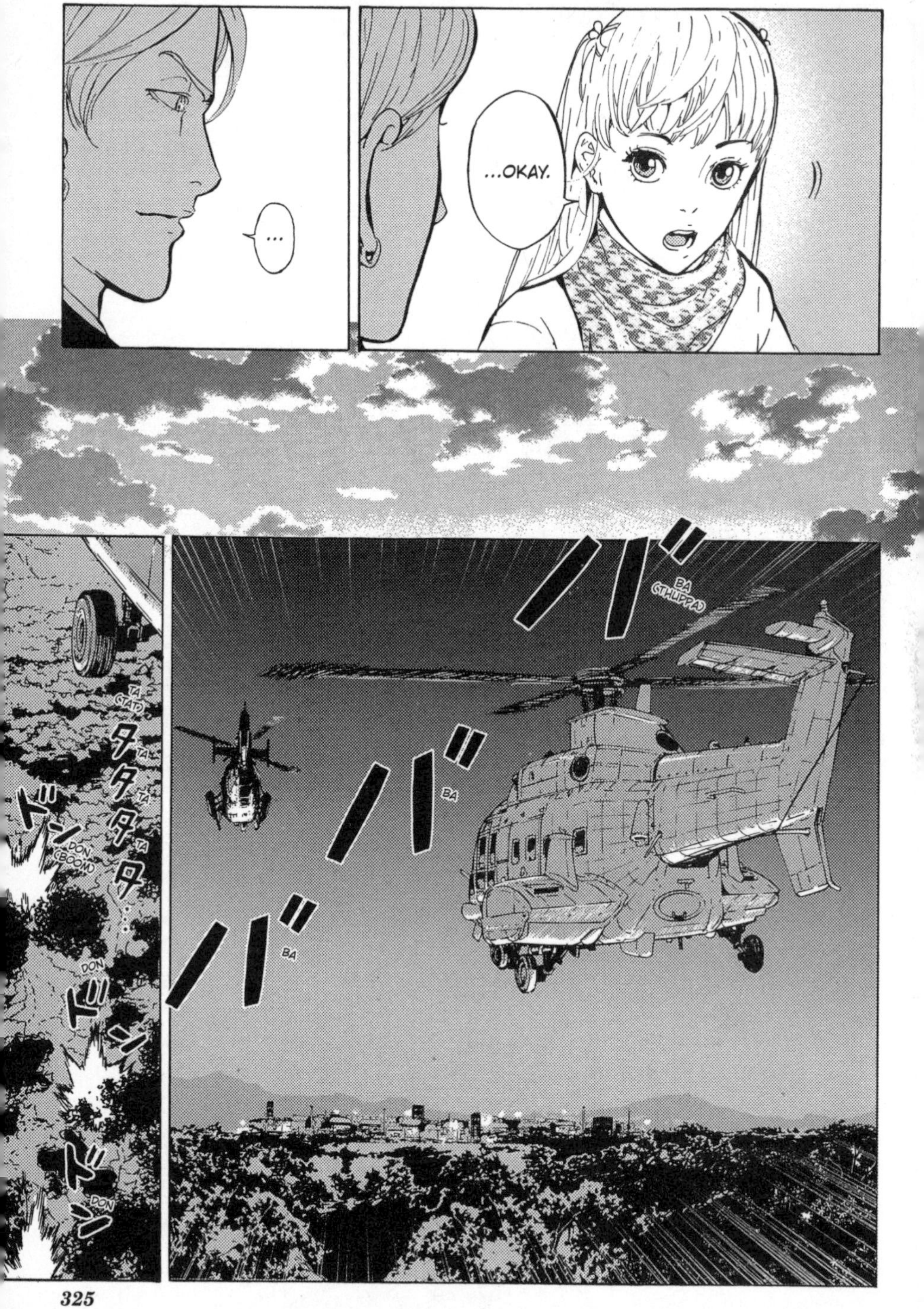
...OKAY.
...
バ
BA (THUPPA)
バ
BA
バ
BA
タタタ…
TA (TAT)
TA
TA
TA
ドン
DON (BOOM)
ドン
DON
ドン
DON

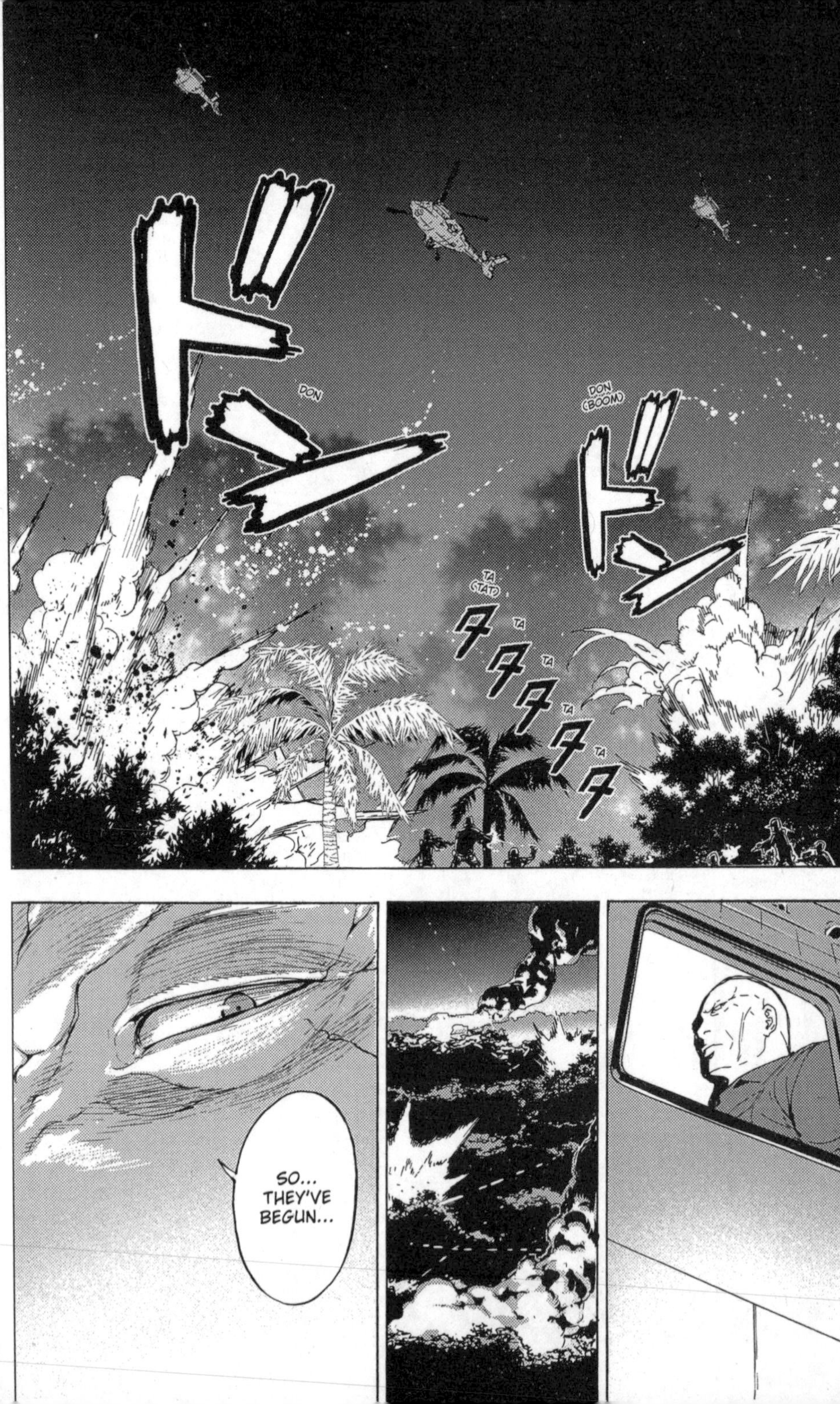
ドドン
DON (BOOM)
ドドン
DON
タタタタタ
TA (TAT) TA TA TA TA
SO... THEY'VE BEGUN...

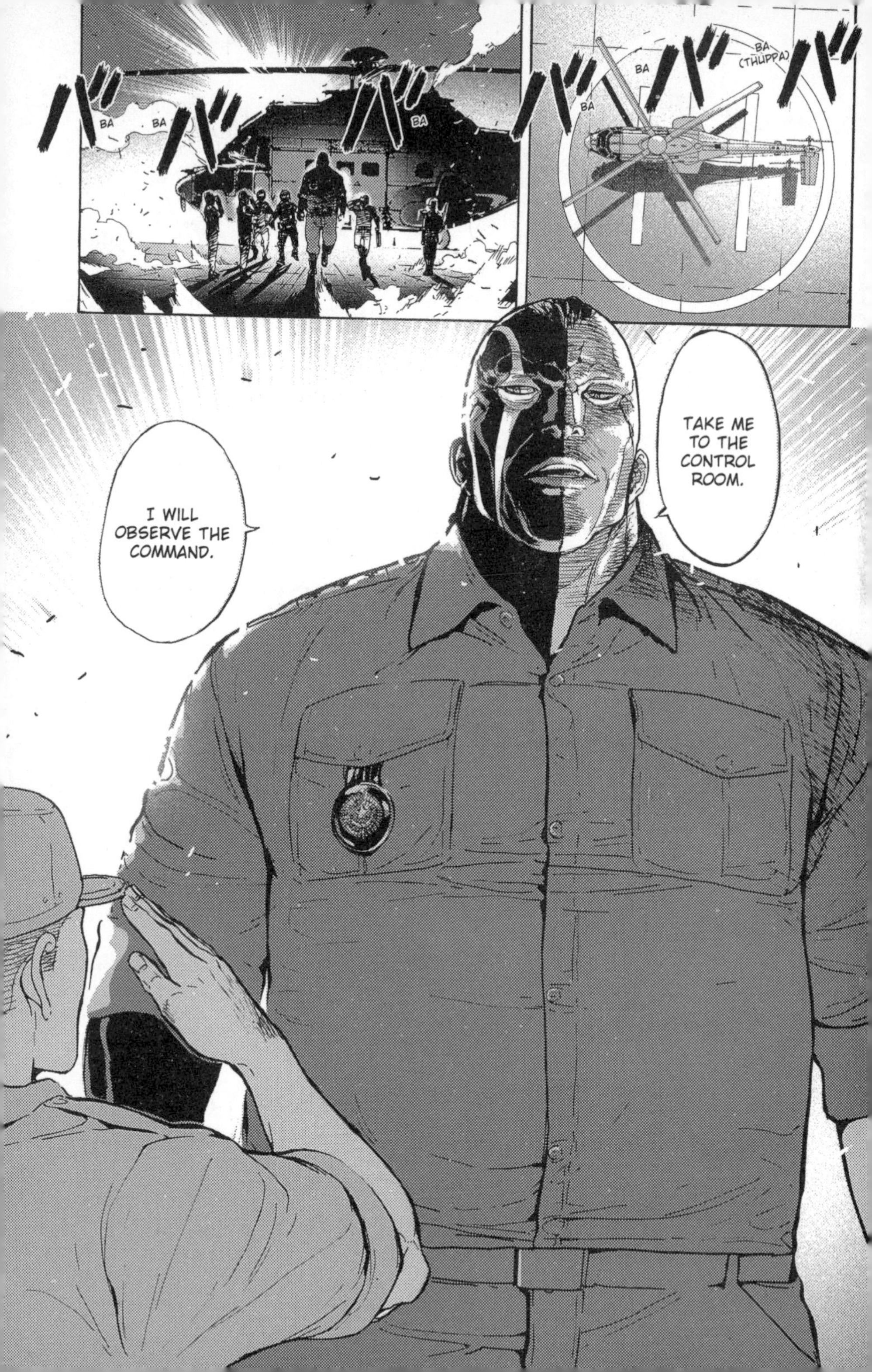
BA (THUPPA)
BA
BA
BA
BA
BA
TAKE ME TO THE CONTROL ROOM.
I WILL OBSERVE THE COMMAND.

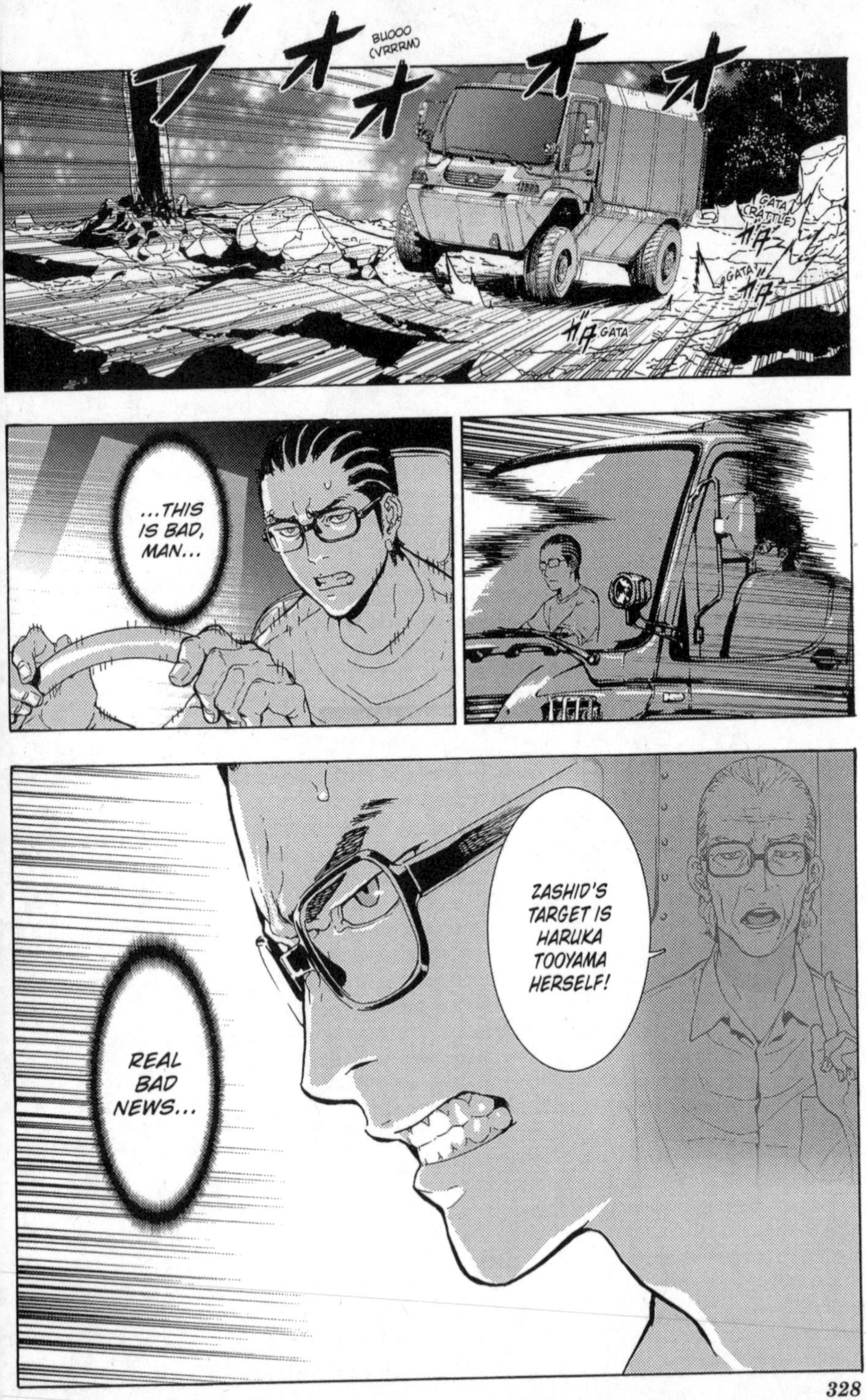
ブオオオオ
BUOOO (VRRRM)
ガタ
GATA (RATTLE)
ガタ
GATA
ガタ
GATA
...THIS IS BAD, MAN...
ZASHID'S TARGET IS HARUKA TOOYAMA HERSELF!
REAL BAD NEWS...

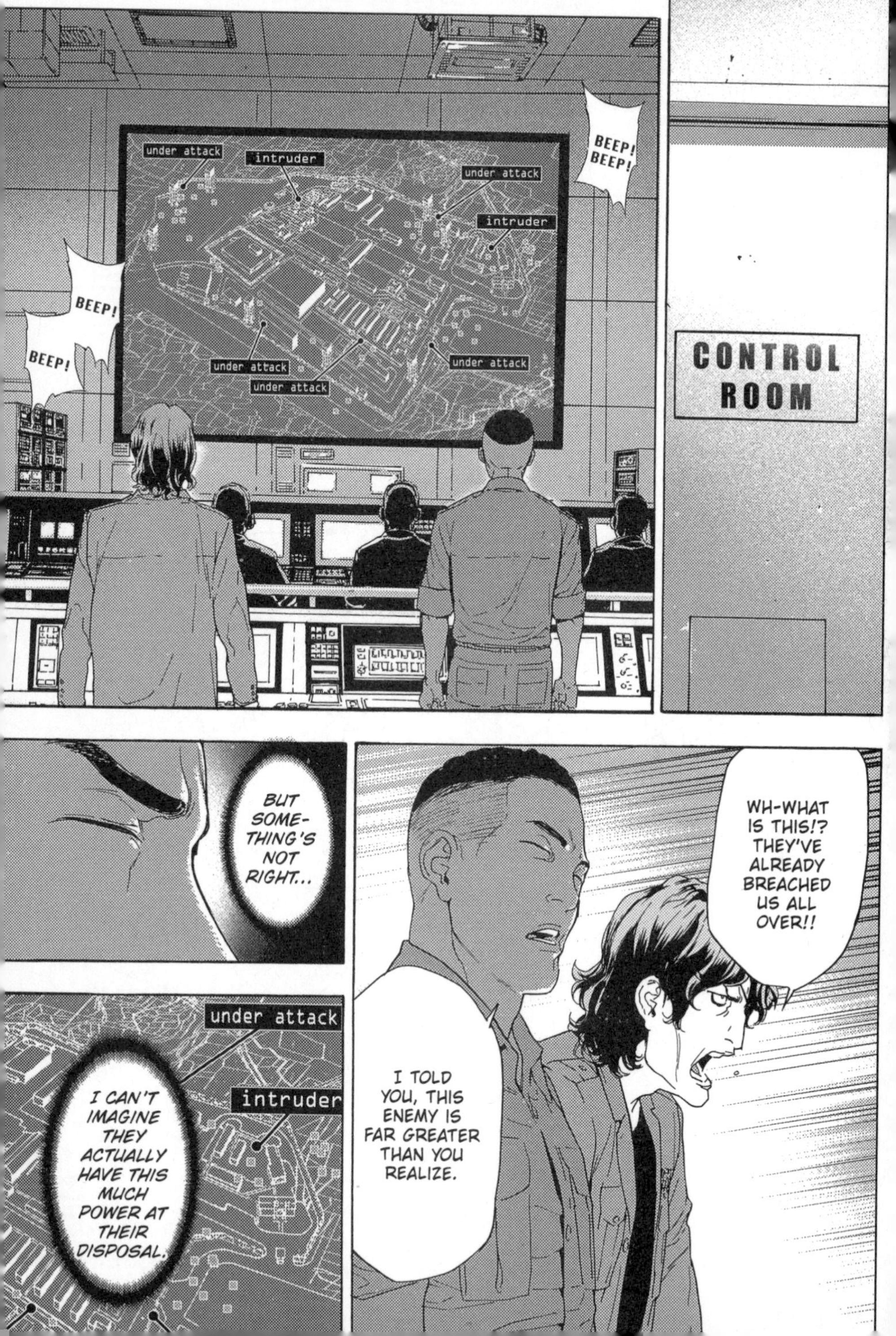
CONTROL ROOM
BEEP! BEEP!
under attack
intruder
intruder
under attack
BEEP!
BEEP!
under attack
under attack
under attack
WH-WHAT IS THIS!? THEY'VE ALREADY BREACHED US ALL OVER!!
I TOLD YOU, THIS ENEMY IS FAR GREATER THAN YOU REALIZE.
BUT SOME-THING'S NOT RIGHT...
under attack
intruder
I CAN'T IMAGINE THEY ACTUALLY HAVE THIS MUCH POWER AT THEIR DISPOSAL.

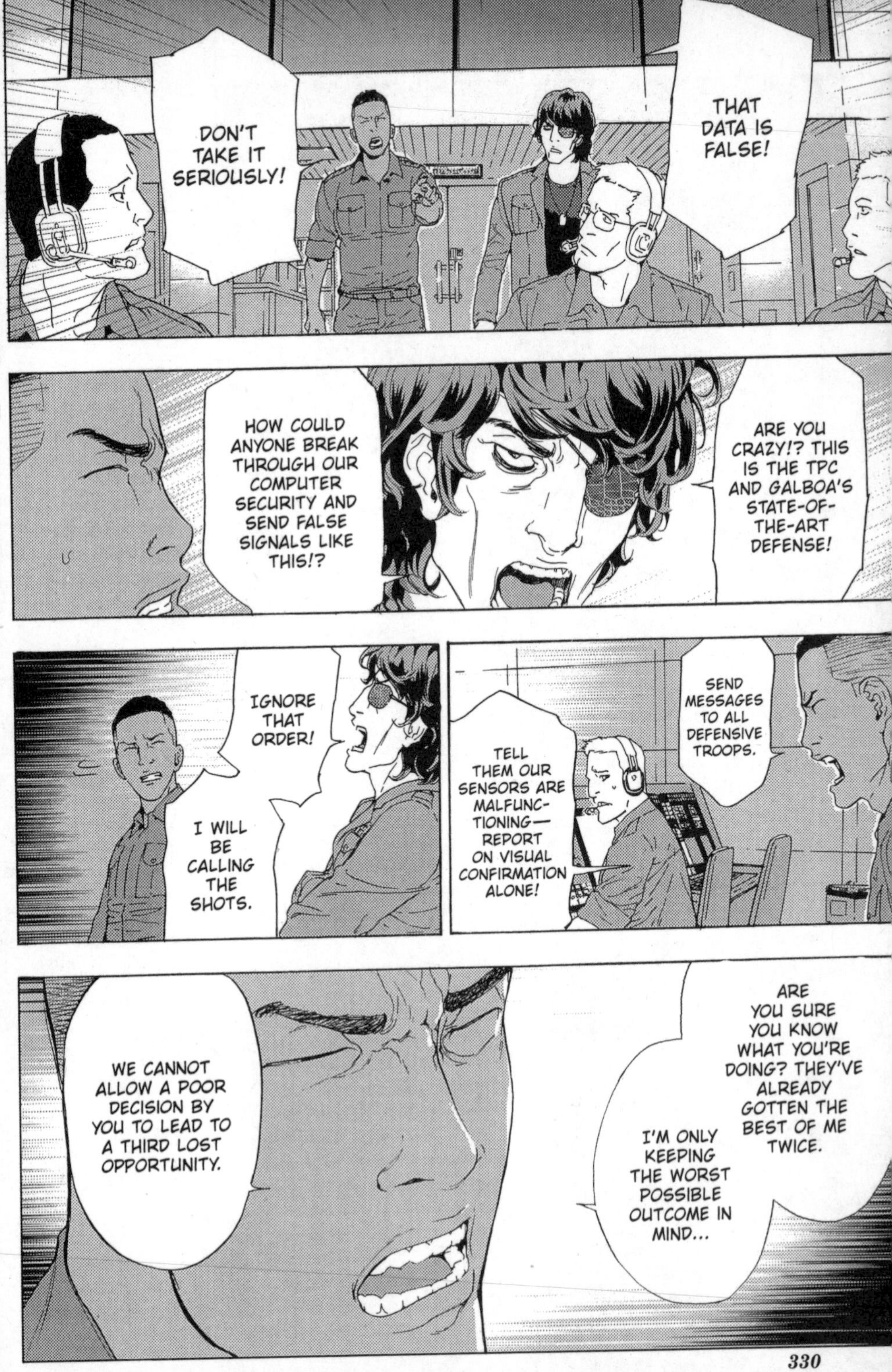
THAT DATA IS FALSE!
DON'T TAKE IT SERIOUSLY!
ARE YOU CRAZY!? THIS IS THE TPC AND GALBOA'S STATE-OF-THE-ART DEFENSE!
HOW COULD ANYONE BREAK THROUGH OUR COMPUTER SECURITY AND SEND FALSE SIGNALS LIKE THIS!?
SEND MESSAGES TO ALL DEFENSIVE TROOPS.
TELL THEM OUR SENSORS ARE MALFUNC-TIONING—REPORT ON VISUAL CONFIRMATION ALONE!
IGNORE THAT ORDER!
I WILL BE CALLING THE SHOTS.
ARE YOU SURE YOU KNOW WHAT YOU'RE DOING? THEY'VE ALREADY GOTTEN THE BEST OF ME TWICE.
I'M ONLY KEEPING THE WORST POSSIBLE OUTCOME IN MIND...
WE CANNOT ALLOW A POOR DECISION BY YOU TO LEAD TO A THIRD LOST OPPORTUNITY.

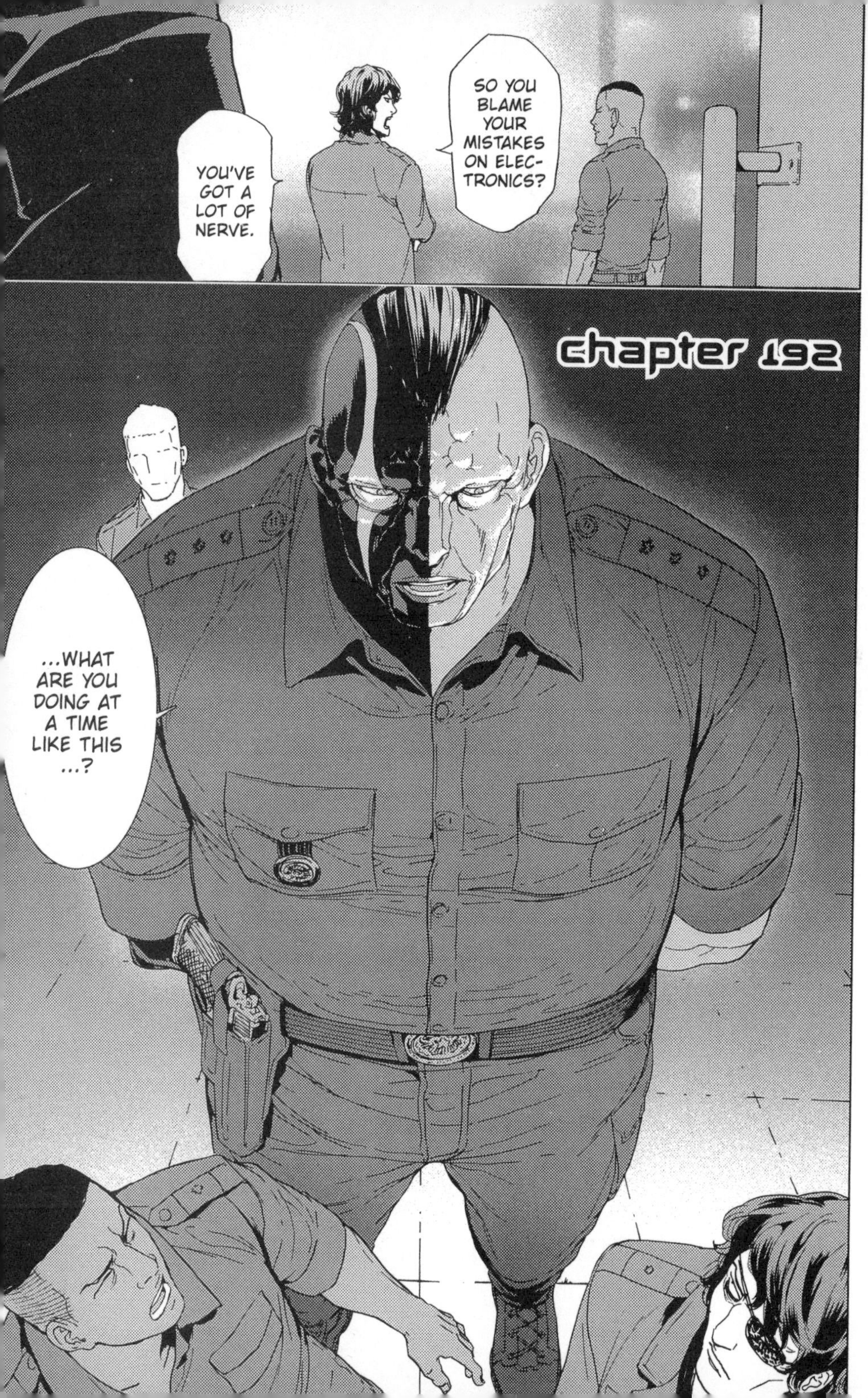
SO YOU BLAME YOUR MISTAKES ON ELEC-TRONICS?
YOU'VE GOT A LOT OF NERVE.
chapter 192
...WHAT ARE YOU DOING AT A TIME LIKE THIS ...?

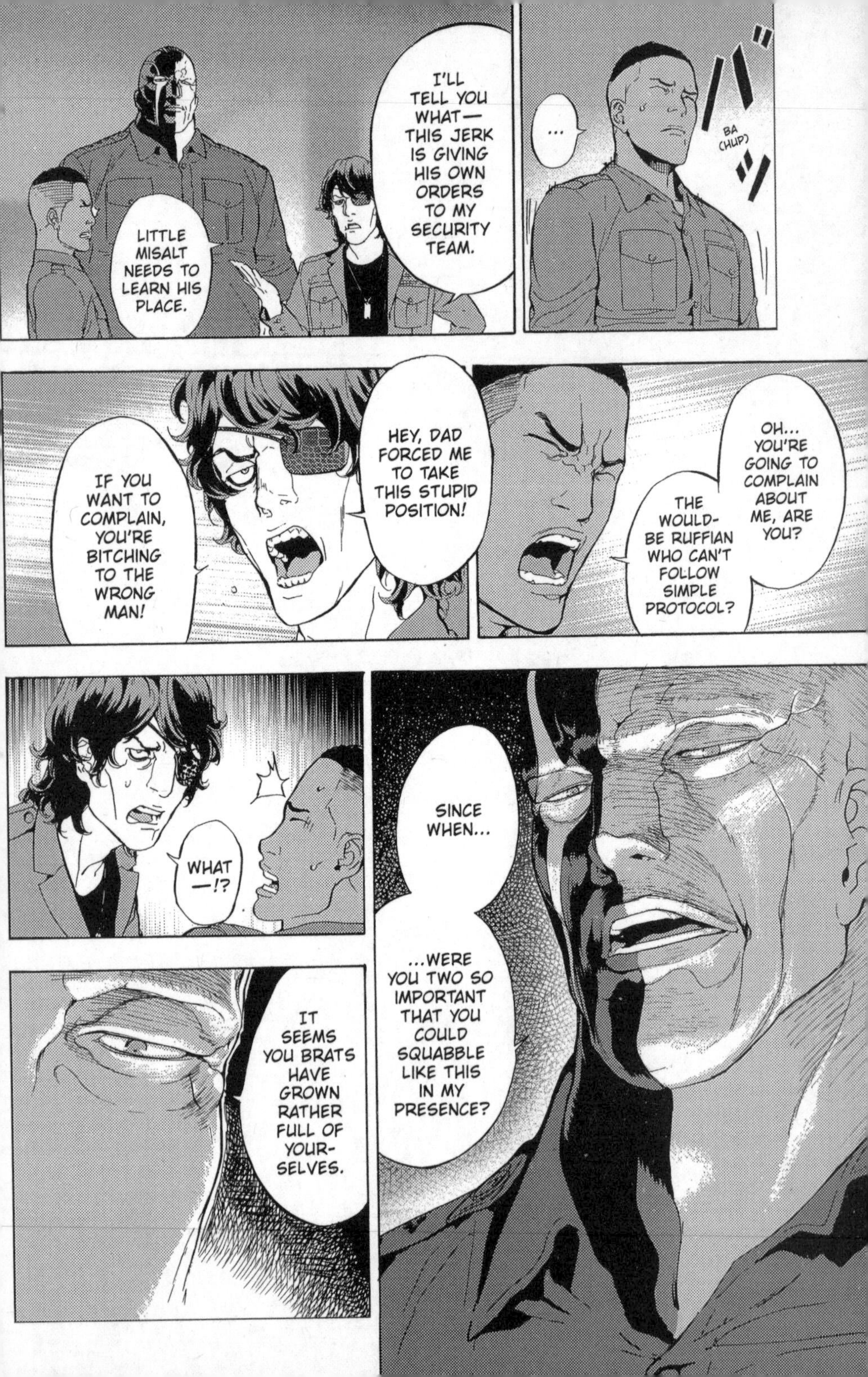
...
BA (HUP)
I'LL TELL YOU WHAT— THIS JERK IS GIVING HIS OWN ORDERS TO MY SECURITY TEAM.
LITTLE MISALT NEEDS TO LEARN HIS PLACE.
OH... YOU'RE GOING TO COMPLAIN ABOUT ME, ARE YOU?
THE WOULD-BE RUFFIAN WHO CAN'T FOLLOW SIMPLE PROTOCOL?
HEY, DAD FORCED ME TO TAKE THIS STUPID POSITION!
IF YOU WANT TO COMPLAIN, YOU'RE BITCHING TO THE WRONG MAN!
SINCE WHEN...
...WERE YOU TWO SO IMPORTANT THAT YOU COULD SQUABBLE LIKE THIS IN MY PRESENCE?
WHAT—!?
IT SEEMS YOU BRATS HAVE GROWN RATHER FULL OF YOUR-SELVES.

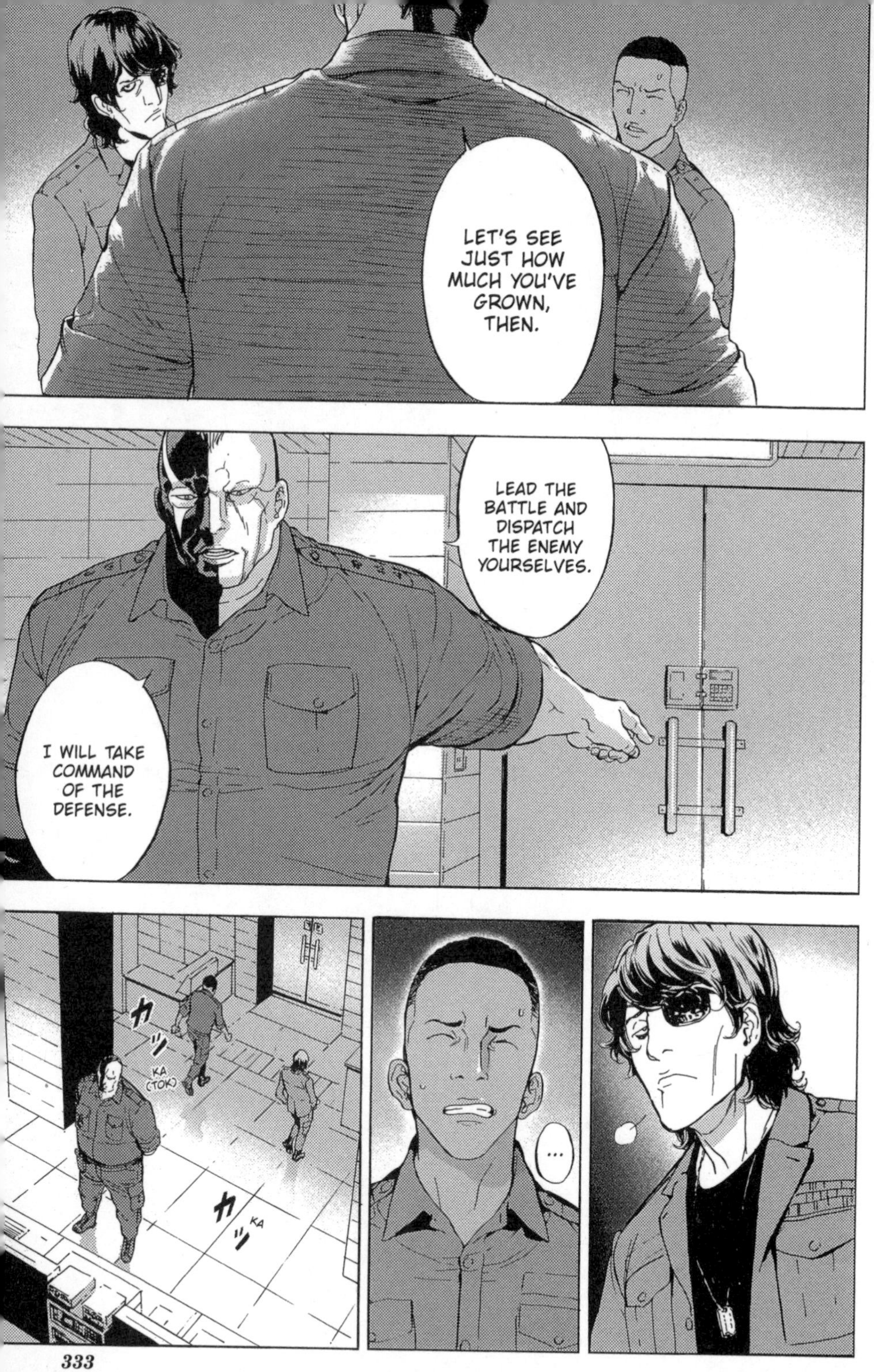
LET'S SEE JUST HOW MUCH YOU'VE GROWN, THEN.
LEAD THE BATTLE AND DISPATCH THE ENEMY YOURSELVES.
I WILL TAKE COMMAND OF THE DEFENSE.
...
カッ
KA (TOK)
カッ
KA

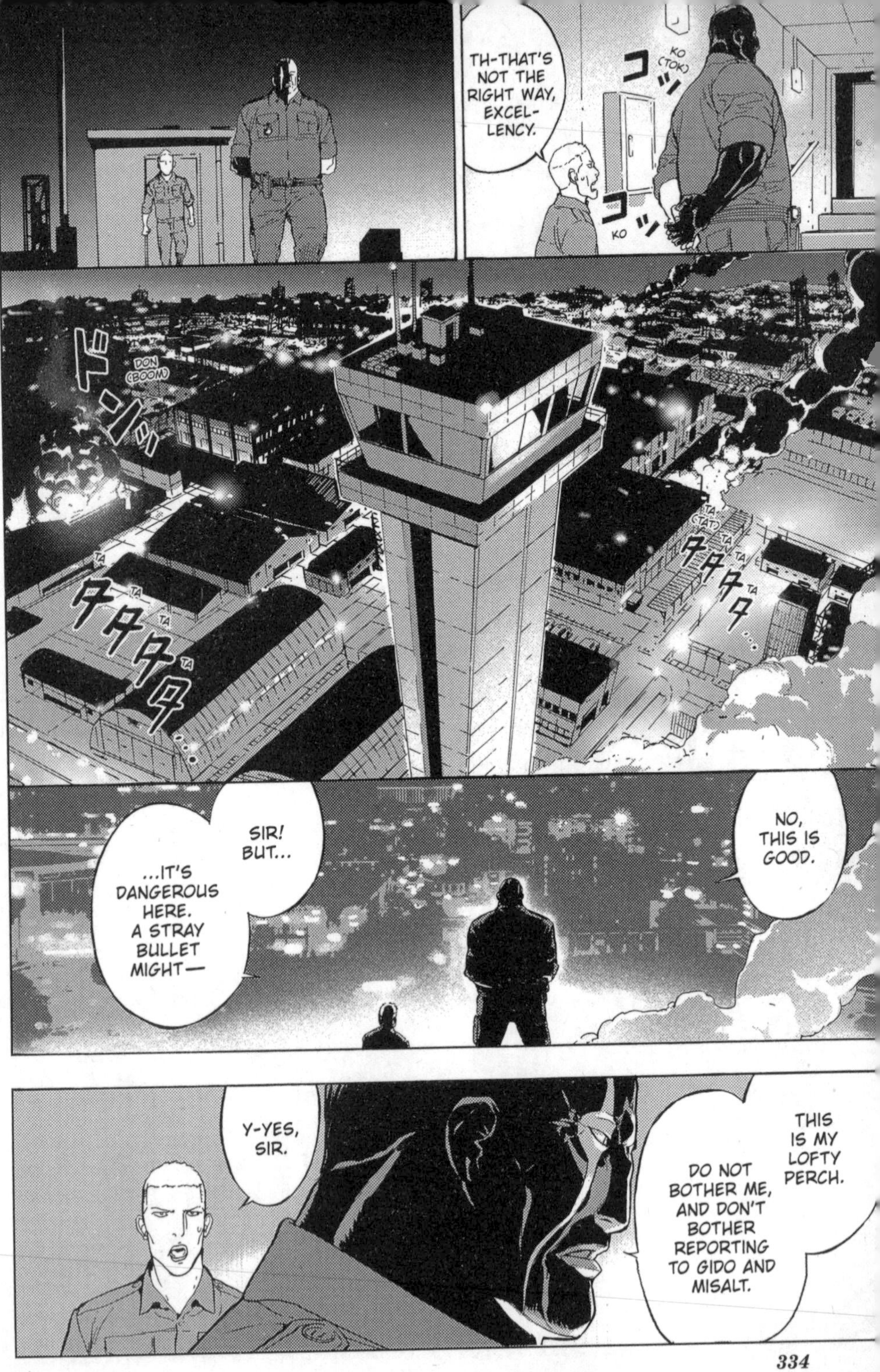

TH-THAT'S NOT THE RIGHT WAY, EXCEL-LENCY.
コッ
KO (TOK)
コッ
KO
ドンッ
DON (BOOM)
タタタタ
TA (TAT) TA TA TA
タタタタ
TA TA TA TA
NO, THIS IS GOOD.
SIR! BUT...
...IT'S DANGEROUS HERE. A STRAY BULLET MIGHT—
THIS IS MY LOFTY PERCH.
DO NOT BOTHER ME, AND DON'T BOTHER REPORTING TO GIDO AND MISALT.
Y-YES, SIR.

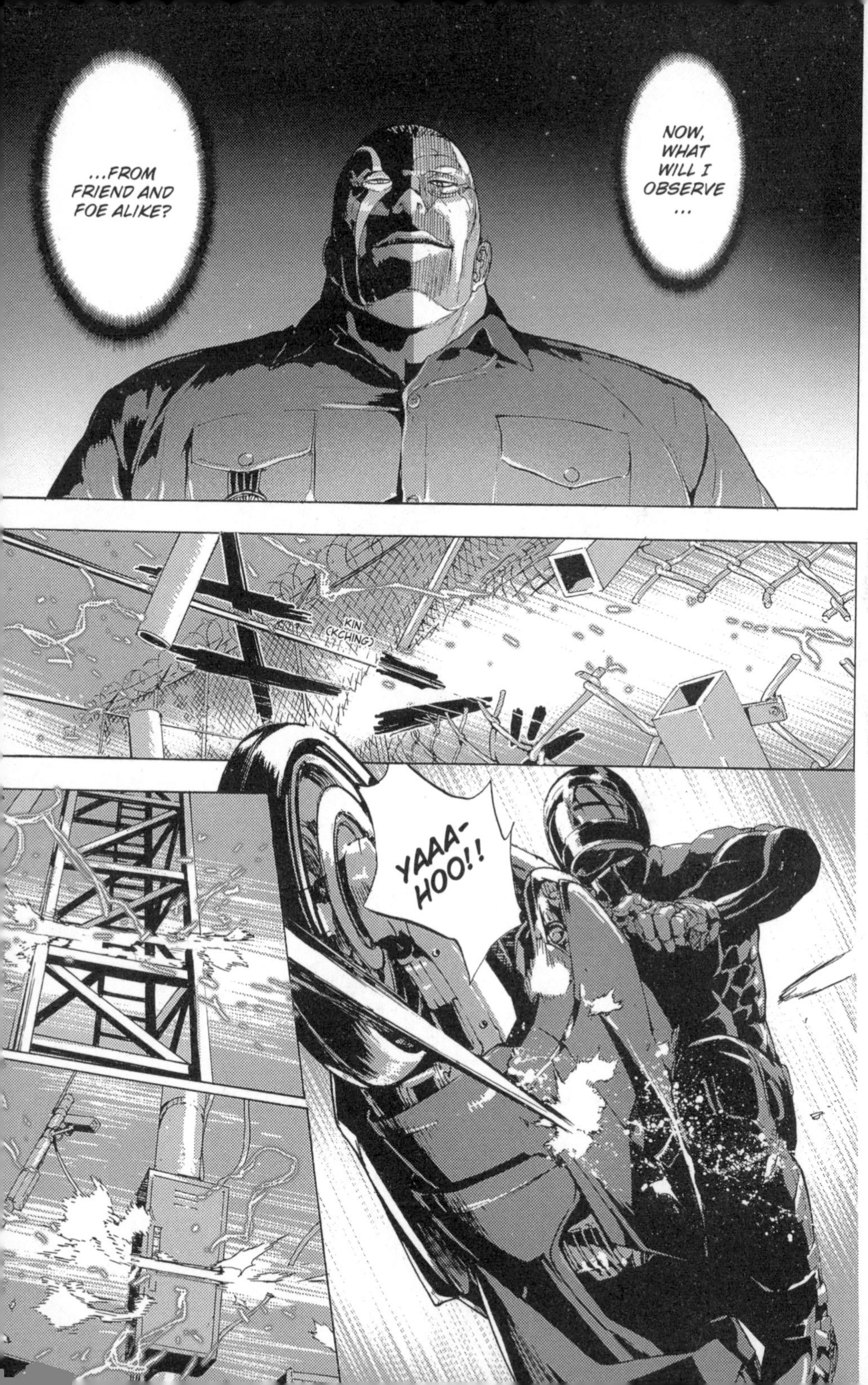
NOW, WHAT WILL I OBSERVE ...
...FROM FRIEND AND FOE ALIKE?
KIN (KCHING)
YAAA-HOO!!

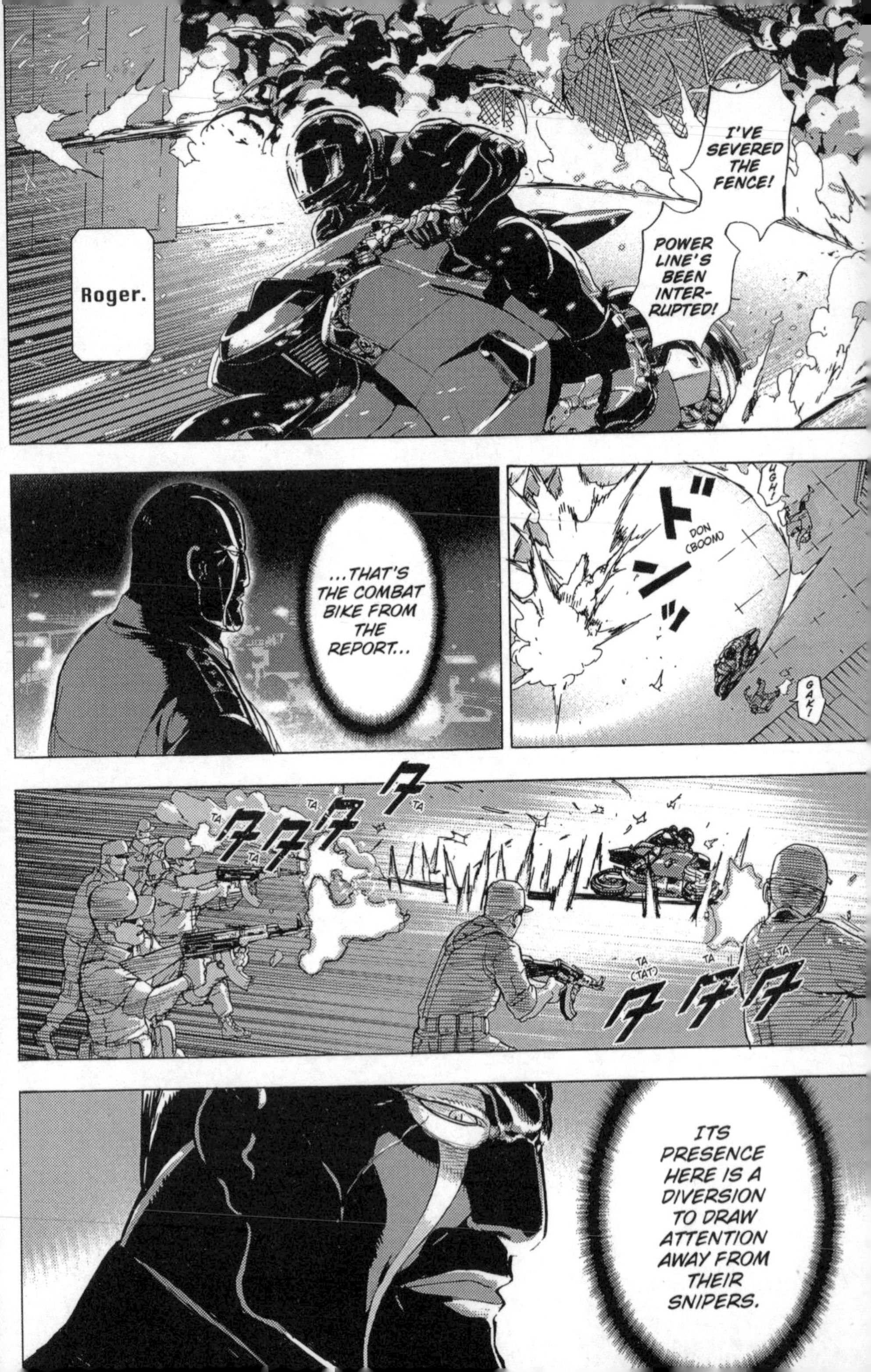
I'VE SEVERED THE FENCE!
POWER LINE'S BEEN INTER-RUPTED!
Roger.
UGH!
DON (BOOM)
GAK!
...THAT'S THE COMBAT BIKE FROM THE REPORT...
TA
TA
TA
TA
TA (TAT)
TA
TA
ITS PRESENCE HERE IS A DIVERSION TO DRAW ATTENTION AWAY FROM THEIR SNIPERS.

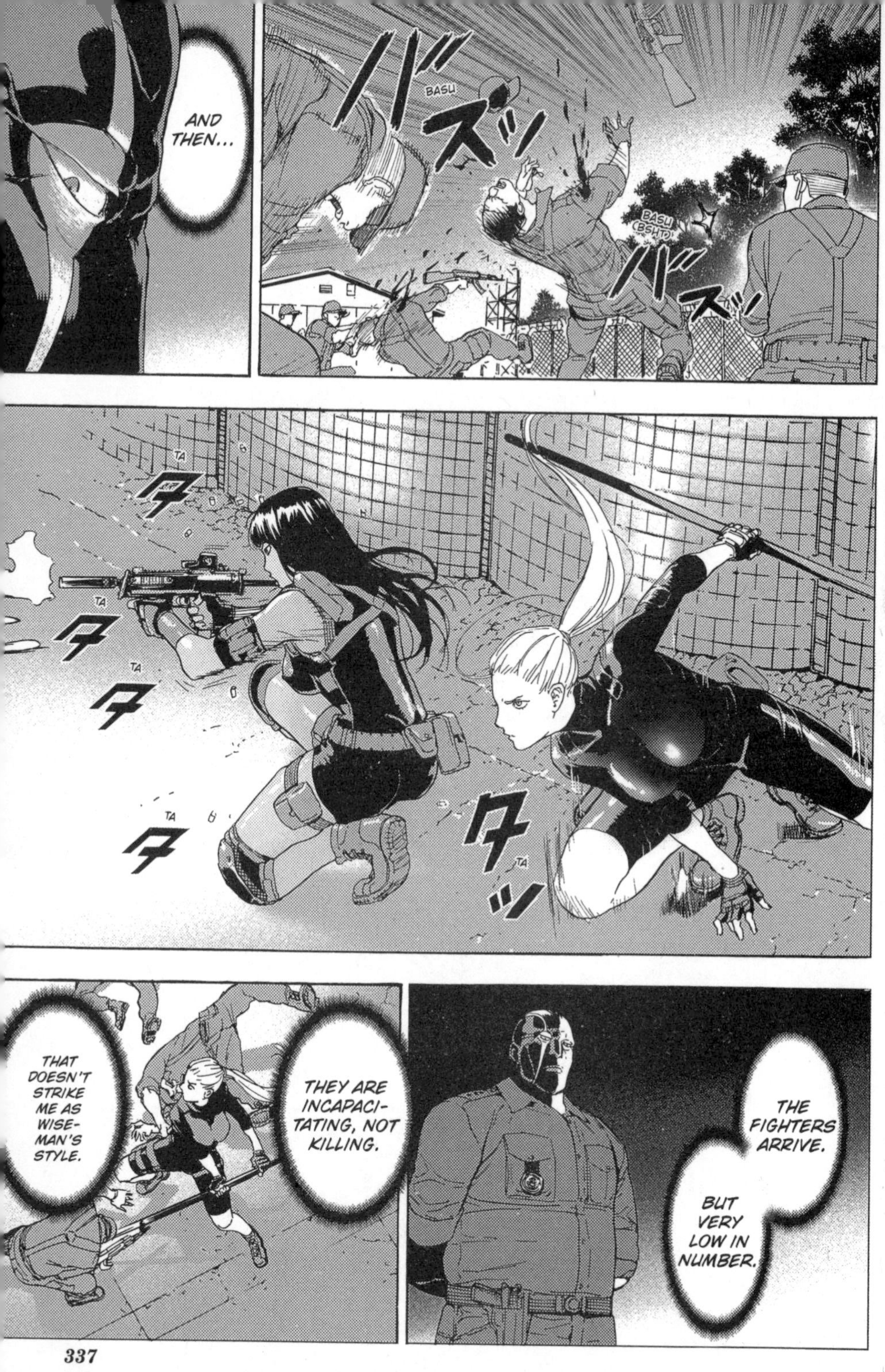
BASU
BASU (BSHT)
AND THEN...
TA
TA
TA
TA
TA
THE FIGHTERS ARRIVE.
BUT VERY LOW IN NUMBER.
THEY ARE INCAPACI-TATING, NOT KILLING.
THAT DOESN'T STRIKE ME AS WISE-MAN'S STYLE.

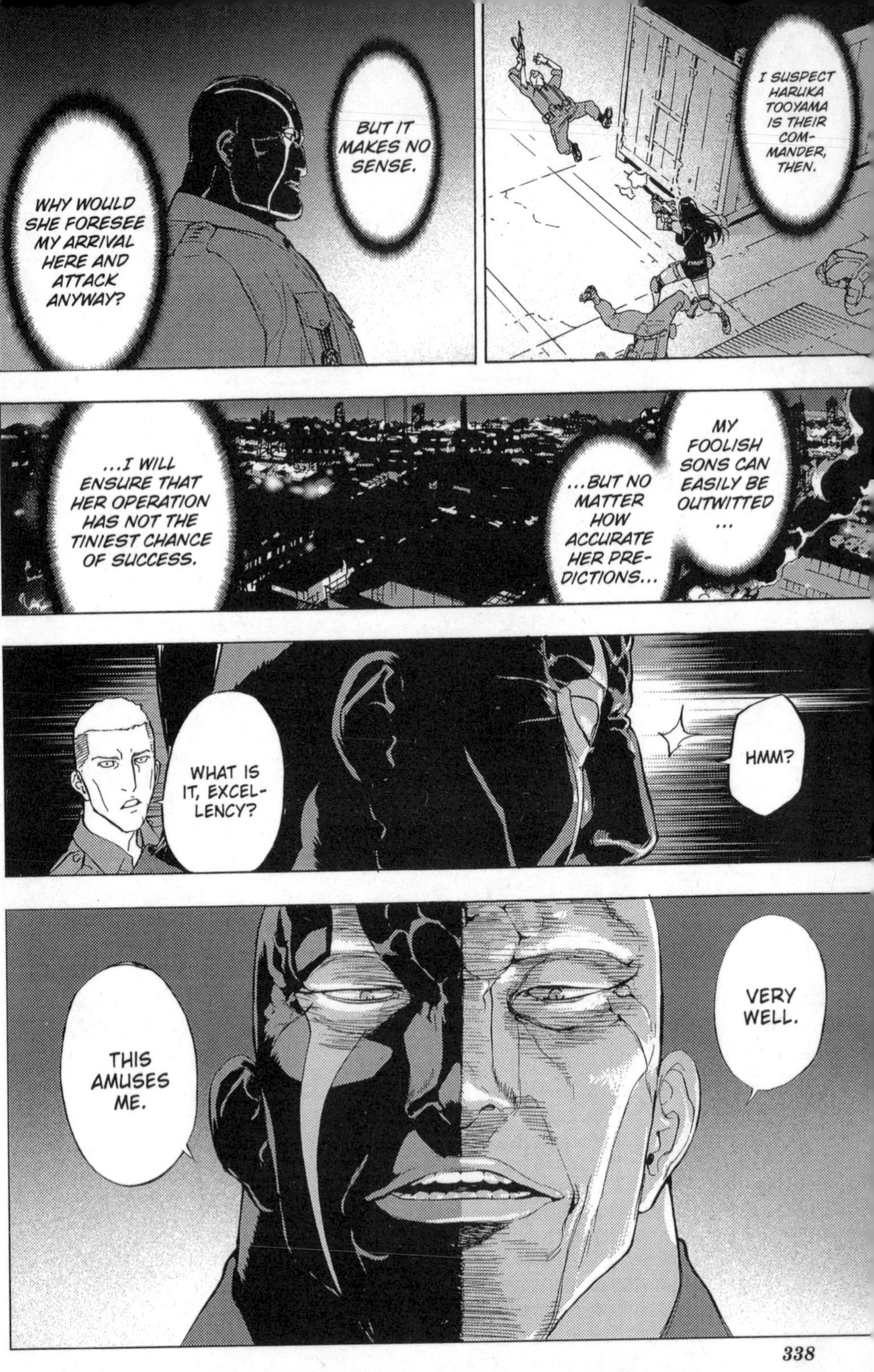
I SUSPECT HARUKA TOOYAMA IS THEIR COM-MANDER, THEN.
BUT IT MAKES NO SENSE.
WHY WOULD SHE FORESEE MY ARRIVAL HERE AND ATTACK ANYWAY?
MY FOOLISH SONS CAN EASILY BE OUTWITTED ...
...BUT NO MATTER HOW ACCURATE HER PRE-DICTIONS...
...I WILL ENSURE THAT HER OPERATION HAS NOT THE TINIEST CHANCE OF SUCCESS.
HMM?
WHAT IS IT, EXCEL-LENCY?
VERY WELL.
THIS AMUSES ME.

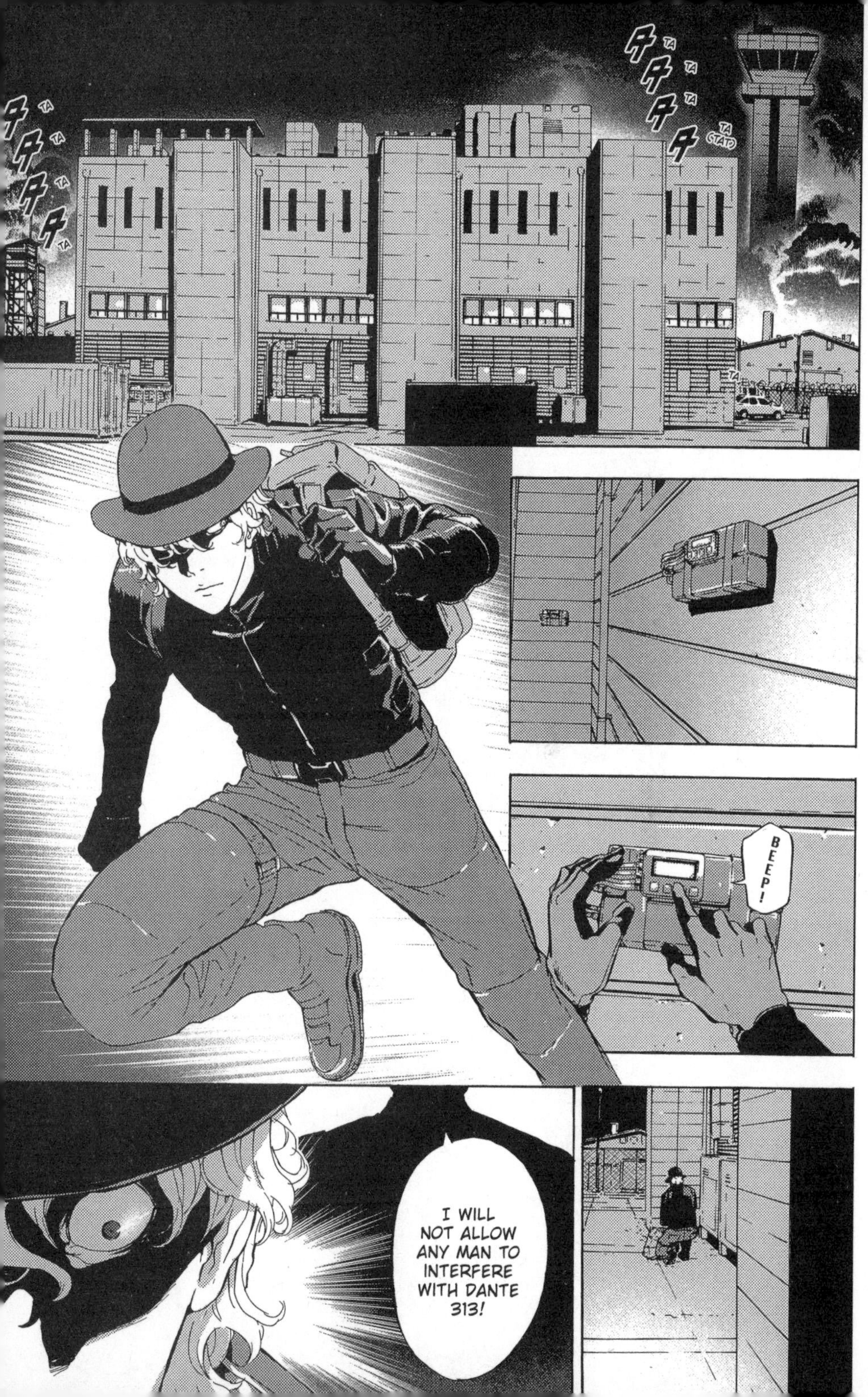
タタタタ
TA TA TA TA (TAT)
タタタタ
TA TA TA TA
TA
BEEP!
I WILL NOT ALLOW ANY MAN TO INTERFERE WITH DANTE 313!

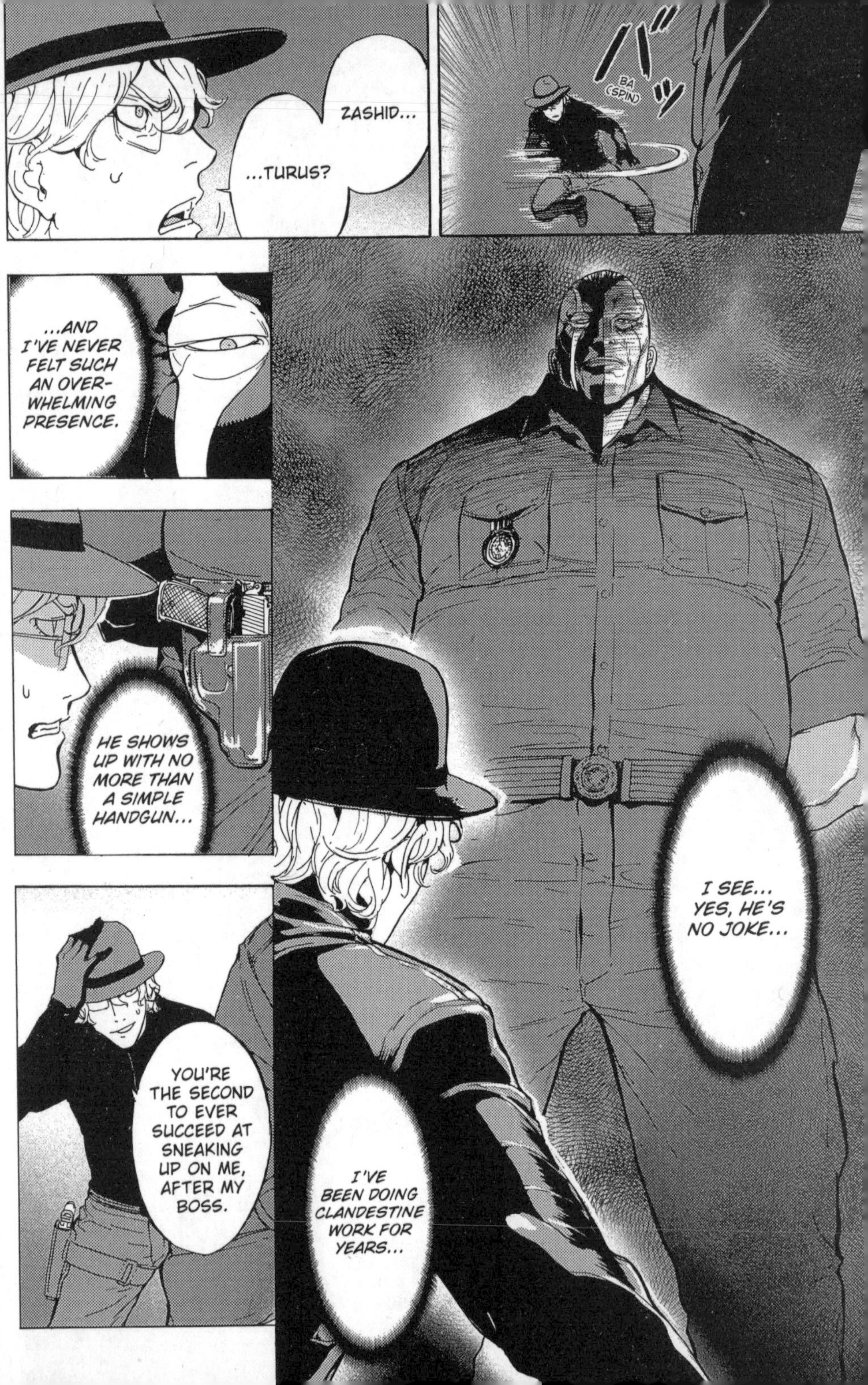
BA (SPIN)
ZASHID...
...TURUS?
I SEE... YES, HE'S NO JOKE...
I'VE BEEN DOING CLANDESTINE WORK FOR YEARS...
...AND I'VE NEVER FELT SUCH AN OVER-WHELMING PRESENCE.
HE SHOWS UP WITH NO MORE THAN A SIMPLE HANDGUN...
YOU'RE THE SECOND TO EVER SUCCEED AT SNEAKING UP ON ME, AFTER MY BOSS.

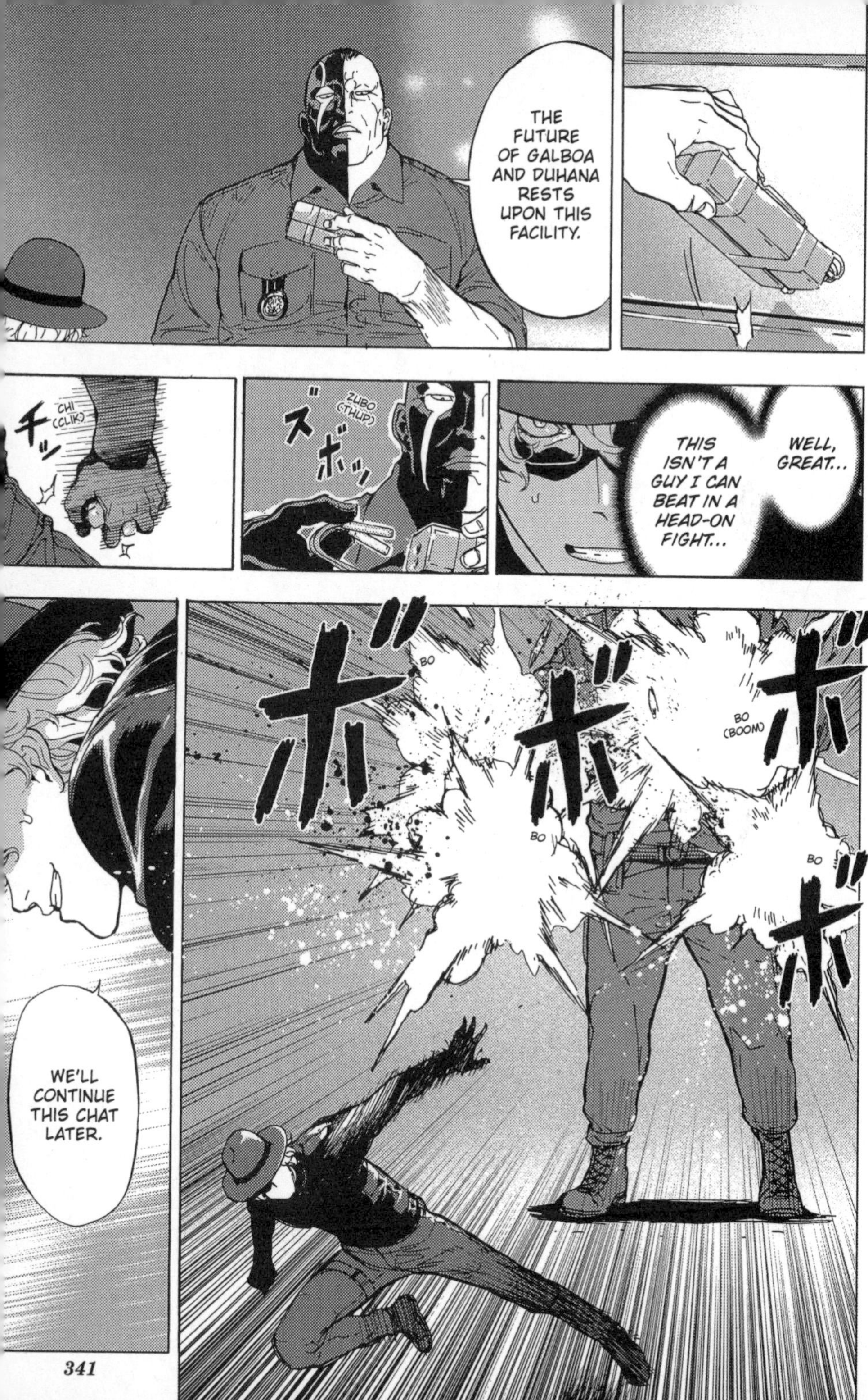
THE FUTURE OF GALBOA AND DUHANA RESTS UPON THIS FACILITY.
WELL, GREAT...
THIS ISN'T A GUY I CAN BEAT IN A HEAD-ON FIGHT...
ズボッ
ZUBO (THUP)
チッ
CHI (CLIK)
ボボボボ
BO
BO (BOOM)
BO
BO
WE'LL CONTINUE THIS CHAT LATER.

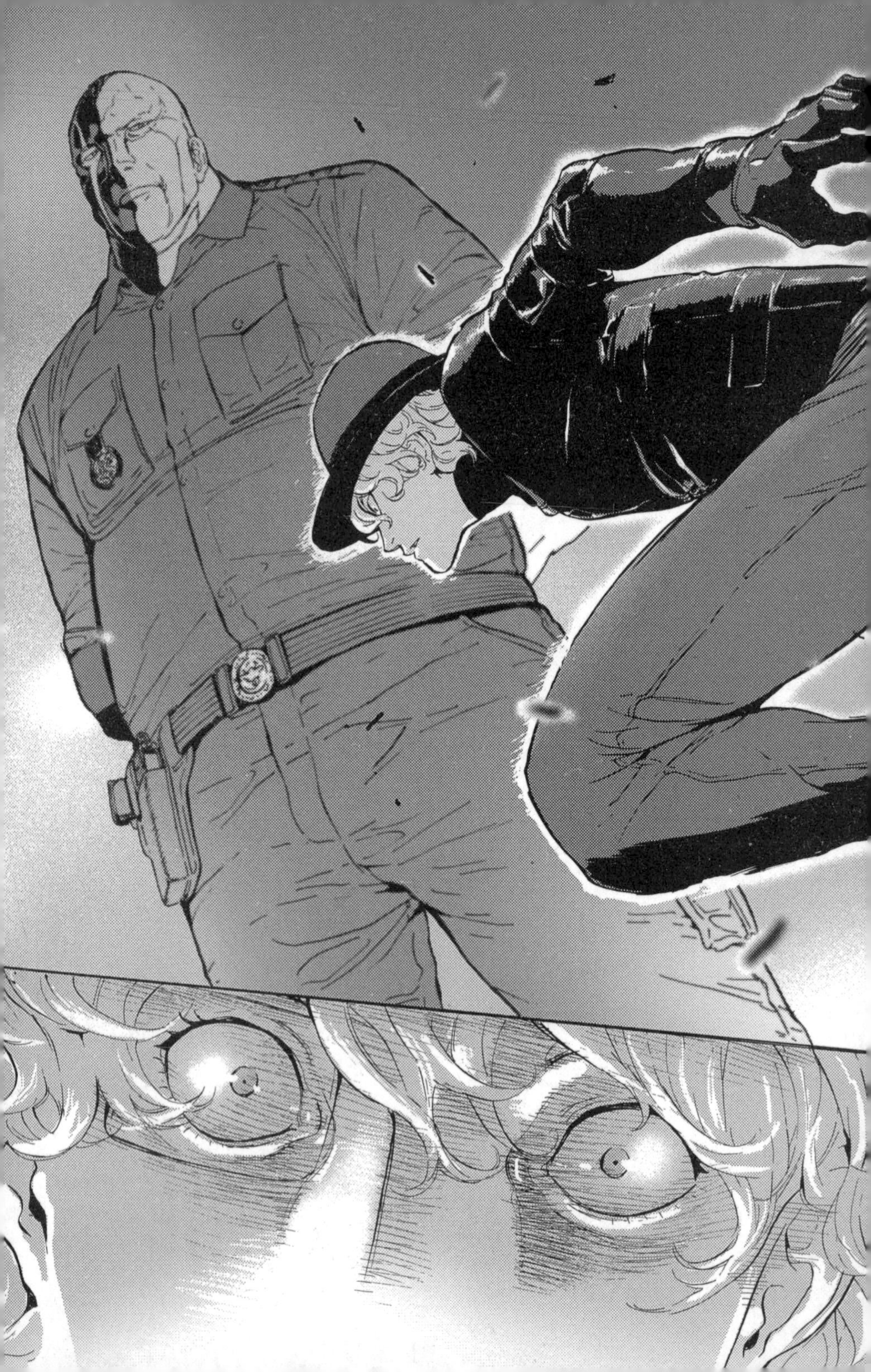

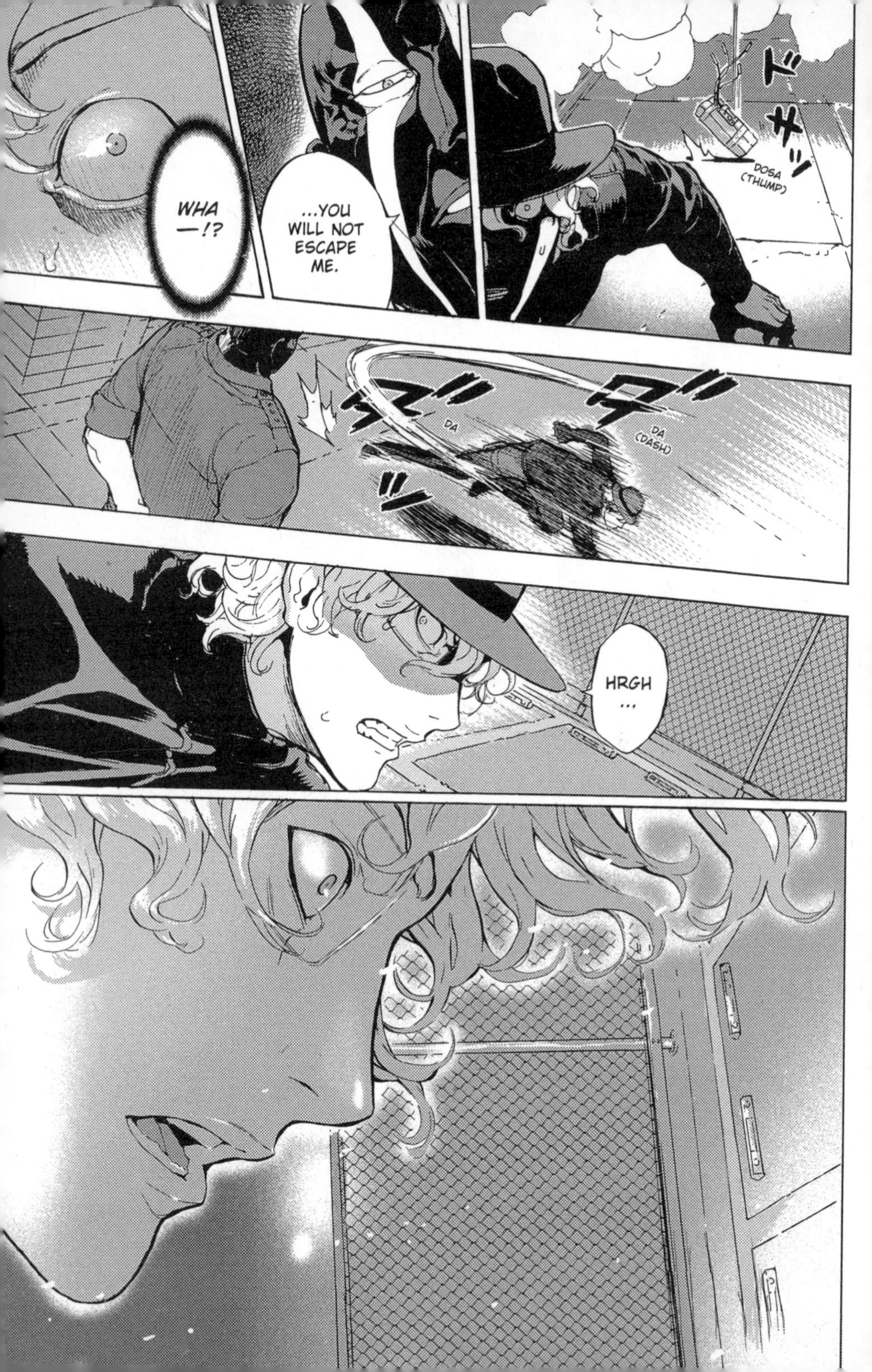
DOSA (THUMP)
...YOU WILL NOT ESCAPE ME.
WHA—!?
DA (DASH)
DA
HRGH ...

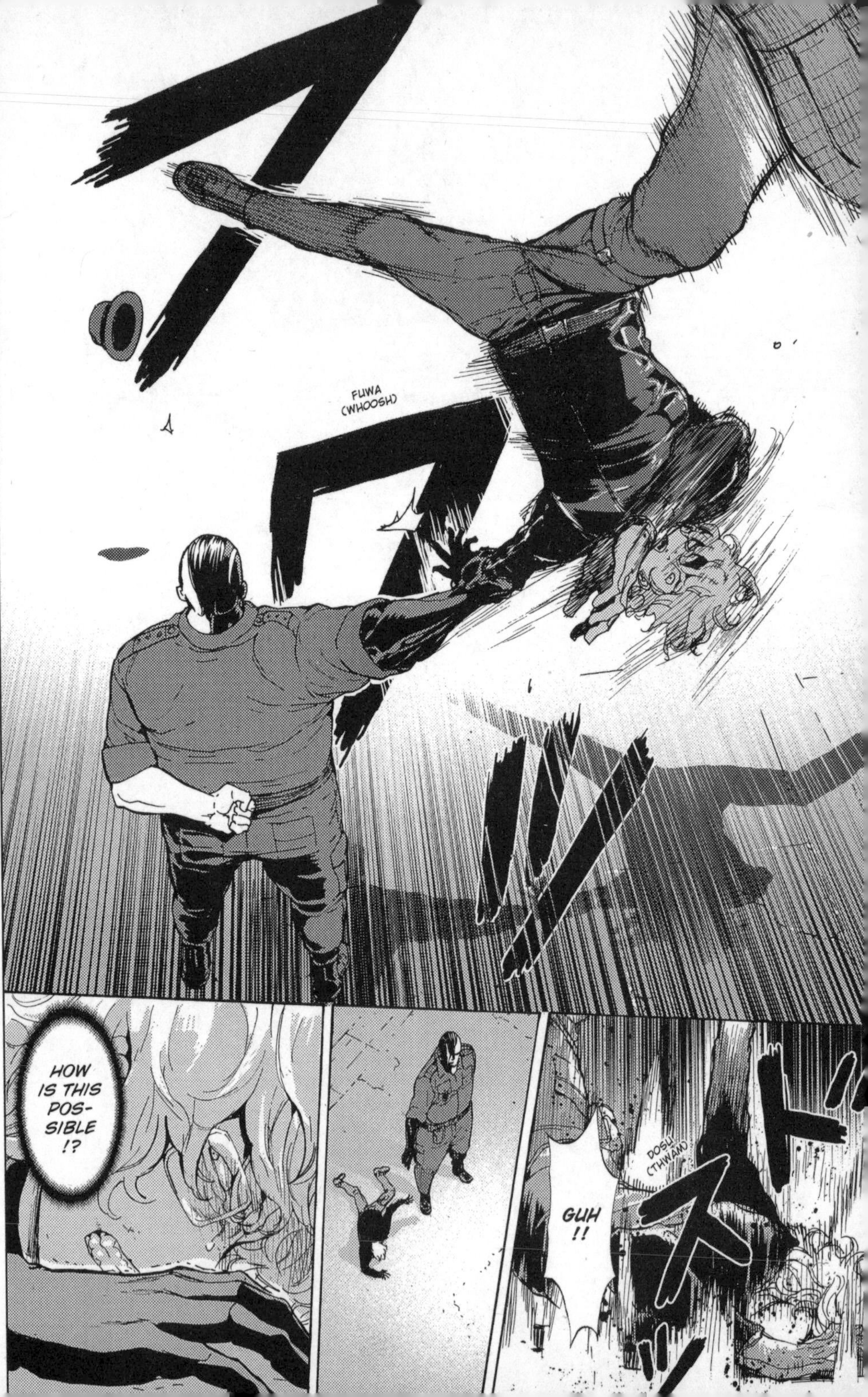
FUWA
(WHOOSH)
DOSU
(THWAM)
GUH !!
HOW IS THIS POS-SIBLE !?

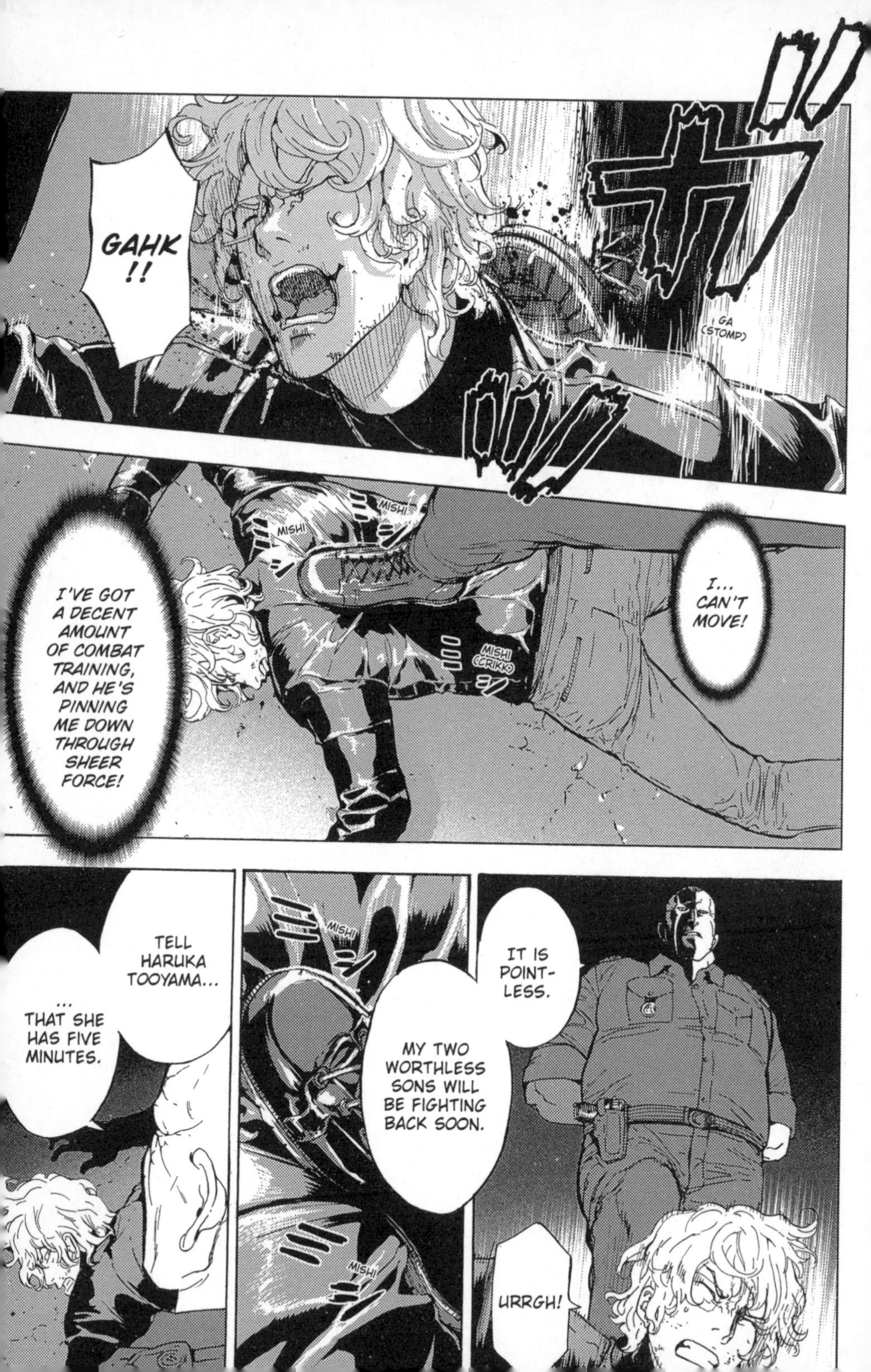
GA (STOMP)
GAHK !!
I... CAN'T MOVE!
MISHI (CRIKK)
MISHI
MISHI
I'VE GOT A DECENT AMOUNT OF COMBAT TRAINING, AND HE'S PINNING ME DOWN THROUGH SHEER FORCE!
IT IS POINT-LESS.
MY TWO WORTHLESS SONS WILL BE FIGHTING BACK SOON.
URRGH!
MISHI
MISHI
TELL HARUKA TOOYAMA...
... THAT SHE HAS FIVE MINUTES.

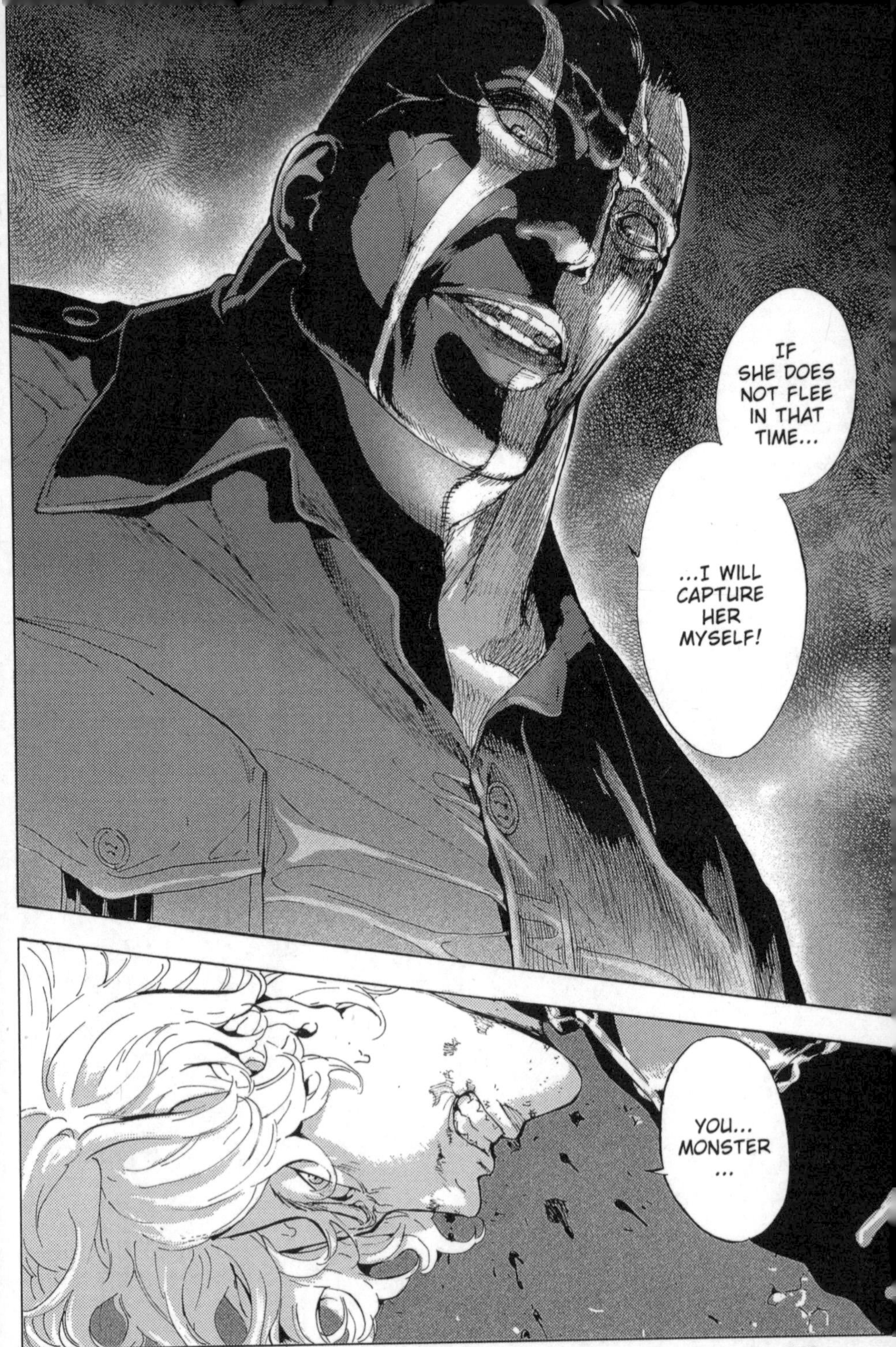
IF SHE DOES NOT FLEE IN THAT TIME...
...I WILL CAPTURE HER MYSELF!
YOU... MONSTER ...

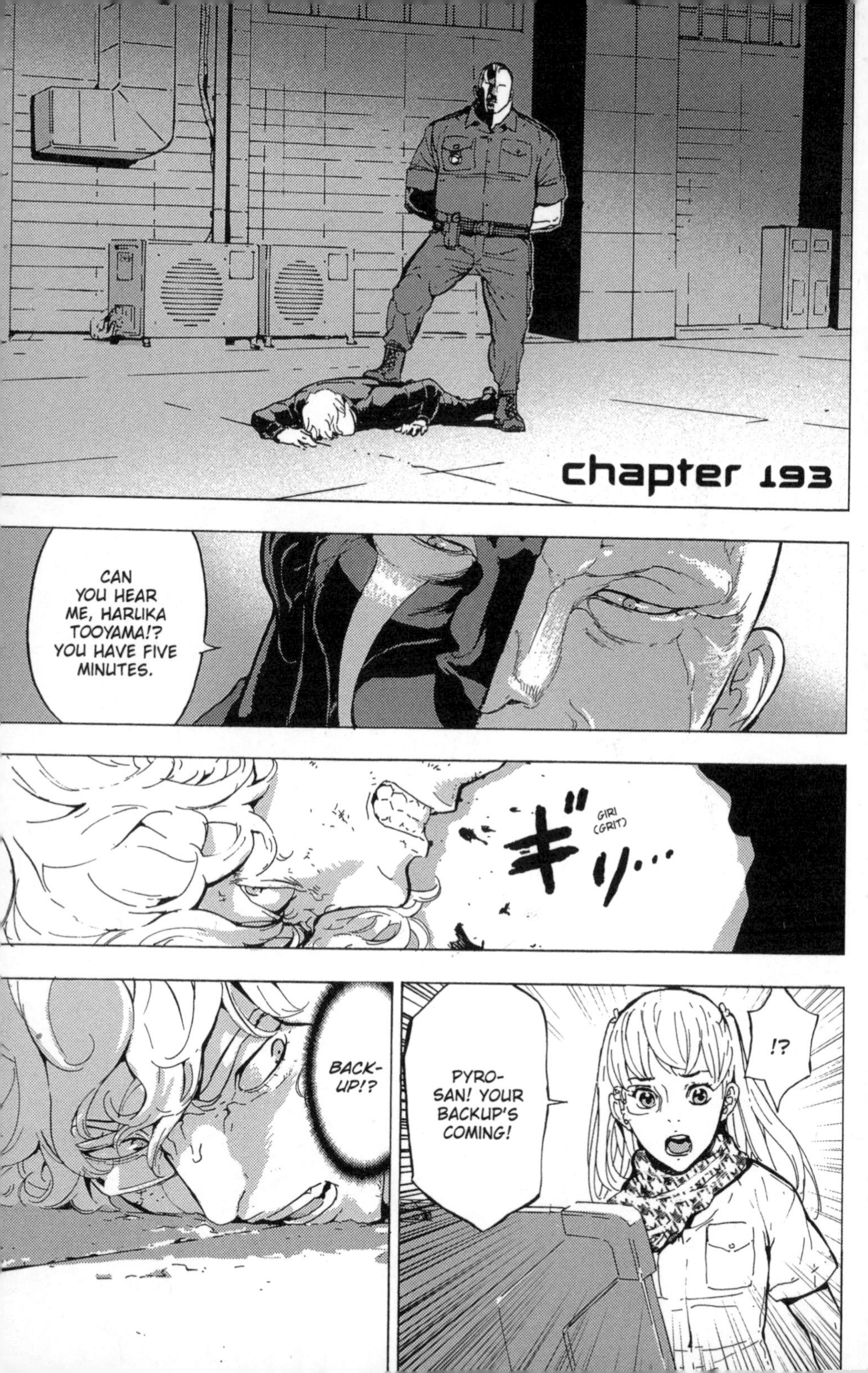
chapter 193
CAN YOU HEAR ME, HARUKA TOOYAMA!? YOU HAVE FIVE MINUTES.
ギリ…
GIRI (GRIT)
!?
PYRO-SAN! YOUR BACKUP'S COMING!
BACK-UP!?

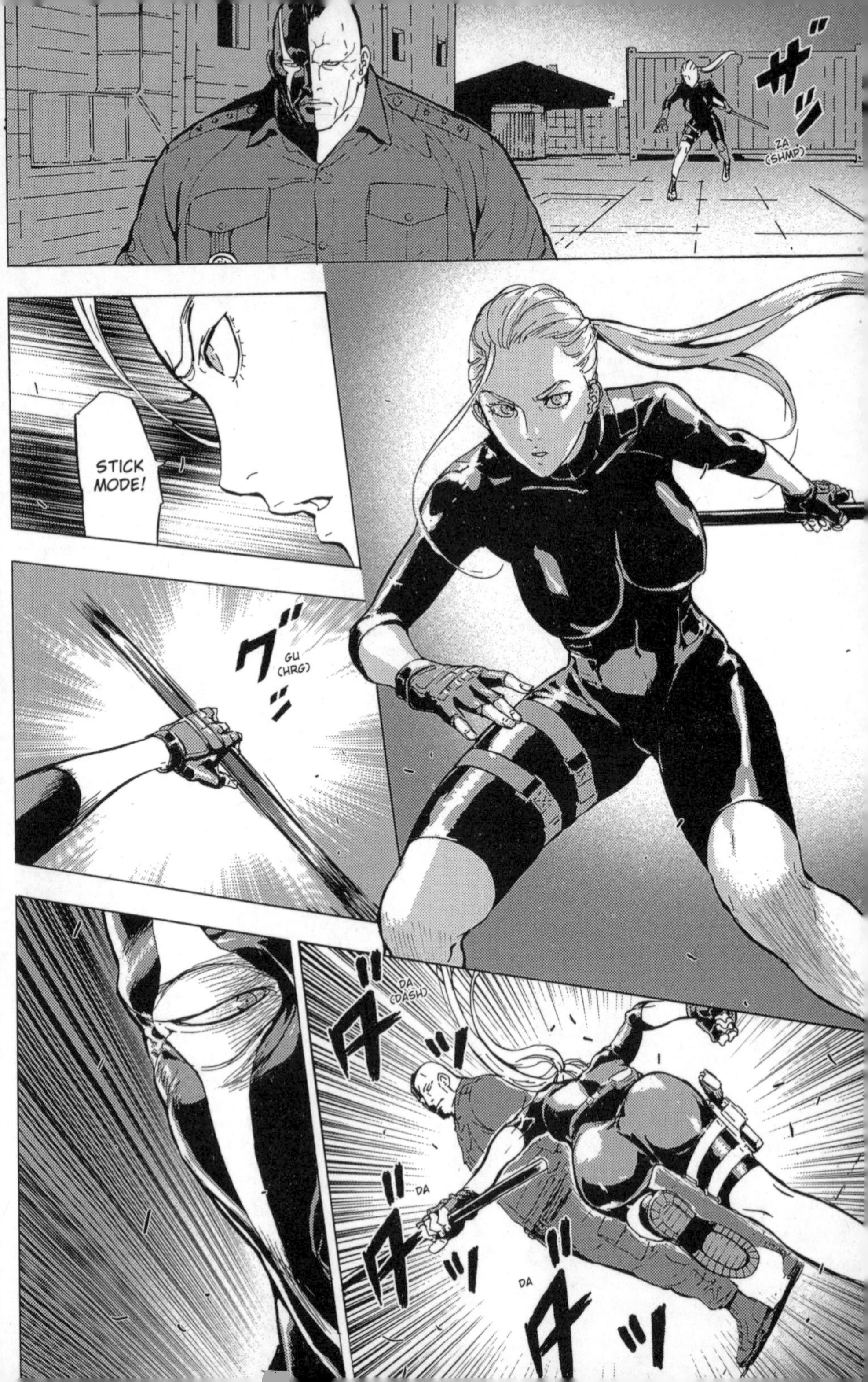

ザッ
ZA
(SHMP)
STICK MODE!
グッ
GU
(HRG)
ダッ
DA
(DASH)
ダッ
DA
ダッ
DA

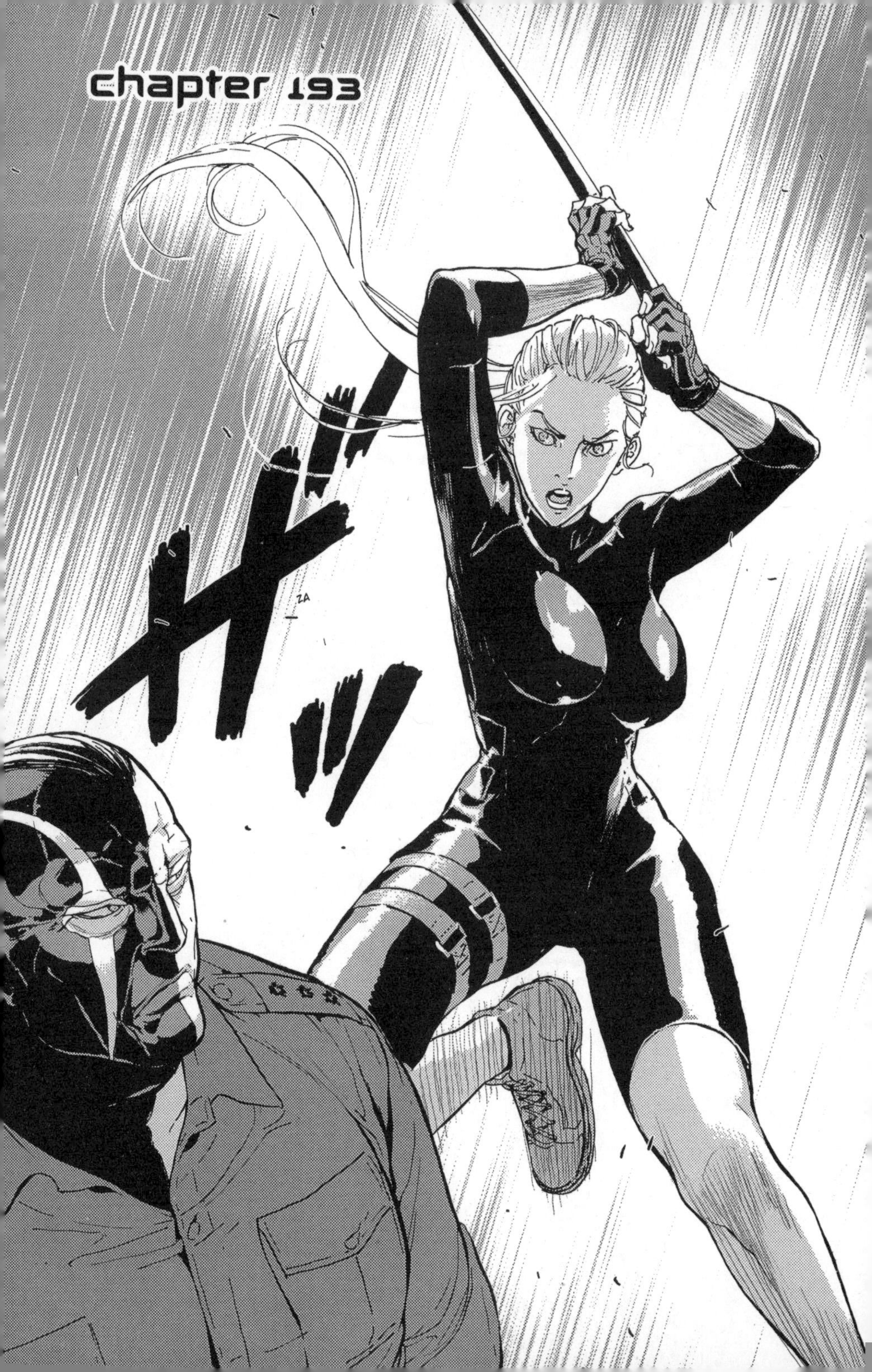
chapter 193
ZA

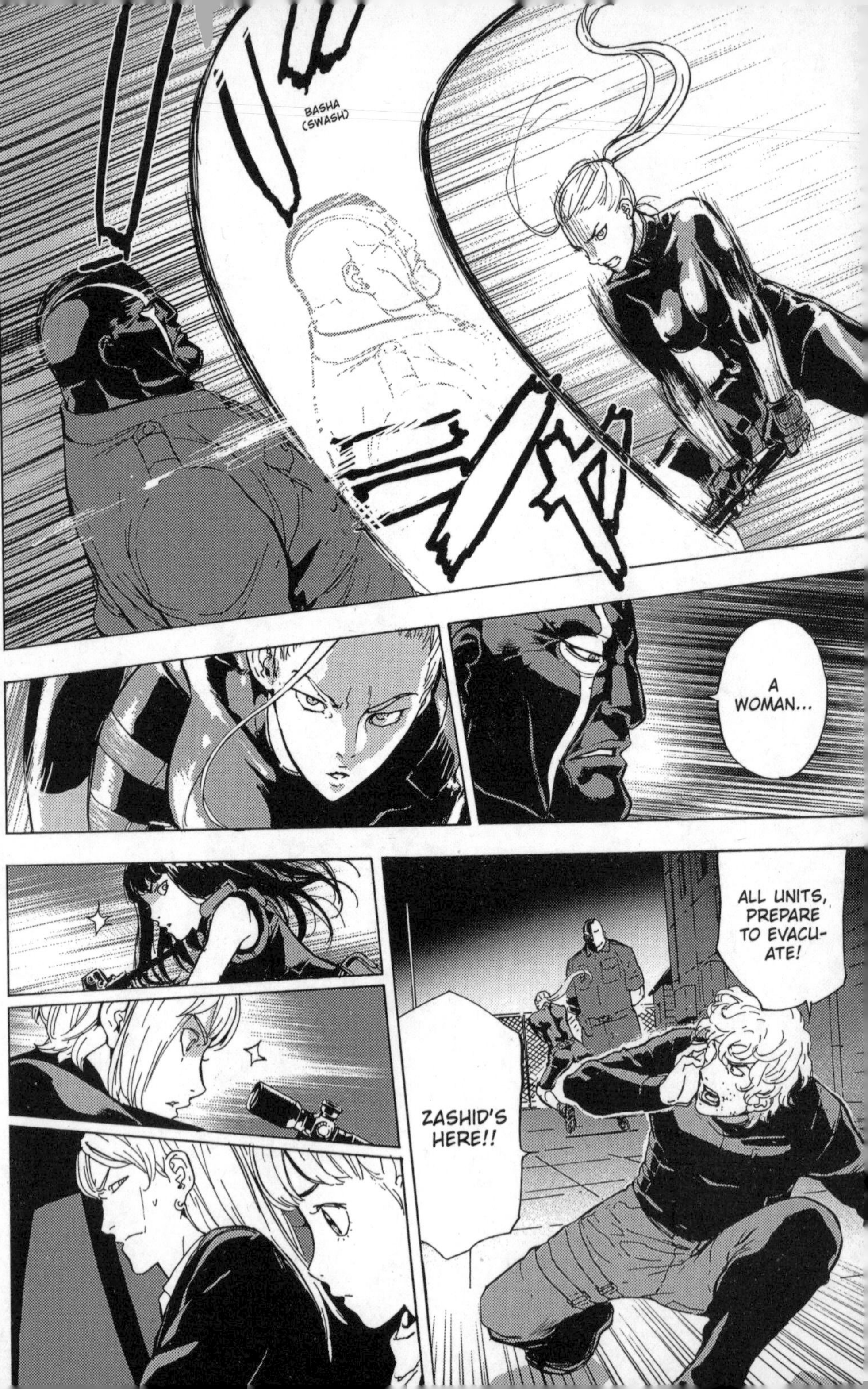
BASHA (SWASH)
A WOMAN...
ALL UNITS, PREPARE TO EVACU-ATE!
ZASHID'S HERE!!

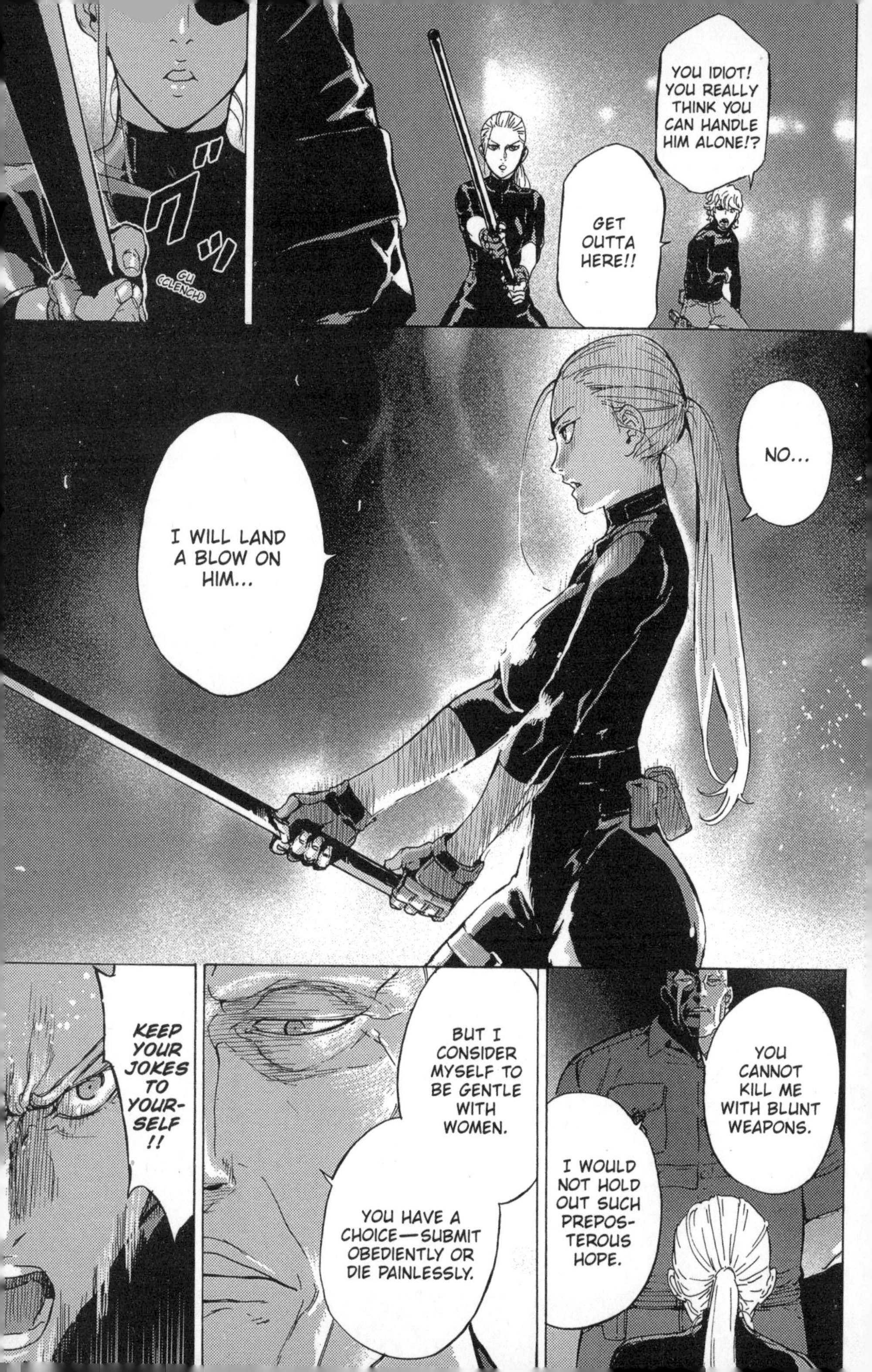
YOU IDIOT! YOU REALLY THINK YOU CAN HANDLE HIM ALONE!?
GET OUTTA HERE!!
GU (CLENCH)
NO...
I WILL LAND A BLOW ON HIM...
YOU CANNOT KILL ME WITH BLUNT WEAPONS.
I WOULD NOT HOLD OUT SUCH PREPOSTEROUS HOPE.
BUT I CONSIDER MYSELF TO BE GENTLE WITH WOMEN.
YOU HAVE A CHOICE—SUBMIT OBEDIENTLY OR DIE PAINLESSLY.
KEEP YOUR JOKES TO YOURSELF!!

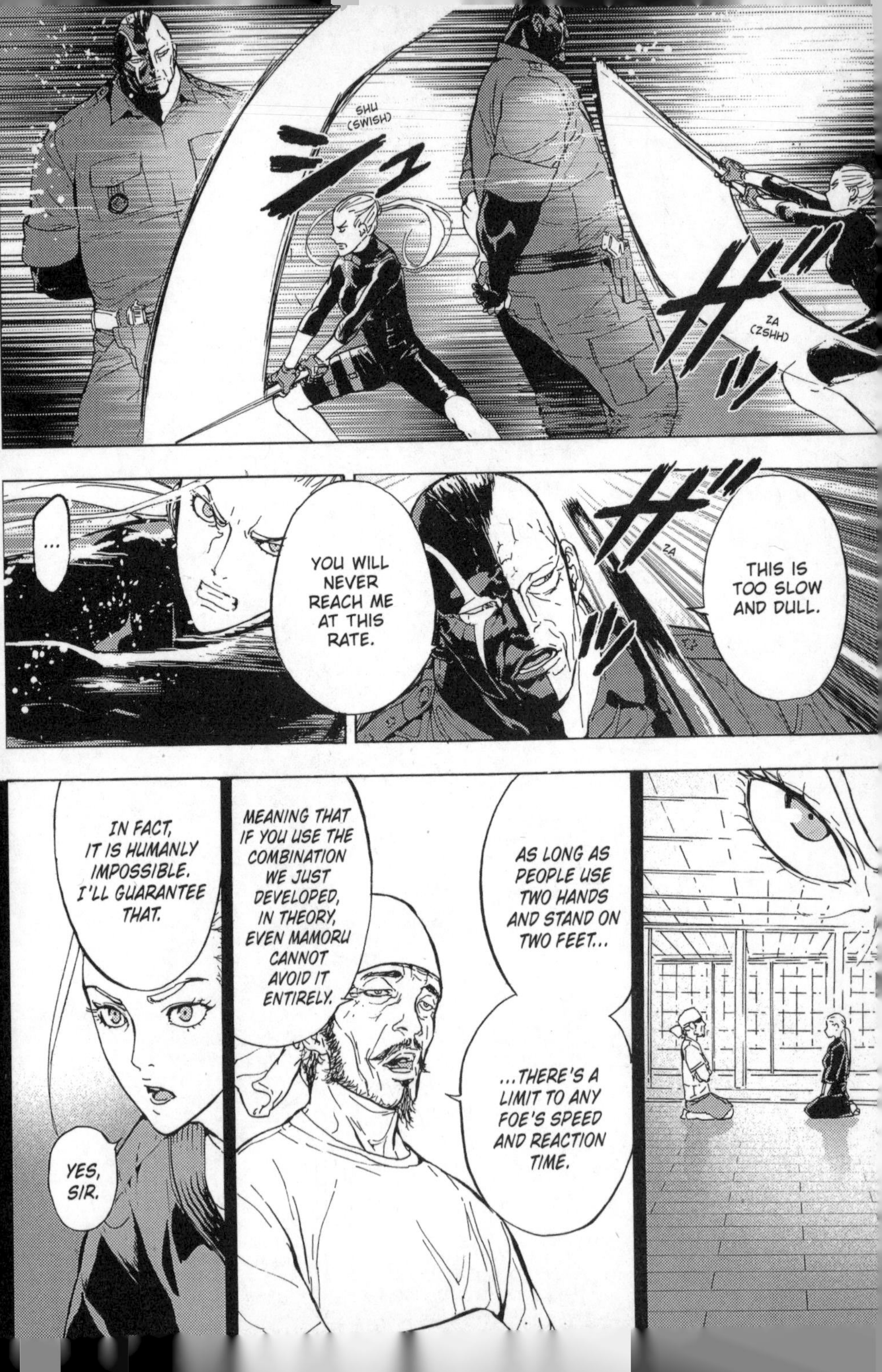
ZA (ZSHH)
SHU (SWISH)
ZA
THIS IS TOO SLOW AND DULL.
YOU WILL NEVER REACH ME AT THIS RATE.
...
AS LONG AS PEOPLE USE TWO HANDS AND STAND ON TWO FEET...
...THERE'S A LIMIT TO ANY FOE'S SPEED AND REACTION TIME.
MEANING THAT IF YOU USE THE COMBINATION WE JUST DEVELOPED, IN THEORY, EVEN MAMORU CANNOT AVOID IT ENTIRELY.
IN FACT, IT IS HUMANLY IMPOSSIBLE. I'LL GUARANTEE THAT.
YES, SIR.

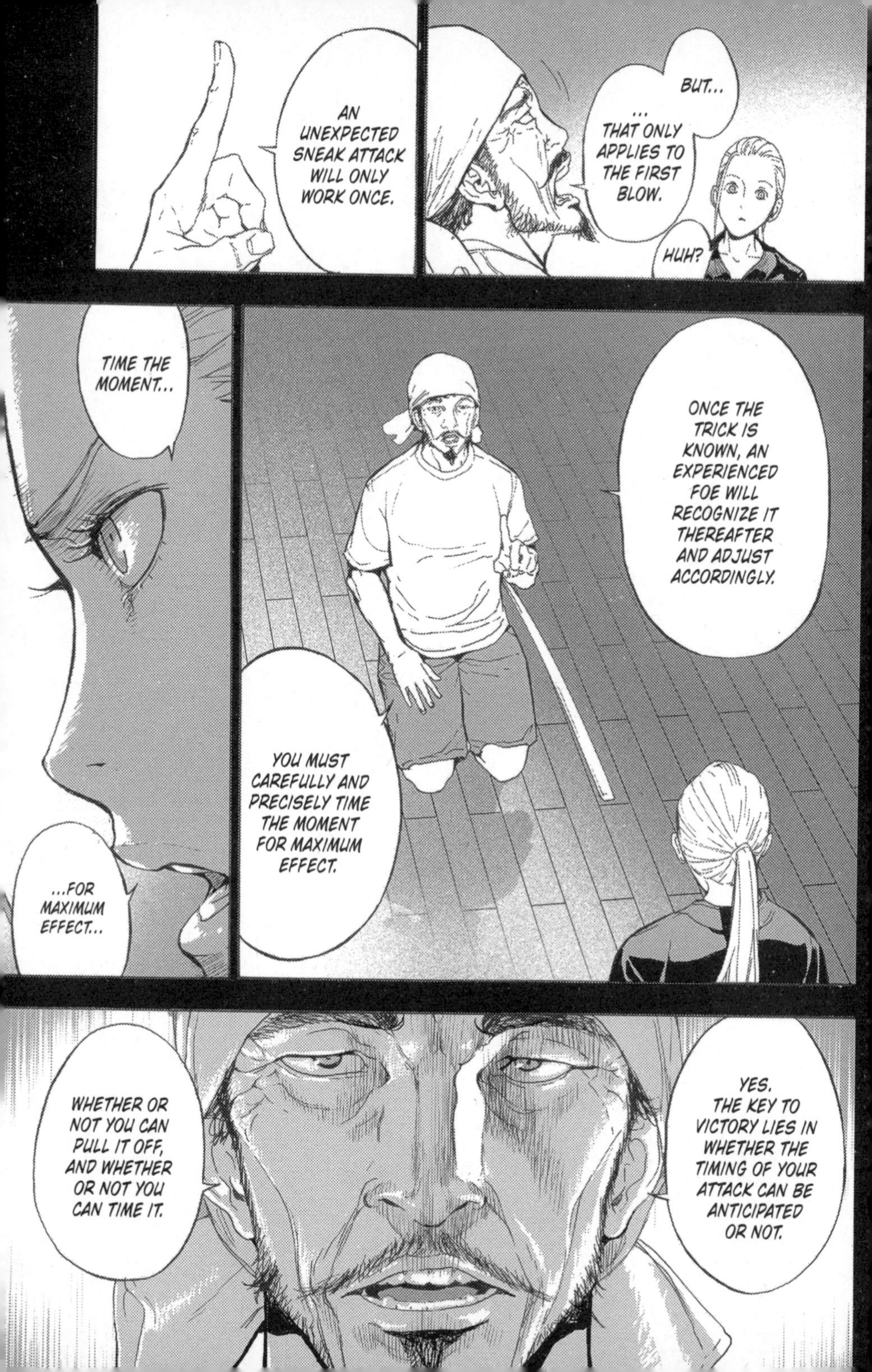
BUT...
...THAT ONLY APPLIES TO THE FIRST BLOW.
HUH?
AN UNEXPECTED SNEAK ATTACK WILL ONLY WORK ONCE.
ONCE THE TRICK IS KNOWN, AN EXPERIENCED FOE WILL RECOGNIZE IT THEREAFTER AND ADJUST ACCORDINGLY.
YOU MUST CAREFULLY AND PRECISELY TIME THE MOMENT FOR MAXIMUM EFFECT.
TIME THE MOMENT...
...FOR MAXIMUM EFFECT...
YES. THE KEY TO VICTORY LIES IN WHETHER THE TIMING OF YOUR ATTACK CAN BE ANTICIPATED OR NOT.
WHETHER OR NOT YOU CAN PULL IT OFF, AND WHETHER OR NOT YOU CAN TIME IT.

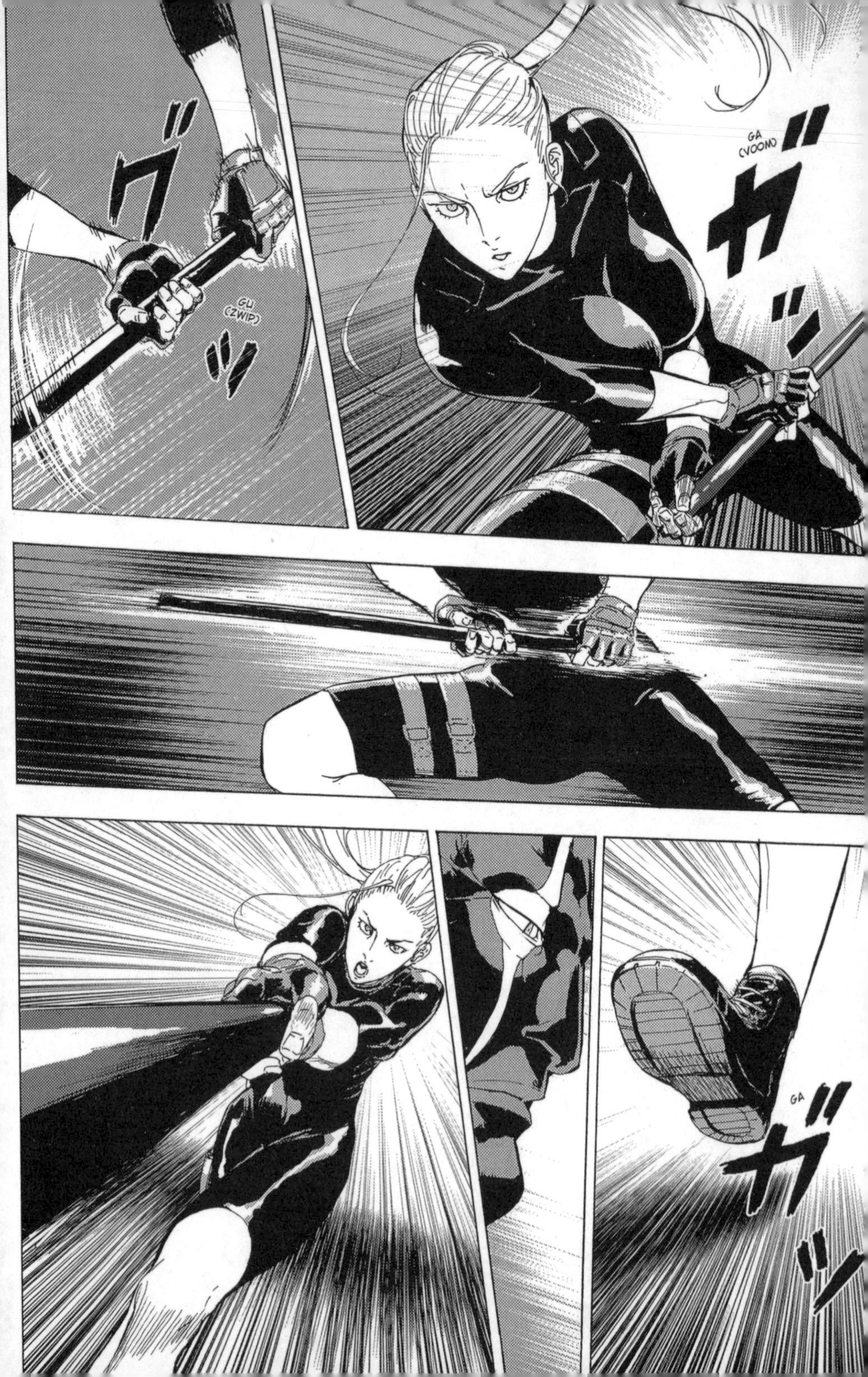
ガッ
GA
(VOOM)
グッ
GU
(ZWIP)
ガッ
GA

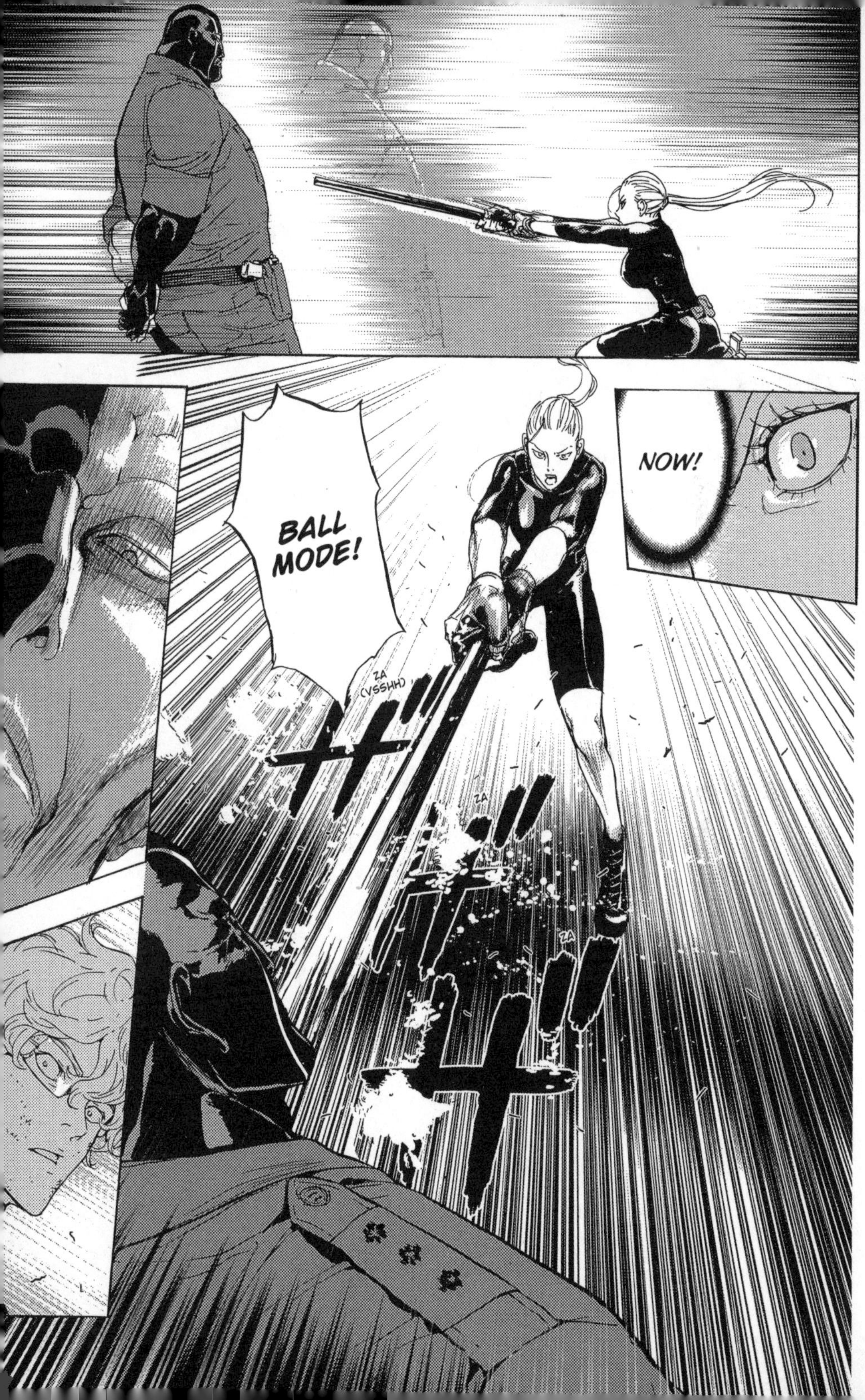
NOW!
BALL MODE!
ZA (VSSHH)
ZA
ZA

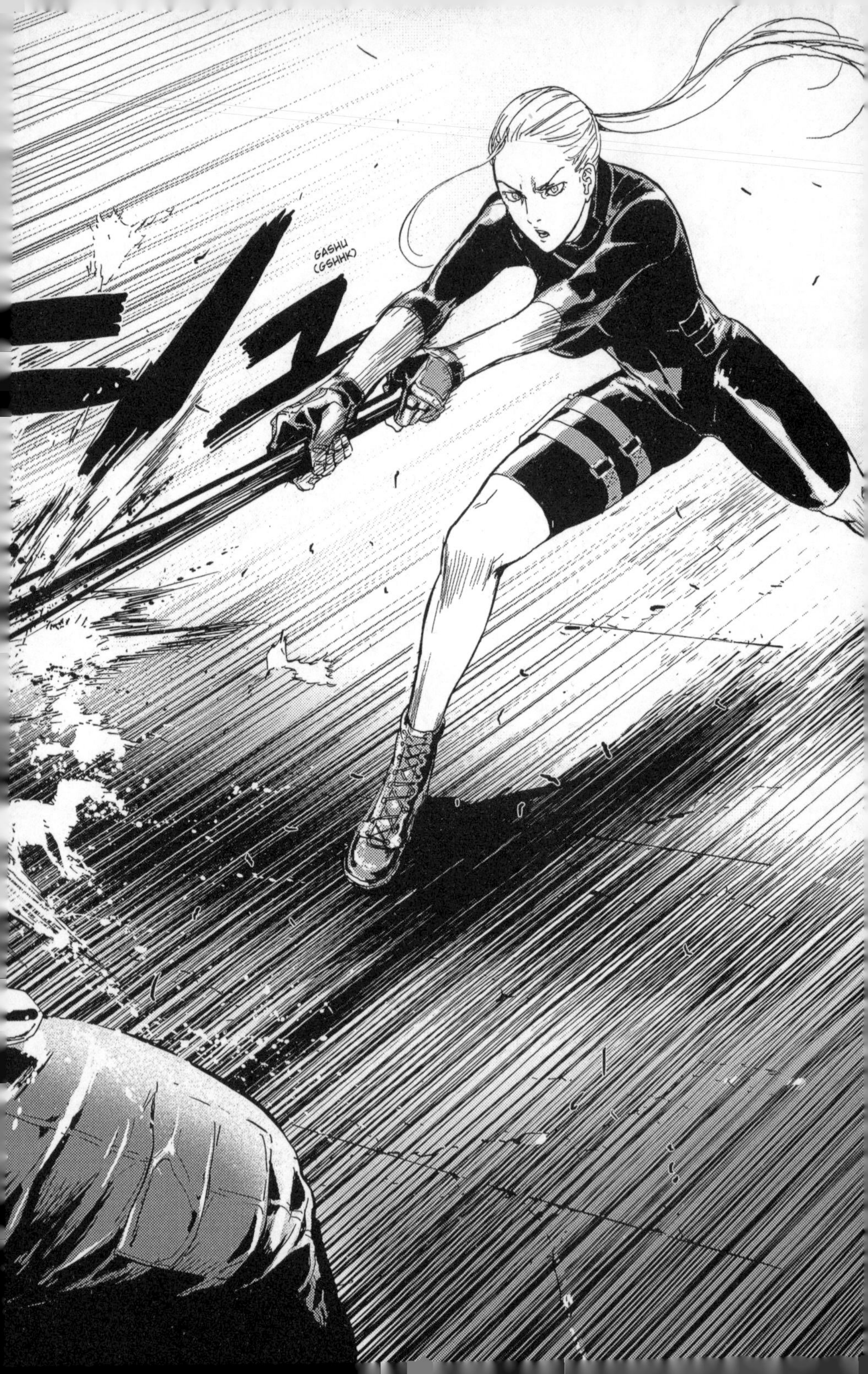
GASHU
(GSHHK)

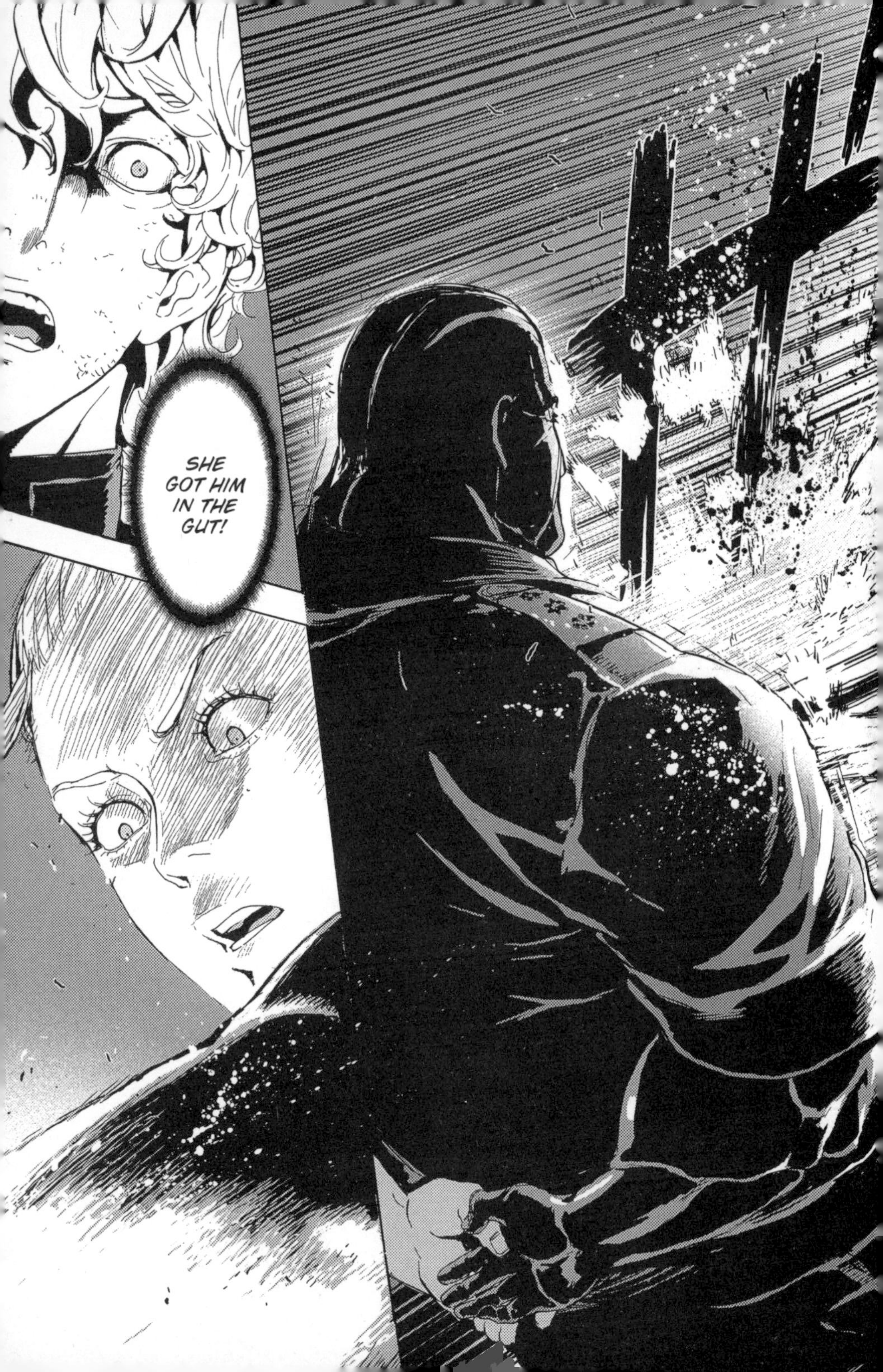
SHE GOT HIM IN THE GUT!

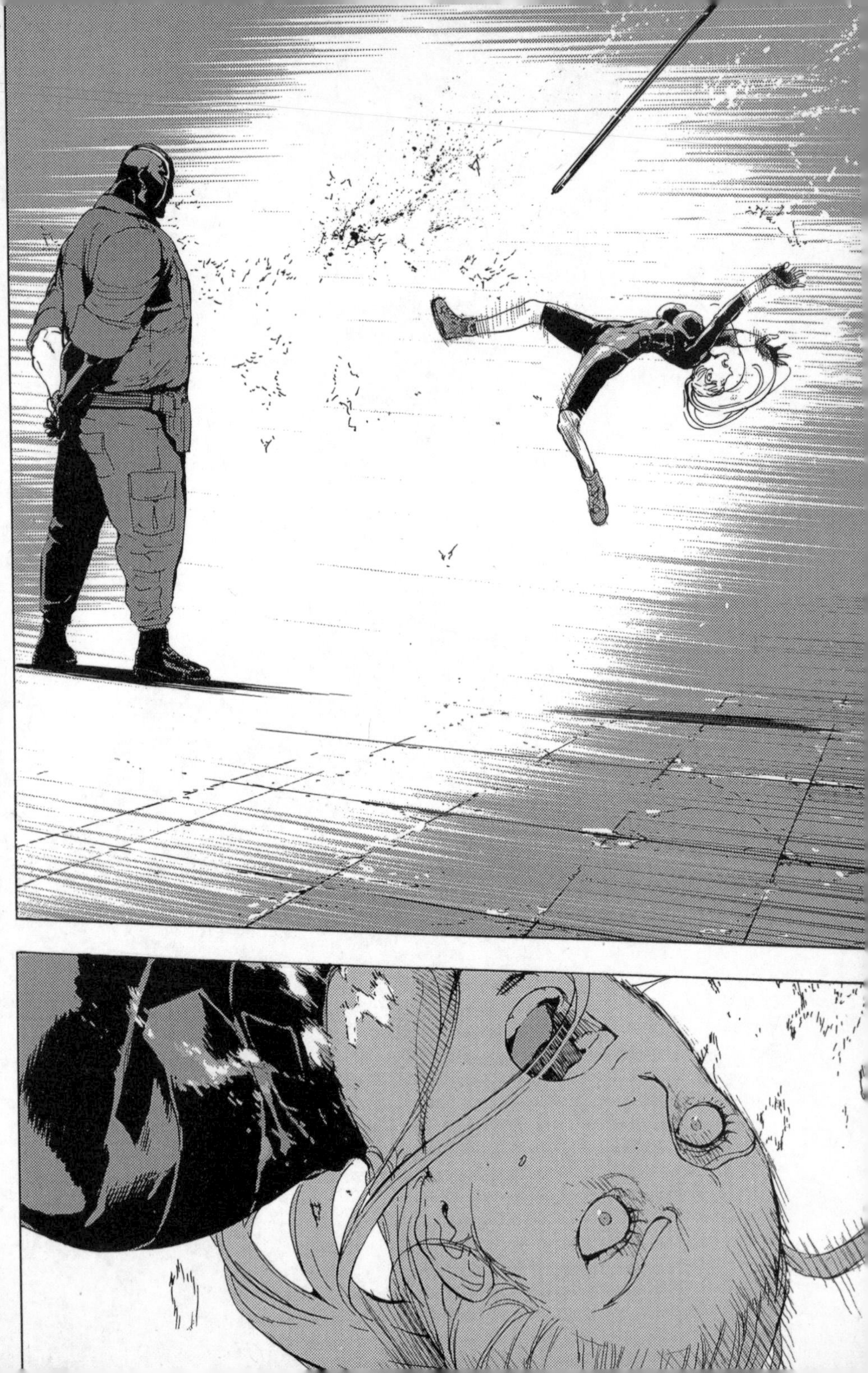

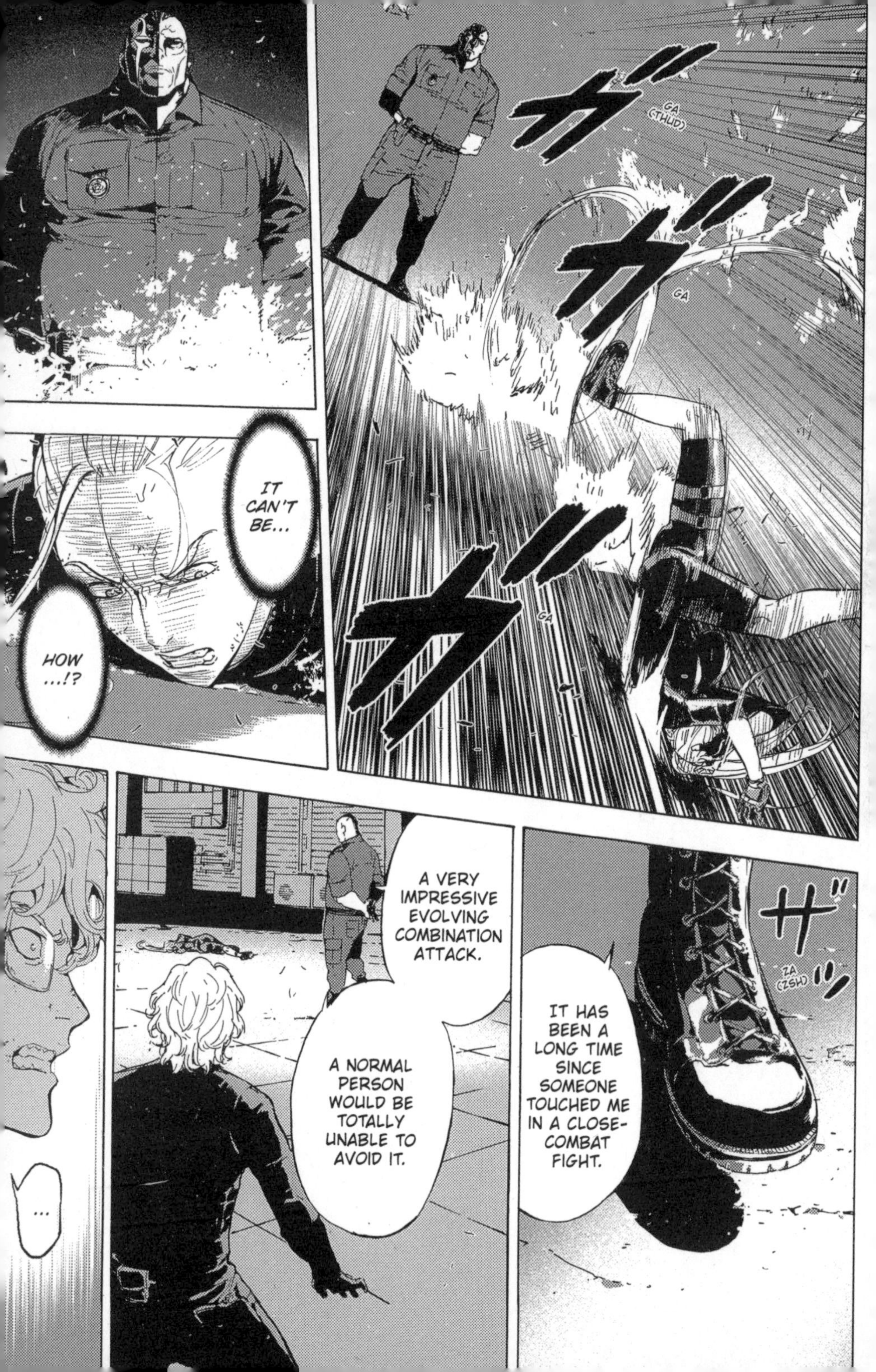

GA (THUD)
GA
GA
IT CAN'T BE...
HOW ...!?
ZA (ZSH)
IT HAS BEEN A LONG TIME SINCE SOMEONE TOUCHED ME IN A CLOSE-COMBAT FIGHT.
A VERY IMPRESSIVE EVOLVING COMBINATION ATTACK.
A NORMAL PERSON WOULD BE TOTALLY UNABLE TO AVOID IT.
...

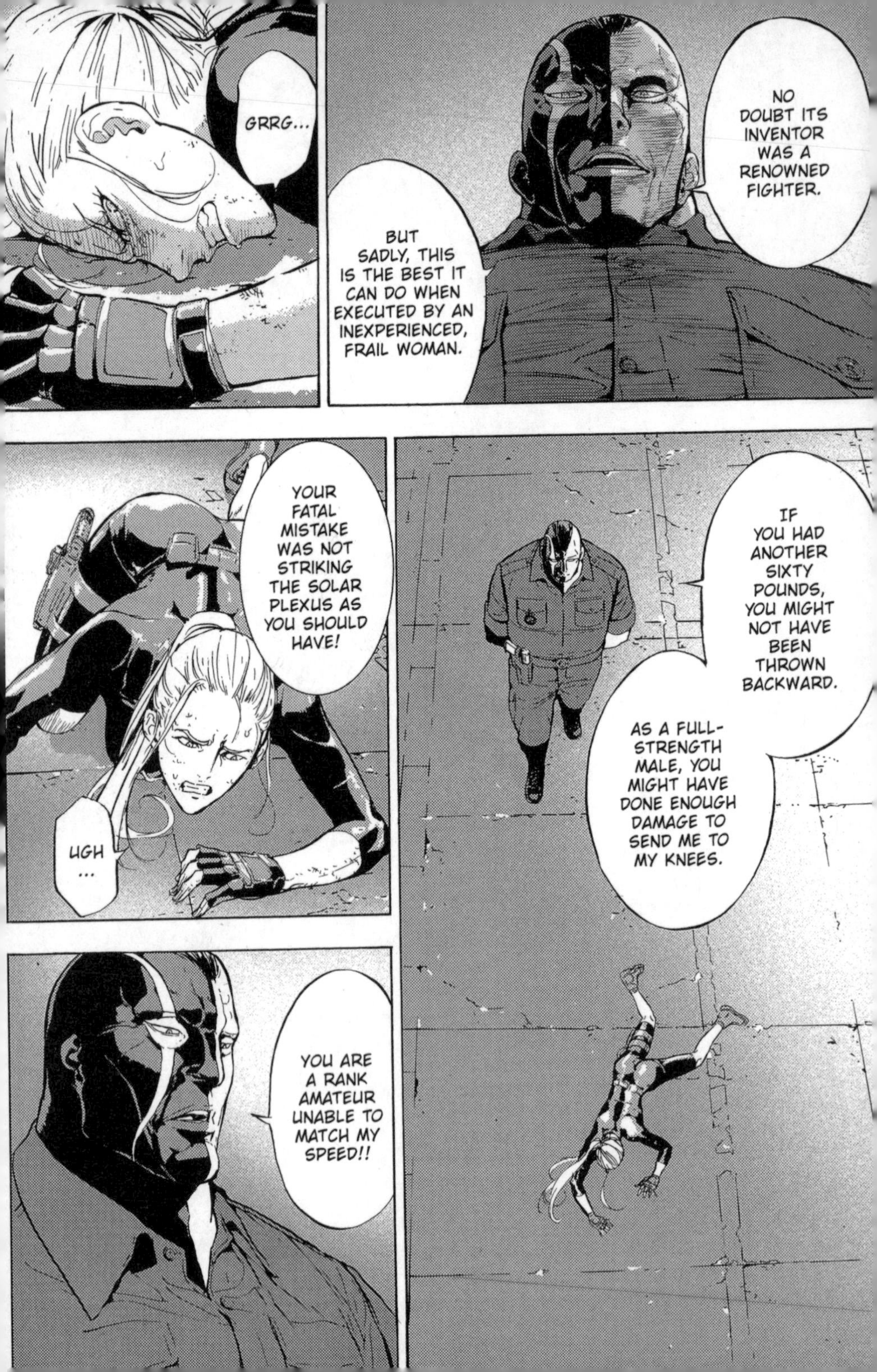
NO DOUBT ITS INVENTOR WAS A RENOWNED FIGHTER.
BUT SADLY, THIS IS THE BEST IT CAN DO WHEN EXECUTED BY AN INEXPERIENCED, FRAIL WOMAN.
GRRG...
IF YOU HAD ANOTHER SIXTY POUNDS, YOU MIGHT NOT HAVE BEEN THROWN BACKWARD.
AS A FULL-STRENGTH MALE, YOU MIGHT HAVE DONE ENOUGH DAMAGE TO SEND ME TO MY KNEES.
YOUR FATAL MISTAKE WAS NOT STRIKING THE SOLAR PLEXUS AS YOU SHOULD HAVE!
UGH ...
YOU ARE A RANK AMATEUR UNABLE TO MATCH MY SPEED!!

I HATE TO ADMIT IT, BUT HE'S RIGHT. AND SOMEHOW HE ASSESSED ALL OF THAT IN THE MOMENT AND TOOK MY ATTACK ANYWAY...

HE'S A TRUE MONSTER!!

WILL IT BE SURRENDER? OR DEATH?

NOW CHOOSE!

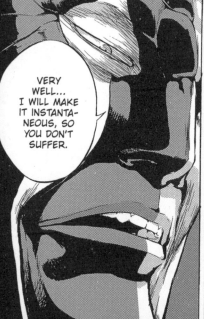

VERY WELL... I WILL MAKE IT INSTANTANEOUS, SO YOU DON'T SUFFER.

...

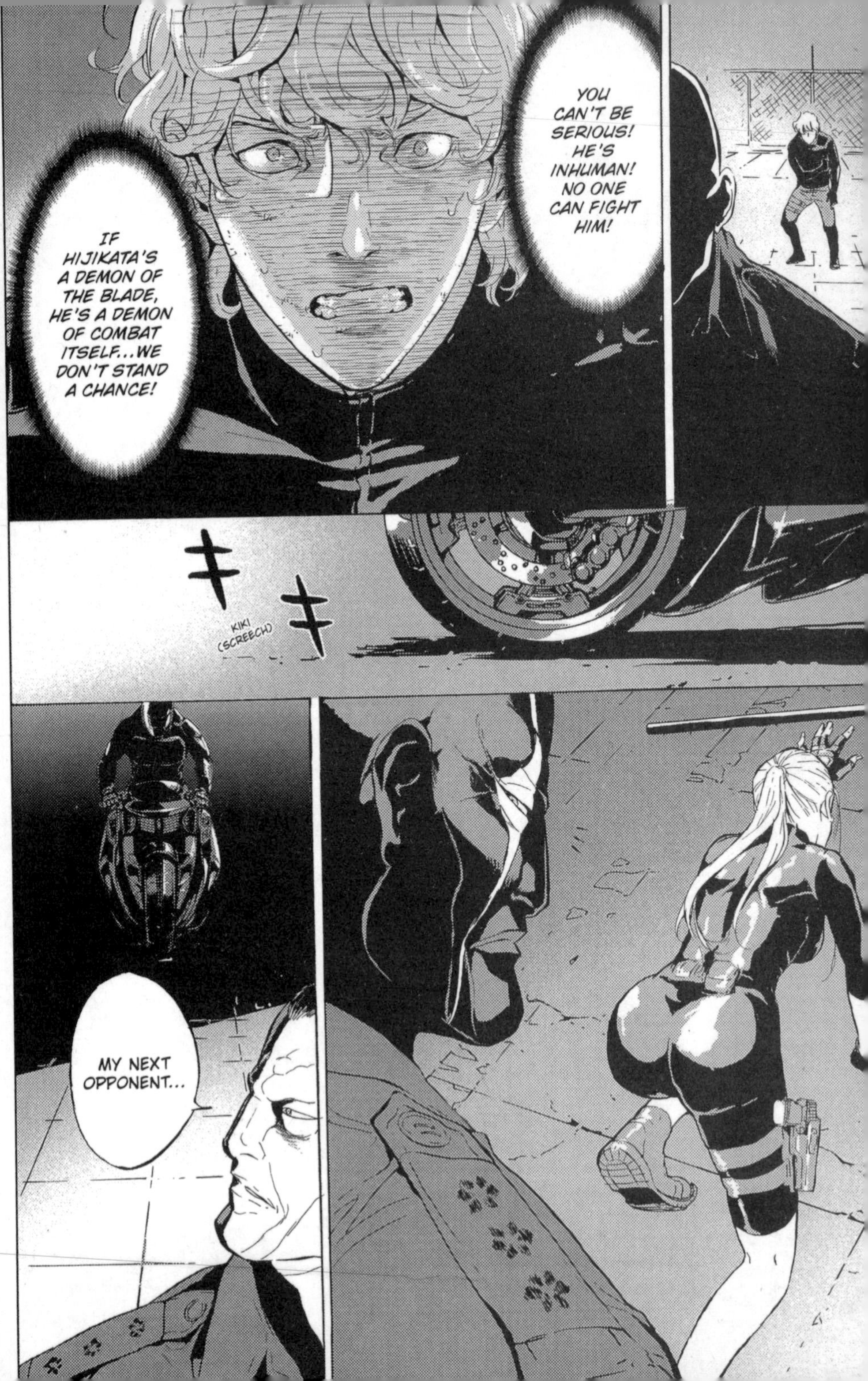
YOU CAN'T BE SERIOUS! HE'S INHUMAN! NO ONE CAN FIGHT HIM!
IF HIJIKATA'S A DEMON OF THE BLADE, HE'S A DEMON OF COMBAT ITSELF...WE DON'T STAND A CHANCE!
KIKI (SCREECH)
MY NEXT OPPONENT...

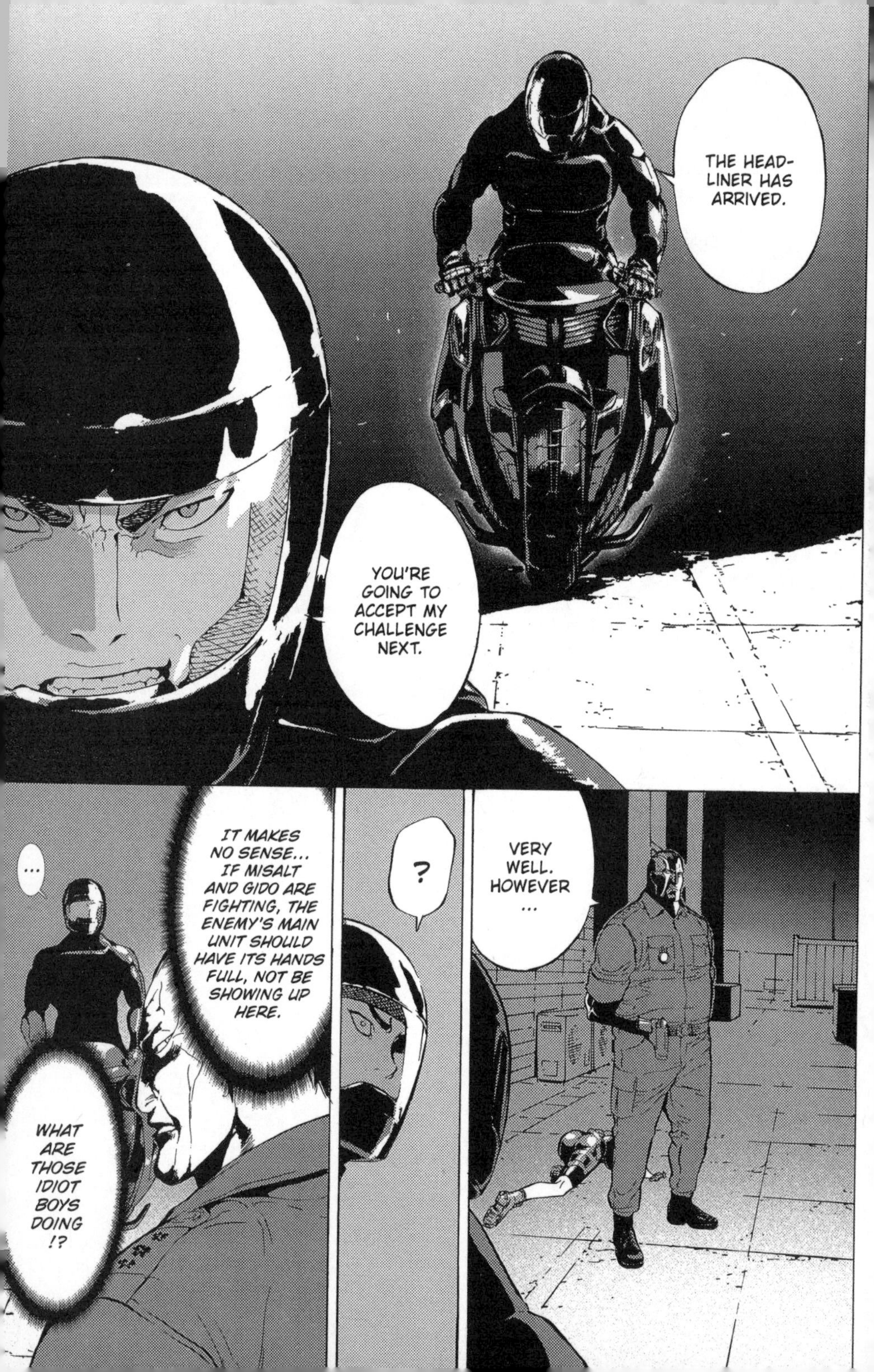
THE HEAD-LINER HAS ARRIVED.
YOU'RE GOING TO ACCEPT MY CHALLENGE NEXT.
VERY WELL. HOWEVER ...
?
IT MAKES NO SENSE... IF MISALT AND GIDO ARE FIGHTING, THE ENEMY'S MAIN UNIT SHOULD HAVE ITS HANDS FULL, NOT BE SHOWING UP HERE.
...
WHAT ARE THOSE IDIOT BOYS DOING !?

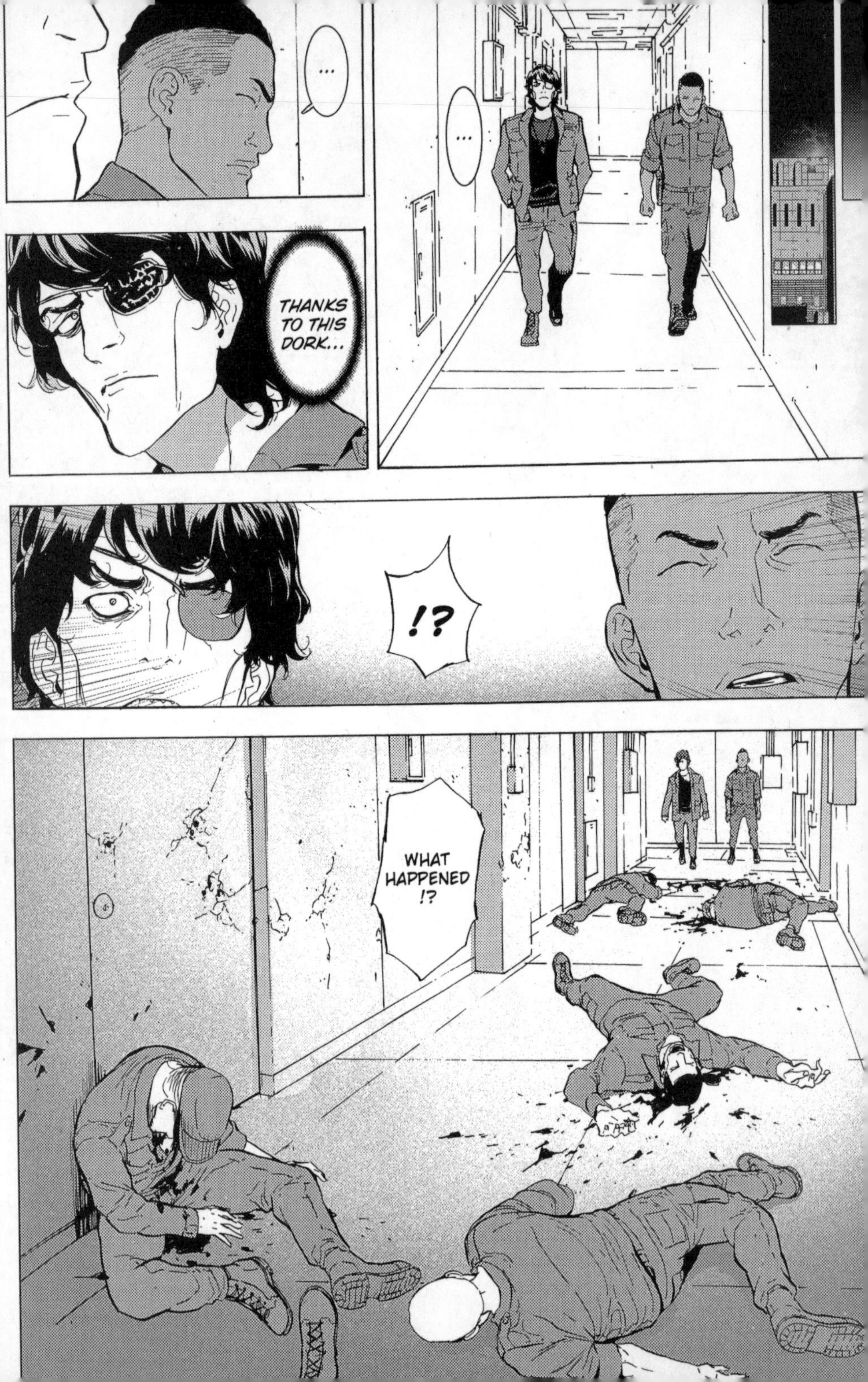
...
...
THANKS TO THIS DORK...
!?
WHAT HAPPENED !?

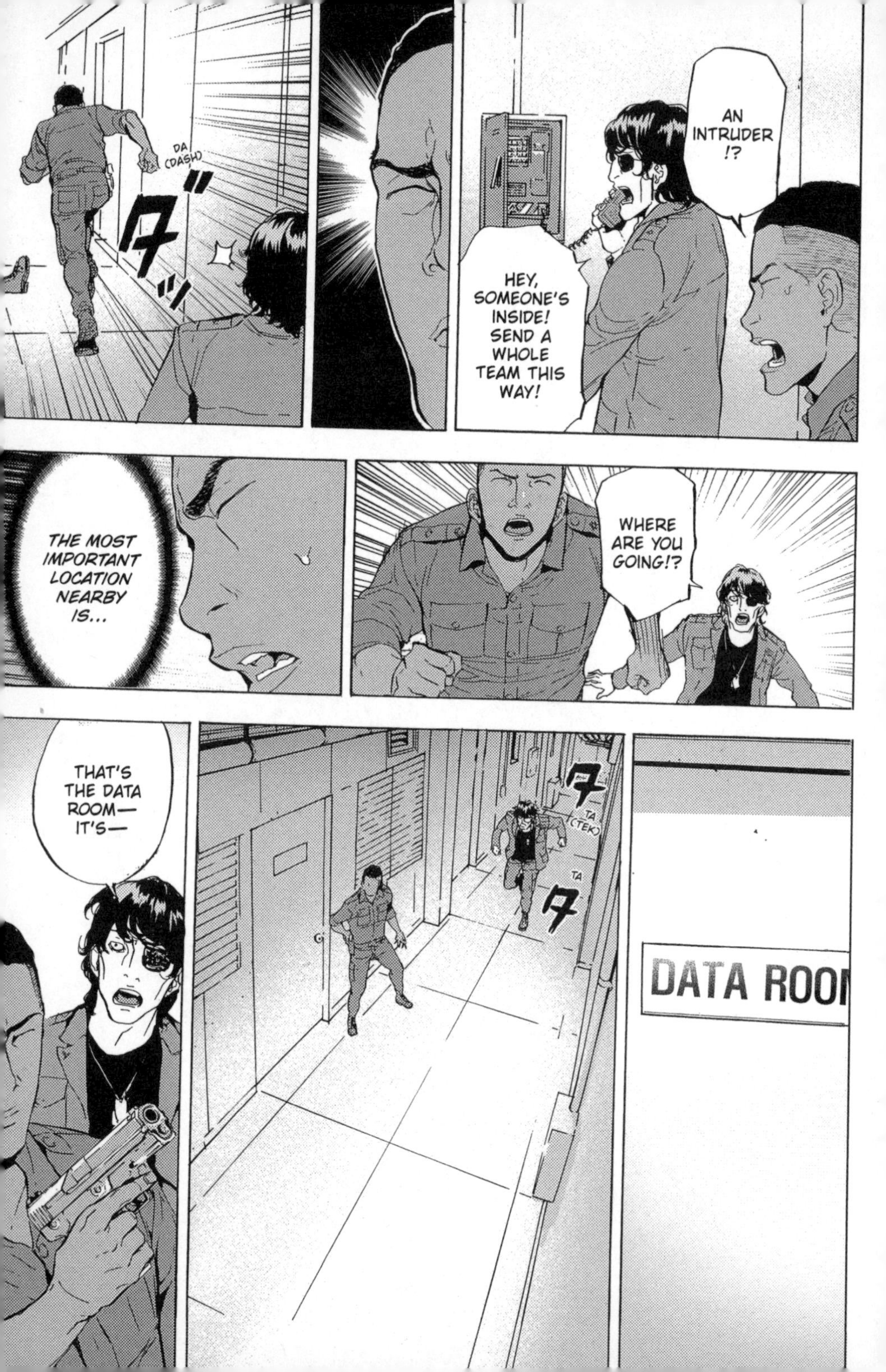
AN INTRUDER !?
HEY, SOMEONE'S INSIDE! SEND A WHOLE TEAM THIS WAY!
DA (DASH)
WHERE ARE YOU GOING!?
THE MOST IMPORTANT LOCATION NEARBY IS...
DATA ROOM
TA (TEK)
TA
THAT'S THE DATA ROOM— IT'S—

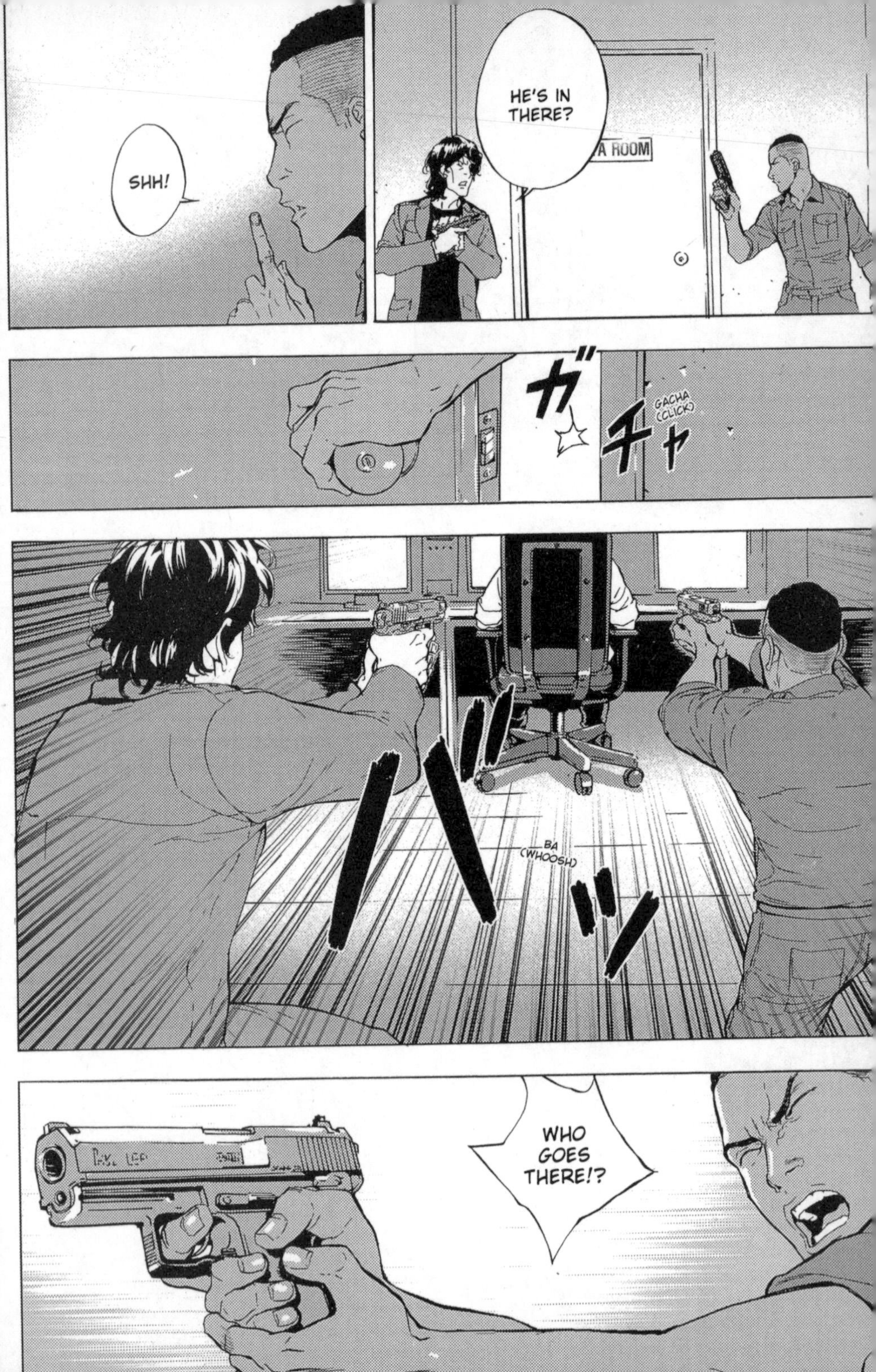
HE'S IN THERE?
A ROOM
SHH!
ガチャ
GACHA (CLICK)
バッ
BA (WHOOSH)
WHO GOES THERE!?

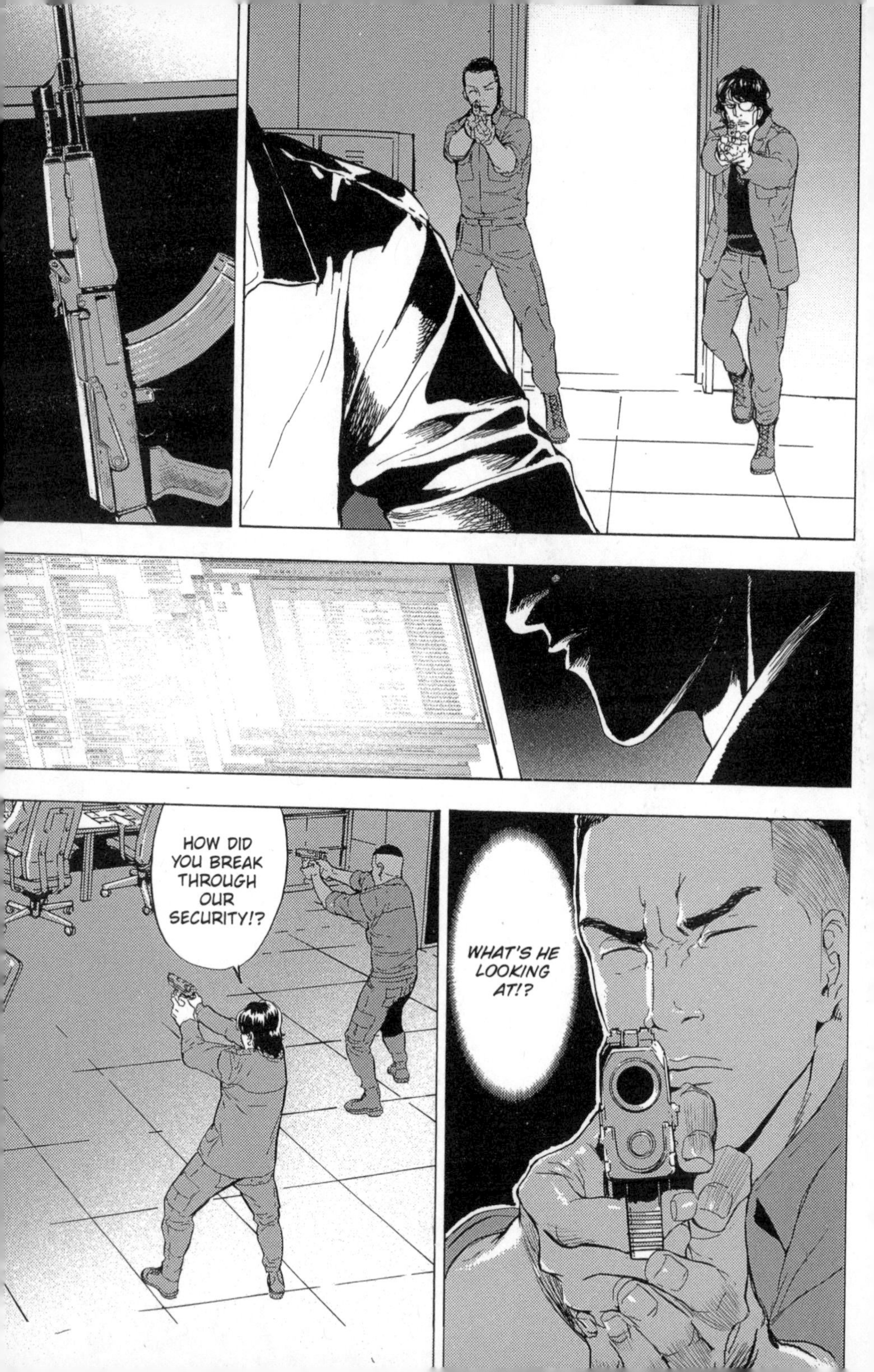
WHAT'S HE LOOKING AT!?
HOW DID YOU BREAK THROUGH OUR SECURITY!?

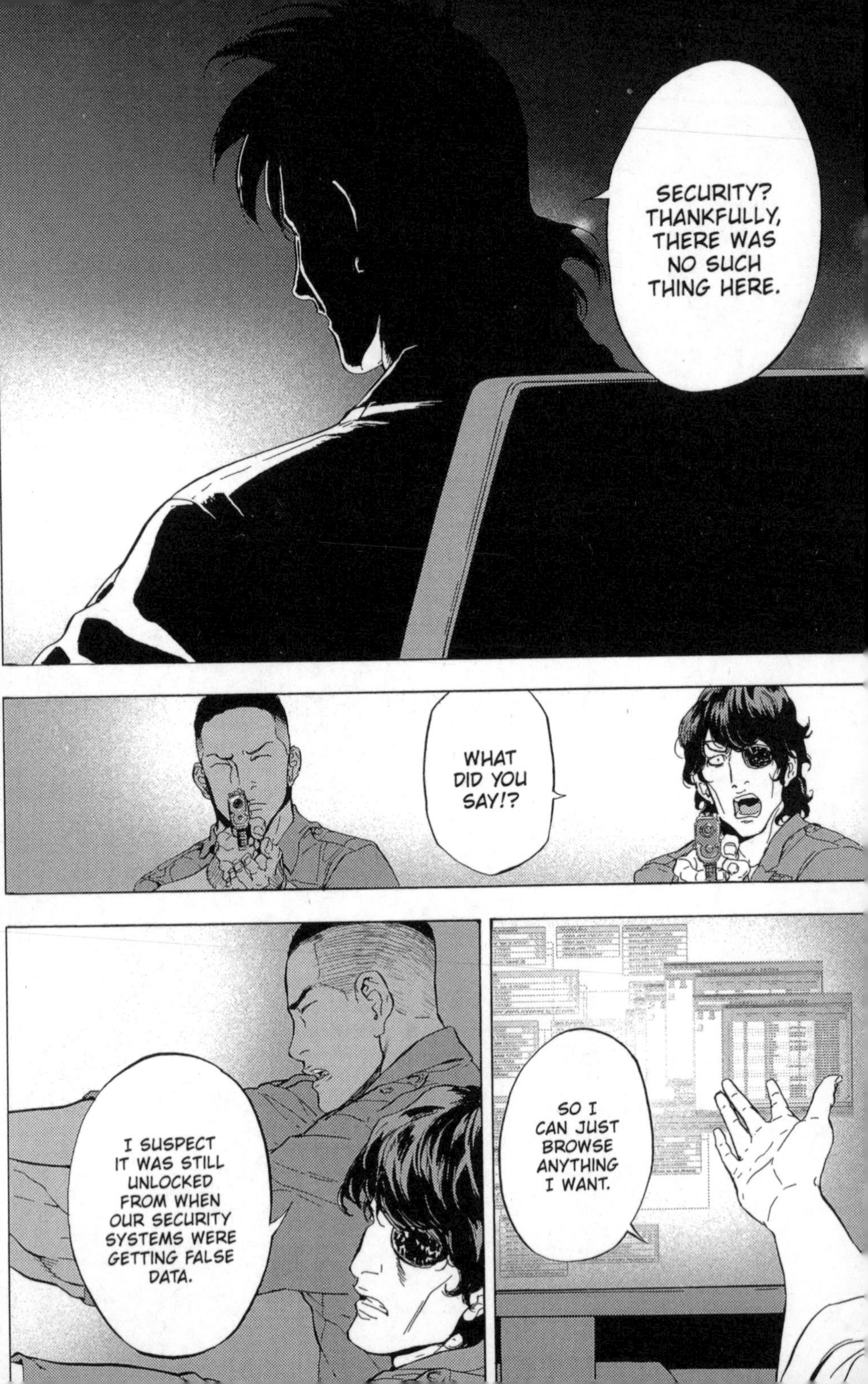
SECURITY? THANKFULLY, THERE WAS NO SUCH THING HERE.
WHAT DID YOU SAY!?
SO I CAN JUST BROWSE ANYTHING I WANT.
I SUSPECT IT WAS STILL UNLOCKED FROM WHEN OUR SECURITY SYSTEMS WERE GETTING FALSE DATA.

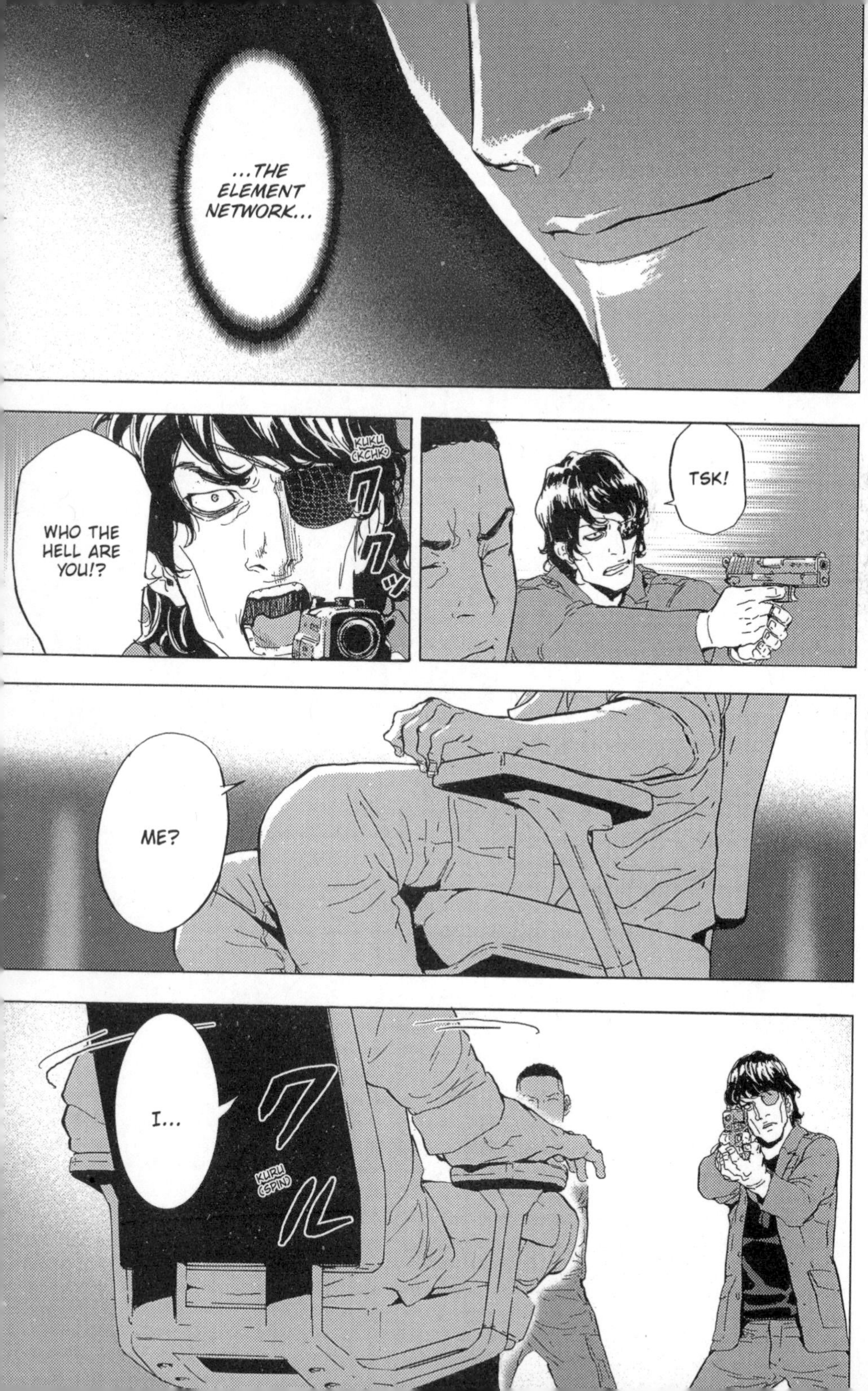
...THE ELEMENT NETWORK...
TSK!
KUKU (KCHK)
WHO THE HELL ARE YOU!?
ME?
I...
KURU (SPIN)

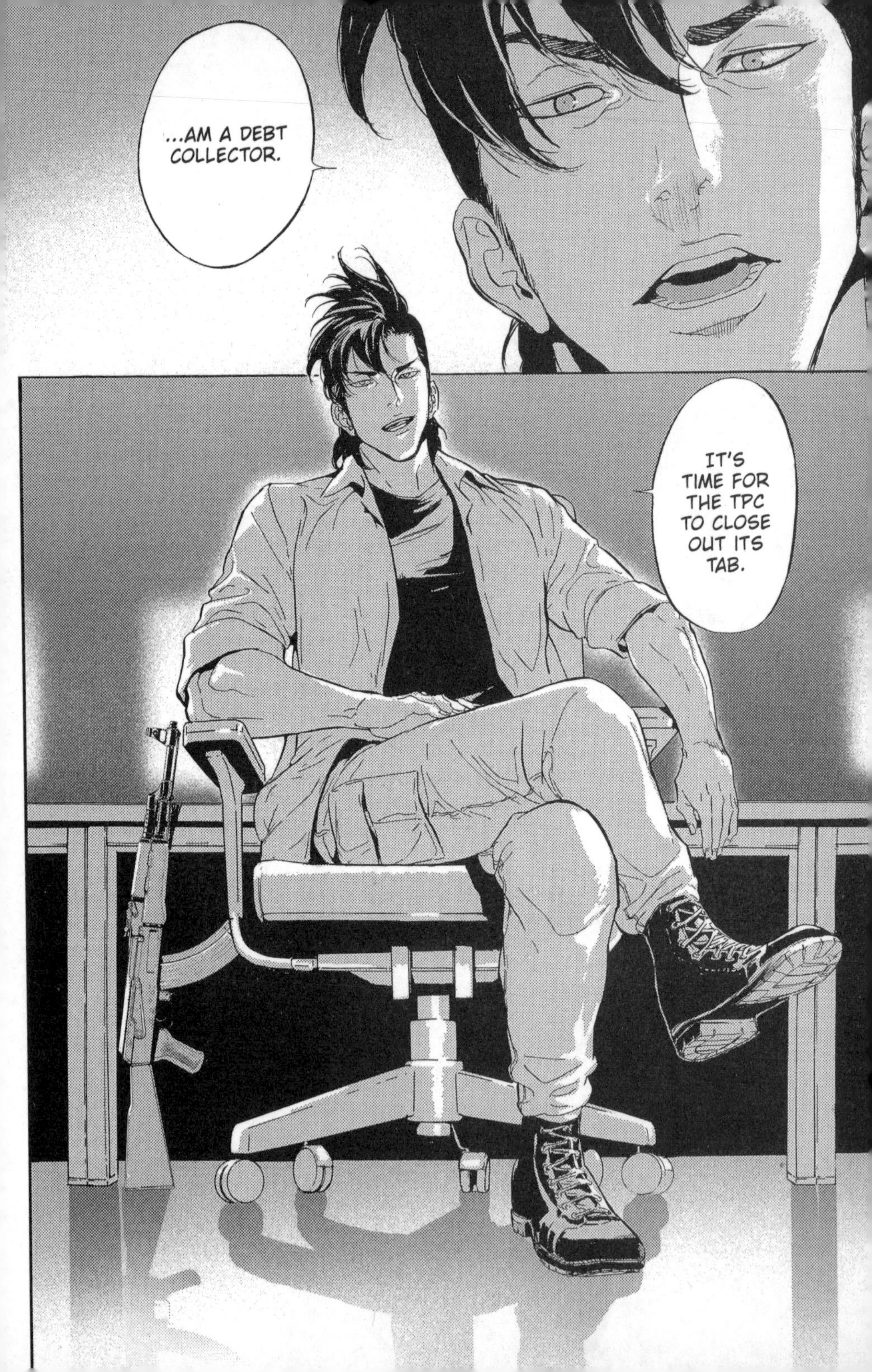
...AM A DEBT COLLECTOR.
IT'S TIME FOR THE TPC TO CLOSE OUT ITS TAB.

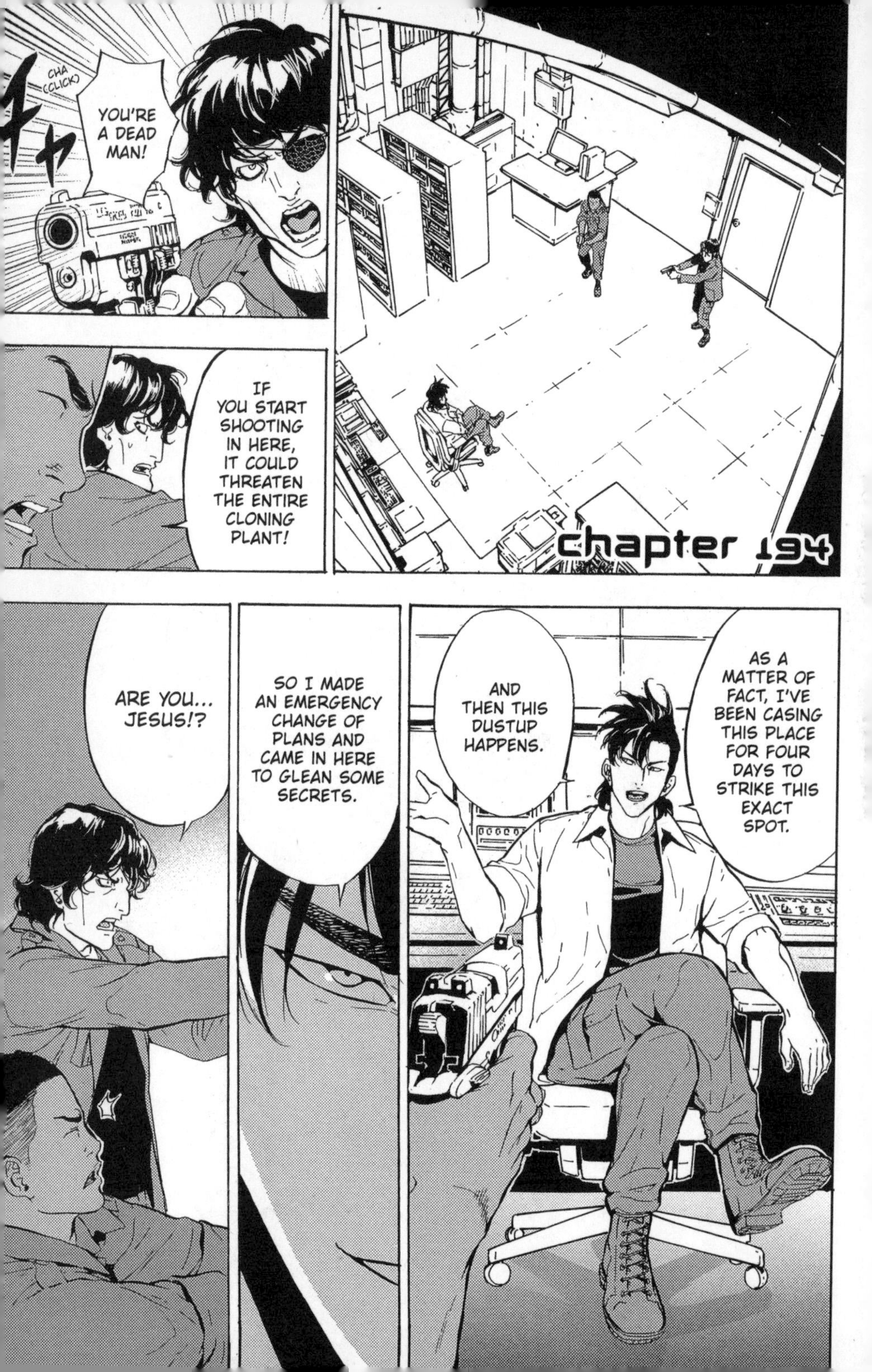
chapter 194
CHA (CLICK)
チャ
YOU'RE A DEAD MAN!
IF YOU START SHOOTING IN HERE, IT COULD THREATEN THE ENTIRE CLONING PLANT!
AS A MATTER OF FACT, I'VE BEEN CASING THIS PLACE FOR FOUR DAYS TO STRIKE THIS EXACT SPOT.
AND THEN THIS DUSTUP HAPPENS.
SO I MADE AN EMERGENCY CHANGE OF PLANS AND CAME IN HERE TO GLEAN SOME SECRETS.
ARE YOU... JESUS!?

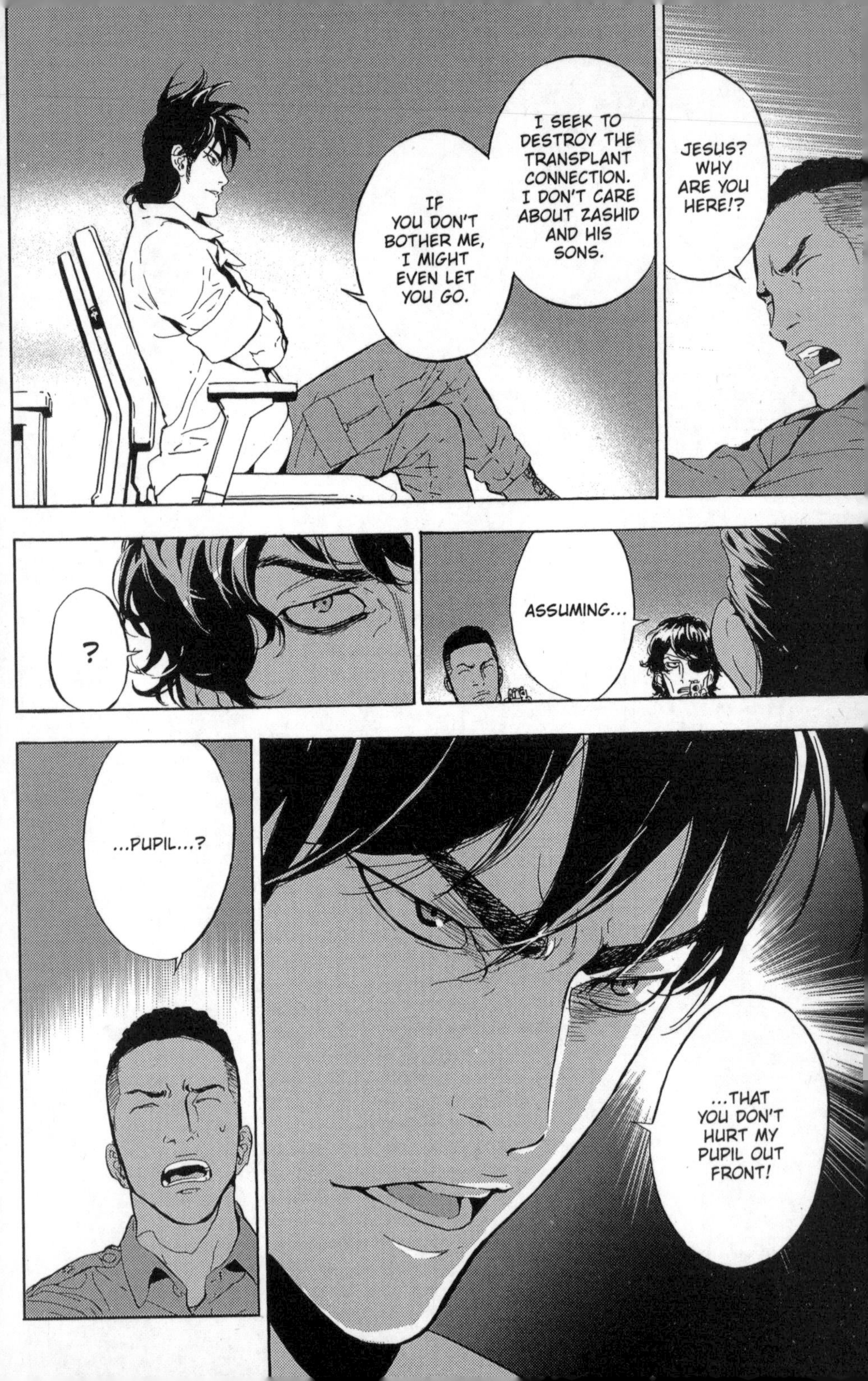
JESUS? WHY ARE YOU HERE!?
I SEEK TO DESTROY THE TRANSPLANT CONNECTION. I DON'T CARE ABOUT ZASHID AND HIS SONS.
IF YOU DON'T BOTHER ME, I MIGHT EVEN LET YOU GO.
ASSUMING...
?
...THAT YOU DON'T HURT MY PUPIL OUT FRONT!
...PUPIL...?

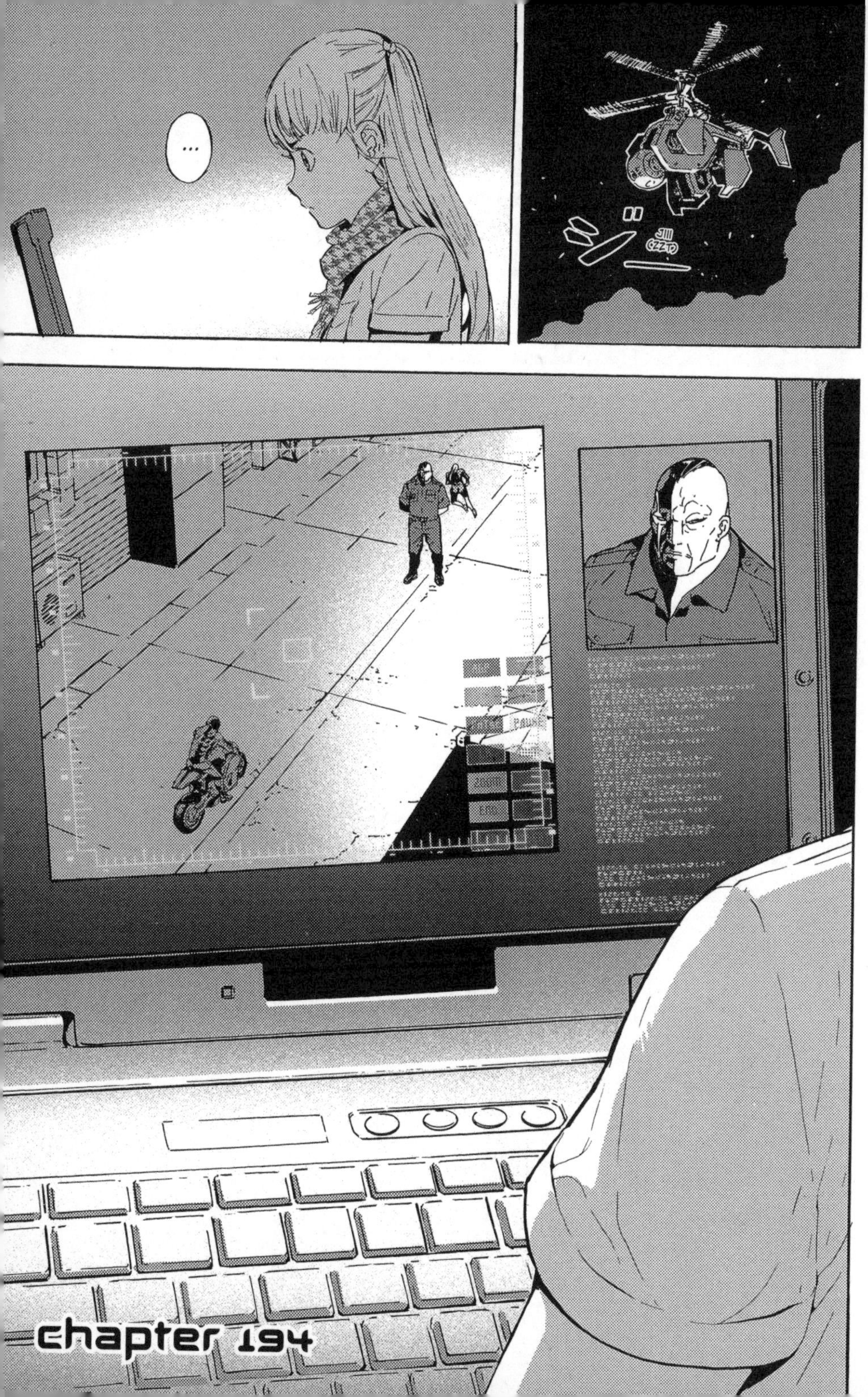
...
PAUSE
ZOOM
chapter 194

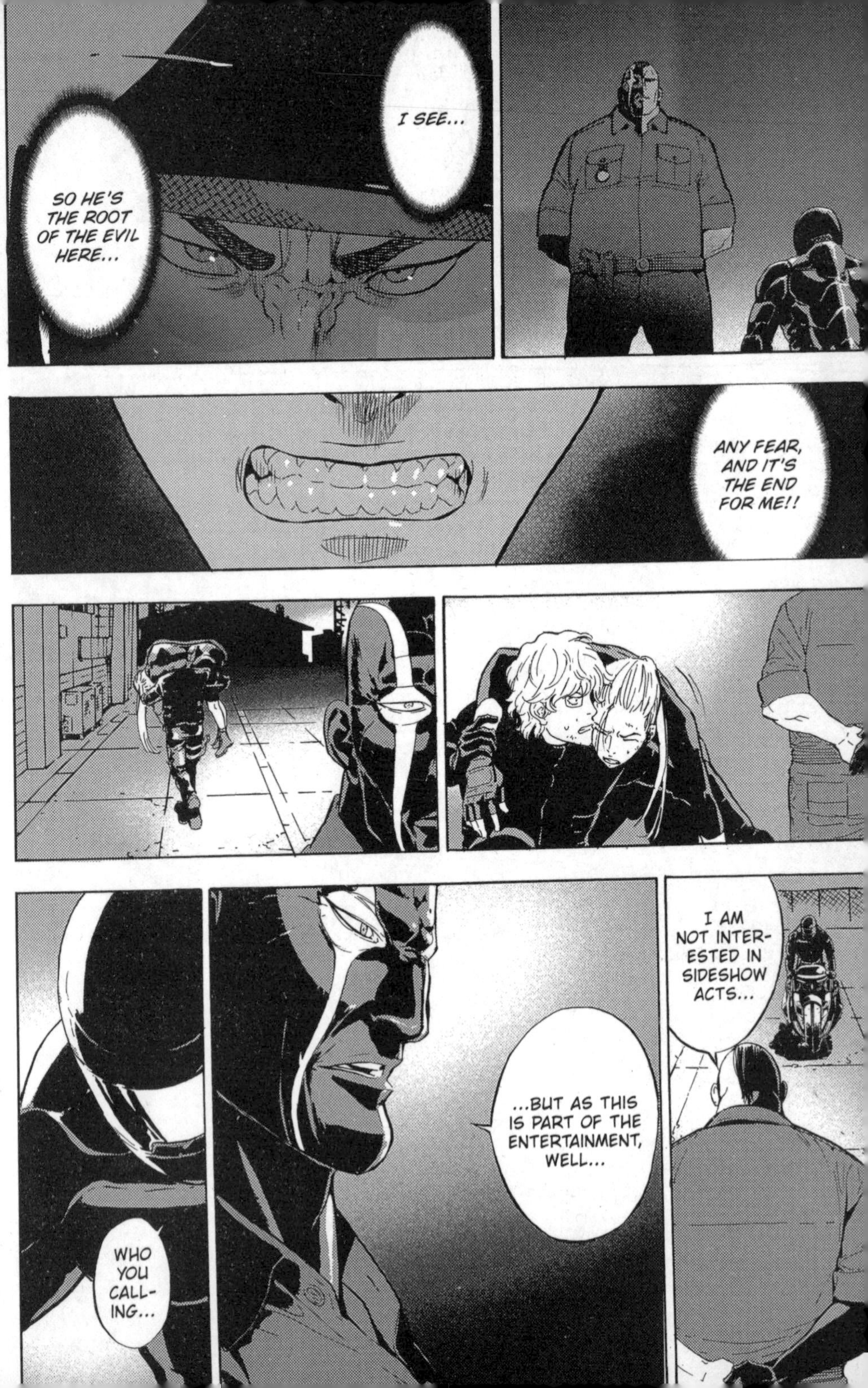
I SEE...
SO HE'S THE ROOT OF THE EVIL HERE...
ANY FEAR, AND IT'S THE END FOR ME!!
I AM NOT INTER-ESTED IN SIDESHOW ACTS...
...BUT AS THIS IS PART OF THE ENTERTAINMENT, WELL...
WHO YOU CALL-ING...

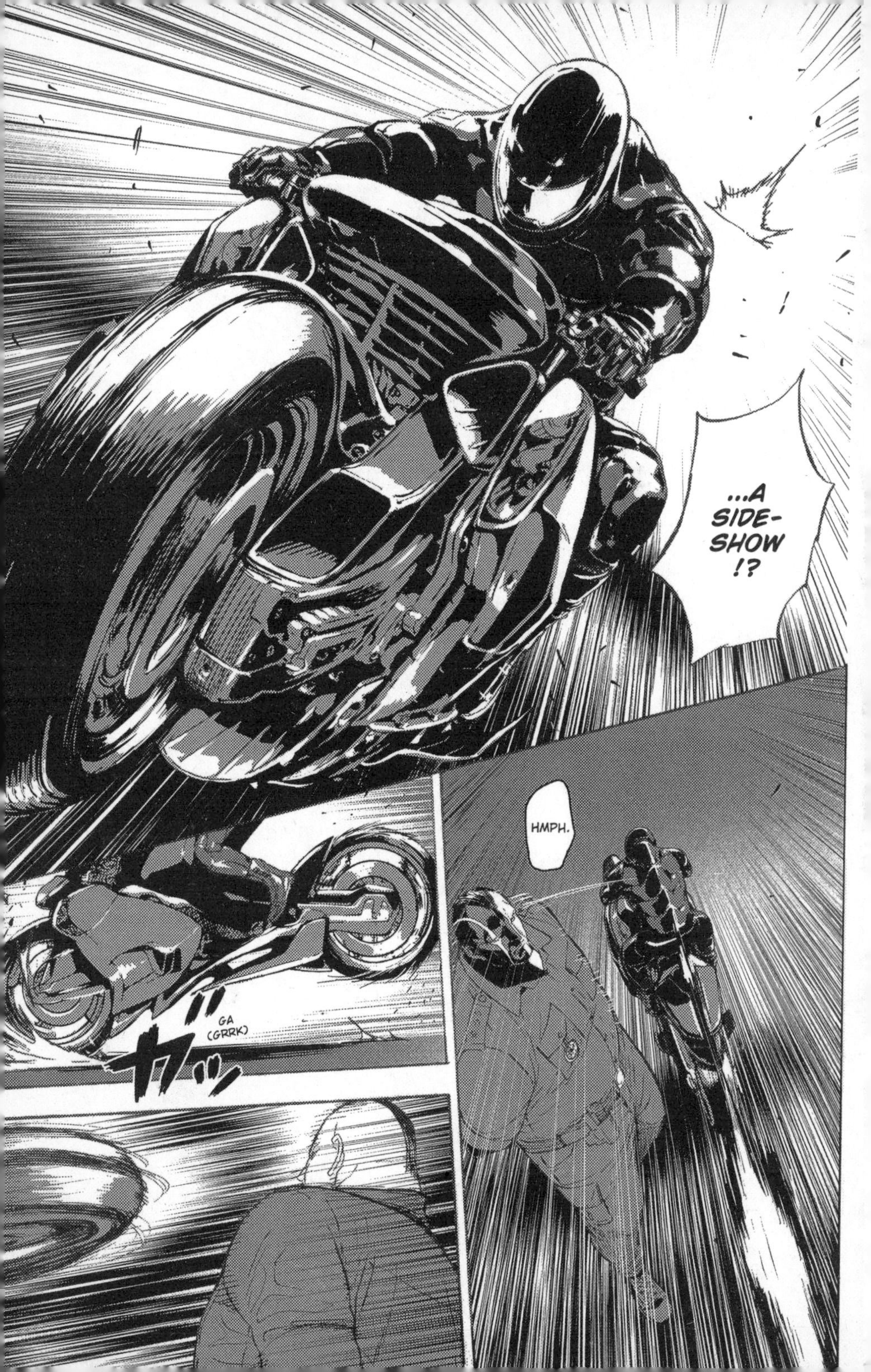
...A SIDE-SHOW!?
HMPH.
GA (GRRK)

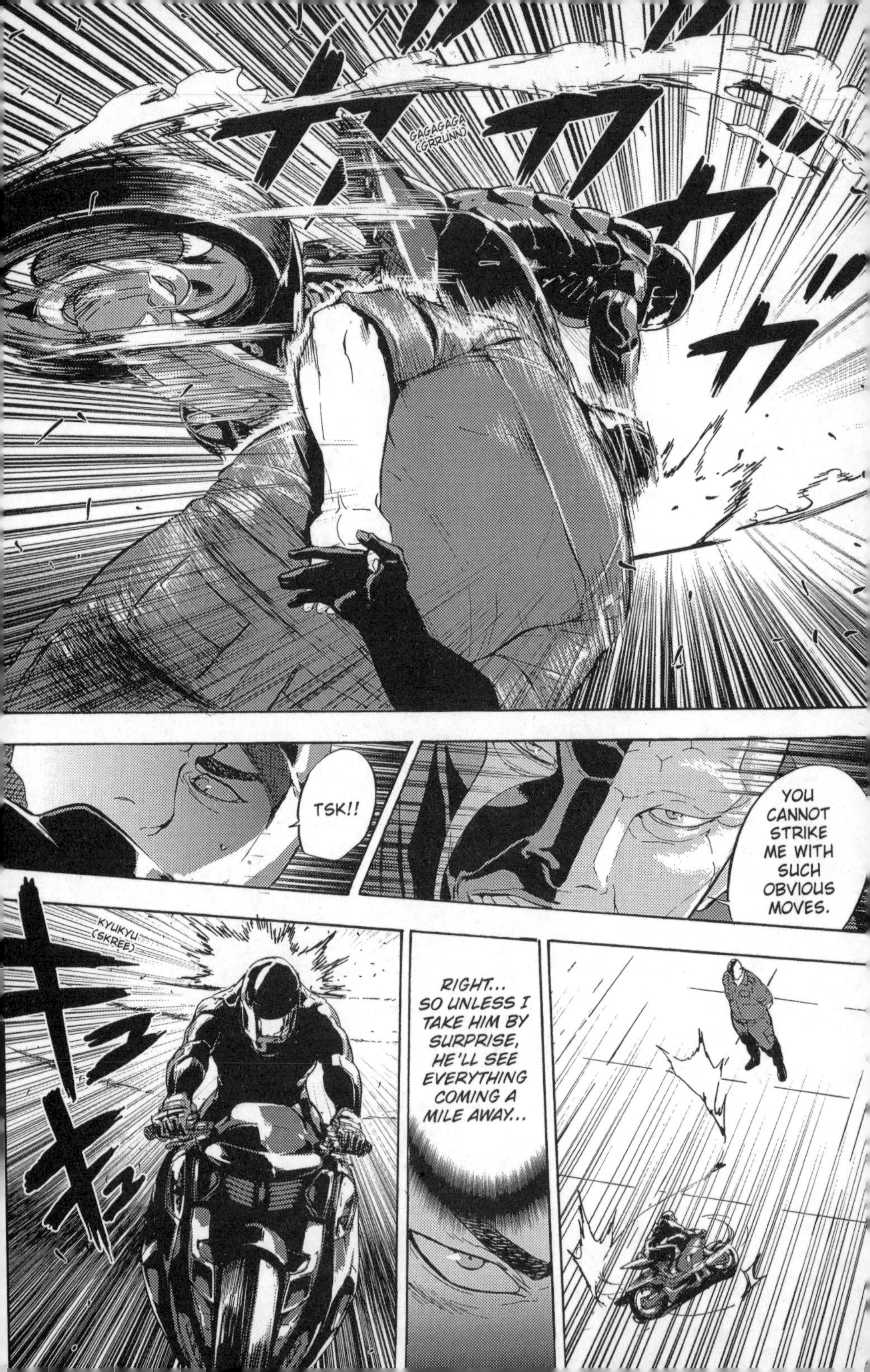
GAGAGAGA (GRRUNN)
YOU CANNOT STRIKE ME WITH SUCH OBVIOUS MOVES.
TSK!!
RIGHT... SO UNLESS I TAKE HIM BY SURPRISE, HE'LL SEE EVERYTHING COMING A MILE AWAY...
KYUKYU (SKREE)

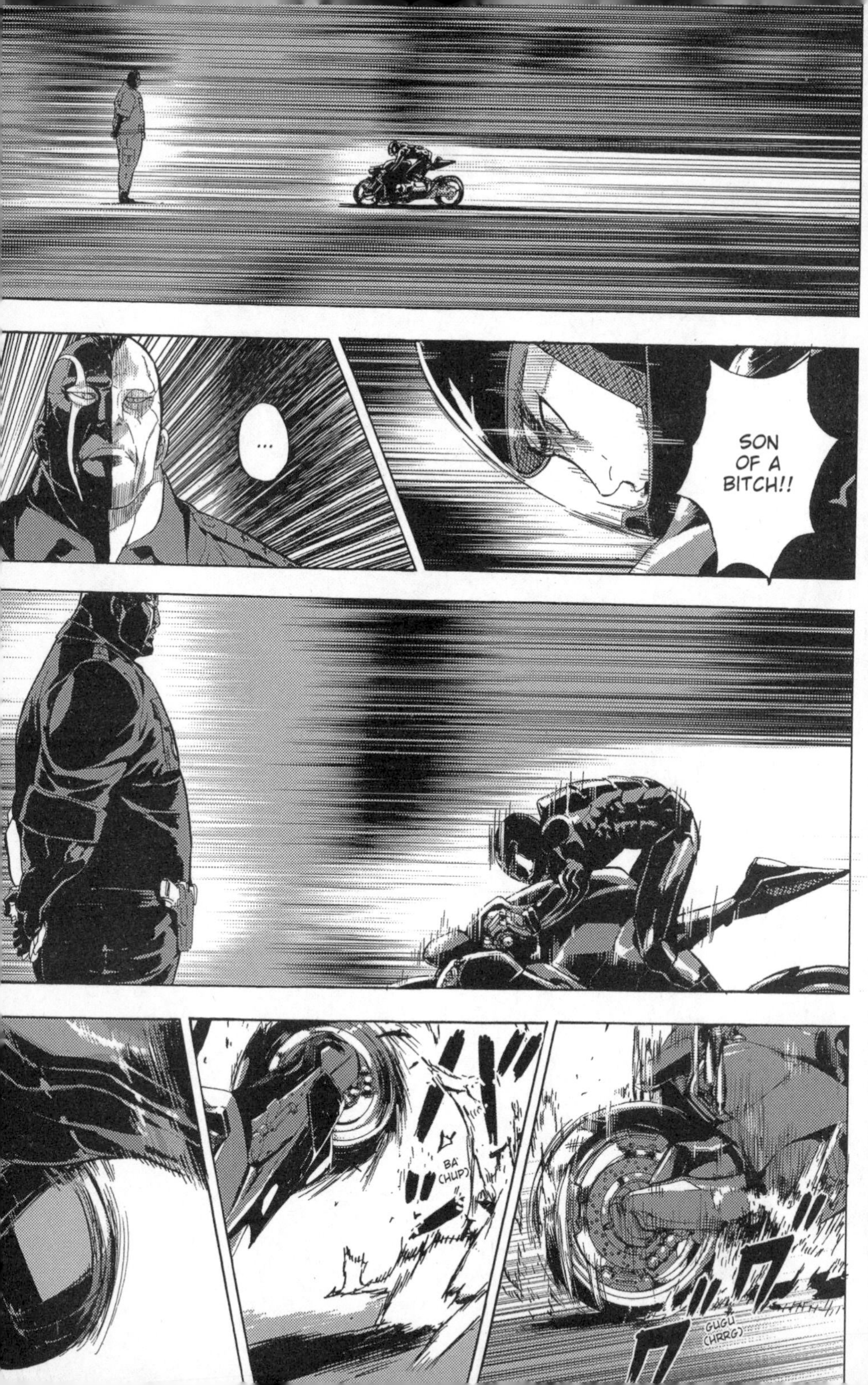
SON OF A BITCH!!
...
GUGU (HRRG)
BA (HUP)

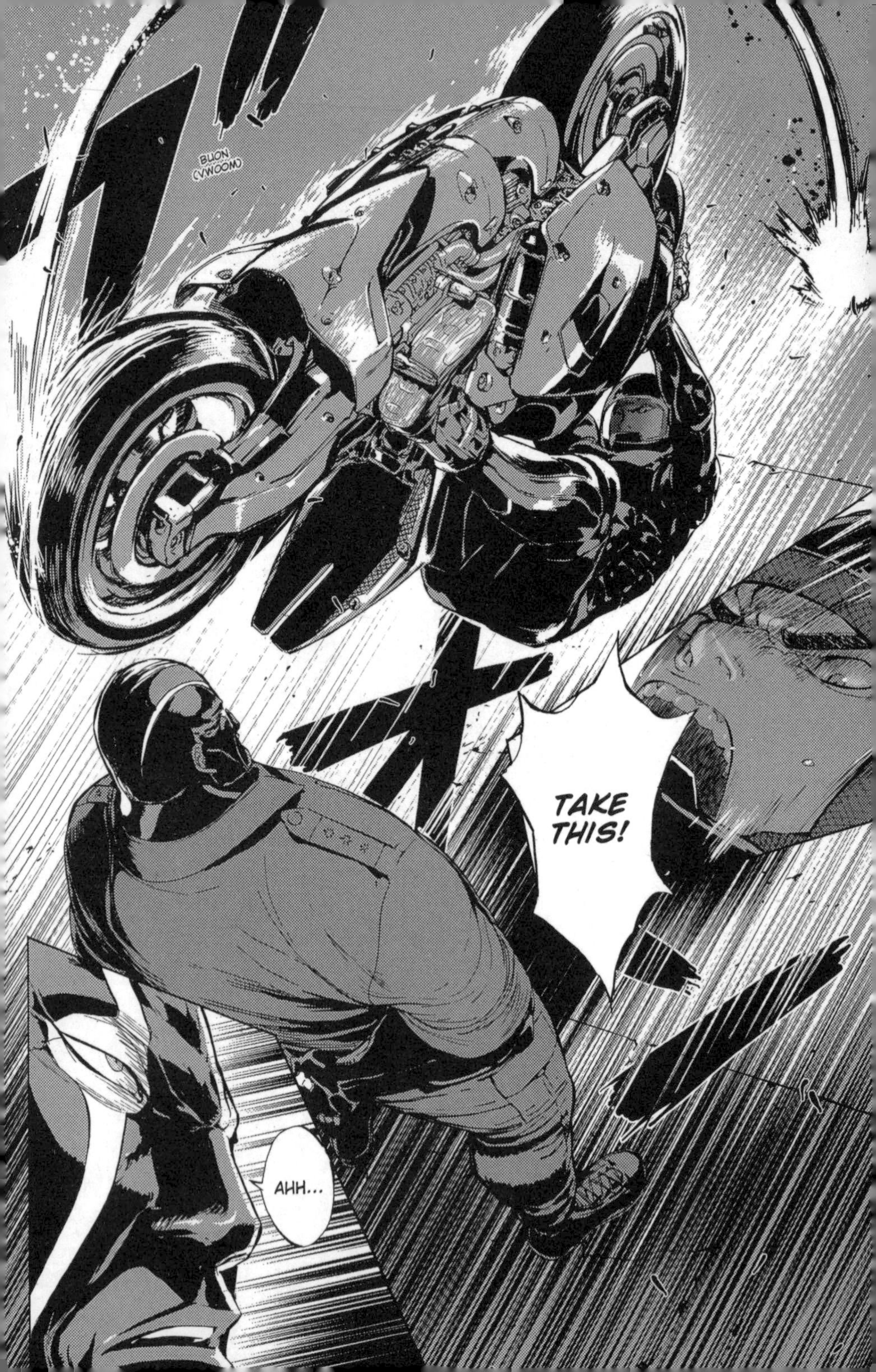
BUON (VWOOM)
TAKE THIS!
AHH...

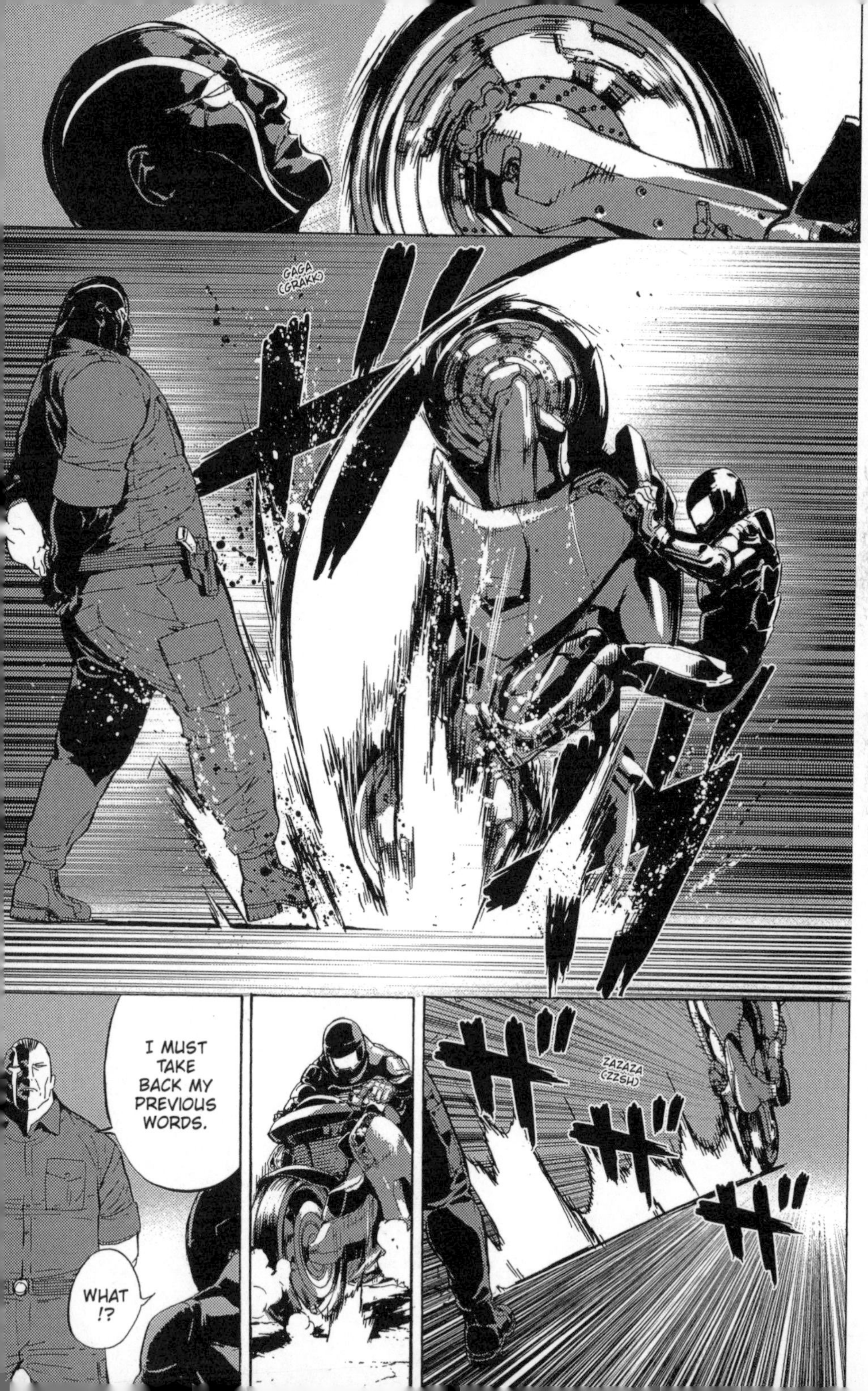
GAGA (GRAKK)
ZAZAZA (ZZSH)
I MUST TAKE BACK MY PREVIOUS WORDS.
WHAT !?

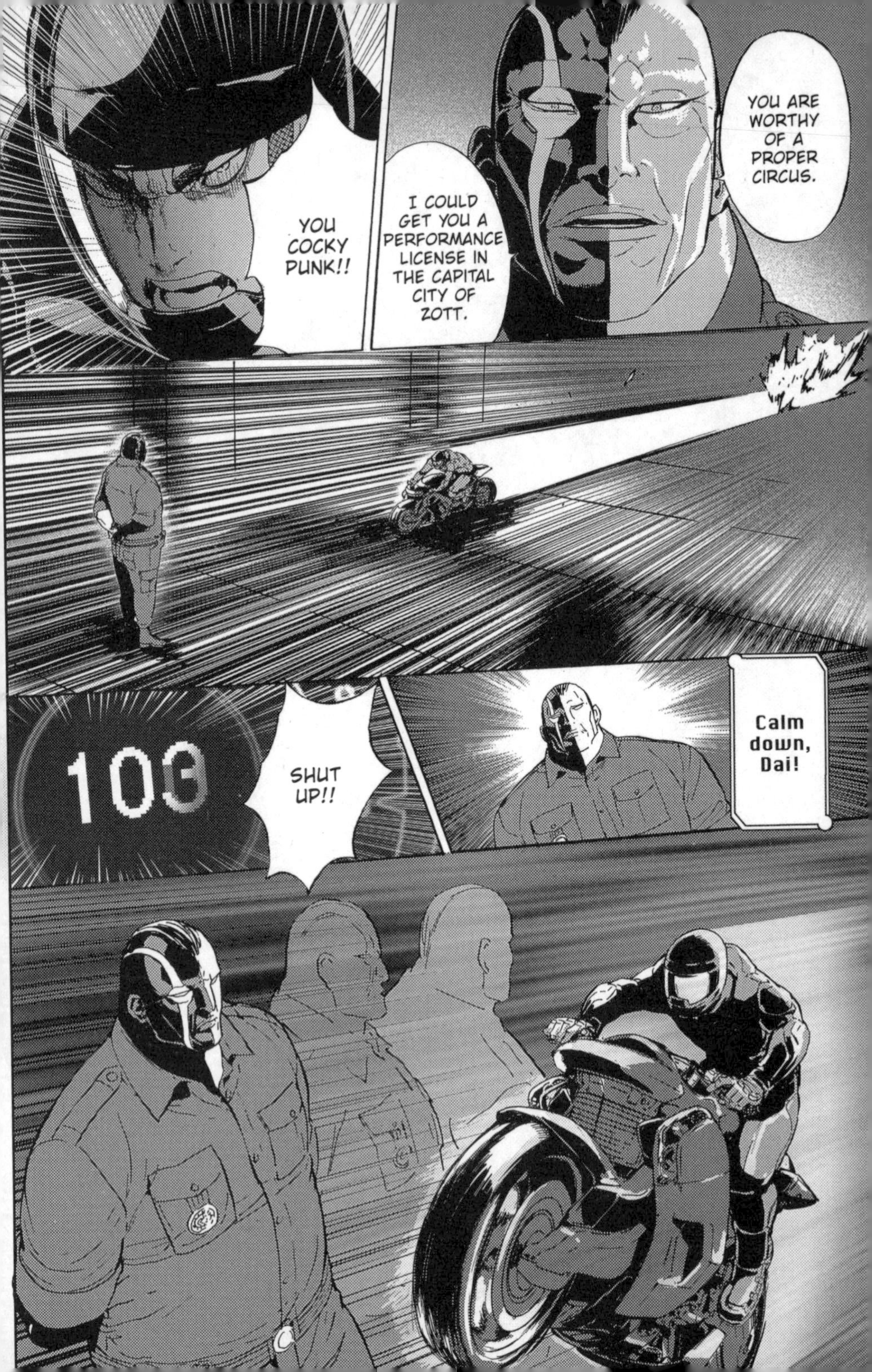
YOU ARE WORTHY OF A PROPER CIRCUS.
I COULD GET YOU A PERFORMANCE LICENSE IN THE CAPITAL CITY OF ZOTT.
YOU COCKY PUNK!!
Calm down, Dai!
SHUT UP!!
103

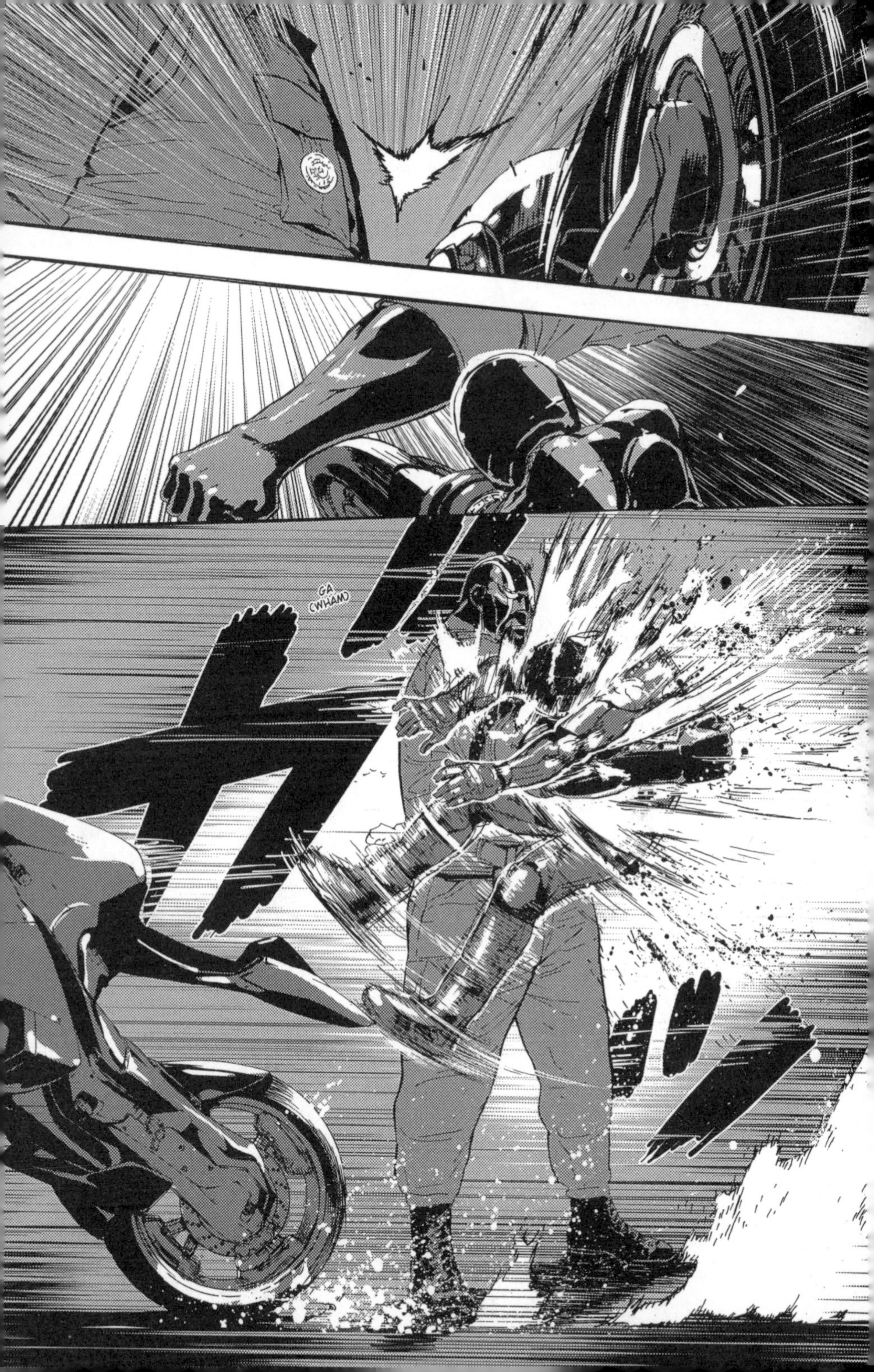
GA
(WHAM)

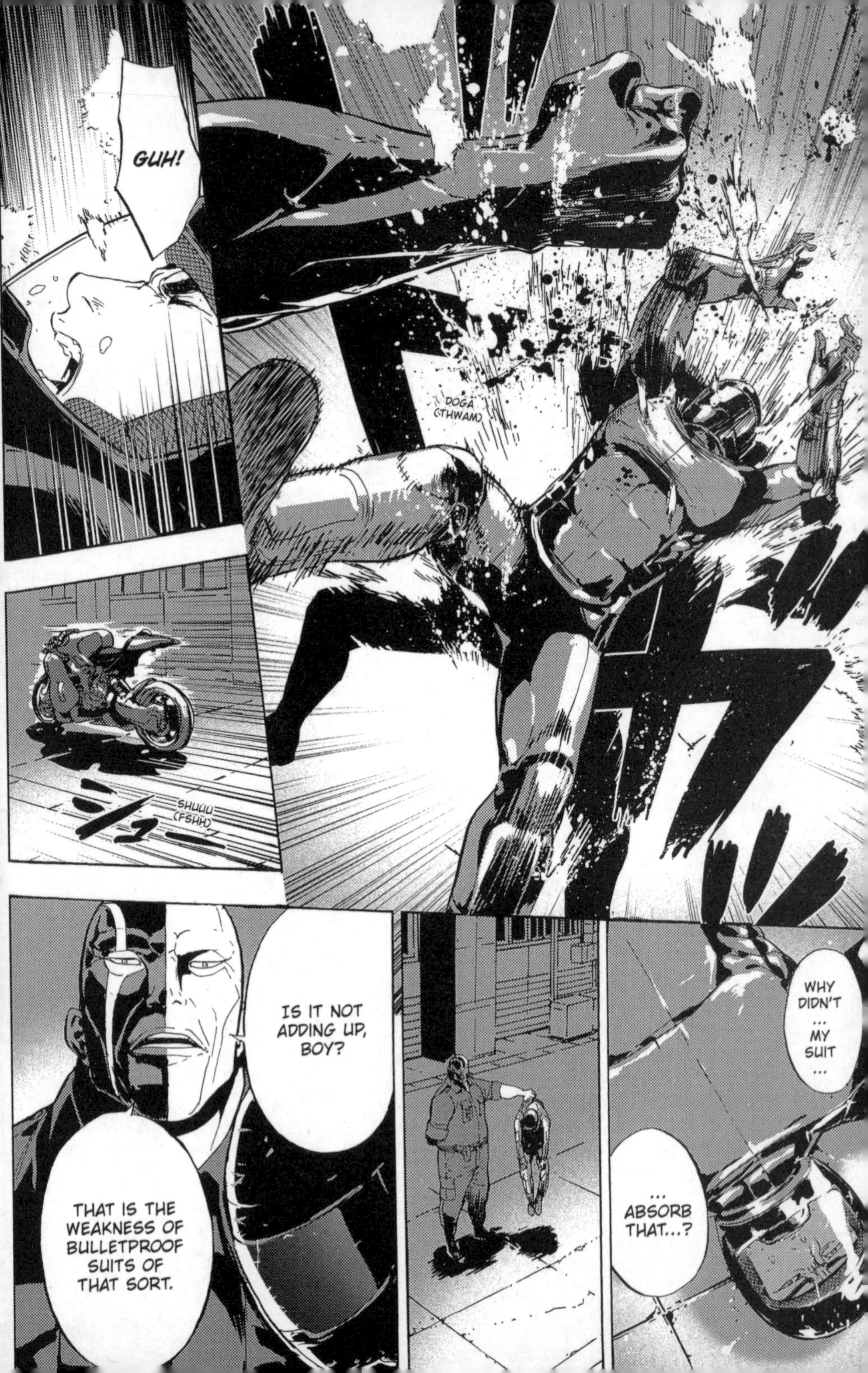
DOGA (THWAM)
GUH!
SHUUU (FSHH)
WHY DIDN'T ... MY SUIT ...
... ABSORB THAT...?
IS IT NOT ADDING UP, BOY?
THAT IS THE WEAKNESS OF BULLETPROOF SUITS OF THAT SORT.

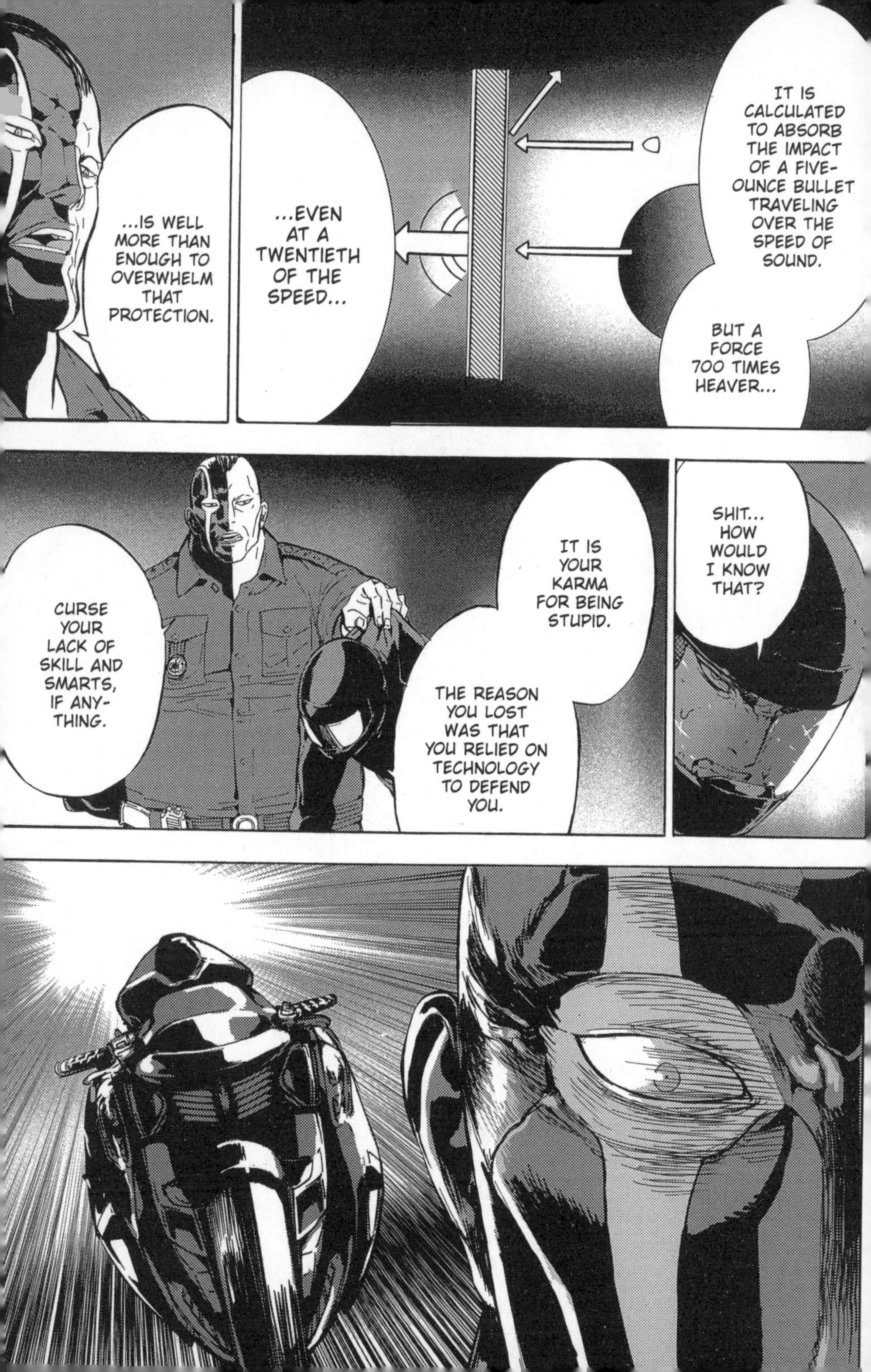
IT IS CALCULATED TO ABSORB THE IMPACT OF A FIVE-OUNCE BULLET TRAVELING OVER THE SPEED OF SOUND.
BUT A FORCE 700 TIMES HEAVER...
...EVEN AT A TWENTIETH OF THE SPEED...
...IS WELL MORE THAN ENOUGH TO OVERWHELM THAT PROTECTION.
SHIT... HOW WOULD I KNOW THAT?
IT IS YOUR KARMA FOR BEING STUPID.
THE REASON YOU LOST WAS THAT YOU RELIED ON TECHNOLOGY TO DEFEND YOU.
CURSE YOUR LACK OF SKILL AND SMARTS, IF ANYTHING.

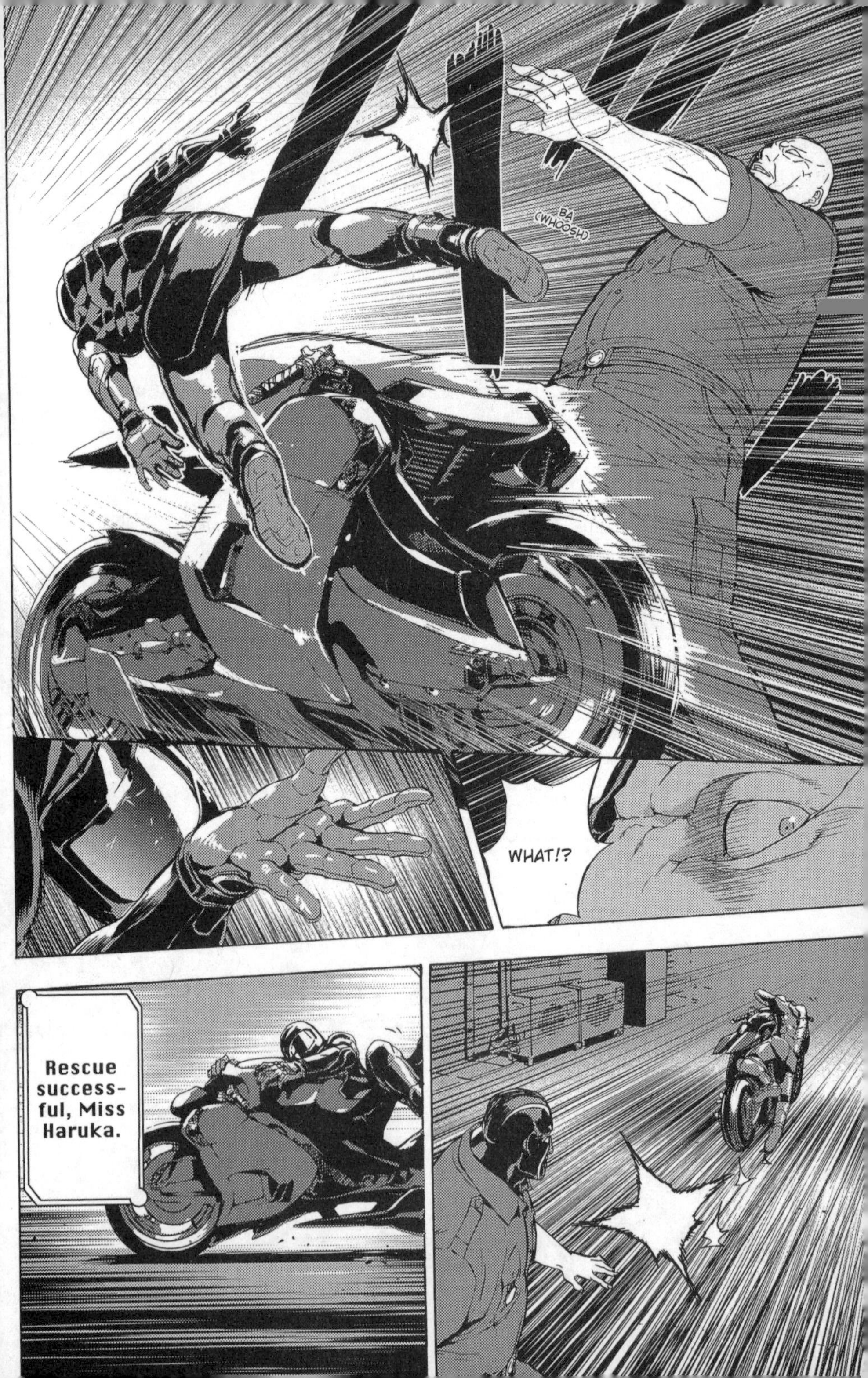
BA
(WHOOSH)
WHAT!?
Rescue success-ful, Miss Haruka.

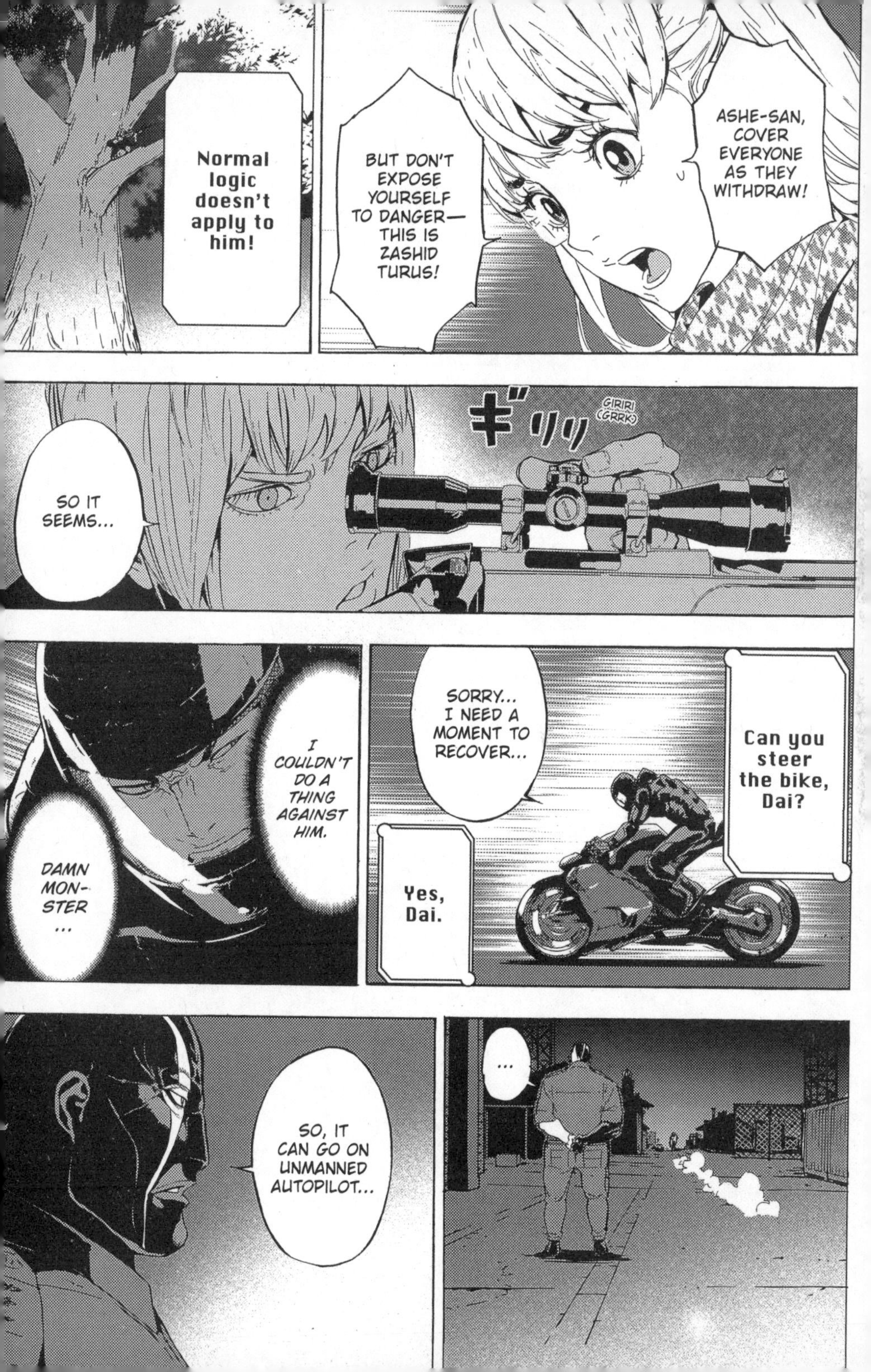
ASHE-SAN, COVER EVERYONE AS THEY WITHDRAW!
BUT DON'T EXPOSE YOURSELF TO DANGER— THIS IS ZASHID TURUS!
Normal logic doesn't apply to him!
GIRIRI (GRRK)
SO IT SEEMS...
Can you steer the bike, Dai?
SORRY... I NEED A MOMENT TO RECOVER...
Yes, Dai.
I COULDN'T DO A THING AGAINST HIM.
DAMN MON-STER ...
...
SO, IT CAN GO ON UNMANNED AUTOPILOT...

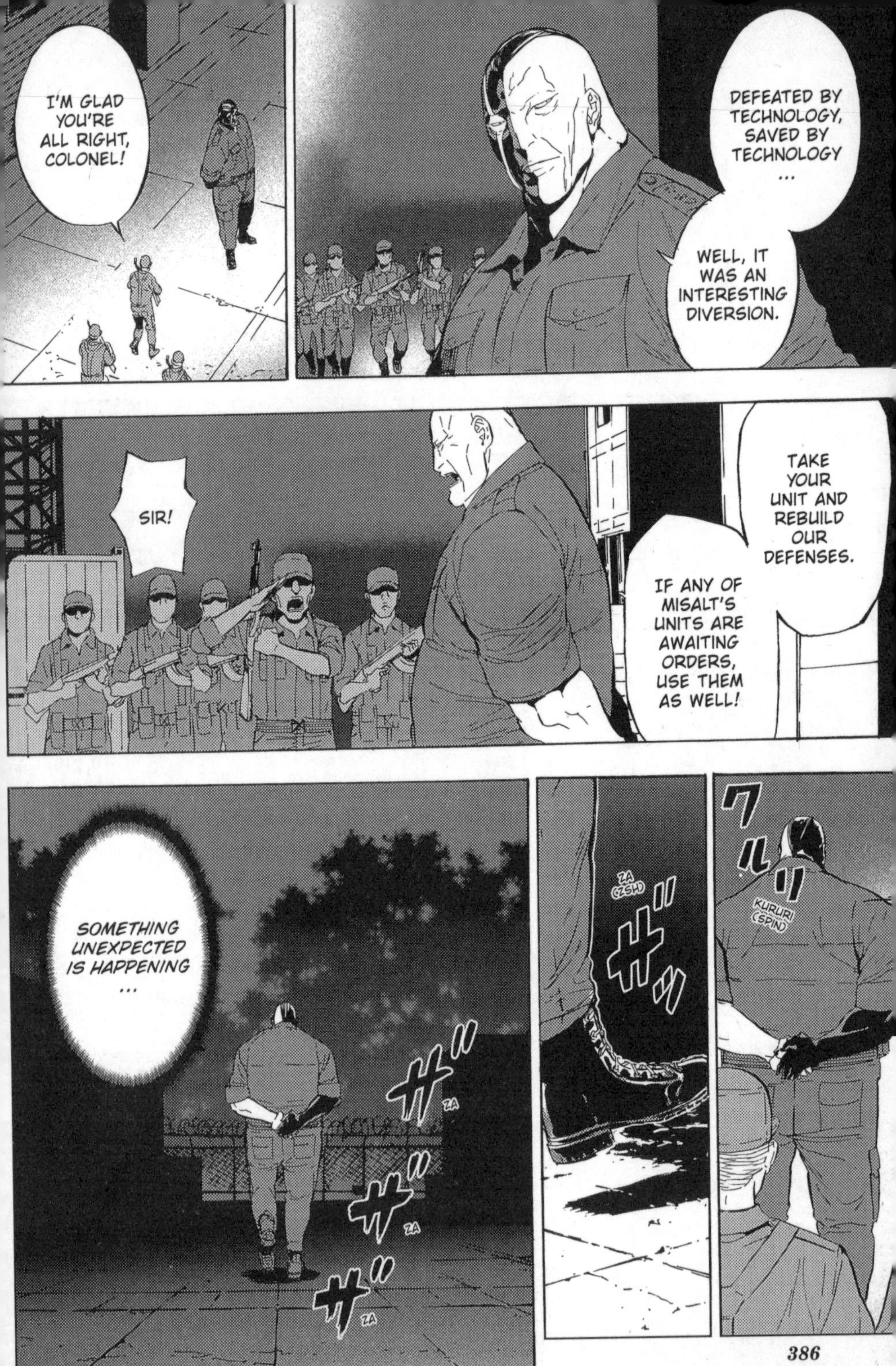
DEFEATED BY TECHNOLOGY, SAVED BY TECHNOLOGY ...
WELL, IT WAS AN INTERESTING DIVERSION.
I'M GLAD YOU'RE ALL RIGHT, COLONEL!
TAKE YOUR UNIT AND REBUILD OUR DEFENSES.
IF ANY OF MISALT'S UNITS ARE AWAITING ORDERS, USE THEM AS WELL!
SIR!
クルリ
KURURI (SPIN)
ザッ
ZA (ZSH)
SOMETHING UNEXPECTED IS HAPPENING ...
ザ
ZA
ザ
ZA
ザ
ZA

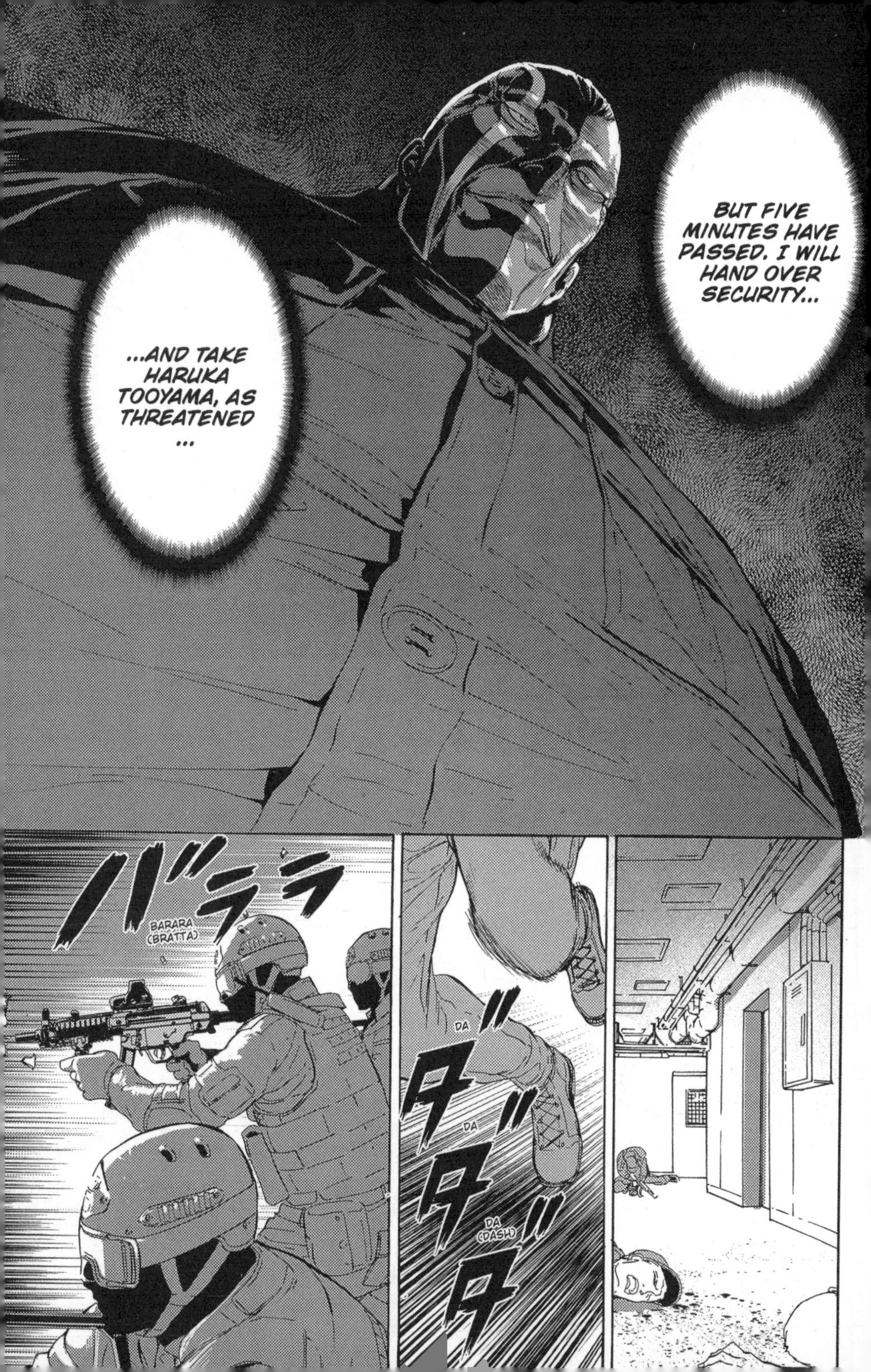
BUT FIVE MINUTES HAVE PASSED. I WILL HAND OVER SECURITY...
...AND TAKE HARUKA TOOYAMA, AS THREATENED ...
DA
DA
DA (DASH)
BARARA (BRATTA)

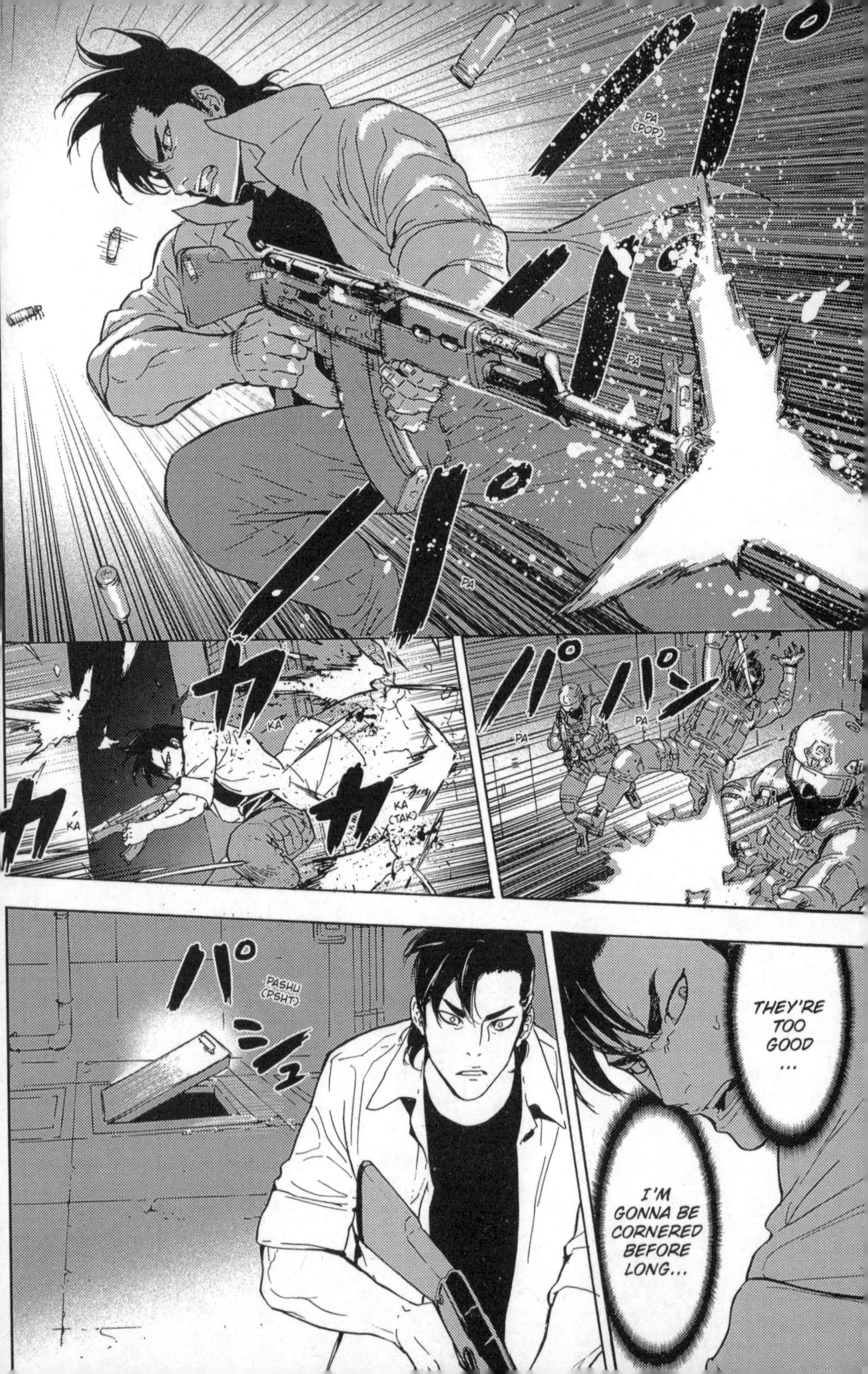
PA (POP)
PA
PA
PA
PA
KA
KA (TAK)
KA
THEY'RE TOO GOOD ...
I'M GONNA BE CORNERED BEFORE LONG...
PASHU (PSHT)

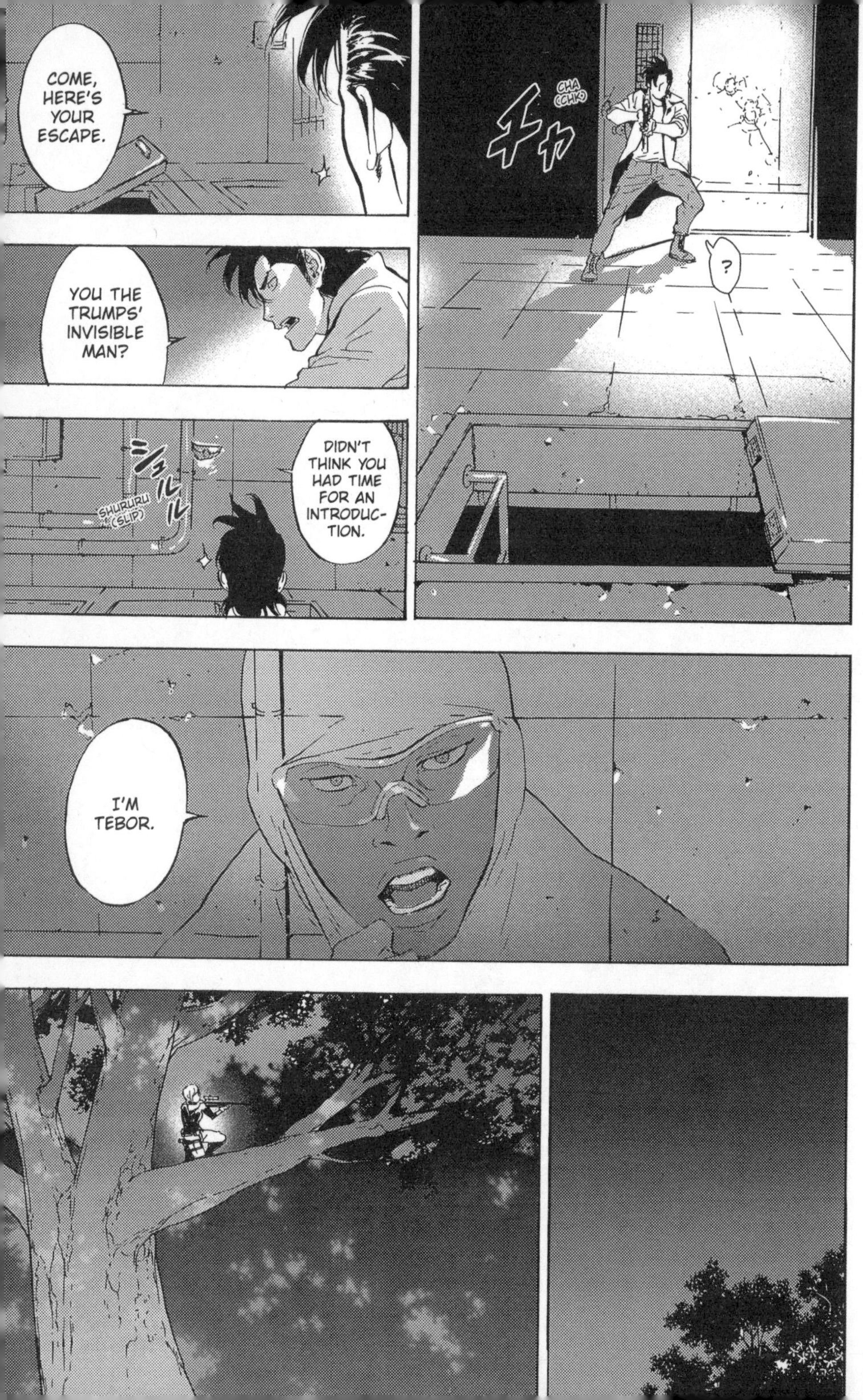
チャ
CHA (CHK)
?
COME, HERE'S YOUR ESCAPE.
YOU THE TRUMPS' INVISIBLE MAN?
DIDN'T THINK YOU HAD TIME FOR AN INTRODUCTION.
シュルル
SHURURU (SLIP)
I'M TEBOR.

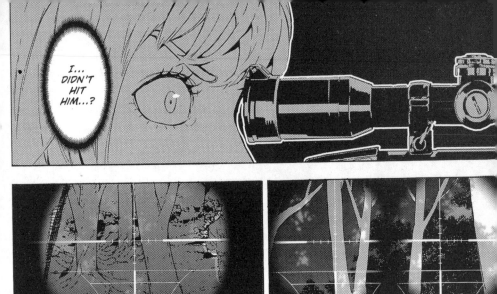

I... DIDN'T HIT HIM...?

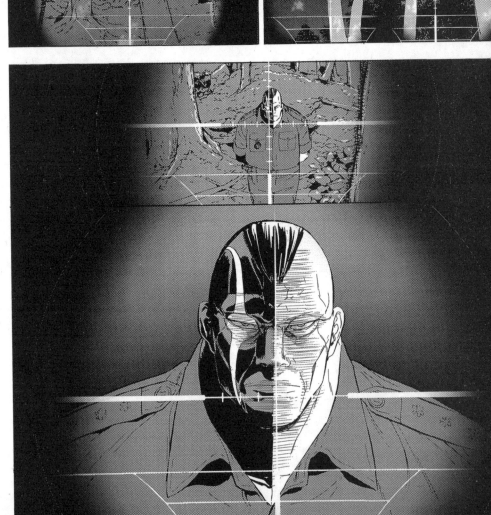

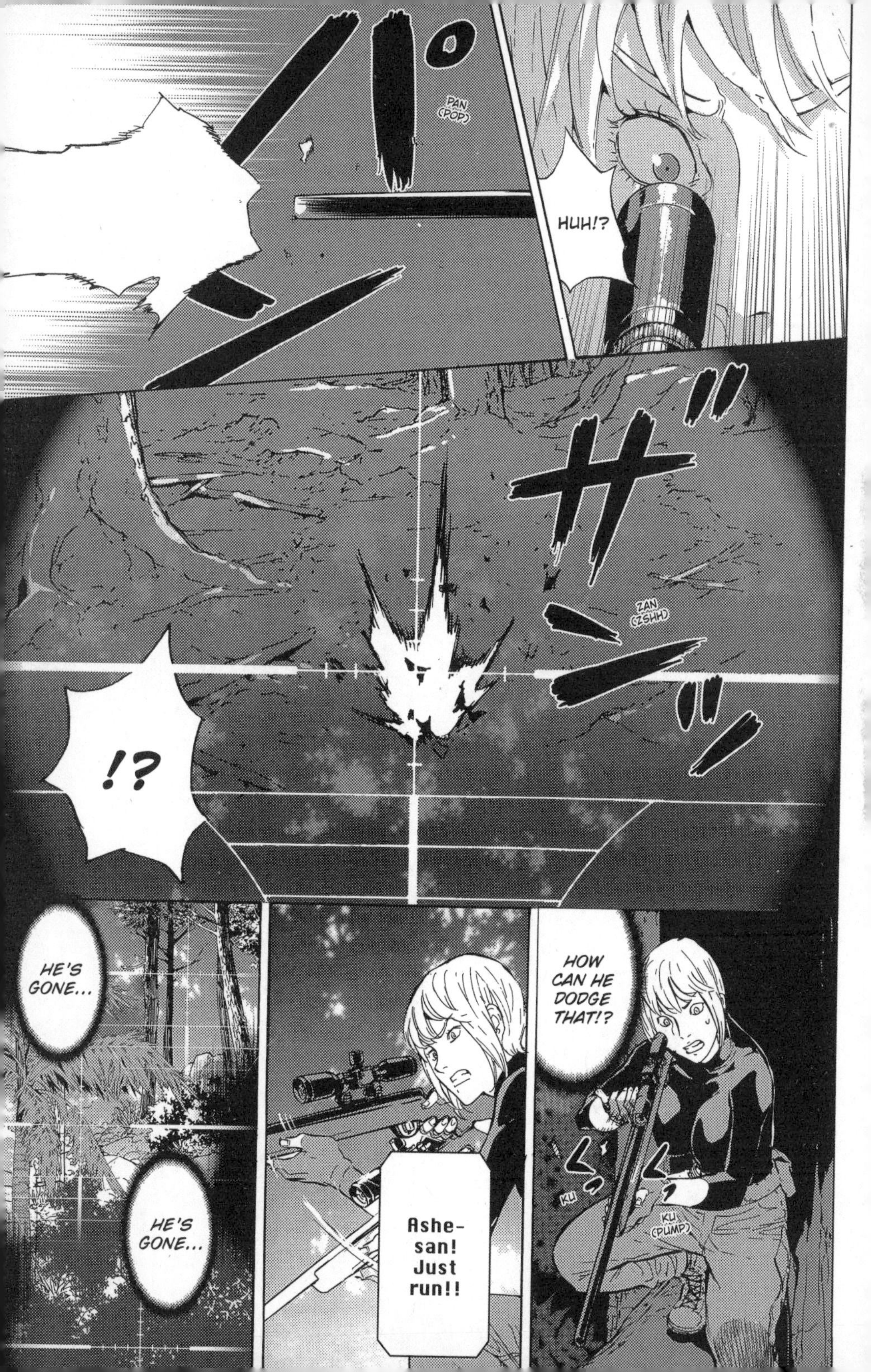
HUH!?
PAN
(POP)
ZAN
(ZSHH)
!?
HOW CAN HE DODGE THAT!?
KU
KU
(PUMP)
Ashe-san! Just run!!
HE'S GONE...
HE'S GONE...

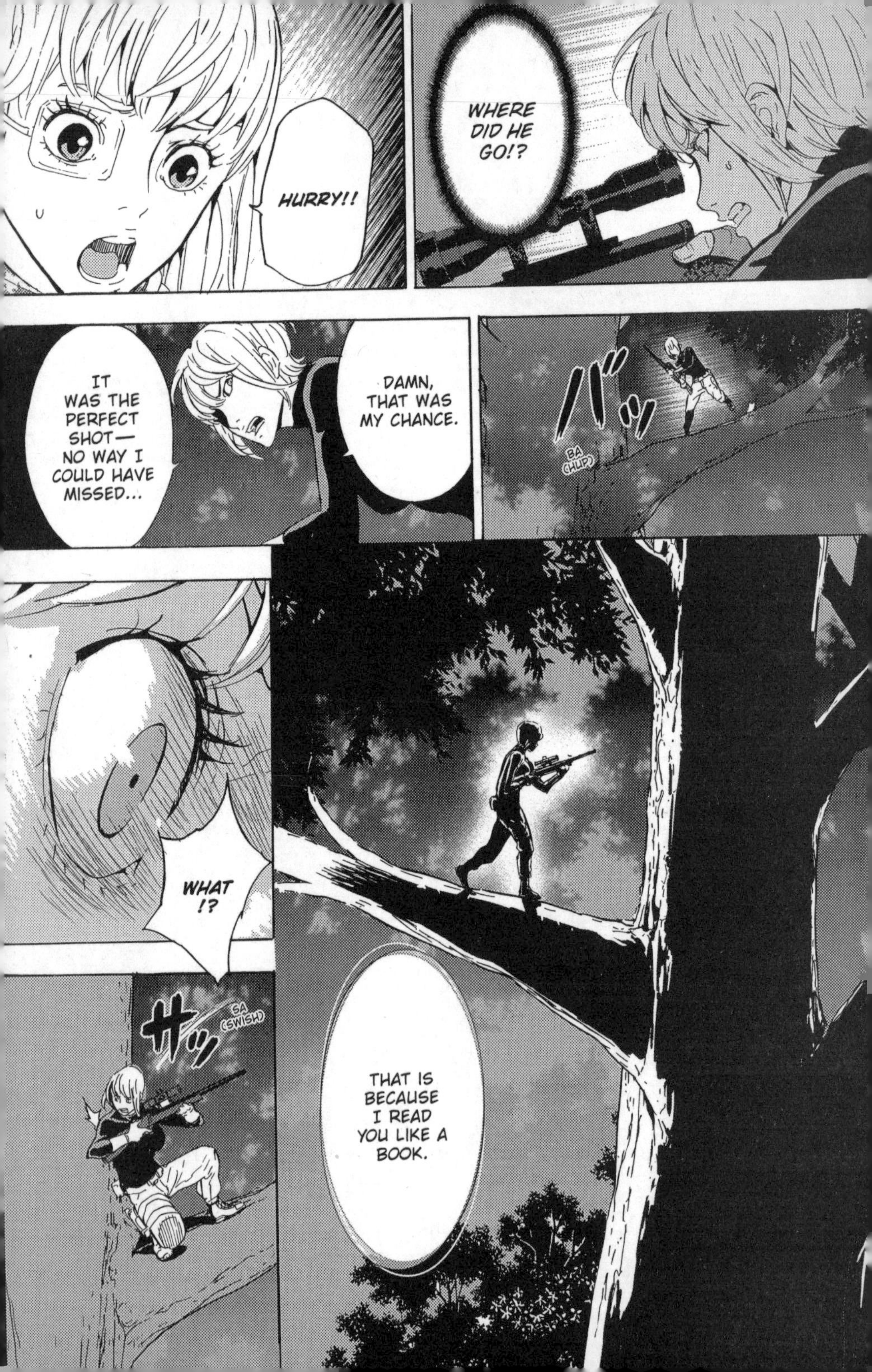

WHERE DID HE GO!?
HURRY!!
BA (HUP)
DAMN, THAT WAS MY CHANCE.
IT WAS THE PERFECT SHOT— NO WAY I COULD HAVE MISSED...
THAT IS BECAUSE I READ YOU LIKE A BOOK.
WHAT!?
SA (SWISH)

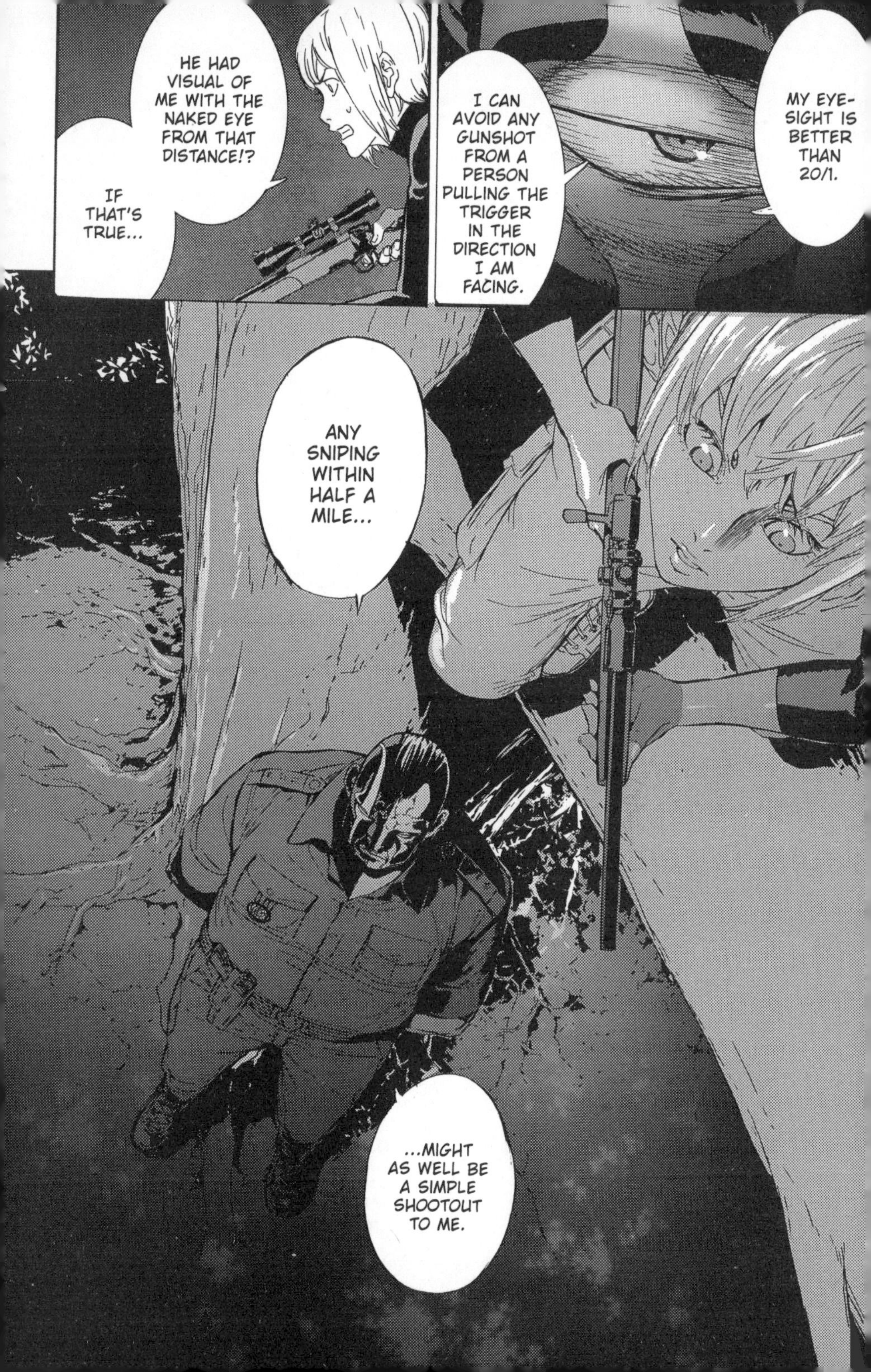
MY EYE-SIGHT IS BETTER THAN 20/1.
I CAN AVOID ANY GUNSHOT FROM A PERSON PULLING THE TRIGGER IN THE DIRECTION I AM FACING.
HE HAD VISUAL OF ME WITH THE NAKED EYE FROM THAT DISTANCE!?
IF THAT'S TRUE...
ANY SNIPING WITHIN HALF A MILE...
...MIGHT AS WELL BE A SIMPLE SHOOTOUT TO ME.

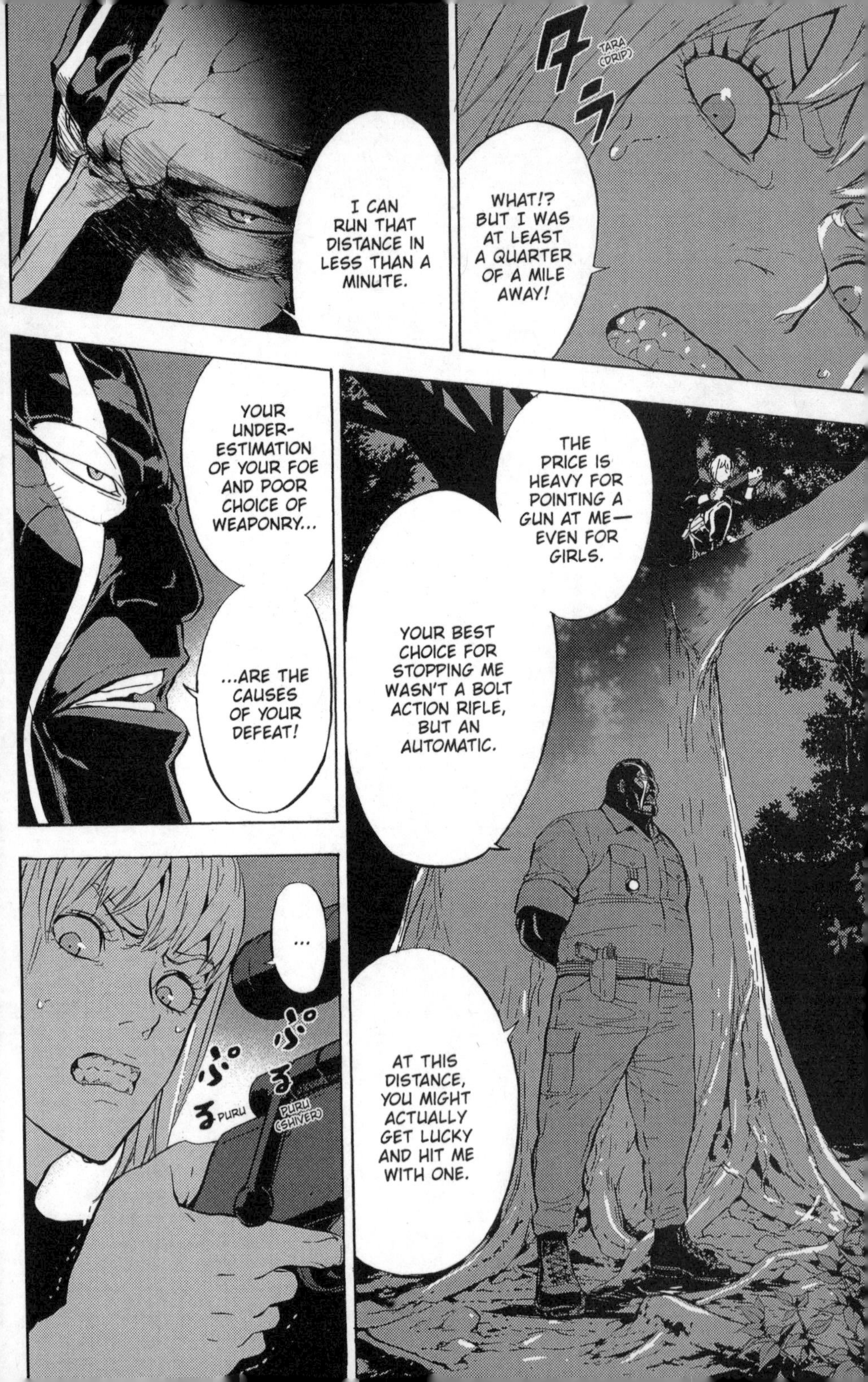
TARA (DRIP)
WHAT!? BUT I WAS AT LEAST A QUARTER OF A MILE AWAY!
I CAN RUN THAT DISTANCE IN LESS THAN A MINUTE.
THE PRICE IS HEAVY FOR POINTING A GUN AT ME— EVEN FOR GIRLS.
YOUR BEST CHOICE FOR STOPPING ME WASN'T A BOLT ACTION RIFLE, BUT AN AUTOMATIC.
AT THIS DISTANCE, YOU MIGHT ACTUALLY GET LUCKY AND HIT ME WITH ONE.
YOUR UNDER-ESTIMATION OF YOUR FOE AND POOR CHOICE OF WEAPONRY...
...ARE THE CAUSES OF YOUR DEFEAT!
...
PURU PURU (SHIVER)

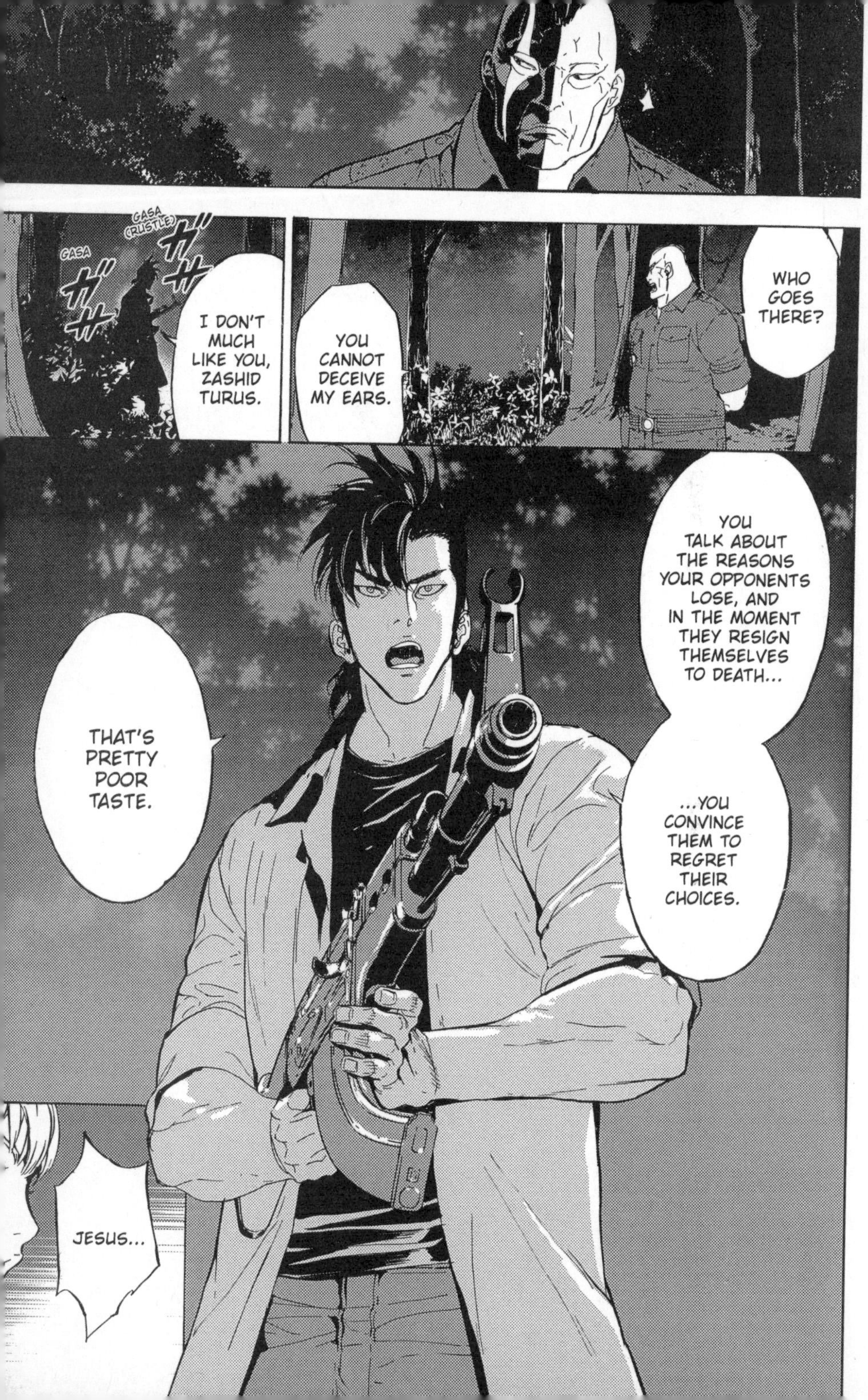
WHO GOES THERE?
YOU CANNOT DECEIVE MY EARS.
GASA (RUSTLE)
GASA
I DON'T MUCH LIKE YOU, ZASHID TURUS.
YOU TALK ABOUT THE REASONS YOUR OPPONENTS LOSE, AND IN THE MOMENT THEY RESIGN THEMSELVES TO DEATH...
...YOU CONVINCE THEM TO REGRET THEIR CHOICES.
THAT'S PRETTY POOR TASTE.
JESUS...

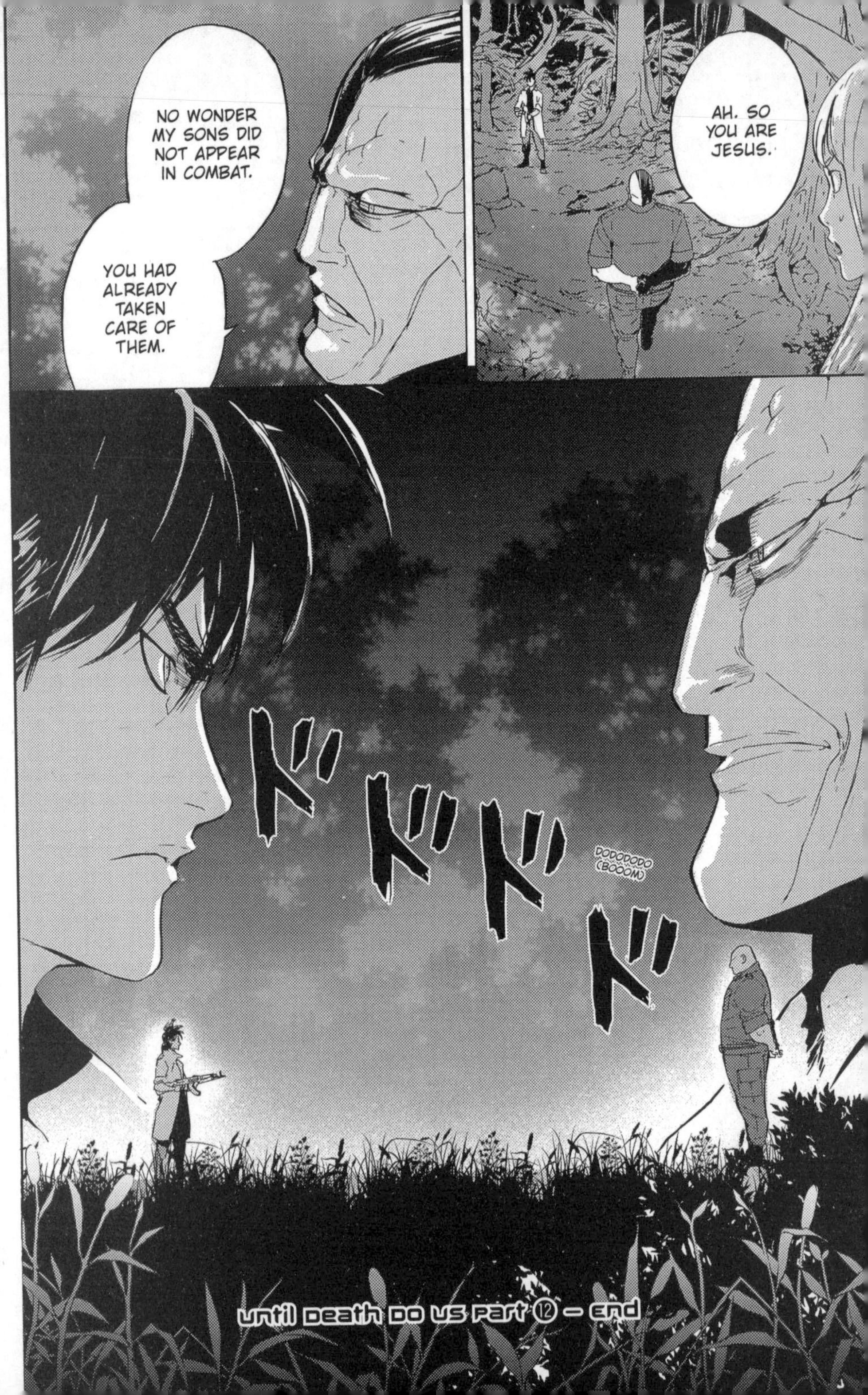
AH. SO YOU ARE JESUS.
NO WONDER MY SONS DID NOT APPEAR IN COMBAT.
YOU HAD ALREADY TAKEN CARE OF THEM.
ドドドド
DODODODO (BOOOM)
until Death do us Part ⑫ - End

Art Staff
hansil ♀: Background Art/Screentone
noeri ♀: Background Art/Screentone

Military Advisor
Lee Hyun Seok (warmania)

Special Thanks
Shingo Takano

Crossover Planning
JESUS—Sajin Kouro, Yami no Aegis, Akatsuki no Aegis
Written by Kyouichi Nanatsuki, Art by Yoshihide Fujiwara
(Shogakukan)

Design Assistance
Hitoshi Fukuchi

Read all your favorite manga titles on your iPad or iPhone!

Download the **YEN PRESS** app for full volumes of our bestselling series!

Yen Press

www.YenPress.com

PRESENTING THE LATEST SERIES FROM

JUN MOCHIZUKI

THE CASE STUDY OF VANITAS

JUN MOCHIZUKI
THE CASE STUDY OF
VANITAS

READ THE CHAPTERS AT
THE SAME TIME AS JAPAN!

AVAILABLE NOW WORLDWIDE
WHEREVER E-BOOKS ARE SOLD!

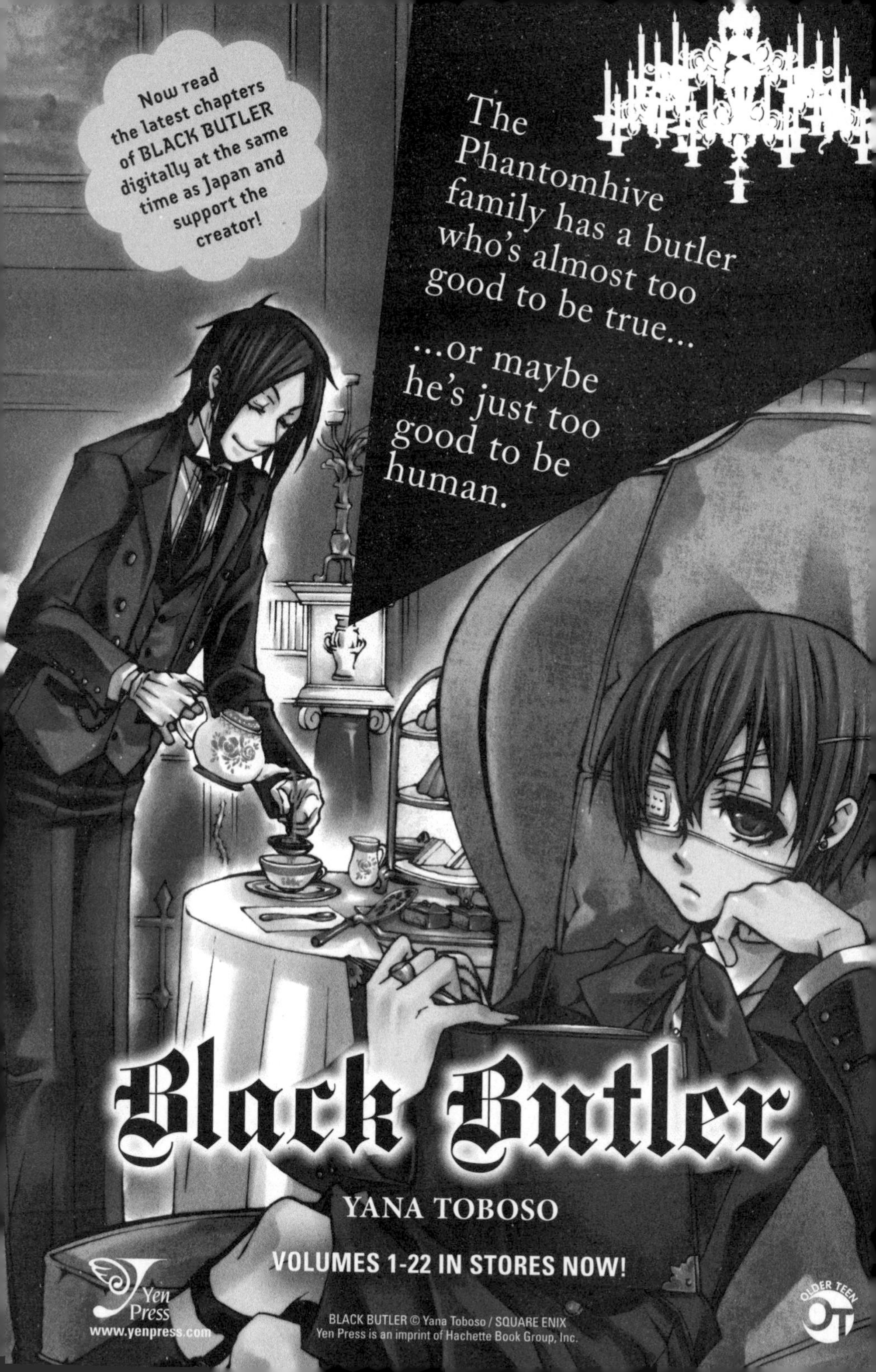

Now read the latest chapters of BLACK BUTLER digitally at the same time as Japan and support the creator!
The Phantomhive family has a butler who's almost too good to be true...
...or maybe he's just too good to be human.
Black Butler
YANA TOBOSO
VOLUMES 1-22 IN STORES NOW!
Yen Press
www.yenpress.com
BLACK BUTLER © Yana Toboso / SQUARE ENIX
Yen Press is an imprint of Hachette Book Group, Inc.
OLDER TEEN
OT

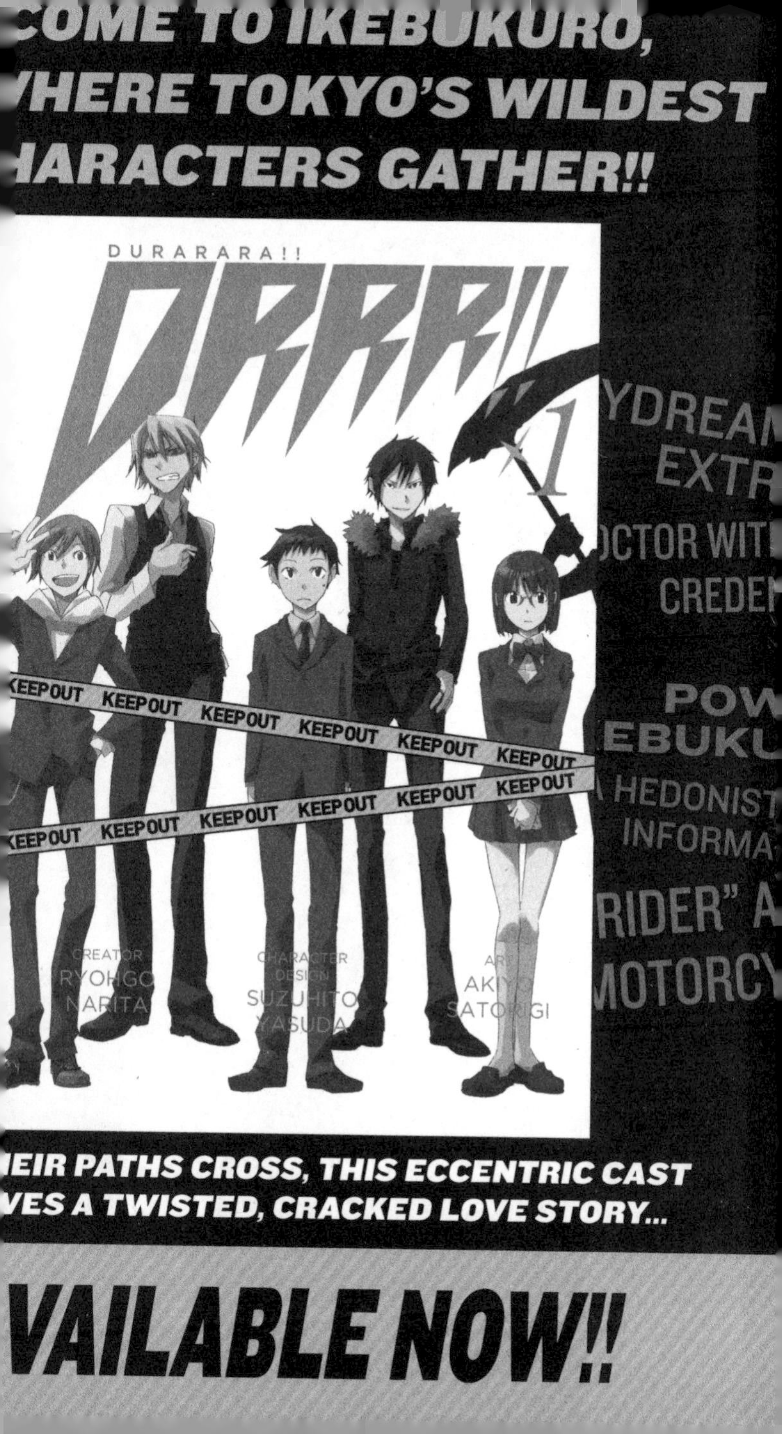
COME TO IKEBUKURO,
HERE TOKYO'S WILDEST
HARACTERS GATHER!!
DURARARA!!
DRRR!!
1
KEEPOUT KEEPOUT KEEPOUT KEEPOUT KEEPOUT KEEPOUT
KEEPOUT KEEPOUT KEEPOUT KEEPOUT KEEPOUT KEEPOUT
CREATOR
RYOHGO NARITA
CHARACTER DESIGN
SUZUHITO YASUDA
ART
AKIYO SATORIGI
YDREAM
EXTR
OCTOR WIT
CREDEN
POW
EBUKU
HEDONIST
INFORMA
RIDER" A
MOTORCY
EIR PATHS CROSS, THIS ECCENTRIC CAST
VES A TWISTED, CRACKED LOVE STORY...
VAILABLE NOW!!

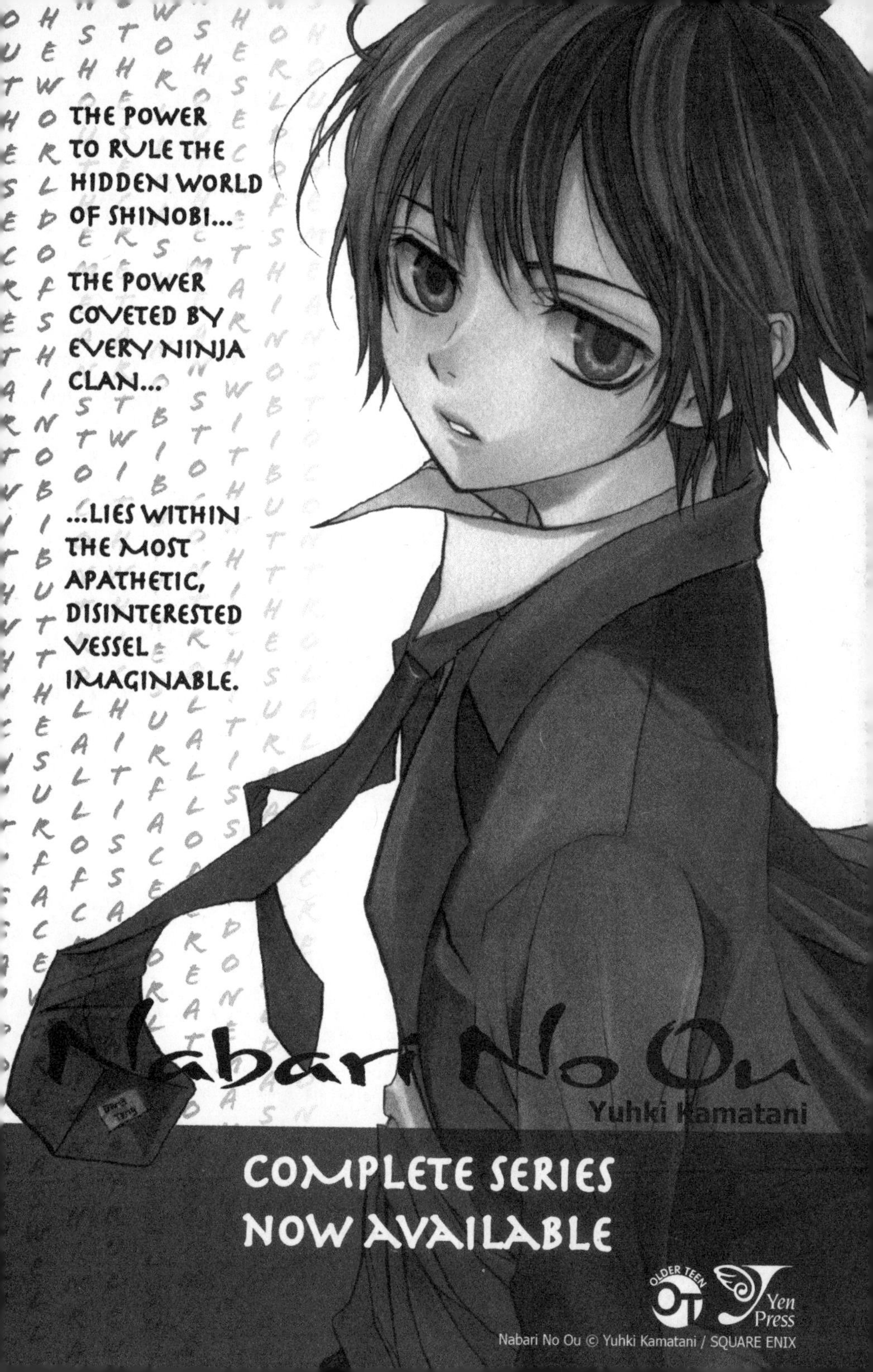
THE POWER TO RULE THE HIDDEN WORLD OF SHINOBI...
THE POWER COVETED BY EVERY NINJA CLAN...
...LIES WITHIN THE MOST APATHETIC, DISINTERESTED VESSEL IMAGINABLE.
Nabari No Ou
Yuhki Kamatani
COMPLETE SERIES NOW AVAILABLE
OLDER TEEN OT
Yen Press
Nabari No Ou © Yuhki Kamatani / SQUARE ENIX

UNTIL DEATH DO US PART ⑫

HIROSHI TAKASHIGE
DOUBLE-S

Translation: Stephen Paul
Lettering: AndWorld Design

UNTIL DEATH DO US PART Vol. 23 and 24 © 2014 Hiroshi Takashige, DOUBLE-S / SQUARE ENIX CO., LTD. First published in Japan in 2014 by SQUARE ENIX CO., LTD. English translation rights arranged with SQUARE ENIX CO., LTD. and Hachette Book Group through Tuttle-Mori Agency, Inc.

Translation © 2016 by SQUARE ENIX CO., LTD.

Yen Press
Hachette Book Group
1290 Avenue of the Americas
New York, NY 10104

HachetteBookGroup.com
YenPress.com

Yen Press is an imprint of Hachette Book Group, Inc. The Yen Press name and logo are trademarks of Hachette Book Group, Inc.

The publisher is not responsible for websites (or their content) that are not owned by the publisher.

Library of Congress Control Number: 2016931014

First Yen Press Edition: May 2016

ISBN: 978-0-316-27216-2

10 9 8 7 6 5 4 3 2 1

BVG

Printed in the United States of America